High-Performance Data Network Design

High-Performance Data Network Design

Design Techniques and Tools

Tony Kenyon

Digital Press
An imprint of Butterworth-Heinemann

Boston • Oxford • Auckland • Johannesburg • Melbourne • New Delhi

Library of Congress Cataloging-in-Publication Data

Kenyon, Tony.
   High-performance data network design : design techniques and tools / Tony Kenyon.
      p. cm.
   Includes bibliographical references and index.
   ISBN 1-55558-207-9 (pbk. : alk paper)
      1. Computer networks. 2. Computer network protocols. 3. Computer networks—Standards.
   4. Computer network architectures. I. Title.

   TK5105.5 .K45 2002
   004.6—dc21   2001058100

British Library Cataloging-in-Publication Data

A catalogue record for this book is available from the British Library.

The publisher offers special discounts on bulk orders of this book.
For information, please contact:

Manager of Special Sales
Butterworth–Heinemann
225 Wildwood Avenue
Woburn, MA 01801-2041
Tel: 781-904-2500
Fax: 781-904-2620

For information on all Butterworth–Heinemann publications available, contact our
World Wide Web home page at: http://www.bh.com.

10 9 8 7 6 5 4 3 2 1

Printed in the United States of America

Contents

Preface   ix

Acknowledgments   xiii

1   A Review of the Basics   1

    1.1   Network design and performance   1
    1.2   An overview of the design process   3
    1.3   Building block 1: The framework   13
    1.4   Building block 2: Protocols   17
    1.5   Building block 3: Hardware   27
    1.6   Building block 4: Physical connectivity   35
    1.7   Summary   39

2   Capacity Planning   41

    2.1   Formal framework for capacity planning   42
    2.2   Understanding application and user behavior   55
    2.3   Understanding traffic characteristics   63
    2.4   Recognizing and analyzing bottlenecks   75
    2.5   Preparing data for modeling   82
    2.6   Summary   89

3   Network Design and Modeling   91

    3.1   Hierarchical design model   92
    3.2   Protocol models   96
    3.3   Review of topology design and optimization   97
    3.4   Spanning trees and shortest-path algorithms   99
    3.5   Modeling   106
    3.6   Summary   137

4 Network Cost Analysis **143**

4.1 Network economics 144
4.2 A general bandwidth charging model 151
4.3 Internet charging model 163
4.4 Private network charging models 166
4.5 Integrated planning and billing tools 179
4.6 Summary 182

5 Physical Topology Design **185**

5.1 Hierarchical network design 186
5.2 Access network design 191
5.3 Backbone network design 198
5.4 Automated design tools 233
5.5 Summary 244

6 LAN and MAN Technologies **249**

6.1 Introduction 251
6.2 Ethernet/IEEE 802.3 268
6.3 High-speed Ethernet and hybrid standards 286
6.4 Token Ring/IEEE 802.5 295
6.5 FDDI/ANSI X3T9.5 309
6.6 Fibre Channel 318
6.7 Wireless LAN/IEEE 802.11 320
6.8 Summary 330

7 WAN Technology and Design **333**

7.1 Wide area network design principles 334
7.2 Encapsulation techniques 354
7.3 Access technologies 363
7.4 Backbone technologies 378
7.5 Summary 427

8 ATM Technology and Design **431**

8.1 Architecture 432
8.2 Operation 451
8.3 Interworking with ATM 467
8.4 ATM network design 484
8.5 Summary 500

9   Designing Bridged and Switched Networks   **503**

9.1   Overview of bridging and switching   504
9.2   Transparent bridging   514
9.3   Source Route Bridging (SRB)   529
9.4   Source Route Transparent Bridging (SRT)   536
9.5   Translation bridging   539
9.6   Encapsulation/tunnel bridging   546
9.7   Virtual LANs (VLANs)   547
9.8   Summary   560

Appendix A: UDP and TCP Port Numbers   **563**

Appendix B: Mathematical Review   **591**

Index   **597**

Preface

In the developed parts of the world virtually all information-based organizations are underpinned by some form of communications infrastructure, and for many companies the communications network is intimately bound with core business operations. For large multinational companies the annual cost of running such an infrastructure may run into millions of dollars, and the unexpected cost of service outages may be equally huge. Good network design and attention to detail is fundamental to providing cost-effective and reliable data networks. It is surprising therefore that there are very few books that deal with the subject of network design from the ground up, combining the theoretical, practical, and financial issues associated with designing real networks.

Today there seem to be two broad classes of network designer: those that know much about routing and virtually nothing about topology analysis, and those who know just the opposite. Unfortunately, knowledge of both is critical in planning and implementing an efficient modern data network. Network design needs to be approached holistically, from the ground up. Networks that are deployed with very little traffic and topology analysis are destined to fail, and nearly always result in substantial and costly redesigns due to gross assumptions made during the design phase. My objective in starting this project was to unite a number of apparently disparate areas of network design, and to provide the balance of theoretical and practical information that practicing engineers would find useful in their day-to-day job. Since network design often receives very fragmented coverage, this book is an attempt to bring together those pieces so that they may be seen in context. In particular, the true cost of deploying networks, and how those costs may be optimized year to year, are often divorced from the network designer. This book is, in part, an attempt to put such issues in focus.

I started this project in an environment where the goalposts are far from static. The speed of change in information technology is simply staggering:

within the last 20 years we have seen a massive shift from large, centralized, host-centric networks to a situation where most of today's computing power resides on desktops. With processing power growing exponentially, and memory prices declining year upon year, we are now witnessing another paradigm shift toward an era of mobile personal computing. We have seen the emergence of distributed architectures and multimedia, and the explosive growth of the Internet and the World Wide Web (WWW), each forcing the development of new protocols and new applications. Network security has become a real force for change in recent years, with massive growth in the firewall market, and completely new models of secure networking, such as the Public Key Infrastructure (PKI) and Virtual Private Networks (VPNs). Businesses are now demanding quality of service guarantees and information privacy, and there is increasing emphasis on Service Level Agreements (SLAs). With overall improvements in the communications infrastructure we have also seen a significant increase in voice communications, new applications for packetized Voice Over IP (VOIP), and the unification of both text and audio messaging systems. Finally, there are radical changes afoot in the field of user interfaces, with the take-up of voice recognition, text to audio translation, and the use of biometrics.

In all areas of technology the boundaries are blurring, between local and wide area networks, data and voice, wired and wireless. All of these technologies are now being provisioned via a new breed of highly integrated hybrid devices with built-in routing, switching, bandwidth management, and security services. In a very short space of time every home will have Internet access via smart integrated digital terminals. There has already been a massive shift in the adoption of mobile wireless computing, and Internet access via a new generation of data-aware mobile phones. Over the next few years we will see the adoption of Java-enabled telephony, with high-resolution color displays, capable of running more powerful applications. This, together with the use of more intuitive user interfaces and voice recognition, will truly mobilize the face of personal computing. We can only guess what changes the next two decades will bring.

About this book

This book is written for practicing engineers and project managers involved in planning, designing, and maintaining data networks. It is also appropriate for undergraduate and graduate students who have taken basic courses in data communications. The content reflects much of my experience in the industry, having worked for several leading network manufacturers in the areas of network design, network security, network modelling, and simulation.

This book represents the first of two complementary books on network design and optimization. It covers the design process, capacity planning, performance analysis, simulation modelling, network topology, financial modelling, local and wide area network technologies, and bridged/switched network design. The book deals with network design systematically, from the ground up, preparing the designer for advanced design topics such as routing, security, quality of service, and network reliability in the second part.

Since this book is concerned primarily with large-scale network design, it focuses heavily on the IP protocol suite, rather than attempting exhaustive coverage of other protocol stacks. Because my primary focus is on the design and performance characteristics of data networks, the approach taken throughout this book is to document technologies only in sufficient depth where they are relevant; for exhaustive information the book cites numerous good references. For more information on TCP/IP many excellent books are available, including *TCP/IP Explained*, by Phil Miller, from Digital Press.

Although the book does include several chapters where numerical techniques are presented, it is not heavily mathematical. The book also makes occasional use of programming code, although the reader may skip these sections. Unfortunately, the use of design algorithms and numerical modelling is an important part of network design and is, therefore, unavoidable. Where appropriate, suitable references are provided. Appendix B provides a brief review of the main numerical techniques used throughout.

About the author

Tony Kenyon is the Chief Technical Officer of Advisor Technologies Ltd. (ATL), based in Berkshire, United Kingdom. ATL develops enterprise security management solutions for multivendor networks. He was formerly Technical Director for Europe, Middle East, and Africa at Nokia Internet Communications, and has worked in the data communications industry since 1983. Tony has designed several international communications networks, and has developed a number of modeling tools, including an award-winning graphical object-oriented network design suite. For comments to the author he can be reached at tonyk@nildram.co.uk.

Acknowledgments

I should start by acknowledging my old high school teacher, David Webster, at the Central High School for Boys in Manchester, U.K. Around 1978, David told me I should concentrate on writing longer essays if I wanted to be successful with my studies—advice that has proved invaluable many times since, and is evidenced here. For painstakingly reviewing the content and making numerous suggestions, I have Brian Hill of Xyplex to thank. For reviews and helpful suggestions on specific topics, I must thank my colleagues Philip Miller, Derin Mellor, Andrew Namboka, and Alex Challis of Nokia Internet Communications. For editing and compiling the final version of this text, I thank Dr. Paul Fortier and Mr. Gurukumar Anantharama Sarma of the University of Massachusetts Dartmouth. I thank Pam Chester and the folks at Digital Press for affording me the opportunity to bring this project to life. Last, I must thank my wife, Amita. This has been a hugely demanding project, and I have lost count of the times that I have told her that the book is "nearly finished." Fortunately for me she is gifted with enormous patience.

This book does not reflect the policy or the position of any organization I have worked for. No financial support, resources, or direction was obtained from these organizations, and the ideas and opinions presented here (rightly or wrongly) are strictly personal. I apologize in advance for any errors I have made which may offend or mislead; no doubt I will have the opportunity to fix them in the next edition. Please forward any constructive input to my e-mail address or Digital Press.

A Review of the Basics

Designing an efficient, cost-effective network that meets or exceeds the requirements is no easy matter. Today's equipment and technologies are becoming increasingly diverse and have the alarming property of becoming "old technology" almost as soon as they are installed. Mistakes can be, and often are, expensive. This chapter provides some basic definitions and introduces the concepts of a design process, the intention of which is to ensure that the design develops in a structured way, with all relevant data exposed during the process so that there are no late surprises. This chapter also introduces the basic hardware and software building blocks used in the construction of modern network designs.

1.1 Network design and performance

No two people agree exactly on what network design is. Network design is a generic and often subjective term that covers a whole range of skills and tasks, from the logical design elements (such as network protocols, addressing, subnetting), down to the physical design elements (such as physical topology, traffic modeling, circuit infrastructure). This book attempts to provide a holistic approach to network design by covering the essential elements from ground up. Whatever your particular perspective, by the end of this book you will get an appreciation of the subject as a whole, at this point in time.

1.1.1 Elements of good network design

The acid test of a good network design is whether it actually works. The fact is that many organizations today rely on networks that either perform suboptimally or cost more than they should, possibly due to poor design or implementation. These networks can soldier on for years, soaking up more and more resources and money. The accumulated costs can be frightening in a badly designed international network, and it is still not unusual for a preferred supplier to be thrown out of an account after installation, simply because the proposed design just does not work, or the equipment doesn't do what it was supposed to. During the mid 1990s, for example, dial-up ISDN technology began to be deployed widely in Europe. Horror stories soon emerged of six-figure quarterly ISDN bills, testament to a number of bad design or poor implementation choices.

A good network design should have the following characteristics:

- It should deliver the services requested by its users.

- It should deliver acceptable throughput and response times.

- It should be within budget and should maximize cost efficiencies.

- It should be reliable.

- It should be expandable without requiring a major redesign.

- It should be manageable and maintainable by support staff.

- It should be well documented.

Above all, a network must meet the application and business expectations of the users; otherwise, it has simply failed to deliver. With today's increasing shortage of skilled engineers it is also vital that even a well-designed network is modular, consistent, and well documented. It's easy to fall afoul of the temptation to design the most elegant network on the planet, only to be brought down to earth when sitting with the support staff trying to explain an overly complex design. If the staff members running the network do not understand your design, you can bet that they will change it sooner or later into a form that they do understand. The golden rule, therefore, is: Keep it simple.

1.1.2   Network performance

Ask a sample of network engineers what they mean by performance, and you are likely to get a range of responses, from abstract queuing theory to explanations of piggybacking in TCP. Ask users about performance, and they will often provide responses such as everything is running too slow today or my machine keeps hanging. Your job is to understand the complexities of performance analysis, and then use that knowledge to build a network that satisfies its users.

In an environment where there is little technical competence it may be important to first educate the users about what they can reasonably expect from the network before moving ahead too quickly. For users who were previously using standalone applications and directly connected printers, installing a fast new network is generally not going to speed things up, often leading to major misconceptions.

With any network design we must focus on what typically concerns the organization most: the performance of the applications and services accessed by its workers and its clients. For network users the most important performance characteristics are those directly experienced, such as response time and delay. However, there are many other aspects of performance, which may directly impact profitability of productivity for the business or organization as a whole. Characterizing performance, particularly on a large heterogeneous internetwork, is a complicated task that requires expertise, since there are many complex interdependencies between systems, protocols, queues, and application software. In this book we examine some of the techniques used to characterize performance and some of the ways in which performance can be optimized.

1.2   An overview of the design process

1.2.1   The life cycle of a design

Network designs are predominantly living entities; they rarely stay the same. Even from inception to initial implementation, a design will often change. The point at which a network is installed often marks the start of a new phase of design rather than the end of the process. Consequently, it is useful to think of network design as a cyclic process, as illustrated in Figure 1.1.

Before the design process can begin, a clear set of requirements should be established to capture what the organization and its users expect from the network and the services to be offered. The requirements should also clearly identify what the budget is and any other constraints that impact the design. The network design process then naturally follows a set sequence:

- Information gathering
- Planning
- Implementation
- Acceptance
- Expansion and modification

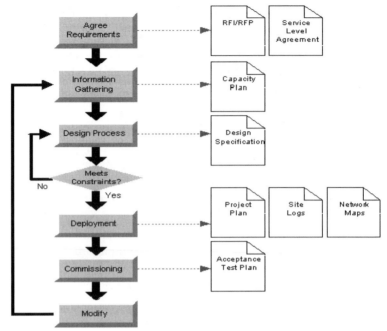

Figure 1.1
Network design process.

Just as with any living organism, networks have a limited life span, becoming increasingly unreliable, inflexible, and unable to cope with the pressures placed on them. Advances in network technology and increases in overall traffic levels render most technology obsolete within a few short years. The lifetime of a network may be extended with the aid of transplants to vital organs (upgrading routers, links, etc.); however, there generally comes a point where the network design itself requires a major overhaul, often resulting in total replacement (at which point the cycle starts over).

Since networks are becoming increasingly inseparable from the organizations, a dynamic organization can put severe strain on a design, forcing radical changes over a much shorter time than a more stable organization. As companies expand and diverge, merge with other companies, and change their product focus and distribution methods, so too must the network.

1.2.2   Establishing requirements

To design and implement any new network or enhance an existing network, there must be two things: a requirement and a budget. At the early stages both may be loosely defined. Large organizations that are very technology aware often have a rolling process of requirements and budgetary planning.

Organizations that are less technically competent may have only the wish to improve matters and a willingness to spend money on it. The job of the network designer is to cooperate with others in translating these wishes into a set of specific requirements, so that expenditure can be justified and appropriate technical choices can be made.

Engaging end users

Network engineering staff and end users may interact only when there is a serious problem. Then the poor engineer often feels outnumbered in a sea of angry users who are not the slightest bit interested in why the ISP router is down, they just expect service. On the other hand, users may have waited for hours to see any sign of progress, while business is being lost, commissions are being eroded, and angry customers are ringing in with complaints.

The design phase of any new network project is, however, a time for engaging user groups. It is important that the real users of the network and its services be involved from the start. Users are best placed to give feedback on how the applications should perform. Without user input you risk making fundamental errors with your design assumptions. It is important that expectations are clearly defined, understood, and realistic.

Translating the requirements

Most reasonably sized networks today are subject to a fairly formal process of specification. Requirements should ideally be specified from the top down. We start with the business objectives, and then refine these objectives by tighter specifications of what the business expects, what users expect, and any constraints that will be imposed on the designer. It will become apparent that the requirement itself will be expressed in very different ways at different levels within the customer organization. At the board level, the requirement may simply be to increase adoption of client/server technology over the next three years to gain competitive advantage and achieve best practice.

While this may be the ultimate truth for a senior executive, it means very little to an engineer. The finance director may have his or her own requirement: to sustain a 35 percent return on investment while minimizing capital expenditure within this fiscal year.

We may have lost a few more engineers by this point. Joking aside, these are genuine requirements and must be translated and formulated into a set of specific requirements, aligned with the application strategy, user expansion plans, site geography, and available technology.

Phasing the requirements

There is always a danger of overspecifying requirements too early, to the point where the requirements are simply unachievable. This is a particular problem if the authors of the requirements have very little knowledge of the networking technology. For example, a customer might express a requirement as follows: It is mandatory that all routers supplied should be supported and upgraded for the next ten years to incorporate new standards-based features and protocols.

Now, if you were investing serious money on this project, this might seem perfectly reasonable, but to most suppliers it appears impossible, or at least highly unattractive, for a number of reasons, as follows:

- The life cycle of such a device may be in reality no longer than five years and more likely three.

- Nobody knows for certain what protocols will emerge in ten years or what resources they will require. In any case it is likely that a future infrastructure will require more CPU and memory than the device offers today.

- The investment in maintaining such a device on the price list is highly questionable. It is not at all certain that even routers (as we know them) will be available in ten years (the router may become a single chip function or may be finally ousted altogether in favor of a better switching technology).

- With the ever-increasing demands made by applications, the traffic requirements in ten years are liable to make this device seem like a toy. Some of today's Personal Digital Assistants (PDAs) have more computing power than early mainframes.

For this reason requirements specification is generally a multistage process, starting with a fairly loose sense of direction and then progressively tightening the requirements as ideas firm up. It soon becomes apparent what is reasonable and what is achievable. These requirements can include the following:

- Request for Information—An initial Request for Information (RFI) document is often generated first. The aim of this document is to solicit responses from all likely candidates so that an initial shortlist can be created of those best able to provide a complete solution and those interested in proceeding. General architectural models may be produced; an overview of product availability is provided, together with information on the supplier's stability and suitability for the project.

- Request for Proposals—Once an initial shortlist of interested parties has been drawn up, the customer may issue a Request for Proposals (RFP) document to those suppliers. The recipients are expected to provide an initial outline design with budgetary costs and are expected to have addressed a number of questions posed by the customer. From the responses received a number of techniques are used to decide the final candidate list, including price, mandatory requirements met, scalability, level of integration, and project management.

- Detailed Requirements Specification—Once a preferred partner and perhaps one other are selected, a more rigorous Requirements Specification, which will include a more expansive and more detailed list of questions, may be produced. In response to this document suppliers are expected to provide a comprehensive design, together with committed costs and draft equipment lists. There will be product demonstrations closely aligned with project functionality. Beyond this phase the customer will have selected the final supplier.

Once a final supplier is chosen, this supplier will be invited to finalize design and to produce final equipment lists and finished schematics for every location. There may be some adjustment of pricing based on functionality. For large networks the supplier is normally responsible for the entire project plan, specifying exactly how and when various components will be installed and tested. Different organizations will approach the process in various ways.

Designing the requirements

The process of developing and gauging responses to requirements specifications is typically done either within the customer organization or between the customer and some third party (e.g., a consultancy group or in some cases even a potential supplier). Large, well-funded organizations tend to employ their own full-time design experts, who are capable of fulfilling this role. For some organizations with financial resources, there are many highly skilled consultancy groups able to take on the task as a contract project. For organizations that have neither the skills nor sufficient budget for external consultancy, often the answer is to pick the safest vendor and use its internal design skills as part of the sales offering. In the latter scenario the customer is really at the mercy of the supplier, and it usually pays to get at least some independent advice during the process as a final sanity check, especially if you are not dealing one of the major suppliers. As we will discuss many times in this book, if the network design is suboptimal, the customer will end up paying for it over and over again.

Requirements should be structured in such a way that associated topics are grouped by function (e.g., network management, routing, cabling, etc.). Individual requirements should be concise and should have a reference number. Once you have a complete set of requirements, go through each item and prioritize, according to the following criteria:

- [M]—Mandatory: Must have. Failure to do so will eliminate the supplier from participating further.

- [H]—Highly desirable: Important but not absolutely essential. Would be very advantageous.

- [D]—Desirable: Not essential but would be nice to have.

- [N]—Note: Not a requirement, but information that the supplier should take note of and acknowledge.

For example:

```
Section 4. Enterprise Routing Requirements

The following requirements are applicable to the enterprise
class router described in section 3.2.

4.1 [M]: The router shall support the routing protocols
RIPv1, RIPv2, and OSPF.
4.2 [H]: The router shall support the routing protocols
EIGRP.
4.3 [H]: The router OS and configuration shall be field
upgradeable via SSH.
4.4 [M]: The router shall support dual load-sharing power
supplies.
4.5 [D]: The router shall support transparent bridging.
```

Take care to ensure that all mandatory requirements are actually achievable; otherwise, you run the risk that no one will meet the basic requirement. In the shortlist stage it is likely that the responses to the highly desirable questions will strongly influence who the preferred supplier will be (assuming that the responders meet all mandatory requirements and all responses are within budget).

Assessing the requirements

In practice, the assessment phase is often part scientific and part instinctive. The process is normally a combination of assessing the true costs of deployment, some form of weighted evaluation matrix, and the much less quantifiable element of whether the customer feels comfortable with the supplier.

The true cost of the network needs to be fully explored in detail. Items for consideration include support and maintenance, depreciation, commissioning costs, project management fees, hardware and software upgrade costs, circuit bandwidth charges, ongoing consultancy charges, whether current prices are fixed against future changes in the pricelist, and so on. What may initially be the cheapest solution may be far from it, when calculated over the lifetime of the network.

In assessing the specific requirements you should create a weighted matrix (e.g., using a spreadsheet) to clarify the responses and provide a quantitative view of the various responses. A simple weighting scheme is shown in Figure 1.2. In Figure 1.2, we weight each response according to its level of compliance (100 for mandatory, 10 for highly desirable, and 1 for desirable). We take into account whether the requirement was met in full, in part, or was noncompliant, using a simple multiplier. Failed mandatory requirements are recorded. The final ranking is calculated by normalizing the final score as a percentage of the total achievable and subtracting it from 100 (i.e., $100 - [100 \times \text{score}/632]$). The supplier with the lowest rank and the highest score will be most compliant. Note that this example is purely for illustration. Superior statistical analysis techniques are widely available and recommended.

In the unfortunate event that all suppliers fail to meet all of the mandatory requirements, you may have to consider whether the requirements were really achievable or whether to reissue the document to a wider set of

Supplier ID: KWPK Micronetworks Associates

Ref	Pri	Description	Status	Mfail	Weight	Mult	Score
1.1	M	Supplier must have approvals for shipping to Europe and USA	FULL	0	100	1.0	**100**
2.1	M	Routers must support RIP, OSPF and BGPv4	FULL	0	100	1.0	**100**
2.1	H	Router must support OSPF unnumbered links	FULL	0	10	1.0	**10**
2.2.1	M	Router must support Ethernet, ATM and Token Ring interfaces	PART	1	100	0.5	**50**
2.2.2	H	Router must support Load balancing over serial links	NONE	0	10	0.0	**0**
3.1	M	PPP and HDLC are required for wide area encapsulation	PART	1	100	0.5	**50**
3.2	M	Modem dialback to be supported for secure remote configuration	FULL	0	100	1.0	**100**
3.2	H	Support for software update mechanisms across the network	FULL	0	10	1.0	**10**
4.1	D	Statistics mainained on routing and spanning tree convergences	FULL	0	1	1.0	**1**
4.2	D	An audit trail must be supported	FULL	0	1	1.0	**1**
5.1	M	Management system must support multi-users plus access levels	FULL	0	100	1.0	**100**
		TOTAL SCORES		2	632	9	**522**
		RANK					**17**

Figure 1.2   *Sample requirements analysis.*

potential suppliers. Either way, with this approach you will be able to measure the best responses systematically.

1.2.3   Information gathering

Once you are clear about the business and user requirements, you must initiate research to characterize the behavior of the users and applications and where they are to be located. Ideally we want to build a database of information, such as the following:

- Where are users to be located, how many per location, which services will they access, and how often?

- How many sites are involved in the new network, and where are they?

- Are there any constraints regarding how traffic can flow between sites (e.g., security, political, or cost-related)?

- Where are the main servers and services located? Do they need to be centralized, distributed, or mixed?

- How much traffic is likely over the key backbone and wide area links?

- What protocols are required to support the applications and services? Should they be routed, bridged, or switched? Is there any requirement for gateway style translation?

- Is there any legacy equipment (routers, hubs, etc.) that must be retained and integrated into the new design?

- Are there any proprietary protocols or legacy services that must be integrated (e.g., SNA or old Wang hosts)?

- Are there any specific availability requirements for the network or its systems (e.g., backup links between key sites, mirrored server sites, online trading floors, etc.)?

- Are there any specific security requirements for the network or its systems?

- What changes in user, application, or service populations are predicted over the next three to five years, and how is the network expected to meet these demands?

- What are the budgetary constraints, by location?

Depending upon whether this is a new design or a modified existing design, you will face different challenges when attempting to collate some of this information, as follows:

- Greenfield site—Installing a brand new network without the constraints of existing infrastructure is often seen as the ideal scenario, but it does have its drawbacks. You may find it hard to determine what the real network loads and stresses are. In order to get these data you are going to have to talk to the potential suppliers, get detailed specifications of the applications and the underlying protocols, and perform some form of simulation or pilot network to gauge the real performance issues and how they will scale.

- Existing site—With an existing site you will have different problems to deal with. Often your access to the site may be limited to unsociable hours, and any testing on a live network may be heavily restricted. On the positive side you may already be aware of the potential bottlenecks, and perhaps some of the services are already in place and can be investigated by putting traffic analyzers onto the network.

It will quickly become clear which information presented here is most important and what level of detail is required. In Chapter 2, we will work through a process of systematically refining and presenting this information to create a formal database called the capacity plan.

1.2.4   Planning

By this stage there should be a database of all relevant information concerning users, services, hosts, and how those entities interwork. The process typically starts with a rough conceptual design, often using a whiteboard. Firm decisions made at this stage generally result in a design that is far from optimal. The conceptual design is repeatedly analyzed and refined until it begins to make sense. Choices in local and wide area technologies, different equipment vendors, and possibly different application vendors can completely change the direction of the design.

Technology choices may be directed by pragmatic issues, such as the geographic relationships between sites, services, and users or the part of the world where the network is to be deployed (e.g., a developing country may have only a single service provider offering low bandwidth leased lines). Such factors often simplify the design, and, although the results are not optimal, such compromises are common in large-scale international network design.

Through an iterative process involving brainstorming sessions, design reviews, and possibly the use of modeling tools, a detailed design will eventually emerge that meets most of the performance and cost constraints and delivers the expected service levels outlined by the requirements specification. This is referred to as the final design (though it tends to be the first draft of the real final design).

The design specification

A network design is just a bunch of ideas in somebody's head unless there is detailed documentation describing that design. The network design specification not only communicates that design, but it also acts as a benchmark for changes made to the design. Design choices made in the final design may lead to changing the design itself. Appropriate justification must be provided in the documentation.

Failure to record the change history (changes in commissioning stages) can have serious consequences for the maintenance staff later on. The problem is that networks change and so do the people designing and maintaining them. Strong project management can help. All key personnel should be updated with current network diagrams and configuration data, and these data should be archived and easily retrievable. An accurate network design specification must be maintained. The design should ideally be presented as a top-down series of schematics, with accompanying documentation explaining the significant overall design concepts and individual configuration aspects. Armed with a network design specification, we can now begin to implement the technology.

1.2.5   Implementation

Successful implementation of the design depends upon many factors. At the outset it is vital that there be a clear project plan identifying all key activities, who will perform them, and when they will take place. Any new technology should be introduced in a phased approach, as follows:

- Educate: Start with a demonstration and presentation to senior representatives of the users. Explain what will happen, when. Ensure that access to floor areas and sites is cleared with the appropriate management team.

- Pilot test: Install a pilot installation for a small group of users, prepared for possible bugs and glitches. For some projects this may be a luxury, but on large projects this is essential to avoid nasty surprises.

- Acceptance: Perform a comprehensive acceptance test to prove that the network performs as intended, and ensure that all outstanding items are resolved. It should be used as a benchmark for subsequent optimizations.

- Deployment: Install the production network. As the network goes live, ensure that you have plenty of support around and make sure that you can invoke fallback plans in the event of critical problems.

Feedback must be taken at each level and resolved either by making explicit changes or by explaining what the limitations are and agreeing on possible future enhancements. It is important to get consent from all interested parties in between phases.

1.3   Building block 1: The framework

The framework for internetworking is based on a set of standards, such as the IAB/IETF, IEEE, ANSI, and ITU; however, the model most often used is the Open Systems Interconnection (OSI) reference model. It presents an abstract seven-layer architecture and should not be confused with the OSI protocol suite; in real-world internetwork designs the TCP/IP protocol suite dominates the market.

1.3.1   Standards organizations

Several key organizations have contributed to internetworking standards, developing formal specifications for today's large-scale, heterogeneous, multivendor internetworks. These include the following:

- International Organization for Standardization (ISO)—ISO is a voluntary body, responsible for a wide range of standards, including many that are relevant to networking. Their best-known contribution is the development of the ISO OSI reference model and the OSI protocol suite.

- Internet Advisory Board (IAB)—IAB is a group of internetwork researchers who discuss Internet-related issues and set Internet policies through decisions and task forces. The IAB coordinates a huge number of Request for Comments (RFC) documents, which are broadly divided into informational, experimental, proposed, drafts, and full standards. Some of the best-known standards include protocols in the TCP/IP suite (e.g., TCP, IP, ICMP, ARP, RIP, OSPF, and SNMP).

- Institute of Electrical and Electronics Engineers (IEEE)—IEEE is a professional organization that defines networking and other standards. It is made up of representatives primarily from the user and equipment manufacturing communities. The IEEE is perhaps best known for the widely used LAN standards, such as IEEE 802.3 and IEEE 802.5.

- American National Standards Institute (ANSI)—ANSI (a member of the ISO) is the coordinating body for voluntary standards groups in the United States. ANSI has developed several communications standards, including the Fiber Distributed Data Interface (FDDI). ANSI attempts to adopt ISO standards, but its specifications may differ to reflect North American requirements.

- Electronic Industries Association (EIA)—EIA is hardware oriented and specifies electrical transmission standards, including those used in networking. The EIA developed the widely used EIA/TIA-232 standard (formerly referred to as RS-232 and first issued in 1962).

- International Telecommunications Union, Telecommunication Standardization Sector (ITU-T)—The ITU-T was formerly called the International Telephone and Telegraph Consultative Committee (CCITT). The ITU-T is now an international organization, made up mainly of the major carriers, that develops communication standards (perhaps the best known is X.25). See reference [1].

- European Computer Manufacturers Association (ECMA)—ECMA is not a trade association as the name might imply; it is a noncommercial organization dedicated to the development of standards applicable for computer and communications technology. ECMA was formed in 1961 and now includes all European computer manufacturers. It works closely with ISO and the ITU-T.

- National Bureau of Standard (NBS)—NBS is another very active international standards committee. The NBS has been active in the upper layers of the OSI standards, including the specification of the Government OSI stack, GOSIP. The NBS also produces the Federal Information Processing Standards (FIPS).

1.3.2   ISO OSI Reference Model

The OSI reference model emerged from early work done by the ISO standards group. The ISO OSI model comprises seven layers, as shown in Figure 1.3. It was originally intended as the benchmark for the international standardization of computer network protocols. It is said to be an open systems architecture, because it enables interworking between different systems over well-defined interfaces and protocols.

Layer 7	Application
Layer 6	Presentation
Layer 5	Session
Layer 4	Transport
Layer 3	Network
Layer 2	Data Link
Layer 1	Physical

Figure 1.3
The ISO OSI reference model.

Each OSI layer represents a discrete function (such as point-to-point connectivity, end-to-end connectivity, data presentation, etc.). However, layers do not necessarily equate to a single protocol; they may comprise a number of protocols. The following is a brief summary of each layer:

- Application Layer—provides a set of services that act as the interface between the user application (such as file transfer, remote terminal access, or e-mail) and the communications protocol stack. The Application Layer communicates with a peer application protocol that resides on a remote system. In true OSI speak the user application sits above layer 7. In the TCP/IP world user applications sit inside this layer, since many IP-based applications (Telnet, FTP, SMTP, etc.) have session, presentation, and application services integrated.

- Presentation Layer—concerned mainly with data manipulation, rather than communications functions. This layer determines how data are to be represented and formatted. When data are being transmitted to it, the Presentation Layer reformats and/or compresses these data before passing them on to the Session Layer.

- Session Layer—manages the process-to-process communication sessions between hosts. It's responsible for establishing and terminating connections between cooperating applications.

- Transport Layer—performs end-to-end error detection and correction and guarantees that the receiving application receives data exactly as they were sent (e.g., OSI transport classes 0–4, TCP, Novell SPX).

- Network Layer—manages network connections. It takes care of data packet routing between source and destination computers as well as network congestion (e.g., OSI IP, DoD IP, Novell IPX).

- Data Link Layer—provides reliable data delivery across the physical network (e.g., LLC 1–3, MAC-Token Ring, MAC-Ethernet, HDLC, LAPB, LAPD, LAPF, and PPP).

- Physical Layer—responsible for transmitting and receiving bits over a physical communication channel (e.g., Ethernet). It has knowledge of voltage levels and of the pin connections to the physical hardware media.

Layers are used to abstract and isolate groups of related functions, so that development and flexibility are promoted through the use of well-defined interfaces (the divide and conquer analogy). Each layer is insulated from the addressing details used by the layer below. For the purpose of this book, the most important protocol suite for internetwork design (especially large internetwork design) is TCP/IP.

1.3.3   Addressing

Addressing is an important concept in network design. In this context, we are primarily interested in Layer 2 (Data Link or MAC addresses) and Layer 3 (Network) addresses, although addresses higher up the stack are becoming more relevant for issues such as quality of service provisioning and network security. Layers 1 through 4 can be described as follows:

- Layer 1—Strictly speaking there are no physical addresses in the OSI model. However, most users associate physical addresses with the term Medium Access Control (MAC) address. Technically the MAC layer is a sublayer of the OSI Data Link Layer (Layer 2), but since these addresses are typically burned into network interface cards and other networking hardware, it is reasonable to informally refer to the MAC address as the hardware address (OSI purists can debate this ad infinitum). MAC addresses assume a flat address space, with a universally unique address for each network device. Addresses are assigned by the original manufacturer of the data communications equipment. MAC addresses have two main parts: a manufacturing (MFG) code and an organizationally unique identifier (OUI).

  - The MFG code is assigned to each vendor by the IEEE. The vendor assigns a unique identifier to each board it produces by burning it in. Users generally have no control over these addresses. Some manufacturers configure MAC addresses dynamically—for example, DEC routing protocols use dynamic MAC addresses, and hub manufacturers may use dynamic indexing for multiple interface chassis.

■ Some vendors have been assigned their own universal addresses that contain an OUI. For instance, IBM has an identifier of 0x10005A, so, for example, all IBM token-ring cards that use IBM token-ring chip sets, have the first six digits of their address begin with 0x10005A.

■ Layer 2—Data Link addresses are called LSAPs in OSI terminology (Link Layer Service Access Points), although this is simply a Layer 2 abstraction and we are generally more concerned with the hardware address of a device (MAC address). As indicated previously, LSAPs are associated with the upper sublayer of the Data Link Layer (i.e., above the MAC layer). LSAPs are typically used to identify different protocol suites running over a common link layer.

■ Layer 3—Network addresses are called NSAPs in OSI terminology (Network Service Access Points). Network addresses are usually assigned by the network administrator (either statically or via DHCP) as part of the overall network design hierarchy. Protocols such as IP, OSI, IPX, and AppleTalk all use Layer 3 addressing. Assigning different network addresses enables better control over routing information. They are usually assigned statically for important resources, such as routers, Web, file, and database servers, whereas user devices are assigned addresses dynamically for ease of administration.

■ Layer 4—Transport addresses are referred to in the OSI world as Transport Service Access Points (TSAPs). In the IP world they are called ports. These addresses have only local significance for hosts but are important in network design, since they are a way of uniquely identifying applications running over the network. By using port numbers, firewalls and routers can deny or allow specific applications, and special bandwidth preferences can be set up to meet different quality of service requirements.

Above Layer 4 there are additional service access points corresponding to each layer in the OSI stack (SSAPs, PSAPS, or equivalents). These addresses are generally of interest only to end systems, security systems, high-level switches, and gateway devices.

1.4   **Building block 2: Protocols**

This section discusses some of the key software components used as building blocks for constructing internetwork designs. The most common protocols running over networks today include Novell NetWare, AppleTalk,

DECnet Phase V, IBM SNA/LU6.2/NetBIOS, and OSI. Over the past decade (especially in the backbone environment) network implementers have largely united around a common protocol stack, based on TCP/IP. Hence, this book focuses mainly on the application of IP-based protocols and services. Specific implementation details of the IP protocol suite are discussed in [2–5].

1.4.1   A review of the IP protocol suite

Today, IP has become universally accepted as the protocol of choice for internetworking. From humble beginnings, IP's widespread adoption is widely attributed to a number of factors, including the following:

- Initial funding from the U.S. Department of Defense (DoD)

- Rapid free development of services and support by many academic institutions

- The development and public domain (PD) distribution of Berkeley UNIX (Free BSD), which included TCP/IP

- Free use of ARPANET, as an experimental WAN created by the U.S. DoD in 1969

IP continues to be successful because it is essentially simple to implement and understand, and no single vendor controls its specifications. Stable specifications and implementations have been available for many years, and practically every serious business application has been ported to run over the IP protocol suite. IP is still considered by many to be somewhat crude, with limitations such as address space limitations (described in RFC 1296 and RFC 1347), lack of security, and limited service support for upper-layer protocols and applications. The approach so far has been to fix problems and add functionality as and when required. This has led in recent years to initiatives such as IP version 6 (which takes care of the addressing problem), and IPSec (which takes care of the security problem).

1.4.2   The IP and the OSI model

The IP stack comprises a suite of protocols used to connect more computers in the world today than any other. IP was originally driven by the needs of the United States government and subsequently by a large community dominated by vendors and users. Most of the advances in IP have been made by individuals and small dynamic working groups, through the publication of Request for Comments (RFCs). IP development is therefore

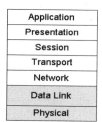

Figure 1.4
*The TCP/IP model
in context.*

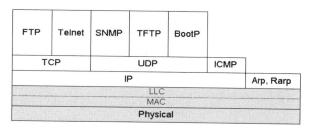

considerably streamlined and based on the ability to provide real implementations and demonstrable interoperability.

In several areas OSI protocols are significantly richer in functionality, more efficient, and generally better thought out than their TCP/IP counterparts. Unfortunately, they are also much more complex and difficult to implement and demand more resources (and were introduced at a time when networking resources were particularly scarce). OSI failed to attract vendors or customers to adopt them in the same way that IP has. Figure 1.4 shows how IP services map onto the layered architecture of OSI. Essentially, IP protocols and services start above Layer 2 and typically sit on top of a media service (such as FDDI, Ethernet, or a wide area stack such as Frame Relay). The following list summarizes five of the layers:

- Application Layer—The Application Layer consists of services to assist applications that peer over the network. In the IP world user applications typically have OSI session, presentation, and application services built in, so it is hard to differentiate between user application and services above the Transport Layer. Example applications include the file-transfer utilities (FTP and TFTP), electronic mail (SMTP), remote virtual terminals (Telnet), and smaller utilities such as the finger program.

- Transport Layer—The Transport Layer provides end-to-end data delivery. The OSI model's Session and Transport Layers fit into this layer of the TCP/IP architecture. A TCP/IP socket is an end point of communications composed of an address and a specific port on a computer. TCP provides reliable data delivery, guaranteeing that packets of data will arrive in order, with no duplicates or data corruption.

- Network Layer—The Network Layer defines the datagram and handles the routing of datagrams. A datagram contains the source address, destination address, and data, as well as other control fields. This layer's function is equivalent to that of the OSI's Network Layer.

IP is responsible for encapsulating the underlying network from the upper layers. It also handles the addressing and delivery of datagrams.

■   Data Link and Physical Layer—TCP/IP does not define the underlying network media and physical connectivity; what is running below Layer 3 is largely transparent. IP makes use of existing standards provided by such organizations as the EIA and Institute of Electrical and Electronics Engineers (IEEE), which define standards such as 802.3, Token Ring, RS232, and other electronic interfaces used in data communications.

1.4.3   The Data Link Layer

The Data Link Layer is not strictly part of the TCP/IP protocol suite; however, it is important to understand some of the key elements involved. As shown in Figure 1.4, it is divided into two sublayers: the Medium Access Control (MAC) layer lies below a Logical Link Control (LLC) layer.

MAC sublayer

The MAC sublayer addresses the requirement for upper-layer insulation from various media types. For example, in an IEEE 802.3/Ethernet LAN environment, features such as error detection, framing, collision handling, and binary backoff are handled at this level. Source and destination station addresses (sometimes called physical addresses) are also contained within the MAC header.

LLC sublayer

The LLC sublayer defines services that enable multiple higher-level protocols such as IP, IPX, XNS, or NetBIOS to share a common data link. There are three classes of LLC, depending upon the quality of service required, as follows:

■   LLC Type 1—offers a simple best-effort datagram service. There is no error control, no sequencing, no flow control, and no buffering. LLC 1 merely provides source and destination LSAPs for multiplexing and demultiplexing higher-layer protocols.

■   LLC Type 2—offers a connection-oriented service and is a superset of LLC 1. LLC 2 features sequence numbering and acknowledgments, buffering, and separate data and control frames. LLC 2 is based on HDLC, designed to run over less reliable point-to-point links.

- LLC Type 3—offers a semireliable service with fewer overheads than LLC 2. It is primarily used on Token Bus for process control applications.

For further information about the Data Link Layer, the interested reader is referred to [6].

1.4.4 The Internet Layer

The Internet Layer corresponds to Layer 3 on the OSI model. It defines the datagram and handles the routing of those datagrams. IP is also considered the building block of the Internet.

Internet Protocol (IP)

IP is a connectionless Network Layer protocol, which means that no end-to-end connection or state is required before data are transmitted (and there are no sequence and acknowledgment numbers to maintain). IP does not guarantee reliable data delivery; packets can arrive at their destination out of order, duplicated, or not at all. IP relies on higher-level protocols, such as TCP, to provide reliability and connection control.

The basic format of the IPv4 datagram is illustrated in Figure 1.5(a). Each datagram, or packet of data, has a source and destination address. Routing of data is done at the datagram level. Fragmentation is the process of breaking the packet into smaller pieces and is a responsibility of the IP layer. IP must also reassemble the packets on the receiving side so that the destination host receives the packet as it was sent.

Figure 1.5
(a) IP version 4 and (b) IP version 6 message formats.

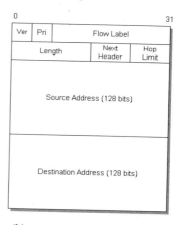

(a)

(b)

A new version of IP is currently being introduced (IP version 6, or IPv6). This version extends the addressing fields of IP and also changes the way Type of Service (ToS) is implemented to assist with Quality of Service (QoS) requirements (see Figure 1.5[b]). For complete details the interested reader is referred to [3, 5].

Address Resolution Protocol (ARP)

Because of the layering of the protocol stack, Physical Layer entities are insulated from Network Layer entities. This means that physical network hardware (such as the Ethernet adapter card in your PC) does not understand how to reach another network-attached system using the remote system's IP addresses, at least not without assistance.

The Address Resolution Protocol (ARP) is used to create a dynamic map of the IP addresses associated with specific physical addresses used by network hardware. ARP operates by broadcasting a message onto the local network, asking for the owner of a certain IP address to respond with its hardware (MAC) address. If the host with the designated IP address is listening, it returns a message to the source, listing its physical MAC address. All other systems that receive the broadcast ignore it. Once the correct addressing details are received, they can be stored locally in an ARP cache, so that future messages can be sent without having to requery the network. Note that ARP operates within a broadcast domain, since broadcasts are not forwarded by routers (at least not by default) [3, 5].

Internet Control Message Protocol (ICMP)

The Internet Control Message Protocol (ICMP) is a low-level diagnostic protocol used primarily by the network to report failures or assist in resolving failures. ICMP runs over IP and is an integral part of IP operations. ICMP must therefore be implemented by every IP-enabled system. ICMP is widely used to perform flow control, error reporting, routing manipulation, and other key maintenance functions. Network engineers make extensive use of the ping utility, which uses ICMP's echo feature to probe remote IP systems for reachability and response times. A successful response from ping indicates that network routing is operational between the two nodes and that the remote node is alive [3, 5].

1.4.5 The Transport Layer

IP is responsible for getting datagrams from system to system. The Transport Layer is responsible for delivering those data to the appropriate program or process on the destination computer. The two most important protocols in the Transport Layer related to IP are User Datagram Protocol (UDP) and Transmission Control Protocol (TCP). UDP provides unreliable connectionless datagram delivery; TCP provides a reliable connection-oriented delivery service with end-to-end error detection and correction. To facilitate the delivery of data to the appropriate program on the host computer, the concept of a port is used. In TCP version 4 a port is a 16-bit number that identifies an end point for communication within a program. An IP address and port combination taken together uniquely identify a network connection into a process (the socket paradigm developed by the University of California at Berkeley makes more intuitive the use of IP addresses and ports).

Services built on top of UDP or TCP typically listen on well-known ports. These are special reserved ports, which are publicly known and enable clients to access common services on servers without having to interrogate some form of directory service beforehand. For example, clients wishing to connect to a server using the Telnet service simply use the destination port 23.

User Datagram Protocol (UDP)

The User Datagram Protocol (UDP) allows data to be transferred over the network with a minimum of overhead. UDP provides unreliable data delivery; data may be lost or duplicated or arrive out of order. UDP is therefore suitable for applications that either do not require a connection state or cannot guarantee it (such as SNMP). UDP is also very efficient for transaction-oriented applications, when error-handling code resides within the application. It may also be used for applications such as IP multicasting. Figure 1.6 shows the simple format of a UDP header. The header contains a 16-bit source and destination port [3, 5].

Transmission Control Protocol (TCP)

Transmission Control Protocol (TCP) is a reliable byte-oriented, connection-oriented transport protocol, which enables data to be delivered in the order they were sent, and intact. TCP is connection oriented because the two entities communicating must first perform a handshake before data

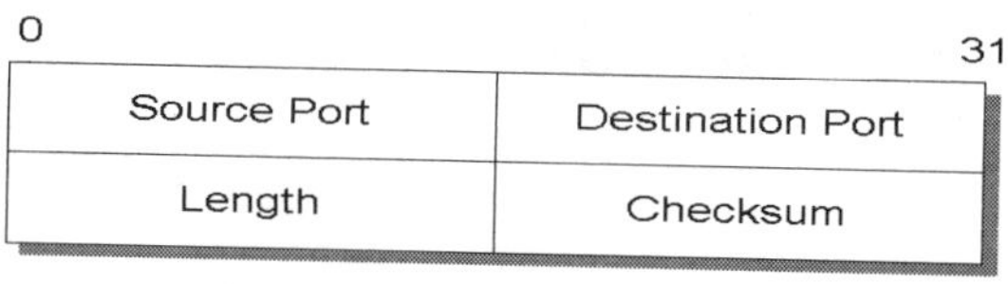

Figure 1.6
UDP header format.

Source Port	Destination Port
Length	Checksum

(0 ... 31)

Figure 1.7
TCP message
format.

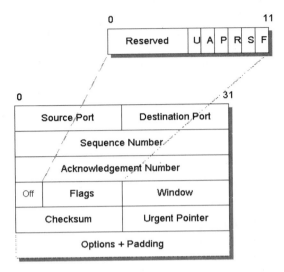

transmission can begin, and the connection state is maintained until explicitly terminated or timed out. The handshake phase is used by the transmitter to establish whether or not the receiver is able to accept data. The flag fields, illustrated in Figure 1.7, are key to connection establishment and release. A connection is initiated with a SYN (S) bit set, responded to with the SYN and ACK (A) bits set, and completed with an ACK bit—hence, the term three-way handshake. Connection release is achieved in the same way, except that the FIN (F) bit is used instead of SYN.

Figure 1.7 shows the format of a TCP header. The header contains a 16-bit source and destination port (as in UDP); however, the header also includes sequence and acknowledgment fields (to assure packet ordering and ensure that dropped packets are identified). Reliable delivery is implemented through a combination of positive acknowledgments (acks) and retransmission timeouts. TCP also includes a checksum with each packet transmitted. On reception, a checksum is generated and compared with the checksum sent in the packet header. If the checksums do not match, the receiver does not acknowledge the packet and the transmitter automatically retransmits the packet. TCP is an end-to-end protocol; therefore, the sender relies on feedback from the receiver to implement congestion control and flow control [3, 5].

1.4.6   TCP/IP applications

TCP is used where a reliable stream delivery is required, especially if an application needs to run efficiently over long-haul circuits. UDP is best for datagram services, such as simple best-effort polling applications (SNMP) or multicast distribution from a news or trading system. If you need more reliability with UDP, then this must be built into the application running over UDP. UDP is also useful for applications requiring efficiency over fast networks with low latency. The following is a brief description of network applications supported over these transport systems.

- Telnet is a widely used virtual terminal protocol, which allows users on a local host to remotely access another host as if they were locally attached. Telnet runs over TCP and is typically invoked by the command-line interface of the host operating system. For example, on the command line the user could type telnet mitch and receive a login prompt from the computer called mitch (alternatively the user could type telnet 193.125.66.2 if the IP address of the remote host is known). Implementations of Telnet are available on many operating systems and interoperability is normally taken for granted. For instance, a Telnet client may be running on a DEC VAX/VMS and a Telnet server on BSD UNIX.

- File Transfer Protocol (FTP) runs over TCP and is widely used. The basic operation and appearance are similar to Telnet but with additional commands to move around directories and send or receive files. The user must be identified to the server with a user ID and a password before any data transfer can proceed.

- Trivial File Transfer Protocol (TFTP) is a file transfer application implemented over the Internet UDP layer. It is a disk-to-disk data transfer, as opposed to, for example, the VM SENDFILE command, a function that is considered in the TCP/IP world as a mailing function, where you send out data to a mailbox (or reader in the case of VM). TFTP can only read/write a file to/from a server and, therefore, is primarily used to transfer files among personal computers. TFTP allows files to be sent and received but does not provide any password protection (or user authentication) or directory capability. TFTP was designed to be small enough to reside in ROM and is widely used in conjunction with BOOTP to download operating code and configuration data required to boot a diskless workstation or thin client.

- Remote Execution Protocol (REXEC) is a protocol that allows users to issue remote commands to a destination host implementing the REXEC server. The server performs an automatic login on a local machine to run the command. It is important to note that the command issued cannot be an interactive one; it can only be a batch process with a string output. For remote login to interactive facilities, Telnet should be used.

■ Remote Procedure Call (RPC) is an API for developing distributed applications, allowing them to call subroutines that are executed at a remote host. It is, therefore, an easy and popular paradigm for implementing the client/server model of distributed computing. A request is sent to a remote system (RPC server) to execute a designated procedure, using arguments supplied, and the result returned to the caller (RPC client). There are many variations and subtleties, resulting in a variety of different RPC protocols.

■ Remote shell ("r" series commands) is a family of remote UNIX commands. These include the remote copy command, rcp; the remote shell command, rsh; the remote who command, rwho; and others. These commands are designed to work between trusted UNIX hosts, since little consideration is given to security. They are, however, convenient and easy to use.

■ Network File System (NFS) was developed by Sun Microsystems and uses Remote Procedure Calls (RPCs) to provide a distributed file system. The NFS client enables all applications and commands to use the NFS mounted disk as if it were a local disk. NFS runs over UDP and is useful for mounting UNIX file systems on multiple computers; it allows authorized users to readily access files located on remote systems.

■ Simple Mail Transfer Protocol (SMTP) provides a store-and-forward service for electronic mail messages (see [7] for details of these messages). Mail is sent from the local mail application (e.g., a Netscape mail client) to an SMTP server application running on a mail server (e.g., Microsoft Exchange mail server). The server stores the mail until successfully transmitted. In an Internet environment, mail is typically handled by a number of intermediate relay agents, starting at the Internet Service Provider (ISP).

■ Domain Name System (DNS) provides a dynamic mapping service between host names and network addresses and is used extensively in the Internet.

■ Simple Network Management Protocol (SNMP) is the de facto network management protocol for TCP/IP-based internetworks. SNMP typically runs over UDP and is used to communicate management information between a network management system (NMS) and network management agents running on remote network devices. The

NMS may modify (set) or request (get) information from the Management Information Base (MIB) stored on each network device. Network devices can send alerts (traps) asynchronously to inform management applications about anomalous or serious events.

■ The X Windows system is a popular windowing system developed by Project Athena at the Massachusetts Institute of Technology (MIT) and is implemented on a number of workstations. The X Windows system uses the X Windows protocol on TCP to display graphical windows on a workstation bitmapped display. X Windows provides a powerful environment for designing the client user interface. It provides simultaneous views of local or remote processes and allows the application to run independently of terminal technology. For example, X Windows can run on OS/2, Windows, DOS, and X Windows terminals.

For further information about TCP/IP and its applications refer to [3, 5]. For detailed internal protocol information about TCP/IP and key applications refer to [4].

1.5   Building block 3: Hardware

In this section, we briefly explore some of the key hardware devices you will encounter when designing networks. In subsequent chapters we will learn how best to use these devices in real network designs. In order to place these devices in context, it is useful to position them using the ISO OSI seven-layer model, as shown in Figure 1.8.

Since the mid 1980s, we have seen a gradual shift in the presentation of networked devices from largely discrete units to highly integrated devices with many hybrid functions (such as multimedia hubs with repeater, bridge, and multiprotocol router interface cards). This is largely the result of functionality becoming a commodity, a general trend toward increased

Figure 1.8
Network devices in context.

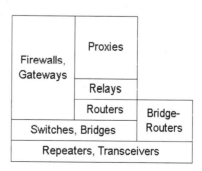

Figure 1.9
*Simplified network
design illustrating
the typical locations
for key hardware
devices.*

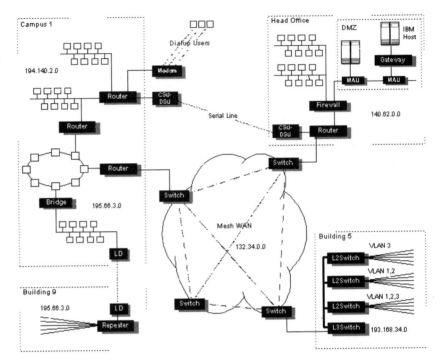

miniaturization, and the need to improve functionality to remain competitive. Scalability, convergence, and traffic optimization are now key driving forces behind today's large-scale network designs. Figure 1.9 is a somewhat simplified network design illustrating where you would typically expect to find these devices in a real network today. Figure 1.9 shows discrete devices, although it is common to see much of the functionality integrated into a single device. The Head Office site uses a firewall and offers a Demilitarized Zone (DMZ) for shared hosts at lower security levels. A gateway is used to convert IBM SNA into TCP/IP protocol for wide area transport. Campus 1 has a number of local area networks (LANs), segregated either via repeaters (LAN extension) or bridges and routers (traffic segregation). Line drivers (LD) are used to extend the campus to a remote office in Building 9. Building 5 is a multistory building with Layer 2 and Layer 3 switches to provide Virtual LAN (VLAN) traffic domains.

1.5.1   Media Attachment Units (MAUs)

MAUs, or transceivers, provide the means of encoding data into purely electrical or light signals ready for transmission onto the physical media. An MAU is responsible for decoding electrical or light signals and converting them back into data for receiving stations. All devices attached to a network will typically have either a built-in transceiver interface (such as an onboard 10 Base T interface provided on a PC network adapter) or will provide a standard AUI interface, which can be mated to a discrete transceiver via a drop cable. MAUs come in various guises, depending on the media technology and the media access control technology (e.g., Token Ring, Ethernet, etc.). MAUs provide a physical connection to LANs and protect against misuse of the LAN.

1.5.2   Repeaters

Repeaters are used to extend LAN segments, either due to the standard distance limitations on the length of a segment or to expand a network because the number of devices attached to a segment is at the recommended limit (e.g., four repeater hops for CSMA/CD). There are various types of repeaters, ranging from single port unmanaged units to multiport devices with full network management support. Repeaters may present a range of interfaces and physical connectors; typical examples are as follows:

- AUI via D type connectors

- 10 Base 2, via BNC connectors

- 10/100 Base T, via multiple RJ45 or bulk RS266 connectors

- 10/100 Base F, via SC, ST (bayonet), SMA (screw), or RJ45 fiber connectors

- Token Ring STP, via IBM connectors

A repeater must regenerate incoming frames to its other port(s) as a frame is received. A typical dumb repeater copies any incoming frames on any port to all other ports, so there is no traffic management capability. The standards documentation also specifies maximum acceptable delays (called bit-budget delays) between the receipt and retransmission of bits in a frame. If these delay thresholds are exceeded, then the device is considered noncompliant and may cause problems in networks where repeaters are chained off in sequence. One special type of repeater, a buffered repeater, not often seen nowadays, is really a hybrid between a bridge and a repeater. This device stores incoming frames temporarily in a memory buffer, prior to regeneration on its other port(s). They can be used in the same way as bridges to segment two or more networks where multiple nonbuffered repeaters are used in series. They also inhibit the regeneration of error frames and collision frames between segments. Repeaters are simple, reliable, and easy to install.

1.5.3   Line drivers, modems, and CSU/DSUs

Line drivers

Line drivers (limited distance modems—LDMs) are used to extend physical circuits over longer distances. They are typically used in designs where point-to-point links would exceed the maximum distance supported by the underlying media and protocols. They are a form of signal amplifier.

Modems

Modulator/Demodulators (modems) are typically used between CPU and a telephone line. This device modulates an outgoing binary bit stream onto the analog carrier, and demodulates an incoming binary bit stream from an analog carrier. Modem standards are defined by the International Telecommunications Union (ITU)

CSU/DSUs

Channel Service Unit (CSU) and Data Service Unit (DSU) functionality is often combined in a single device called a Digital Data Set (DDS). A DSU is a low-speed device used to terminate digital circuits, providing protocol translation and signal formatting. A CSU provides additional features, such as filtering, line equalization and conditioning, signal regeneration, circuit testing, and error control protocol conversion (e.g., B8ZS). Standard CSUs offer a T1/E1 circuit interface. Combined CSU/DSUs can also support Extended Super Frame (ESF) monitoring and testing, together with the ability to multiplex traffic from multiple interfaces into a single point-to-point or multidrop circuit, and some can now offer T3/E3 support via the High-Speed Serial Interface (HSSI). Some support SMDS via the Data Exchange Interface (DXI) and include functions beyond the scope of a traditional DDS (including segmentation, protocol conversion, etc.).

1.5.4   Bridges

Bridges provide Layer 2 Data Link Layer functionality and are protocol independent of Layer 3 protocols and higher. They can, therefore, transparently connect multiple 802.x-compliant networks (either locally or remotely). Bridges operate at the Data Link Layer and do not examine protocol information that occurs at the upper layers; they may forward different types of protocol traffic (e.g., DECnet, IP, or Novell IPX) between two or more networks. Bridges offer filtering and forwarding capabilities based on Layer 2 fields, which are used to create discrete traffic domains to optimize backbone efficiency. Bridges may have filters and offer some traffic management capability by associating node MAC addresses with particular interfaces and forwarding them (at the Data Link level) semi-intelligently. They are responsible for preserving topology integrity by stopping the formation of network loops by using protocols such as Spanning Tree or proprietary variants.

1.5.5   Switches

The increasing power of desktop PCs and the growth of client/server and multimedia applications have driven the need for higher-bandwidth, shared-access LANs. Consequently, network designers are replacing older repeaters and bridges in their wiring closets with intelligent LAN switches to increase network performance and protect their existing wiring investments. Switches are basically high-speed bridges, usually with a significant hardware assist to ensure low latency and high throughput. They are divided into LAN switches and ATM switches. LAN switches can reduce congestion in existing shared-media hubs while using new backbone technologies, such as Fast Ethernet and ATM. Gigabit Ethernet and ATM switches and routers offer greater backbone bandwidth required by high-throughput data services.

1.5.6   Routers

WAN operations were historically performed by hosts. However, in the early 1980s these tasks started to migrate into dedicated Layer 3 devices called routers. The first routers were single protocol only and did not offer any concurrent bridge operations. As both memory and CPU power increased and became much less expensive, more functionality was added, with routers becoming the ubiquitous general-purpose multiprotocol network tool. Routers forward traffic based on the destination Network Layer address rather than the MAC address. They form discrete broadcast domains and are commonly used to extend LANs (both locally and remotely). They typically communicate with one another, learning neighbors, routes, costs, and addresses, and select the best path routes for individual packets.

Multiprotocol bridge routers have become the preferred tool used to create large scalable internetworks. They offer effective bandwidth utilization and security advantages. Router networks are functionally more robust than those provided by bridges; they do not suffer issues such as LLC timeouts, susceptibility to broadcast storms, and poor congestion control. Routers are much more scalable and can support very large internetworks in terms of

Figure 1.10
*Architecture of a
multiprotocol
bridge router.*

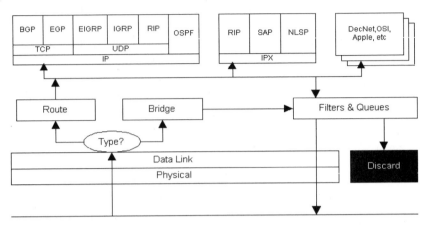

both load and addressing; they do, however, require more skilled support
and maintenance staff. (See Figure 1.10.)

1.5.7   Gateways

The term gateway is used as a generic term in networking; the only thing
that defines it is that there is some functional or protocol conversion or
translation implied. In this broad sense we will also include devices such as
transport relays, since, as far as we are concerned, these are all gateways.
Many of the older IP standards documents (RFCs) use the term gateway to
mean a router. In this book router means router, and gateway means some
form of protocol translator.

1.5.8   Comparing bridges, switches, and routers

It is useful to briefly summarize the various issues and benefits of using
these three complementary technologies in a network design.

Bridge benefits

The key advantages of using bridges in designs are as follows (note that
most of these features also apply to switches):

■ Bridges are largely plug-and-play devices that require relatively little
  expertise to install and maintain.

■ Bridges enable you to automatically isolate traffic domains, which can
  have instant benefits to overall network performance. Local network
  traffic is contained within learned interfaces.

- Bridges extend LANs and eliminate local node limitations on cable segments.

- Bridges are in the main transparent to higher-layer protocols and therefore are truly multiprotocol. This allows them to forward packets of protocols that are not routable.

- Bridges are generally transparent to end systems. Routers require end systems to be aware of the router's addresses, either by static configuration or by running a limited routing protocol.

- Bridges typically have better price/performance than routers. Since bridges have much less work to do on a packet basis, they can operate at higher speed, with much lower latency, and can be constructed using cheaper components. Router performance has, however, improved significantly in recent years.

Bridge issues

Bridge issues include the following:

- Layer 2 incompatibilities make some MAC-to-MAC implementations quite complicated.

- Interworking issues across end-to-end WAN links may require both bridges to be from the same vendor.

- Manageability becomes an issue in large networks.

- Learning table sizes can get large and overflow on very large networks, making traffic management ineffective.

- Bridges can reconfigure around topology changes, but the process is typically much slower than for routers.

- Different implementations of STA do not interwork and can cause stability problems. Underpowered Spanning Tree bridges in particular (i.e., those capable of dropping packets under load) can cause serious stability problems if STP packets are being lost. Spanning Tree configurations can also be expensive for resilient WAN configurations, and there are no standards for load sharing over multiple paths with separate bridges.

- Transparent bridges use only a subset of network topology at any one time, since only a single path can exist at any time between two points in a bridged internetwork. Routers, however, can use the best path that exists between source and destination and can readily switch paths as better ones become available.

- Bridges offer little protection against broadcast storms. In forwarding broadcast packets, bridges are only carrying out their normal function, but in doing so they can impact internetwork performance and function. This is a particular problem with remote bridges, where broadcasts have to traverse interbridge serial links.

- Bridges must drop packets that are too large for their attached networks. Routers, because they support the Network Layer, have the capability of fragmenting packets to accommodate networks with a smaller MTU.

- Bridges have no capability to provide congestion feedback to other bridges or to end nodes. This can lead to the need to discard packets, with consequent impact on end-system performance. Routers provide congestion feedback using the capabilities of the Network Layer protocol.

- Bridges cannot distinguish applications or higher-layer protocols. They cannot, therefore, prioritize application traffic or offer QoS guarantees.

Router benefits

Because routers use Layer 3 addresses, which are typically hierarchical, routers can use techniques such as address summarization to build networks that maintain performance and efficiency as they grow in size. Routers can use redundant paths and determine optimal routes even in a dynamically changing network. Routers are necessary to ensure scalability as the network grows and expands. They provide the following capabilities, which are vital in network designs:

- Broadcast and multicast control

- Broadcast segmentation

- Security

- Quality of Service (QoS)

- Multimedia support

Since routers operate at Layer 3, they can enforce a hierarchical addressing structure. Therefore, a routed network can tie a logical addressing structure to a physical infrastructure—for example, through IP subnets for each segment. Traffic flow in a bridged or switched (flat) network is, therefore, inherently different from traffic flow in a routed (hierarchical) network. Hierarchical networks offer more efficient traffic flows than flat networks because they can use the network hierarchy to determine optimal paths and contain broadcast domains. Routers offer several advantages over bridges and switches, as follows:

- Scalability—Routed networks can be much larger than bridged networks, and the traffic engineering capabilities are much more efficient.

- The Data Link Layer packet header has very little useful information to determine optimal routing; routers offer real least-cost routing. Routers are much more sensitive to protocols and traffic conditions.

- Topological reconfiguration is much faster in routers during failure conditions. For example, OSPF can reconverge around a link failure in several seconds.

- Routers contain broadcasts and so prevent the possibility of broadcast storms.

- Routing is much better suited for uniting dissimilar networks.

Router issues

Router issues include the following:

- IP network multicasting may introduce broadcast storm–like problems.

- Network headers are more complex to parse than a Data Link Layer header (checksums, variable length fields, and options); hence, more CPU and latency are required. Packet latency is generally an order of magnitude higher for routers than bridges.

- Single-protocol routers lack flexibility in multivendor environments. Routers must encapsulate if bridging is not supported.

- Routers are generally not quite so plug-and-play as bridges.

- In campus environments high-speed switches are generally preferred to routers for better performance, lower cost per port, and ease of use.

1.6   Building block 4: Physical connectivity

In this final section, we briefly discuss ways in which all of the previous elements can be physically interconnected. Over the decades this infrastructure has evolved from the centralized mainframe architecture, with terminals attached via RS.232, RS.422, or some proprietary means, through to a wide armory of local and wide area connectivity options.

1.6.1   Connectivity

Today there are many ways to interconnect network elements, each with its own particular strengths and weaknesses. The following list is far from exhaustive:

- Low-speed, direct-attached serial lines (RS.232, RS.422, etc.)
- Dial-up serial lines (analog and digital)
- Local Area Networks (Ethernet, Token Ring, AppleTalk, ATM)
- Metropolitan Area Networks (FDDI, SMDS, ATM, SONET/SDH)
- Wide Area Networks (Frame Relay, ATM, ISDN, X.25, leased lines, satellite links)
- Wireless LANs and WANs (802.11, Bluetooth, GSM, GPRS, UMTS)

There are marked differences among these technologies; some of the key differentiators are as follows:

- Packet, cell, or circuit switching
- Wired or wireless
- Distances supported
- Performance
- Bandwidth
- Quality of Service (QoS)
- Availability

1.6.2   Switching

One of the key differentiators between data network connectivity is whether the technology is circuit or packet switched. (See Figure 1.11.) There is a variety of packet-switched (ps), circuit-switched (cs), and point-to-point (pp) technologies, each applicable for the LAN, MAN, WAN, or all environments. Although most of these technologies have a range of bandwidth offerings, the choice has continued to expand vertically and horizontally over the last 40 years, beginning with simple leased circuits back in the 1960s.

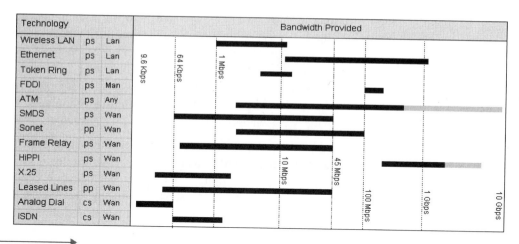

Figure 1.11 *Sample media and bandwidth choices available today.*

Circuit switching

Circuit switching has its history firmly rooted in voice networks. In the telephone network Pulse Code Modulation (PCM) is used to transmit digital information by sampling voice at 8,000 times per second (corresponding to 125 μs per sample), where each sample is encoded as an 8-bit number (note that this is where the magical 64 Kbps circuit multiplier originates: 8 × 8,000 = 64,000 bps). Unlike packet switching, this digital information does not require a protocol header and addressing information to be routed. In order to transfer data between two locations a call is made to the destination node. This call reserves a discrete set of physical resources (circuits or channels) across the network; only when these resources have been allocated can data be transferred. Routing is therefore implicit in the physical path. Although the circuit is dedicated, on large trunk connections traffic can be interleaved with other users' traffic through strict timing control (called multiplexing). Once the data transfer is complete, the call may be disconnected. Note that this model supports permanent calls if required, and either packetized data or digitized voice can be carried over circuit-switched networks. Examples of circuit-switching technologies include voice calls, analog dial-up circuits, and ISDN.

Packet switching

Packet switching covers packet, frame, or cell switching (the main difference being that cells have fixed length, and both packets and frames are variable). In packet-switched networks each packet is an autonomous unit (called a datagram), with source and destination address information placed in a header preceding each packet. When data are transferred between two nodes, each packet traverses the network following logical paths created by intermediate nodes (such as routers or switches). Packets are normally interleaved with traffic from other sources, although there is no strict timing required, and packets can travel autonomously down different routes to reach their destinations. Examples of packet-switching technologies include X.25, Frame Relay, ATM, and SMDS.

There are fundamental differences in the way the circuit- and packet-switched networks behave under load. In essence, with circuit switching, network resources are either utilized or they are not. While a circuit and associated switch ports are in use, the subscriber has exclusive access to that resource; the circuit is effectively dedicated. In heavy subscription periods it is therefore possible that all resources will be allocated (referred to as a period of oversubscription). In this event new subscribers are blocked from making new calls until circuits are freed up, even though in practice many circuits could be underutilized (i.e., any spare bandwidth is locked up). A circuit-switched network, therefore, needs to have sufficient circuit and switching equipment capacity to cope with heavy use periods in order to keep customers satisfied. This can lead to substantial resource waste and cost inefficiencies during average/low use periods, leading to a practice referred to as overprovisioning.

By contrast, with a packet-switched network, traffic is generally competing for shared circuit resources. As more users subscribe to the network, circuit utilisation increases and performance gradually degrades. As resources approach saturation, packets are simply discarded (either because they cannot be serviced or because they are aged out of queues); new users are not explicitly blocked. Overall, the network can be better optimized through traffic engineering techniques, enabling service providers to provision the network more cost-effectively. To enable different service classes to be supported, soft policy control can be imposed over the whole network (in which case best-effort packets could be discarded prior to saturation to alleviate congestion problems).

Note that these two switching techniques are applicable to both wired and wireless network solutions. We will discuss these issues in more depth later in the book.

1.6.3   Bandwidth

Providing connectivity, whether packet or circuit switched, is only half of the problem. To satisfy traffic requirements we also need to provide an appropriate level of bandwidth. The technologies we have introduced so far operate at different speeds, and the methods used to access the physical media, the quality of the media, distances traveled, and the protocols used to transfer data all have a part to play in determining the effective rate at which data can be transferred. The unique operational characteristics of these technologies often mean that different design techniques must be used in each case. The various design implications are discussed in detail later in the book.

1.7   Summary

This chapter discussed the building blocks for internetworking design and the key components of the software and protocols running over such networks. We can summarize these as follows:

- Network design is an iterative process of continuous refinement. A good network design is logical and consistent and should deliver acceptable performance and cost metrics.

- IP is the dominant protocol suite today. Its role is now central to all Internet application delivery. IP protocols and services are independent of the underlying network hardware. Each host on an IP network should have a unique IP address, which universally identifies the device. IPv4 addresses are becoming depleted. A new version of IP, IPv6, is being introduced to provide scalability for the next-generation Internet.

- Networks can be constructed from a wide variety of local and wide area media interconnected using devices such as repeaters, bridges, switches, routers, and gateways. All of these devices have different uses depending upon the scale of the network and the protocols in operation. The boundary between devices such as switches, routers, and bridges is becoming blurred. Current trends indicate that further integration and greater performance are likely as these technologies mature.

- LAN switches are best used to provide simple connectivity for local workgroups, server clusters, and LAN backbone applications. Bridges can be used for similar applications, but they are dying out, largely replaced by higher-speed switches (unless they are required for specific applications such as bridging between different media technologies). Switches and bridges are useful on sites where there is limited technical and management support available and are best suited for environments where it is undesirable or impractical to configure end systems for operation with routers. Bridges and switches may also be the only option when some of the protocols in use are nonroutable (e.g., DEC LAT or IBM SNA).

References

[1]   www.itu.ch, International Telecommunications Union (ITU) home page.

[2]   U. Black, *TCP/IP and Related Protocols* (New York: McGraw-Hill, 1992).

[3]   D. E. Comer, *Internetworking with TCP/IP*, vol. I: *Principles, Protocols, and Architecture* (Englewood Cliffs, NJ: Prentice Hall, 1991).

[4]   D. E. Comer, *Internetworking with TCP/IP* vol. II: *Design, Implementation, and Internals* (Englewood Cliffs, NJ: Prentice Hall, 1991).

[5]   P. Miller, *TCP/IP Explained* (Woburn, MA: Digital Press, 1997).

[6]   W. Stallings, *Data and Computer Communications* (Englewood Cliffs, NJ: Prentice Hall, 1997).

[7]   D. Crocker, Standard for the Format of ARPA Internet Text Messages, RFC 822, August 13, 1982.

2

Capacity Planning

This chapter discusses identifying and collating raw data required for network design and techniques for presenting those data for analysis. Capacity planning lays the foundations of the design phase; if the foundations are bad, then cracks will quickly begin to appear in the design and the costs of repair will start to spiral. It is surprising how many commercial network operators simply throw more technology and money at the problem in an effort to make that problem go away, rather than start with a solid capacity plan. In order to perform useful modeling and produce an effective design it is clearly important that the initial traffic assumptions and estimates you make are meaningful and have at least some resemblance to what is likely to happen on the network. Since these data may also be used to predict future expansion, it is even more important that these data are a reasonable reflection of reality.

Having said all this, nobody ever claimed that capacity planning was easy. In designing a new network, a considerable amount of theoretical and empirical test data must be gathered, sanity checked, and analyzed. More often than not there is already a network in place, and the proposed new design must migrate existing users and services. On a large existing internetwork with many sites and many services this task can be daunting. This task is time consuming, calls for good communication and coordination between interested groups, and requires skilled staff and sophisticated traffic capture tools. We should also remember that capacity planning is a dynamic process; it merely produces a snapshot of the network at any particular time. Therefore, data capture and analysis should be carried out periodically and whenever significant changes in the user base or application base take place. Close attention should be given to accurate capacity plans for network traffic, host utilization, and application performance, and these plans must be updated religiously and then scrutinized to see if they affect the existing design. This chapter addresses these issues by outlining a capacity management framework from which you can build.

2.1   Formal framework for capacity planning

2.1.1   Capacity planning defined

Capacity planning is primarily concerned with understanding and quantifying the following items, in order of relative priority:

- User response times

- Application behavior and performance characteristics

- Network utilization

The bottom line for any network lies ultimately with the users. In an ideal world the user should be completely unaware of the network. If the users accept the level of response offered and can access the services they require and you are within budget, then you probably have achieved a good design. As part of our capacity plan we must assess how much delay is tolerable to the current user groups for the relevant applications. Applications and services are fundamental to the business and have a direct impact on the network. As part of our capacity plan we must examine the key applications and attempt to quantify their behavior. If we are introducing new services, how do they affect existing services? Are any existing services likely to be degraded or compromised? Only when we have quantified the application and user components of the plan can we start to look at the design of our network.

2.1.2   Need for capacity planning

As described previously, without any formal capacity planning we run the risk of some serious potential business failures when a network is badly sized. These include the following:

- Network downtime—intermittent or even catastrophic failure of business-critical services

- Inability to service customers and consequent loss of customers

- Paying for equipment and services that are not necessary

- Costs and resources to fix a system already in production

- Bad press—competitive advantage used by rivals

Business-critical services might include customer response centers, trading floors, or even the entire telephone network. Network availability is becoming increasingly important as businesses rely on networking for the majority of their operations. Several current trends in the industry are making capacity planning an increasingly vital part of network design. These include the following:

- E-commerce—Web-based access to business applications and electronic mail are now a critical part of the way many organizations function. Traditional assumptions about traffic behavior have had to change with this new breed of application, and network outages and performance degradation can have a significant impact on a company's bottom line. Capacity planning is now vital to the implementation of any successful design.

- Centralized services—Early networks were largely deployed around large centralized mainframes. With the emergence of local area networks in the 1980s, there was a shift to distribute resources and computing power to the desktop. Subsequent improvements in wide area bandwidth availability, coupled with the need for tighter control, mean that the current trend is to centralize application, file, database, and Web servers into large server farms. While this makes sense from a management standpoint, this tends to concentrate traffic and leads to bottlenecks. There are also vulnerability issues when servers are all located in a single location.

- Use of Internet, intranet, and extranets—Most medium to large businesses now have Internet access. Increasingly companies are deploying intranets and extranets to disseminate corporate information and peer with suppliers. Users want rapid access to high-quality graphical information. All of this places huge burdens on carriers and service providers to provide more capacity at more competitive prices. The only way to scale this level of provisioning is via smarter traffic engineering.

- Increased remote access—Many companies are distributing more and more information to remote offices, and we already see an increasing number of dial-in users. Access to remote information and services requires greater bandwidth over wide area connections and the use of dynamic bandwidth technologies such as ISDN. Recent advances in high-bandwidth access media, such as xDSL and cable modems, mean that remote access via the Internet is becoming increasingly commonplace as these new services are rolled out.

- Multimedia applications—After several years of hype, multimedia is now starting to appear in production network environments. Streaming video and audio traffic can place huge demands on even a well-designed network. Toll bypass for long-haul packetized voice is finally here. The latest generation of bandwidth management, quality of service, multicast, and real-time protocols is finally enabling much of this technology.

- Security—Because of the need for external and remote access to corporate sites and the increasing use of e-business applications, a requirement for tighter network security has emerged. This has led in recent years to the deployment of new technologies, such as firewalls and Virtual Private Networks (VPNs). These technologies have profound effects on the traffic dynamics of the network.

- Wireless networking—The introduction of the Wireless Application Protocol (WAP), together with new mobile phone and Personal Digital Assistant (PDA) technologies, is expected to further fuel demand for Internet and intranet access over the next few years. Already we are seeing substantial mobile phone take-up in Europe and Japan (the United States lags behind mainly because of the lack of consistent digital access standards).

All of these changes mean that the traditional assumptions in networking are being overturned, and longstanding rules, such as the 80/20 split between local and remote traffic, are no longer valid. In many companies one of the most important resources is the corporate Web server, typically centrally located. For an international company this means a larger proportion of remote internal traffic. Companies are also forming new extranets with partners and cooperating organizations, again breaking the 80/20 rule. The rise of distributed application architectures such as CORBA and EJB and the increased use of technologies such as caching mean that it is becoming increasingly difficult to generalize about application traffic flows. These changes require a more rigorous approach to network design and close attention to detail.

2.1.3   Top-down framework

Capacity planning should be broken down into logical steps, each requiring the cooperation of a number of interested parties. The following process is recommended:

- Form a discussion group.

- Quantify user behavior.

- Quantify application behavior.

- Baseline the existing network.

- Make traffic projections.

- Summarize input data for the design process.

We discuss each step in detail in the following text. Once you have completed the first four steps, you will be in a position to make meaningful calculations of network capacity and application performance. You need to quantify the expected volume of traffic the network infrastructure must accommodate and the typical performance end users will experience. Then more detailed studies can be undertaken to properly model the design and to examine strategies.

Form a discussion group

The first step should be to initiate a formal discussion group, which should comprise members of the relevant parts of the organization who can actually deliver the information you need. Specifically, you will need the following representatives:

- Representatives from the user groups, who can comment on expected levels of service and potential changes or expansion of the user base.

- Representatives from the application groups, who can provide input on current application behavior and the likely changes in the way these services are to be deployed in the future.

- Representatives from the network management and design groups, who can comment on what is actually possible and provide input on any traffic modeling.

Without this forum, the capacity planning process is likely to be flawed, and critical information is likely to be missed. What you are looking for is a clear understanding of what is and is not acceptable to users, a map of where all services and users are and will be, and how they behave on the network. You can start off with some simple questions, such as the following:

- What applications are running over the network, from where and to where?

- Does the current application scenario make sense; is it likely to change?

- Where are the users, how many are there, how do they access the network?

- Are the users happy with the service they are currently receiving?

- What are the perceived expectations of users (if any) and senior management?

- What are the busy periods?

- What are the likely plans for growth, in applications and users?

This list is by no means exhaustive, but you get the general drift. Basically we should start by asking some common-sense questions about key locations, sizes, and behavior. There are several techniques that can be used to quantify these items. Here are some of the most important:

- Gather user and service sizing data from the appropriate staff.

- Perform regular statistical snapshots from existing data capture and network management tools.

- Perform detailed traces of key services on different parts of the network using a network protocol analyzer.

- Build a small pilot network; try to scale up traffic levels to simulate the final behavior of the design.

The last technique is useful to reassure yourself that the behavior you anticipate is actually happening, or likely to happen. For meaningful data capture you will need to get representative samples hourly, daily, and at least for one typical week. You will be looking for average and peak loads and a breakdown of all protocols in operation, together with an assessment of the busiest periods. The busy period is a vital feature to track, since this represents the worst-case scenario (i.e., the worst conditions your design will have to cope with). For example, if the network is affected by fast market conditions (such as a trading floor), you must establish what the likely traffic levels and flow are on the busiest day of the year. Failure to meet the worst-case conditions will mean that your network will cope for the majority of the time but collapse at key times of stress.

Quite often you will be starting from scratch, so it is a good idea to build a traffic profile of some of the key traffic characteristics expected both now and in the future. This can be done either by hand or, more typically, by using a database or spreadsheet, such as Microsoft Access or Excel.

Quantify user behavior

The first basic item to capture here is the location and population of the user base. Ideally we need the following:

- User populations by site, building, floor, and so on

- A summary of the major user groups (e.g., functional organizations, business units, etc.)

- Application use by user group (e.g., the MKT group uses applications DBASE-2 and SPREAD-1)

- Site location data (country, grid reference, town/city name, post/zip code, and telephone exchange codes)

- Expansion or change of plans (number of new users per location, planned moves for certain groups, etc.)

Clearly, if we know the user populations by site and their application use, we can use these data to scale the demand data. It is also important to understand how users interact with the various applications and services and what their expectations are. We need to know, for example, if all users log in between 8:30 A.M. and 9:00 A.M. every morning and download all their data. Interviews with end users will establish what services and response times are important to them. For example, if a network operator performs a database query on average 300 times per hour during a production process, then that query must have a worst-case response time of 12 seconds ([60 × 60]/300) otherwise, productivity will be lost. Since we are talking about average transaction rates here, in practice we may need the capability to service transactions much faster in order to cope with worst-case scenarios.

Site location data can be extremely useful (and often mandatory) when using automated design tools, since many of the service choices we will make later on depend on physical location, distance between sites, and proximity to various points of presence. For example, sites that lie within the same exchange area (e.g., same area code) are likely to be cheaper to connect than sites in different exchange areas, even though they may be the same distance apart. As another example, access circuits in rural areas may be more expensive than in major cities, because they tend to require longer circuits (in rural areas there is a lower density of exchange locations). These location-based design issues are covered in detail in Chapters 4 through 6.

Quantify application behavior

It is important to understand all of the key applications that are running over the proposed network. Basically there should be no surprises when you run these applications on your final design, and in order to achieve this you need to do the following:

- Identify all applications likely to affect network performance.

- Identify the location and performance characteristics of all servers.

- Identify the location and performance characteristics of all clients.

- Identify key constraints on performance (response times, timeouts, buffer sizes, etc.).

- Define application behavior during periods of data loss (retransmissions).

- Define addressing mechanisms (broadcast, multicast, or unicast).

- Define packet characteristics (min, max, and average frame size, and by direction).

- Identify routable and nonroutable services (e.g., IP and DECnet versus NetBIOS and DEC LAT).

A network analyzer is a powerful tool for understanding detailed application transaction behavior, since typically this information will not be readily available in the application documentation. If some of the applications are as yet undefined, think about the various models of application architecture and application partitioning, as follows:

- Thin clients or distributed applications—Do you put most of the CPU cycles on the server or on the clients?

- Centralized or distributed data—in the branch offices or in the data center?

Baseline the existing network

It is important early on in the life of a network to build a complete behavioral profile of both the network and its services as a whole; we call this information the baseline database. This database is a fingerprint of your network and is likely to be invaluable later on when the inevitable performance problems occur; without this information you will have nothing to compare.

Baselining activities

Here are some of the key activities you should include to create the baseline database:

- Run packet traces at key points in the topology, and also gather evidence from statistics and accounting logs on key devices, such as routers, firewalls, switches, and bridges.

- Talk to application vendors and build a profile of the expected transaction rates they would expect in your environment. Take some sample traces to back this up.

- Examine router event logs and statistics/accounting data. Often this will expose very detailed information about bytes/packets in and out, with breakdowns by protocol and possibly application. Make a note of the expected forwarding rates supported by these devices. Note any queuing advanced mechanisms you intend to use.

- Copy all router access control lists (ACLs) and firewall rulebase settings to ensure you know what traffic was being allowed or disallowed.

- Make an inventory of the hardware and software revisions used at the time the network was installed. Some performance issues could be the result of an OS upgrade that does not perform as well as its predecessor.

Traffic profiles

The traffic dynamics of the stable working network are particularly important to capture for future reference. Taking baseline measurements periodically enables the network designer to monitor the health of the network and also ensures that sufficient historical data are available to provide input for trend analysis and growth projections. This means that future bottlenecks could be avoided by provisioning appropriately in good time. In particular, you should aim to capture the following information on key locations in the network (backbone links, private server segments, mission-critical wide area links, etc.):

- Bandwidth utilization, split by broadcast, multicast and unicast traffic—Pay special attention to the level of broadcasts, since increased or anomalous levels may indicate application or routing issues.

- Bandwidth utilization, split by protocol type (e.g., IP, DECnet, IPX, etc.)—In the enterprise environment it is often surprising to see protocols that you did not expect to be running on your network. Check settings for client software and networking devices to ensure that unnecessary traffic is not activated by default (e.g., NetBIOS broadcasts, BOOTP requests, DEC MOP requests, etc.).

- Packet/frame size distribution—Often this will be bimodal, meaning that there are often two peaks in the distribution, either side of the average frame size. Usually this is seen as a relatively large proportion of large and small packets, reflecting data transfer and acknowledgment traffic, respectively.

- Background error rates (e.g., runts, pygmies, CRC errors, lost tokens, retransmission rates, etc.)—Undersized or oversized packets should not occur and are indicative of equipment or cabling problems. High retransmission rates indicate underlying problems, which should be investigated.

- Collision rates where appropriate (Ethernet shared media)—Excessive collisions may indicate cabling or equipment problems.

For example, our capture device may provide us with the following data for an Ethernet LAN backbone segment:

```
CAPTURE: SEG_A      Time Started: 12:07   Time Stopped: 14:03
UTILIZATION         Peak   : 93%          Average   : 34%
PROTOCOLS           FRAME STATS           ERRORS
IP          61%     1,514 byte:  27%      Jabbers   : 0
IPX         15%       512 byte:  13%      Runts     : 1
AppleTalk   12%       256 byte:   7%      Pygmies   : 0
NetBIOS      7%       128 byte:  22%      CRC Errors: 23
LAT          1%        64 byte:  41%      Collisions: 349
Other        4%
SUMMARY STATS
Unicast   : 83%
Broadcast : 17%
Avg Size  : 549 bytes
```

While this information is a useful for a top-level view, it provides data for only one part of the network, and at this level there is no visibility of where traffic is coming from or going to. More detailed analysis should follow, with a breakdown of all major traffic flows.

Tools for baselining

There are several tools and techniques you can use to capture baseline data, including the following:

- Network and protocol analyzers

- SNMP management stations and SNMP agents

- RMON probes

- Basic operating system tools (e.g., ps under UNIX)

- Application probes (if available)

- Monitoring and reporting tools on server utilization (for CPU, disk, and memory)

- Device-specific CLI status commands (e.g., show interfaces, show processes, show buffers)

- Diagnostic programs, such as Traceroute, Ping, etc.

- Auto-discovery protocols (e.g., Cisco Discovery Protocol—CDP)

For servers, numerous commercial tools are available to gather performance data. UNIX, for example, provides traditional applications such as iostat and mpstat to gather status information about machine use. Microsoft NT Server has similar tools, but for Windows clients there is a significant lack of standardized, accurate reporting tools to examine client performance issues dynamically. Figure 2.1 illustrates two relatively simple tools available under Windows: SysMeter is available as part of the Microsoft Windows Resource Kit, and on specific hardware platforms (such as a Dell personal computer) there may be vendor-specific tools available, such as Dell's System Monitor.

Figure 2.1
Simple Windows OS performance monioring tools. System Monitor (on the left) is provided with Dell personal computers running Windows, and SysMeter (on the right) is part of the Microsoft Windows Resouce Kit.

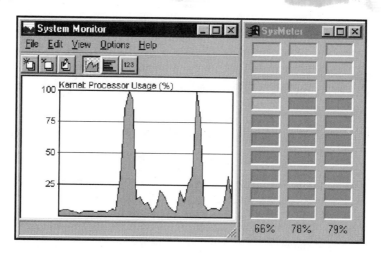

NetWare can be monitored using tools such as ServerTrak and TrendTrak from Intrak. These tools provide useful information on CPU utilization, NetWare I/O, and memory use. BMC NetTUNE also monitors physical disk I/O so you can distinguish cache memory I/O from disk requests. Software agents such as HP MeasureWare provide centralized monitoring of host performance. When using SNMP to gather data, you should be careful to use evenly distributed short interval scans; otherwise, you may inadvertently skew the traffic measurements with bursts of additional management traffic, especially on a large network. RMON is a much more efficient way to collate agent data.

Sample interval and duration

The more data you capture, the more granular your traffic database will be. The amount of data captured will depend upon the sample interval and sample duration. For troubleshooting problems you really need to sample large amounts of traffic in real time, so that complete application flows can be analyzed systematically. Often the volume of data captured is so large that you will need to set filters on capture devices to discard extraneous information. This level of detail would be inappropriate for baselining and long-term trend analysis; the volume of data would require huge amounts of storage space, and without statistical postprocessing tools you would not be able to derive much useful information. Imagine capturing Ethernet traffic averaging 3 Mbps for just ten minutes. This would require approximately 215 MB of uncompressed disk space $[(3 \times 60 \times 10)/8]/1.048576$.

For baseline purposes it is reasonable to use a sample interval of between five and ten minutes, capturing data for perhaps two to three minutes. You would aim to capture a number of samples that are representative of both quiet and heavy utilization periods during the day. For longer-term trend analysis you might use a sample interval of between 15 and 30 minutes, capturing data for perhaps five minutes. These data would be used to track busy days during the month, as well as busy months. All of these data need to be regularly archived and properly labeled. It is likely that you will want to export these data into some form of database or spreadsheet-friendly format, such as .CSV (comma-separated variable), where these data can be subsequently processed and analyzed using statistical methods.

Make traffic projections

Given application and end-user needs, and the existing network baseline data, you can determine the projected network utilization with new users and/or new applications. There are several complementary ways to go about this, including the following:

- By hand, using some of the performance estimation techniques described later in this book

- Using commercial analytical modeling tools, which will allow you to project network utilization

- By using a class of modeling tools known as discrete event simulation tools (such as CACI's COMNET tool and Cadence Systems' BONeS tool)

Simulation tools give the most detailed view of projected network utilization and the impact of the network on application performance. It is essential that probes be set up to monitor network traffic, preferably by application. Without this step, you will never know how accurate your capacity planning has been. We will discuss simulation and modeling tools in more detail in Chapters 3 and 5.

Summarize input data for the design process

At this stage we should now be in a position to produce various inputs for the design phase, including the following:

- The budget for the design

- A database of all user sites and populations by location, grid reference, post/zip code, and telephone area codes

- A list of all key applications and a good understanding of their behavior

- A traffic matrix, summarizing all data to and from sources and sinks on the network.

Based on this matrix of requirements we can begin to examine different network topologies and technologies and play with a number of traffic models. We need to consider factors such as these:

- How static is the bandwidth requirement? Do we need to consider static or dynamic allocation for all or parts of the network (leased circuits, Frame Relay, SMDS, ISDN, ATM, etc.)?

- What kind of delay can we tolerate on average? What is the maximum number of hops we can tolerate between any two sites?

- How important is resilience? How much site meshing is required? What are the availability targets?

Many of these issues are contradictory. For example, if we determine that delay is critical and there must be no more than one hop between any two backbone sites, then we end up with a star topology. This may be much more expensive than a partial mesh or tree topology, because of longer overall circuit lengths, and we may exceed the budget. As we will see in Chapters 4 through 6, network design is often a compromise between many conflicting demands.

2.1.4   Other information that requires collation

As well as capturing user application data, it is important to collate all other data that could ultimately impact the overall cost or the final network design and its deployment. These factors should all be fed into the final project plan. Broadly speaking, these include the following:

- Environmental data for any proposed or existing networking equipment

- Equipment room locations, sizes, power outlets

- Any special restrictions on access times to buildings, floors, and so on

- Any activities onsite that could affect deployment (e.g., contractors refurbishing parts of the building)

As a network designer it is often your responsibility to collate data on the environmental and physical attributes relevant for any network equipment. These attributes do not directly impact the modeling process but are, nevertheless, important in determining overall costs and feasibility. Given their importance we will briefly outline the key data you need to collate.

Environmental data

You should aim to establish the following information about all network equipment to be deployed and any already installed:

- Heat dissipation (output in BTU/hour) per device

- Power consumption per device, AC or DC

- Restrictions on operating temperature and storage temperature

- Equipment weight—old buildings may have tight limitations on load bearing

- Vertical rack space required, per device, for standard 19-inch wide rack equipment. Vertical height is usually indicated as a standard multiple of U, where 1 U = 1.75 inches. Check the depth of equipment also; some equipment may require especially deep cabinets, which may be very expensive and not fit into small equipment rooms.

- Any special restrictions on air quality

- Any other installation restrictions (position in racks, front or back facing, gaps required above or below equipment for airflow, etc.)

While these data may seem mundane, it would be a mistake to overlook them. Equipment rooms and communication cabinets are often starved for space, and if you have to provide additional space this could be expensive and could impact the design (e.g., if the only other space available happens to be three floors away from the main computer room!). A typical floor-standing rack (sometimes called the distribution frame) can accommodate 42 U of equipment. Typical open rack dimensions (height × width × depth) are 84 × 15 × 20.4 inches, although many variations are available. Remember to leave room for patch panels, fan trays, and so on, since these can take up considerable space. Heat dissipation and air quality are other potentially serious problems in small equipment rooms. Typical operating temperatures are 32°–104°F (0°–40°C), with relative humidity between 10 and 90 percent, noncondensing. Failure to meet the manufacturer's environmental requirements could lead to intermittent equipment failure and the installation of expensive air-conditioning units.

A good approach to handling these data is to build a spreadsheet indicating the power outlet, rack space, and floor space available per communications room. You can use this spreadsheet to automatically calculate power requirements, total heat output, and total rack space required. Whenever the kit list changes, make sure that this database is updated so there are no surprises for the installation team.

Now that we have a formal framework in place, let us examine some of the techniques used in capacity planning in more detail.

2.2 Understanding application and user behavior

2.2.1 Application bandwidth requirements

Applications require very different amounts of storage space for their data. A color graphic image is likely to require significantly more storage than a text file, since the amount of data required to build a graphic image is several orders of magnitude greater than that required to display a text message on the screen. Applications also may be more or less sensitive to network delays. For example, multimedia applications are much more sensitive to

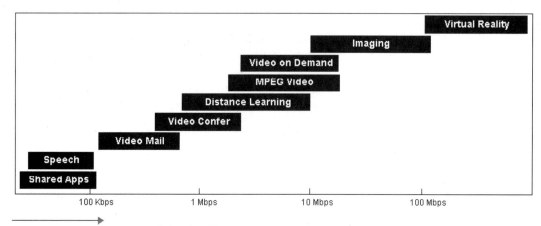

Figure 2.2   *Network bandwidth use.*

delay than basic file transfer, and they place significant bandwidth requirements on the network, ranging anywhere from 100 Kbps to 70 or 80 Mbps. Figure 2.2 shows the amount of bandwidth that various types of multimedia applications require. It follows, therefore, that different applications will exhibit very marked differences in the way they impact the network, and it is wise not to generalize or take things for granted in this respect.

As Figure 2.2 indicates, the type of application has a direct impact on the amount of LAN or WAN bandwidth required. Given that on any network bandwidth is finite (largely constrained by cost), the designer may have to compromise between a lower-quality video application that works within the available bandwidth or modifying the network to deliver more effective bandwidth.

Table 2.1 illustrates the typical best-case transmission times for various applications. Note that I say best-case times, because these figures do not take into account any time delays in acknowledgments and buffering; they do, however, give a good idea of relative worst-case impacts on the network for various traffic types. Note that we assume here an MTU of 1,514 bytes (the maximum frame size on Ethernet, minus the four-byte FCS) and protocol overhead of 54 bytes (14 bytes MAC, 40 bytes of TCP/IP). Maximum-sized Ethernet frames should be accommodated easily over wide area links such as PPP and Frame Relay, but remember there may be some circumstances where fragmentation is required, making the data sent even larger due to replicated header overheads (e.g., X.25 networks typically support a 256 or 512 maximum packet size). Be aware that the four-byte FCS should be included in bandwidth calculations when Ethernet is the transport medium, but it will not be included over wide area links.

Table 2.1 *Application Data Rates for Various Link Speeds*

Application	Msg Size (KBytes)	FrameSize (Bytes)	Overhead (Bytes)	Frms/Msg	Total Bits (Kbps)	Link Speed (Kbs)	Time (secs)
Terminal Display	4	1,514	54	0.003	33.2	64	0.518
(Character based)	4	1,514	54	0.003	33.2	2,048	0.016
Approx 4KB	4	1,514	54	0.003	33.2	10,000	0.003
	4	1,514	54	0.003	33.2	100,000	0.000
Web Page	10	1,514	54	0.007	83.0	64	1.296
(with simple JPEG/GIF graphics)	10	1,514	54	0.007	83.0	2,048	0.041
Approx 10KB	10	1,514	54	0.007	83.0	10,000	0.008
	10	1,514	54	0.007	83.0	100,000	0.001
Spreadsheet	25	1,514	54	0.017	207.4	64	3.241
Approx 25KB	25	1,514	54	0.017	207.4	2,048	0.101
	25	1,514	54	0.017	207.4	10,000	0.021
	25	1,514	54	0.017	207.4	100,000	0.002
Diagram	200	1,514	54	0.137	1,659.2	64	25.925
(e.g. Visio)	200	1,514	54	0.137	1,659.2	2,048	0.810
Approx 200KB	200	1,514	54	0.137	1,659.2	10,000	0.166
	200	1,514	54	0.137	1,659.2	100,000	0.017
Word Processing Doc	350	1,514	54	0.240	2,903.6	64	45.368
20 Page, Text Only	350	1,514	54	0.240	2,903.6	2,048	1.418
Approx 350KB	350	1,514	54	0.240	2,903.6	10,000	0.290
	350	1,514	54	0.240	2,903.6	100,000	0.029
Graphic	1,000	1,514	54	0.685	8,295.9	64	129.623
(screen clip)	1,000	1,514	54	0.685	8,295.9	2,048	4.051
Approx 1MB	1,000	1,514	54	0.685	8,295.9	10,000	0.830
	1,000	1,514	54	0.685	8,295.9	100,000	0.083
Graphical Display	2,300	1,514	54	1.575	19,080.5	64	298.134
(1024x768, 24-bit colour)	2,300	1,514	54	1.575	19,080.5	2,048	9.317
Approx 2.3MB	2,300	1,514	54	1.575	19,080.5	10,000	1.908
	2,300	1,514	54	1.575	19,080.5	100,000	0.191
Fax	3,000	1,514	54	2.055	24,887.7	64	388.870
Approx 3MB	3,000	1,514	54	2.055	24,887.7	2,048	12.152
	3,000	1,514	54	2.055	24,887.7	10,000	2.489
	3,000	1,514	54	2.055	24,887.7	100,000	0.249
CAD/CAM	10,000	1,514	54	6.849	82,958.9	64	1,296.233
Approx 10MB	10,000	1,514	54	6.849	82,958.9	2,048	40.507
	10,000	1,514	54	6.849	82,958.9	10,000	8.296
	10,000	1,514	54	6.849	82,958.9	100,000	0.830
Colour Graphic Image	50,000	1,514	54	34.247	414,794.5	64	6,481.164
(high resolution, print quality)	50,000	1,514	54	34.247	414,794.5	2,048	202.536
Approx 50MB	50,000	1,514	54	34.247	414,794.5	10,000	41.479
	50,000	1,514	54	34.247	414,794.5	100,000	4.148
Video/Multimedia	100,000	1,514	54	68.493	829,589.0	64	12,962.329
(compressed)	100,000	1,514	54	68.493	829,589.0	2,048	405.073
Approx 100MB	100,000	1,514	54	68.493	829,589.0	10,000	82.959
	100,000	1,514	54	68.493	829,589.0	100,000	8.296
Database Archive	1,000,000	1,514	54	684.932	8,295,890.4	64	129,623.288
Approx 1GB	1,000,000	1,514	54	684.932	8,295,890.4	2,048	4,050.728
	1,000,000	1,514	54	684.932	8,295,890.4	10,000	829.589
	1,000,000	1,514	54	684.932	8,295,890.4	100,000	82.959

The rightmost column in Table 2.1 shows the time taken to send data, assuming a specific link speed. We can see that even for a typical, small Microsoft Word document without diagrams, we will take up at least 45 seconds of bandwidth on a wide area link running at 64 Kbps. For a compressed video file we will need at least 3.6 hours to send data over the same 64-Kbps link. Note also that we have only illustrated the raw data rates involved; factors such as queuing delays (discussed in the next chapter) will make these data transfer times even longer. Equally important are the traffic flow characteristics of the application. We need to consider several key points here for each application, as follows:

- Where are data held? Centrally or distributed?

- Are data downloaded to each user at startup time?

- When the user interacts with the application, how much data are sent to and from the application server? How symmetrical is the data flow?

- What are the critical performance criteria for the application to function well? Can it timeout if responses are not received in a timely manner, and if so how does the user recover the session?

- When the user closes the application what is the data flow?

- How many concurrent users can the application support? What are the busy periods?

These very complex interactions will all play a part in degrading the network performance, and it is important that you try to quantify, as best you can, any significant data impacts on the network at the early stage of design. As we will see, there are equally important issues for the underlying transport protocols, such as windowing, acknowledgments, checksums, encryption, and compression.

2.2.2   Determining application thresholds and limitations

If applications are already running on the network, then you should create application maps, as described in Section 2.5.1. You should take measurements and packet traces to identify where possible problems are likely to be for each specific application. Tools such as protocol analyzers and probes can be used for this purpose. You need to collect data such as the following:

- Packet arrival rates

- Packet size distribution

- Any session limitations

- Host turnaround times

- Slow I/O features such as database or disk access

All of these features could be useful in locating bottlenecks later on.

2.2.3 Quantifying end-to-end transaction delays

The elapsed time for a particular transaction may be milliseconds, seconds, or even minutes. This response time is important to users and should be minimized. We can break down this time into the following components:

- The time it takes for packets to traverse the network

- The time it takes for a server to process the request and, if necessary, retrieve data

- The time it takes for the client to accept these data

The network component is referred to as network delay. The server and client delays are also referred to as host turnaround, or think, times. The delays can be measured for the whole transaction or per packet. The important point is to determine the relative fractions of the transaction delay attributed to network delay, Tn; server processing time, Ts; and client processing time, Tc. The network delay itself may have to be broken down if several subnetworks are traversed, and any significant delays introduced by intermediate devices should be included (e.g., router latency). Where there is a WAN link involved, the LAN propagation delays can typically be ignored, since the WAN delay is usually orders of magnitude higher. On high-bandwidth media (such as 10/100 Mbps Ethernet), networking delay is likely to represent a very small fraction of overall delay. If packet sizes differ in each direction, then we should break the network delay into a client/server part, $Tncs$, and a server/client part, $Tnsc$. To simplify matters we also assume that Ts is the total time for the server to process and respond to a request, whereas Tc is the time to either issue or receive a request at the client (assuming that these times are roughly equivalent).

For a simple client/server scenario, you need to make measurements on both the client segment and the server segment. The assumption is that the client issues a request to the server, the total delay includes two network traversals (client to the server and back again), and the client must process the received transaction. We assume here that packet size in both directions is the same. We then have the following calculation to make:

Total transaction delay = $2 \times Tc + Ts + 2 \times Tn$

In the more likely case, packet size will differ significantly in each direction, and we would then use the following calculation:

Total transaction delay = $2 \times Tc + Ts + Tncs + Tnsc$

Measurements can be made in off-peak hours to establish baseline equipment and network performance. Measurements in peak periods will demonstrate if additional bottlenecks are likely. For example, let us assume that a client and server are to be remotely connected across a 64-Kbps link, via local switched Ethernets running at 100 Mbps. Some local users are to be moved to this remote site, so what can they expect in terms of performance? Let us assume an average client think time of 1 ms, a server think time of 5 ms, a request packet of 100 bytes, and a response packet of 1,024 bytes. First, we can ignore the local network delays, since they are insignificant compared with the shared WAN link:

$$\text{Total transaction delay} = 2 \times Tc + Ts + Tncs + Tnsc$$
$$= 2 + 5 + 12.5 + 128$$
$$= 147.5 \text{ ms}$$

Even with this rough calculation, we can see that if users are expecting the same response time for remote access as they experienced locally, then clearly they are going to be disappointed; 86.8 percent of the network delay is due to the return packet from the host.

There is a fair body of evidence to suggest that interactive users (i.e., those using remote virtual terminal protocols such as Telnet) are prepared to accept delays of between 100 ms and 150 ms before these delays become obtrusive and affect productivity. Ideally the delay should be approximately 90 ms to allow a good typist to continue unhindered.

2.2.4   Understanding use patterns

As we indicated at the start of this chapter, it is critical to understand use patterns for applications and services on the network, especially since we typically need to identify the worst-case scenario in order to ensure that the network can cope. The following text discusses some example trace summaries showing network utilization over time for various applications.

Use profile: equipment supplier

The use profile in Figure 2.3(a) illustrates a typical daily use profile for a typical production network. Staff members arrive between 8:00 A.M. and 9:30 A.M. and log into their systems. At around 12:00 A.M. there is a dip in

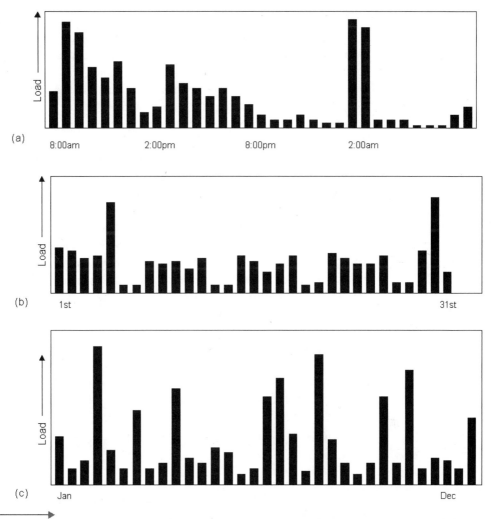

Figure 2.3   *Average utilization profiles. (a) Daily and (b) monthly use profile for typical production network. (c) Monthly use profile for an online brokerage.*

use as staff members take time for lunch. By 8:00 P.M. most of the staff have left the office and only background network maintenance traffic is visible, punctuated at 2:00 A.M. by the regular daily server archive. The use profile in Figure 2.3(b) illustrates a typical monthly use profile for the same network. The two main spikes coincide with regular monthly conference calls (using video conferencing) between the sales teams (on the fifth of every month) and the support teams (on the last week of the month).

Use profile: online brokerage

The use profile in Figure 2.3(c) illustrates a typical yearly use profile for an online financial trading floor. Notice that there are several spikes and little apparent order to the traffic profile. These spikes may coincide with fast market conditions or market meltdowns and are, by their very nature, difficult to predict. Worse still, the scale of activity during these busy periods can dwarf normal trading conditions, and missed opportunities could represent literally millions in lost revenue, so planning capacity for the average case is clearly not going to work here. We need to offer some sympathy for the designer who has to cope with this kind of profile—the design must accommodate near worst-case scenarios; this is likely to prove expensive and bandwidth inefficient. If we do not design for worst case then business will suffer, to the point where transactions are effectively barred during high-volume trading conditions, and the high levels of congestion anticipated could further aggravate the situation. There are techniques and technologies we can use to design around these effects, but this is one reason why many financial networks are heavily overprovisioned, to ensure that they can cope with just such events.

2.2.5   Busy hour, busy day analysis

Try to identify the worst-case scenario for the network. The worst-case scenario will depend on the nature of the business—for example, it may be as follows:

- 9:30 A.M. Monday morning, with all customers ringing in with complaints

- A fast-market condition for a financial trading institution, such as a major share collapse, or following the announcement of an interest rate change

- The last week of every month, 3:00 P.M. on a Friday, when all remote international users log in for a complete database download

- End-of-quarter sales activity

Understanding the worst-case scenario will to a large degree influence the kind of design you put in place, and this in turn will be constrained by the amount of funding available. Specifically, you should include the following:

- Identify the worst-day, worst-time scenario for the network over the year.

- Quantify max packet rates and link utilization on critical parts of the network (i.e., the backbone, key WAN links between sites, etc.).

- Quantify server performance during this scenario.

Once you have identified the worst-case scenario, you can decide whether you can afford to cope with it. With certain applications this will not be optional—for example, a utility, transport, healthcare, or financial organization may have no choice but to design the network around the worst-case scenario. A less-critical application may only justify smooth operation for 80 percent of the load and live with poor performance or degraded service on the odd day where demand outstrips supply. Clearly, having expensive wide area lines lying idle or underutilized for long periods is a dilemma. Fortunately there are dynamic services such as ISDN and Frame Relay we can consider; we cover these in Chapter 7.

2.3   Understanding traffic characteristics

The traffic flow over networks, and the kinds of features and problems it demonstrates, is remarkably similar to the road traffic problems encountered on any developed country's highway system. Networks have fat pipes (motorways or freeways) and thinner pipes (urban and country roads) together with a variety of large and small packets (trucks and cars). Traffic can be bursty and even oversubscribed in peak hours, and occasionally cars crash, or get lost, and may be late for their destinations. Private networks (like toll roads) may offer a better quality of service, although even here things can go wrong.

On real networks there may be a wide variety of packet sizes and many different protocols operating concurrently. Some packets may be addressed for many targets (broadcasts and multicasts) and others for specific targets (unicasts). Some protocols may require special handling, and often there are timing issues that become increasingly important as the end-to-end distance between nodes increases or the bandwidth utilization between nodes becomes so high that congestion occurs. The network designer must be aware of all of these issues when putting together a design. Failure to understand these subtleties may result in a design that looks great but simply doesn't work. In this section we will cover some of the basic characteristics of traffic that you should be aware of.

2.3.1 Basic network performance definitions

Bandwidth

This is sometimes called the signaling speed and is the rate at which individual bits can be transmitted across the media. On wide area networks bandwidth is an expensive resource, and it is important that you partition the network in order to make the best use of it. Bandwidth is determined by the Physical and Data Link Layers of the network infrastructure. So, for example, standard Ethernet can transfer bits at a rate of 10 Mbps. A T1 link can transfer bits at a rate of 1.536 Mbps.

Throughput and capacity

Throughput is the quality of error-free data that can be transmitted over a specific unit of time (e.g., packets per second [pps], frames per second [fps], cells per second [cps] and bits per second [bps]). It may be expressed for the whole network, for a specific link, or down to an individual session. Capacity is the amount of data a network or link can theoretically service within a specific unit of time. In an ideal world throughput and capacity would be the same, but this is not the case with real networks for several reasons. Theoretically, throughput should increase as the offered load increases up to the maximum capacity of the network. However, in reality, throughput tends to increase linearly; it reaches a peak below capacity and then falls off (because of factors such as inability of intermediate devices to process incoming

Figure 2.4
Ideal and realistic throughput under offered load.

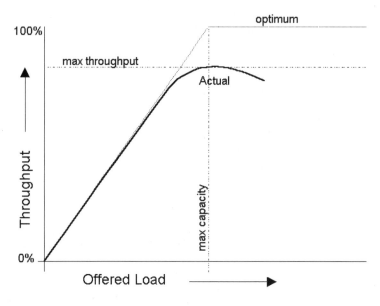

packets quickly enough, causing further delays). (See Figure 2.4.) If we are expressing throughput in terms of actual user data (rather than just bits per second transmitted), then throughput will always be less than capacity because of factors such as protocol encapsulation overheads, media access delays, queuing delay, server latency, and so on.

Latency

Latency is the accumulated delay, or end-to-end delay, experienced by packets as they traverse the network. Each network component in the transmission path will add to the overall latency. It is important to understand that throughput and latency are not the same. It is quite possible to have the same throughput over two different media but very different latencies (i.e., data can be sent at the same rate, but on one medium it may start to arrive later). Bandwidth and latency combine to determine the overall throughput of the communication channel. The network contributes to latency in several ways, as follows:

- Propagation delay—the theoretical time it takes for bits to travel the length of the media. This is typically the speed of light, or a large fraction of it, and therefore propagation delay is not a significant contributor to network latency.

- Transmission delay—the time a packet takes to traverse a specific medium type, determined by the speed of the medium and the size of the packet.

- Store-and-forward delay—the time taken for an internetworking device (i.e., a bridge, switch, or router) to buffer a packet and then forward it.

- Processing delay—the time taken by a networking device to process an incoming packet and decide what to do with it. This includes activities such as routing lookups, filtering, modifying headers, checksums, incrementing hop counts, encapsulating, and so on. Each of these steps will contribute to the processing delay.

Voice applications are notoriously sensitive to delay; we have all experienced a frustrating conversation over satellite links where both parties start talking just as the last person's response is delivered. Telephone networks are therefore engineered to provide less than 400 ms round-trip latency. Interactive virtual terminal protocols, such as Telnet, are also sensitive to delay. Users can normally tolerate a round-trip latency of up to 100 ms before the effects becoming annoying. Real-time interactive applications, such as video conferencing, are also very sensitive to latency. Multimedia networks that

support desktop audio and video conferencing must be engineered with a
latency budget of less than 400 ms per round trip.

Jitter

Jitter is a measurement of the variability of latency. No jitter means that the
delays experienced are constant. The last thing you need in a telephone conversation are delays that vary, causing speech to essentially speed up and
slow down, with pops and clicks that are noticeable to the user. Many multimedia applications are designed to minimize jitter, so that a constant
stream of data is transmitted. The most common technique is to store
incoming data in a buffer, and then retrieve those data at a uniform rate.
Figure 2.5 shows a typical buffering strategy to minimize jitter.

Buffering is typically performed within the network itself. Consider a
client that connects to a video server. During the video playback session,
data moving from the video server to the client can be buffered by the network interface cards and the video decompressor. In this case, buffering acts
as a regulator to offset jitter during transmission. Even though the traffic
transmitted over the network may be bursty, the video image is not
impaired, because the buffers store incoming data and then regulate the
flow to the video display card. Network buffers are not usually large enough
to accommodate the entire audio or video file and so cannot guarantee jit-
ter-free delivery. For that reason, multimedia networks should also make use
of techniques that minimize jitter.

Media access delay

Media access delay can be particularly important when considering LANs,
where there can be a number of factors influencing the total delay. There is
the nominal delay inherent in the particular medium—for example, Ethernet uses CMSA/CD, and Token Ring/FDDI use a token-passing scheme to

Figure 2.5
*Hardware
buffering.*

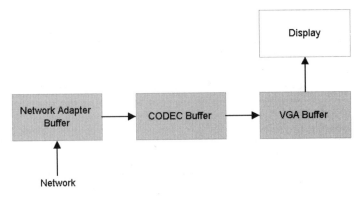

access media. Media access time for CMSA/CD is five to ten times faster than for Token Ring, although this differential is eroded as load is increased (due to increased collisions on shared Ethernet). Media access delay is also affected by the number of devices contending for the media. The more competition there is, the higher average delay experienced. Again, Ethernet tends to degrade more quickly than Token Ring, and Ethernet access times are said to be non-deterministic.

Accuracy

The term accuracy is sometimes used to express the difference between data offered to the network and data received from the network. Ideally, data should be identical, but because of features such as noise, interference, crosstalk, bad connections, power surges/spikes, and device failures there is a probability that some data will be corrupted during transmission. Usually these problems are taken care of by higher-layer protocols such as TCP, but the effects of data corruption ultimately mean retransmissions and inefficiency, lowering effective throughput. For wide area links the accuracy threshold can be expressed as the Bit Error Rate (BER). An error rate above the specified BER value is considered unacceptable. On local area networks a BER is not explicitly used, but a general rule of thumb is no more than one corrupted frame in 10^6 byes of data transmitted. We cover BER in more detail in Section 2.3.3.

2.3.2   Frames, packets, and messages

The literature is inconsistent in naming the messages that are transferred between networked systems. The terms frame, packet, Protocol Data Unit (PDU), segment, message, and several others have all been used at various times with no real clarity. For the sake of simplicity we will attempt to use the following definitions, although frankly I don't adhere religiously to any. The context in which the term is mentioned is usually sufficient to illustrate what we are talking about; nevertheless, here goes:

- Frame—denotes variable-length information units whose source and destination are Data Link Layer entities.

- Cell—denotes fixed-length information units whose source and destination are Data Link Layer entities.

- Packet—denotes variable-length information units whose source and destination are Network Layer entities.

- Message—denotes an information unit whose source and destination entities exist above the Network Layer.

Where other terms or meanings are used they will be specifically indicated.

Units of Measurement

Traffic is measured using various metrics, including the following:

- Size—Measured in bits, bytes, octets, messages, blocks, and files, with flow rates measured in bits, bytes, kilobytes, and megabytes per second/minute/hour/day

- Packaging—Measured in messages, cells, frames, and packets, with flow rates measured in messages, frames, packets, or cells per second/minute/hour/day

Throughout this book I refer to bytes using a capital B, and bits using a lowercase b, so ten kilobits per second will be shown as 10 Kbps, and five megabytes per second as 5 MBps. You should also be aware of the potential confusion over terms such as mega and kilo, as these are frequently misused. The term mega can mean either 2^{20} or 10^6, while the term kilo can mean either 2^{10} or 10^3, and we need to be careful which context we are using, as the various definitions are often intermixed.

When we talk about message size, we often use the term megabyte (MB) and kilobyte (KB). Since data are stored in computer memory, based on powers of 2, the M in MB is generally understood to mean 2^{20} (or 1,048,576), and likewise the K in KB means 2^{10} (or 1,024).

Network bandwidth, however, is typically governed by the speed of a clock, which controls the timing of bit transmissions over a link. For example: a 10-Mbps link will be controlled by a 10-MHz clock. Since the M in MHz means 10^6 (or 1,000,000) hertz, we also define Mbps as 10^6 bits per second. Similarly, Kbps is 10^3 (or 1,000) bits per second.

So it is quite reasonable to say that we are sending a 60-KB message over a 2-Mbps circuit, but we should be clear in interpreting this as sending $60 \times 1,024 \times 8$ bits over a $2 \times 1,000,000$-bits-per-second circuit. There is a 4.9 percent difference if we misinterpret mega, and a 2.4 percent difference if we misinterpret kilo. Luckily, for most rough-and-ready calculations the difference is not significant enough to cause too many surprises, but, nevertheless, be aware of the difference.

Message size

Typically a message unit is called a Protocol Data Unit or PDU (terminology used in SMDS and ATM). PDUs vary in both size and format between

Table 2.2   *Frame and Cell Sizes for Various Network Media Types*

Media	Minimum (bytes)	Maximum (bytes)
ATM	53	53
ATM LANE	64	1,518
ATM Classical IP	64	9,180
SMDS	53	53
BISDN	53	53
Ethernet (DIX V2)	64	1,500
Ethernet (802.3)	64	1,492
Fast Ethernet	64	1,518
FDDI	32	4,352
Token Ring (4Mbps)	32	4,464
Token Ring (16Mbps)	32	17,914
Hyperchannel		65,535
Serial HDLC	14	4,500
PPP	4	1,500
X.25		576
Frame Relay	12	8,096

applications and the underlying protocols used. When attempting to understand traffic flow over internetworks, it is important to consider the Maximum Transmission Units (MTU) allowed on any of the intermediate local and wide area links. The MTU determines the maximum packet size you can transmit over a particular link. Table 2.2 lists various frame characteristics for a number of media technologies. Note that Ethernet (802.3) assumes 802.2 plus SNAP encapsulation. Note also that ATM, SMDS, and BISDN use fixed-length ATM cells. Token Ring, running at 4 Mbps, recommends an MTU of 2,002 bytes in practice. Ethernet (DIXv2) and IEEE 802.3 have different MTU sizes, because the data part of the 802.3 frame contains an eight-byte 802.2 header. With PPP an MTU of 296 bytes is recommended for interactive use.

It follows that we cannot transport a packet that is longer than a medium's MTU in its original form. Therefore, if a packet's MTU exceeds the MTU supported on an intermediate circuit, the packet must be fragmented (i.e., broken up into smaller packets) at the point of ingress. At the point of egress (or more typically at the receiver) these packets must be reassembled back into the original PDUs. If fragmentation is not supported, then the packet must be discarded and an alternate route must be found. Clearly, fragmentation and reassembly can limit throughput and can degrade performance, depending upon the relative differences in MTU. Remember that every fragment must contain valid headers as well as the newly sliced up data, so there are considerable overheads in addition to the aggregate packet delays involved.

Routed networks can generally accommodate different MTUs along any particular end-to-end transmission path, since most Layer 3 protocols can fragment and reassemble packets where the packet size is too large for a particular subnetwork. Conversely, end systems on switched LANs of different media types must negotiate an MTU that is the lowest common denominator of all the intermediate switched LANs. This can limit throughput and affect performance more seriously, since the entire end-to-end transmission path is compromised.

Payload

Payload is the amount of real data we can transfer over a particular medium, and has been shown to be a very significant factor in determining perceived performance. Payload is limited by two main factors: the MTU of the medium, and the protocol overhead in each packet. So, for example, on Ethernet, using TCP/IP to transfer data, our maximum payload will be:

$$
\begin{aligned}
\text{Payload} &= MTU - (TCP_{overhead} + IP_{overhead} + MAC_{overhead}) \\
&= 1{,}518 - (20 + 20 + 18) \\
&= 1{,}460 \text{ bytes}
\end{aligned}
$$

If you have applications on your network that can make use of the maximum MTU available, then it is clearly worth considering media with very high MTUs. For example, in the LAN environment 16-Mbps Token Ring could offer much better performance than 100-Mbs FDDI, even though FDDI offers 6.25 times the bandwidth!

In practice, payload is often limited further by the applications themselves. For example, a database engine may transfer read responses according to the record size of a table rather than the table size. Instead of trying to transfer a 3-MB table the application could in reality be transferring 256-byte chunks of data (assuming a record size of 256) even though the MTU available is much higher. These subtleties are important to understand, as it would seem apparent initially that Token Ring at 16 Mbps and a much higher MTU should offer much better performance than Ethernet. However, since the media access time of Token Ring is much slower (five to ten times) than Ethernet, Ethernet will offer better performance with small to medium packet sizes.

2.3.3   **Key performance relationships**

Calculating maximum packet rate

Maximum packet rate is a useful measurement to highlight potential bottle-necks and assess whether the assigned capacity is adequate for a particular application. It can be calculated as follows:

$$PPS_{max} = Channel\ speed/(8\ bits \times PDU\_size)$$

For example, let's assume we have a 64-Kbps circuit, and a client wishes to send 128 bytes across this link from an Ethernet LAN:

$$PPS_{max} = 64,000/(8 \times 128)$$
$$= 62.5\ pps$$

So we can at most send 62.5 packets per second. However, this does not account for protocol overhead for the link itself, and the fact that some encapsulation protocols will strip off the MAC header. Assuming the link is using PPP encapsulation, for example, we need to account for the additional four-byte PPP header and the loss of the 14-byte MAC header, so the revised calculation is:

$$PPS_{max} = 64,000/[(8 \times 114) + (8 \times 4)]$$
$$= 67.797\ pps$$

With smaller packet sizes it is clearly even more important to consider the encapsulation effects, especially with protocols such as X.25 where the encapsulation is much heavier. Still using PPP, but with a packet size of 64 bytes, we see that PPS_{max} is 125 pps without the effects of encapsulation, and 148 pps with the correct encapsulation. This difference is significant, so it is important that what we are modeling is based on reality.

We saw that the maximum frame rate for small packets is much greater than for larger packets (148 pps for a 64-byte packet, and only 68 pps for 128-byte packets). So it looks like we are getting better performance by using smaller packets. However, what may not be immediately obvious here is that larger packets are much more efficient. For example, assuming a 1,500-byte Ethernet frame we can see that the max frame rate drops to a mere 5.37 pps. However, assuming these are TCP/IP packets, the total encapsulation overhead is 44 bytes (20-byte TCP, 20-byte IP, and 4-byte PPP). This represents a measly 2.95 percent on a 1,500-byte frame and a massive 81.48 percent on a 64-byte frame.

Table 2.3   *Link Saturation Matrix*

Link Speed (Kbs)

		9.6	56	64	128	256	512	1,544	2,048	10,000	34,000	44,480	100,000
	64	18.8	109	125	250	500	1,000	3,016	4,000	19,531	66,406	86,875	195,313
	128	9.4	55	63	125	250	500	1,508	2,000	9,766	33,203	43,438	97,656
Frame Size (Bytes)	256	4.7	27	31	63	125	250	754	1,000	4,883	16,602	21,719	48,828
	512	2.3	14	16	31	63	125	377	500	2,441	8,301	10,859	24,414
	1024	1.2	7	8	16	31	63	188	250	1,221	4,150	5,430	12,207
	1514	0.8	5	5	11	21	42	127	169	826	2,807	3,672	8,256

The relationship between packet rate and link speed

As we discussed previously, for various packet sizes there will be a point above which the link is saturated. Table 2.3 shows the relationship between line speed and maximum frame rate for a range of packet sizes. The point about this illustration is to understand and anticipate where the underlying bottlenecks in the network could be. For example, if you have a super-slinky trading floor application, which can happily churn out 1,000-byte Ethernet frames at 150 pps, there is no point in expecting it to perform over a 64-Kbps leased line. The only options here would be either to provide more bandwidth, say a T1 or E1 link, or use hardware compression between the two routers on the link. Since bandwidth is often the most expensive resource, it is often this that determines the performance of applications rather than vice versa. In an ideal world we would always like more band-width, but in the real world your company may not be able to afford to install anything higher than a 64-Kbps circuit, so prepare to do some serious compromising.

The relationship between error probability and frame size

We previously indicated that large packets were more efficient for transmit-ting data. This is true; however, the larger the packet sizes the more likely there will be a transmission error, and this is especially true in packet switching. For any given Bit Error Rate (BER) the probability of the frame generating an error increases with frame size, to a point above which you could almost guarantee an error in every frame. To test the BER on serial links you can use specialized test equipment called a Bit Error Rate Tester (BER tester). Table 2.4 illustrates the bit error rate for typical media types in use today. Note that analog wide area links have a BER of about 1 in 10^5;

Table 2.4   *Bit Error Rates for Common Media Types*

	Data Rate Mbps	Bit Error Rate	Bandwidth
Twisted Pair	10	1.0E-05	250kHz
Coax	100	1.0E-06	350MHx
Fibre	1000	1.0E-09	1GHz

digital circuits are much better, with some fiber circuits quoting a BER of 10^{11}.

It is important to understand that there are several factors that affect the data and error rates: bandwidth, media type, the method of data encoding, and the length of the link (hence its susceptibility to noise, echoes, crosstalk, and nonlinear distortions). For example, twisted-pair cables run at 10 Mbps for up to 300 ft for balanced transmissions (e.g., with Manchester Encoding). After 300 ft the data rate drops to 1 Mbps, and after 3,000 ft it drops to 100 Kbps. Hence the need for repeaters to perform signal regeneration.

Since the bit error rate increases with packet size, there will be an optimum packet size above which protocol efficiency will start to fall. The relative efficiency of a protocol can be expressed as follows:

$$E = S_{data}/[R(S_{data} + S_{prot} + S_{ack})]$$

where

E = the relative protocol efficiency

R = the expected number of retransmissions per message

S_{data} = the data size

S_{prot} = the protocol overhead

S_{ack} = the acknowledgment size

If R is zero, then clearly we can get maximum efficiency by making the data size as large as possible. However, since R will increase with S_{data}, E will be maximized for a particular value of S_{data}, as illustrated in Figure 2.6.

This is partly why a default 128-byte packet size was chosen as a compromise for packet-switched networks in the days of X.25. X.25 was designed to incorporate a significant number of recovery procedures to ensure that X.25 packets could be delivered reliably over relatively unreliable circuits. Today, with the increased use of cleaner fiber-optic channels,

Figure 2.6
*Protocol efficiency
versus data size.*

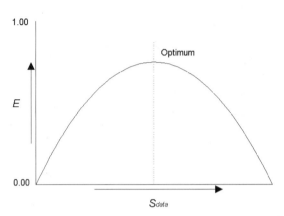

this has led to the introduction of stripped down packet-switching protocols such as Frame Relay (strictly speaking, a frame-switching protocol),
where the error correction features have been excluded. (See Figure 2.7.) For
older, noisy lines (i.e., where PTOs are still running FDM on old analog
backbones) you can improve performance by decreasing the frame size (say
to 64 bytes). The increased encapsulation overhead is offset by fewer
retransmissions.

Compression

Compression can be a useful technique for improving performance, especially in wide area circuits where bandwidth is at a premium. Clearly, compressing data at the source would be optimum for all concerned; this may
require user intervention or end-to-end agreement on the compression
techniques used. The most common use of compression in internetworks is
for relatively low-speed wide area links, usually activated automatically by

Figure 2.7
*Theoretical delay
for packet-switched
and frame-switched
transmissions.*

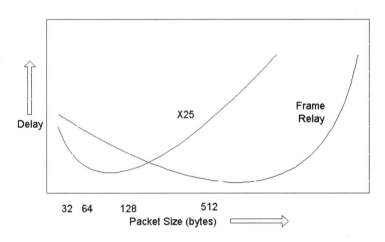

intermediate devices, such as routers, switches, and multiplexers. Compression is not generally used above 64 Kbps, as it may begin to impact performance detrimentally (often the algorithm performing compression cannot maintain pace with higher circuit speeds). Widely used compression techniques include the following:

- V.42bis link compression (typically negotiated as a PPP option)

- Van Jacobson TCP header compression

- Proprietary algorithms (usually variants of Lempel-Ziv)

- Repetitive Pattern Suppression (RPS), sometimes called Data Frame Multiplexing (DFM) or Run-Length Encoding (RTE)

Compression is a relative measure of the amount of data input versus the amount of data output. This is expressed by the term compression ratio, calculated as follows:

Compression ratio = Size of output stream/Size of input stream

For example, if we have an input stream of 100 KB and manage to compress this down to an output stream of 60 KB, we have achieved a compression ratio of 0.6 (i.e., output data are only 60 percent of the size of the original data). A compression ratio greater than one indicates negative compression (i.e., expansion of the original data). This can occur where the original data are either truly random or have already been compressed (in which case these data will appear random). Note that the term compression factor is the inverse of the compression ratio.

2.4   Recognizing and analyzing bottlenecks

As part of the full design process it is worthwhile identifying any potential bottlenecks early in the design process. By identifying potential weak spots early, you can choose to either design around them or simply monitor them. This knowledge may also be invaluable later on when debugging performance problems or optimizing the design. Locating bottlenecks is very much dependent on the topology employed, circuit speeds, routing protocols, and the nature of the services running over your network. This section should help you focus your attention on key areas in the infrastructure.

2.4.1   Typical bottlenecks

On internetworks most bottlenecks fall into a shortlist of usual suspects. As with any line up, some of these suspects may appear to place the blame elsewhere, so the trick is to find the suspect who is really culpable. In general you should focus on the following possible targets for investigation (in no particular order):

- Shared services (centralized server farms, Web farms, etc.)

- Multiuser applications and shared databases

- Low-speed network interface cards (e.g., parallel port cards)

- Internet access points

- Shared LAN segments (10 Base 5, 10 Base 2, Token Ring, and FDDI)

- Bandwidth-constrained WAN links

- Core routing and switching components

- Firewalls (especially public facing)

Figure 2.8 illustrates just some of the potential problems likely to impact performance in an internetwork. If you have data from traffic analysis or simulation studies, these data may already indicate areas of stress in the design. It is advisable to take a holistic view of the design and the implications of any potential changes before wading in and attempting to fix a problem locally; otherwise, you might just be simply shifting the problem elsewhere. For example, let's assume that users are complaining about the database server's response time. The servers are attached to a shared 10-Mbps Ethernet segment, and this segment is running at an average 65 percent load, peaking regularly at well over 90 percent. Packet traces reveal application timeouts that are causing excessive retransmissions (responsible for a large proportion of the loading). Without any further evidence it would seem appropriate to upgrade the shared segment to a switched 100-Mbps connection. However, the problem is far from resolved; the response times are actually worse and the server occasionally crashes. Further investigation reveals that the server has not had the planned processor upgrade, and memory has been removed from it without your knowledge. Sixty additional users from the marketing department have also been using this server instead of their local database due to a routing fault. Both CPU and memory are extremely overloaded; the server is simply unable to cope with demand. By upgrading the network you have effectively given it even more to do and failed to solve the problem.

This type of problem can be avoided early on by taking an end-to-end view of the problem, avoiding potentially expensive and unnecessary refits. Make sure you have all the pertinent information, and be sure to analyse the

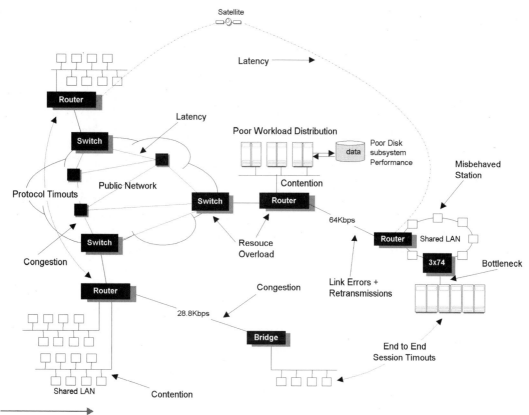

Figure 2.8   *Examples of bottlenecks and potential performance problems in an internetwork topology.*

complete path between client and server application. Take detailed readings so you can see what the response times actually are and whether there are features such as retransmissions, lost frames, error packets, and so on. Work out what the slowest device is in the end-to-end path. Note any shared paths.

2.4.2   Client and server issues

As indicated previously, bottlenecks are not always in the network. If you have nice fat pipes everywhere, then clearly the applications and host systems themselves are more likely to limit performance. Both client and servers are subject to the same potential bottlenecks, as follows:

■ Memory

■ CPU cycles

- I/O (network and disk)

- System bus throughput

When designing scalable networks with a simple server-oriented application scenario, server performance is inherently more important than client performance (server performance must scale as the network grows, clients typically support only one user). Many high-end servers today are hard pressed to transmit more than 300–400 Mbps through their Network Interface Card (NIC), and there are substantial differences in the throughput available from various bus architectures (e.g., the 32-bit PCI bus is inadequate for gigabit applications and has been superseded by the 64-bit PCI bus). For high-bandwidth interfaces such as Gigabit Ethernet, this may be a significant limitation. There are also occasions where client performance can be a limiting factor, and processor, RAM, or I/O upgrades should be considered. With a distributed application scenario the bottlenecks may be a little more difficult to diagnose, since the complete transaction path may be convoluted and hard to trace.

All of this information can be reviewed to assess potential bottlenecks, and decisions can be made about whether more detailed analysis is needed. In cases where the bottlenecks are application or host limited, any upgrades to the network are clearly a waste of money.

2.4.3   Network performance issues

Network transmission paths are limited by two fundamental constraints: bandwidth and latency. However, the devices used to deliver the network (i.e., routers, switches, and bridges) are also limited to some degree by internal resources (such as CPU cycles, memory access speeds, and network I/O performance). In a large internetwork these factors can be just as important and contribute significantly to end-to-end latency. We can use a simple model to illustrate the effects of network delay when transmitting a large segment of information, broken into several blocks of data, each of size W bytes (where W is the smaller of the transport protocol window or the application block size). The file is transmitted over the network of bandwidth Bw from the server to the client. Each block transmitted is followed by an acknowledgment from the client to the server (for the sake of simplicity we will ignore windowing operations). The data rate for this transaction can be expressed as follows:

Data rate = $W/(W/Bw + 2 \times Tn + Ts + Tc)$

where

Tn = network latency

Ts = server think time

Tc = client think time.

Bw = bandwidth available

Data rate = actual performance achievable

W/Bw = amount of time required to transmit a block of data over the transmission media.

Data rate, therefore, is effectively the block size divided by the total time to send, receive, and acknowledge the block. Note that network delay, Tn, appears twice in this equation. Client and server think times appear only once. Since we are interested here in network latency effects, we will assume that Ts = Tc = 0, and can, therefore, normalize our equation as follows:

Data rate = $W/(W/Bw + 2 \times Tn)$

This very simple equation calculates the real network throughput achieved and is also a measure of efficiency. For example, let is assume you have installed an E1 link (2.048 Mbps) with 10 ms one-way network delay, and the host equipment supports a 1,500-byte window size (12,000 bits). We can, therefore, calculate effective data throughput as follows:

$$Data Rate = 12,000/(12,000/2,048,000 + 2 \times 0.010)$$
$$= 12,000/0.0258593$$
$$= 464,050 \text{ Kbps}$$

This represents only 23 percent of the available bandwidth! Applications that move large amounts of data around (such as Web/HTTP applications) are especially vulnerable to network latency, and you should consider block sizes and windowing in any traffic models used.

The effects of contention and protocol overhead on shared LANs

The traffic characteristics of shared LANs are important to understand. Maximum frame rates for common LAN types are illustrated in Table 2.5.

Ethernet

A 10-Mbps shared Ethernet has a maximum forwarding rate of 14,880 frames per second. This is derived from the knowledge that Ethernet has a minimum frame size of 64 bytes, a 64-bit preamble, and an interframe gap of 9.6 ms as follows:

$$10,000,000/[(64 \times 8) + 64 + 96] = 14,880.9$$

Table 2.5 *Maximum Frame Rates at Various Packet Sizes on LAN Media*

Frame Size (Bytes)	Ethernet 10Mbps	Token Ring 16 Mbps	FDDI 100 Mbps
64	14880	24691	152439
128	8445	13793	85616
256	4528	7326	45620
512	2349	3780	23585
768	1586	2547	15903
1024	1197	1921	11996
1280	961	1542	9630
1518	812	1302	8138

For maximum-sized Ethernet packets (1,514 bytes) the maximum frame rate is only 814.8 frames per second (although the protocol efficiency is much higher at 99.08 percent instead of 78.1 percent for small packets, since the Ethernet header is a much smaller proportion of the overall frame size). Unfortunately, both of these figures assume that the transmitter has exclusive access to the media. On shared media Ethernet performance drops significantly, as more stations contend for access, and the rate of collisions increases. Studies performed by the IEEE suggest that at approximately 37 percent load on a shared Ethernet segment with 50 nodes, Ethernet frames experience more delay than token-ring frames due to the increased level of collisions. This study compared 10-Mbps Ethernet with 10 Mbps token passing using 128-bye frames (although results are essentially the same with either 4- or 16-Mbps Token Ring). This has led to a widespread misconception that Ethernet starts to fail at 37 percent load.

On a real 10-Mbps shared Ethernet LAN we might be happy to accept a more realistic aggregate throughput of between 3 and 4 Mbps. On a point-to-point full-duplex Ethernet segment with only a single client and server we would expect to be able to carry a sustained load of almost 100 percent (since there will be no collisions); the limiting factor is likely to be server processing delays.

Token Ring

Token Ring shared media are deterministic, since access is controlled by tokens; unlike Ethernet there is no "free for all." On a 4-Mbps Token Ring LAN we would expect an aggregate throughput of approximately 3.9 Mbps. On a 16-Mbps Token Ring LAN we could expect an aggregate throughput of approximately 15.9 Mbps. Ideally we should aim for average utilization of approximately 70 percent to allow traffic bursts to be handled with minimal performance degradation.

FDDI

FDDI is essentially similar to Token Ring, in that it is a shared deterministic medium. On a 100-Mbps FDDI MAN we could expect an aggregate throughput of over 95 Mbps. As with Token Ring, ideally we should aim for average utilization of approximately 70 percent to allow traffic bursts to be handled with minimal performance degradation.

The effects of TCP/IP protocol inefficiency on media types

Most current data communication protocols used in the internetwork environment are general-purpose protocols and therefore exhibit many compromises in design and efficiency in order to cope with an extremely varied range of media characteristics. TCP/IP is no exception. When TCP/IP is run over different media types, its performance is very much dependent upon a number of factors, including the following:

- The implementation/protocol stack used

- The operating system and host platform

- Packet size distribution of the application

- Background traffic characteristics of contended paths

- LAN, MAN, or WAN media properties, overheads, and bit error rates

- Intermediate device-forwarding characteristics

- TCP's sliding window behavior

The effects of buffering on shared WAN links

The use of shared wide area circuits is commonplace, because conventional WAN bandwidth is both expensive and in relatively short supply (usually bandwidth an order of magnitude less than that of conventional LAN technologies). In a routed internetwork, routers at the WAN interface must handle bursty LAN traffic that is intended for remote sites. There is usually a large speed differential between the LAN and WAN interfaces supported by the router, and if all LAN traffic were to go over the wide area, then either much of it would be lost or a large number of WAN circuits would be required to provide sufficient capacity. Fortunately, in most networks only a proportion of LAN traffic is destined for remote sites (usually less than 20 percent, although this is increasing with the emergence of more distributed types of computing). Because LAN traffic is also bursty, it makes sense to deal with the overall load by using buffers at each WAN interface rather than multiple expensive WAN circuits. Router buffers (queues) are therefore used to smooth out bursty traffic over relatively low-speed WAN circuits. It is important that sufficient buffer space is available for worst-case bursts; otherwise, traffic is likely to be dropped, causing retransmissions, which in turn may increase the overall load. Fortunately, memory prices have dropped rapidly over recent years. For multiple flows running over a WAN router link an accepted level of efficiency for queuing is approximately 80 to 90 percent. For example, on a 128-Kbps circuit we should expect a throughput of approximately 115 Kbps. Ideally, we should aim for average utilization of approximately 70 percent to allow traffic bursts to be handled with minimal performance degradation, but given the cost of wide area bandwidth there is always a temptation to maximize utilization.

Another factor to consider where there is a large speed differential is the time packets spend in queues and overall contribution of queuing to end-to-end latency. Real-time and mission-critical applications may not tolerate the latency or jitter introduced by end-to-end buffering, forcing timeouts and retransmissions. Some applications may even condition traffic before transmission, to regulate the end-to-end flow in such a way that jitter is artificially constrained (e.g., by purposely introducing a high initial delay in transmission and then using this delay window to even out jitter). Another factor is that packets that remain in queues for too long will age out and be discarded (low-priority packets are particularly vulnerable, especially in periods of congestion). This also leads to retransmissions, often aggravating the situation further.

2.5   Preparing data for modeling

By this stage we should have enough information to build detailed maps of application use, identify what the major application flows are, and be able to summarize traffic by using traffic matrices. First, let's start with application maps.

2.5.1   Application maps

In any reasonable-sized network it can be extremely useful to characterize application use by generating a series of application maps. These can be drawn logically or as physical maps, as shown in Figure 2.9. In the example shown we can plot user populations together with the physical distribution

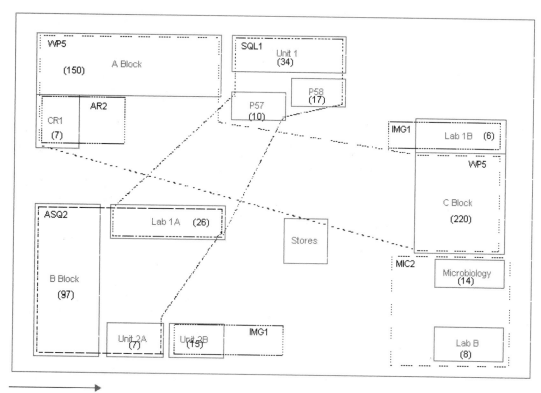

Figure 2.9   *Application map at the campus level.*

of various applications over a campus site. This example can be expanded hierarchically to include as much detail as is deemed appropriate. In Figure 2.9, we see five applications (WP5, SQL1, ASQ2, IMG1, and MIC2) superimposed over the physical site layout. In brackets we also include current user populations. This diagram is useful to begin flow analysis of each application.

In a real network design there may be several maps per site, showing not just the different types of applications, but also projected changes and growth in use over time. This kind of schematic is particularly useful when presenting ideas to senior management, since it is visual and readily understandable.

2.5.2   Characterizing flows

There are a number of different application architectures, such as centralized, client/server, peer-to-peer, and fully distributed. It is clear, therefore, that network traffic can be characterized by different types of flow, and it is important to both recognize and capture these differences so that adequate provisioning is provided. We can broadly classify flows into the following groups:

- Terminal-host traffic—for example, Telnet. The traffic profile is typically bidirectional and asymmetrical with most traffic coming from the host to the terminal (i.e., screen updates). The terminal typically sends no more than a few characters at a time as users type on the keyboard.

- Client/server traffic—for example, remote database access, FTP, NFS, Web traffic (HTTP). The traffic profile is typically bidirectional and asymmetrical with most traffic coming from the server to the client. Client traffic comprises mainly small packets but occasionally may be larger as data are pushed up to the server.

- Peer-to-peer traffic—for example, routing traffic, peer workgroup resource sharing, HTTP, and NFS. The traffic profile is typically bidirectional and symmetrical. Essentially, with this model several cooperating entities may act as both client and server simultaneously for multiple applications.

- Server-to-server traffic—for example, DEC VAX cluster communications, management applications, directory services, caching systems, and information feed-processing subsystems. The traffic profile is typically bidirectional and usually symmetrical, but asymmetrical flows are also possible, depending upon the application (e.g., there may be a hierarchy of servers leading to some asymmetry).

- Distributed entity traffic—for example, CORBA or EJB distributed object interaction, distributed NFS components. Some objects or systems may interact heavily; some may communicate infrequently. The traffic profile here is very much application dependent.

As discussed previously, for each application it is important to understand how the underlying components interact, since this directly affects the kinds of flows imposed on the network. The old adage of 80 percent local traffic, 20 percent remote still works in legacy client/server environments, but with the increased use of distributed components and corporate intranets it may be more realistic to expect a 50:50 split, or even a 20:80 split. At the highest level we should identify the major sources and sinks of data in the network. Using the example network in Figure 2.9, we can further refine this schematic with the flow data, as illustrated in Figure 2.10. Each flow can be quantified separately and subsequently broken down.

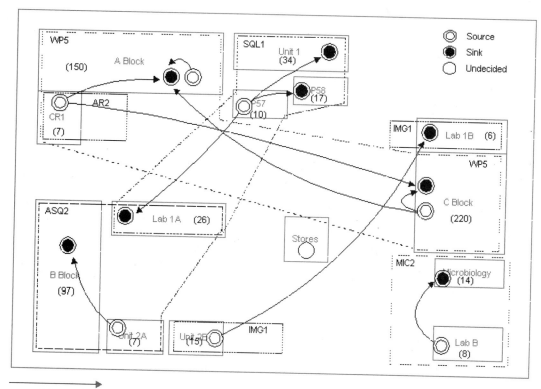

Figure 2.10   *High-level application flow map at the campus level.*

As we begin to refine these data, we can eventually develop, for each class of user on the network, a picture of the applications each class is using and the kind of behavior to be expected. We must ultimately quantify traffic flows by direction, size, and the physical source and destinations. To characterize individual flows we can build simple spreadsheets, as illustrated in Figure 2.11. In general, many applications are asymmetric in operation; FTP file transfer or Telnet/VTP (virtual terminal protocol) are typical. In highly asymmetrical applications you can often ignore acknowledgment traffic, since it is often insignificant (typically less than 5 percent). In any case you should always quantify the worst-case flows. Capture both flow directions if the application is symmetrical (since this represents double the load).

As well as building user profiles, quantify any significant system or server interaction, such as server-to-server communication disk mirroring or inter-process communication (e.g., DEC VAX cluster behavior). You may find that some of this activity is extremely time sensitive and may influence your

Node Type:							Client	X
							Server	
							IMP	

Application	Activity	Flow	Message Size (Bytes)	Frame Size (Bytes)	Frms/Msg	Frequency (frms/hour)	Bit Rate (bps)
FTP	File Transfer	Tx	100,000.000	1,514.000	66.050	3.000	666.667
		Rx	64.000	64.000	1.000	3.000	0.427
DTP	Print Graphics	Tx	4,000,000.000	1,514.000	2,642.008	1.000	8,888.889
		Rx	64.000	64.000	1.000	1.000	0.142
W P	Print Doc	Tx	2,048.000	1,200.000	1.707	5.000	22.756
		Rx	64.000	64.000	1.000	5.000	0.711
NetScape	Web Access	Tx	128.000	128.000	1.000	200.000	56.889
		Rx	12,800.000	1,500.000	8.533	200.000	5,688.889
Aggregate Traffic (bps)							15,325.369

Figure 2.11 *Simple application profile for a networked client. Note that if the application is running over Ethernet, four bytes should be appended to the message size for the Ethernet Frame Check Sequence.*

design. Once you have a profile for all of the major user and server groups, you can use the population data to scale up the demands placed on the network. From these aggregated data we can start to produce traffic matrices, as we shall see shortly.

For the interested reader, reference [1] provides a systems-based approach to network design that makes good use of application mapping techniques.

2.5.3   Building the traffic matrix

Once application flows have been established, we need to overlay all of these flows on some form of network data map. Typically we will use a traffic matrix to represent composite (aggregated or summarized) traffic flows, as illustrated in Figure 2.12. The traffic matrix is a common way to summarize and represent network data, such as traffic flows, link capacities, and performance data. In network modeling traffic matrices are widely used, and if you are planning to use automated design tools as part of the design process, then producing a good traffic matrix is key to starting the design process. As we can see in Figure 2.12, there are two characteristic flow distributions: symmetrical and asymmetrical.

Symmetrical

Symmetrical traffic is typical of networks with distributed resources, where traffic flow is broadly the same in any two directions. We could expect this

	A	B	C	D	E	F	G
A	0	2	1	10	34	0	8
B	1	0	5	5	4	46	7
C	24	3	0	19	2	4	0
D	65	4	3	0	1	2	5
E	3	17	10	0	0	1	23
F	37	20	4	44	6	0	2
G	17	3	26	33	1	5	0

(a)

	A	B	C	D	E	F	G
A	0	34	30	29	34	44	30
B	21	37	25	28	34	46	32
C	24	32	0	19	28	19	30
D	35	42	43	0	23	20	25
E	31	19	26	41	0	25	23
F	37	20	4	44	27	0	34
G	17	27	26	33	43	38	0

(b)

	A	B	C	D	E	F	G
A	0	2	32	2	1	1	4
B	2	0	34	3	5	2	6
C	67	72	0	78	103	65	98
D	9	3	37	0	2	3	1
E	2	4	56	4	0	3	1
F	5	7	37	3	6	0	4
G	4	1	45	2	8	2	0

(c)

Figure 2.12   *Traffic matrices for a network of seven sites: (a) simple traffic matrix, (b) symmetrical traffic matrix, (c) asymmetrical traffic matrix.*

kind of flow where services are handled at the local level, and the only inter-site communication is for communication such as e-mail or file transfer. A typical symmetrical flow matrix is shown in Figure 2.12(b). Notice that the traffic flows are roughly the same in each direction, and this reflects the relative democracy of the application use between sites.

Asymmetrical

Asymmetrical traffic is typical of networks with centralized resources. In reality most networks will exhibit asymmetrical traffic flow, since it is common for at least some of the main business applications to be managed and housed centrally for cost, security, and maintenance reasons. A typical asymmetrical flow matrix is shown in Figure 2.12(c). Notice here that there is a clear focus of traffic to and from site C. In this case site C may be where a central mainframe or server farm is housed.

To build a matrix from your raw data you could simply create a number of linked tables in this form, one for each class of user, and use the final table to add together all of the application traffic per cell. The units in each of these cells are arbitrary and could represent packets, bits, or calls per second. The letters A through G in this diagram typically indicate sites. For example, the aggregate traffic coming from site E to site A is 34 units. The traffic from site A to site E, on the other hand, is only three units. More complex multiprotocol and multimedia traffic may require N-dimensional matrices to take into account features such as priority, delay, and throughput.

For the interested reader, references [2, 3] describe an architecture for measuring and reporting traffic flows, with particular reference to the Internet. This architecture is intended to provide a starting point for the Real-time Traffic Flow Measurement Working Group.

2.5.4   Modeling the data

The ideas presented so far have been rather simplistic and do not take into account the fact that there is going to be contention for both the server and network resources. Users will be making simultaneous demands on servers, and at the same time stations will be competing for bandwidth on both LAN and WAN links. In these events a queue of requests will form, as individual messages wait in line to be processed. Queuing is another key concept that must be considered in capacity planning.

To illustrate this point, suppose that a database server is capable of servicing user requests for data records in 2 ms (this level of response would typically be observed if data are already in cache). So how many transactions per second will this system support? The simple answer is: 1/0.002 = 500 transactions per second. Assuming that transactions occur regularly, at a rate of one every 2 ms, then the server will be able to respond to all of them, and each will get 2-ms response time per record. However, let's assume that all requests occur at exactly the same time; clearly the server will have to queue these requests and deal with each one in turn. Assuming a FIFO queue, then the first user will experience a 2-ms response time; however, the last user in the queue will get a huge one-second response time.

Whenever resources are contended for, additional performance hits will be incurred due to queuing, and these delays are strongly dependent on the time distribution of requests being made by the users. Clearly, queuing has an important part to play in the capacity planning of network designs; there is a large body of queuing theory, and there are several commercial simulation tools that can be used. The next chapter covers the subject of queuing and modeling in depth.

2.6   **Summary**

In this chapter we covered the following:

- The penalties of poor or nonexistent capacity planning are likely to be financially disastrous on any medium to large network. The key to successful network capacity planning is to understand the needs of the users and the behavior of networked applications and services.

- Use a top-down approach, and then refine your data. Start with simple estimates of capacity of the various elements in your system. Map out user communities and the locations of key sites and buildings. If possible take baseline measurements of the existing environment. This information is invaluable for future trend analysis and network optimization.

- Terms such as mega and kilo are frequently misinterpreted, depending upon whether we are talking about link speed or message size. Make sure you are consistent.

- Traffic flows may be uni- or bidirectional, asymmetrical or symmetrical. Different types of applications tend to exhibit characteristic flow patterns. Traffic matrices give us a useful visual map of the traffic flows and form the basis for the design and modeling phases. It is important to identify the major sources and sinks of information.

- By identifying potential bottlenecks in the design early on, these areas can be monitored over time and dealt with proactively. Bottleneck analysis can also be extremely valuable later, since this information can focus remedial attention more effectively should performance problems emerge.

- Simulation tools can assist you in modeling the end-to-end performance of your applications and in removing potential bottlenecks to expansion.

References

[1]   J. McCabe, *Practical Computer Network Analysis and Design* (San Mateo, CA: Morgan Kaufmann,1998).

[2]   Traffic Flow Measurements: Architecture, RFC 2063, January 1997.

[3]   Traffic Flow Measurements: Meter MIB, RFC 2064, January 1997.

Network Design and Modeling

The introduction of new kinds of network applications, such as the World Wide Web (WWW), multimedia, and e-commerce, has made it increasingly difficult to accurately predict traffic behavior on large communications networks. The complex interaction between multiple protocols and applications, different vendor devices, sophisticated queuing strategies, and mixed media types all make this a complicated task.

Before investing valuable time and money in deploying a new network infrastructure, it is often worth investing some effort in trying to predict just how that network will behave. Careful design and a solid understanding of the appropriate tools to use can reduce many pitfalls associated with growth. We will examine both the general approach you should take when tackling a design and some of the underlying theory and tools you should be aware of. Discussions focus on the following topics:

- Hierarchical design models

- Topology designs

- Resilient design techniques

- Multiprotocol or single-protocol models

- Shortest path algorithms

By creating better models of network traffic we are more able to design better protocols, better network topologies, better routing and switching hardware, and better services to users. Apart from providing the predictive models it also provides an overview of key design methodologies, together with some of the key terminology used. Once the design has been decided, there are several techniques that can be employed to model network and system behavior. Generally these techniques fall into three broad categories, in increasing order of accuracy, as follows:

- Analytical models

- Simulation models

- Empirical models

Networks naturally expand to offer more service or reflect the current trend toward business consolidation. Network planners, therefore, have to accommodate expansion into their designs.

3.1 Hierarchical design model

When approaching any large task it is natural to break it down into manageable pieces. The most favored strategy for an internetwork design is the hierarchical model, where we attempt to isolate different layers of the model into discrete tasks, with defined interfaces between each layer. The main functional layers in a hierarchical model are the access, distribution, and backbone layers, as illustrated in Figure 3.1.

The backbone (or core) layer provides optimal transport between sites via Backbone Nodes (BNs).

Figure 3.1
The hierarchical design model.

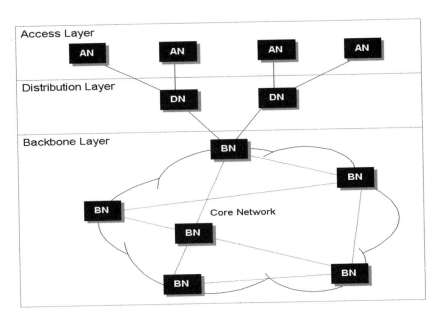

The distribution layer provides policy-based connectivity via Distribution Nodes (DNs).

The access layer provides workgroup and user access to the network via Access Nodes (ANs).

By using a layered approach we can simplify this enormous task and in many cases treat each layer as an individual design project, or subnetwork, and even hand this out to different design groups. Hierarchical designs also facilitate scaling of internetworks, because new subnetwork modules and internetworking technologies can be integrated into the overall scheme without necessarily disrupting the existing backbone. This approach enables the network traffic, capacity, and node placements to be more easily managed. Figure 3.1 shows a high-level view of the various aspects of a hierarchical network design. This model enables traffic and topology problems to be solved independently. In the diagram, the blocked objects would typically be routers.

3.1.1 Backbone layer

The backbone layer (sometimes referred to as the core) is typically a high-speed switching network optimized for packet or cell switching and forwarding. These networks are generally deployed as a collection of high-capacity trunk circuits, interconnecting a number of large backbone switches located in major population centers. The physical topology employed should offer some degree of fault tolerance to avoid major service outages, and so a degree of circuit meshing is likely. Backbones are generally constructed from Frame Relay or ATM meshed networks or private high-speed leased circuits and satellite links. Since these circuits often cover large distances (possibly spanning countries or even continents), it is important to get the design of the backbone as near to optimal as possible.

The backbone layer is concerned with huge volumes of traffic and is designed to do simple things very quickly. To assist this, backbones are generally single-protocol entities—today almost exclusively based on IP.

3.1.2 Distribution layer

The distribution layer is effectively the glue between the access and backbone layers, and this is typically a concentration point where multiple Local Area Networks (LANs) from a campus or metropolitan area are collapsed into a central distribution node. In this layer we would expect to see a range of medium-speed circuits and perhaps less redundancy (depending upon how mission-critical the application is). Packet manipulation may take place at this layer, since we are effectively feeding large concentrations of traffic into the backbone, and this traffic may be of mixed protocol types or require address translation. In the noncampus environment, the distribution layer is typically a redistribution point between routing domains, or the demarcation between static and dynamic routing protocols.

3.1.3 Access layer

The access layer is the interface layer through which end users and services are allowed access to the network. Typically this is the domain of the Local Area Network (LAN). Switching nodes within the access layer may employ access lists (i.e., packet filtering) to control traffic, and resource-intensive applications such as protocol and address translation are not uncommon. In the campus environment this layer is responsible for shared/switched bandwidth provisioning, MAC layer filtering, and microsegmentation. In the noncampus environment, this layer may provide remote access capabilities via wide area technology such as Frame Relay, ISDN, leased lines, and dial-up analog modem circuits.

3.1.4 Advantages of a hierarchical design

For a network to function well and to remain in control, it is desirable that some degree of hierarchy be maintained. Although other design strategies are possible, there are several real advantages that favor a hierarchical approach, as follows:

- Scalability—Hierarchical designs are modular and enable changes at one layer to be isolated from the rest of the network. Adding a new distribution node, for example, becomes a straightforward task, and new circuits can be easily deployed in the backbone to accommodate additional traffic.

- Manageability—Problems in a hierarchical design can be quickly identified, and traffic management becomes easier within clearly defined boundaries and interfaces.

- Broadcast traffic segmentation—Broadcast and multicast domains are constrained so that bandwidth and packet replication issues become more manageable.

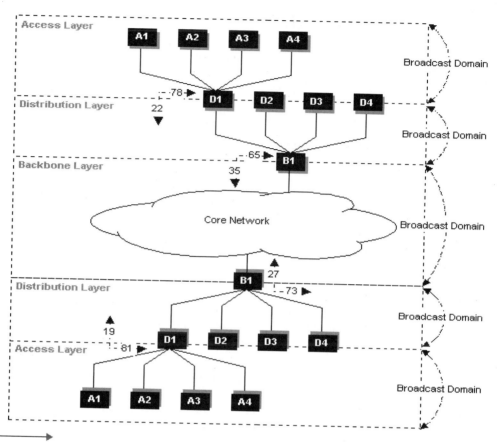

Figure 3.2 *Traffic flows and broadcast/multicast segmentation in the hierarchical model.*

Figure 3.2 illustrates traffic flows and segmentation in the hierarchical model. At each major interface there is a local and remote component of the traffic flow (shown as horizontal and vertical arrows, respectively). These numbers represent the percentage of a layer's traffic that is destined for local or remote users. Remote traffic is injected into the distribution layer and into the backbone layer. Local traffic is handled by the distribution and backbone nodes internally (i.e., by switching traffic between ports). Each layer also acts as a self-contained broadcast/multicast domain. As we will see later on, different routing protocols are applicable for each layer.

The discussions that follow outline the capabilities and services associated with backbone, distribution, and local access internetworking services.

3.2   Protocol models

Given that today's networks still harbor significant islands of legacy protocols, when you are designing an internetwork you must consider whether to
implement a multiprotocol or single-protocol network. The following discussions outline the characteristics and properties of these two strategies.

3.2.1   Multiprotocol design

For many years backbone networks often had no choice but to carry different protocol traffic in their native format, often by building parallel networks, limiting functionality, or by performing protocol conversion on
gateways and host systems. Today, a multiprotocol network design may
adopt one of the following routing strategies, depending on the routing
protocols involved:

- Integrated routing—requires a single routing protocol to build the
  shortest path topology, routing tables and forwarding different protocols. For example, Cisco's proprietary EIGRP routing protocol
  supports several protocol stacks concurrently. The standards-based
  protocol Integrated IS-IS supports both OSI and TCP/IP traffic concurrently. With this approach different protocols are routed over the
  backbone without any additional encapsulation, so the packets from
  different protocol stacks effectively coexist on the same physical link.
  The key advantage is that routing tables are unified and there is likely
  to be fewer resources required (i.e., CPU, RAM) on the router.

- "Ships-in-the-night" routing—involves the use of a different routing
  protocol for each network protocol. Again, with this approach different protocols are routed over the backbone without any additional
  encapsulation, so the packets from different protocol stacks effectively
  coexist on the same physical link. A router would run multiple routing protocol instances concurrently. For example, IP could be routed
  with OSPF, and DECnet Phase V traffic could be routed via ISO IS-
  IS. Each of these network layer protocols requires separate routing
  processes and resources to handle each traffic type.

- Encapsulation routing (tunneling)—involves the use of a single routing protocol, which either routes native traffic directly or encapsulates
  foreign traffic inside native traffic. This router could, for example, be
  a pure IP router. It would either forward native IP packets or wrap
  any foreign protocols inside IP before forwarding. Clearly, other rout-

ers would need to decapsulate packets elsewhere in the network. This way the core network remains a pure IP environment.

Multiprotocol routing is inherently inefficient and resource intensive, especially when we see three independent routing protocols handling traffic like "ships in the night." Network troubleshooting can also be a nightmare. Of these two approaches integrated routing is easier to manage and deploy; however, this approach may not be available for all protocol stacks you need to transport. Tunneling may be the only option for some protocols if you wish to limit the number of protocols running on the distribution or core network.

3.2.2 Single-protocol design

If we have fewer protocols running on the internetwork, then more resources will be available for actually forwarding traffic, and less overhead traffic will be present on the wire. In a single-protocol backbone, all routers can run a single routing protocol instance, and there is a common routing table. If multiple protocols are to be passed over the backbone, then these foreign protocols must be encapsulated within the backbone protocol or they will simply be dropped. Consider, however, that this additional encapsulation will add overhead to traffic on the backbone (e.g., an additional 20 bytes per packet for IPv4 encapsulation). This is a small price to pay for simplicity.

3.3 Review of topology design and optimization

Within all three levels of the network hierarchy—backbone, distribution, and access—you are free to decide upon the best physical topology to suit your needs. The simplest topology could be a star topology at all three levels, so there would be a central backbone node, acting as a concentrator for all the main distribution nodes, which in turn feed all the access nodes. In reality this is rarely done or even achievable for many reasons, as we shall see. When designing any internetwork, whether it is based on packet-switching services or point-to-point interconnections, there are essentially three design patterns you can adopt, as follows:

- Star topology

- Fully or partial meshed topology

- Tree topology

It is typically only at the local area environment where we get to choose bus style topologies, so we will not discuss them in this section.

3.3.1 Techniques for improving performance and resilience

Once a basic network design is established, it is likely that you will want to assess both the reliability and the performance characteristics of the network and make improvements where appropriate. This includes techniques such as the following:

- Load sharing over multiple paths and dynamic link aggregation

- Backup or dial-up links

- Network segmentation

We will briefly review these techniques in the following text.

Load balancing

Load balancing is a generic technique that can be employed at various levels of the design hierarchy. The level of meshing within the backbone network provides potential opportunities for delivering traffic over multiple paths, and at the local access layer it is quite common to load balance traffic over multiple lower-speed, point-to-point circuits.

Routers and routing protocols often provide support for load balancing over multiple links and paths. For example, the OSPF protocol has an optional feature called multilink, where multiple paths of equal cost can support traffic sharing. In some routing implementations (such as IGRP and EIGRP) unequal cost load balancing is also possible within certain metric ranges, and traffic can be shared in proportion to the offered capacity. There are also a number of service-oriented and clustering techniques. With many of the Layer 3 (and above) software load-sharing techniques you will find a range of distribution algorithms available, such as round robin, source-destination hash, or destination hash.

Alternate paths

Large internetwork backbones generally carry at least some mission-critical data. Many businesses and organizations that use these backbones will expect a high degree of protection and are prepared to pay for it. Unfortunately, a totally resilient design is often not possible, as the costs of total fault tolerance are likely to be prohibitive. The trade-off here is between cost and risk. The main techniques of importance include the following:

- Alternate paths—for example, ISDN dial-up

- Standby devices that can come online automatically whenever a failure occurs (using VRRP, HSRP protocols)

- System hardware fault-tolerance—load-sharing power supplies, split buses, duplicate routing processors

Most medium to large networks should protect mission-critical segments by using backup or dial-up links. To be truly effective these backup links should terminate at routers different from the original link termination points. Although backbone routers may be completely fault tolerant (no single points of failure), the interface into the packet-switched network may itself be a single point of failure.

Network segmentation

One of the main tasks on any internetwork design is to contain all unnecessary traffic, and we can achieve this by limiting the scope of traffic (particularly broadcast and multicast traffic) to the domains for which they are applicable. Fundamental to this concept is a thorough understanding of where the traffic is actually flowing. At the highest level of the design, segmentation is provided automatically by access routers and switches. These devices implement local policies and are configured to drop all unnecessary traffic. As we move further in toward the core, routers tend to do much less packet manipulation and will support fewer protocols in an effort to maintain optimum throughput.

3.4   Spanning trees and shortest-path algorithms

The problem of identifying shortest paths is fundamental to network design. The term shortest path implies quickest and cheapest, which is generally what we are aiming for with most network designs, although we may have more subtle requirements based on performance, delay, and resilience. Algorithms used to determine shortest paths are heavily dependent on the granularity of the metrics used. This section covers some of the key concepts of path-finding algorithms, trees, and some of the data structures you should consider when implementing such techniques in design tools.

3.4.1   Complexity analysis—Big "Oh"

The performance characteristics of these algorithms are fundamental to many aspects of network design because of the following performance issues:

- Network design tool performance—In network design we are often dealing with what are termed N-P complete or N-P hard problems [1]. These problems (such as least-cost topology design with multiple constraints) are basically very tough to resolve (mathematically intractable) and require repetitive, greedy heuristic algorithms to search for near-optimal solutions. Since these algorithms may be run many times in the inner loops of design tools, it is important to understand and quantify their performance characteristics. For practical purposes, if we were modeling a very large network, then we would typically wish to see 90 percent optimal solutions within at most a few hours (enabling us to try out a few different scenarios), rather than a 99 percent optimal solution after a week.

- Real-time implementation performance—We may have to run these algorithms within the critical tight time constraints of a real-time system. For example, we might be running a shortest-path algorithm in real-time software embedded within a router, operating in a large internetwork domain. This algorithm will need to converge quickly, in order that the network as a whole can converge and reestablish packet forwarding.

For engineers without a computer science background some of the terminology used in the literature may seem impenetrable at times. Often we will see phrases such as the algorithm has a time complexity of $O(\log N)$. This phrase has a very specific meaning, and once understood, you can easily translate it into language you understand. The following list describes common terminology, called Big "Oh" notation, which is used to characterize algorithm complexity (e.g., worst-case performance bounds). In practice you may also see these terms applied to other areas of data communications (such as routing table growth, memory utilization, etc.). Big "Oh" is essentially a form of shorthand used to characterize growth.

Big "Oh" Meanings

$O(1)$	Constant
$O(\log N)$	Logarithmic
$O(\log^2 N)$	Log-squared

Big "Oh" Meanings

$O(N)$	Linear
$O(N \log N)$	N log N
$O(N^2)$	Quadratic
$O(N^3)$	Cubic
$O(2^N)$	Exponential

When applied to algorithms these terms are most frequently used to characterize the worst-case growth rate applied to the time taken for the algorithm to complete a task, based on input data of size N objects. For example, we could characterize the time taken for an algorithm to work out the shortest path in a graph, based on a network of N nodes. This growth rate may simply be unacceptable for a large population of N, especially if the algorithm is intended as part of the inner loop of a more complex program. Much of the attention in algorithm design is, therefore, aimed at reducing time complexity.

3.4.2   Minimum Spanning Tree

The next problem we will consider is that of finding a Minimum Spanning Tree (MST) in an undirected graph (a graph where edge costs are symmetrical). Informally, a minimum spanning tree of an undirected graph, G, is a tree formed from graph edges that connect all the vertices of G at the lowest total cost. A minimum spanning tree exists if, and only if, G is connected. In Figure 3.3 the second graph is a minimum spanning tree of the first (it happens to be unique—but this is not always the case, since there may be

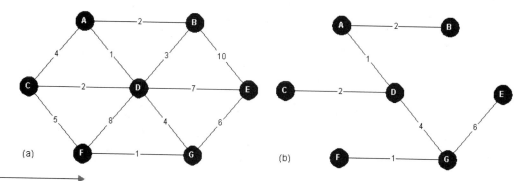

Figure 3.3   *(a) A weighted graph, G, and (b) its minimum spanning tree.*

more than one MST within the same topology). The number of edges in the minimum spanning tree is $|V| - 1$. The minimum spanning tree is a tree because it is acyclic; it is spanning because it covers every edge; and it is minimum because the sum of all edge costs connecting each node is minimized, or $\Sigma C_{ij}\, min$.

Note that graphs may have more than one minimum spanning tree. Spanning trees are used in many aspects of network design. For example, if we need to design a physical network topology with a minimum of cable, then an MST problem needs to be solved. Spanning trees are commonly employed in routers and bridges to resolve logical topology issues and ensure that loops are not formed (which could create traffic meltdown).

3.4.3 Dijkstra's algorithm

Dijkstra's algorithm is a greedy algorithm, which basically performs a breadth-first traversal to create a single spanning tree from the perspective of each node in the topology. The algorithm can be stated as follows: Find the shortest paths from a given vertex to all other vertices by processing the paths in order of increasing path length. Dijkstra is perhaps most notably implemented by the OSPF Link State routing protocol. The algorithm proceeds as follows:

- Mark each node as unscanned, and assign each node a label equal to infinity (where the label indicates the distance to the root node).

- Assign the root node a label equal to zero. Set the predecessor of the root node to itself.

- Loop until all nodes have been scanned.
    - Find the node n with the smallest label (d_min).
    - Mark the node as scanned.
    - Scan through the adjacent nodes, m, to see if the distance to root through n is better than the distance stored in the label of m. If so, update the label with the shorter distance and set *pred* [m] = n.

When the loop terminates, we will have a tree stored in predecessor format, anchored at the root node. The predecessors are as follows:

Predecessors:

0 : 0

1 : 0

2 : 4

Predecessors:

3 : 0

4 : 3

5 : 4

The complexity of Dijkstra is $O(N^2)$. It is most suitable for dense networks and is especially appropriate for parallel implementation, where the scan operation can be carried out independently, and results in linear $O(1)$ rather than quadratic running times. Dijkstra does not take good advantage of sparse networks and requires positive metrics.

3.4.4   Prim's algorithm

In each stage, one node is picked as the root, to which we attach the lowest-cost adjacent edge (and thus an associated vertex) to the tree. At any point in the algorithm, we can see that we have a set of vertices that have already been included in the tree and a set of vertices that have not. The algorithm finds, at each stage, a new vertex to add to the tree by choosing the edge (u, v) such that the cost of (u, v) is the smallest among all edges where u is in the tree and v is not.

We can see that Prim's algorithm is almost identical to Dijkstra's algorithm for shortest paths. As before, for each vertex we keep values dv and pv and an indication of whether it is known or unknown. dv is the weight of the shortest arc connecting v to a known vertex, and pv, as before, is the last vertex to cause a change in dv. The rest of the algorithm is exactly the same, with the exception that since the definition of dv is different, so is the update rule. For this problem, the update rule is even simpler than before: After a vertex, v, is selected, for each unknown w adjacent to v, $dv = min(dw, cw, v)$. Be aware that Prim's algorithm runs on undirected graphs, so when coding it, remember to put every edge in two adjacency lists. The running time is $O(|V|2)$ without heaps, which is optimal for dense graphs, and $O(|E| \log |V|)$ using binary heaps, which is good for sparse graphs.

3.4.5   Kruskal's algorithm

Kruskal's algorithm is another greedy strategy that iterates by selecting edges in order of smallest weight, accepting an edge only if it does not cause a cycle, until all edges have been tested. The algorithm is typically implemented by maintaining a forest (a collection of trees), with initially $|V|$ single-node trees. Adding an edge forces two trees to merge, and when the algorithm terminates, there is only one tree, the Minimum Spanning Tree (MST). The algorithm proceeds as follows:

- Check that the graph, G, is connected; if not, abort.

- Sort the edges of G in ascending order or weight.

- Mark each node as a separate component.

- Loop through the edges until we have accepted $|G| - 1$ edges. Let e be the candidate edge.

- If the two ends of e are in different components, merge those components and accept the edge; then increment the number of edges accepted by one.

An edge consists of three pieces of data (source, destination, cost); it is typically more efficient to implement the priority queue as an array of pointers to edges, rather than as an array of edges (so only pointers, not large records, need to be moved when rearranging the heap). The worst-case running time of this algorithm is $O(|E| \log |E|)$, which is dominated by the heap operations. However, since $|E| = O(|V|^2)$, the running time is actually $O(|E| \log |V|)$. The algorithm completes much faster than this time bound would indicate in practice [2].

3.4.6   Floyd-Warshall algorithm

The Floyd-Warshall algorithm [3] computes the shortest paths between all pairs of nodes. The algorithm is used in some networks that deploy centralized routing (such as TYMNET). The route matrix (Table 3.1) is structured so that node R[i][j] is the number of the next last node along the path ij. For example, the optimal path from node 0 to node 5 can be found by first

Table 3.1   *Simple Route Matrix*

	0	1	2	3	4	5
0	0	0	4	0	3	4
1	1	0	1	1	3	4
2	3	2	0	4	2	4
3	3	3	4	0	3	4
4	3	3	4	4	0	4
5	3	3	4	4	5	0

looking at R[0][5], which indicates that node 4 is the preceding node. Node 4 is preceded by node 3 (R[0][4]), which in turn is preceded by node 0 (R[0][3]). So the complete path from node 0 to node 5 is 0,3,4,5.

The complexity of Floyd-Warshall is $O(N^3)$, since at each of N steps the algorithm must be executed for $O(N^2)$ node pairs. This is the same as running Dijkstra to find the same optimal route set.

3.4.7   Bellman-Ford algorithm

The Bellman-Ford algorithm is a greedy algorithm and can be implemented as a breadth-first search; it is based on Bellman's principle of optimality [4, 5]. It was originated by Bellman [6] and subsequently refined by Ford [7] and Moore [8]. The algorithm is sometimes referred to as the Ford-Fulkerson algorithm [9]. The algorithm can be stated as follows: Find the shortest paths from a given vertex subject to the constraint that the paths contain at most one link, then find the shortest paths with a constraint of paths of at most two links, and so on.

Bellman-Ford is perhaps most notably implemented by the RIP distance vector routing protocol. This algorithm will find optimum routes even where some costs are negative, as long as there are no loops where the total distance is negative. The algorithm works well either for working out the optimal paths from a source node to all destinations or for working out optimal routes to a specific destination from all other nodes. Essentially the algorithm scans nodes in the order they are labeled, eliminating the requirement to find the smallest label. It is possible to enhance the implementation with an array to manage nodes that are already in the queue, avoiding the need to have duplicate copies in the queue.

Experiments indicate that in large, sparse networks this modification of the Bellman-Ford algorithm is faster than almost any other known algorithm for finding optimal paths from a specified source node to all destinations. In reality many telecommunications networks exhibit this form of topology. The computational requirements can be estimated as follows. For a network of N nodes, a path contains at most $N-1$ links. Therefore, there can be at most $N-1$ iterations for convergence. With each iteration a minimisation is done over at most $N-1$ alternatives. Hence, the worst-case computation is in the order of $O(N^3)$. In practice the complexity can be shown to be $O(mE)$, where E represents the number of edges (links) and m the number of iterations required for convergence. This is considerably faster than $O(N^3)$.

3.4.8 Distributed asynchronous Bellman-Ford

There are two basic problems with a synchronous implementation: getting all nodes to start the algorithm at the same time, and figuring out a method of aborting calculation should a link state change occur while in the middle of a computation. The simpler alternative is to run the algorithm asynchronously at regular intervals. The algorithm converges to correct distances in a finite time, providing no changes occur within this time, regardless of the initial conditions. Even if several changes occur in a short interval, the algorithm will converge if the time before the next change is sufficient.

The algorithm is more suited to datagram traffic than virtual circuit traffic, since packets may travel via different paths and arrive out of order when the algorithm is adapting to changes, and long delays are possible. The algorithm is also prone to looping.

3.4.9 Stability issues with shortest path routing

There can be significant stability problems with shortest path routing where metrics are affected by traffic on links. In cases where delay is dynamically calculated it is possible to achieve oscillating paths, as traffic is switched from one path to another in response to increasing delay. There can be a positive feedback mechanism induced, since link arrival rates depend upon routing and vice versa. Various techniques such as dampening or bias factors can be employed to control this (as employed on the original ARPANET), although they may not solve all potential issues. Other techniques are commonly used, such as hold downs or staggering the intervals at which nodes recalculate routing tables.

3.5   Modeling

For serious network design a combination of the analytical, theoretical, and prototyping methodologies can be tremendously helpful in identifying potential limitations of the design. At least some time should be devoted to analytical or simulation tools, since these can reveal obvious bottlenecks in the design and highlight performance thresholds that were not anticipated. Pilot tests can often be achieved at very little cost or exposure to the customer, generally with the assistance of the supplier (who is usually only too willing to get involved). There may be issues with implementation, or there may be specific bugs that occur only under heavily stressed conditions. It is very useful to try to simulate both the traffic dynamics of the expected network utilization and the upper bounds of the equipment's performance curve.

A good model can predict, within reasonable limits, what will happen most of the time. It is no substitute, however, for the real thing, and you need to concern yourself with the task of identifying where the model is likely to go wrong and whether the design you choose to implement meets the financial or performance constraints placed on it.

3.5.1 Analytical modeling

Analytical models are purely theoretical, relying heavily on mathematical techniques. The advantages of analytical models are that they are very fast (usually several orders of magnitude faster than simulation) and can sometimes offer greater insight. The disadvantages are a tendency to oversimplify; there is a danger of building a model that does not reflect reality if too many shortcuts are taken.

Overview of analytical traffic models

In this section we give a brief overview of three broad classes of stochastic models for packetized traffic, as follows:

- Classical or short range dependent models (Poisson models)

- Packet train models

- Long-range dependent models (self-similarity and fractal models)

For an overview of basic probability theory and distribution models refer to [10, 11]. Several recent studies [12], however, question the validity of these distribution models for modern circuit-switched networks. The question of why and how traffic dynamics have changed is still an active area of research and has led to the introduction of new traffic models, which have profound implications for network designers. We will now review the classical model.

Classical queuing analysis (short-range dependent memory model)

Although Erlang's theories used to model both circuit-switched traffic and packet-switched traffic were first outlined in the 1920s, the concepts of queuing theory are still relevant for today's more complex devices, such as multilayer switches and multiprotocol routers.

Markovian queuing systems have been widely documented and used for several decades to model network traffic. These models are sometimes referred to as short-range dependent (SRD) processes, assuming Poisson packet arrival rates and an exponential distribution of message lengths. Studies on data traffic indicated that external data sources in communication networks were often bursty in nature (i.e., relatively short periods of activity followed by longer idle periods). These models make several assumptions for the following data sources:

- Message interarrival times are exponentially distributed.

- Message lengths are exponentially distributed.

- Processes described by $T(i)$ and $L(i)$ are stationary and independent.

The last assumption is not realistic, since intuitively it is clear that interarrival times and message lengths for message streams entering a packet switch node are statistically dependent. For example, if we consider two messages arriving one after the other at a switch, the second message cannot get into the switch before the first message has arrived completely.

Queuing models

The arrival or input process is analogous to the arrival of data frames into a receive buffer. The server process performs operations on these frames (such as unpacking protocol layers), and the output process is responsible for transmitting frames to the next node. If the arrival rate exceeds the service rate for any period, then a queue will form (sometimes referred to as a waiting line), assuming buffers are available. If a queue is never formed, then this implies that the service is either idle or has more than sufficient capacity (i.e., it has a faster frame-processing speed than can ever be met by the input feed).

The queuing models can be one of the following four types:

- Single channel, single phase (see Figure 3.4[a])

- Multiple channel, single phase (see Figure 3.4[b])

- Single channel, multiple phase (see Figure 3.4[c])

- Multiple channel, multiple phase (see Figure 3.4[d])

An example of a multiple-phase system would be a device that receives frames, processes them, and then hands them off to other systems for further processing before releasing onto a communication link. In effect all networks are multiphase when considered as a whole. However, such networks can be discretely modeled, using the single-phase model on a point-

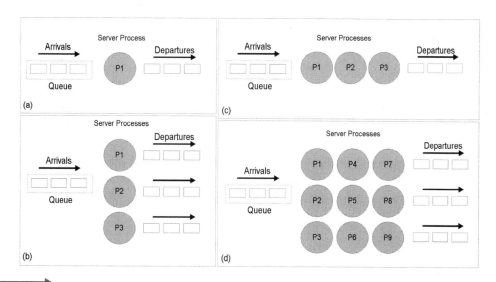

Figure 3.4   *Queuing models.*

to-point basis, by taking each node in isolation and modeling the output of one device as the input for the next device.

Statistical distribution functions

In order to quantify arrivals and service times, we must use a distribution function to model the probabilities of both the distribution of frame arrivals and time to service; these outcomes are represented by random variables. There are two types of distribution functions that control queuing systems: discrete and continuous. There are many statistical functions for determining the probability distribution for random variables, including (but not limited to) the following:

Normal	Log-Normal
Uniform	Poisson
Exponential	Beta
Binomial	Negative
Gamma	Triangular
Geometric	Hypergeometric
Erlang F	Weibull
Students t	Chi-squared
Laplace	Pareto

For further information about their derivations and applications refer to [13, 14]. For more general information about statistical distributions refer to [15].

Poisson distribution   As indicated previously, for packet-switched networks the distribution of arrivals is typically a Markovian process, represented by a Poisson distribution. Poisson is a discrete distribution, which assumes that an arrival is independent of previous arrivals, and the probability of more than one arrival is negligible compared with that one arrival. The PDF for a Poisson distribution is as follows:

$$P(x) = \frac{\lambda^x e^{-\lambda}}{x!}$$

where:

$P(x)$ = probability of n arrivals

λ = mean arrival rate

e = exponent function (2.7182818)

$x!$ = x factorial

Figure 3.5(a) illustrates the Poisson distribution profile.

Exponential distribution   The distribution function for modeling interarrival times in a Poisson process is the exponential function (an example of a continuous distribution function). The PDF for an exponential distribution is as follows:

$$P(x) = \xi e^{-\lambda x}$$

Figure 3.5(b) illustrates the exponential distribution profile.

The Poisson system is the simplest and best-known distribution function for traffic modeling [16]; however, many authors now believe that the Poisson process is inappropriate for today's data traffic [17]. Nevertheless, Poisson systems are referenced many times in network simulation and modeling, and they are essentially the benchmark against which all other models are compared.

Queuing metrics

Queues can be characterized by a number of metrics. These metrics summarise the status and performance of queues in a steady state and are often

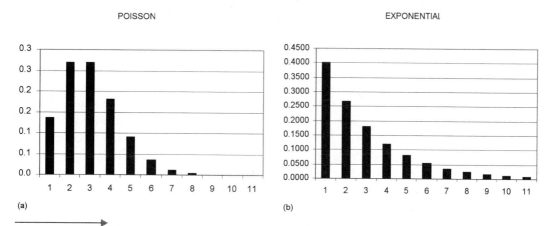

Figure 3.5 *(a) Poisson distribution with a mean arrival rate of λ = 2. (b) Exponential distribution with a mean arrival rate of λ = 0.4.*

used to form part of the output of a theoretical model or simulation. In the case of packet-switched networks the term customers equates to packets, frames, or cells.

Waiting time is a measure of the total time spent queuing and being serviced and is expressed as:

Waiting time = time in system = queuing time + service time

Traffic intensity indicates the capacity of the server to cope with arrivals. It provides a measure of how many servers are occupied on average (measured in Erlangs) and is expressed as:

$$\text{Traffic intensity} = \frac{\text{mean service time}}{\text{mean interarrival time}} = \frac{\text{mean arrival rate}}{\text{mean service rate}}$$

Utilization factor indicates the server utilization and is closely related to traffic intensity. Low traffic intensity implies that the server is lightly loaded and hence has low utilization. Since a server cannot be utilized more than 100 percent of the time, the utilization factor is at most 1, and for most systems utilization is below 1. Arrival and departure rates are effectively the same where server utilization is less than 1 (since it has spare capacity and therefore is not acting as a bottleneck). Utilization is expressed as:

$$\text{Utilization} = \frac{\text{traffic intensity}}{\text{number of servers}}$$

Throughput is a measure of the amount of work done in a specified period of time. In simulation this would normally be the period of simulation. Throughput is expressed as:

$$\text{Throughput} = \frac{\text{total customers served}}{\text{time interval}}$$

Mean queue size is a measure of the number of customers waiting in front of a server process (i.e., in the queue), averaged over a time period that is relatively long compared with the interarrival time. If traffic intensity is less than 1, then the queue size will have a well-defined mean value. If traffic intensity is greater than 1, then the queue size never stabilizes and continues to grow as more arrivals occur. Mean queue size is expressed as:

Mean queue size = mean number in system − traffic intensity

Little's result

Little's result is one of the key elements of queuing theory and was formulated in 1961 (with some later enhancements). It states that if L_q is the average number of customers in the queue and W_q is the average queuing time, then both the following relationships hold true:

$$L_q = (\lambda)W_q$$
$$L = (\lambda)W$$

and

$$W = W_q + T_{avg}$$

where

T_{avg} = the average service time (effectively T_p in an M/M/1 queuing system with one transmission line).

Buffer utilization in packet-switched networks

In packet-switched networks it is often important to calculate when a buffer will overflow, since in these circumstances data will be lost. Devices such as bridges and routers typically support a variety of interface speeds, which dictates that buffers must be used to solve the problem of speed matching. This is most evident on remote bridges and routers, where relatively low-speed WAN links may be fed by very fast LAN links. Without buffering, these devices would simply drop packets due to the wide area link's inability to service LAN-speed traffic. On some products users may be allowed to configure buffer sizes, timers for holding frames in the buffer, and possibly even add more memory to provide the system with more buffers. This section examines how queuing theory can be used to estimate buffer memory utilization in such devices.

If we denote the mean length of a queue as Lq, we can multiply by the mean frame size to determine the average buffer size required. Clearly, this is not too helpful, as we can conclude that half of the time we will need more buffers. In order to determine worst-case buffer size we need to compute the probability of different numbers of frames in the system. The probability that there will be n packets in the M/M/1 queue is approximated as:

$$P_n = (\lambda/\mu)^n (1 - \lambda/\mu) = \rho^n(1 - \rho)$$

We can use this to calculate the probability of overflowing a buffer capable of holding k packets of variable length $P_{[n \leq k]}$, in a single-server system as follows:

$$P_{[n \leq k]} = (\lambda/\mu)^k = \rho^k$$

Assuming that we want a 99.9 percent probability of not overflowing the buffer, we can calculate the thresholds for minimum queue size for various levels of server utilization. For example, Table 3.2 and Figure 3.6 illustrate the utilization and queue lengths for Ethernet and Token Ring, at various packet sizes. We calculate queue length as:

$$\rho^n(1 - \rho)$$

that is,

$$[(Util/100)^2]/[1 - (Util/100)]$$

We calculate buffer requirements as:

(Queue length × Frame length + 0.99)

since we are looking for $P_{[n \leq 99.9]}$.

From Table 3.2 and Figure 3.6 we observe that as the level of server utilization increases, so does the queue length. We can see also that at 50 percent utilization the queue length is 0.5, but above 70 percent we start to see a steep climb in queue length. In fact, in a single-server system, once the utilization exceeds 50 percent we start to see notable increases in the queue length. As the utilization approaches 100 percent, particularly in the final 10 percent, we see substantial increases in the queue length. Since the mean queue length is directly related to the mean waiting time, this is a good reason to consider increasing network capacity when utilization exceeds

Table 3.2   *Growth in Buffer Requirements for Ethernet and Token Ring as Utilization Increases in a Single-Phase, Single-Channel System (M/M/1)*

Utilisation (%)	Queue Size (Frames)	Ethernet 10Mbps	Token Ring 4Mbps	Token Ring 16Mbps
0	0.0000	0	0	0
10	0.0111	17	50	200
20	0.0500	75	225	900
30	0.1286	193	579	2315
40	0.2667	400	1200	4800
50	0.5000	750	2250	9000
60	0.9000	1350	4050	16200
70	1.6333	2450	7350	29400
80	3.2000	4800	14400	57600
85	4.8167	7225	21675	86700
90	8.1000	12150	36450	145800
91	9.2011	13802	41405	165620
92	10.5800	15870	47610	190440
93	12.3557	18534	55601	222403
94	14.7267	22090	66270	265080
95	18.0500	27075	81225	324900
96	23.0400	34560	103680	414720
97	31.3633	47045	141135	564540
98	48.0200	72030	216090	864360
99	98.0100	147015	441045	1764180
Frame Size =		1500	4500	18000

50 percent. Recent studies [17] indicate that traffic models based on heavy-tailed distributions, such as the Pareto distribution [18], are required when dealing with small buffer sizes.

Figure 3.6
Growth in buffer requirements as utilization increases in a single-phase, single-channel system.

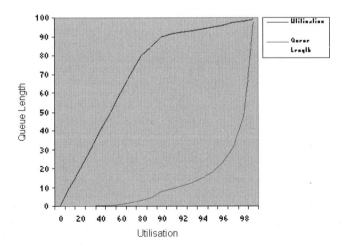

Networks of M/M/1 queues

In real data networks we are mostly concerned with the performance of traffic over multiple hops, where multiple queues are entered and exited and traffic streams merge and split repeatedly. This raises the problem of how to model packet interarrival times in store-and-forward communication networks after the first queue has been traversed, since subsequent interarrival times become strongly correlated with packet lengths. Packets enter the first queue randomly, but the exit distribution is controlled by the time required to process a packet, which is determined by the length of the packet, and this distribution becomes the next queue arrival distribution. A very large packet traveling around the network maintains its size, and therefore introduces nonrandom gaps in the arrival pattern. This would appear to invalidate queuing models based on Poisson distribution.

Kleinrock [19] observed this problem and resolved it by introducing the Kleinrock independence assumption (or independence approximation). This proposes that in systems with multiple data sources, the effects of merging multiple packet streams over a network restore the independence of arrival times. Kleinrock proposed that when a message is received at a packet-switch node, it loses its identity, and a new length can be chosen from an exponential distribution. This implies that the message length varies from hop to hop, and therefore the service time (i.e., the link propagation delay) will differ for the same message as it traverses the network. Obviously this assumption does reflect reality, but its mathematical consequences have led to models that fairly accurately describe the behavior of store-and-forward communication networks. By using this approximation we can derive the average number of packets in the system as if each queue were M/M/1.

An open network of M/M/1 queues can be analyzed as if each queue were isolated, and this analysis is due to Jackson's theorem [20]. The output of one channel becomes the input of another, and in many cases several M/M/1 queues are being multiplexed and demultiplexed, reinforcing the Poisson distribution. It is useful in these circumstances to quantify a number of metrics, including the mean number of hops per packet and the mean queuing delays experienced overall, on a per-circuit basis. Assuming capacity, C_i, of a communications circuit, we can calculate the aggregate delay of both the queuing and transmission delay, T_i, as follows [21]:

$$T_i = 1/(\mu C_i - \lambda_i)$$

Table 3.3   *Network of Queues Base Data: (a) End-to-End Traffic Matrix for a Six-Node Network (b) Link/Circuit Capacity Assigned (c) Routing Table (d) Aggregated Traffic Flows Calculated by Imposing the Routing Table on the Basic Traffic Matrix*

	A	B	C	D	E	F
A	-	65	20	5	55	25
B	65	-	65	28	44	5
C	20	65	-	25	15	10
D	5	28	25	-	15	20
E	55	44	15	15	-	120
F	25	5	10	20	120	-

(a) Traffic Matrix (pps)

	A	B	C	D	E	F
A	-	AB	ABC	ABFD	AE	ABF
B	BA	-	BC	BFD	BFE	BF
C	CBA	CB	-	CD	CE	CEF
D	DFBA	DFB	DC	-	DCE	DF
E	EA	EFB	EC	ECD	-	EF
F	FBA	FB	FEC	FD	FE	-

(c) Routing Matrix

	A	B	C	D	E	F
A	-	128	-	-	128	-
B	128	-	128	-	-	128
C	-	128	-	64	128	-
D	-	-	64	-	-	64
E	128	-	128	-	-	256
F	-	128	-	64	256	-

(b) Capacity Matrix (Kbps)

	A	B	C	D	E	F
A	-	115	-	-	55	-
B	115	-	85	-	-	107
C	-	85	-	40	40	-
D	-	-	40	-	-	53
E	55	-	40	-	-	174
F	-	107	-	53	174	-

(d) Aggregate traffic (pps, via routing table)

For example, for an arrival rate of 10 pps over a 64-Kbps circuit, and a mean frame size of 500 bytes (4,000 bits), we calculate T_i as follows:

$$T_i = 1/(64,000/4,000 - 10) = 167 \text{ ms}$$

To illustrate the calculation of mean queuing delay, consider the example in Table 3.3. We assume a partially connected graph of six nodes: A

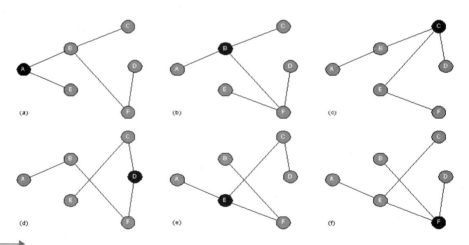

Figure 3.7   *Shortest path routes for a six-node example topology. Each graph shows the shortest path tree calculated via the routing matrix for each source node, A through F.*

Table 3.4 *Delay Analysis for a Network of Queues*

Line	AR(λ_i)	Ci	μCi	Ti	Tavg
AB	115	128	123.1	123.8	10.6
BC	85	128	123.1	26.3	1.7
CD	40	64	61.5	46.4	1.4
AE	55	128	123.1	14.7	0.6
EF	174	256	246.2	13.9	1.8
FD	53	64	61.5	117.1	4.6
BF	107	128	123.1	62.2	5.0
EC	40	128	123.1	12.0	0.4
TOTAL	669	1024	984.6	416.4	26.1

through F. Table 3.3(a) shows the end-to-end traffic requirements for each node. Table 3.3(b) shows the assigned capacities for physically connected circuits (hence this is also an adjacency matrix). Table 3.3(c) shows the routing table to be used for directing traffic flows, which results in six logical topologies (shortest path trees per source node), illustrated in Figure 3.7. When the end-to-end traffic flows are superimposed over the routing topology, we arrive at a set of aggregated traffic between each node, illustrated in Table 3.3(d). For example, the total traffic on link AB comprises four flows: AB, ABC, ABFD, ABF. Hence, total arrival rate (AR) for link AB = 65 + 20 + 5 + 25 = 115 pps.

Table 3.4 provides a simple delay analysis using a network of M/M/1 queues based on this example network. We assume an average frame size of 130 bytes (1,040 bits). From this analysis we can see that worst-case delay of 123.6 ms is experienced by link AB, hardly surprising since this 128-Kbps circuit carries 119.6 Kbps of aggregated traffic (115 × 1,040 bits per packet). The arrival rate is summarized traffic listed in packets per second. Capacity *(C)* is listed in Kbps; μC is listed as packets per second. Link delay and mean delay per line, T_{avg} are measured in milliseconds.

The mean hop per packet is 1.29, and the mean packet delay for the entire network is found to be 67.49 ms. These metrics are calculated as follows:

Total traffic between nodes:

$$y = \sum_{i=1}^{n}\sum_{j=1}^{n} y_{ij} = \text{Sum of all traffic in Table 3.2(a)} = 1{,}034 \text{ pps}$$

Total arrival rate (TAR) $\lambda = \sum \lambda_i = 669 \times 2 = 1{,}338$ pps

$$\text{Mean hops per packet } H_{avg} = \lambda / y = 1,338/1,034 = 1.294 \text{ hops}$$

$$\text{Mean line delay (ms) } T_{avg} = \sum_{i=1}^{m} (\lambda_i \times T_i / \lambda)$$

$$\text{Mean packet delay (ms) } T = H_{avg} \sum_{i=1}^{m} T_{avg} = 1.29 \times 26.1 \times 2 = 67.49 \text{ ms}$$

In this example we assigned circuit capacities statically. Additional material and a more rigorous mathematical treatment of these subjects can be found in [10, 21].

Modeling packetized traffic

In packet-, frame-, or cell-switched networks we need to build a model that incorporates the concept of queuing, since packets are generally dealt with on a best-effort basis and dynamically held in buffers to cope with congestion and mismatches in line speeds. It is easy to see why it emerged: A telephone conversation requires a constant steady flow, in-sequence transmission, and a guaranteed connection. If small fragments of the voice transmission are lost, it is often still possible to make sense of most of what is being said. It is, however, difficult to make sense of a conversation that fluctuates in speed markedly or delivers information out of sequence.

Packet-switched networks make extensive use of buffering, and in the following sections we will concentrate on the use of simple M/M/1 queues to model a number of networking scenarios. We will also use some of the queuing metrics previously discussed. In these examples we are particularly interested in analyzing the following:

- The impact of circuit bandwidth on the throughput of devices such as bridges, routers, and switches

- The estimation of buffer sizes best suited to different channel size scenarios

- The optimization of response time and queuing delays

In general we should be aiming for optimum performance without overspecifying the service facility or its resources. In packet-switched networks it is often accepted that you will drop some packets; it is up to the applications to pick up the pieces—besides, wide area bandwidth is expensive.

Example 1: X.25 packet switch   In this example we have an X.25 packet switch that has four users, each transmitting 128-byte frames (including ten

Table 3.5 *X.25 Queuing Model—Single Channel, Single Phase*

Queuing Theory Example:		
X25 Switch, 56Kbps Trunk Single Channel, Single Phase		Buffer = M/M/1

Input

Average Day	7.5	hours
Number of Users	4	
User Frame Rate	12.00	frames per second per user
Aggregate Frame Rate	1296000	total frames per day
Average Mesage Size	118	bytes (frame size at arrival)
Frame Overhead on Trunk	10	bytes (protocol overhead)
Average Frame Size on Trunk (Fw)	128	bytes (frame + overhead)
Trunk Speed (Cs)	56000	bits per sec

Output

Average Arrival Rate λ (AR)	48.000	frames per sec
Arrival Bit Rate (AR * Fw * 8)	49152.000	bits per sec
Expected Service Time (EST)	0.018	secs
Mean Service Rate μ (MSR)	54.688	frames per sec
Utilization of Server (p)	87.771	%
Probability of no Frames in Router (Po)	12.229	%
Mean Frames in System (L)	7.178	frames
Mean Queue Length (Lq)	6.300	frames
Mean Frames on Channel (L-Lq)	0.878	frames
Mean Loading of Channel ((L-Lq) * Fw/Cs)	1.605	%
Mean Waiting Time in Queue (Wq)	0.131	secs
Mean Waiting Time in System, i.e. Response Time (W)	0.150	secs

bytes of protocol overhead) at a rate of 12 frames per second. This gives us an arrival rate, λ, of 48 frames per second. Traffic is forwarded over a 56-Kbps circuit.

The results of our queuing analysis are illustrated in Table 3.5. We deduce that there is an average response time of 150 ms; this could be a problem for virtual terminal applications (such as Telnet or an X.25 PAD), since users are likely to see a noticeable delay on the screen while typing at the keyboard. Actually the problem is even worse, since during echoplexing the character generated by the keystroke must traverse the link twice in order to be processed by the remote application server, so our real response time is going to be 300 ms plus host turnaround time.

Note also that the queuing delay, at 131 ms, is much greater than the transmission delay, at 18 ms, and we can see that the utilization of the trunk, at 1.6 percent, is directly influenced by the queuing delay. As system utilization increases, so does the delay through the system (W), as shown in

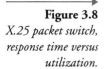

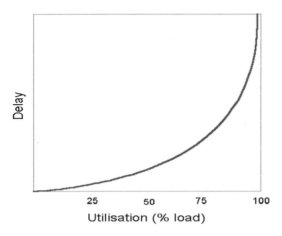

Figure 3.8. If the delay due to queuing becomes excessive, then we can either remove some users or add more circuits to the switch.

Example 2: Interconnecting remote LANs   In this example we have two remote local area networks with an active population of 80 users (i.e., live traffic sources), which we intend to connect. We have the usual pressure to limit costs but also an additional constraint to achieve a mean response time *(W)* of less than 100 ms. We also know that at some point in the near future the number of active users is predicted to rise to 145. From our initial data-gathering phase we estimate that there will be a worst-case scenario of 216,000 frames sent between the two sites in an average day (7.5 hours), with an average frame size of 548 bytes (including protocol overheads).

Initially we do not know what size circuit we should provision between the two sites, but let us start off by assuming a 64-Kbps leased line. In our example we assume also that the link is full duplex and offers symmetrical bandwidth (it could be running different speeds in either direction if the service was ATM). In either case it is generally sufficient to take the worst-case scenario. With 80 users transmitting we can see that the 64-Kbps line copes reasonably well, but the main concern is that latency incurred in the system results in a mean response time of 152 ms, exceeding our delay constraint. (See Figure 3.9.)

If we subsequently increase the number of users to 145, we can see that the effects of queuing significantly degrade performance. There is a less than 1 percent chance of having no frames queued. There is an average of 146 frames in the queue and a server utilization of over 99 percent. The response time and the queuing time exceed ten seconds. This latency is likely to cause buffer timeouts (i.e., frames age out and are flushed from the

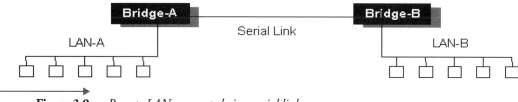

Figure 3.9   *Remote LANs connected via a serial link.*

queue), and the acknowledgment timers of many protocols may also be exceeded. These factors are likely to induce more retransmissions and thereby aggravate the situation further by increasing the load.

Let us see what happens when we upgrade our serial link to 128 Kbps. This increases our ability to service frames and should alleviate the queuing backlog. Clearly, things are looking better. Server utilization has dropped to under 50 percent, and response time has dropped. We also see that there is an approximate 50 percent chance of having no packets queued at all. To illustrate the point further, we can model these inputs across a range of circuit speeds to get the results shown in Table 3.6.

By examining these data we can see that there is little point in installing a link slower than 64 Kbps, since the delays become exponential and server utilization, ρ, exceeds 100 percent (i.e., impossible). To meet our ideal average response time of less than 100 ms we should install a 128-Kbps link or higher. We can also see that the benefits of higher bandwidth tail off quite rapidly, and to meet our cost constraints it would appear unnecessary to install additional bandwidth above 128 Kbps at this stage. In Table 3.7, traffic comprises 145 users sending 548 byte frames at 14.5 frames per second. Utilization (ρ) values of 1 or greater are untenable, since queuing at this level simply breaks down through exponential delays.

Modeling circuit-switched traffic

Circuit-switching networks are historically associated with telephony, although access technologies such as ISDN are now widely used to transport both data and voice. Circuit switching operates differently from packet switching, in that traffic cannot flow until a call has been made and a circuit established. Furthermore, systems that terminate calls (i.e., switches) have finite resources for handling calls. Unlike packet networks, where we are concerned primarily with queuing models, with circuit-switched networks it is important to understand how to provision circuits and analyze the effects of blocking (when no further calls can be received until resources are released).

Table 3.6   *Queuing Analysis for a Remote LAN with a 64-Kbps Serial Line. Traffic Comprises 80 Users Sending 548-Byte Frames at Eight Frames per Second*

Queuing Theory Example: Bridged LAN to LAN, 64 Kbps Trunk, Single Channel, Single Phase		Buffer = M/M/1
Input		
Average Day	7.5	hours
Number of Users	80	
User Frame Rate	0.10	frames per second per user
Aggregate Frame Rate	216000	total frames per day
Average Mesage Size	540	bytes (frame size at arrival)
Frame Overhead on Trunk	8	bytes (protocol overhead)
Average Frame Size on Trunk (Fw)	548	bytes (frame + overhead)
Trunk Speed (Cs)	64000	bits per sec
Output		
Average Arrival Rate λ (AR)	8.000	frames per sec
Arrival Bit Rate (AR * Fw * 8)	35072.000	bits per sec
Expected Service Time (EST)	0.069	secs
Mean Service Rate μ (MSR)	14.599	frames per sec
Utilization of Server (p)	54.800	%
Probability of no Frames in Router (Po)	45.200	%
Mean Frames in System (L)	1.212	frames
Mean Queue Length (Lq)	0.664	frames
Mean Frames on Channel (L-Lq)	0.548	frames
Mean Loading of Channel ((L-Lq) * Fw/Cs)	3.754	%
Mean Waiting Time in Queue (Wq)	0.083	secs
Mean Waiting Time in System, i.e. Response Time (W)	0.152	secs

Circuit-switched traffic modeling is the domain of Erlang analysis. This refers to the statistical estimate of user demand based on random call arrival, measured in units called Erlangs. One Erlang is equivalent to 36 Call Century Seconds, or CCS (a rather archaic measurement arrived at by Bell Labs, where a camera recorded pictures of call peg counters on the electro-mechanical switches every 100 seconds). The formula used to calculate Erlangs is as follows:

$$E = lt$$

where

E = one Erlang

l = mean arrival rate (calls/hour)

t = mean holding time (hours)

Table 3.7 *Remote LANs, Single Channel, Single Phase*

Channel (bps)	AR λ	EST	MSR μ	Po	p	L	Lq	W	Wq	Load %
4,800.000	14.50	0.913	1.095	-12.243	13.243	-1.082	-14.325	-0.075	-0.988	1209.56
9,600.000	14.50	0.457	2.190	-5.622	6.622	-1.178	-7.800	-0.081	-0.538	302.39
19,200.000	14.50	0.228	4.380	-2.311	3.311	-1.433	-4.744	-0.099	-0.327	75.60
56,000.000	14.50	0.078	12.774	-0.135	1.135	-8.400	-9.535	-0.579	-0.658	8.89
64,000.000	14.50	0.069	14.599	0.007	0.993	147.148	146.155	10.148	10.080	6.80
128,000.000	14.50	0.034	29.197	0.503	0.497	0.987	0.490	0.068	0.034	1.70
256,000.000	14.50	0.017	58.394	0.752	0.248	0.330	0.082	0.023	0.006	0.43
384,000.000	14.50	0.011	87.591	0.834	0.166	0.198	0.033	0.014	0.002	0.19
768,000.000	14.50	0.006	175.182	0.917	0.083	0.090	0.007	0.006	0.001	0.05
1,536,000.000	14.50	0.003	350.365	0.959	0.041	0.043	0.002	0.003	0.000	0.01
2,048,000.000	14.50	0.002	467.153	0.969	0.031	0.032	0.001	0.002	0.000	0.01
8,192,000.000	14.50	0.001	1868.613	0.992	0.008	0.008	0.000	0.001	0.000	0.00

This measurement was originally introduced for analyzing analog voice communications. Calls arrive at a switch at a rate, λ, and their total transmission time is τ hours. For example, assume five users at a switch. If each user calls every 50 seconds and talks for 30 seconds before disconnecting, the total utilization of the circuit is 0.6 Erlangs:

$$1/50 \times 30 = 0.6$$

Obviously it is possible to offer one Erlang (one circuit) to every user, but since statistically not all users will be calling at the same time, it is much more cost-effective to provide a lower number of circuits. The utilization of an access line is, in practice, much less than one Erlang. Obviously this formula is very simplistic, and in most cases call duration will vary. Therefore, we use the following formula:

$$\sum_{n=1}^{k} \tau n = \text{average Erlangs}$$

where

k = total calls completed in one hour

τn = length of the calls in hours

Since all blocked calls are cleared, we should calculate blocking from the above formula, where the probability of blocking (B) is:

$$B = \frac{E^N/N!}{\sum_{n=1}^{k=N} E^k/k!}$$

where

B = B(N,E) = (the percent of blocking as a function of the number of lines available and the number of affected Erlangs)

$N!$ = N factorial (i.e., $N(N-1)(N-2)\ldots$)

As the call arrival rate increases, the probability that the call will be blocked or dropped increases. Most packet-switching design books include Erlang B (lost calls cleared) tables, which demonstrate blocking versus Erlangs for various levels of traffic. For further information on this topic the interested reader is referred to [22].

Call abandonment   A more subtle issue in determining optimal capacity in circuit-switched networks is characterizing real user behavior in the advent of call blocking and its revenue impact. This is a particular issue for call center applications, where businesses need to know whether to install more lines, employ more reception staff, or assume callers will retry later. The revenue impact of abandoned calls is difficult to assess. The interested reader is referred to [23], where a mathematical model is presented to analyze this issue. A model is presented demonstrating the impact of the probability that an abandoned call is reattempted on the fraction of calls handled by the service. The fraction of calls handled is directly proportional to the revenue obtained. The outputs of the model show that the fraction of abandoned calls reattempted has only a small impact on the fraction of calls handled, provided that the probability that a call is reattempted after abandonment lies between 0.0 and 0.5. The reason for this is that served reattempted calls increase the average time to answer of subsequent calls, both new and reattempted. This tends to increase the fraction of abandoned call attempts. The results also suggest that service improvements that reduce abandonment probabilities result in increased revenue regardless of the fraction of calls reattempted. Therefore, the decision to increase staffing levels or not is best made by comparing anticipated extra revenue with anticipated extra cost.

Packet train model

The classical Poisson queuing model can be thought of as the car model (where a car is analogous to a packet) in that it assumes that packets are autonomous. Even if all packets are traveling to the same destination, independent routing decisions are made at each major junction in the network. This typically results in some overhead, and on computer networks we see this as extra per-packet decision processing at intermediate nodes (e.g., routers). During the last decade the size of data objects moved over communications networks has increased dramatically, and this has caused several researchers to reexamine the nature of traffic flows more closely. Clearly, when a large object is transferred between two nodes, this means that many more packets are likely to be flowing down the same path in succession over a relatively short period of time. In the packet train model (which emerged in the mid-1980s, see [24]), packets are considered to travel together in groups, like carriages in a train. The traffic on the network is viewed as a number of packet streams (or flows) between multiple pairs of nodes on the network. Each node-pair stream comprises a number of trains. Each train holds a number of packets (cars) going in either direction. Unlike the classical model, the locomotive (the first packet of the train) may determine the routing decision, in which case all other packets in the train could simply follow it (see Figure 3.10). The intercar time (Tc) is small relative to the intertrain gap (Tt), so trains are effectively terminated and restarted when Tc exceeds the maximum allowed intercar gap (MAIG).

The packet train model is a source model in that it applies only when we look at the packets coming from or going to a single node. Furthermore, unlike the Poisson processes, packet trains are not additive, so the sum of several trains is not a train. Another important observation is that the packet arrivals exhibit a source locality, in that successive packets tend to belong to the same train. If a packet is seen on the network going from A to B, the probability of the next packet going from A to B or from B to A is

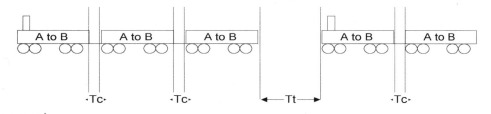

Figure 3.10 *Packet train model.*

very high. In the packet train model the intercarriage gap is assumed to be relatively large (compared with packet transmission time) and random. The intertrain time is assumed to be much larger. Clearly, a model based on the assumption of packet train arrivals would differ significantly from one based on independent arrivals. In order to allow analytical modeling with a simplified form of train model, a two-state Markovian model, where the source can be either in a generation (train) state or an idle (intertrain) state, and the transitions between these states are memory-less, has been suggested [24]. The duration of the two states is exponentially distributed, with intertrain arrival times usually on the order of several seconds, and intercar times inside the trains on the order of a few milliseconds.

The implications of the packet train arrivals and of source locality on the design of network equipment (bridges, routers, and gateways) and reservation protocols are significant, and there are several open problems still requiring development of analysis techniques for systems with train arrival processes [24, 25].

Self-similarity (long-range dependent memory model)

In the past, broadband networks were used for a relatively small number of file transfer or remote terminal applications, and the resulting traffic dynamics were thought to be well understood using classical queuing models. However, the nature of packetized data over broadband communications has now changed considerably to embrace a much broader set of mixed-media applications (e.g., video conferencing, file transfer, packetized voice, and Web browsing). This heterogeneous traffic mix has led many researchers to challenge the use of traditional traffic models. This view has been confirmed in recent years, largely through extensive and highly accurate traffic measurements [26], where traffic distribution in LANs and WANs [27] exhibited very close correlation over a range of time scales (not predicted in classical queuing models). This new distribution model is more formally referred to as the Long-Range Dependent (LRD) or long-memory model [28]. Furthermore, traffic distribution patterns in LANs were discovered to be self-similar (i.e., fractal, see [26]).

One of the most remarkable features exhibited by present-day traffic is the high degree of burstiness of traffic over almost all time scales (i.e., the traffic profile is not smoothed out as expected over large time scales or as the number of stations increases). This long-range burstiness is not predicted by the traditional traffic models, such as the Poisson process, and implies a long-range dependency. There are several methods that can be used to estimate the Hurst parameter; these are outside the scope of this book and the

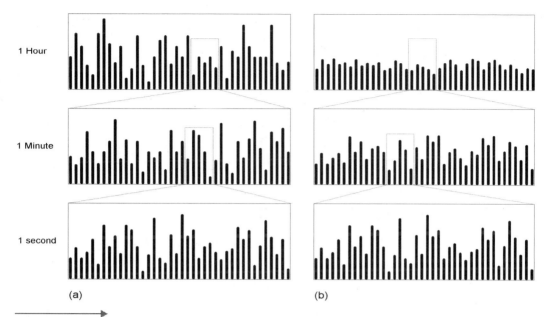

Figure 3.11   *Comparison of long- and short-range dependent models. (a) The long-range dependent model displays a high degree of self-similarity in the traffic profile, and burstiness is maintained over a wide range of time scales. (b) Traffic modeled using the Poisson process exhibits short-range dependence; over time the burstiness is averaged out.*

interested reader is referred to [29]. There have been several methods proposed to generate and simulate self-similar traffic; for example, traffic can be synthesized by superimposing packet trains produced by multiple on-off sources or by using the fast Fourier transform techniques. (See Figure 3.11.) Refer to [30] for further information.

Cell loss is of major significance for network designers and is an active area of research; for example, the first generation of ATM switches were designed using traditional Poisson assumptions, and these devices experienced a higher than anticipated level of cell loss [31], forcing a redesign.

Analytical modeling tools

Advances in analytical modeling techniques mean that analytical modeling is now more capable of handling large-scale, sophisticated network designs. Queuing models in particular have been actively researched for decades and are more precise for network traffic modeling than other analytical techniques (which model performance based on average values). For the network designer a good analytical queuing model could be used as the starting point for the network design or to create snapshots of the network in progress. Queuing models are generally easier to set up, require less CPU and RAM, run much faster than discrete-event simulations, and can therefore be applied to very large network studies. Simple analytical models can be constructed using basic spreadsheet tools. More sophisticated models can be created using specialized languages such as SLAM and Simscript. In order to relieve the user from much of the complexities, there are now commercial analytical modeling tools available, such as NAC WinMind and CACI's COMNet Predictor. WinMind uses analytical modeling methods to give you a picture of your entire WAN and also includes network pricing data.

3.5.2 Simulation modeling

The highly variable, bursty nature of today's packetized mixed-media traffic makes it very difficult to predict the use levels at which queuing delays become a significant component of end-to-end delay. Added to this is the increasing sophistication of bandwidth management and Quality of Service (QoS) systems employed on modern data networking hardware, as well as a whole array of new routing and signaling protocols, all interacting and affecting traffic dynamics in a highly complex manner. For these reasons we often turn to simulation modeling to help us better understand the traffic dynamics. First we outline the problem and gather data from the capacity-planning phase. Using these data we can build an abstract model of the system under test. The simulation activates entities within the model for a period of time and then outputs results. For a sanity check we must be sure to verify that the model behaves as expected and also validate the model against known inputs. Unexpected or anomalous behavior can be corrected and fed back into the model design. (See Figure 3.12.) Applications for these models include (but are not limited to) the following:

- Abstract system design through to detailed component design

- LAN and WAN capacity planning

- Delay modeling in packet-switched networks

- Blocking models for circuit-switched networks

- Protocol design and tuning

- Routing strategy and design

- Availability and survivability modeling

The outputs of the simulation are basically the same as we saw earlier with queuing theory; we are still essentially interested in waiting times,

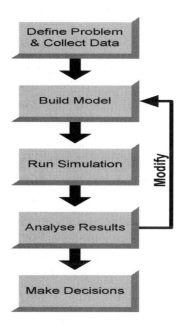

Figure 3.12
*Simulation
modeling process.*

queue lengths, and the utilization of resources. With a simulation, however, there is typically much better granularity: We may wish to see queuing statistics per interface, per circuit, per protocol, per application, or per storage subsystem. We may wish to model a specific networking device from a particular vendor, with a particular CPU/RAM configuration and a specific queuing strategy enabled. The complexity of these systems dictates that automated tools are preferred. In the following sections we will review both the tools available and the processes required to build simulation models.

Simulation methods

There are essentially three broad classes of simulation models in widespread use today, as follows:

- Discrete models—are a collection of abstract system objects called entities. Entities hold data pertinent to them and have associated functions. With event-driven models, actions on these entities occur on event boundaries (i.e., the status of an entity can change only on an event). Typical events include customer arrivals, customer departures, start of service, and end of service. The modeler defines not only the entities but also the events and the relationships between events. With process-driven models the entities themselves are effectively process objects with associated data. The modeler not only defines the entities but also the behavior associated with them and the interaction with other entities.

- Continuous models—are essentially mathematical models where the model changes state based on the computations of equations and their relationships with one another. The modeler must determine what equations are appropriate for describing the system being studied and define the relationships and interactions between these equations.

- Queuing models—were dealt within the previous section from an analytical standpoint. There are specialized languages available, however, to build queuing systems, and these will be described shortly.

Often several methods (possibly some proprietary) are employed in commercial tools to solve different problems in the same simulation package. From the network designer's perspective, there are several methodologies and tools available to model networks, depending upon the level of sophistication and flexibility required and the budget. These include the following:

- Spreadsheets and database tools (e.g., Microsoft Excel)

- Mathematical applications (e.g., MathCAD, MatLab, Mathematica, and Maple)

- Commercial discrete event simulation packages (e.g., BONeS Designer, OPNET, PlanNet, COMNET)

- Simulation programming languages (e.g., Simula, GSS, GPSS, Simscript)

- General-purpose programming languages (e.g., C, C++, Delphi, BASIC, Pascal, SmallTalk, PLI)

Many of these tools hook into live traffic collection systems, support auto-discovery features, and incorporate detailed equipment libraries containing object models of industry hardware (such as routers, switches, etc.). For total control you may choose to develop your model using either a specialized or general-purpose language (this approach is not recommended for the novice).

Since the analysis of modern data network operations is becoming so complex, discrete-event simulation, rather than queuing theory, has traditionally been the preferred methodology for understanding complex network performance. Discrete-event simulation analyzes the operation of a network over a period of time by scheduling the arrivals and departures of customers (i.e., messages, packets, frames, cells, etc.) within a software model of the network under scrutiny. Discrete-event simulation can be broadly classified into the following three main strategies:

- Two-phase event scheduling—processes entities at key event boundaries defined by the modeler. These models comprise an A-Phase, which identifies the next set of bound events to execute in the calendar, and a B-Phase, where those events are activated.

- Three-phase event scheduling—is essentially the same as the two-phase event model with an additional C-Phase. During the C-Phase an additional set of conditional events is scanned after the B-Phase. These events can be activated during the C-Phase, depending upon the state of the system.

- Process interaction—this strategy is similar to the three-phase model; however, attention is focused on the behavior of individual entities in the system rather than events. Here the A-Phase identifies the next bound events to execute, the B-Phase activates these entities, and the C-Phase scans for blocked entities ready to be executed.

Regardless of the strategy employed, a discrete-event simulation maps real-time activities onto its own simulated time using a private scheduler. Simulated time is said to be asynchronous, in that events are processed according to a calendar of waiting events, and the clock ticks that separate calendar intervals may be of unequal duration. It may, for example, take four seconds to process a number of events that are all expected to occur simultaneously in real life (so-called bound events), because in simulated time they must be processed sequentially (unless parallel processing is available). For a large-scale simulation of today's backbone or enterprise networks it can be impractical to use packet-level or cell-level discrete-event simulation for capacity planning purposes, since the run-time requirements could be prohibitive (especially if you need to simulate long periods of network activity to get statistically significant results). With this in mind we may need to compromise the scale of the simulation and focus only on the most sensitive aspects of the design [13].

Simulation modeling tools

Commercial modeling tools can give you a more detailed picture of performance issues, often presented through a graphical user-friendly interface. These products can be used to great effect if the designer takes the necessary care and attention when building the simulation model. In a large complex network they can highlight issues early in the design process, enabling you to make significant design trade-offs with some degree of confidence before committing serious time and money on deployment.

To get an idea about some of the concepts just discussed refer to [32, 33]. OPNET is a widely used commercial simulation modeling tool, particularly favored by the research community, while BONeS (Block-Oriented Network Simulator) Designer is a sophisticated modular simulation and modeling software package that operates on Sun workstations under UNIX, a typical high-end commercial product from Cadence Systems.

Simulation languages

For the experienced network designer with programming skills, there are a number of specialized languages developed specifically to handle simulation and queuing models. These languages have many built-in functions and facilities specifically designed for the generation of simulation tools, and so they greatly speed up development. These languages typically provide user transparency to tasks such as queue management, simulated time management, random number generation, scheduling, data collection and analysis, and statistical functions. The development of specialized languages started back in the 1950s. They are designed to eliminate much of the programming effort by focusing purely on the construction of the model. Although there have been many languages developed, only a few have gained wide acceptance. The most commonly used languages include GPSS, Simscript, Simula, GASP, SLAM, SIMON, and RESQ. They can be described as follows:

- GPSS (General-Purpose Simulation System) is the most commonly used special-purpose simulation language. GPSS is an interpretative, discrete-event simulation language developed at IBM and first published in 1961.

- Simscript is also very widely used and again is a special-purpose language for discrete-event simulation, first developed at the Rand Corporation in the early 1960s. Simscript is based on FORTRAN and is more of a general-purpose language than GPSS.

- Simula is a special-purpose simulation language based on ALGOL-60 and was developed in the early 1960s. It has a wide range of applications, not limited to simulation. Simula was widely used in Europe and Australia but never gained acceptance in commercial environments due to its complexity. Simula is essentially object based and had a significant influence on the development of several programming languages, such as Concurrent Pascal, ACT, and SmallTalk.

- SLAM (Simulation Language for Alternative Modeling) is yet another FORTRAN-based simulation language, first introduced in 1972. SLAM was based on GASP IV and Q-GERT (Queues' Graphical Evaluation and Review Techniques). It has three structures: process, event, and continuous. Later versions include animation and graphics support. SLAM provides a relatively simple and yet highly flexible way to build queuing models.

- RESQ (RESearch Queuing) package is a product of IBM research and is a software tool for developing queuing network models. RESQ offers a hierarchical modeling approach, and later versions include graphs support.

- GASP is a set of extensions to the general-purpose FORTRAN language and was first developed in the early 1970s. It is essentially a collection of FORTRAN subroutines specially designed for modeling discrete, continuous, and hybrid simulations.

- SIMON is a set of extensions to the general-purpose ALGOL language. It is essentially a collection of ALGOL subroutines designed to perform event-oriented simulation and results analysis.

While special-purpose languages are extremely useful for queuing models, it is also possible to develop simulation models in a general-purpose language such as FORTRAN, C, C++, Pascal, Ada, and PL/1. The advantages of a general-purpose language are primarily flexibility and the ability to understand and maintain the model without specialized language skills. Reference [1] provides a simple example of an event-driven simulation programmed in C and using linked lists. A more sophisticated approach is to use a general-purpose language such as C or C++ linked to a special simulation library. The interested reader is referred to [13], which provides an excellent treatment of this subject and complete source code for a working simulation library. Reference [34] provides an online catalog of simulation products and tools with links and references.

3.5.3 Empirical modeling

Network staging, or pilot testing, can be very helpful in determining network equipment or application performance thresholds and to iron out bugs in the system early on. From the customer perspective, a pilot test can avoid making serious errors in the network design or the choice of vendor equipment. From a vendor or system-integrator perspective, it is therefore advisable (if practical) to first test the main features of the network away from the customer site. This approach has several benefits to both parties, as follows:

- The customer's time is not wasted.

- It is not a good idea to make mistakes in front of the customer (especially in a competitive situation).

- More importantly, there will be no surprises.

More practically, you may have very little flexibility on site to do live testing, especially if the customer's business is network sensitive. Empirical modeling also has the very real benefit of allowing you to stress test the design on real network equipment to the absolute limits. The customer also can get a real appreciation of just how easy the equipment will be to configure, deploy, and diagnose in the real environment. As part of this process work can be started on developing training tools and installation guidelines for the subsequent mass deployment. The main drawbacks of empirical modeling are that it costs time and money, but any organization implementing a large network would be foolish to omit this stage in the design process.

Designing a prototype testbed

It would generally be impractical and prohibitively expensive to try to build a complete replica of the entire network prior to installation (although some customers may insist on something pretty close!). Figure 3.13 illustrates a testbed design for a regional Frame Relay network. Here we have a subset of the main design with traffic generators (TG-x) placed at strategic locations. Traffic could be taken from the live network and played back, or it could be generated from predicted models. We must also inject routes (RG-x) to simulate many additional routes. We will also want to run network analyzers (NA-x) at strategic points to record key performance data. This kind of testing can reveal basic functional and performance problems not anticipated in the theoretical design or simulation phase and can, therefore, provide valuable input into the final design. We can also stress the lab network well beyond anticipated thresholds to establish worst-case operating scenarios. It is not uncommon for this phase of testing to be used as part of the final selection criteria for the networking equipment, so it is important from the vendor perspective to anticipate any problems and resolve them beforehand.

Traffic generation

Once a basic testbed design has been established, the next problem you will encounter is how to scale up the traffic to simulate real working conditions on the live network. If you cannot physically prestage as many devices as are in the final network design, then the only real option is to use traffic generators to simulate the load (see Figure 3.13). Several options are available, as follows:

- Play back live traces—If possible get a live trace from the existing or proposed applications (as part of the capacity planning phase). For example, if we know that one of the services is a database query application, then get a packet trace of that application, capturing the key events. It should then be possible to edit that trace and build up a replay trace, which can simulate many more connections at the same

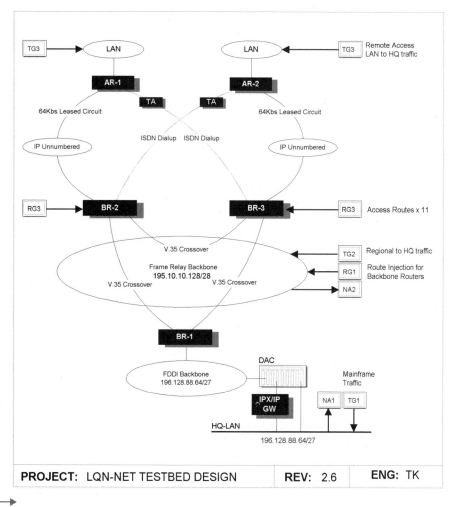

Figure 3.13   *Example testbed design for a regional Frame Relay network with ISDN backup links.*

time. This trace would be overlaid with other application flows. You may need to globally edit timestamps and modify addressees (and checksums) to simulate many flows and increase packet frequencies.

- Specialized packet generation and testing equipment—Use specialized low-level packet generators to both inject load and test for packet loss between send and receive ports. Examples include NetCom Systems' SmartBits tester [35], which is widely used for network performance analysis over a range of protocols and media types (10/100-Gigabit Ethernet, 100/1,000-Mbps Ethernet over Copper, ATM, VoIP, Packet over SONET, Frame Relay, xDSL, cable modem, multicast IP, and TCP/IP).

- Specialized application simulators—Use advanced application-profiling traffic generation suites, such as Ganymede Software's Chariot package. This class of product creates representative flows of application transactions between specified hosts, using supplied or custom transaction data profiles (supplied profiles include Web traffic, FTP, Telnet, etc.). This makes it relatively easy to reuse the same transaction scenarios for before-and-after analysis of changes in the real network or relative performance tests across a number of devices.

- Customized tools—Some users prefer to develop customized traffic generation or automated test tools. These can be readily developed under LINUX, UNIX, or Windows using standard Application Programming Interfaces (APIs) such as BSD Sockets or WinSock.

Application simulators are a relatively new class of product and can be extremely useful, provided they support the underlying protocol stacks used on your network. Networking devices such as routers may include facilities for packet generation or capture (e.g., via RMON).

Populating routing tables

To simulate a large router network you may have to build large routing tables. Again, with this process it is well worth exceeding what you would expect under normal operating conditions to see if there are any serious issues when routing tables exceed key thresholds. Since routers generally learn routes dynamically from neighboring routers, you must fool the test-bed routers into believing that many other routes exist. A common practice is to build additional routes statically (usually through some form of scripted automation), and use edge routers to import these routes into dynamic routing protocols, such as OSPF or EIGRP, and then inject these routes into your test network by peering the edge routers with the main test routers. Some products may allow you to handle this through network management interfaces or the CLI (check with your equipment vendor).

While route importing allows you to build large routing tables, one of the problems with this approach is that it does not test resource utilization as the number of peer routers increases. For link state protocols such as OSPF this is well worth exercising, since the number of adjacent routers consumes CPU and RAM resources and therefore affects scalability. To achieve this you may have to resort to using application simulators, custom software, or more equipment.

Simulating links

LAN links are easy to simulate by using standard LAN cabling and small switching hubs. Generally there is no issue with this part of the design. WAN links can be more difficult to simulate, since they often rely upon external switching or clocking equipment; they may, therefore, require specialized cables or test equipment in lab situations. Since vendors often like to test equipment in lab situations, there are often facilities built into equipment specifically to allow back-to-back testing without the use of expensive WAN links. For example, Frame Relay interfaces can often be programmed in either DCE or DTE mode on routers and bridges specifically for this purpose. All you need is a cross-over cable; for example, V.35 crossover cables are commonly employed to simulate a range of WAN interfaces. Note that for X.21 interfaces (used primarily in Europe) you will need to use a relatively cheap external clocking device to generate timing signals for the link.

3.6   Summary

We are still learning about the way traffic behaves in complex data communication systems. To date there are no absolute models for predicting behavior, and this is an active area of research. In this section we covered the following:

- Any medium- to large-scale network design should be broken up into manageable pieces. This simplifies and insulates the different phases of design and ensures modularity and clear interfaces between the various design layers. We use a three-tiered model comprising the backbone layer, distribution layer, and access layer.

- Shortest-path determination is fundamental to many applications of networking and data communications. We have examined several key algorithms and discussed their relative merits based on network size and density. For large, sparse networks the Bellman-Ford algorithm performs well; for smaller, dense networks Dijkstra performs better. For centralized routing we used the Floyd-Warshall algorithm.

- Various topologies are available for designing internetworks, each with their own strengths and weaknesses. The main categories include mesh, partial mesh, tree, and star.

- When determining the type and number of protocols supported on the network, it is wise to restrict the number of active protocols as we move from the access layer through to the core (backbone). This can be achieved either through protocol conversion or tunneling at the distribution and access nodes. At the backbone layer routing and switching resources need to be optimized for high-speed switching and forwarding above all else. There is simply no time for exotic packet manipulation or protocol conversion.

- Once the network design has been decided upon, the various models (queuing, analytical, and empirical) could be used to test and predict the performance of the design before installing the real network.

- Queuing models have been used successfully for decades to predict performance on packet-switched networks. New research suggests that traffic dynamics have changed sufficiently on modern data networks to challenge the accuracy of some of the classical systems. For circuit-switched networks we turn to Erlang analysis.

- Regardless of the traffic correlation that exists in open queuing systems, it turns out that networks of queues can be modeled as if each queue were independent, using Kleinrock's independence approximation.

- In order to predict buffer utilization effectively, different distribution models are applicable depending upon the buffer size. Small buffers can be modeled using heavy-tailed distributions such as the Pareto distribution; for larger buffer sizes traffic models that exhibit Long-Range Dependence (LRD) are appropriate.

- Simulation models can be used to examine the behavior of very complex systems. They can be constructed using dedicated simulation packages, special-purpose languages, or general-purpose languages. Regardless of the modeling platform, bad data in get bad data out, so be prepared to spend the time and effort to build a representative model.

- Simulation packages vary in cost, complexity, and credibility. There are three main strategies for discrete event simulation in widespread use today: two-stage event scheduling, three-phase event scheduling and process interaction. Each has relative strengths and weaknesses.

- Empirical modeling is a mandatory part of any large-scale network design and implementation. It allows you to iron out any glitches in the design, uncover any bugs or implementation issues in the network equipment, and test out issues such as interoperability in a multivendor solution.

- A combination of modeling techniques is strongly recommended to get a balanced view of the planned network design. A purely theoretical approach will almost certainly expose you to many unwanted surprises and failures on the day that the real equipment and real applications are installed.

References

[1]   Y. Langsam, M. Augenstein, and A. Tenebaum, *Data Structures Using C and C++*, 2nd ed. (Englewood Cliffs, NJ: Prentice Hall, 1990), 220–224.

[2]   M. A. Weiss, *Data Structures and Algorithm Analysis in C*, 2nd ed. (Reading, MA: Addison-Wesley, 1997).

[3]   R. W. Floyd, "Algorithm 97: Shortest Path," *Communications of the ACM* 5 (1962).

[4]   R. Bellman, *Dynamic Programming* (Princeton, NJ: Princeton University Press, 1957).

[5]   R. Bellman, and S. Dreyfus, *Applied Dynamic Programming* (Princeton, NJ: Princeton University Press, 1962).

[6]   R. E. Bellman, "On a Routing Problem," *Quarterly of Applied Mathematics* 16 (1958).

[7]   L. R. Ford, Jr., "Network Flow Theory," Report P-923, Rand Corporation, Santa Monica, CA, August 1956.

[8]   E. F. Moore, "The Shortest Path through a Maze," in *Proceedings of International Symposium of the Theory of Switching*, Part II (Cambridge, MA: Harvard University Press, 1959).

[9]   L. R. Ford, Jr. and D. R. Fulkerson, *Flows in Networks* (Princeton, NJ: Princeton University Press, 1962).

[10]   D. Bertsekas and R. Gallager, *Data Networks* (Englewood Cliffs, NJ: Prentice Hall, 1987).

[11]   W. Stallings, *High-Speed Networks: TCP/IP and ATM Design Principles* (Englewood Cliffs, NJ: Prentice Hall, 1998).

[12]   D. E. Duffy, A. A. McIntosh, M. Rosenstain, and W. Willinger, "Statistical Analysis of CCSN/SS7 Tra_c Data from Working CCS Subnetworks," *IEEE Journal of Selected Areas in Communication* 12 (April 1994).

[13]   K. Watkins, *Discrete Event Simulation in C* (New York: McGraw-Hill, 1993).

[14]   M. A. Pollatschek, *Programming Discrete Simulations* (R&D Books, 1995).

[15]   E. Kreyszig, *Advanced Engineering Mathematics* (New York: John Wiley & Sons, 1999).

[16]   D. Gross and C. M. Harris, *Fundamentals of Queuing Theory*, in *Wiley Series in Probability and Mathematical Statistics*, 2nd ed. (New York: John Wiley & Sons, 1985).

[17]   F. Huebner, D. Liu, and J. M. Fernandez, *Queuing Performance Comparison of Traffic Models for Internet Traffic*.

[18]   J. J. Gordon, "Pareto Process as a Model of Self-Similar Packet Traffic," *IEEE GLOBECOM* (November 1995): 2232–2236.

[19]   L. Kleinrock, *Communication Nets: Stochastic Message Flow and Delay* (New York: Dover Publications, 1964).

[20]   J. R. Jackson, "Networks of Waiting Lines," *Oper. Res.* 5 (August 1957).

[21]   A. S. Tanenbaum, *Computer Networks* (Englewood Cliffs, NJ: Prentice Hall, 1981).

[22]   S. Keshav, *An Engineering Approach to Computer Networking* (Reading, MA: Addison-Wesley, 1997).

[23]   A. B. Bondi, *An Analysis of the Revenue Impact of Retried Abandoned Calls in an Operator Service* (Holmdel, NJ: AT&T Labs).

[24]   R. Jain and S. Routhier, "Packet Trains—Measurements and a New Model for Computer Network Traffic," *IEEE Journal of Selected Areas in Communications* SAC-4 (September 1986): 986–995. Reprinted in *Integrated Broadband Networks*, ed. A. Bhargava (Norwood, MA: Artech House, 1990).

[25]   G. Babic, B. Vandalore, and R. Jain, "Analysis and Modeling of Traffic in Modern Data Communication Networks," Ohio State University Department of Computer and Information Science, February 5, 1998.

[26]   W. E. Leland, M. S. Taqqu, W. Willinger, and D. V. Wilson, "On the Self-Similar Nature of Ethernet Traffic," *IEEE/ACM Transactions on Networking* 2 (February 1994).

[27]   S. M. Klivansky, A. Mukherjee, and C. Song, "Factors Contributing to Self-Similarity over NSFNet," Technical Report, 1994.

[28]   D. R. Cox, "Long-Range Dependence: A Review," in *Statistics: An Appraisal*, ed. H. A. David and H. T. David (Iowa City, IA: Iowa State University Press, 1984).

[29]   J. Beran, *Statistics of Long-Memory Processes* (New York: Chapmen & Hall, 1994).

[30]   P. Ramakrishnan, "Self-Similar Traffic Models," CSHCN Technical Report 99-5 (ISR Technical Report 99-12).

[31]   M. Csenger, "Early ATM Users Lose Data," *Communication Week* (May 16, 1994).

[32]   www.cadence.com, Cadence Design Systems, Inc., BONeS Simulator.

[33]   www.opnet.com, Home page for OPNET Technologies' OPNET modeling package.

[34]   www.nmsr.labmed.umn.edu/~michael/dbase/comp-simulation.html, The Comp.Simulation software archive, maintained by Michael Altmann.

[35]   www.netcomsystems.com, Home page for NetCom Systems' SmartBits test equipment.

4

Network Cost Analysis

Network economics and financial modeling are key facets of the design process but are probably given proper attention only by service providers, operators, and research institutions. From the text presented previously, this may seem like a contradiction, since the most common constraints of a network design are performance, reliability, and cost. Nevertheless, in practice there is disproportionately little time spent planning the topology, capacity, and traffic flows with respect to cost. This may be partly due to the lack of relevant skills in the design community, the lack of cost-effective modeling tools, or the difficulty in finding and analyzing the relevant tariffs and cost data. The focus for network designers, even in the area of backbone design, all too often appears to be on the choice of routing and switching equipment, which wide area protocols to implement, and the initial cost of the system. Unfortunately, a full financial analysis may demonstrate that the most cost-effective solution in the short term may turn out to be far less attractive in the long term. There could be several reasons for this, including the following:

- In the majority of internetworks, wide area costs represent a substantial proportion of the financial upkeep.

- High maintenance, training, and support costs can seriously erode annual budgets.

- Poorly chosen equipment could lead to early obsolescence, impacting network longevity.

- A design that works today but is underspecified for the future may be very expensive to upgrade later.

Since a number of these hidden costs are recurring, the penalty for making the wrong decision at the outset will be compounded year after year. Clearly, a holistic approach needs to be taken that includes a full cost analysis over the lifetime of the network, and the network designer must have a firm grasp of the key financial components of the design. A lack of awareness may exclude designers from high-level discussions within the organization, and the decisions taken at that level may be ill advised without informed technical input. Most books about network design tend to focus almost exclusively on the technology; the reader is encouraged to become familiar with the basic economic factors in order to make better design decisions.

As we have seen in previous chapters, attention should be focused on the core applications used by the business, the optimum topology of the network, and the most appropriate technology choices (ATM, Frame Relay, etc.). These factors can be determined only after a capacity plan has been produced, together with a model of the traffic and application behavior. Based on these data and detailed tariff information, you may find, for example, that part of your Frame Relay network would benefit from dynamic bandwidth technology such as ISDN, and this could dramatically reduce overall costs. Perhaps your network is to be deployed in an area where ATM is priced very competitively against leased lines. In any event choosing the edge equipment before selecting the most appropriate backbone service for your business makes no sense. In most cases the network will still be growing in five years and the equipment will most likely be obsolete.

Note: All pricing information used in this chapter is purely for illustration. The prices were accurate at the time of writing and may have changed since publication. They are included purely as a guide for comparing different service models.

4.1   Network economics

In this section, we will briefly review some of the terminology and theory behind network economics and present some general concepts applicable to network engineering.

4.1.1   Basic economics terminology

The network designer should become familiar with basic economics terminology. A number of useful terms are as follows:

- Amortization: A fund that is set up for settling debt-financed assets.

- Breakeven point: The level of cash flow at which the company is breaking even (i.e., income and expenditure are the same so no profit or loss is being made).

- Budget line: The line linking together all possible combinations of expenditures within a given income.

- Capital assets: In economic terms this means any material resource, including money held, debt owed, plant and machinery, and all stock held by a company. In this book we concentrate on physical assets used by the organization to produce goods or provide services. Examples include PCs, routers, and printers.

- Capital budget: A statement of the company's planned investments (typically based on future sales projections, production requirements, and the availability of capital).

- Capital gain/loss: The difference between the original cost of an asset and its final selling price. A capital gain or loss can be realized only when the asset is sold.

- Cash flow: The difference between the income generated and the expenditure paid out. This term is inherently dynamic; it represents a snapshot of the organization's financial status and will vary over time.

- Compound interest: Interest charges are an exponential of the principal. Compounding is standard practice in the business world.

- Cost of capital (also called interest or cost of money): The interest rate charged by the lender to the borrower to secure a loan to finance a project or investment. Clearly the rate of return on an investment should at least equal this percentage.

- Depreciation: Money offset annually from company income, a percentage of the initial cost of a capital asset subtracted over the lifetime of the asset. Typical examples include five years for small equipment such as PCs and modems and seven years for larger equipment such as a PBX or an FEP.

- Economies of scale: The reduction in production costs per unit output gained by increasing the size of the plant, organization, or industry.

- Factoring: The activity in which a specialized company (the factor) undertakes debt collection on behalf of another organization for a fee.

- Future value: The projected value of money at some point in the future (as opposed to present value). If the future purchasing power of money invested is to remain the same as its present value, then the interest rate needs at least to match inflation for the investment period.

- Inflation: The rise in the general level of prices.

- Lease: A contract between the lessor and the lessee. The lessee pays a regular (typically monthly) fee for the loan and use of an asset owned by the lessor. There is also typically an initial one-off charge.

- Net lease: A lease where the lessee pays all maintenance costs associated with the asset.

- Opportunity cost: The cost of an alternative forgone. For example, lost sales due to switchboard outages.

- Payback period: The length of time over which an asset generates sufficient cash flow to cover the initial cost of outlay.

- Present value: The value of money at the present time. Money today is always more valuable than money in the future (due to inflation, the possibility of investing that money and earning interest, and future uncertainty).

- Prima facie: On the face of it. First impression.

- Principal: The sum of money on which interest is paid by the borrower. The principal decreases according to the amortization schedule.

- Sale and leaseback: Where the owner of an asset sells it and then leases it back from the new purchaser.

- Salvage value (sometimes called residual value): The value of an asset after it has come to the end of its useful lifetime (i.e., the amount for which the organization could expect to sell that item).

- Simple interest: Interest charges are a linear function of the principal.

- Tender: To offer to supply some goods or undertake some work at a stated price.

- Third-party lease (sometimes called a leveraged lease): In this case the lessor does not own the asset offered on lease, and may have borrowed funds to cover all or part of the purchase price of the asset, owned by a third party.

- Utility: The satisfaction derived from goods or services.

For further details on these terms refer to [1, 2]. The latter provides an excellent treatment of financial modeling as applied to networks.

The value of money

One of the key concepts to understand in economics is the difference between the present and future value of money, and this is critical for the long-term financial analysis of network design projects. As indicated previously, money today is worth more than the same quantity of money in the future, due to factors such as inflation, uncertainty, and the possibility to invest that money today. Future value (the real value of a specific sum of money today, projected into the future) is calculated as:

$$F = P \times (1/(1 + i)^n)$$

where

P = present value

F = future value

i = interest rate (i.e., inflation)

n = number of years.

For example, if we had $1,000 today, and a flat inflation rate of 10 percent, this would be eroded by nearly two-thirds in ten years' time:

$$F = 1000 \times (1/(1 + 0.10)^{10})$$

$$F = \$386$$

In the next section we will see how present value calculations can be used with a relatively simple example.

4.1.2   Decision models

In network design projects there are relatively straightforward financial decisions that need to be made regarding the cost merits of a number of technology choices. These decisions involve calculations that can be built into a simple spreadsheet and reused as and when required. There are several widely used decision methods that can be used to build comparative financial models for network engineering projects, where the outputs are simply numbers that can be used to rank alternate solutions. These include the following:

- Net Present Value (NPV) method: This involves calculating the net cash flow created by the project—that is, project revenues minus expenses (other than depreciation), capital expenditure, and taxes. A positive NPV means that the project produces a rate of return that exceeds the cost of capital. When comparing projects we would look for the highest NPV value that was also positive.

■ Internal Rate of Return (IRR) method: This gives the rate of return for a project. If the rate of return exceeds some value (say the cost of capital), then the project is selected.

■ Payback period method: This method is used to compare projects to determine which has the shortest payback period. This is the length of time required to recover the initial investment.

■ Accounting rate of return method: This method (also called the Return on Investment method—ROI) is defined as the annual after-tax profit divided by the initial expense.

The NPV method is generally considered the best approach, and we will see an example shortly. The IRR method is inferior to the NPV method, since it is useful only when comparing projects of equivalent outlay costs. For example, the IRR of 25 percent on a project costing $1 million is much lower than an IRR of 50 percent on a project costing $20,000. However, the first project produces $250,000, whereas the second project produces only $10,000; hence, the first project is clearly more attractive even though its IRR is lower. The payback period method is also inferior to NPV, since it is limited in scope to cash flows up to the payback time. The ROI method is inferior also, since it does not analyze cash flows or take the cost of money into account.

An example using NPV

To illustrate the NPV method let us assume that you have the option to either lease or purchase a router. You can amortize this equipment over three years, at a cost of capital (interest rate) of 10 percent. You have the following options:

■ Purchase option: The router costs $20,000 to buy, and the salesman offers a 7 percent discount. After three years the router is worth only $1,200 if you resell it.

■ Lease option: The router costs $850 per month to lease. You don't own the device after three years.

Without some detailed analysis it is not at all obvious which solution is preferable, so we need to run these figures through an NPV model, taking into account what our money will be worth over a three-year period. The main calculations for the model are illustrated in Figure 4.1. Key calculations are as follows:

1.   NPV is the sum of all present values: (Purchase Price – Discount).

2.   Present value is calculated as: Net $\times$ $(1/(1 + \text{Cost of Capital})^{\text{Year}})$.

3.   Depreciation is calculated as: (Purchase Price – Salvage Price)/ Years.

4.   Expenses are calculated as: (Lease Cost $\times$ 12 months).

We can see that the best option in this case is to buy the equipment, since the NPV for the purchase option is $15,393 (as opposed to $11,638

ITEM	LEASE OPTION		PURCHASE OPTION	
Cost of Capital	10%		10%	
Purchase Price	0		20000	
Lease Cost (Monthly)	850		0	
Discount	0%		7%	
Company Tax Rate	40%		40%	
Amortization Period (years)	3		3	
Salvage Value	0		1200	
Fixed Yearly Revenue	18,000		18000	
Depreciation	0		6267	
Expenses	10,200		0	
Revenue	18,000		18,000	
Expenses (other than depreciation)	10,200		0	
Tax				
Revenue Minus Expenses	7,800		18,000	
Less Depreciation	0		6267	
Taxable I	7,800		11,733	
TAX	3,120		4,693	
Net Cash Flow for a year	4,680		13,307	
Cash Flow	Net	Present Value	Net	Present Value
Year 1	4,680	4,255	13,307	12,097
Year 2	4,680	3,868	13,307	10,997
Year 3	4,680	3,516	14,507	10,899
NPV		**11,638**		**15,393**

Figure 4.1   *NPV calculation for a lease and purchase option.*

for the lease option). By remodeling the initial purchase price we would find that the equipment cost would have to exceed $26,275 for the lease option to become attractive (we could also model a lower rental cost and improve our NPV that way).

The NPV model presented here is a good starting point for comparative modeling; however, all of the models proposed are effectively static, in that they assume that complete information is available at the time of calculation, and future uncertainty is not considered. In reality interest rates, inflation rates, and exchange rates all fluctuate. The other issue our model does not take into account is risk. For example, if we choose to purchase the equipment rather than lease it, and the router subsequently dies, what is the likelihood of failure and the financial impact of replacing it? Risk analysis and probability theory are used in more sophisticated models to manage variability [2, 3].

4.1.3   Currency exchange rates and taxes

It goes without saying that in any large international network the designer should be aware of currency rate fluctuations and localized taxes (such as VAT in the United Kingdom or TVA in continental Europe). In a network

Table 4.1   *Exchange Rates*

Country	Currency	Exch Rate	Country	Currency	Exch Rate
US	US$	1.0000	Hungary	HUF	104.7379
UK	UK£	0.6161	Hong Kong	HK$	8.0797
South Africa	R	4.4140	Greece	Dr	228.9674
Singapore	S$	1.4125	Germany	DM	1.6297
Switzerland	SFr	1.4676	France	FFr	5.5025
Sweden	SEK	7.2338	Finland	FM	4.4113
Spain	Pts	137.1203	Estonia	EEK	13.7888
Slovenia	SIT	156.2079	Europe	Ecu	0.8401
Portugal	Esc	172.6000	Denmark	DKr	6.2249
Norway	NKr	6.6969	Czech Republic	CZK	30.7770
Netherlands	Fl	1.8276	Cyprus	CY£	0.4839
Luxembourg	LFr	35.5510	Canada	C$	1.4267
Japan	Y	120.6580	Belgium	BFr	33.5592
Italy	L	1602.9511	Austria	Sch	9.7093
Ireland	IR£	0.5941	Australia	AUS$	1.1244
Iceland	ISK	61.7645			

that spans several countries there will typically be a number of service providers involved, and service charges will fluctuate over time with exchange rates. The network designer should be acquainted with the relevant currency rates (even if just to avoid being startled when adding circuits in Italy, for example, where $1,000 is over 1 million lire!). Table 4.1 illustrates exchange rates for most of the major currencies at the time of writing, in relation to U.S. dollars. Note that throughout this book all costs are shown in U.S. dollars using these exchange rates, unless specified otherwise.

4.2 A general bandwidth charging model

In this section, we will develop a general cost model, which should give you a clear idea of how circuit bandwidth costs are structured. Later on in this chapter, we will work through specific circuit cost models by technology.

4.2.1 Types of charge

In order to tariff network services it is important to distinguish four types of charge, as follows:

- A fixed, connection, or access charge

- A use charge

- A congestion charge

- A service quality charge

The fixed charge is a monthly subscription fee for access to the network, where access can be unlimited or limited to certain times of the day. The fee is independent of the number of connections made or the amount of data sent or received. Ideally this charge should equate network cost and user benefit. It should cover just the additional cost incurred to provide network access. For example, the fixed monthly fee charged by a telephone company should cover the cost of the local loop connection to the central office.

The use charge is based on each connection made, the amount of data sent, or the call duration of the circuit. It may also be a function of the distance or destination of the call or circuit. For example, an ISDN connection will be charged according to the duration of the call, the distance (local, regional, national), or the country destination (if international). Note that call duration will usually be rounded up and charged to the nearest integer threshold, so, for example, a 15-second ISDN transaction could be charged as a full 30-second call if the provider tariffs calls in 30-second blocks. Use charges should also equate cost with benefit: More network resources are consumed by high-use subscribers, and therefore costs should reflect this proportionally. Ideally the use charge should equal the cost of the additional resources that a call or connection needs, over those provided by the fixed charge.

The congestion charge is dependent upon the load carried by the network at the time of the user's connection. When the network is heavily congested, charges are higher, and there will be no congestion charge if there is no congestion on the network. The rationale for this is that quality of service degrades rapidly as congestion increases. For example, in networks that use statistical multiplexing (such as the Internet and ATM), congestion increases queuing delay and packet loss through buffer overflow. In circuit-switched networks congestion increases the probability of blocking. The congestion charge allows users to decide whether or not to make a call during busy periods or postpone it, and this in effect discourages less-valued connections. The charge should be set at a level sufficient to prevent congestion. If the charge is too low, then congestion will still occur. If the charge is too high, then there will be spare capacity and the service providers' revenue will be suboptimal.

The service quality charge reflects the fact that different users may elect to use more network resources as part of the service-level agreement made with the service provider. At present most networks do not offer more than one type of quality of service, but with the growth in high-bandwidth applications (such as video or voice over IP, which require guaranteed delay bounds) there is considerable pressure to offer differentiated service qualities. We should, therefore, expect the quality charge to become more commonplace over the next few years.

Although we have discussed the four components of the network-pricing model, in practice many services may impose only a subset of these charges, either for practical, technical, historical, or economic reasons. In the next section, we see how these charges can be used in various combinations to develop a service.

4.2.2   Charging models

Figure 4.2 illustrates a general model of charging structures. The Points of Presence (PoP) are gateways, switches, or exchanges that normally form part of the service provider's own private backbone, and their physical locations may or may not be public knowledge (for either competitive or security reasons).

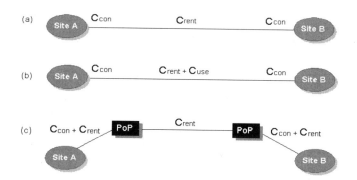

Figure 4.2
Generalized tariff models for (a) leased line services, (b) ISDN services, and (c) Frame Relay and ATM services.

Figure 4.2(a) is typical for leased line services, Figure 4.2(b) is typical for ISDN, and Figure 4.2(c) is typical for ATM, Frame Relay, and SMDS services. Note that these models are truly generic; individual service providers may choose more complicated charging structures or even obfuscate their model. Table 4.2 illustrates how the various service types are typically charged. Charges may be based on site-to-site (s-s) distance, site-to-PoP (s-p) distance, or a combination. Other charges may be based on time (length of call, according to the time of day or day of week) or the amount of data sent (packets, bytes, segments, etc.). Complex services such as Frame Relay and ATM may also factor in tariff multipliers based on burst ratio, peak, sustained, or excess rates (this varies by service provider). Note that in some countries there may be unique schemes based on regional boundaries or urban/rural locations, such as in Sweden.

Table 4.2 *Tariffs Charges Breakdown by Service Type*

Service	Connect	Rental	Usage
Leased Line	s-s	bw	
Satellite	s-s	bw	
ISDN	s-s	bw	time
Voice	s-s	bw	time
ATM	s-p	bw	data
SMDS	s-p	bw	
Frame Relay	s-p	bw	data
X.25	s-p	bw	data

4.2.3   Key information required for tariff calculations

In order to make any useful tariff calculations you will need to know the following information about your network.

- The precise location of the sites to be interconnected. Usually this will be based on a site's grid reference in latitude and longitude (L&L) and the host country in which the site is located. There may be localized coordinate variants, such as Ordinance Survey (OS) grid references, used in the United Kingdom, or the vertical and horizontal (V&H) system used in the United States. As a general rule it is best to normalize all of these coordinates to latitude and longitude for international network designs, since these are universal.

- Distances between sites and from sites to the nearest points of presence (PoP)—that is, the nearest switch, gateway, or exchange.

- The telephone exchange number (area code) and postal/zip code of the sites. Some services, such as ISDN and voice, may allocate the nearest PoP by dial code (nearest area code) rather than distance.

- The bandwidths required for all interfaces and the number of interfaces required (based on the traffic matrix).

- The expected duration of the contracts you want to sign up for. Generally the longer the commitment period the better the discount you can expect.

Distance calculations

For an international network it may be desirable to use a consistent coordinate system, and the only system that is globally accepted is that based on latitude and longitude (L&L). To calculate distances (in kilometers) between locations, based on their latitude and longitude, you can use the following algorithm (coded in C). This code simplifies the calculation by assuming that the earth is a perfect sphere (the earth is in reality an oblate spheroid, slightly flattened at the poles due to centrifugal force). The code also does not take the height above sea level into account. These issues are negligible for most network designs. More accurate methods of calculating distances along a spherical surface are available, but they tend to get somewhat complex and are, perhaps, overkill for our purposes.

```
double GetDistanceByLatLong(double Xlat, double Xlong, double Ylat, double Ylong)
{
    static double circumf = 40077.0;            // Earths circumference
    static double pi = 3.1415926535;            // PI
```

```
static double radianCF = 3.1415926535/180;      // Convert degrees to radians
double distanceKm;                              // result placed here
double w1, w2, w3, w4, w0;                      // working variables

w0 = fabs(Xlong - Ylong);
if((360.0 - w0) < w0)                           // Ensure less than 360 degrees
   w0 = 360.0 - w0;
w0 = w0 * radianCF;                             // convert to radians
w1 = (90.0 - Xlat) * radianCF;                  // ditto
w2 = (90.0 - Ylat) * radianCF;                  // ditto
w3 = cos(w2) * cos(w1) + sin(w2) * sin(w1) * cos(w0); // Spherical geometry
w4 = pi * 0.5 - asin(w3);
distanceKm = circumf * w4/(2 * pi);

return (distanceKm);
}
```

In the United States, a vertical and horizontal (V&H) system of curves was devised by AT&T to break up the United States into a regular grid pattern, and this is still commonly used to calculate national distances for North American tariffs. The V&H coordinates of most cities and switching centers are readily available. The algorithm used to calculate the distance between two cities, in locations ($v1$, $h1$) and ($v2$, $h2$), is as follows:

Distance = ceil {sqrt((dv × dv + 9)/10 + (dh × dh + 9)/10)}

where

dv = abs($v2 - v1$)

dh = abs($h2 - h1$)

The function sqrt() returns the square root. The function ceil() returns the smallest integer greater than or equal to the real number—for example, ceil[7.25] = 8. The function abs() returns the absolute value regardless of the sign—for example, abs(77 − 80) = 3. As an example, the distance between New York (4,997, 1,406) and Boston (4,422, 1,249) can be calculated as follows:

Distance = ceil{sqrt((575 × 575 + 9)/10 + (157 × 157 + 9)/10)}

Distance = ceil(sqrt (33,063.4 + 2,465.8))

Distance = 189 miles

This is almost the same result as achieved through the L&L method. Over longer distances the two methods produce variations in their results (e.g., Los Angeles to Boston yields 2,587 km with V&H and 2,603 km with L&L). However, since the difference here accounts for less than 1 percent, the cost impact is negligible at such great distances.

4.2.4 The importance of location for circuit cost modeling

Many services impose charges based on the distance between sites and, optionally, the site-to-exchange distance. It is rare to find distance-based tariffs using simple linear costing; almost always the tariff will be piecewise linear (there will be linear charging but within a number of fixed distance thresholds). Using the example shown in Figure 4.3, we see a service that starts with a fixed (one-off) access charge of $1,800, plus one of four linear multipliers to be applied on a per-kilometer basis to calculate monthly rental charges, as follows:

- Multiplier, m1, applicable to distances less than 15 km

- Multiplier, m2, for distances between 15 and 55 km

- Multiplier, m3, for distances between 55 km and 100 km

- Multiplier, m4, for distances over 100 km

As indicated previously, site information such as post codes (zip codes in the United States) and area codes can be extremely important in tariff analysis, and you should aim to gather these data as part of the site plan. For example, networks deployed in large metropolitan areas such as London or New York may be able to take advantage of special discount schemes based

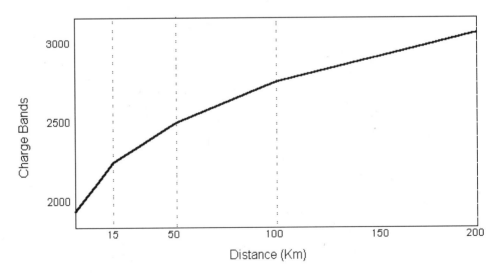

Figure 4.3   *Piecewise linear charging model. This service imposes a fixed access charge plus one of four linear monthly rental charges (applied per kilometer) based on site-to-site distance.*

on zip code or area code. A key point to appreciate here is that tariffs for some services may be more closely attuned to area code than distance, so least distance does not always mean least cost.

In Figure 4.4, for example, we have a new London office based in Fulham that requires 2-Mbs access to the backbone. Using a least-distance strategy we would intuitively connect into the PoP at Hammersmith, approximately 4 km away. Using a BT megastream service, with price breaks for sites in the 0171 area, this would be the wrong strategy. The connection cost for both circuits would be approximately $14,981, but the rental cost for the Millwall circuit is almost half the rental cost of the Hammersmith circuit ($6,655 versus $11,686). So the solution would be to use a circuit nearly four times longer than necessary at a saving of approximately 20 percent. Clearly, these anomalies in service tariffing are well worth observing; if you intend to connect lots of short-distance circuits in large metropolitan areas, the cost savings could be substantial.

Building on some of the work we have already covered, we saw that traffic also plays an important role in least-distance circuit cost modeling. In Figure 4.5 we show a simple three-node problem, where an existing BT kilostream 64-Kbps service is installed between Birmingham and London at a cost of $11,891 ($1,688 connection and $10,203 annual rental). A new site in London expects to send up to 64 Kbps of traffic to Glasgow, so the

Figure 4.4
A remote office in Fulham has two choices for accessing the backbone network.

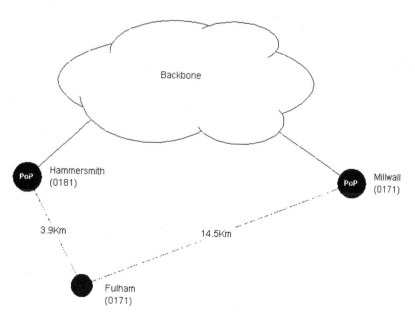

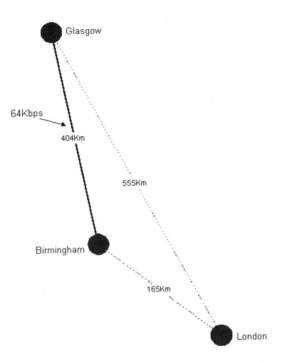

Figure 4.5
*A 64-Kbps leased
circuit between
Birmingham and
Glasgow.*

intuitive least-distance solution would be to add another 64 Kbps between London and Birmingham; however, this would require the existing circuit to be upgraded to 128 Kbps. The total cost of this solution would be approximately $38,000. In fact, it would be cheaper to leave the existing circuit and add a direct 64-Kbps circuit between London and Glasgow, for a total cost of approximately $25,000. Clearly, we must consider traffic flows in any cost modeling exercise.

In some countries tariffs are not quoted in distance but by regions, or zone information. Luxembourg, for example, is divided into seven regions, and each region is subdivided into exchange areas. There is a different price structure depending upon whether a circuit terminates both ends: within the same exchange area, different exchange areas in the same region, different exchange areas in different but adjacent regions, or different exchange areas in different nonadjacent regions. Belgium, Italy, and Sweden operate similar schemes, and this can make life tough when attempting tariff analysis, especially if key information on exchange areas or zones is not made available.

Some services also impose maximum costs once a circuit reaches a certain distance (e.g., in Norway services reach a maximum charge at 300 km).

Again, the site geography needs to be examined carefully to see if a least-distance topology makes sense financially. If a circuit length exceeds the distance threshold, then it may be appropriate to connect sites directly rather than using intermediate hops, if there is no cost handicap.

There are other anomalies with international circuits you should be aware of. For example, traditionally it would seem intuitive to collapse regional site traffic from a country onto a central site and then via a single fat pipe internationally. In some cases, however, it may be cheaper to add multiple international circuits from each site. For example, between Germany and London it could be cheaper to run discrete 256-Kbps circuits from each site internationally rather than collapse them into large circuits, with the additional benefit of reduced hops.

4.2.5   Peak load pricing

Observations of traffic dynamics show that they exhibit strong cyclical behavior over a day and over a week. During the working day, traffic usually peaks between 9:00 A.M. and 5:00 P.M. There are typically slack periods around lunch time and dinner time, and traffic tends to pick up after 11:00 P.M. when cheaper telephone rates become available. The fact that there are cheaper rates during unsociable hours is no accident, but is the result of the operator having analyzed use patterns and implemented peak load pricing. Peak load pricing is a traffic management technique used to shift some of the demand away from really busy periods and to even out the daily traffic profile. In effect the additional cost imposed on the peak rate period is a congestion charge, as described previously.

Without this technique the operator would have to significantly over-provide capacity, which would be heavily utilized for only a small portion of the day and therefore would not be cost-effective. Alternatively, users would be faced with delays and congestion during certain periods, which does not make for a happy customer base. Figure 4.6 shows a demand curve of network utilization. If the network is built with capacity B, all users are satisfied, but the service provider is overpaying, since the network is underutilized. At capacity A the service provider is satisfied, but the users will experience delays during peak periods.

By making later time slots less expensive the operator plans to move a certain portion of users outside the traditional peak periods. (See Figure 4.7.) For example, users who would typically Web browse for several hours during the afternoon are encouraged to browse late at night. Peak load pric-

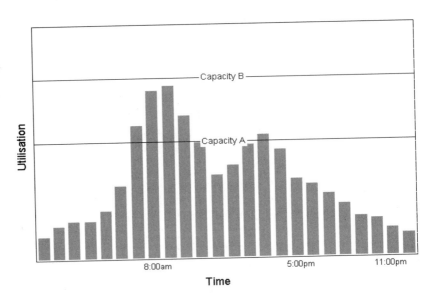

Figure 4.6
Typical aggregate demand curve of network utilization over time.

ing can also be applied at the scale of a week, and you will see even more attractive rates for weekend use with some services. The overall capacity of the network can now be maintained at capacity A, and both the users and the service provider are satisfied.

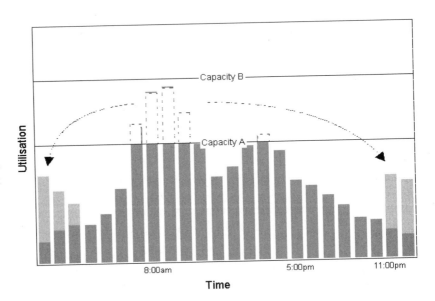

Figure 4.7
The service provider moves some of the demand from the peak periods over to slack periods by introducing low-rate tariffs or increasing tariffs for peak periods.

Charging time bands

In order to implement peak load pricing operators have defined several time bands during which tariffs will differ. Typically the following time bands are defined:

- Peak

- Off-peak

- Weekend and holidays

In some countries you may encounter much more granularity in time periods (e.g., French PTTs define eight different time bands throughout the day). For services such as leased lines this is irrelevant, but for service charges by time of day (such as voice and ISDN) these time bands are important. For example, if you do a weekly two-hour database archive between your sites in London and Paris via an ISDN link, you may want to take special care of both the time slot in which you perform the file transfer and the country from which you open up the link. It may be cheaper, for example, to open up the link from Paris during a weekend. Over the duration of a year the cost savings could be significant.

Modeling relative utility

In Section 4.1.1 we defined utility as the satisfaction derived from goods or services. So how does a service provider determine what tariffs to charge for peak and off-peak periods, without causing customer dissatisfaction? There is a considerable amount of literature on this subject [4, 5]. The general consensus is as follows:

- Off-peak users should be charged only for operational costs plus the profit.

- Peak users should be charged in addition for capital depreciation and the costs associated with capacity expansion.

We can present a simple charging model by the use of two relative measurements: the user utility, U_u, and the network utility, N_u. These are basically measurements of the user and service provider's level of satisfaction, and modifying one will directly affect the other.

The user utility is calculated as:

$$U_u = (-\text{Total Tariff} - \text{Overload})$$

The network utility is calculated as:

$$N_u = (\text{Revenue} - \text{Off-Peak Slack})$$

In effect, the revenue accrued by the network operator and the tariff levied on the user are equal and are calculated as follows:

(Peak Demand × Peak Rate) + (Off-Peak Demand × Off-Peak Rate)

Assuming a capacity, C, overload is simply the peak demand minus C, and off-peak slack is C minus the off-peak demand (i.e., the idleness in the system during off-peak periods).

Using the example data in Table 4.3, starting with the top row, let us assume that we have a network of capacity 100, and a pricing strategy of one cent per unit for both peak and off-peak use. Initially the peak demand is 100, and the off-peak demand is only 10. Our revenue (or cost to the user) is 110, giving a network utility, N, of 20, and a user utility, U, of –110. At this point we can assume that both the users and the operator are relatively unhappy. The network is saturated at peak times, so response times may be poor, and the operator has to provide costly high-speed circuits with no spare capacity at peak periods. During off-peak periods the network is hardly being utilized. Clearly it would be advantageous to shift some demand to the off-peak period, enabling the operator to either downgrade circuit capacity (to save money) or increase the number of users (to make more money). There are a number of strategies for achieving this; we will concentrate on changing just the circuit capacity and pricing model.

We start by dropping the off-peak rate to 0.8; this allows us to cut capacity to 90, with the result that peak demand drops to 90 and off-peak demand goes up to 15. The network is still saturated, and revenues have gone down, but even so both operator and users are relatively happier with

Table 4.3 *Modeling Relative Utility*

Capacity	Peak Demand	Offpeak Demand	Peak Rate	Offpeak Rate	Revenue /Tariffs	N	U
100	100	10	1.0	1.0	110	20	-110
90	90	15	1.0	0.8	102	27	-102
80	80	20	1.0	0.6	92	32	-92
70	70	30	1.0	0.4	82	42	-82
60	60	40	1.0	0.3	72	52	-72
60	55	45	1.1	0.2	70	55	-65
60	52	48	1.2	0.2	72	60	**-64**
60	50	50	1.4	0.1	75	**65**	-65

$N = 27$ and $U = -102$. In effect, the operator is paying less for circuits, and the user is getting a slightly better deal. We can see from the last two rows in the table that when capacity is dropped to 60 and the operator sets the peak tariff between 1.2 and 1.4 and the off-peak tariff between 0.1 and 0.2, both parties are much happier (relatively). What is interesting is that this is true even when over 30 percent of the operator's revenue has been eroded. In effect, the operator is paying even less for circuits, the user is getting a better deal, and there is now spare capacity in the system, meaning that response times are likely to be improved. The network operator (N) and user (U) are most happy at the values indicated in bold in Table 4.3.

We could play around with this model forever given the number of permutations present; however, it is instructive to see that revenue is not the only measure worth optimizing. By changing the pricing model we can perform traffic engineering over time, affording us the opportunity to better optimize capacity.

Clearly, peak load pricing can be used to increase the customers' utility without affecting the networks' utility if required. In practice any changes in the pricing model and capacity offered need to be implemented with care; it is important to have regular and accurate feedback on shifts in customer demand. We cannot accurately predict what customers will do under these circumstances, so changes need to be handled incrementally. For example, even if we lowered the off-peak rate, we would not want to remove real capacity until a shift in use from peak to off-peak is proven.

We will now examine service models for public and private network services in more detail.

4.3 Internet charging model

4.3.1 Flat-rate pricing

The Internet currently differs from private networks in that it is essentially a shared medium, providing access to both business and residential subscribers, all competing for the same resource. The charging model most commonly adopted to date is therefore one of flat-rate pricing (a fixed access charge regardless of use). This pricing mechanism is clearly at odds with the different classes of users accessing the network, the patterns of use throughout the day, and user needs. Business users may be willing to pay more for a premium service, and fluctuations in use mean that the network may often be oversubscribed with low priority or non–mission-critical traffic at peak

Figure 4.8
*Tariff model for
Internet access
based on flat-rate
pricing.*

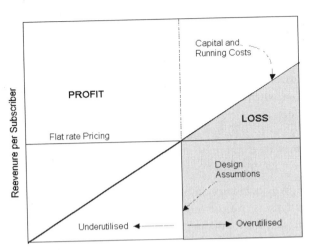

Capacity Consumed per Subscriber

Figure 4.8
Tariff model for Internet access based on flat-rate pricing.

periods. In order to implement such features, quality of service and a degree of privacy are required over the Internet.

From the service provider's perspective there are two key competing variables in the business model that determine profitability: revenue per subscriber and capacity consumed per subscriber.

As illustrated in Figure 4.8, the diagonal cost line represents the break-even point for the business, where revenue per subscriber equals the cost to provide network capacity to the subscriber. The cost of capacity in this model includes not only capital equipment expenditure, but also the cost of maintaining and operating the service. Above the cost line the business is profitable; below the cost line there will be a loss. In order to build a business, an ISP must make assumptions regarding the capacity consumed by the typical subscriber. In most network designs the capacity of the transport is oversubscribed, assuming subscribers utilize only a small fraction of their connection.

The flat rate per connection is set to accommodate the cost of the provided capacity, plus profit. This rate is also extremely sensitive to competitive pressure (there are now several thousand ISPs competing for the same users). Unfortunately, fluctuations in a subscriber's utilization pattern above the anticipated capacity violate the static design assumptions and can destroy the delicate balance between the charge rates and capacity offered. These burst events occur most frequently during peak periods of the day, where the planned capacity is exceeded, causing both residential and business users to experience poor performance. When multiplied over the entire subscriber base, even relatively small deviations from the design assumptions can damage overall business profitability. Although there is excess capacity during other parts of the day, it cannot be used to help out during the peak period. The only solution in today's Internet is to add more capacity to the network, thereby creating an even larger amount of unused capacity during nonpeak times. The excess capacity outside the peak period represents a valuable asset that is not generating any revenue.

4.3.2 Multi-tiered pricing

With the emergence of bandwidth management and traffic prioritization tools in edge devices, service providers are now offering multi-tiered pricing strategies, with several levels of service based on different subscription rates. (See Figure 4.9.) Traffic can now be classified and marked at the edge according to characteristics such as explicit addressing or application type. This marking is then used when the traffic enters the core of the network to manage congestion. When there is no congestion, all traffic passes through the network with no preference, while during periods of high congestion premium traffic can be allocated priority.

In addition to classifying traffic and providing priority during periods of high congestion, the intelligence of the edge of the network can also limit the flow of subscriber traffic into the core (referred to as admission control). Admitting traffic is very flexible and can be based on customizable criteria such as application type or percent of connection utilization. Multiple service tiers enable Internet service providers to differentiate traf-

Figure 4.9
Tariff model for Internet access based on multi-tiered pricing.

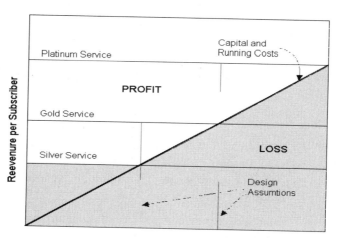

fic by customer and offer advanced service structures designed to meet the needs of different classes of user, while maintaining control of available network resources. Within a single customer site it would be possible to differentiate between different applications (e.g., Web traffic could be treated as standard and mission-critical traffic as premium). At the time of writing it is fair to say that this pricing model is a statement of intent rather than the norm, since the relatively immature state of QoS provisioning over public networks is holding back the ability of providers to achieve this kind of differentiation.

4.4   Private network charging models

Private network tariffs are the published rates for various communication services offered by carriers. Larger service providers, such as Cable & Wireless and British Telecom, will supply multivolume publications containing their tariffs, which can run into thousands of pages of detailed service breakdowns and discount structures. Costs typically include both monthly and one-time setup charges (such as installation costs). Some services are use sensitive, and there will be additional monthly costs accrued depending upon either the amount of data sent or the time for which a circuit is open. Different services have different tariff models, and different service providers will potentially have models different from other carriers. Since the goal for a carrier is to make as much money as possible, while providing a service that can meet the service-level agreements it undertakes, there may be subtly different agendas depending upon the size of the carrier and its relative position in the market. One carrier may play to its strength in coverage and support, and a challenger may consistently try to undercut the market leader for some services and possibly overprice services for which it does not have sufficient coverage (to avoid the embarrassment of oversubscription).

Tariffs are typically very sensitive to location and distance. Often it is enough to know the area code of the site to work out the nearest exchange or point of presence (PoP). In some cases you will need the grid reference to work out site-to-site or site-to-PoP distances. For interstate tariffs in the United States a location's Local Access and Transport Area (LATA) may be required. In some European countries you may need to know the region or zone of the country where the site is located for regional tariffs or international tariffs.

Some service providers publish all the information you need to calculate line costs accurately; many do not. Often there are specific services for which charges are not publicly available, and key information such as PoP locations or zoning information may not be freely available. Even with published information there is a whole range of factors that tend to obfuscate the charging model, such as complex discount structures, time band variations, and varying terms according to contract duration. For example, for even a simple leased line service there are likely to be several charging models available depending upon bandwidth, destination, location, distance from a major city or specific area code, and duration of contract commitment. For long-term contracts the carrier often may waive the initial setup charge and charge a reduced monthly fee. Discounts may also be available on the number of interfaces installed, the number of channels per interface, or bulk use.

To emphasise the differences in service cost structures, we will now examine how common services such as ISDN, leased lines, Frame Relay, X.25, and ATM are typically modeled.

4.4.1 Leased line and satellite services

Leased (terrestrial cable) and satellite links are usually closely aligned in their pricing structure. These services are the easiest to understand. The main characteristic of these services is a fixed bandwidth point-to-point link that is always available. Typically there is a single interface to attach to at each site per circuit, so a three-node network will require two physical interfaces per site to form a triangular topology.

Tariff structure

Typically there is a one-off connection charge scaled by interface speed and a recurring rental charge scaled by interface speed. For national circuits the cost is generally applied to one end of the circuit only, although there may be exceptions in certain countries. For international circuits, both sites will typically incur a half-circuit connection and rental charge and may have to use different service providers. Some service providers may vary connection based on distance to a nearest gateway or Point of Presence (PoP).

Examples

For a United Kingdom–based 100-km or 400-km national leased circuit, you could expect to pay the charges shown in the following chart. This assumes a committed 12-month contract period.

Service	Link Speed	Connection	Rental 100 km	Rental 400 km
BT Kilostream	9.6 Kbps	$1,688	$6,432	$9,704
BT Kilostream	64 Kbps	$1,688	$6,887	$10,159
BT Kilostream N	128 Kbps	$9,739	$10,193	$18,958
BT Kilostream N	256 Kbps	$9,739	$13,894	$31,423
BT Megastream	2 Mbps	$14,981	$50,803	$123,843
BT Megastream	8 Mbps	$22,902	$151,695	$370,813
BT Megastream	45 Mbps	$66,417	$379,156	$1,109,551

Notice that we would be paying over a third of a million dollars per annum for less performance than basic Ethernet over a 400-km wide area link!

For short-haul circuits the rental prices may drop significantly, and there are also discounts on longer-term commitments. For example, an 8-Mbps circuit over 1.5 km, with a committed contract for 60 months, would incur the same $22,902 connection charge but a $28,925 rental charge, representing an annual difference of over 92 percent over the 400-km circuit.

Charges for international circuits are considerably higher—for example, an international 128-Kbps Kilostream circuit between London, England and Boston, Massachusetts would incur no connection charge, but would incur an annual rental charge of $86,674 via BT from the United Kingdom and $74,400 via AT&T from the United States (a total of $161,074). You can see why circuit topology optimization is important for wide area international network design, since the costs really start to escalate.

An example of a monthly DS1/T1 tariff in the United States is provided in the following chart using the Pacific Bell FasTrak HiCap service [6]. This is a dedicated, point-to-point service that operates as a 1.544-Mbps full-duplex digital channel and provides multiplexing capabilities (up to 24 64 Kbps voice or data digital channels) without the need for additional CPE equipment.

Service	Link Speed	Connection	Rental	Notes
PacBellT1	1.544 Mbps		$118.53+ per minute $23.75	Mileage Charge

Service	Link Speed	Connection	Rental	Notes
		$600.69	$165.94	Channel Termination
		$600.69	$71.12	Channel Termination IEC PoP
		$600.69	$308.17	T1 Multiplexed to 24 channels

For nonchannelized service, the customer must provide a Channel Service Unit (CSU). Typical costs for T1 CSUs range from approximately $800 to $2,500, depending on features and capabilities.

4.4.2 Frame Relay

Frame Relay is a switched or permanent virtual circuit topology (although many providers currently supply only PVCs). Each physical interface into the Frame Relay cloud can carry multiple virtual circuits, and each circuit has the capability to switch data to any destination with a Frame Relay SVC. If SVCs are not available, PVCs are used and provide fixed data paths throughout the Frame Relay network, similar to leased lines. Each Frame Relay circuit can have its own speed and excess bit rate setting.

In Frame Relay, CIR means that the information rate is committed or guaranteed, whereas EIR is excess information. Data that burst over the CIR into the EIR are tagged as discard eligible and may or may not get to their destination, depending upon the current network loading.

Tariff structure

Packet-switched service provider tariff metrics

When you take out a contract with a Frame Relay service provider, there are several metrics that are important to understand, since they affect the level of service offered by the Frame Relay network. These metrics are as follows:

- Committed Information Rate (CIR)—is measured in bits per second over a time interval, T, and is the key tariff parameter. CIR is the maximum permitted (guaranteed in normal operating conditions) traffic level that the carrier will allow on a specific DLCI into the packet-switching environment. CIR can be anything up to the capacity of the physical limitation of the connecting line. Anything above the CIR rate is considered best effort.

- Committed Burst Size (Bc)—is the number of bits that the Frame Relay internetwork is committed to accept and transmit at the CIR over a time interval, T. In effect, Bc represents traffic that will probably be delivered, although the switch is allowed to set the Discard Edible (DE) bit of frames at this level.

- Excess Burst Size (Be)—sometimes called Excess Information Rate (EIR) sets the absolute limit for a DLCI in bits. This is the number of bits that the Frame Relay internetwork will attempt to transmit after Bc is accommodated, over a time interval, T. In effect, Be determines a peak or maximum Frame Relay data rate (R_{max}), where:

R_{max} = (Bc + Be)/Bc × CIR (in bits per second)

- The switch will set the Discard Edible (DE) bit of frames at this level.

It is important to understand that CIR is a *probabilistic* threshold, not a guarantee. Many service providers overprovision their Frame Relay networks in order to meet this commitment, but under extended periods of congestion even CIR frames may be discarded. Traffic that exceeds the CIR is more likely to be dropped in higher-load conditions (where all other CIR commitments are met simultaneously). Therefore, CIR represents traffic that should be delivered most of the time; Be represents traffic that will probably be delivered some of the time—anything that exceeds this level will definitely be dropped.

Pricing model

Frame Relay is one of the more complicated services to cost, and pricing structures vary significantly. Typically there is a one-off connection charge, scaled by interface speed; a recurring rental charge, scaled by interface speed; and dynamic charges based on PVC or SVC use, scaled by speed attributes. Connection and rental costs are normally charged at each physical interface (port). Individual virtual circuits may have rental charges applied according to the bandwidth and possibly use charges.

Typically the user gets a larger physical interface bandwidth than required (and pays a proportional cost), over which several concurrent PVCs or SVCs can be run to multiple destinations. Bandwidth charges are typically applied to individual or aggregated CIR and, optionally, EIR speeds. For both national and international circuits the cost is generally applied at both ends as a half-circuit cost and may be through different suppliers. Some suppliers may charge at one end only for national circuits.

The connection charge may vary based on distance to a nearest gateway or Point of Presence (PoP). An end-to-end circuit distance cost may also be applied. Frame Relay providers may offer oversubscription charges (an interface could, for example, be oversubscribed to 200 percent of the available bandwidth for busy period traffic). There may be limitations as to how much of the interface can be used for aggregate CIR. Some suppliers limit total CIR to 75 percent of the available interface bandwidth. Some service providers do not currently support EIR.

Certain service providers allow you to oversubscribe the network interface to allow for different activity levels on each PVC/SVC. For example, you may have a 128-Kbps trunk with three PVCs, each configured with a 48-Kbps CIR and a 16-Kbps EIR. You would rely on the fact that not all circuits will be transmitting data at the same time, and therefore the 128-Kbps trunk would provide sufficient bandwidth for your requirement. It is worth noting that Frame Relay effectively operates similar to classical statistical multiplexing, since bandwidth allocated to an idle virtual circuit can be claimed as part of the Bc/Be of another virtual circuit—that is, until the owner of that bandwidth wants the guaranteed bandwidth back. If you do not wish to use, or are not provided with, an oversubscription option, you should ensure that the aggregated CIR settings do not exceed the access speed for the network interface. If you oversubscribe an interface, you will see a warning message indicating that the interface is oversubscribed. Some service providers restrict aggregate bandwidth to a percentage of the network interface speed. For example, C&W's Frame Relay service allows up to 75 percent of the network interface bandwidth to be used by aggregate CIR.

Note that some service providers may not let you set Be or Bc, and some will not even let you set CIR. In these cases the service offered may be based on simple access speeds (similar to a channelized leased line interface). In cases where the CIR is effectively zero, then only a best-effort service is provided (presumably at a much cheaper rate then a dedicated leased circuit).

Examples

Using a C&W Frame Relay service in the United Kingdom, we would be offered a choice of interface speeds between 64 Kbps and 2,048 Kbps, a subset of which are shown in the following chart. For each interface we would expect to pay a one-off connection charge, plus an annual rental.

These charges give us access to the Frame Relay network, but no traffic. Over each interface we select, we can add one or more circuits, specifying

Service	Link Speed	Connection	Rental
C&W datalink 64 K	64 Kbps	$4,869	$15,660
C&W datalink 128 K	128 Kbps	$16,231	$16,065
C&W datalink 256 K	256 Kbps	$16,231	$17,591
C&W datalink 1,024 K	1,024 Kbps	$16,231	$26,843
C&W datalink 2,048 K	2,048 Kbps	$21,425	$34,471

CIR and EIR for each, up to the maximum threshold allowed for the interface speed (this varies by provider, as indicated previously, and with C&W this would mean an aggregate CIR of no more than 75 percent of the interface speed). Interface speeds and CIR and EIR settings do not have to match at each end, so we can set up symmetrical or asymmetrical circuits based on the expected traffic plan (a very attractive feature of both Frame Relay and ATM). So, for example, let's suppose we had a 256-Kbps interface in London, and a 64-Kbps interface in Manchester, and we add an asymmetrical circuit between these cities with CIR = 64 Kbps, EIR = 32 Kbps at the London interface, and CIR = 32 Kbps, EIR = 32 Kbps at the Manchester interface. The cost breakdown would be as shown in the following chart.

Location	Service	Link Speed	Connection	Rental	Bw Charge
Manchester	C&W datalink 64 K	64 Kbps	$5,031	$15,659	$487
London	C&W datalink 256 K	256 Kbps	$16,393	$17,591	$974

At the time of writing C&W did not charge for EIR (since it was not supported), so we can ignore this in the final cost. Note also that the one-off connection charge also incurs an additional $162 (£100) for each circuit added, just to complicate matters.

4.4.3   Switched Multimegabit Data Service (SMDS)

Switched Multimegabit Data Service (SMDS) is a technology that can be used as an alternative to leased lines, typically at speeds of 0.5 Mbps to 45 Mbps (DS-3). SMDS is offered by most telephone companies in the United States and Europe, although in the United States it is often priced higher than Frame Relay and is therefore less popular. SMDS operates as a full-mesh topology. Similar to Frame Relay, SMDS is typically accessed via a single physical interface, over which many logical connections to different destinations can be enabled. Each interface into the SMDS cloud has the capability to dynamically switch data to any destination with an SMDS port. Separate multicast groups may be configured within the cloud to enable closed user group scenarios.

Tariff structure

The tariff model used will vary by service provider. For example, British Telecom uses a simple model where connection and rental costs are charged at each physical interface. Costs vary by the size of the access channel required, typically from 0.5 MB upwards. More sophisticated models will incur costs characterized by the sustained information rate, maximum burst size, and the maximum number of interleaved messages.

Examples

The following chart shows example costs for SMDS service between London and Edinburgh (a circuit distance of approximately 534 km). For this service a flat rental charge is levied based on interface speed, node-to-PoP distance, and PoP-to-PoP distance. There are no specific use or circuit charges. Other SMDS services may impose a more granular tariff model.

Service	Link Speed	Connection	Rental
BT SMDS	0.5 Mbps	$14,608	$13,390
BT SMDS	2 Mbps	$14,608	$25,969
BT SMDS N	4 Mbps	$53,562	$69,793
BT SMDS	10 Mbps	$53,562	$89,270

At the time these costs were compiled BT had installed only a small number of SMDS gateways. Since node-to-gateway charges are part of the calculation, overall costs improve if the number of gateways is increased, especially for networks with a significant proportion of remote nodes located outside major population centers.

4.4.4   Asynchronous transfer mode

ATM is one of the most complicated services to cost, and pricing structures vary significantly; some tariff models are extremely simple, others completely opaque. A one-off connection charge is scaled by interface speed. A recurring rental charge is scaled by interface speed. Use charges, based on PVC or SVC use, are scaled by speed attributes. Typically the user pays for a large physical interface bandwidth (ATM is available on DS-1, DS-3, and OC-3c transmission facilities) over which several concurrent PVCs or SVCs can be run to multiple destinations. Services offered include Constant Bit Rate service (CBR), non–real-time Variable Bit Rate service (nrt-VBR), and Unspecified Bit Rate (UBR). Bandwidth charges are typically applied to individual or aggregated Peak Cell Rate (PCR) and, optionally, Sustained Cell Rate (SCR) and Maximum Burst Size (MBS). Speeds can be different at each end of the circuit. Circuits can be half duplex. For both national and international circuits the cost is generally applied at both ends as a half-circuit cost and may be billed through different suppliers. Some suppliers may charge at one end only for national circuits.

Tariff structure

The connection charge may vary based on distance to a nearest gateway or Point of Presence (PoP). An end-to-end circuit distance cost may be applied. Complex multipliers may be used based on the burst ratio, maximum burst size, and difference in speeds at ends of a circuit.

As with Frame Relay, ATM is a switched or permanent virtual circuit topology. Each physical interface into the ATM cloud can carry multiple virtual circuits, and each virtual circuit has the capability to switch data to any destination with an ATM SVC. If SVCs are not available, PVCs are used and provide fixed data paths throughout the network, similar to leased lines. Each ATM circuit can have its own Peak Cell Rate (PCR), Sustained Cell Rate (SCR), and Maximum Burst Size (MBS).

The Burst Ratio (BR) is the relationship between SCR and PCR. For example, an SCR of 10 Mbps with a PCR of 20 Mbps gives a burst ratio of 2. A PCR of 120 Mbps with a burst ratio of 1.5 gives an SCR of 80 Mbps.

ATM circuits typically specify the peak cell rate and, optionally, the sustained cell rate. PCR-only circuits are called CBRs (Constant Bit Rates), and PCR-SCR circuits are called VBRs (Variable Bit Rates). Even more confusing is the fact that circuits in ATM can be full-duplex symmetrical, full-duplex asymmetrical, or half-duplex.

Connection and rental costs are normally charged at each physical interface (port). Individual virtual circuits may have rental charges applied according to the bandwidth and possibly use charges. ATM is always costed or optimized based on the configured PCR, SCR, and MBS settings for each circuit. There may be incremental costs based on overall circuit length, node-to-switch distance, or a combination.

Examples

The following chart shows example costs for ATM services in the United States (available online from Pacific Bell [6]). Note that PacBell is very straightforward and does not impose any use or distance charges. Discounts are available for three-year and five-year term contracts.

Service	Link Speed	Connection	Rental
UNI DS1	1.544 Mbps	$1,500	$750 per month
UNI DS3	20 Mbps	$3,000	$4,200 per month
UNI DS3	40 Mbps	$3,000	$5,000 per month
UNI OC-3c	50 Mbps	$3,000	$6,000 per month
UNI OC-3c	100 Mbps	$3,000	$6,500 per month
UNI OC-3c	148 Mbps	$3,000	$7,000 per month
PVC Virtual Paths			$30 each (no charge for the first path)
PVC Virtual Channels			$15 each (no charge for the first channel)

User Network Interface (UNI) prices

A UNI includes the ATM port and the transmission facility.

The Permanent Virtual Connection (PVC) service is based on the number of connections on each port.

4.4.5   X.25 Packet-switched network

X.25 is a switched or permanent mesh, similar to Frame Relay. Each interface into the X.25 cloud can carry multiple circuits, and each circuit has the capability to switch data to any destination with an X.25 SVC. If SVCs are not available, PVCs are used and provide fixed data paths through the X.25 network; the topology is similar to point-to-point leased lines, or permanent ISDN circuits.

Note that some providers offer the option of running X.25 over ISDN, on both B-channels and D-channels. The D-channel option is a way of accessing additional low-cost bandwidth for background applications such as mailbox status checking (since the D-channel is effectively live and does not require a B-channel call to be established). Another application that could be supported is credit card transactions, using the X.25 Fast-Select feature. X.25 Fast-Select enables up to 128 bytes of user data to be piggy-backed onto the X.25 Call Request Packet (CRP). The receiving DTE can respond with a clear request (returning up to 128 bytes of data if required). This enables short transactions to take place without the overhead of the full X.25 call setup. Note that this option is not available from all providers, and, even if supported, many providers simply have no charging mecha-nism in place to date.

Tariff structure

Connection and rental costs are normally charged at each physical interface (port). Individual circuits typically have use charges applied based on the data passed. Normally the charges are applied at the end of the circuit that made the X.25 call (both send and receive traffic). Use charges are generally the most significant factor.

4.4.6   Voice services

Voice is a circuit-switched technology, essentially based on calls that can be placed dynamically and consume a circuit for the duration. Each call into the voice network has the capability to switch to any destination with a voice port. In a circuit-switched network resources are blocked until they are freed up by terminating the call, so the challenge is to design the net-work with sufficient circuit capacity to deal with enough incoming calls at any one time, without annoying users by presenting them with a network busy signal. A special analytical technique called Erlang Analysis is used to model call behavior in circuit-switched environments.

A more subtle issue in circuit-switched networks is characterizing user behavior in the advent of call blocking, and its revenue impact. This is a particular issue for call center applications, where businesses need to know whether to install more lines, employ more call staff, or assume callers will retry later. The revenue impact of abandoned calls is notoriously difficult to assess. The interested reader is referred to [7], where a mathematical model is presented to analyze this issue by demonstrating the impact of the proba-bility that an abandoned call is reattempted on the fraction of calls handled by the service. The model shows that the fraction of calls handled is directly proportional to the revenue obtained and that the fraction of abandoned calls reattempted has only a small impact on the fraction of calls handled, (provided that the probability that a call is reattempted is between 0.0 and 0.5). The reason for this is that served reattempted calls increase the average time to answer of subsequent calls, both new and reattempted. This tends to increase the fraction of abandoned call attempts. The results also suggest that service improvements that reduce the probability of call abandonment result in increased revenue, regardless of the fraction of calls reattempted. Therefore, the decision to increase staffing levels or not is simply a matter of comparing anticipated extra revenue with anticipated extra cost.

Tariff structure

The charging model typically comprises three main components: a connection charge, a rental charge, and a use charge. Use charges typically include a call setup cost (often dependent on the destination) and different rates for the duration for which calls are open (at a specific time of day, day of week, destination country, or regional zone). Often there are special rates for large metropolitan areas such as London (typically based on area code).

4.4.7   ISDN

Topology

ISDN uses a model similar to leased lines for the basic connection and rental cost structure, although the actual costs imposed are generally very low in comparison. The main difference is that a use charge is applied dynamically, based on the duration of the call. Both voice and data are supported, and, in fact, this is exactly the same model as a voice network and is illustrated as Figure 4.2(b). For a data network the final cost of the network is difficult to predict, since it is largely based on application use and the specific time of day and day of week during which there is activity. Time zones for peak, off-peak, and other periods may vary between suppliers and can vary significantly between countries.

Tariff structure

Connection and rental charges may scale according to the number of channels purchased and whether a Basic Rate Interface (BRI) or Primary Rate Interface (PRI) is selected. Channel speeds vary according to the multiplexer hierarchy of the country. In Europe channel speeds are in increments of 64 Kbps, including half E1 (1,024 Kbps), up to 1,920 Kbps (PRI). In the United States channel speeds are 56 Kbps, fractional T1 (128 Kbps, 192 Kbps, 256 Kbps, 384 Kbps, 512 Kbps, and 768 Kbps), and full T1. Note that ISDN also supports a special signaling channel called the D-channel, which normally carries control information but can in some circumstances be used to carry data (hence you may see the terminology 2B+D and 30B+D).

Use charges are scaled according to the number of channels opened on the circuit, the duration for which they are open, the time of day, and the destination country or regional zone. For both national and international circuits the cost is generally applied at both ends as a half-circuit cost and may be sourced through different suppliers.

Service providers in some countries (e.g., Germany) promote ISDN as a viable alternative to leased lines and thus make ISDN pricing very attractive (e.g., it would be feasible to run ISDN circuits in so-called nailed-up mode). Providers in other counties (such as the United Kingdom) appear to want to restrict ISDN use for niche applications such as circuit backup or home dial-up use (generally, after three or four hours utilization per day it would be wise to consider alternative technologies such as leased lines). Providers in other countries (e.g., France) have such complex tariffs that it can be worthwhile to use multiple service providers for traffic at different times of the day or week (e.g., a customer may use a different dial prefix over the same local loop to access different providers' ISDN services using time-of-day rules programmed for the cheapest tariff options).

For data applications ISDN circuits are typically demand or backup in nature, since use charges for permanent ISDN circuits can be excessive in some countries and by the blocking nature of an ISDN circuit-switched call. Variations or malfunctions in the application can dramatically affect the final cost of the network, since the longer the circuits are held open, the higher the bills will be. It is vital that ISDN devices be robust and configured to automatically shut down links in the event of excessive use. Call charges should be monitored at regular intervals to ensure that expensive trends are not emerging.

Examples

A United Kingdom national ISDN basic rate service between London and Bristol (approximately 170 km), with approximately 90 minutes peak utilization per day (Monday–Saturday), would incur connection costs of approximately $320, rental charges of $878 per annum, and use charges of approximately $4,638 per annum. Note that a variety of discount schemes may be offered for connection costs, but the key thing to watch is use rates. If the ISDN link stayed open all day, then you could expect an annual use charge of $32,455 (roughly three times the cost of a BT Kilostream 64-Kbps circuit!).

A permanent ISDN call from London to San Francisco would cost a massive $452,322 per annum in use charges. Clearly, it is important with ISDN equipment to minimize call duration and to ensure that calls are torn down when data/voice traffic is no longer active.

4.5   Integrated planning and billing tools

4.5.1   The need for automated tools

Manual tariff analysis can be extremely tedious, and few of us would actually enjoy wading through a provider's price book for longer than a few minutes. Attempting to design and cost a topology manually can be extremely time-consuming and is also prone to error. Even a relatively small ATM network could take several hours to cost, due to the number of calculations involved. This process can be further hindered by additional factors: some tariff information is not published, discount schemes are often obfuscated, important information such as switch locations may not even be published (making distance calculations guesswork), and tariffs change all the time. Since the network designer is paid to design networks, and is usually motivated by the technology, not the cost, looking into volumes of tariffs and figuring out the intricacies of the latest discount scheme in a supplier's price book usually rates low on the list of priorities (far better to carry on tweaking revision 37 of the network design). Unfortunately, we cannot get off that easily; this area represents potentially up to 80 percent of the network cost, and this is recurring cost.

One answer to this problem is to use automated tools to do the hard work, leaving the designer to get on with the job. There are several integrated planning tools on the market (see Table 4.4). At the top end of the market there are fully fledged modeling tools with built-in tariff databases for a whole range of services. The key features of these products are their ability to model more complicated services such as Frame Relay, ATM, and circuit-switched networks, as well as the ability to handle discount schemes, time-of-day/day-of-week charging, and so on.

At the lower end there are simple tariff calculators, which let you put in a source and destination, pick a service type, and then calculate the distances and costs involved. Figure 4.10 shows an example of one such tool. These products tend to focus on leased-line and satellite links, since they are

Table 4.4   *A Sample List of Automated Tariff Tools.*

Tool	Description	Services	Vendor
IPT-NetSolv	Full design & modelling suite	EUR,INT	Salford Networking Insitute
LinkWare	Full design & modelling suite	EUR,INT	Grid Technologies Ltd
LYNX GTD	Basic Pricing Tool	US,INT	LYNX
NetTool	Full design & modelling suite	US,INT	Make Systems Inc
PRICER	Basic Pricing Tool	US,INT	NAC Corp
Tarrifica Pricer	Basic Pricing Tool	EUR,INT	Tarrifica
T-Calc	Comprehensive Pricing Tool	EUR,INT,US	Eurodata (via Telegen Ltd)
WinMIND	Full design & modelling suite	US,INT	Network Analysis Centre Inc
WinPRICER	Basic Pricing Tool	US,INT	Network Analysis Centre Inc

Note that service coverage is indicated as Europe (EUR), North America (US), and international circuits (INT).

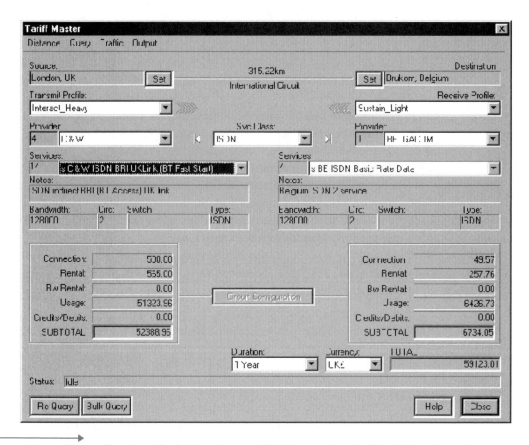

Figure 4.10   *Simple tariff calculator showing ISDN charges from the United Kingdom to Belgium.*

the easiest to work with, although some tools may also include more complex service such as ISDN if they can cope with traffic profiles and time-of-day/day-of-week charges. Note that traffic profiles are required to generate use costs, and this calculation will take into account time-of-day charges at each end of the circuit (defined in this case within the traffic profile).

Clearly, the vendors of such products still have a hard task in keeping their tariff databases up-to-date. It is also a nontrivial task to integrate many different pricing models into a consistent database schema. Nevertheless, a key benefit of automated tools is that they allow the user to play what-ifs with many technologies in a very short time (seconds or minutes rather than weeks), and, hence, the technology focus for the basic design can be settled early on and subsequently refined as the design firms up.

4.5.2   Sources of raw tariff data

Raw tariff data are available from many of the larger service providers. For example, British Telecom provides copious volumes of tariff data about many of its services to its registered list of consultants. BT also provides summary tariff information online, through its Web site [8]. However, some providers may not readily provide tariffs for all services they offer, or they may withhold (or charge for) key information critical for accurate cost calculations (such as switch locations). Typically, established services such as voice, leased line, satellite, and X.25 are widely available, but you may experience some difficultly obtaining tariffs for highly competitive newer services such as Frame Relay, SMDS, and ATM. For other examples of major operators' price availability refer to [6, 9–11].

There are also organizations such as Eurodata [12], Tarifica [13], and Lynx Technologies [14] that sell consolidated tariff information. These companies perform the arduous task of presenting a whole range of services from different providers in a normalized and abridged form (providers tend to present tariff data in a variety of formats, making it very difficult to make quick comparisons). Eurodata, for example, consolidates tariff information from over 150 carriers and produces a number of text publications, a CD-ROM, and a simple tariff calculator. Tarifica offers a similar range of products. Lynx Technologies offers a comprehensive database providing tariff coverage for over 350 carriers in more than 200 countries. All of these products vary in price, service coverage, and the level of detail offered. In my experience U.S.-based companies tend to provide more detailed coverage for North America than for Europe and vice versa. When evaluating these products, you should investigate how often the suppliers update their databases and how these data are validated to ensure that you are dealing with accurate, up-to-date tariff information.

4.5.3   Billing systems

The ability to collect data and bill according to use is obviously a core function of service providers, but this facility is also becoming of interest in private networks and enterprises. This has been partly assisted by the migration toward a unifying TCP/IP transport stack. In order to bill against use charges in a TCP/IP network, the system must meter the traffic for each connection (i.e., statistics on packet/byte counts in each direction, connection attempts, and source and destination must be maintained). In order to accommodate congestion charges the billing system must also monitor the state of the network (utilization, delay, packet loss, etc.) and provide real-time feedback on price changes to the users. A billing system must therefore embody the following features:

- Transparency—Because of the sheer size of the install base, a billing system must work with existing protocols and devices without requiring any modifications.

- User interaction—In order to bill individual users and provide feedback on price changes the billing system must be able to identify, interact, and obtain approval for price changes in a secure manner.

- Real-time monitoring—The state of the network must be monitored in real time in order to offer the possibility of congestion charges.

- Resource sharing and identification—Billing systems must be able to identify users and bill them accordingly, even when remotely accessing applications offered on the WWW. This is fundamental to e-commerce and is typically achieved via a trusted third party.

In reality the data collection part of this solution is often handled by specialized real-time applications, and the billing component is a separate entity, which is interfaced to the data collector.

4.6   Summary

In this chapter we discussed the following:

- Wide area network charges are often the most expensive part of the network cost, and they are recurring. Failure to pay enough attention to optimizing the wide area design, and poor choice of wide area technology, can result in a significant waste of money and bandwidth.

- Tariff models in network economics distinguish four types of charge: a fixed connection charge, a use charge, a congestion charge, and a service quality charge.

- Physical site location, site-to-PoP, and site-to-site distances are very important in many charging schemes. Dial codes and post codes also play an important role in determining circuit costs, and least-distance topologies are not necessarily least cost. Use this knowledge to best position your major sites and call centers.

- Time of day and day of week are important for many use-based charging schemes. These are key considerations for your application use, especially with international calls where schemes at either end may vary markedly. Use this knowledge to tune dial-up access appropriately with services such as ISDN.

- Wide area technologies often implement charging models in very different ways, resulting in a wide range of charging schemes, which are extremely difficult to understand or apply by hand. On even a relatively small network of ten nodes it is often extremely time consuming to build an accurate cost model without automated tools. A key benefit of automated tools is that they allow the user to play what-ifs with many technologies in a very short time (minutes rather than weeks), and, hence, the technology focus for the basic design can be settled early on and subsequently refined as the design firms up.

References

[1]   G. B. Richardson, *Economic Theory* (Hutchinson & Co., 1964).

[2]   D. Minoli, *Broadband Network Analysis and Design* (Norwood, MA: Artech House, 1993).

[3]   J. L. Riggs, *Engineering Economics* (New York: McGraw-Hill, 1977).

[4]   E. Bailey and E. Lindenburg, "Peak Load Pricing Principles: Past and Present," New Dimensions in Public Utility Pricing, MSU Public Utilities Studies, 1976.

[5]   I. Pressman, "A Mathematical Formulation of the Peak Load Pricing Problem," in *Bell Journal of Economics and Management Science*, vol. 1, Autumn 1970.

[6]   www.pacbell.com, Pacific Bell's home page, includes online tariff information.

[7]   A. B. Bondi, *An Analysis of the Revenue Impact of Retried Abandoned Calls in an Operator Service* (Holmdel, NJ: AT&T Labs).

[8]   www.bt.com, British Telecom's home page.

[9]   www.att.com, AT&T's home page.

[10]   www.cw.com, Cable & Wireless's home page.

[11]   www.energis.com, Energis's home page.

[12]   www.telegen.com, Telegen's home page (the commercial representative of the Eurodata Foundation).

[13]   www.tarifica.com, Tarifica's home page.

[14]   www.lynxtech.com, Lynx Technologies' home page.

5

Physical Topology Design

In this chapter, we will look at the techniques and issues associated with designing a physical network topology (the physical arrangement of the nodes and the connectivity offered by links). Designing an optimum topology is a nontrivial task on any medium to large internetwork; in fact, it is intractable. We must, therefore, rely heavily on specialist algorithms and heuristic techniques (for the uninitiated, a heuristic is an algorithm that is not guaranteed to find the best solution, generally produces good results, but can sometimes fail). To get an idea of the scale of the problem, consider the following. If there are N locations to consider, then there are $N(N-1)/2$ possible links, and since links can be either present or absent, there are $2^{N(N-1)/2}$ potential topologies. This means that even for a relatively small backbone of, say, only 25 nodes, we are presented with 2×10^{90} possible topologies to consider when designing a least-cost network!

To design a network topology we must start with supporting data (specifically, node locations, traffic flows, and cost matrices). Perhaps as much as 80 percent of the design process is concerned with data preparation in some form or other. This information should be collated during the capacity-planning phase. When designing the topology, we must usually satisfy a number of constraints (such as reliability, delay-throughput, and overall budget); these need to be clearly understood at the outset—otherwise, valuable time will be lost exploring inappropriate solutions. The designer will also rely on techniques presented earlier, such as queuing theory, graph theory, and shortest path algorithms. Armed with all this information we can begin to offer various solutions to the problem by generating topologies, assigning capacities to links, and distributing traffic flows over those links. Our goal is to produce a design that minimizes cost while satisfying overall performance and reliability constraints. When designing network topologies, it is important that we remain aware of both the physical and logical elements in play. The physical network topology provides the physical paths through which traffic flows. A point sometimes misunderstood by those with a rudimentary understanding of networking is that having a physical path between devices does not automatically mean that they can communicate. In order that devices communicate we must provide a logical path between devices, and this path might not traverse the most obvious (e.g., shortest) physical path. Because of the inherent complexity of network design, there are few specialist tools available to assist in the design process. These tools are often very expensive and difficult to use and tend to specialize on particular technologies. To illustrate some of the concepts we will generate some example designs using a simple design tool I developed called iSIM+.

Topology optimization is a huge subject, highly theoretical, and littered with jargon about algorithms, complexity analysis, and software engineering. Unfortunately, for any sizable network, design algorithms are fundamental to the overall efficiency and cost and cannot simply be ignored. Most current books about topology design are almost impenetrable for the novice and tend to focus on very specialized areas of design. This chapter is one of several intended to bridge the gap between high-level design texts and those devoted exclusively to design algorithms. It is impossible within the constraints of a few chapters to fully explore such a complex subject; however, you should have a clear idea about what the key issues and techniques are, and the following text will provide a springboard for further research. We should keep in mind that we are concerned largely with theoretic analysis of topology and performance. In real networks the physical topology will be overlaid with many logical topologies, created by switching components and routing protocols, which we will touch on in this chapter. This infrastructure may itself be overlaid with Virtual Private Networks (VPNs), which we will discuss later in the book.

5.1 Hierarchical network design

5.1.1 A divide-and-conquer approach

Given the complexity of the problem already outlined, we know that topological design is generally subdivided into discrete, manageable tasks. We will use a widely accepted approach of attacking the problem hierarchically, by separating the design process into an access network design and a backbone network design. The techniques employed in the access layer are equally applicable to the distribution layer, so we will group all such techniques under the general heading of access network design. Access and backbone are described as follows:

- The access network is the part of the network where hosts and terminals feed into the closest backbone node. There are several basic subproblems to tackle, such as concentrator location, the assignment of sites to concentrators, and node layout within a site. Note that I use the term node here to be synonymous with the term *terminal*, typically found in the literature, since I find the use of the word *terminal* misleading if taken literally. The access network determines the input traffic flows for the backbone.

- The backbone is arguably the most important piece of any network design; if done badly, then the whole network suffers and any application traffic crossing the backbone will experience delays and congestion. In large national or international networks there may also be a large price to pay for a badly executed network design, since wide area links are usually expensive and offer restricted bandwidth. This section covers some of the theoretical aspects of designing a topology that meets the traffic demand, as well as many of the protocol and routing issues of importance in this topic.

Each of these subproblems requires different specialized techniques in order to arrive at a solution and should be tackled in a specific order. First, we solve the access design, and then we solve the backbone design (in Figure 5.1 this is illustrated by working from right to left). The reason for this approach is that the output of the access design will be a set of summary traffic matrices, which form the input into the backbone nodes and subsequent backbone design. As we see in Figure 5.1, within individual sites there are one or more access nodes (ANs), typically hosts, and local routing/switching equipment. These are connected together in a variety of topologies (including spanning tree, star, or meshed layouts). At the egress point of a site there is a site concentrator (SC), typically a router. Site concentrators are collapsed into a larger distribution concentrator (DC), typically a larger router, and then further collapsed into a backbone node (BN).

5.1.2   Key techniques used in backbone design

Backbone design is inherently more complex than access design, as we shall see shortly. The problems associated with optimizing backbone designs have their origins in the classic traveling salesperson problem (TSP) [1]. This problem introduces a number of cities spaced geographically at different

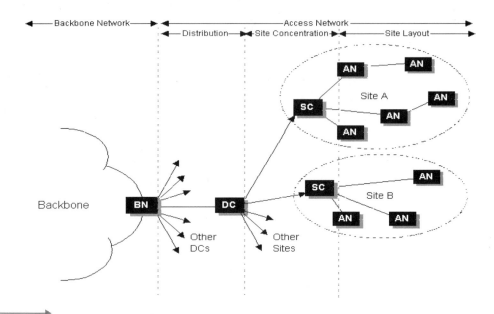

Figure 5.1   *Three-level model for hierarchical network design.*

distances from each other. The problem for the salesperson is how to plan a tour starting at a particular city, visiting each other city only once, and returning to the origin using the shortest possible route. While simple in concept, this problem has proved very difficult (mathematically intractable: NP-Hard) to optimize because of the huge number of paths available as the number of cities increases. If this problem were not hard enough, real backbone design also embodies traffic, routing, performance, and congestion problems, which are equally intractable.

There are several optimization techniques that have been adopted specifically to solve (well, at least provide satisfactory results for) large-scale backbone topology problems, mainly focusing on iterative improvement algorithms [1]. Some of these techniques are applicable only to specific problem domains; others are generic techniques, which must be customized to some extent around a specific problem. Considering the potential size of the search space (i.e., the total number of possible solutions) in large-scale topology optimization, a number of these techniques may be extremely inefficient. Current known methods fall into the following categories:

■ Random (enumerated) search: This is effectively a brute-force approach for solving difficult functions. Points in the search space are selected randomly. This is a poor strategy for this size of problem and very expensive computationally.

- Gradient methods: These methods are generally referred to as hill-climbing or gradient-descent methods and perform well on functions with only one peak/trough. There are several drawbacks with these methods—for example, when hill climbing is used on functions with many peaks, the first peak encountered will be climbed and selected as the best solution, whether it is the highest peak or not. In this event no further progress will be made, and we refer to this as being trapped inside a local maxima. Gradient-descent methods have the converse problem of being susceptible to local minima.

- Random-restart gradient methods: Random search and gradient search may be combined to give an iterated hill-climbing or gradient-descent search. For example, with hill climbing once one peak is encountered, the results are cached and the hill climb is started again, this time using a random starting point. However, since each random trial is performed in isolation there is no coordinated picture of the problem domain, and trials are randomly allocated over the entire search space. This leads to overall inefficiency, since many suboptimal solutions will be evaluated unnecessarily.

- Simulated annealing: This is essentially a modified version of hill climbing. To avoid the problem of local maxima, negative (downhill) moves are allowed but constrained (too many negative moves would lead the search away from the maxima). Simulated annealing deals with only one candidate at a time; as with random search, it does not build an overall picture of the search space, and no information from previous moves is used to guide the selection of new moves. Nevertheless, this technique has been successful in many applications—for example, Very Large Scale Integration (VLSI) circuit design and optimization models for market data networks [2].

- Dynamic programming: This is a method for solving sequential decision problems developed in the late 1950s by Richard Bellman. It can be used only where the overall fitness function is the sum of the fitness functions for each stage of the problem, and there is no interaction between stages.

- Genetic algorithms (GAs): This is a general-purpose technique that can be applied to topology and design problems. The base data structures operated on are a translated representation of the fundamental design data (typically a chromosome string encoded with a finite alphabet to represent a topological design). GAs can deal effectively with a broader class of functions than many other techniques, and performance evaluation (such as design cost, average delay, etc.) is achieved using objective payoff information. The search domain is, therefore, transparent to the GA, and there is an upper bound to its performance potential. The parallelism inherent in GAs avoids stagnation in local maxima or minima, especially if some diversity is maintained in the chromosome population (some candidates may become trapped; others will not). In the design context each chromosome string could (in its simplest form) be a coded representation of an adjacency matrix, and a population of chromosomes is regularly interbred and manipulated in such a way that fitter designs emerge over time. Since this method is general purpose, it is essentially left to the designer to customize representation, breeding, and population maintenance to the associated problem.

- Swarming algorithms: This is another relatively recent general-purpose method applied to solving tour and routing problems by modeling the behavior of certain cooperative insects (such as ants, termites, bees, wasps, etc.). Although it provides near-optimal solutions relatively quickly [3], this method is also highly flexible, similar to the GA method, and may be applied to other classes of problems.

The remainder of this chapter is dedicated to access and backbone design, although we will revisit some of the concepts just described in more detail. For the interested reader, this chapter should form the starting point for further research. Topological analysis is the subject of entire books and numerous research papers.

5.1.3 Availability analysis

A key issue with network design is fault tolerance and the level of service outages you are prepared to accept on a particular network. We group these concepts loosely under the heading availability analysis. Tolerance of network outages tends to decrease as we move down the three-tier design hierarchy and approach the core network, although even at the access layer there are mission-critical components (such as server farms) that dictate very high availability. Examples of factors that could affect availability include the following:

- Breaks in backbone fibers

- Denial-of-service security attacks

- Server disk subsystem failure

- Device failure (router, switch, firewall, concentrator, etc.)

- Network meltdown through broadcast storms or equipment malfunction

- Corrupted DNS or routing tables

The cost of network outages can, in most cases, be quantified financially. For example, let us assume that there is a publishing company with annual revenues of $550 million. Operating hours are eight hours per day, five days per week. The company depends on its network and computer systems for 70 percent of its operations. We can, therefore, calculate that:

Revenues per hour = 550,000,000/(8 × 5 × 52) = $264,423,000

Cost per hour of downtime (lost revenue) =
(0.70 × revenues per hour) = $185,000

Therefore, if the network sustains a full day's outage, the cost to the company in lost revenue is almost $1.5 million. Note that this does not take into account the damage to customer loyalty and market credibility.

Availability analysis should, therefore, be an integral consideration of the design process. You should have a clear idea about what the specific availability targets are for any particular aspect of the design, because availability costs money to provision. There could be a substantial difference in the cost and resources required to maintain a network uptime of 99 percent (a maximum outage of 3 days, 15 hours, 36 minutes per year) as opposed to 99.999 percent uptime (a maximum outage of five minutes per year). Some of the more sophisticated network design tools (described in Section 5.4) include tools specifically for analyzing and modeling the survivability and availability of a given topology.

5.2   Access network design

You may remember that the techniques used in access design are applicable for both the access and distribution layer. Access design involves decisions on where to place distribution concentrators, how sites should be assigned to those concentrators, and how individual access nodes (sometimes referred to as terminals) within sites should be attached to site concentrators. This three-tiered hierarchy is illustrated in Figure 5.1. For any access network design, the first stage is to identify which traffic is truly local. This traffic can be back-hauled behind the access nodes and is of no consequence for the backbone or distribution layers. Only the remote component is of interest, and once this has been identified you can begin to decide how many access nodes are required per site. We need to scale the size and number of the access nodes according to the number of users and volume of remote traffic from a region. We will now examine how to tackle these sub-problems in detail.

5.2.1   Collapsing sites in distribution concentrators

Typically a real network design would start with the customer providing a list of the locations of various sites. Sites could comprise almost anything: manufacturing plants, transport depots, air force bases, gas stations, university campuses, and so on. Each site will comprise one or more nodes; typically there will be a range of site sizes, and the customer may already have classified these, since this is often related to site use. For example, a gas/chemical company may have a main headquarters (thousands of nodes), a manufacturing plant (hundreds of nodes), several transport depots (tens of nodes), and thousands of gas stations (one node). For each site we would typically need to have a breakdown of information as follows:

Site	ID	Nodes	Location	Country	Latitude	Longitude	Area Code
HQ	1	300	Edinburgh	United Kingdom	55.95	–3.2	0131
MKT_1	8	60	Boston	United States	42.34	–71.08	02116

From the concentrator perspective, each site is either a source or sink for data, and at this level of the design hierarchy it is irrelevant to the concentrator where it plugs into the backbone; we are simply concerned with collapsing all of the user sites onto the nearest concentrators. I mention the term nearest, because the real problem is deciding what nearest means in terms of the most cost-effective topology and the available bandwidth and port density available at each concentrator. Nearest may not equate to closest geographically. Refer to Figure 5.2.

The problem can be expressed as a zero-one programming problem. There are n customer sites, numbered 1 to n, and m concentrators, numbered 1 to m, plus the backbone node itself (typically the central site), designated as location 0. The cost of connecting customer site i to concentrator j is c_{ij}. Let x_{ij} be 1 if we have assigned site i to concentrator j, and 0 if the site is unassigned. The total cost of a particular assignment is, therefore:

$$\text{Total Cost} = \sum_{i=1}^{n} \sum_{j=0}^{m} x_{ij} c_{ij}$$

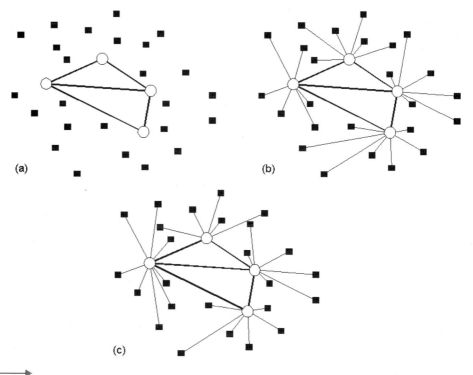

Figure 5.2 *(a) A number of customer sites (squares) and concentrators (circles) and a backbone (thick solid line). (b) and (c) represent two of many possible node assignments to the concentrators.*

There are two constraints we have to impose on the solution, x_{ij}. First each customer site is connected to exactly one concentrator:

$$\sum_{j=1}^{m} x_{ij} = 1 \qquad (i = 1, 2, \text{K}, n)$$

Second, concentrator j can cope with a maximum number of sites, k_j:

$$\sum_{i=1}^{n} x_{ij} \leq k_j \qquad (j = 0, 2, \text{K}, m)$$

This limitation may be due to the number of ports, the processing time required for each interrupt, or some other limit. If there is no limit, then k_j can be set to infinity.

A simple node assignment heuristic

We need to assign 1s and 0s to x to satisfy the design constraints while minimizing cost. There are $2^{(m+1)n}$ possible assignments of x, so clearly a full search of the search space is unworkable for any reasonable-sized network. So now we can find some simple heuristics for good, but not necessarily optimal, solutions. For details of an optimal algorithm see [4].

A very simple heuristic, put forward by [5], is simply to scan rows of costs to connect site x to each concentrator, choosing the cheapest cost, fol-

Table 5.1   *Basic Cost Assignments*

(a)

Site	CS	C1	C2	C3	C4	C5
A	9	5	6	6	12	9
B	1	4	5	8	5	7
C	15	3	2	8	19	8
D	12	8	4	3	15	5
E	3	2	17	10	5	8
F	14	3	20	4	7	9
G	3	8	17	6	4	14
H	9	9	1	5	7	2
I	6	7	4	4	1	2
J	9	9	1	5	7	2
K	7	7	11	10	14	7
L	1	5	6	4	8	12

(b)

Site	CS	C1	C2	C3	C4	C5	Scan Order
A	9	5	6	6	12	9	1
B	1	4	5	8	5	7	2
C	15	3	2	8	19	8	3
D	12	8	4	3	15	5	4
E	3	2	17	10	5	8	5
F	14	3	20	4	7	9	6
G	3	8	17	6	4	14	7
H	9	9	1	5	7	2	8
I	6	7	4	4	1	2	9
J	9	9	3	5	7	2	10
K	7	7	11	10	14	7	11
L	1	5	6	4	8	12	12
Total	4	7	3	7	9	9	39.000

(c)

Site	CS	C1	C2	C3	C4	C5	Scan Order
A	9	5	6	6	12	9	7
B	1	4	5	8	5	7	6
C	15	3	2	8	19	8	4
D	12	8	4	3	15	5	8
E	3	2	17	10	5	8	3
F	14	3	20	4	7	9	2
G	3	8	17	6	4	14	11
H	9	9	1	5	7	2	10
I	6	7	4	4	1	2	1
J	9	9	3	5	7	2	9
K	7	7	11	10	14	7	12
L	1	5	6	4	8	12	5
Total	2	5	8	13	5	4	37.000

(d)

Site	CS	C1	C2	C3	C4	C5	Scan Order
A	9	5	6	6	12	9	7
B	1	4	5	8	5	7	6
C	15	3	2	8	19	8	4
D	12	8	4	3	15	5	8
E	3	2	17	10	5	8	3
F	14	3	20	4	7	9	2
G	3	8	17	6	4	14	11
H	9	9	1	5	7	2	10
I	6	7	4	4	1	2	1
J	9	9	3	5	7	2	9
K	7	7	11	10	14	7	12
L	1	5	6	4	8	12	5
Total	2	5	3	9	5	9	33.000

(a) Cost assignments from sites A through L for connection to Central Site (CS) or concentrators 1 through 5.
(b) Suboptimal cost of 39 achieved with scan order 1, 2, 3, 4, 5, 6, 7, 8, 9, 10, 11, 12. (c) Improved cost of 37 achieved with random scan order 7, 6, 4, 8, 3, 2, 11, 10, 1, 9, 12, 5. (d) Improved cost of 33 achieved by checking for ties and shifting existing assignments if the costs are improved.

lowed by some randomization. Let us assume a cost matrix, with 12 sites (A–L), a Central Site (CS), and a set of five concentrator nodes. We will assume for simplicity that k_j is 2 (i.e., we can connect no more than two sites to any concentrator). Table 5.1(a) shows the basic costs for all possible assignments. The basic idea is to scan each row and assign the least-cost path to a concentrator. If a concentrator is fully connected, then the next cheapest site cost should be chosen, and so on. The diagrams in Table 5.1 show that by simply rerunning the heuristic with different row orders we can achieve better total costs. Table 5.1(b) uses a sequential row scan to get a cost of 39, Table 5.1(c) randomizes the scan order, and a better cost of 37 is found. We could do this several times to check for even better costs.

As a further refinement, we can keep track of any concentrators where there was excess demand, resulting in a site having to choose another concentrator at a higher cost. Wherever there is a situation where a site cannot choose its concentrator of preference, we examine existing assignments to see if a reassignment would be cheaper, as in the case of Table 5.1(d). Here we see that site A was originally assigned to concentrator C2 for a cost of 6. When the scan for site H was in progress, C2 was the cheapest option by far (at a cost of 1) but already fully subscribed. By simply reassigning site A to C3 we save cost. A more sophisticated heuristic would improve on this and may even assign sites to more expensive concentrators if the overall cost is to be reduced.

5.2.2   Locating distribution concentrators

Now that we have figured out a simple way to assign sites to concentrators we can examine methods for locating the concentrators themselves. We will assume that there are m possible locations for concentrators. Since the number of concentrators is a variable, we introduce a new term to our cost equation:

$$\text{Total Cost} = \sum_{i=1}^{n}\sum_{j=0}^{m} x_{ij}c_{ij} + \sum_{j=0}^{m} y_i f_j$$

where,

y_j = 1, if at least one user is using concentrator j

y_j = 0, if nobody is using concentrator j.

The cost of the concentrator is f_j.

This problem has been extensively studied by people in the field of operations research, where it is known as the warehouse location problem. There are two well-known heuristics, ADD and DROP. These are discussed in the following text.

The ADD heuristic

The algorithm proceeds as follows:

1. Begin with all customer sites attached directly to the central site and work out the cost.

2. Introduce concentrator site 1 and assign each customer to either the central site or concentrator 1. We can simply use the cheapest option. If the total cost is cheaper than simply having a central site, then we should note this solution as being of interest.

3. Eliminate concentrator 1 and work through each concentrator–central site combination to find out which is the cheapest combination.

The result will be that we find a concentrator, say $c1$, which is the minimum cost solution when combined with the central site.

Now repeat steps 1 through 3, using $c1$ together with each concentrator in the remaining $m - 1$ list of concentrators, plus the central site, to find the minimum cost solution for three concentrators, $c1$ plus $c2$. Use this result to work out the cheapest solution for four concentrators and so on. Continue the search while the costs continue to decrease. At some point the costs will increase as the trade-off between line costs and the cost of adding a new concentrator become prohibitive. The previous solution to this point will be the desired minimum cost solution.

The DROP heuristic

The DROP heuristic is the reverse of ADD. We start by using all concentrators available, attaching each customer site with one of the $m + 1$ concentrators, and then calculate the total cost. The DROP algorithm works by discarding uneconomical concentrators one at a time. The algorithm proceeds as follows:

1. Start with concentrator 1. Tentatively remove it and reassign each customer to one of the remaining m possible concentrators, and calculate the new cost.

2. Reattach concentrator 1, and repeat the same procedure with concentrator 2 and so forth, each time calculating the cost of a concentrator's removal. The largest cost saving is associated with the concentrator that should be disconnected.

3.   In the same way, repeat the whole process for all the remaining nodes, detaching costly concentrators until the point where costs start to increase. A cost increase will occur when the concentrators are spread so thinly that the line costs start to go up dramatically.

5.2.3   Site layout

So far we have treated a site as a single concentrator. This is fine if the site contains only a large central server with no other nodes; however, in reality a site may comprise many devices laid out over a building or campus LAN. We now need to consider how access nodes on the local site (sometimes referred to as terminals) are to be collapsed to these site concentrators. There are many strategies available for this part of the design, including the following:

- If each access node has very little traffic to flow in/out of the site, then it may make sense to attach all access nodes to a shared line to the site concentrator.

- If better performance is required and the site is relatively small (say a single floor of a building), then each access node could be star-wired from the site concentrator.

- A larger campus network may require a more cost-effective topology; this could be achieved with a spanning tree topology.

The actual topology selected depends on a number of factors, including budget, site geography, number of nodes, and performance constraints. One good place to start would be to consider using spanning tree algorithms such as Prim or Kruskal's algorithms [6]. In reality, however, we also need to consider constraints on the design, such as the following:

- Maximum traffic allowed on any access node to site concentrator link.

- Maximum traffic allowed on any site concentrator to distribution concentrator link. (In the case where the site concentrator to distribution concentrator link were to overflow, then another site concentrator is required, as well as another site concentrator to distribution concentrator link.)

- Links that are mandated to be present regardless of cost (perhaps they already exist).

■ Links that are not allowed regardless of cost (e.g., two buildings that cannot physically be connected due to physical or contractual limitations).

Neither algorithm will work on constrained designs without modification, although it is fairly easy to insert checks in the link selection parts of the code to check valid edge choices. Reference [7] provides details of heuristics applicable to constrained spanning tree design.

5.3   Backbone network design

Backbone topologies are easy to design badly—just join a few sites together, install the biggest pipes between them that you can afford, then switch on and see if the lights dim! I would hazard a guess that a surprising proportion of mission-critical networks in operation today would, if analyzed systematically, be far from optimal in either performance or cost terms. This is not necessarily the fault of the designer. The techniques available for backbone network design are extremely demanding, and automated tools are in short supply, very expensive, and often inflexible, incomplete, and very hard to use. The skills required to do this work are also extremely rare and often misunderstood, and the science supporting topology optimization is still very much an area of active research, as illustrated by relatively new biological modeling techniques discussed later in this section.

The factors that influence the choice of an optimal backbone topology are quite varied, sometimes incomplete or inexact, and often mutually dependent. Furthermore, the requirements placed on a backbone usually vary by time of day, week, month, and over the years as the network expands. It is, therefore, extremely difficult to produce an exact solution with any reasonable-sized network, and what we generally aim for is a set of good-fit solutions that at least address worst-case traffic conditions. Modeling tools in this area typically require large amounts of time and processor bandwidth to produce near-optimal solutions, since the number of potential solutions (the search space) can grow alarmingly as the number of nodes increases.

Given the potential financial gains for improvements in this area it is surprising that there are so few commercial design tools on the market. This is partly a reflection of the state of the science and also of the attitude within organizations regarding network design. Aside from a small number of major telcos, network design is still viewed as a black art, and the specific area of topological optimization is often overlooked in favor of what looks right because of the obvious difficulty of using these techniques. Topological optimization is, however, an increasingly key issue for PTTs, ISPs, and corporate organizations running their own international backbones. The increasing complexity of networking and tariff structures means that significant cost savings are available for the smart designer. What we must do is take the best of the approaches available today, and, where necessary, use some short cuts. It is also a reasonable approach to get at least 80 percent of the way toward a good solution and then start to get some installation feedback. Further gains are likely to be increasingly hard to realize, and by the time we've got all the way to a 90 percent optimal solution the network requirements will have probably changed!

5.3.1 The design process

Backbone design requires knowledge of the aggregate traffic requirements feeding into the backbone nodes and the cost metrics used for various media speeds between potential backbone nodes (this information is derived from the access network design discussed previously). The classical approach to the backbone design problem is to iterate through trial and error. Effectively we could generate a topology and continuously modify it, checking at each stage whether we are making a good move or a bad move by examining factors such as overall delay and cost. This is rather like playing chess with a search depth of one position. If a move results in a key piece being taken, or an obviously poor position being reached, we reset the position back and move a different piece. This is likely to produce a reasonable game but unlikely to produce the best game possible and is clearly very inefficient. By moving incrementally and in isolation we never see the big picture, and our incremental changes are likely to lead us down one of many suboptimal positions.

Input data

To generate an initial topology we need the following sets of data:

- A list of nodes, with location information to calculate relative distances and host countries

- A traffic matrix

- A cost matrix

- Constraints such as cost, delay, throughput, and connectivity

In the case of backbone design we are assuming that the access design has already been completed, so our node list refers to backbone nodes, and the traffic matrix is summarized traffic at the ingress points into the backbone (derived from the aggregate access design flows). Constraints are important, in that there should be some tangible targets used to direct the design process; at the very least the aim should include a performance and cost constraint.

A basic design algorithm

A general algorithm for optimizing the backbone design is expressed in the following C code. Don't be fooled by the simplicity of this code; as with many aspects of network design the devil is in the detail.

```
GetOptimalTopology()
{
  bestCost = 0;
  previousCost = INFINITE;
  bestTopology = NULL;
  currentTopology  = CreateStartingTopology();
  while ( NotFinished )
  {
    AssignTrafficFlows();
    AssignLinkCapacities();
    currentCost = GetCost( currentTopology );
    If ( feasableTopology )
    {
      if ( currentCost < previousCost )
      {
      bestTopology = currentTopology;
        bestCost = currentCost;
        previousCost = currentCost
      }
    }
  }
}
```

The general process is illustrated in Figure 5.3. After the starting topology is generated, the process loops around, continuously modifying (perturbing) and improving the design until an acceptable or near-optimal solution is found, some threshold has been exceeded, or the user terminates the process. To decide what an improvement is we may examine several factors to assess relative fitness, such as cost, average delay, throughput, and resilience. Each new topology must also satisfy the basic constraints (i.e., be feasible), which at the very least will involve a basic test of connectivity to exclude nonsensible topologies (such as disconnected graphs). It should not be underemphasized that some of these intermediate steps are nontrivial (to put it mildly). The misleadingly simple functions AssignTrafficFlows() and AssignLinkCapacities() could fill a chapter in themselves. It is important that these procedures be implemented efficiently, since this loop will have to be run many times on a large network.

Although the heuristic is well understood and reasonably successful, there are also seemingly impossible issues to resolve. The reason that routing and capacity assignment are shown interlocked in Figure 5.3 is because they should ideally be optimized simultaneously. It is clearly difficult to determine routing paths for traffic flows without prior knowledge of the available capacities, and we would typically not assign capacities until we know the routing paths and traffic flows! Furthermore, in real life there are many

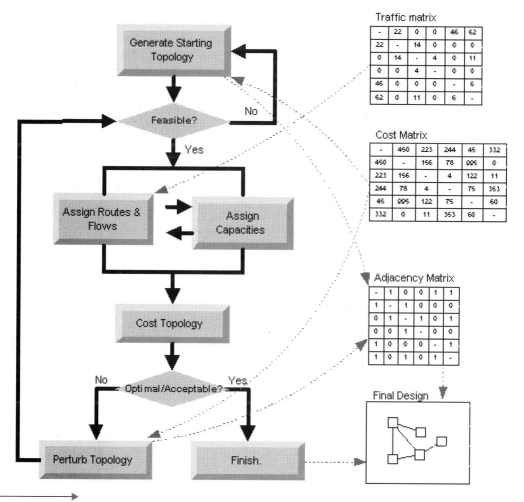

Figure 5.3   *Backbone design process, showing relationships between key steps and databases.*

examples of routing protocols that behave dynamically, automatically rerouting based on traffic congestion or utilization. All is not lost, however. Most dynamic protocols will behave as static protocols in a relatively stable network with well-distributed traffic flows. If the network has a few very large clients capable of dynamically saturating bandwidth whenever they feel like it, then this assumption does not hold true; however, this is fortunately not the norm.

In the routing process there are several techniques available, including static routing (using either the shortest path or a combination of shortest path and some cost scalar). We will examine some of the techniques that can be used to closely couple the flow, routing, and capacity assignment processes.

Another factor in determining what is optimal is that different users and applications have different requirements and priorities with respect to constraints such as delay and throughput (e.g., the latency requirements for file transfer and voice are very different). In fact, there are often different priorities within different parts of the network for either better throughput or lower delay. We could, therefore, embellish the algorithm further to take account of local requirements; however, all of this adds complexity and processing overhead. There is a trade-off between reality and simplicity at the expense of execution time. Clearly, a tool needs to produce useful results within a reasonable time frame; there is not much demand for a tool that produces fantastic results after a ten-year execution cycle on a Cray supercomputer; most networks simply don't last that long.

Drawbacks of this approach

One of the possible limitations of a localized iterative approach is that we are likely to get stuck in some local minima (see Figure 5.4), and the choice of starting topology may play a big part in limiting the scope of the solution space examined. The choice of perturbation algorithms is also quite critical. Due to the limited scope we employ (i.e., we take a very systematic single-step-then-look-around approach) it is very likely that this process will move toward a good solution, where it will stagnate because any move away from that solution is viewed as a backward step, even though five moves later we may start to approach a better solution. In Figure 5.4, a Ping-Pong ball is released from the seabed and must negotiate a path upward around icebergs. There are several positions where the ball will become trapped, and in this case only one optimal case where the ball will reach the surface. Clearly, we must either direct the ball explicitly or use some technique to dislodge the ball and attempt another route.

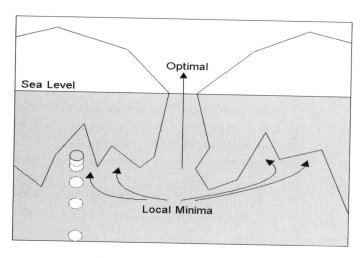

Figure 5.4
*Illustrating the
concepts of
suboptimal local
minima.*

As we will see later, there are refinements we can make and entirely different approaches to solving this problem. One obvious improvement would be to have the whole program run continuously, allowing it to store best-fit solutions and use the previous best-fit solutions to eliminate local minima or maxima (depending upon the objective).

5.3.2   Starting topology algorithms

There is some debate over the relative merits of putting much effort into a sensible starting topology; this really depends upon the algorithms you intend to employ for backbone design and their ability to escape suboptimal traps. An initial topology of the network could be one of the following:

- Unconnected

- Fully meshed

- An entirely random topology

- Some form of spanning tree based on useful starting criteria

- An initial best estimate of the optimal design based on some fast heuristics

Common sense tells us that the closer we are to a good solution at the start, then the faster we are likely to converge. However, if we ignore what appear to be less attractive starting points, then we may in fact avoid going down a path that would lead to even better solutions. The algorithms used to perturb this topology play an important part in deciding how much effort you should put into the starting topology, since these should ensure that you avoid local minima or maxima. Many of the classic backbone design algorithms are quite sensitive to the starting topology, so it is probably worth investing at least some time in the initial topology generation, using a fast algorithm such as MENTOR (described in Section 5.3.7). At least this way you will have one feasible design if all else fails!

When creating an initial topology, we must at least meet the connectivity constraint and use some combination of the remaining constraints to measure the fitness of the solution proposed. Clearly, we could always meet the connectivity constraint by simply connecting all nodes together (i.e., a full mesh), but factors such as cost should guide us toward much leaner solutions. Where the primary constraint is to minimize delay at the expense of cost, we will tend to produce more meshed topologies in order to reduce the average hop count (in a fully meshed network there are no hops between nodes).

We will now discuss an algorithm historically associated with starting topology, the link deficit algorithm. As already mentioned, we could also opt to use a more sophisticated but fast algorithm such as MENTOR to achieve similar results.

Link deficit algorithm

This is a fairly general heuristic [8]. It takes a reasonable approach in providing a starting topology based on connectivity alone (using Whitney's theorem). If we constrain the network into providing a k-connected topology, then we must assume that every node has at least k links. Nodes are selected at random, and this allows us to create many topologies from the same input data. The basic algorithm runs as follows:

1.   Renumber all nodes randomly (1 through N).

2.   Allocate the number of required links to each node (the link deficit, initially k).

3.   Add links one at a time until the link deficits are all zero.

     a.   Find the node with the highest deficit. In the event of a tie choose the lowest node ID.

     b.   Find the node not already adjacent with the highest deficit. In the event of a tie choose the node the least distance away. In the event of a tie choose the lowest node ID.

In step 3b we use the term distance loosely. This could be geographic distance, cost, or some other metric. In general this heuristic is unlikely to fully satisfy the connectivity constraint, and with odd numbers of nodes we get negative link deficits. It is up to the perturbation heuristics to provide properly connected topologies.

5.3.3   Determining routing and traffic flows

Assuming we have a starting topology we need to figure out how traffic will be routed over this topology, and what the resulting traffic flows will be. This may appear premature in the design process, since we have not assigned capacities yet, and most dynamic routing algorithms use metrics derived from link speeds to determine least-cost routing paths. However, we cannot assign capacities at this stage either, since this would presuppose traffic flow data, which also cannot be determined until a routing topology has been generated!

Ideally, routing, flow assignment, and capacity assignment need to be optimized simultaneously, or at least in a tightly coupled manner, and clearly these nontrivial processes need to be implemented very efficiently, since they will form the inner loops of our design heuristic. Having said that, there is a temptation by designers to optimize the routing algorithm to the point where it no longer produces results that bear any resemblance with what happens in the real world. Thus, we may have a very fast heuristic that produces unrealistic topologies. For example, if the routing protocol chosen to run on our backbone is OSPF, then there is little point in our design algorithm assuming that traffic from a source to a destination can be arbitrarily distributed along multiple paths of varying bandwidths. OSPF either routes traffic down shortest paths or requires load-sharing paths to be of equal aggregate cost between a source and destination. There are clearly trade-offs between complexity, speed, and realism to deal with during this process.

Types of routing algorithms

Our choice of routing algorithm can be broadly classified into one of the following groups:

- Flooding—a robust, simple, and fast algorithm to implement. Traffic is flooded throughout the network; at each receiver traffic is forwarded through all interfaces except the source interface. There is no need for topological knowledge or state synchronization. Traffic is likely to be replicated (several times), so the probability of delivery is high, but there are clearly bandwidth and performance overheads. Mechanisms need to be in place to prevent loops (either by limiting hop counts, time to live, or recording status at each node). Flooding is widely used in military and mobile networks.

- Shortest path—again, relatively simple and often effectively static. Each link has a length assigned to it (often a metric derived from the link speed), and a shortest path algorithm is run to determine a set of shortest paths. Some implementations may use dynamic metrics (e.g., OSPF), where link status can affect the metric and hence force dynamic routing changes based on factors such as congestion or link availability. If link metrics are all fixed at 1, then we are effectively using minimum-hop or distance-vector routing (e.g., RIP). This form of routing is likely to produce ties between link paths and sub-optimal topologies (since it takes no account of link speed). In some cases the metric may be a real cost (derived from tariff data), which may be used to preserve expensive bandwidth.

- Explicit—is a highly specific form of routing where routes are configured based on source, destination, and full or partial path information. There is consequently little or no computational complexity, and network bandwidth can be highly optimized. The downside is that traffic flows on real networks can vary significantly over time, and changes in subscriber populations or topology can lead to inconsistencies and high maintenance overheads.

- Adaptive—is a more sophisticated form of routing where route calculations are highly dynamic, based on factors such as CPU loading on intermediate nodes, link congestion, link and protocol failures, and error levels. The dynamic nature of adaptive routing requires that up-to-date routing data are highly synchronized throughout the network, so that routing loops and load-induced instabilities are avoided. The distribution frequency of this state information may itself cause congestion problems, so real implementations tend to approximate status by distributing information at reasonable intervals.

- Distributed—is a form of adaptive routing that avoids its potential instability problems by maintaining state information centrally. Intermediate nodes forward congestion data to a central manager node, which then performs route computation and redistributes the results. There is clearly some overhead in the distribution mechanism, and the computational requirements on the central node can be significant (consequently some implementations may offload the route calculation to another device). This was originally the mechanism used by ARPANET.

If you are using an automated design tool to produce network designs, then there will typically be a selection of routing algorithms available to you. These algorithms may be variants of the above or (most likely) highly optimized algorithms that produce designs deemed to be close enough to the real thing.

Routing metrics

Routing algorithms find paths based on one or more metrics. Metrics are parameters that describe the state of the topology and include the following:

- Hop count is commonly used by distance vector algorithms (such as Bellman-Ford) and represents the distance between routing nodes as a number of physical hops. This is perhaps the crudest type of metric and has the drawback of not reflecting differences in link capacity (e.g., two parallel links between two routing nodes will be treated as equally attractive in the shortest path calculation, even if one offered a capacity of 64 Kbps and the other offered a capacity of 1.54 Mbps).

- Abstract cost is commonly used by conventional routing algorithms (such as Dijkstra) to represent a cost using an arbitrary integer value (positive in the case of Dijkstra). In effect this allows paths to be weighted so as to make them more or less attractive. Normally low values are most attractive.

- Bandwidth is commonly used in metric calculation, since it refers to the available capacity of a circuit, and faster circuits are inherently more attractive than slower circuits. Although bandwidth indicates the maximum throughput attainable on a circuit, high bandwidth paths do not necessarily offer optimal routes (since they often attract most of the traffic!). Factors such as congestion and delay need to be used in tandem.

- Load can be used to influence metrics and may be attributed to a number of components in the path, including circuit utilization, router CPU utilization, and packets processed per second. Monitoring these parameters on a real-time basis can itself be CPU and bandwidth intensive.

- Reliability is useful in metric calculation. Factors such as the bit-error rate (BER) are sampled on each link, and link state changes are monitored. Reliability ratings may be assigned to network links by network administrators as arbitrary numeric values.

- Delay (characterized by features such as latency, jitter, or round-trip time) is a useful factor for metric calculation since it is indicative of many factors in the overall path, including circuit bandwidths, queuing issues, congestion, and the actual distance traveled.

■ Monetary cost is important in that it is a real reflection of the tariffs accrued by a circuit. In some companies performance may be subordinate to operating expenditures. Organizations may prefer to send packets over their own circuits (even though delays might be longer) rather than via more expensive public lines, given the choice.

Metric classes

It is useful to formally characterize metrics. We can group metrics into three classes: additive, multiplicative, and concave [9]. Assuming that n_1, n_2 ..., and n_j represent network nodes, let $d(n_1, n_2)$ be a metric for link (n_1, n_2). For any path, $P = (n_1, n_2, \ldots, n_i, n_j)$, metric m is:

Additive: if $m(P) = m(n_1, n_2) + m(n_2, n_3) + \ldots + m(n_i, n_j)$

Multiplicative: if $m(P) = m(n_1, n_2) \times m(n_2, n_3) \times \ldots \times m(n_i, n_j)$

Concave: if $m(P) = \min[m(n_1, n_2), m(n_2, n_3)], \ldots, m(n_i, n_j)$

Using this definition, delay, jitter, cost, and hop count are additive (e.g., the delay of a path is the sum of the delay of every hop). Reliability (1 – loss rate) is multiplicative [where $0 < m(n_i, n_j) < 1$]. Bandwidth is concave (the bandwidth of an end-to-end path is determined by the link with the minimum available bandwidth).

Multipath-Constrained (MPC) routing problems

With conventional shortest-path routing (using algorithms such as Dijkstra or Bellman-Ford) paths are typically selected using only a single metric, such as an abstract cost or hop count. In more sophisticated routing implementations such as Constraint-Based Routing (CBR), routing algorithms select paths that optimize one or more of these metrics; and the more metrics used, the harder the combinatorial problem we must solve. Calculating optimal routes subject to constraints of two or more additive and/or multiplicative metrics belongs to a class of problem referred to as NP-Complete. For example, algorithms that use two or more from the set of additive metrics (delay, jitter, hop count, loss probability) and attempt to optimize them simultaneously are said to be NP-Complete, whereas a computationally feasible combination of metrics would be bandwidth plus one additive metric, such as delay.

NP-Complete problems can be solved in polynomial time, if all other NP-Complete problems can be solved in polynomial time. Unfortunately, this has not yet been proven [10]). However, the proof of NP-Completeness is based on the assumptions that all metrics are independent, and link delay and jitter are known a priori. Although these assumptions may be true for circuit-switched networks, metrics such as bandwidth, delay, and jitter are not independent in packet networks. Consequently, polynomial algorithms for computing routes with hop count, delay, and jitter constraints exist [11]. The complexity of such algorithms is:

$$O(N \times E \times e)$$

where

   N = the hop count

   E = the number of links of the network

   $e \leq E$ = the number of distinct bandwidth values among all links

Nevertheless, the theorem can tell us qualitatively the complexity of a routing algorithm; a complex algorithm in circuit-switched networks is still complex in packet networks, although it may not be NP-Complete.

To resolve multiple path constraint problems that are NP-Complete we must make use of heuristic techniques, possibly including the use of sequential filtering (where metrics are attacked sequentially in order of importance; a set of viable routes is created using the first metric, and then successively reduced by each further metric computation until the routes satisfy all). Such techniques do not guarantee optimal solutions—just, hopefully, good ones—within an acceptable time period. Fortunately, algorithms for finding routes with bandwidth and hop-count constraints are much simpler [12], and the Bellman-Ford algorithm or Dijkstra algorithm can be used. For example, to find the shortest path between two nodes with bandwidth greater than 64 Kbps, all the links with residual bandwidth less than 64 Kbps can be pruned first. Either the Bellman-Ford algorithm or Dijkstra algorithm can then be used to compute the shortest path from the pruned network. The complexity of such algorithms is $O(N \times E)$.

We will now briefly review a specialist algorithm frequently used to solve the topology routing problems in practice, the Flow Deviation (FD) algorithm. Further information on routing algorithms applicable for network topology design can be found in [7, 13–15].

Flow Deviation algorithm

The Flow Deviation (FD) algorithm finds a set of routes that minimize the average end-to-end delay, given a topology and a set of traffic requirements. In this case link delay is calculated using M/M/1 queuing formulae (although other strategies could be used), and we assume that packets arrive independently and message sizes are exponentially distributed. We know that arrivals in a network are far from independent, but, in practice, with a reasonable mix of transmitters and receivers, this has been demonstrated to be effectively close enough [16]. To make the problem simpler, this algorithm assumes that traffic can be bifurcated (i.e., distributed) over multiple paths. As described earlier, some routing protocols allow this and some do not. Those that do may have quite specific requirements (such as equal cost metrics), which may make these methodologies questionable. Nevertheless, the algorithm is well known and fairly successful in determining routing and traffic flows efficiently.

The algorithm uses the simple observation that total delay (and hence average delay) can be decreased when small amounts of traffic are moved from paths with high delay to those with smaller delays. In this case we compare the incremental delay on paths (i.e., the sum of all incremental delays in all links that form the path). The algorithm proceeds as follows:

1. Assign lengths to links based on incremental delay.

2. Find the shortest path from each source to each destination based on these lengths.

3. Load links based on these paths.

4. Superpose flow patterns iteratively (the new flow pattern is merged with the previous flow patterns using paths that minimize delay).

In order to maintain feasible designs link capacities are scaled up to begin with, so they are slightly larger than the flows assigned to them; thus, links that would be initially overloaded will simply appear congested until flows are subsequently displaced. Once flows have been optimized, capacities can be reassigned to meet the final flow configuration. The algorithm terminates when no further progress can be made (i.e., when no path can be found that decreases incremental delay). To illustrate the concept consider the simple example in Figure 5.5. We have a traffic requirement, r, of 8, and two links between nodes A and B of capacity 10 and 20, respectively.

Figure 5.5
Two nodes connected via two links with a flow requirement of 8 from A to B.

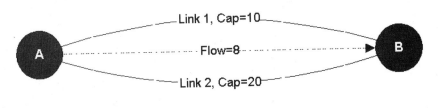

Initially all traffic is flowing over link 1 (capacity 10). In this example we use an arbitrary delay function:

$$T = (f/c)2$$

where

f = the flow over a link

c = the link capacity

The resulting flow pattern, F, is calculated by adding the new flow pattern, F_n, with the existing global or aggregate flow pattern, F_g, so:

$$F = xF_g + (1 - x) F_n$$

where

x = the total flow over the path

Combining this with our delay function we can reduce this down to:

$$T = f_1(f_1/c_1)^2 + f_2(f_2/c_2)^2$$

where

f_1 and c_1 = the flow and capacity for link 1

f_2 and c_2 = the flow and capacity for link 2

So in this example, we start with f_1 = 8, and since there is no flow over link 2, our delay is calculated as:

$$T = (8)(8/10)^2 + (0)(0/20)^2$$

$$= 5.120$$

Now, if we move some of the traffic (say 0.2 units) from link 1 to link 2 we should see an improvement in overall delay:

$$T = (7.8)(7.8/10)^2 + (0.2)(0.2/20)^2$$

$$= 4.74554$$

At some point we will move sufficient traffic to reach the minimum delay achievable. If we continue to move traffic incrementally in 0.2 units, we can plot overall delay to find the optimum value (as illustrated in Figure 5.6). Flow is bled from link 1 to link 2 in 0.2-unit increments. When link 1 reaches approximately 2.6 units of flow (i.e., 5.4 units have been moved to link 2), total delay reaches the optimum of approximately 0.569. Beyond this value there is no payback in displacing further traffic. In this case we stop moving traffic from link 1 to link 2 when a total delay of about 0.569

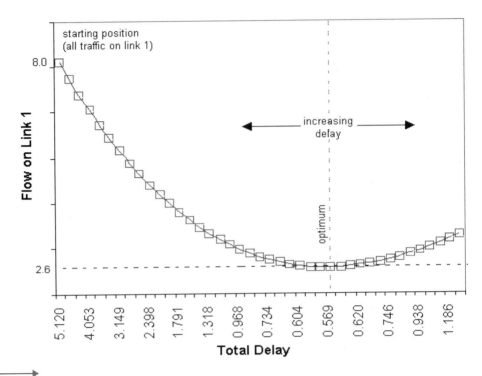

Flow on Link 1

starting position
(all traffic on link 1)

8.0

←——— increasing ———→
delay

optimum

2.6

5.120 4.053 3.149 2.398 1.791 1.318 0.968 0.734 0.604 0.569 0.620 0.746 0.938 1.186

Total Delay

Figure 5.6   *Flow deviation, with a flow of eight units over two links.*

is reached. Only 32.5 percent of traffic remains on the slower link 1 (as one would expect); the rest has been shunted to link 2. Any further traffic shifts mean that overall delay starts to increase again.

The complexity of this algorithm is:

O(*kNE*)

where

   k = the number of flow patterns examined

   N = the number of nodes

   E = the number of edges

Note that *k* can get quite large, and after initially good progress the algorithm converges very slowly as it approaches the optimum, since it is forced to move flow from all requirements at the same time. For further information on the algorithm, ways to improve convergence, and sample source code see [7]. Another alternative approach is to use the Bertsekas-Gallager (BG) algorithm, described in [7, 14, 15]. This algorithm offers faster convergence by considering node pairs one at a time, but has its own draw-backs.

5.3.4 Assigning capacities

At this point we have a physical topology with logical routing established and a map of aggregated traffic flows over each link. As we saw in the previous section, there will have been some manipulation of capacities to maintain a feasible design, but our task now is to optimize these capacities based on the flow map, within the constraints of cost and average delay. Once again M/M/1 queuing is traditionally used to describe delay. An important subproblem to resolve is whether to allocate continuous or discrete capacities. It is clearly much easier and faster to assign capacities from a range of contiguous bandwidths; however, in reality bandwidth is usually available at discrete speeds (e.g., 64 K, 128 K, etc.). This presents us with a difficult integer-programming problem, which requires specialized techniques to resolve [7]. There are several strategies we can employ to assign link capacities, as follows:

- Equal—Capacities are assigned to equal flow.

- Proportional—Capacities are assigned in proportion with the link flows.

- Square root—Capacities are assigned to match flows, and excess capacity is allocated in proportion to the square root of the flows.

- Min-cost—Capacities are assigned to minimize cost.

- Minimax—Capacities are assigned to minimize delay.

The first two strategies are fair but unlikely to meet the delay constraints. We will illustrate this process with the example shown in Figure 5.7.

In Figure 5.7 we see a graph with five nodes. By this stage we know what the flows are (shown by arrows) and what the routing paths are; tentative capacities (solid links) are assigned but need to be optimized. Note that we also assume asymmetrical flows for simplicity. Our job at this stage is to refine capacities based on the traffic flows and routing matrix to the point where delay and cost constraints are met.

For the purposes of this example we will assume a uniform packet size. We also assume a simple cost model, where a specific cost per bandwidth multiplier is used for specific links (see Table 5.2). We can use these data to

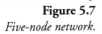

Figure 5.7
Five-node network.

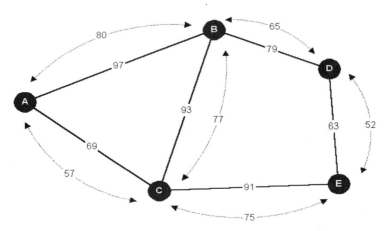

optimize capacities based on average total delay and cost, using simple M/M/1 queues. We will use several simple methods to illustrate how capacity may be allocated, as follows.

- Proportional—Capacity is allocated in proportion to the flow on a specific link, f_i, plus the total capacity constraint, C:

$$c_i = C\left(f_i / \sum f_i\right)$$

- Square root—Capacity is allocated as the current link flow, f_i, plus the total capacity constraint, C, according to a square root assignment law with the sum of all flows:

$$c_i = f_i + \sqrt{f_i\left(C - \sum f_i\right)} / \sum \sqrt{f_i}$$

- Min-cost—Capacity is allocated due to a relaxed version of the capacity formula (termed Lagrangian Relaxation), which takes into account delay power, p; the cost per link, d_i; and a total budgetary cost, D. The purpose is to minimize delay, given a fixed budget:

$$c_i = f_i + \left(f_i / d_i\right)^{(1/p+1)}\left(D - \sum f_i d_i\right) / \sum \left(f_i d_i^p\right)^{(1/p+1)}$$

- Equal cost—Capacity is allocated by simply dividing total capacity, C, by the number of links, L:

$$c_i = C/L$$

For the interested reader these formulae and their derivations are described in detail in [5, 7]. The results of these calculations are shown in Table 5.2. M/M/1 queuing is assumed, so Delay is calculated as 1/(Capacity

Table 5.2   *Capacity Assignments Based on the Result of the Flow and Routing Procedure*

Link	Cost/Cap	Flow	Capacity	Util /	Delay	Cost
AB	800	80	100.89	0.793	0.0479	$80,709.36
AC	1500	57	71.88	0.793	0.0672	$107,822.66
BC	1500	77	97.10	0.793	0.0497	$145,655.17
BD	1000	65	81.97	0.793	0.0589	$81,970.44
CE	500	75	94.58	0.793	0.0511	$47,290.64
ED	1200	52	65.58	0.793	0.0737	$78,691.63
Total		**406**	**512.00**		**0.0566**	**$542,139.90**

(a) Proportional Assignment of Capacity   p= 1

C= 512

Link	Cost/Cap	Flow	Capacity	Util /	Delay	Cost
AB	800	80	99.27	0.806	0.0519	$79,415.30
AC	1500	57	73.27	0.778	0.0615	$109,897.52
BC	1500	77	95.90	0.803	0.0529	$143,856.57
BD	1000	65	82.37	0.789	0.0576	$82,368.96
CE	500	75	93.66	0.801	0.0536	$46,828.63
ED	1200	52	67.54	0.770	0.0644	$81,042.32
Total		**406**	**512.00**		**0.0563**	**$543,409.30**

(b) Square Root Assignment of Capacity   p= 1

C= 512

Link	Cost/Cap	Flow	Capacity	Util /	Delay	Cost
AB	800	80	102.41	0.781	0.0446	$81,930.03
AC	1500	57	70.82	0.805	0.0724	$106,224.03
BC	1500	77	93.06	0.827	0.0623	$139,586.96
BD	1000	65	83.07	0.782	0.0553	$83,069.57
CE	500	75	102.45	0.732	0.0364	$51,224.82
ED	1200	52	66.75	0.779	0.0678	$80,104.49
Total		**406**	**518.56**		**0.0550**	**$542,139.90**

(c) Lagreangean Relaxation with Cost constraints   p= 1

D= $542,139.90

Link	Cost/Cap	Flow	Capacity	Util /	Delay	Cost
AB	800	80	85.33	0.938	0.1875	$68,266.67
AC	1500	57	85.33	0.668	0.0353	$128,000.00
BC	1500	77	85.33	0.902	0.1200	$128,000.00
BD	1000	65	85.33	0.762	0.0492	$85,333.33
CE	500	75	85.33	0.879	0.0968	$42,666.67
ED	1200	52	85.33	0.609	0.0300	$102,400.00
Total		**406**	**512.00**		**0.0943**	**$554,666.67**

(d) Equal Cost Assignment   p= 1

C= 512

(a) Proportional allocation. (b) Square root allocation. (c) Lagrangian Relaxation, where a fixed budget is used as a constraint. (d) Equal cost assignment, where capacity is simply divided by the number of links.

– Flow). Utilization is calculated as Flow/Capacity. Total Delay is calculated by summing Flow × Delay for each link and dividing by the total flow.

We can make several observations about these various models, as follows:

- When capacity is constrained uniformly at 512 Kbps, utilization for each link is uniformly 79.3 percent (see Table 5.2[a]). Individual delays vary between 47.9 and 73.7, a variation of 35 percent. Average delay is 56.6 ms, and the total cost of this design is $542,139.90.

- When we apply the square root law (Table 5.2[b]), we notice three things. Average delay has improved by 0.53 percent, delay variation (51.9 to 64.4 ms) has been reduced to 19.4 percent, and cost has risen slightly by 0.2 percent (but this may go up or down depending upon how traffic is redistributed and the various link costs). Note also that the links with larger flows have increased utilization, while those with smaller flows have decreased utilization. Since links with larger flows are assigned larger capacities, they have smaller service times, and thus increasing utilization on larger links does not increase delay by as much as it would on links with smaller flows. If an M/M/m queuing model were used (i.e., a multiple server model), then these effects would be less pronounced.

- In Table 5.2(c) we attempt to optimize by cost. In this case we have constrained total cost to be no more than $542,139.90 (we use this number to make comparisons with our uniform capacity assignments; in real life you would set the appropriate project budget). Average delay has dropped by 2.9 percent, and delay variation (36.4 ms to 72.4 ms) is now at 49.7 percent.

- Finally, we spread the bandwidth evenly across all links. Total cost increases, but the most noticeable change is that total delay increases to 94.3 ms, an increase of 40 percent. Delay variation is extreme (30 ms to 187.5 ms), a difference of 84 percent. Utilization is, as we would expect, worst on high-flow links, reaching nearly 94 percent.

We could increase the delay objective, p, to high values such as 100. This would minimize our maximum delay. What is noticeable is that all of these models work reasonably well, and differences are not so marked as one might imagine. Clearly, this is a rather simplified view of capacity optimization, but these procedures are still extremely useful and can be implemented as either algorithms or as spreadsheet macros. This section should raise your awareness of how capacity models can be developed. Given the space we could introduce more sophisticated models to minimize overall delay and address the problems of discrete bandwidth assignment and more realistic piecewise-linear costing models [7].

5.3.5   Costing the design

At this stage we can run our cost analysis on the design and, assuming it remains feasible, decide whether the current topology is an improvement on what we already have. Costing can be relatively simple, using piecewise-linear modeling or by accessing a real tariff database (which would be more accurate but very slow unless data are precharged into the design database).

If the cost and performance characteristics of this topology are better than previous models, then we would cache this model and either exit (if the user requests or if constraints or running time thresholds have been met) or perturb (modify) the topology further as described in the next section.

5.3.6   Perturbation algorithms

At this stage we have at least one workable design, which has cost and performance data associated with it. Our task now is to modify the design somehow to (hopefully) improve performance and cost. Again, there are well-known algorithms for solving the topology perturbation problem. The specific aim of all these algorithms is to improve the existing topology, preferably by balancing improved performance, lower delay, and lower cost. Since these algorithms are run many times within the main body of the optimization code, much research has gone into providing the most efficient solutions to a very tough problem. There is still plenty of room for improvement, however, and this topic is still very much in its infancy.

Branch exchange

Branch exchange is a simple heuristic, summarized as follows:

- Select two links from four nodes, ideally local to each other.

- Delete these links.

- Add two new links using a different combination of the original nodes.

For example, with a set of four nodes there are 15 ways to draw a two-link topology (see Figure 5.8); however, since we are doing link swapping in pairs we are only concerned here with the first three topologies.

Figure 5.8
*Permutations with
two links and four
nodes.*

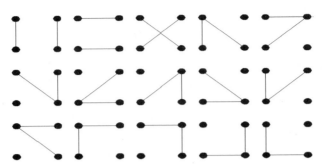

Essentially the heuristic drives the topology locally to be less expensive and offer better performance. The criteria for selecting link pairs are typically low utilization on the links, heavy traffic between unconnected node pairs, high costs for the selected links, and low costs for potential links. The sequence shown in Figure 5.9 illustrates how this might operate. We start out by selecting links DF and EG for exchanging. We delete these links and add DE, FG, and then test for fitness. We then try DG, FE, and again test for fitness. Remember that each time we swap links we must recalculate traffic flows and assign capacities to represent how the new network will operate. We may find in this case that solution (a) in Figure 5.9 remains the best choice once cost, delay, and throughput have been assessed for each alternative.

Branch exchange is a very general approach and still quite widely used. It is open to modification and enhancement. For example, we can incorporate additional constraints, such as the following:

■ Checking that the maximum hop count lies within a specified constraint

■ Checking that the resulting topology is still fully connected

■ Checking that the topology is always biconnected

If any exchange violates these requirements, then the heuristic would disallow it.

Since branch exchange is incremental, it can be used to test and perhaps improve existing designs (i.e., it can be applied to a real-life topology or an artificially created topology). These improvements can be locally restricted or applied to the whole network. There are, however, two main drawbacks with branch exchange, as follows:

■ It requires traffic flows (routing) to be done in the inner loop of the exchange process. Since routing is itself typically $O(N^3)$, this tends to

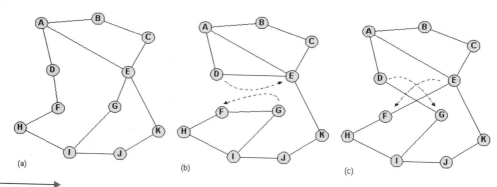

Figure 5.9   *Branch exchange operations. (a) Starting topology. (b) First swap. (c) Second swap.*

make branch exchange O(N^5), which is generally unacceptable for medium to large networks due to the additional processing time needed as N increases.

- Since, by definition, branch exchange operates locally within the topology, it tends toward local minima, rather than the optimal solution, and is very sensitive to the quality of the starting topology. A poor initial topology often results in a poor solution.

One approach to solving this [5] is to run the whole design process several times, each with a different starting point. This tends to ease the problem of local minima but again may be unacceptable for any reasonable-sized network. One approach to expedite the process is to drive the link selection process by an algorithm faster than rerouting. This method is called cut saturation algorithm and is explained in the following text.

Cut saturation algorithm

The cut saturation algorithm was proposed in 1974 by Chou and colleagues [17]. This heuristic is more sophisticated than branch exchange, and the authors claim this gives better results with less computation on larger networks. The heuristic is based on the observation that in a network with effective routing, congested links form cuts (i.e., if a link becomes congested, it is because it is the preferred path for the traffic flowing over it).

A cut across a point in the network where the links are all heavily loaded is referred to as a saturated cut. For the purpose of identification, we define a saturated cut as a cut whose links are at least as heavily utilized as the links in any other cut. This can be realized quite easily using Kruskal's minimum spanning tree algorithm. When Kruskal's algorithm is run, we add $N - 2$ links to the tree and form two components. The links in the cut dividing these two components are the ones we are interested in. A simplified summary of this heuristic is as follows:

- Sort all links by percent utilization (i.e., traffic/capacity).

- Starting with the highest utilized links, remove links until the network has been divided into two parts.

- Minimize this cut by putting back each link in turn, testing whether or not each link reconnects the network. If a link does not reconnect the network, then do not install it, since it is clearly not part of the minimal cut.

- Mark all nodes that are vertices for the minimal cut links as primary nodes.

- Mark all nodes adjacent to the primary nodes as secondary nodes.

Let us use an example of a small network with nodes A through S. The matrix in Table 5.3 shows utilization on the various links; for the sake of simplicity we will assume a symmetrical traffic pattern so that utilization is the same in both directions.

From this table we can see that the heaviest utilized links are CD, GH, and QL. We sort all links in order of utilization and start removing them until the network is cut in two, in this case after CD, QL, and then GH are

Table 5.3 *Link Utilization Matrix for Sites A through S*

	A	B	C	D	E	F	G	H	I	J	K	L	M	N	O	P	Q	R	S
A	0	23	0	0	0	56	0	0	0	0	15	0	0	0	0	0	0	0	0
B	23	0	45	0	0	0	0	0	0	0	0	0	0	0	0	0	0	0	0
C	0	45	0	90	0	0	34	0	0	0	0	0	0	0	0	0	0	0	0
D	0	0	90	0	42	0	0	38	25	0	0	0	0	0	0	0	0	0	0
E	0	0	0	42	0	0	0	0	37	0	0	0	0	21	0	0	0	0	0
F	56	0	0	0	0	0	27	0	0	0	0	0	0	0	0	0	32	0	0
G	0	0	34	0	0	27	0	87	0	48	32	0	0	0	0	0	32	0	0
H	0	0	0	38	0	0	87	0	44	0	0	41	33	0	0	0	0	0	0
I	0	0	0	25	37	0	0	44	0	0	0	0	25	0	0	0	0	0	29
J	0	0	0	0	0	0	48	0	0	0	54	0	0	0	53	0	0	0	0
K	15	0	0	0	0	0	32	0	0	54	0	0	0	0	0	19	0	0	0
L	0	0	0	0	0	0	0	41	0	0	0	0	0	0	0	0	76	26	0
M	0	0	0	0	0	0	0	33	25	0	0	0	0	0	0	0	0	0	16
N	0	0	0	0	21	0	0	0	0	0	0	0	0	0	0	0	0	0	0
O	0	0	0	0	0	0	0	0	0	53	0	0	0	0	0	54	0	0	0
P	0	0	0	0	0	0	0	0	0	0	19	0	0	0	54	0	45	0	0
Q	0	0	0	0	0	32	32	0	0	0	0	76	0	0	0	45	0	0	0
R	0	0	0	0	0	0	0	0	0	0	0	26	0	0	0	0	0	0	23
S	0	0	0	0	0	0	0	0	29	0	0	0	16	0	0	0	0	23	0

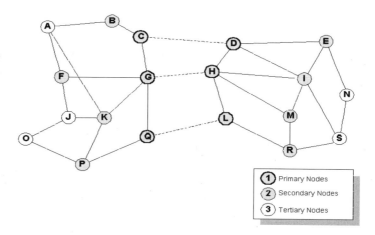

Figure 5.10
Cut saturation process. Note that in this topology tertiary nodes on either side of the cut are at least five hops apart.

removed and the network becomes disconnected. We can then mark up the node classes, as illustrated in Figure 5.10. The heuristic is fairly flexible; you can start with a very sparse topology and start adding links, or a very rich mesh and start deleting links, or a good initial topology and do both. Reference [18] describes the use of cut saturation in guiding branch exchange more effectively. Specifically, links are added across saturated cuts and deleted on one side of the cuts. This should lead either to an increase in throughput, a decrease in mean delay, or both.

Link addition

When adding a link, one end should be a left tertiary node, and the other should be a right tertiary node. There are two alternatives for making the link selection, as follows:

- Rule 1—Select the cheapest link.

- Rule 2—Select the pair of nodes whose best path is the most saturated.

Rule 1 drives the design to a cheaper cost, while rule 2 improves performance. Note that the heuristic can occasionally fail and there may be no tertiary nodes available on one or both sides of a cut.

Link deletion

When deciding which links to remove use the percent underutilization multiplied by the cost of the link, on each link as a metric. This gives a measurement of how much money is being wasted. Select a link with the highest waste regardless of its position in the topology.

A combined heuristic

The full heuristic uses both addition and deletion. If a topology gives a smaller delay than is specified in the constraints, try deleting a link to reduce cost. If the delay is higher than required, try adding a link to improve performance (at additional expense). The heuristic is unlikely to oscillate, since new links added are always long ones that are either less expensive or badly needed for additional capacity and hence are not usually good candidates for removal later on. This is a very simple heuristic, which considers each node pair in turn. If a link exists between them, it is deleted; if not, one is added. The resulting topology is costed, and if an improvement is found then the new topology is maintained, as shown in the following code segment.

```
for( AllNodePairs( A, B))
{
    if ( ExistsLink(A,B) )
        DeleteLink(A,B);
    else // (No link between A and B)
        AddLink(A,B);
    if ( ConstraintMet() AND Cheaper())
        AdoptNewTopology();
}
```

Link swapping

Link swapping is another technique available that utilizes swap transformations. Suppose there are three nodes—A, B, and C—and there is a link AB but not a link AC or BC. Several transformations may be tried in the search for cost savings. The nodes considered must lie in the neighborhood of A, the neighborhood of B, or the global neighborhood of AB. Increasing neighborhood sizes thus increases the number of swap options evaluated. However, this has a corresponding impact on the processing time required. Good results can generally be obtained with small neighborhoods (3 to 5 nodes), since these lead to the consideration of modifications most likely to result in cost savings. The addition of links is also restricted by the use of neighborhoods. The addition of link AB is considered only if either A is in the neighborhood of B or B is in the neighborhood of A. Link deletion is not restricted at all. The operation of an unrestricted pass is as follows:

```
for( AllNodePairs( A, B))
{
    if ( ExistsLink(A,B) )
    {
        DeleteLink(A,B);
```

```
            if ( ConstraintMet() AND Cheaper())
               AdoptNewTopology();
            else
            {
               ReplaceLink( A,B)
               SwapLink( A,B)
               if ( ConstraintMet() AND Cheaper())
                  AdoptNewTopology();
            }
         }
         else // (No link between A and B)
         {
            AddLink(A,B);
            if ( ConstraintMet() AND Cheaper())
               AdoptNewTopology();
            else
               ReplaceLink( A,B)
         }
      }
```

Link elimination

The link elimination algorithm starts with a fully meshed network, and uneconomical links are gradually pruned until an acceptable cost is achieved. This approach was investigated by Gerla and colleagues [13].

5.3.7 A hybrid algorithm—MENTOR

From what we have seen so far, it would appear that most of the heuristics we have examined would solve mesh topology problems in at best $O(N^5)$ time. We can deduce this because a mesh network will require $O(N^2)$ candidates to be considered, and each link requires routing to be considered, which is an $O(N^3)$ problem itself. For even very small to medium networks (even a modest 50 nodes) this becomes a serious computational problem. Worse still, if such a technique is expected to be employed iteratively, inside a more sophisticated tool, then we can assume that such a tool will not be interactive in any useful sense.

However, there is a very fast algorithm called MENTOR (MEsh Network Topology Optimization and Routing), which performs in the order of $O(N^2)$ [7, 19]. This level of performance is achieved by doing implicit routing inside the inner loop of the procedure, which evaluates links, and by so doing this heuristic becomes very useful for examining many feasible topologies when embedded within larger tools. In fact, MENTOR is used in a number of commercial tools including IBM's design tool called

INTREPID. I have some experience with this algorithm and have coded up a variant of the algorithm inside a design tool called the Interactive Network Simulator (iSIM+). We will explore a case study using this tool to develop a good topology for a United Kingdom–based network at the end of this chapter.

MENTOR is based on generic network design principles and is appropriate for designing many types of communication networks. MENTOR aims to find networks with the following characteristics:

■   Traffic requirements are routed on relatively direct paths.

■   All links are expected to have a reasonable level of utilization, since high utilization implies possible performance degradation, and low utilization implies cost inefficiencies.

■   Relatively high capacity links are chosen, enabling the benefits of economy of scale.

Of course, these objectives are somewhat contradictory, and part of what MENTOR does is trading off these aims.

Operation

The algorithm proceeds as follows:

1.   First we find the center of mass in the network, node M—that is, the node best suited to which to bring all traffic. We call this the median node.

2.   We identify all potential backbone nodes. MENTOR employs a simple threshold algorithm based on node weights.

3.   All nodes with a specified radius from each backbone node are assigned as local nodes to those backbone nodes.

4.   The center of mass is again retested, this time using only the backbone node list. If necessary, it may be appropriate to select a new median node.

5.   A minimal spanning tree is calculated that interconnects all backbone nodes. Actually, MENTOR attempts to minimise both the tree length and the path length to the median node.

6.   Given a tree of backbone nodes, centered at node M, we test adding links between each pair of nodes if they have sufficient traffic to justify deviating from the spanning tree topology.

7.   Wherever links are added, a decision is made regarding how many channels to add and how much traffic is to be carried. Routing is done implicitly at this stage in our test for suitable direct links. Traffic that is not routed down direct paths is overflowed via detour points.

Results are generally good and achieved in very fast operation times. The interested reader is strongly encouraged to read the excellent book by Aaron Kershenbaum [7], which provides complete details of this and many other network design algorithms.

One of the main problems with MENTOR is that the routing algorithm it uses does not behave like real-world routing protocols (such as OSPF). MENTOR works well for relatively sparse networks and trees, but the routing algorithm breaks down with highly meshed topologies. In these situations MENTOR simply does not distribute traffic flows like a real routing protocol, and this renders many of these topologies useless for real-world applications. There are workarounds, but these greatly increase the complexity of the algorithm. For this reason Cahn [20] developed the MENTOR algorithm a stage further, leading to an enhanced algorithm called MENTOR-II. MENTOR-II makes more intelligent decisions on traffic distribution and when to add direct links by running an incremental shortest path (ISP) algorithm. It also includes several other refinements, which as a whole make the outcomes closely aligned to protocols such as OSPF. The time complexity of MENTOR-II is the same as for MENTOR, with the exception of direct-link addition between backbone nodes, b, which is $O(b^4)$. Hence, for large numbers of backbone sites (relative to n, the total number of nodes), MENTOR-II is considerably slower. Generally speaking the number of backbone nodes is at least an order of magnitude lower than the number of distribution/access nodes, so this is usually not a problem.

5.3.8 Genetic algorithms in topology optimization

Genetic algorithms (GAs) represent a new approach to solving problems in topological design. Much of the work done in this area is still experimental. As already discussed in some detail, traditional approaches to the topology optimization problem tend to focus on greedy hill-climbing algorithms, starting with a single network and then iterating its topology until a good solution is achieved. These methodologies on their own rarely lead to optimal solutions in dense networks; however, they generally lead to good results within reasonable time scales, but they are not always optimal since there is a tendency to get stuck in some local minima. Furthermore, these techniques usually start off with one sample and then modify that sample until a good fit is achieved, without examining the search space with a wider perspective. They do not examine or allow for the possibility that several good-fit solutions may coexist and that one of these may be optimal. GAs are, however, a general-purpose tool and as such require customization to attack topological problems [21]. Using a pure GA in a simple implementation can demonstrate several potential problems, including the following.

- It may be computationally expensive.

- Data structures need very careful planning to optimize performance while maintaining the appropriate level of granularity. It is initially tempting to encode chromosomes as a simple link matrix. While this is very inefficient in terms of storage (quadratic in n) and clearly does not scale, this still yields encouraging results. Such an example is outlined in reference [22]; however, the encoding used is so simple as to preclude the use of aggregated capacity or multiple parallel links. Berry and colleagues assume that links are symmetrical, while real networks are rarely so.

- Population size and maintenance and crossbreeding and mutation require careful implementation and experimentation. If done in a simple manner, this can lead to situations where near-optimal solutions are easily destroyed by out-of-context transformations. If tightly directed, then exchanges could lead to good but not optimal solutions (similar to the problems encountered by hill-climbing techniques). Techniques such as grouping might be worthy of research [23].

Consequently, GAs must be adapted to this problem by utilizing hybrid techniques (such as in combination with linear programming [22]) and a certain degree of trial and error. Concepts of elitism and at least some directed breeding should be considered. By using GAs multiple samples of the population (i.e., topologies) are evaluated and interbred concurrently. In the real world there may be no absolute best solution, since the constraints on the design are often contradictory. There may be several good outcomes of value to the designer, each relatively fit in terms of the original design constraints but possibly meeting different criteria better than others. For example, a simulation might yield one least-cost solution and three close solutions, which differ in factors such as throughput, delay, and resilience but still are within the constraints imposed. The user may wish to examine all of these alternatives, and in a real-world situation might not choose the least-cost solution if a close second is available with better performance and reliability attributes.

Several differences separate genetic algorithms from more conventional optimization techniques, including the following:

- Population search, not a point search—By maintaining a population of well-adapted samples, the probability of reaching single suboptimal minima is reduced, and sensitivity to the starting topology is diminished.

- Direct manipulation of a coding—Genetic algorithms manipulate control variable representations at a string level to exploit similarities among high-performance strings. This gives an overview of the problem and the capability for parallel processing. Other methods usually deal with functions and their control variables directly.

- Insulation from derivative data—GAs are general techniques and achieve much of their breadth by ignoring information except that concerning payoff. Other methods rely heavily on derivative information, and in problems where the required information is not available or difficult to obtain, these other techniques can fail.

- Search using stochastic operators rather than deterministic rules—GAs use random choice to guide a highly exploitative search. Other methods often use simple random walks, which are essentially undirected.

There are several key features to consider when adapting a GA for use in topology design, as follows:

- Chromosome encoding

- Initial population generation methods

- Population sizes, maintenance and pruning techniques

- Selection schemes, fitness evaluation

- Crossover operators plus repair mechanisms

- Elitism/directed mutation/ enforced diversity

These terms are explained further in the following text.

Chromosome encoding

The obvious initial starting point is to simply encode the link matrix of each network organism as a single chromosome strand [22]. Note that the use of the term matrix here does not imply that the data structures used should be matrices; in a real implementation for large network modeling purposes, some form of linked adjacency list would be preferable. For the

Figure 5.11
*Conversion of a
simple eight-node
topology into an
adjacency matrix
and then
conversion into a
chromosome string
by direct bit
encoding.*

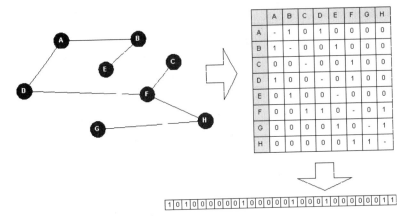

purpose of simplification we will assume that a two-dimensional matrix is used. This has the advantage that the matrix truly is the blueprint for the network, and changes to its genes are exactly the kind of changes required to iterate a network topology (i.e., breaking some links and adding others). Figure 5.11 shows an eight-node topology with the simplest way of transforming an adjacency matrix into a chromosome string. In this example the matrix is symmetrical and indicates a connection between two nodes by the value 1. The matrix is then stretched out into one long string of 1s and 0s to form the bit string.

This very rudimentary encoding is easy to understand, has linear lookup times (since data are simply indexed by source and destination and no searches are required), and can produce useful results. However, the disadvantages are fairly obvious, as follows:

- For a large population in the gene pool, and large node populations, there are storage implications (quadratic in n). However, since a cost-constrained network is typically quite sparse (and many cells in the matrix will therefore be unused), these chromosome data structures could be compressed for efficient storage.

- Manipulating this structure during breeding is, if handled simply, likely to lead to out-of-context transformations that constantly destroy the possibility of reaching optimal solutions.

There is clearly a trade-off in the chromosome encoding between search efficiency, storage space, and data granularity. I would suggest that a richer structure be chosen and then optimized, in preference to selecting a minimal scheme that achieves fast but essentially useless results. Consider the possibilities, for example, with multiple symmetrical and asymmetrical

ATM virtual circuits of different bandwidths between nodes. A simple matrix is inadequate for real-world networking representations. A predecessor node encoding has been successfully tested [24].

Population generation

GAs will generate several network entities as a starting ecosystem. Fitter networks will interbreed and randomly mutate. It is important that the algorithm converges efficiently toward useful designs. Some careful research is necessary to investigate whether the initial populations should be seeded using greedy heuristics (generating initially useful designs to a starting population) or simple and possibly poor designs. It would seem intuitive that the former will speed up convergence, but we must be cautious here not to discard superficially unpromising designs that could fall into the trap of local minima. One approach would be to use a combination of techniques to generate a variety of starting organisms, some strong contenders and some weak contenders, where we know the tool will start with at least a small population of useful designs. The same care needs to be taken in the mutation and interbreeding stages.

Fitness evaluation

The measurement of fitness will be a combination of one or more variables, such as cost, delay, throughput, and availability. Interestingly, Berry and colleagues [22] suggest a pruning technique to detach zero-traffic links to avoid a tendency toward highly meshed designs after repeated crossover and mutation. This suggests that the fitness test is possibly not sufficiently developed to avoid such problems implicitly.

Clearly, some of these constraints are contradictory, but they represent demands placed on real network designs. Some network designs may have a very specific budget, and perhaps only one solution (or even none) might lie within this budget; others may have a window of cost and be more concerned with performance and resilience. The implication here is that there may be several solutions that could be considered as attractive, and a solution that is attractive to one user might be less attractive to another. This indicates that a dynamically weighted measurement of fitness is required, configured by the user at run time. It is likely that other techniques, such as linear programming, will be needed to establish the traffic and cost measurements. Note also that these constraints could be both global and local in scope. For example, there may be a global requirement for no specific resilience but a local requirement at a specific node for alternate paths. This again somewhat complicates the problem.

Current research often oversimplifies the more subtle issues of traffic routing, delay, and throughput and the concepts of channelised capacity and resilience. While this is clearly a benefit in simplifying the problem and achieving efficient code, there is a real danger that the results obtained are of no value whatsoever in the real world. Significant work will be required in this area to develop hybrid techniques that are fast enough but remain true to reality. The advances in CPU performance and reductions in memory costs for general-purpose workstations will also greatly improve matters.

Elitism

It might be interesting to investigate whether or not maintaining a small, very fit (i.e., elite) chromosome population is of value and what percentage of the population these entities should comprise. In this way the design process will always yield good solutions at any point in time (after the initial startup phase). If this is not done, then it is possible for the population to oscillate in terms of absolute fitness, with some promising entities being lost. Conversely, care needs to be taken not to overstock the breeding pool with so-called elite chromosomes, precluding less obvious designs by arriving at local minima.

Selection scheme

GAs typically select a chromosome for breeding randomly, with the probability of selection based on its fitness value. Berry and colleagues [22] suggest using a linear scaling technique for weighting the probability of selection so that clearer differentiation is achieved as the organisms converge. This is worthy of further investigation as are other techniques such as logarithmic scaling or more granular attributes. A consideration not addressed is the individual weighting of a more sophisticated set of constraints (i.e., the measurement of fitness itself). This must be user selectable, since different users will place different importance on features such as cost and delay.

Crossover and mutation

In order to breed new designs we need to choose a point at which to break two chromosome strings and then splice them together: This process is called a crossover operation and can be achieved in several ways. Berry and colleagues [22] suggest a very simple crossover, an example of which is illustrated in Figure 5.12. In order to introduce some element of chance (to avoid stagnation through local minima) it is also useful to impose some small random changes in the string, and this process is termed mutation.

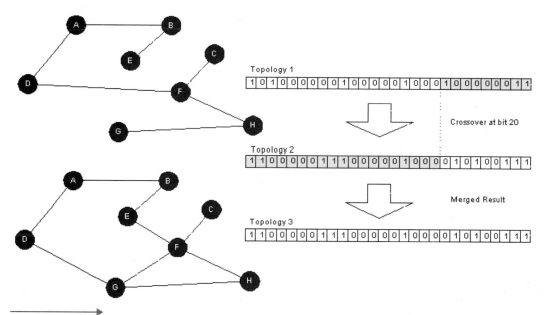

Figure 5.12 *Crossover and merging of two topologies at bit 20. The result of the merge is a new network, Topology 3.*

Using these techniques, a starting population can be crossbred iteratively, and the best designs (the most successful genes) are maintained within the population until as more and more successful designs emerge. One feature that I suggest might be useful to research is the presence of good genes in the chromosome string. For example, if a link within an adjacency matrix consistently appears in all of the fittest designs, then this could be classified as a good gene (a backbone link between two central sites in a large mesh network might always be desirable and always cheaper; or policy rules may dictate that it should always be included—overriding any crossover or mutation effects). This could be implemented by maintaining a fitness value with each gene over time or by statically configuring certain genes to be mandatory. The benefit of this approach would be faster convergence, but, again, care must be taken to reward only consistent behavior and avoid local minima.

Active research

Some success using a hybrid integration of linear programming and GAs with topology optimization on both 10-node and 50-node networks has been reported [22]. With a 10-node network an exhaustive search would require examining 2^{45} possibilities (over 35 billion). The GA they implemented found solutions (on average) after examining only 350 possibilities and managed to converge on optimal cost solutions within only 34 generations. This represents a difference between five minutes and 950,000 years on a typical Pentium PC. On a 50-node network the solution converges after 230 generations. Note that the researchers chose a very small population pool, limited to 15 chromosomes.

5.3.9 Swarming algorithms in topology optimization

Just to illustrate that researchers are still actively searching for creative ways to improve topology optimization techniques, Bonabeau and Theraulaz [3] cite research work where ant movements are modeled in software in an attempt to solve the traveling salesperson and traffic routing problems. Computer scientists frequently use ants and other social insects (bees, termites, wasps, etc.) to solve complex problems because of the way they introduce randomness and group cooperation (so-called swarm intelligence) to solve real-world problems. In the case cited here, ants are modeled as they forage for food from their nest (analogous to the source node). Ants lay a trail of pheromones as they traverse a particular route from their nest to a food source. If a route is shorter, then the amount of pheromones along that particular path increases more quickly, since ants can traverse that path more frequently. This attracts other ants from less "smelly" routes and thereby increases pheromone levels even more. This process is analogous to a route metric being decreased over time as that particular route is discovered to be more optimal. Note that in the real world these pheromone levels decay slowly over time, so the model artificially speeds up this decay to ensure that old, long routes are abandoned if new shorter routes are subsequently discovered.

This work has been extended at the Free University of Brussels to solve the classic traveling salesperson problem, introduced earlier. In this problem ants travel from city to city, essentially randomly, but favoring nearby cities, eventually returning home. The amount of pheromone left is inversely proportional to the length of the tour. Subsequent tours continue to reinforce shorter paths to cities close by in preference to long paths (analogous to short-haul links being preferred to long-haul links). When repeated over time, eventually the better links survive. While this method has proved to be successful for finding short routes, it does not necessarily find the shortest route, so a near-optimal solution is generally achieved but in a reasonable time. This model also has the advantage of flexibility (if a particular path is impassable, then good alternatives will be selected quickly) [25, 26].

5.4   Automated design tools

Designing optimal backbones for medium to large networks is really not achievable without at least some degree of automation. This section describes some of the tools available today.

5.4.1   Publicly available tools

For the researcher, or engineers interested in building a modeling application, there is very little code available publicly, limited primarily to a few university sites. Both Cahn [20] and Kershenbaum [7] include many useful examples in pseudocode and C code that can be incorporated into a modeling tool, and a basic but useful educational tool called Delite (DEsign tool LITE) by Robert Cahn is available with source code [27]. This program enables hierarchical networks to be built and then analyzed for utilization, delay, and reliability. A number of algorithms can be used to design the network, including Prim, Prim-Dijkstra, Esau-Williams, MENTOR, MENTOR-II, and various Tour-based algorithms. An algorithm tutorial is also included. Figure 5.13 shows the main design view of the Delite tool. For

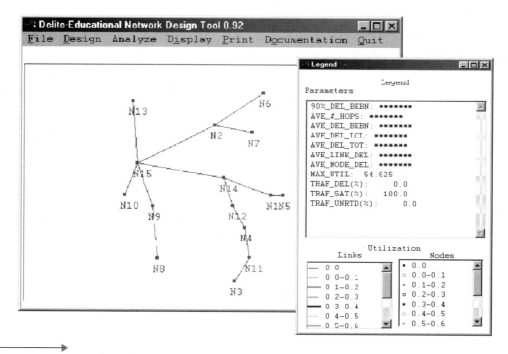

Figure 5.13   *Delite, a basic design and modeling application.*

more serious work you will almost certainly require a commercial modeling tool, and there is a substantial leap in both technology and cost.

5.4.2   Commercial tools

Developing a design tool from scratch is nontrivial, and you may want to consider buying or leasing a commercial design tool. There are several products of interest; they are listed in Table 5.4.

These products have been developed over many years, starting life as in-house tools to solve specific problems on a particular network and then being spun off and enhanced to make the functionality more generic. These products incorporate functionality to assist with activities such as the following:

- Traffic baselining

- Capacity planning

- Network topology modeling and optimization

- Application deployment

- Availability analysis

- Network documentation/inventory management

- Service pricing and financial analysis

None of these products is especially cheap (the starting price is around $10,000, and several products are well over $100,000). This should not really be surprising, since we have seen that the techniques used to analyze

Table 5.4   *Commercial Topology Modeling Tools*

Tool	Vendor
AUTONET Designer	Network Design & Analysis Corp.
IPT-NetSolv	Salford Networking Insitute
INTREPID	IBM
LinkWare	Grid Technologies Ltd
MIND	Network Management Inc.
NETConnect	Connections Telecommunications
NETTOOL	Make Systems Inc
Network Design & Analysys System	NET Inc.
NPAT (Network Planning and Analysis Tools)	WANDL
WinMIND	Network Analysis Centre Inc

design, performance, and costing are not exactly trivial, and the financial rewards for getting the design right are huge (one international circuit change alone could pay for the software). These products use a mixture of classic and closely guarded techniques to obtain near-optimal designs. Several of these products include links to complete tariff databases and may also include specific device modeling software.

We will briefly review two products that are fairly representative of the applications available. You should investigate all leading suppliers before deciding which tool to buy, since they all have particular strengths and weaknesses (not the least of which is cost), which will depend very much on what you are trying to model.

WANDL NPAT

WANDL Network Planning and Analysis Tools (NPAT) are a sophisticated integrated suite of network design tools targeted for high-end wide area network design. The manufacturer claims NPAT has been used to plan and analyze networks ranging from 30 to well over 300 backbone nodes; WANDL's customer base therefore includes the likes of supercarriers, Fortune 500 companies, and government organizations. The main features of NPAT include incremental least-cost access and backbone design, availability and survivability analysis, and network analysis capabilities (including bandwidth utilization and bottleneck analysis). A U.S. domestic and international tariff database, with capability for customized tariffs is also provided. The product incorporates a packet-level discrete event simulator, which estimates network queuing delay, throughput, and cell drop percentage. NPAT also includes hardware device libraries, for modeling vendor-specific equipment (e.g., TDMs, routers, and Frame Relay/ATM switches). This includes equipment models from companies such as Cisco, NorTel, IBM, and NET and incorporates device-specific details such as bandwidth allocation and routing algorithms, as well as custom features. Network data can be imported directly from Ascend and NET products, and Cisco's Stratacom NMT can create NPAT-formatted files. NPAT runs on a Sun SPARCstation (SunOS, Solaris 1.1, or higher), or an IBM RS/6000 (AIX 3.x or higher). It requires at least 8 MB of RAM and 64 MB of disk space. Interestingly, NPAT supports a Java client to access the GUI. The interested reader should see reference [28] for further information.

Make Systems NetMaker

NetMaker MainStation is a modular, integrated suite of network planning tools that enables you to perform a wide range of network planning, engineering, and traffic analysis activities. NetMaker is also designed to scale designs up to very large enterprise and carrier-class networks. The main features of NetMaker include topology modeling and optimization, inventory management, application and network traffic analysis, baselining link and network utilization, application deployment modeling, tariff modeling and financial analyses, network performance modeling, and reliability analysis. The system runs on an Ultra SPARC model with Solaris 2.5.1 or Solaris 2.6, a 2.1-GB internal disk drive, and at least 96 MB of RAM (128 MB recommended). The interested reader should see reference [29] for further information.

5.4.3 Case study using iSIM+

In this section we attempt to pull together many of the ideas already presented, by examining the results we can obtain by using a relatively simple automated tool (a home-grown application called iSIM+) to develop some solutions for a backbone topology problem. iSIM+ implements a modified version of the MENTOR algorithm (described in Section 5.3.7).

Site list

I have chosen 22 sites in the United Kingdom, although the location is arbitrary; the sites could be located in any country or even across national boundaries. The full site list is given in Table 5.5. Note that the grid references (in latitude and longitude) are also listed; these are normally required for topology modeling calculations, since node positions almost always have a direct impact on circuit costs (described in Section 5.2.3).

Cost matrix

For the purpose of this experiment we will model line costs as a fixed cost plus a rental charge based on distance (i.e., $c + r \times d$) and a fixed bandwidth of 64 Kbps. This works reasonably well for a medium to large well-distributed network, and many leased line tariffs use this kind of model. The model will, however, be less accurate if the network comprises many shorter circuits (due to piecewise linear price breaks for short circuits and circuits connected to the same exchange). Table 5.6 illustrates the resulting cost matrix.

To keep this example simple we are provisioning only 64-Kbps circuits, so if more bandwidth is required, then additional 64-Kbps circuits are added rather than stepping up the circuit size. Multiple circuits between sites in the resulting topology diagrams could easily be replaced by single,

Table 5.5 *Site List for 22 Node United Kingdom Network*

Name	Town	County	Country	Lat	Long
Doncaster_1	Doncaster		UK	53.533	-1.117
Liverpool_1	Liverpool	Merseyside	UK	53.417	-3
Sunderland_1	Sunderland		UK	54.9	-1.367
Edinburgh_1	Edinburgh	Lothian	UK	55.95	-3.2
Cardiff_1	Cardiff	South Glamorgan	UK	51.5	-3.2
Newbury_1	Newbury	Berkshire	UK	51.4	-1.317
Reading_1	Reading	Berkshire	UK	51.433	-1
Leicester_1	Leicester		UK	52.633	-1.133
Colchester_1	Colchester	Essex	UK	51.883	0.9
Birmingham_1	Birmingham	West Midlands	UK	52.467	-1.917
Alloa_1	Alloa		UK	56.117	-3.8
Manchester_1	Manchester	Lancashire	UK	53.5	-2.217
Leeds_1	Leeds	West Yorkshire	UK	53.8	-1.583
London_1	London	London	UK	51.5	-0.117
Glasgow_1	Glasgow	Strathclyde	UK	55.833	-4.25
Bristol_1	Bristol	Avon	UK	51.45	-2.583
Exeter_1	Exeter	Devon	UK	50.7	-3.533
Portsmouth_1	Portsmouth		UK	50.767	-1.083
Brighton_1	Brighton	East Sussex	UK	50.833	-0.15
Norwich_1	Norwich	Norfolk	UK	52.633	1.3
Saint Ives_1	Saint Ives		UK	50.2	-5.5
Hull_1	Hull	North Humberside	UK	53.717	-0.333

higher-bandwidth circuits. I have chosen to constrain the circuit size so we can better see the effects of traffic and the related circuit dimensioning. Clearly, a more representative model will take account of the incremental circuit speeds and the possible price breaks available, although this is a difficult integer-programming problem in itself (not all providers offer identical bandwidths, bandwidths may not increase logically, and the price of a large circuit may not always be cheaper than multiple lower-bandwidth circuits). Note that the cost of connecting any site to itself is simply the fixed cost of 1,040, since there is no distance involved.

Traffic matrix

Again, to simplify matters we will assume that the traffic requirement is symmetrical; each node sends exactly 8 Kbits of traffic to every other node. Table 5.7 illustrates the resulting traffic matrix.

Due to the locations of these nodes and the fact that the lowest circuit speed available is 64 Kbps, the resulting topology is never likely to be fully

Table 5.6   *Partial Cost Matrix for 22-Node Network Based on 64-Kbps Circuit Distances*

Design Database										
Global Cost Matrix										
Cost Matrix										
	0	1	2	3	4	5	6	7	8	9
0:	1040	8944	3474	5851	6017	7037	5452	6198	4742	227
1:	8944	1040	9185	6807	5819	3288	4751	10513	7104	826
2:	3474	9185	1040	4393	5006	6984	5482	8631	3422	451
3:	5851	6807	4393	1040	2029	4613	3784	10317	2152	619
4:	6017	5819	5006	2029	1040	3627	2979	10053	2625	612
5:	7037	3288	6984	4613	3627	1040	2637	9626	4856	657
6:	5452	4751	5482	3784	2979	2637	1040	8529	3601	508
7:	6198	10513	8631	10317	10053	9626	8529	1040	9333	528
8:	4742	7104	3422	2152	2625	4856	3601	9333	1040	515
9:	2279	8261	4513	6197	6121	6577	5086	5287	5150	104
10:	2938	7495	4847	5962	5741	5898	4477	5394	4996	184
11:	6239	11048	8668	10560	10356	10074	8911	1672	9545	544
12:	3658	6350	4312	4320	4002	4427	2868	7095	3492	328
13:	4340	8308	2355	3103	3819	6063	4712	9342	2269	509
14:	3015	7126	3501	4207	4151	5106	3509	7177	3196	303
15:	4907	6205	4132	2378	2153	3961	2685	9045	1963	502
16:	5029	5879	4421	2584	2123	3638	2358	8977	2297	505
17:	5738	4288	6022	4416	3569	2418	1686	8337	4239	520
18:	5669	10897	8090	10091	9932	9798	8566	2040	9055	494
19:	3253	9921	5642	7929	7935	8373	6918	4182	6843	288
20:	3727	6989	5544	6241	5874	5602	4346	5244	5374	258

Table 5.7   *Actual Traffic Requirement Matrix for 22-Node United Kingdom Network*

Design Database									
Global Data Traffic									
Global Traffic Matrix									
	0:	1:	2:	3:	4:	5:	6:	7:	
0:	0	8000	8000	8000	8000	8000	8000	8000	8000	800
1:	8000	0	8000	8000	8000	8000	8000	8000	8000	800
2:	8000	8000	0	8000	8000	8000	8000	8000	8000	800
3:	8000	8000	8000	0	8000	8000	8000	8000	8000	800
4:	8000	8000	8000	8000	0	8000	8000	8000	8000	800
5:	8000	8000	8000	8000	8000	0	8000	8000	8000	800
6:	8000	8000	8000	8000	8000	8000	0	8000	8000	800
7:	8000	8000	8000	8000	8000	8000	8000	0	8000	800
8:	8000	8000	8000	8000	8000	8000	8000	8000	0	800
9:	8000	8000	8000	8000	8000	8000	8000	8000	8000	
10:	8000	8000	8000	8000	8000	8000	8000	8000	8000	800
11:	8000	8000	8000	8000	8000	8000	8000	8000	8000	800
12:	8000	8000	8000	8000	8000	8000	8000	8000	8000	800
13:	8000	8000	8000	8000	8000	8000	8000	8000	8000	800
14:	8000	8000	8000	8000	8000	8000	8000	8000	8000	800
15:	8000	8000	8000	8000	8000	8000	8000	8000	8000	800
16:	8000	8000	8000	8000	8000	8000	8000	8000	8000	800
17:	8000	8000	8000	8000	8000	8000	8000	8000	8000	800
18:	8000	8000	8000	8000	8000	8000	8000	8000	8000	800
19:	8000	8000	8000	8000	8000	8000	8000	8000	8000	800
20:	8000	8000	8000	8000	8000	8000	8000	8000	8000	800

5.4 Automated design tools

Table 5.8 *Simulated Traffic Requirement Matrix for 22-Node United Kingdom Network*

Design Database

 Global Live Voice Traffic

Aggregate Traffic Matrix

	0	1	2	3	4	5	6	7	8	9
0:	0	8000	8000	8000	8000	8000	8000	8000	8000	3200(
1:	8000	0	8000	8000	16000	168000	24000	8000	8000	1600(
2:	8000	8000	0	8000	8000	16000	16000	8000	8000	5600(
3:	8000	8000	8000	0	168000	8000	16000	8000	40000	5600(
4:	8000	16000	8000	168000	0	32000	16000	16000	24000	3200(
5:	8000	168000	16000	8000	32000	0	152000	8000	24000	800(
6:	8000	24000	16000	16000	16000	152000	0	64000	16000	2400(
7:	8000	8000	8000	8000	16000	8000	64000	0	8000	1600(
8:	8000	8000	40000	24000	24000	48000	16000	8000	0	1200(
9:	32000	16000	56000	32000	8000	24000	16000	120000	32000	3200(
10:	16000	8000	16000	16000	24000	16000	112000	16000	16000	3200(
11:	8000	16000	16000	8000	8000	8000	8000	168000	8000	1600(
12:	16000	16000	8000	8000	16000	8000	507200	72000	24000	1200(
13:	8000	8000	168000	16000	16000	32000	16000	8000	320000	5600(
14:	8000	8000	80000	56000	72000	8000	8000	80000	216000	800(
15:	8000	8000	32000	32000	32000	64000	32000	16000	456000	1600(
16:	24000	8000	24000	56000	320000	112000	379200	40000	8000	800(
17:	16000	8000	8000	8000	8000	320000	456000	16000	8000	4800(
18:	16000	24000	24000	16000	8000	32000	72000	136000	8000	800(
19:	24000	8000	32000	24000	8000	8000	8000	128000	24000	5760(
20:	8000	8000	8000	8000	8000	16000	32000	8000	8000	800(

meshed, since this would be very expensive. As a result, our traffic requirements must be folded onto the current paths available, according to the current routing table. This will result in a simulated traffic matrix based on aggregate flows, as illustrated in Table 5.8. Based on the original traffic requirements, the resulting topology means that traffic must be aggregated down the chosen circuits. So, for example, 16 Kbps of traffic is flowing between nodes 1 and 4, which indicates that two flows have been aggregated.

Design variables

Within the backbone-modeling tool in iSIM+ there are several parameters we can experiment with to generate promising topologies. Primarily we will look at the following:

- Circuit size (variable)—is the capacity of the circuit. In the example model we will assume only 64-Kbps circuits are available for the sake of simplicity.

- Circuit utilization (0–100)—a measure of how much of the provided circuits we can effectively use before we have to add another circuit. For our example we will assume quite a high utilization of 90 percent. When the routing calculation is performed, any circuits that exceed

90 percent utilization will cause additional circuits to be added in parallel (of course, with a more sophisticated approach you could just add a larger pipe, but this requires an integer programming solution).

- Spare circuit capacity (0–100)—is the minimum amount of bandwidth that must remain available on each circuit. If any circuit traffic flow violates this requirement, then a new circuit must be added in parallel. We will use a value of 5 percent.

- Topology constraint (0–100)—provides dramatic changes in the topology between highly meshed topologies (with a value of 0) through to star network topologies (with a value of 100). We use this parameter to act as a trade-off between higher-cost networks with very little delay and fewer hops (star) and cheaper, more reliable topologies (meshed).

Design output

We will run iSIM+ on the 22-node network using a circuit speed of 64 Kbps, maximum circuit utilization of 90 percent, and spare capacity of 5 percent. We will leave these values fixed and simply vary the range of topology constraint values from 99 percent through to 0 percent. The model assumes a one-year contract and uses BT's 64-K Kilostream service. Figures 5.14 through 5.17 show key snapshots of the main topology changes. In a more sophisticated model we would vary several of these parameters inside a loop, and iterate through thousands of feasible topologies to get the best possible performance/cost result. Even so we can demonstrate here that minor changes in these constraints can have a dramatic effect on the resulting network topology.

In Figure 5.14, the cost of 63 circuits for one year is $614,435. All node-to-node communication (unless to the median node) incurs 2 hops. The median node is a single point of failure.

In Figure 5.15, the cost of 69 circuits for one year is $657,148. Most node-to-node communication (unless to the median node) incurs two hops. The median node is a single point of failure for much of the network. Performance has improved.

In Figure 5.16, the cost of 101 circuits for one year is $880,163. Node-to-node communication is now in many cases direct. Resilience is good; the median node is no longer a single point of failure. Performance has improved.

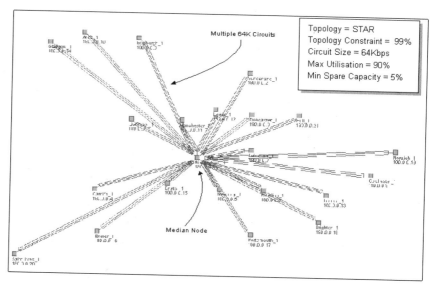

Figure 5.14   *iSIM+ generated topology for 64-Kbps circuits; circuit utilization = 90 percent, circuit spare capacity = 5 percent, and a topology constraint is set to 99 percent.*

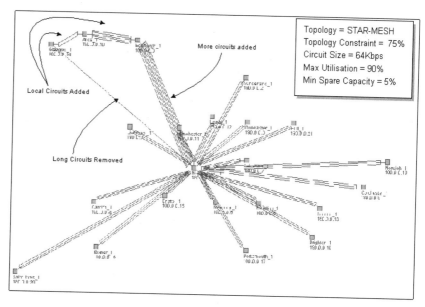

Figure 5.15   *iSIM+ generated topology for 64-Kbps circuits; circuit utilization = 90 percent, circuit spare capacity = 5 percent, and a topology constraint is set to 75 percent.*

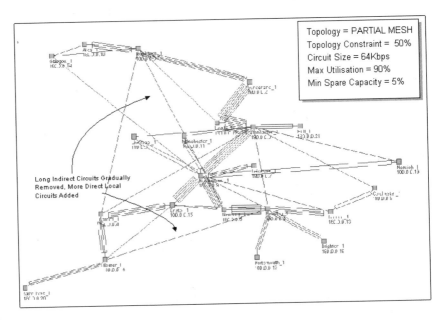

iSIM+ generated topology for 64-Kbps circuits; circuit utilization = 90 percent, circuit spare capacity = 5 percent, and a topology constraint is set to 50 percent.

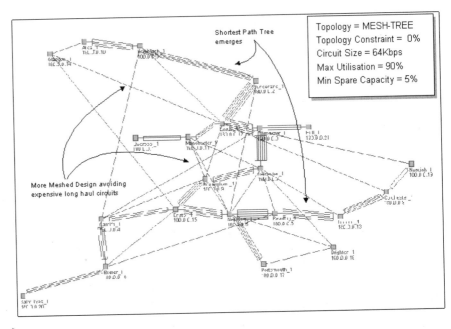

Figure 5.17 *iSIM+ generated topology for 64-Kbps circuits; circuit utilization = 90 percent, circuit spare capacity = 5 percent, and a topology constraint is set to 0 percent.*

In Figure 5.17, the cost of 103 circuits for one year is $892,394. Note the emergence of the minimum spanning tree in the design (the bulk circuit concentrations follow the shortest path tree). Performance is degraded; resilience is still high.

The central node (the median) in the star is chosen as the least-cost sink point for transit traffic between each node. This node will almost always be centrally weighted geographically, since this decision is largely constrained by the way circuits are charged by distance. By varying just one parameter (the topology constraint) we can see a definite transition from a simple star network through to a partially meshed topology, and ultimately a tree-like topology. As a result, the cost increases from $614,435 to $892,394 as the total number of circuits increases from 63 to 103. However, the average hop count is initially reduced, as many long-haul circuits are replaced by shorter, more direct circuits. This results in decreasing delay as the amount of meshing increases, until a point beyond which delay begins to increase again, and the average hop count also increases.

In the final topology we can begin to see the Minimum Spanning Tree (MST) emerging within the design (notice where most of the trunk capacity is being added). In fact, if we momentarily change the minimum circuit

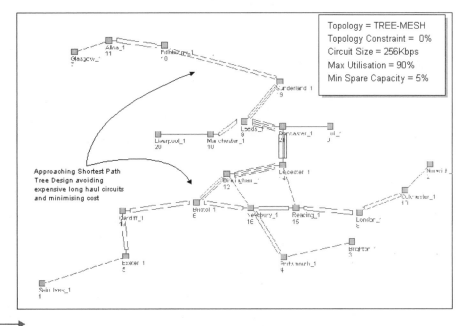

Figure 5.18   *iSIM+ generated topologies for 256-Kbps circuits; circuit utilization = 90 percent, circuit spare capacity = 5 percent, and topology constraint is set to 0 percent.*

speed to 256 Kbps and rerun the algorithm, we end up with a topology that is very close to the MST (since by increasing capacity we have forced the actual circuit utilization to be very low), as illustrated in Figure 5.18.

The MST topology imposes more variation in delay as the number of hops between nodes increases on average. In Figure 5.18 the worst-case path length is 11 hops (Glasgow to St. Ives). The other major point of interest is that resilience is better with a meshed design; both the star and MST topologies introduce single points of failure, which compromise network availability. MST designs are generally only suitable for networks with a small number of sites and high trunk reliability.

What is particularly useful about the MENTOR algorithm is that by using its embedded capacity-routing algorithms these topological results are available in a matter of seconds, so the design tool can be highly interactive and very educational. Another major benefit of this speed is that the algorithm can be embedded within more sophisticated heuristics to examine thousands of potential topologies very rapidly. The best designs can be cached until either an acceptable network is arrived at or some external interrupt occurs (such as the program running out of time or the user halting progress).

5.5   Summary

This chapter examined some of the key techniques used in topological design. A good topological design is fundamental to cost-effective wide area networks, especially international networks, since the costs involved are potentially enormous. We saw that this design problem is best divided up, by employing hierarchical design concepts. The main division of labor is between access network design and backbone network design, and it may be appropriate in large networks to insulate the access layer further from the core via a distribution layer. There are currently no techniques guaranteed to solve large topological problems in realistic time scales. Many of the techniques currently available employ clever heuristics to arrive at near-optimal designs. Specifically, we have discussed the following:

■ Backbone design is a nontrivial task, and there are various algorithms and heuristics that can be employed to approximate optimal solutions in real time. Backbone designs have a fundamental impact on network cost and performance; therefore, backbone design should be a key area of focus. In large internetwork designs it may be appropriate to use automated tools to model various designs to expedite the design process.

- Access design is less complicated than backbone design and, again, uses a number of algorithms and heuristics to approximate optimal solutions in real time. The results of access designs can be fed into backbone design through a clearly defined interface.

- To optimize forwarding, memory, and maintenance, multiple protocols on the backbone should be avoided. Almost all service providers today are focussing on IP as the main carrier protocol over the core. Non-IP protocols are either converted at the edge or tunneled through the core.

- New mathematical and programming techniques are required for solving topological problems, and this is an area of active research. This chapter introduced the reader to the relatively new field of genetic programming, an area recently adapted for use to solve topological problems. As networks grow in size and complexity, the task of building near-optimal networks will become increasingly difficult. No doubt over the next 20 years we will see further exciting developments in algorithms and design techniques to assist the process.

As stated at the beginning of this chapter, topological design is a huge subject, and the interested reader is encouraged to study the material in the reference section.

References

[1]   S. J. Russel and P. Norvig, *Artificial Intelligence, A Modern Approach* (Englewood Cliffs, NJ: Prentice Hall, 1995).

[2]   Adaptive Simulated Annealing (ASA) is a powerful optimization algorithm for nonlinear and stochastic systems developed by Lester Ingber. The latest code can be retrieved via WWW path http://www.ingber.com/ or using anonymous FTP from ftp.ingber.com.

[3]   E. Bonabeau and G. Theraulaz, "Swarm Smarts," *Scientific American* (March 2000): 55–61.

[4]   A. Kershenbaum and R. Boorstyn, "Centralized Teleprocessing Network Design," in *Proceedings of the NTC* (December 1975): 27.11–27.14.

[5]   A. S. Tanenbaum, *Computer Networks* (Englewood Cliffs, NJ: Prentice Hall, 1981).

[6]   B. R. Preiss, *Data Structures and Algorithms with Object-Oriented Design Patterns in C++* (New York: John Wiley & Sons, 1999).

[7]   A. Kershenbaum, *Telecommunications Design Algorithms* (New York: McGraw-Hill).

[8]   K. Steiglitz, P. Eeiner, and D. J. Kleitman, "The Design of Minimum-Cost Survivable Networks," *IEEE Transactions on Circuit Theory* CT-16 (November 1969): 455–460.

[9]   S. Chen, "Routing Support for Providing Guaranteed End-to-End Quality of Service" (Ph.D. diss., University of Illinois, May 1999).

[10] E. Horowitz, S. Sahni, and S. Rajasekaran, *Computer Algorithms in C++* (Computer Science Press).

[11] Q. Ma, "QoS Routing in the Integrated Services Networks" (Ph.D. diss., January 1998).

[12] R. Guerin, S. Kamat, A. Orda, T. Przygienda, and D. Williams, "QoS Routing Mechanisms and OSPF Extensions," Internet Draft draft-guerin-QoS-routing-ospf-03.txt (January 1998).

[13] M. Gerla, L. Fratta, and L. Kleinrock, "The Floe-Deviation Method: An Approach to Store and Forward Communication Network Design," *Networks* 3 (1973): 97–133.

[14] E. Gafni, D. Bertsekas, and R. Gallager, "Second Derivative Algorithms for Minimum Delay Distributed Routing in Networks," *IEEE Transactions on Communications* 32 (1984): 911–919..

[15] D. Bertsekas and R. Gallager, *Data Networks* (Englewood Cliffs, NJ: Prentice Hall, 1987).

[16] L. Kleinrock, *Queuing Systems,* vol. 1, *Theory* (New York: Wiley-Interscience, 1975).

[17] W. Chou, M. Gerla, H. Frank, and J. Eckl, "A Cut Saturation Algorithm for Topological Design of Packet-Switched Communication Links," in *Proceedings of the NTC* (1974): 1074–1085.

[18] J. Suruagy Monteiro, M. Gerla, and R. Pazos, "Topology Design and Bandwidth Allocation in ATM Networks," *IEEE JSAC* 7 (1989): 1253–1262.

[19] G. Grover, A. Kershenbaum and P. Kermani, "Mentor: An Algorithm for Mesh Network Topological Optimization and Routing," *IEEE Transactions on Communications* 39 (1991): 503–513.

[20] R. S. Cahn, *Wide Area Network Design, Concepts and Tools for Optimization* (San Mateo, CA: Morgan Kaufmann, 1998).

[21] D. E. Goldberg, *Genetic Algorithms in Search, Optimization, and Machine Learning* (Reading, MA: Addison-Wesley, 1989).

[22] Berry, Murtagh, McMahon, Sugden, Welling, *An Integrated GA/LP Approach to Communication Network Design* (RMIT University, 1998).

[23] E. Falkenauer, *Genetic Algorithms and Grouping Problems* (New York: John Wiley & Sons, 1998).

[24] Berry, Murtagh, Sugden, *Optimization Models for Communication Network Design*, (RMIT University).

[25] E. Bonabeau, M. Dorigo, and G. Theraulaz, *Swarm Intelligence: From Natural to Artificial Systems* (Oxford University Press, 1999).

[26] iridia.ulb.ac.be/dorigo/ACO/ACO.html, Marco Dorigo's Web page on ant-based shortest path topology optimization at the University of Brussels.

[27] ftp.mkp.com/wand and www.mkp.com/wand.htm, Morgan Kaufmann's FTP and Web sites. Source code for various design algorithms and the Delite tool.

[28] www.wandl.com, Home site of Wide Area Networks Laboratory (NPAT design suite).

[29] www.makesystems.com, Home site of Make Systems, Inc. (Net-Maker design suite).

6

LAN and MAN Technologies

During the 1980s Local Area Networks (LANs) and the applications that emerged to run over them revolutionized business operations fundamentally. One could argue that LANs prepared businesses for the further revolution to come in the 1990s, in the form of e-business over the Internet. The ability to communicate via e-mail, the use of shared office applications, and the ability to transfer image-based documentation in seconds are now taken for granted. In the early 1980s the first home computers were only just emerging, and the personal computer was slow and relatively expensive and relied on command-line input and menu-driven, character-based applications. The first LANs were relatively slow and unreliable and were more of an academic curiosity than a mission-critical resource. Today the LAN is now as valuable a resource as the phone system, and many modern businesses could not operate effectively without both; in fact, the network is becoming the phone system.

During the early 1980s, there were a variety of access technologies vying for dominance, including Ethernet, Token Ring, Token Bus, ArcNet, and Apple's LocalTalk. By the mid 1980s there were still no clear winners, and a religious debate was being waged between the Token Ring and Ethernet camps. A typical customer visit would not be complete without the customary discussion about their respective merits. What subsequently emerged was a vote for simplicity and cost-effectiveness, and it is generally accepted that Ethernet won. Token passing offered a very reasonable and apparently compelling argument in the form of deterministic performance, which should have secured its future. Unfortunately for token passing, many networks at that time were not short of bandwidth, and the mere sight of an IBM cabling system tended to make customers weak at the knees. The relative simplicity, vendor independence, and lower cost of ownership of Ethernet became the key factors. According to IDC, by the end of 1996, 83 percent of all network connections were Ethernet (over 120 million connections). The development community and standards bodies have also rallied strongly behind Ethernet, and we have witnessed a 100,000-fold improvement in Ethernet performance over the last decade, with the latest incarnation of Gigabit Ethernet. In effect Ethernet has become the IP of local area networking.

With the rapid emergence of newer and faster technologies during the 1990s, and the ability to drive data over greater distances, there is an increased blurring of the distinction between local and wide area technologies. This middle ground between LANs and WANs is referred to as the Metropolitan Area Network (MAN). This is a rather loose distinction based on distance, with MANs generally represented by campus-type environments and LANs generally represented by office or building environments. As already noted, technologies such as Ethernet and Token Ring are practically synonymous with LANs. Technologies such as FDDI and SMDS are more commonly associated with MANs, although they may support distances of hundreds of miles and their applications are quite different (FDDI can be thought of as a kind of LAN-MAN technology, whereas SMDS is more of a MAN-WAN technology). Other technologies such as ATM make no useful distinction. Enhancements to conventional LAN technologies, such as Gigabit Ethernet, make the distinction even less precise. LANs are at present almost exclusively privately owned; MANs may simply be extended LANs (as in the case of FDDI) or may be public or private networks offered by service providers (as in the case of SMDS). It is, therefore, unwise to associate the LAN/MAN/WAN function with any particular technology. Personally I have never found the concept of MAN particularly useful, since its definition is usually ambiguous; suffice it to say that I consider it the LAN-WAN interface.

This continual blurring of the boundaries is to be expected, as the LAN and WAN environments become ever more tightly integrated, in the hope of providing a more seamless high-speed communication infrastructure. This chapter discusses some of the key local and metropolitan area media technologies for constructing network designs. It is not my intention to cover all of the possible options; we will focus on those you will encounter on major network design projects. The following subjects are covered:

- Media and carrier technologies: topologies, media types, and design issues

- Structured Cabling Systems (SCS)

- Local and campus network protocols and design: Ethernet/802.3, Token Ring, 100BaseX, 100VG-AnyLAN, FDDI, Gigabit Ethernet

- Wireless LANs (including IEEE 802.11 and Bluetooth)

We will also briefly review operational and performance details that pertain to design, without attempting to provide complete details, since this is beyond the scope of this book. There is a wealth of information available about specific protocol details [1–3].

6.1   Introduction

In local area networks there are several driving forces that have influenced the evolution of cabling, topologies, and bandwidth provision. Most notably, application developers have a habit of using whatever bandwidth is made available to them. As bandwidth has increased, this has led to a new breed of applications, capable of greatly increased function but at the cost of increased bandwidth. In particular, applications such as scientific modeling, network backup, publications, data warehousing, real-time video conferencing, and multimedia are all contributing to the need for more resources. Traditionally, shared media approaches have gradually given way to dedicated media per user, in an effort to reduce contention and avoid network latencies. This in turn leads to many more network segments with many more nodes per segment, significantly increasing complexity by introducing more intricate topologies with many more components (notably, the appearance of various LAN-switched products that address the clustering and management of local bandwidth). All of these factors affect cost of ownership and network reliability. Today we are on the brink of yet another revolution in the form of wireless networking, in both the local and wide area environments.

6.1.1   Key LAN standards

The majority of the LAN standards in existence today have been created by the IEEE, under the project designation IEEE 802, with several standards subsequently standardized by the ISO. Table 6.1 summarizes the main standards of interest for LANs and MANs. Other relevant standards of interest include ANSI X3T9.5 FDDI and the ATM Forum's ATM.

In this chapter we are concerned primarily with the key technologies used in commercial networks today, including Ethernet, Token Ring, FDDI, Wireless LANs, Gigabit Ethernet, Fast Ethernet, and 100BaseVG.

Table 6.1   *IEEE LAN and MAN Standards*

Standard	Description
IEEE 802 .0	LAN and MAN Overview and Architecture
IEEE 802 .1	Higher level interface standards for management and bridging
IEEE 802 .1 B, K	LAN and MAN management standards
IEEE 802 .1 D	MAC Bridge operations and resilient Spanning Tree operations
IEEE 802 .1 E	System Load Protocol
IEEE 802 .2	Logical link Control (LLC) standard.
IEEE 802 .3	Collision Sense Multiple Access with Collision Detection (CSMA/CD) Access Method and Physical Layer Specifications (i.e. Ethernet style LANs)
IEEE 802 .3 u	100Mbps Fast Ethernet/100 Base-X
IEEE 802 .3 x	Full Duplex Operations
IEEE 802 .3 y	100Mbps 100 Base-T2
IEEE 802 .3 z	1000Mbps Gigabit Ethernet
IEEE 802 .3 ac	Frame extensions for VLAN tagging on 802.3 networks
IEEE 802 .3 ad	Aggregation of Multiple Link Segments
IEEE 802 .4	Token-Passing Bus Access Method and Physical Layer Specifications
IEEE 802 .5	Token-Passing Ring Access Method and Physical Layer Specifications (i.e. Token Ring style LANs)
IEEE 802 .6	Distributed Queue Dual Bus (DQDB) Access Method and Physical Layer Specifications (i.e. MAN operations)
IEEE 802 .7	Broadband Technical Advisory Group
IEEE 802 .8	Fiber Technical Advisory Group
IEEE 802 .9	Integrated Services (for Voice/Data on LAN)
IEEE 802 .10	Interoperable LAN/MAN Security
IEEE 802 .11	Wireless LAN
IEEE 802 .12	Demand Priority Access Method, Physical Layer and Repeater Specifications (i.e. 100Base-VG/AnyLAN style LANs)
IEEE 802 .14	Cable-TV-Based Broadband Communications Networks
IEEE 802 .30	100Base-X

We will also discuss some of the Structured Cabling System (SCS) standards introduced by collaborative efforts between bodies such as the International Organization for Standardization (ISO), the American National Standards Institute (ANSI), Telecommunications Industries Association (TIA), and the Electrical Industries Association (EIA).

6.1.2   **LAN topologies**

LANs can be formed in a number of different physical topologies. This section briefly discusses the common topologies seen today. The term topology refers to the way in which network devices are interconnected, and LAN topologies fall into the following basic classifications: bus, ring, tree, star, and mesh.

The physical connections of these networks may look confusingly similar in practice. For example, a Token Ring network has a logical ring topology but may appear physically to resemble a star topology, and bus networks can quickly resemble tree networks as they grow.

Bus topology

Bus topologies are very common for local area networks. Nodes are all attached to a common transmission medium (often a single cable) called a bus, and data are broadcast across the medium. A popular protocol used with bus topology is CSMA/CD (Carrier Sensed Multiple Access with Collision Detection). Such networks are very democratic: There is no controlling station since all control and error handling and bus arbitration functions are distributed and handled by each node. When a node transmits a frame, propagation on the bus occurs in both directions (away from the node), and the frame will be seen by all other nodes on the LAN. At each end of the cable is a terminating resistor (called a terminator). An electrical signal is passed along the cable between these two terminators. When a node transmits a frame onto the wire, the bus propagates a frame from one end of the cable to the other. Frames are effectively broadcast at the electrical level (not to be confused with the term broadcast when discussing addressing mechanisms). When the frame reaches other nodes, each node checks the destination address on the frame, and if the address matches the receiving node address, then the node will copy the message into a local buffer.

Each node on the bus can in theory transmit data whenever it is ready. Since this is a shared medium, this means that two nodes could potentially transmit simultaneously, causing a collision. In fact, collisions are guaranteed to occur on this type of shared medium. To deal with this special collision-detection hardware is implemented by the network hardware for each node. When the transmitting node detects a collision, a special jamming signal is generated on the wire. This aborts the current frame and warns all other nodes that any data they are seeing are bad. Both colliding nodes will back off and try to retransmit the frame.

Advantages of bus technologies are that bus technology is typically passive, in that nodes only listen for data being propagated on the wire, and are not responsible for moving data from one node to the next. If one node fails, it doesn't affect the entire LAN, since it is not a relay point. Bus technology is generally easy to install and uses simple, inexpensive technology. It is readily understood and maintained and therefore requires less skilled maintenance staff.

The main disadvantages of bus technologies are that if a cable breaks, the entire cable segment (the length between the two terminators) loses its connectivity, so that the entire segment isn't functional until the cable can be repaired. If a station misbehaves (e.g., by causing continuous broadcasts), then all nodes are potentially affected. Bandwidth is shared between all nodes, and all nodes are assumed to behave fairly. If one node is particularly aggressive, then other nodes will be unfairly affected. Troubleshooting can be difficult, since there is no easy way to isolate problems. As more nodes are added to the network, more collisions are likely, and hence more retransmissions take place. The overall network performance will degrade. Performance cannot be guaranteed (it is said to be nondeterministic). Examples of bus topology include ArcNet, which relies on the IEEE 802.4 Token Passing bus standard. Perhaps the best-known example of a bus technology is Ethernet/IEEE 802.3, available in two bus formats: 10Base5 (thicknet) and 10Base2 (thinnet). Ethernet buses were widely used in the 1980s to construct many local area networks because they were cost-effective and relatively simple to install. Thinnet is still used today for small networks and lab environments, although for serious network designs star-wired multi-access switched Ethernet is much more common, primarily due to the advances in structured cabling systems and the need for greater flexibility and better traffic management.

Tree topology

The tree topology is simply a variation of bus topology (e.g., a tree topology can be formed in Ethernet networks by simply joining together multiport repeaters). Transmitted frames are electrically broadcast to all stations active on the shared medium, down all branches of the tree. As with the bus topology, there is no controlling station on the LAN. The tree topology is used by the IEEE 802.3 10Broad36 standard, a broadband signaling specification that is rarely used nowadays.

Ring topology

In a ring topology, each node is attached to its adjacent node by point-to-point links, forming a physical ring. The network adapter in each node regenerates the signal as it retransmits a data packet that is circulating on the ring. A popular protocol used with ring topology is token passing, in which access to the medium is controlled by possession of a circulating token. Different token-passing access protocols are defined for ring topology LANs, although token passing is also applicable to a bus local area network. In token-passing ring networks, data frames (called tokens) are continually being passed around the ring from one node to the next. To transmit data, a node must wait for the circulating token to arrive, where it can examine the contents of the token to see whether it is empty. If it is empty, the node may append data to the token and address the packet to a destination. When the token reaches the destination node, it recognizes the destination address and copies these data (in technologies such as Token Ring the node will flip the state of the address recognized bit (A) and copied bit (C) in the frame to indicate these actions). The token then continues around the ring and eventually reaches the original sender, which then strips off the data from the frame and releases a new free token. The token-passing scheme is in direct contrast to the bus topology, where any computer can send freely and the physical-level protocols must detect collisions.

Advantages of ring technologies are that Ethernet-style collisions cannot occur on a ring network and performance can be guaranteed and predicted (i.e., deterministic), since the performance characteristics are readily calculated using the number of nodes on the ring and the length of the ring. The main disadvantage of ring technologies is sensitivity to single link failure. If one connection between two stations fails or a bypass for a particular inactive station is malfunctioning, the ring traffic is down. Examples of ring technologies include Token Ring and FDDI. Token Ring is found on many local area networks, particularly those with IBM mainframes. Both 4- and 16-Mbps variants are available. FDDI is a common ring network used primarily for campus fiber backbone applications. FDDI is available as 100 Mbps dual or single rings (a logical star topology is also available).

Star topology

The star topology is perhaps the earliest incarnation of the local area network, with its origins in the mainframe environment. There are two subtle variants of star topology, corresponding broadly to carrier-sense technologies such as Ethernet/IEEE 802.3 and token-passing technologies such as Token Ring. The former is a logical bus network, whereas the latter is a variation of a ring topology, also referred to as radial hierarchical wiring (although the cable layout closely resembles a star topology, the physical and logical topology is still a ring). In the star network, each node is connected to a central controlling device (also called a switch, hub, relay, or concentrator) via point-to-point lines. The structure of a star network is very simple, and to extend the star network, hubs can be interconnected, forming multiple stars. The hub provides a common physical connection for all nodes, and all communication between nodes is relayed via the hub. Each node is connected to a hub with transmit and receive paths.

Advantages of star technologies are that they are simple to implement, expand, and manage. The major disadvantage of star networks is the reliance on a central device (i.e., there is a single point of failure). If the hub fails, then the entire network is broken. To overcome the disadvantage, the central switch must use very reliable components and typically provides some form of local redundancy. Examples of star technologies include Ethernet/IEEE 802.3, Token Ring, StarLAN, and the PBX.

Mesh topology

This topology involves considerable cabling overhead, since every node is directly connected to all the other nodes. Furthermore, each station needs $N-1$ interfaces (physical or logical), where N is the number of nodes in the network. The advantages of mesh technologies are that a mesh network topology has excellent fault tolerance, since, when a link fails, message traffic can be routed through an intermediate node. Higher-level protocols may also be able to use multiple paths to provide better aggregate throughput. The main disadvantages of mesh technologies are cabling/interface overheads and cost, they do not scale, and they introduce potentially complicated routing issues. For these reasons it is common to employ partial meshes in large routed networks.

6.1.3   LAN media characteristics

Several different types of media can be used for the physical wiring infrastructure for a LAN or MAN. The main types of media in use today include unshielded twisted pair (UTP), coaxial, shielded twisted pair (STP), and fiber-optic. Media can be broadly categorized as baseband or broadband, depending upon the transmission characteristics, and each medium has individual topology and environmental characteristics that make it suited for particular applications. Before describing specific media we will quickly review some of the important features of transmission lines relevant to the network designer.

Characteristics of transmission lines

Wire sizes

Wiring is defined partly by size. In the United States the standard sizing system is called the American Wire Gauge (AWG). The AWG system specifies the diameter of the wire, although the higher the gauge, the thinner the cable. Small-diameter wires offer greater resistance to the signal propagated, resulting in a decreased bit transfer rate over that medium (see Table 6.2). They also offer less cross-sectional area for the signal, resulting in increased signal loss. Larger-diameter wires offer a greater cross-section, allowing for greater signal intensity. Common examples [4] used in structured cabling systems and telephone networks include the following:

- 19 AWG—Cross-sectional area of 1,288.0 circular mils

- 22 AWG—Cross-sectional area of 624.4 circular mils

- 24 AWG—Cross-sectional area of 404.0 circular mils

- 26 AWG—Cross-sectional area of 254.1 circular mils

The smaller the diameter of the wire, the greater its resistance, resulting in a lower bit transfer rate. Smaller wires also produce greater signal loss than those with a larger cross-sectional area.

Propagation velocity

Table 6.2 illustrates the minimum propagation velocities of various media. These velocities ultimately constrain the speed with which bits are transmitted, and hence they also constrain the maximum media distances allowed for various LAN technologies.

Crosstalk

Crosstalk is an interference phenomenon caused by the inductive (magnetic field) coupling from one transmission line to another and is most pronounced in bidirectional transmission when the conductors are held in the same sheath (as is the case with twisted pair). Crosstalk is measured in decibels (dB) and is expressed as follows:

$$dB = 10\log_{10}(PowerOut/PowerIn)$$

or

$$dB = 20\log_{10}(VoltageOut/VoltageIn)$$

For example, if the input power is 10 W, and the output power is measured at 6.5 W, the loss due to crosstalk would be: $10[\log_{10}(6.5/10)] =$

Table 6.2   *Minimum Propagation Velocities of Various Media Types (expressed as a fraction of the speed of light. c = 300,000 km per second)*

	FDDI - Fibre Optic	FDDI - Copper
FDDI Cable type	Optical Fibre	Twisted pair
Data Rate	100Mbps	100Mbps
Max Length Between Repeaters	2000m	100m
Max No of Repeaters	100	100
Signalling Technique	4B/5B/NRZI	MLT-3
Max Transceiver cable length	50m	50m

−1.87 dB. Often this loss may be expressed in relation to a reference power of 1 mW or a reference voltage of 1 mV, as follows. Using these formulae the loss is expressed as either decibel milliwatts (dBm) or decibel millivolts (dBmV).

$$dBm = 10\log_{10}(\text{Power}/1 \text{ mW})$$

or

$$dBmV = 20\log_{10}(\text{Voltage}/1 \text{ mV})$$

Crosstalk disrupts the signal between the generator and receiver and may lead to errors and retransmissions at higher-protocol layers; it is therefore imperative to keep crosstalk as low as possible and the signal-to-noise ratio as high as possible. The best way to achieve this is to keep metallic cables clear of potential sources of interference (such as heavy electrical equipment). Note that fiber-optic cables do not suffer from this phenomenon, so in heavy industrial environments fiber may be preferable.

Noise

The term noise in this context refers to any unwanted signal that affects the transmission line from an external source-impairing communications. There are two basic types of noise: Radio Frequency Interference (RFI) and Electromagnetic Interference (EMI). Typical RFI sources include television and radio transmitters; typical EMI sources include fluorescent lighting, arc welders, motorized fans, and electric light dimmers. The effects of noise are measured in decibels (dBs) and are expressed as follows:

$$\text{Noise (dB)} = 10\log_{10} S/N$$

where

S and N = the signal and noise powers measured in watts or milliwatts

Balanced and unbalanced transmission

The terms balanced and unbalanced are often used when describing transmission lines.

- A balanced line (sometimes referred to as differential mode) has the characteristic that the current flowing between the signal generator and receiver in a two-wire system are equal in magnitude but flowing in opposite directions. The voltages in these wires, with respect to ground, are also equal in magnitude but opposite in polarity (technically, 180 degrees out of phase), so a ground potential difference may exist between the generator and receiver. In twisted-pair systems the twisting of each pair is staggered evenly so that the radiated energy from the current flowing in one direction is largely canceled out by the return flow (minimizing the effects of crosstalk). Examples of balanced transmission cables include copper twisted pair and twinaxial cable (twinax).

- With an unbalanced line the current flowing in the signal conductor returns via a ground (earthed) connection, which may be shared with other circuits. Both the current and voltage in the signal conductor are measured with respect to this return conductor. Coaxial cable is an example of an unbalanced transmission line.

In some cases it is necessary to convert between balanced and unbalanced modes, and in this event a special transformer, called a balun (short for balanced to unbalanced) is required. Baluns were commonly used to migrate from coaxial to twisted-pair Ethernet to preserve investment in cabling, but they are much less common in network designs today.

We will now discuss some of the more important media types used in network design. For further information on transmission characteristics refer to reference [5].

6.1.4   LAN media types

Coaxial cable

Coaxial cable (sometimes called coax) comprises a central core with a shield around it and can be used for both baseband and broadband transmissions. It is an unbalanced medium (the two conductors have a different impedance to ground) with the shield being used as one of the conductors. Coax has low attenuation characteristics and can drive signals at high data rates for relatively long distances. It generates less Radio Frequency (RF) noise than UTP at high data rates. Early Ethernet networks were based on coax buses, but it is not a supported medium in the cabling standards and is not an option for LANs above 10 Mbps. The 50-ohm coaxial cable is not generally recommended for new installations, and it is rarely used in enterprise or campus design due to its relatively high cost and inflexibility for installation.

Unshielded twisted pair (categories 3, 4, 5)

Significant effort has been put into improving the performance of UTP media for higher-speed data applications. Unshielded, voice-grade twisted-pair cable can be used for data transmission over limited distances if the data signal strength is filtered. This type of medium is used by many PABX manufacturers to carry voice and data, and it tends to suffer from high attenuation (loss of signal strength due to inherent media characteristics) and is very susceptible to noise if located near strong electromagnetic fields (such as power cables). Attenuation results in a reduction in the drive distance, number of attachments, and bandwidth potential of the LAN using this medium. When used for high rates of data transmission (1 Mbps or higher), it will radiate RF emissions. Filters can be used to reduce this; however, filters increase loss in signal strength and add to the cost of the cabling and attachments. UTP wire also suffers from crosstalk between adjacent twisted pairs.

The cable classifications were introduced specifically to differentiate existing voice-grade cables from later high-speed data cables. The type 3 specification for 100-ohm twisted pair was the first to provide high-frequency capabilities. It has no crosstalk specifications and no attenuation specifications above 1 MHz. It was basically designed for customers who wanted to use existing cabling for Token Ring transmission. The next advance came in 1991 with the development of EIA/TIA 568, Commercial Building Telecommunications Wiring Standard. The specifications in this standard were developed with input from the IEEE Project 802 Local Area Network Standards committees. The UTP specifications are much more comprehensive than the type 3 specifications in that both crosstalk and attenuation characteristics through 16 MHz are specified.

Shortly after these specifications were adapted, cabling manufacturers developed higher-performance UTP cables. The EIA/TIA issued the Technical System Bulletin TSB-36, which defined categories 3, 4, and 5 UTP cables (often referred to as Cat-2, Cat-4, and Cat-5). Cat-1 and Cat-2 are for voice and low-speed data and are beyond the scope of this book (these are in any case made obsolete by TIA 568-B). Cat-4 and Cat-5 cables, in addition to being specified at higher frequencies (up to 20 and 100 MHz, respectively), have lower attenuation and crosstalk.

Shielded Twisted-Pair Cable (STP)

Data-Grade Media (DGM) Shielded Twisted-Pair Cable (STP) has one or more twisted pairs within a shield. The shielding reduces its susceptibility to low levels of noise and its own generation of radio frequency interference, thus making it more suitable for data transmission. Shielded data-grade cable can be used with data rates in excess of 20 Mbps over most distances encountered within buildings. The cable can be constructed with two twisted pairs within a shield, while maintaining a low level of crosstalk due to the shielding and the way in which the pairs are twisted around each other. In addition to providing two data paths, the twisting and shielding of DGM cable provides greater immunity to external interference than coaxial cables, which use the shield as one of the conductors. Data-grade twisted-pair cable is a balanced medium better suited to the differential encoding schemes used by some LANs. While this type of cable can be used for base-band and broadband transmission, it is primarily used for baseband.

STP cable, 150 ohm, was designed back in the early 1980s; each of the two twisted pairs are shielded from one another by a signal-grounded poly-ester aluminum tape shield. The whole package is further shielded in copper braid. STP is still a good choice for high-speed data transmission. Its high characteristic impedance is fundamental in achieving low transmission attenuation. The shield is needed to transmit the highest possible data rates while staying within country emission standards. Token Ring operation, 16 Mbps, on shielded 150-ohm cable has been a standard since 1989. Fiber Distributed Data Interface (FDDI), 100 Mbps, also runs over STP for at least 100 m from the workstation to the wiring closet. IBM also announced the F-Coupler in 1991, which enables STP to be used for broadband trans-missions in the 50- to 550-MHz band while simultaneously running 4- or 16-Mbps Token Ring signals.

Fiber-optic cable

Fiber-optic cable presents an attractive solution for high-speed transmission rates used in backbone local area networks, particularly since installation costs have fallen significantly over recent years. Fiber-optic cable is normally used for baseband transmission. Optical fiber offers several distinct advantages over traditional copper cable, such as the following:

- Reliability—Optical fiber is inherently immune to the types of electrical noise and grounding trouble that can plague metallic conductors in some environments. Thus, it is also an ideal medium for outdoor connections or for factories or locations in which cabling has to run near higher-voltage wiring.

- Speed and drive distance—Optical fiber cable has extremely high data transfer capability (hundreds of megabits per second, terabits per second) with very little signal attenuation (signal loss due to the medium). Because of the high data rates and the distances that fiber-optic cables can carry a signal without regeneration, its use in telephone networks, channel extenders on mainframe computers, and backbone LANs is rapidly increasing (e.g., with the use of Enterprise

System Connection (ESCON)–capable mainframes and communications devices).

■ Security—In comparison with transmission of electrical signals on copper media, it is difficult to tap an optical signal from a fiber-optic cable without the inherent optical signal loss being detected. Therefore, fiber-optic cable has potential for greater security than metallic conductors.

Optical fiber is produced in varying sizes. Typically these are 62.5/125 μ (10^{-6} m), 50/125, and 9/125. The dimensions refer to the diameter of the core and of the cladding. The core is the central solid element within the fiber. The cladding is the fiber wall. Individual fibers are normally bundled together into a sheathed cable, strengthened internally to protect the weak contents. There are basically two types of fiber: multimode and single-mode (better known as monomode). Multimode fibers are suitable for using Light Emitting Diodes (LEDs) as the light source and can handle data rates in the order of hundreds of megabits per second. They are suitable for general-purpose LAN configurations, over distances of two kilometers. Because LED technology is relatively cheap, the cost of the transmitters is also kept at a minimum. Monomode fiber requires the use of lasers as a light source. These devices are more expensive than LEDs, but drive distances can be longer. This technology is normally found within the long-haul networking environment (e.g., as used by the public telephone companies for high-speed trunk links).

It is generally recommended to use the 62.5-μ optical fiber for most establishment cabling applications. This 62.5/125-μ fiber specification is patterned after the fiber specification in the Commercial Building Wiring Standard (developed by the TIA 41.8.1 and by the ISO SC25/WG3 working groups) for meeting most intrabuilding and campus link requirements. It is expected to become the accepted multimode standard for government and commercial buildings and will meet future FDDI application requirements. The FDDI standard also provides information for attaching FDDI cable plants using 50/125-μ, 100/140-μ, and 85/125-μ multimode optical fibers as alternatives. Several vendors also recommend 62.5/125 multimode optical fiber for FDDI connection. In Japan and other countries 50/125 is the preferred fiber. Each cable specification parameter must be met over the full range of operating temperatures. A suggested temperature range of 0°C to 52°C is an appropriate choice for many installations. Maximum summer and minimum winter temperatures may differ from this range, particularly in installations where the fiber cable will be installed in poorly insulated and unheated areas.

Customers should select a grade of fiber that will perform to specification in those instances where the temperature may exceed the suggested range (refer to the SP-2840 Commercial Building Telecommunications Cabling Standard [ANSI/TIA/EIA] for recommendations). Some vendors also recommend that customers should install single-mode fiber along with multimode for future high bandwidth applications. Although fibers are normally installed using prepackaged bundles (cables), there is a relatively new technology available known as blown fiber. With blown fiber, installation is achieved by forcing (using compressed air) optical fibers through tubes or microducts that have been previously installed between points in the building or on the campus site. This approach allows optical fibers to be quickly installed or replaced as required, with minimum disruption to the customer's facilities. Blown fiber is available from British Telecom (who invented this technology), Corning Incorporated, and Sumitomo. Optical fiber technology requires specialized skills to install and commission an installation. It requires special connectors, jumper cables, and fiber-splicing techniques, as well as careful handling, of both the fibers themselves and the patch panel. Its use is now widespread and growing.

6.1.5   Structured cabling standards

The standards for structured cabling in the United States were developed through a collaborative effort between the American National Standards Institute (ANSI), the Telecommunications Industry Association (TIA), and the Electronic Industries Association (EIA). The current standard (SP-2840) has been prepared by the Working Group TR-41.8.1 and replaces the ANSI/EIA/TIA-568-A standard of July 1991. This standard covers additional specifications for categories 3, 4, and 5 UTP cables and connecting hardware, as well as additional specifications for 150-ohm STP cables and connectors. New specifications for 62.5/125-μm optical fiber and single-mode optical fiber cables, connectors, and cabling practices have also been included. Outside the United States the relevant standards are ISO/IEC 11801 and EN (and BS-EN) 5017. These are the international/european/United Kingdom standards for building cabling. Cable system designers should be using the country-relevant standard for all new designs. Figure 6.1 illustrates the basic concepts of the structured cabling.

Structured cabling is essentially based on a hierarchical topology. At the core of the tree is the Campus Distributor (CD), which feeds one or more Backbone Distributors (BDs), which in turn feed one or more Floor Distributors (FDs). Ultimately cables are terminated at the Telecommunications Outlets (TOs), where fly leads in the work area are used to attach user

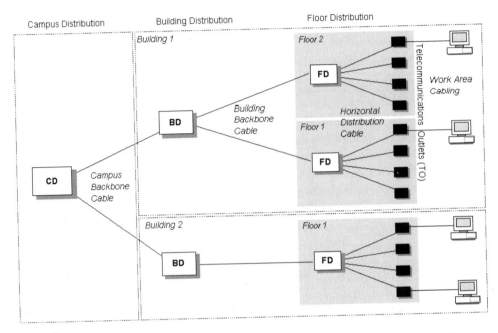

Figure 6.1   *Structured Cabling System (SCS) hierarchy based on ISO/IEC 11801 terminology.*

devices. At each of the three main distribution points there will be appropriate cable distribution/patching facilities to facilitate cable management, as well as associated transmission equipment (hubs, concentrators, etc.). Note that in ANSI 568A terminology floor distributors are referred to as the telecommunication wiring closet, the backbone distributor as the intermediate crossconnect, the campus backbone as the interbuilding backbone, and the campus distributor as the main crossconnect.

The purpose of the SCS standards is to specify the minimum requirements for telecommunications cabling within a commercial building, including the telecommunications outlet and connections between buildings in a campus environment.

Horizontal cabling

The current standard specifies this as the portion of cabling extending from the desk port to the wiring closet (floor distributor). It is important to get the cabling design right at this level, since it is often more difficult to replace than a backbone cable. The following types of cables are recognized for the horizontal cabling system:

- Two-pair, 100-ohm balanced UTP, Categories 3, 4, and 5 (ISO/IEC 11801)

- Four-pair, 100-ohm UTP/FTP, Categories 3, 4, and 5 (ANSI/EIA/TIA 568A)

- 120-ohm star quad, Categories 4+ or 5+ (ISO/IEC 11801)

- Two-pair, 150-ohm STP (ISO/IEC 11801 and ANSI/EIA/TIA 568A)

- 62.5/125-μ optical fiber (ISO/IEC 11801 and ANSI/EIA/TIA 568A)

Note that the maximum distance between the floor distributor and telecommunications outlet for all media types is 90 m (295 ft). There is also an additional 5 m allowed for patch chords at distribution points and fly leads in the work area, making the total length between user and hub equipment 100 m. Coaxial cable (50 ohm) is not recommended for new installations. Hybrid cables, which comprise more than one type under a common sheath, may also be used.

Backbone cabling

This is basically the wiring that connects the wiring closets to each other within a building via crossconnects (backbone distributors) and interconnects buildings via the main crossconnect (campus distributor). All of the horizontal cable specifications are available for backbone wiring, plus an additional fiber-optic specification:

8/125-μ optical fiber (ISO/IEC 11801 and ANSI/EIA/TIA 568A)

Note that the maximum distance for building backbone cabling (excluding patch chords) for all media types is 500 m (1,640 ft). The maximum patch chord length allowed is 20 m. The maximum distance for campus backbone cabling (excluding patch chords) for all media types is 1,500 m (4,921 ft). When added to the maximum building backbone length this gives a total backbone length of 2 km.

For further information on each of the recommended cabling systems (supported media, distance limitations, or mechanical features such as attenuation, capacitance, termination, and cabling practices) consult the country-relevant standards listed previously. Reference [1] also provides a good review of the LAN cabling plant and Structured Cabling Systems (SCS).

6.1.6   Centralized versus distributed cabling design

So far we have talked about the choice of cabling medium, but not about physical topology. Topology is partly controlled by the specific LAN protocol chosen, but nowadays almost all LAN protocols will happily run over a structured cabling system (the difference being in how the cables are terminated and patched into LAN equipment). Essentially there are two design philosophies to consider, as illustrated in Figure 6.2. They are described as follows:

- Centralized wiring topology—where all cabling inside buildings is wired back to a central communications room, usually in the basement or on the ground floor where external cabling also enters the building. On a campus environment all buildings may be star-wired back to a specific building, which acts as the focal point for all external wide area communications.

- Distributed wiring topology—where cabling and equipment inside buildings may be distributed so that floors run autonomously and are interlinked to other floors. In campus environments there may be a ring backbone between all buildings, with some or all buildings sharing responsibility for services and wide area connectivity.

There are advantages and disadvantages to each approach, and in reality most networks are hybrids of the two approaches. The centralized approach has the main advantage of being more manageable. Moves and changes can be handled in central locations; it is therefore generally easier to debug problems, and resources can be concentrated cost effectively. The disadvantages are that cabling can be more expensive (longer runs back to central locations), and functional working groups may need resources and services

Figure 6.2
Wiring topology approaches. (a) Centralized model, where hubs are star-wired back to concentrators both at the building and campus level. (b) Distributed model, where hubs are largely autonomous through the use of ring or shared bus topologies.

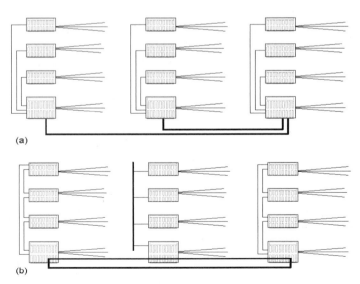

in close proximity, for either performance or pragmatic reasons (e.g., file and print servers). The distributed approach is typically less manageable, but the wiring costs are likely to be cheaper (shorter cable runs and fewer runs overall). This approach suits a more autonomous campus network. There may be a significant amount of duplication in resources such as servers and WAN links.

Figure 6.3 illustrates a hybrid cabling plan for a two-story building, which is part of a campus network. Since this building was built several years ago, there are some remaining legacy cables in place on the second floor, so the wiring infrastructure is in a state of transition. The first floor has been completely flood-wired with 100-ohm, four-pair UTP, apart from a small test lab area (room 124), which has a 50-ohm coax backbone. Multicore fiber-optic cable is run up the central riser to floor 2, where a mixture of new UTP wiring and legacy coax cabling is in place.

Figure 6.3
Part structured cabling in a two-story building complex. A range of copper and fiber-optic cabling is required, all terminated at patch panels (PP) in the main equipment rooms close to the building risers (e.g., W1, E1).

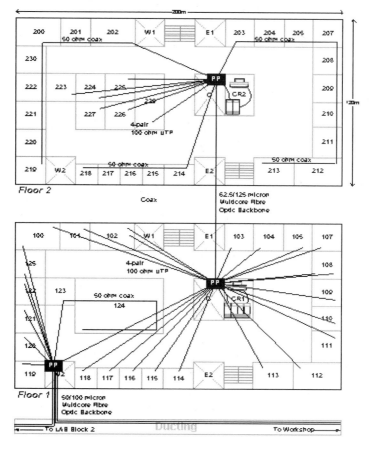

Most of the equipment (hosts and servers) is centralized in the main computer room (CR1) on the first floor. However, local print services are installed in computer room CR2 on the second floor for convenience. External multicore monomode fiber enters the building on the ground floor and comes up riser W2 to be terminated at a patch panel. Monomode is required because this building is part of a large industrial complex; the distances between adjacent buildings are several kilometers. Fiber is also preferable in these environments to avoid problems such as grounding issues and signal interference from heavy machinery.

6.2   Ethernet/IEEE 802.3

6.2.1   Background

Ethernet was developed by Xerox Corporation's Palo Alto Research Center (PARC) in the 1970s as the follow-up to some research done at the University of Hawaii. Ethernet was designed to fill the gap between long-distance, low-speed networks and specialized, computer room networks carrying high-speed data over very short distances. It became commercially available in 1975 as a 2.94-Mbps network able to connect up to 100 computers spread over a 1-km cable. Xerox Ethernet soon became popular, and work was done with the Intel Corporation and Digital Equipment Corporation to extend Ethernet's capability to 10 Mbps. This consortium jointly developed and released an Ethernet version 2.0 specification (often called DIX). They also published the architecture and presented it to the IEEE to have it accepted as an international standard. The IEEE ratified the Ethernet DIX V2 standards with some slight modifications as IEEE 802.3. The 802.3 standard has since been approved by a number of other organizations, including the American National Standards Institute (ANSI) and the International Organization for Standardization (ISO 8802-3). Today both Ethernet and 802.3 LANs are widely implemented across all areas of the marketplace. Although Ethernet and 802.3 are not identical, the term Ethernet is often used to refer to all Carrier Sense Multiple Access/Collision Detection (CSMA/CD) LANs that generally conform to Ethernet specifications, including IEEE 802.3. Although Ethernet can be run in baseband or broadband mode, we will only concern ourselves with baseband Ethernet, since broadband use is extremely limited. Ethernet is well suited to applications that generate bursty, occasionally heavy traffic at high peak data rates. Ethernet (802.3) is currently the most widely used LAN protocol in the world, and today 100-Mbps Ethernet is gaining in popularity.

6.2.2   Frame formats

The frame formats for Ethernet and IEEE 802.3 are not identical, although the difference is minor, restricted to the length/type field. However, since both protocols use the same medium and access method, LAN stations running these protocols could share a common bus, but they would not be able to communicate directly. Ethernet and IEEE 802.3 frame formats are shown in Figure 6.4. Note that the LSAP, DSAP, and CNTRL fields shown in Figure 6.4(b) are, strictly speaking, part of IEEE 802.2 Logical Link Control (LLC) specifications. These fields will not be present if IEEE 802.3 is used in raw mode (e.g., with early Novel NetWare implementations). It is also common to see SNAP encapsulation used together with IEEE 802.2 LLC.

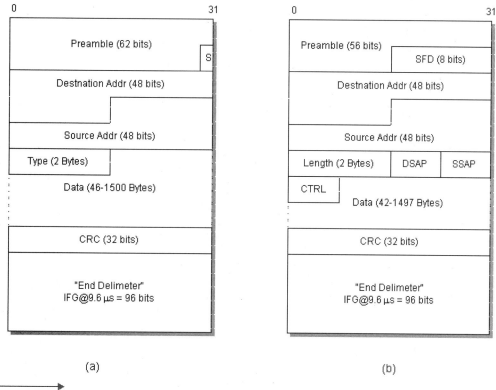

Figure 6.4   *Frame formats for (a) Ethernet and (b) IEEE 802.3.*

6.2.3 Operation

Both Ethernet and IEEE 802.3 LANs are broadcast networks. All nodes on
the network receive every frame and must examine each frame to see if the
frame is destined for them. The protocol used to access and control an
Ethernet bus is called Carrier Sense Multiple Access with Collision Detection (CSMA/CD). When a node wishes to transmit data on the CSMA/CD
bus, it first listens (senses) to see if the bus is available (i.e., no other node is
transmitting), and if so begins transmitting data immediately. If the bus is
not free, then the node will wait until all activity on the bus stops and a predetermined period of inactivity follows. If, during transmission, another
node transmits at the same time, then a collision occurs. In this event both
nodes will stop transmitting immediately and send a special jamming signal
to warn all other nodes about the collision. The transmitting nodes both
use a binary exponential backoff algorithm to determine how long to wait
before attempting to transmit again (in effect this causes each node to back
off for a random period of time). If a node's subsequent transmission
attempt causes another collision, then its wait time will be doubled, and so
on. This process can be repeated up to 16 times, at which point the transmission attempt is aborted and the frame is typically discarded. The driver
will report a transmission error to the higher-layer protocols (usually
reported as excessive deferrals).

Field definitions

- Preamble—56 bits (802.3) or 62 bits (Ethernet). Both Ethernet and
  IEEE 802.3 frames begin with an alternating pattern of 1s and 0s
  (i.e., 1010101010 . . .) called a preamble. The preamble tells receiving stations that a frame is coming and allows the Physical Layer Signaling (PLS) circuitry to synchronize with the receive frame timing
  circuitry.

- SFD (Start Frame Delimiter)—8 bits (802.3) or 2 bits (Ethernet)
  Indicates that the data portion of the frame will follow. In Ethernet
  this is more correctly called the SYNC (Synchronize) field. This field
  ends with two consecutive 1 bits (i.e., 10101011), which serve to synchronize the frame reception portions of all stations on the LAN.

- DA (Destination Address) and SA (Source Address)—48 bits (six
  bytes), Media Access Control (MAC) addresses. The least significant
  bit of the most significant byte of this field is called the I/G (Individ-
  ual/Group) bit. The type of address used is indicated by the state of
  this bit, as follows:

- Unicast: The DA contains the unique address of one node on the network. I/G bit is not set.
- Multicast: A group destination, where multiple devices will be listening on this address. I/G bit is set.
- Broadcast: When the DA field is set to all 1s (hence the I/G bit is also set), it indicates a broadcast. A broadcast is a special form of multicast. All nodes on the network must be capable of receiving a broadcast.

- TYPE (Type field, Ethernet) or LF (Length field, 802.3)—16-bit field, defined as follows:

  - The Type field (Ethernet) identifies the upper-layer protocol that is used. Vendors must register their protocols with the Ethernet standards body if they wish to use Ethernet version 2.0 transport. Each registered protocol is given a unique two-byte type identifier. Since this field is used as the length field by the 802.3 frames, the value assigned to the type field in Ethernet is always higher than the maximum value in the length field for the 802.3. This is to ensure that both protocols can coexist on the same network.
  - The Length field (802.3) indicates the number of data bytes (excluding the PAD) that are in the data field (preceding the Frame Check Sequence [FCS] field). In the case of IEEE 802.3, the upper-layer protocol must be defined within the data portion of the frame, via the SAP fields.

- DATA (Data field)—This contains the actual data being transmitted and is 46–1,500 bytes in length. Both IEEE 802.3 and Ethernet specify a minimum packet size (header plus data) of 64 bytes. Ethernet assumes that the upper layers will ensure that the minimum data field size (46 bytes) is met prior to passing data to the MAC layer. However, 802.3 permits the data field to be less than 46 bytes and requires the MAC layer to add pad characters to the LLC data field before transmission.

- FCS—A 32-bit field, containing a Cyclic Redundancy Check (CRC) value, calculated by the transmitting node and recalculated by the receiver to ensure that no damage has occurred during transit. The CRC algorithm is a polynomial executed on the DA, SA, length, information, and pad fields.

In order to detect collisions, a transmitting node must monitor the network for a safe period of time, termed the slot time, before attempting transmission. The slot time at 10 Mbps is specified as 51.2 ms (or 512 bit times). The slot time is the period during which a collision might occur and is the maximum delay allowed for a transmission to reach the furthest point of the network plus the time for a collision to propagate back. This time limit dictates a maximum length for the network plus a minimum frame size for transmission (64 bytes, excluding the preamble). The process of collision detection varies according to medium type, and the probability of a collision occurring is proportional to several factors, including the number of nodes, frequency of transmissions, frame size distribution, and length of the LAN. Since high numbers of collisions represent wasted bandwidth, clearly you should attempt to minimize them in your network design. If you have a very busy network, you can start by restricting node populations and using switches or bridges to extended LANs. You must ensure that individual segment lengths and total length of the LAN do not exceed specified limits, as defined by the 802.3 standards.

In Ethernet all nodes have equal access rights to the bus. Although inherently fair, this lack of priority control is seen as an increasing problem for some applications, especially when the network is heavily loaded. Since Ethernet is also broadcast based, potentially sensitive data are received by all attached stations, which could be seen as a security risk. Ethernet is a contention-based protocol and for relatively low traffic volumes and short messages Ethernet can produce very good response times and low latency. However, Ethernet is nondeterministic, and under heavy utilization the instability introduced by collision handling causes response times and performance to degrade, and services become unpredictable. These performance considerations make IEEE 802.3 10-Mbps shared-access LANs undesirable for backbone LANs or mission-critical applications, although, as we will see later, higher-speed, full-duplex options now exist.

Both Ethernet version 2 and IEEE 802.3 frame types can coexist on the same LAN simultaneously; however, nodes using one frame encapsulation cannot interoperate directly with nodes using the other frame encapsulation unless the node is configured to support both frame types. In general, Ethernet version 2 tends to be the encapsulation of choice for TCP/IP, while most other protocols tend to use IEEE 802.3 plus IEEE 802.2 encapsulation (with or without SNAP). Both Ethernet and IEEE 802.3 are usually implemented in hardware. For further details of Ethernet operations refer to reference [1].

Transceiver operation

Transceivers (strictly speaking Media Attachment Units [MAUs]) provide the mechanical, electrical, and functional interface between the DTE and the particular media used on the Ethernet (802.3) bus. Therefore, there is a different type of transceiver for each media type. Transceivers perform the following functions:

- Transmit and receive data—The transceiver will transmit data from the DTE onto the segment. It is also responsible for receiving data from the segment and passing it on to the DTE.

- Collision detection—It is the transceiver's responsibility to detect collisions and to inform the DTE of their occurrence. It does this by constantly monitoring the segment via a 10-MHz signal that is sent on the Control In (CI) pair of the AUI cable. The collision detection mechanism used by the transceiver varies according to the type of medium used. In a coax network (thick or thin), since all the DTEs are connected to the center conductor of the cable, the transceiver can detect two or more devices simultaneously transmitting on the network by just monitoring the voltage level on the center conductor. If the voltage seen is more than the allowed threshold (-1.6 V nominally), there is a collision on the network. In a 10BaseT network, there are two pairs of twisted copper between the DTE and the hub. One pair is for transmit and the other is for receive. During the normal transmission, the receive pair is idle. If the transceiver detects activity on the receive pair while it is transmitting, it will report a collision to the DTE.

- Jabber protection—Jabber occurs when a DTE transmits a frame greater than 1,518 bytes. This is typically caused by hardware failure or a software bug within the DTE. The transceiver must prevent DTE from effectively monopolizing the network by monitoring the time taken to transmit a frame. The 802.3 specification states that a transceiver must stop the DTE transmitting after 20–150 ms, and indicate a collision on the Control In (CI) pair of the AUI cable. The transceiver should remain in this state until the DTE stops transmitting data on the Data Out (DO) pair of the AUI cable.

- Link integrity—On a coaxial network, during a normal transmission, a transceiver will receive its own transmissions (since all the nodes are connected to the same central conductor on the cable). The transceiver will return this to the DTE on the Data In (DI) pair of the AUI cable. This signal will be used by the DTE as an indication of transmit-to-receive integrity. Networks such as 10BaseT and 10BaseF have a separate transmit and receive path and can therefore perform a more explicit link integrity check. 10BaseT transceivers transmit a sequence of idle (IDL) link pulse signals whenever there are no data to transmit. 10BaseFx transceivers use a defined light level to achieve the same result.

- SQE testing—Also known as heartbeat, the SQE test is a 10-MHz burst that is sent to the DTE by the transceiver after each frame is transmitted. The purpose is to inform the DTE that the transceiver is working properly. The SQE test signal is sent on the Control In (CI) pair of the AUI cable. Note that SQE is an Ethernet-specific feature, not supported by IEEE 802.3, and is normally enabled on transceivers when they ship. If repeaters must be attached to the network by transceivers, then SQE test must be disabled; otherwise, the repeater will eventually partition the offending port, believing that it is seeing excessive collisions (a repeater cannot discriminate between an SQE test and real collisions).

However, it is still necessary in these networks to ensure that a break in the transmit or receive path is detected. To do so, the MAU will start transmitting a link test pulse as soon as it has no data to transmit. If the MAU at the other end does not see either data packets or a link test pulse within a predefined time known as link loss time (50–150 ms for 10BaseT), the transceiver will enter the link test fail state. This will disable the transmit, receive, loopback, collision presence, and SQE test functions. During the link test fail, the transmission and reception of the link test pulses will continue. Receiving a minimum of two consecutive link test pulses or a single data packet will cause the transceiver to exit the link test fail state and reestablish the link.

Quality of service

Unlike protocols such as FDDI and Token Ring, Ethernet does not offer any useful priority facilities. Only the two levels of priority (high or low) can be recovered, based on the value of priority encoded in the Start Frame Delimiter (SD). To address this problem Ethernet may be used with an extended tag header format (defined by IEEE 802.1p and 802.Q).

6.2.4   Designing Ethernet networks

Over the last decade the media and physical topology over which Ethernet can be implemented has been enhanced significantly from the early simple thicknet bus. These enhancements (such as improved manageability, star-wiring over UTP, dedicated full-duplex paths per end system, and higher speeds) have taken some of the perceived benefits offered by competitive technologies such as Token Ring under the guise of Ethernet. Ethernet networks can now be designed using a variety of different media types and physical topologies. The most common specifications for Ethernet are as follows:

- 10Base2—which uses thin coaxial (thinnet or cheapernet) cable up to approximately 607 feet in length.

- 10Base5—which uses thick coaxial (thicknet) cable up to 1,640 feet in length.

- 10BaseT—which uses unshielded twisted-pair (UTP) cable up to 328 feet between a host and a hub.

- 10BaseFL—which uses either mono or multimode fiber-optic cable up to several kilometers in length (10BaseFL supersedes the older Fiber Optic Inter-Repeater Link (FOIRL) standards).

Coaxial cable acts as the bus to which the DTEs (nodes) are attached. With 10Base5 the transceiver is an external device, while 10Base2 relies on transceivers embedded in the host interface card. Coax-based networks do not require structured wiring, which makes them suitable for use in simple networks, small offices, or single-floor networks. Since coax-based networks are not centrally distributed, they can be difficult to manage and offer very little in the way of fault isolation—a single break in the cable will cause the whole network to fail and can be difficult to trace.

10BaseT offers full support for structured wiring. 10BaseT provides a point-to-point link between the DTE (node) and a central concentrator over twisted-pair wiring. The hub contains a Medium Access Unit (MAU) function on each of its ports. It also contains a repeater function, which allows these point-to-point segments to communicate with each other. The hubs can also be connected to extend the size of the network and the number of stations that can be attached to them. Since the network is centrally distributed, and each node attaches to a single port on the concentrator, a 10BaseT network provides much better management and fault isolation than coax-based networks. (See Table 6.3.)

There are several standards for fiber-optic media in an Ethernet environment, FOIRL perhaps being the most common. FOIRL offers fiber-optic media for point-to-point links and is generally used for backbone interconnections between concentrators. It can be used to provide a vertical building backbone, to interconnect buildings, or to link campus networks across long distances. In some cases fiber-optic cables can provide direct connections for hosts, via fiber-optic transceivers, although this is an expensive option and only typically justified for mission-critical services or environments where there is a serious electrical noise problem.

Table 6.3   *Coax and Twisted-Pair Ethernet Specifications*

	10Base5	10Base2	10BaseT
Data Rate	10Mbps	10Mbps	10Mbps
Max Segment Length	500m	185m	100 meters (point-to-point)
Transeiver Interval	2.5m	0.5m	-
Max Transeivers/Segment	100	30	2
Max Stations/Network	1024	1024	1024
Max Transceiver cable length	50m	50m	
Transeiver Cable	4-strand, twisted-pair conductors plus overall shield and insulating jacket	4-strand, twisted-pair conductors plus overall shield and insulating jacket.	
Ethernet Cable type	50 ohm PVC or teflon FEP coaxial	RG-58A/U, 50 ohm coaxial cable	2 unshielded twisted-pairs 0.4 mm AWG 26 0.5 mm AWG 24 (most common) 0.6 mm AWG 22 RJ-45
Connectors	N-series	BNC type	No external terminators required
Termination	50 ohm terminators (if not attached to repeaters)	50 ohm terminators (if not attached to repeaters)	
Impedance	50 ohms (+2)	50 ohms (+/- 2)	85 - 111 ohms (nominal 100)
Attenuation	8.5 dB for 500 meters at 10 MHz	8.5 dB for 185 meters at 10 MHz	8.5 - 10 dB for 100 m at 10 MHz
Max Propagation delay/segment	2165 nanoseconds	950 nanoseconds	1000 nanoseconds
DC Resistance	5 ohms per segment	10 ohms per segment	

Generic design rules

Before examining media-specific design details, generic design guidelines are as follows:

- The maximum number of stations allowed in a collision domain is 1,024. Beyond this you must use bridges, switches, or routers to extend the network. The collision domain is the maximum LAN radius allowed beyond which the time to transmit a minimum size frame is shorter than the time required to detect collisions.

- Repeaters can be attached at any position on the coax segments but should preferably be at the ends of a link segment. Each repeater takes one attachment position on the segment and should be counted toward the maximum number of stations allowed on that medium. With 10-Mbps Ethernet repeaters, port partitioning occurs on reception of 30 or more collisions.

- Some vendors offer extended distance working by boosting the transmission signal and increasing the reception sensitivity. While this may increase overall cable lengths by as much as 40 percent, there are no guarantees on signal quality, and performance is largely dependent on the quality of cable, connectors, and patching facilities used. In general you should avoid exceeding the standard specifications, since this could preclude you from upgrading the technology in the future without an expensive rewiring exercise.

- You can have many segments and repeaters within a single collision domain as long as no two DTEs in the same collision domain are separated by more than four repeaters (unless using FOIRL, where the limit is five).

- No two DTEs in the same collision domain can be separated by more than three coax segments. The other two segments in a maximum configuration must be link segments.

- Inter-Repeater Links (IRLs) are typically implemented with 10BaseT, 10BaseFL and 10BaseFB, depending upon the length required and environmental characteristics. Although not recommended, 10Base2 and 10Base5 segments can be used for this application so long as the round-trip delay is factored into calculations.

- 10Base5, 10Base2, 10BaseT, and fiber segments can be mixed in a single collision domain, allowing you to take advantage of the facilities offered by the most appropriate medium for different parts of your network.

10Base5

10Base5 (thick Ethernet or thicknet) specifies 10-Mbps operation over baseband Ethernet with a maximum segment length of 500 m (1,640 ft). The topology is bus based, extended via repeaters. 10Base5 uses a high-quality, 50-ohm RG8 (Belden 9880) coaxial cable, either 9.53 mm or 10.28 mm in diameter, which makes it difficult to install and handle. Special termination resistors must be used at both ends of the segment to prevent the signal from being reflected back, and the cable must be grounded at one point along its length. Cable segments may be joined via screw-fit N type barrel connectors. Because of the cable's size, weight, and inflexibility, it is recommended that segments be deployed in what are referred to as lambda lengths of 23.4 m (76.8 ft) or odd multiples of lambda lengths. This length is an approximation, derived from 10Base5's propagation velocity (0.77 c). A single wavelength, λ, at 10 MHz can be calculated as:

= (Speed of Light/Frequency) × Propagation Velocity

= 300,000,000/10,000,000 × 0.77 = 23.1 m

Installers generally try to minimize the number of join bends to avoid the possibility of reflections, which can affect network traffic and require skillful diagnosis. If the cable must be bent, then a minimum bend radius of 203 mm (8 in) is recommended. To reduce the likelihood of Electromagnetic Interference (EMI) it is also recommended that the cable not be

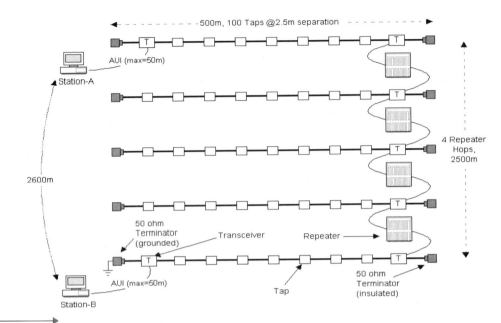

Figure 6.5   *10Base5 cabling system and topology.*

installed within 1 m of fluorescent lighting or power cables. Figure 6.5 and
Table 6.3 illustrate the basic design principles and physical characteristics.

The cable is typically coated in yellow PVC or orange Teflon and is
marked with black bands every 2.5 m (8.2 ft) to indicate points for transceiver attachment (these are guides only, and up to 100 taps can be installed
per 500-m segment). Hosts attach to transceivers via a 10-Mbps AUI cable
(as illustrated in Figure 6.5). The transceivers used with this type of installation come in two formats, as follows:

- Nonintrusive piercing tap connectors (sometimes called vampire taps
  or bee stings). These are the most common types of transceivers used
  on 10Base5 networks and they may be installed while the network is
  operational. The connection is made by piercing through the outer
  shield and dielectric of the cable (hence the term vampire) and inserting a tap screw. This is a skilled task, and if incorrectly done may
  adversely affect the whole segment until the fault is remedied.

- Intrusive N-type connectors. The connection made is effectively the
  same as a cable join via a barrel connector, and therefore requires the
  network to be broken prior to installation to enable N-type screw
  connectors to be fitted to the cable ends. Because of the work and
  downtime involved, these transceivers are less common than the vam-

pire tap; however, several manufacturers now offer segmented 10Base5 cables preterminated by N connectors, which may be joined together via N-type transceivers.

For most modern office environments the 10Base5 bus topology is impractical. The difficulties of manipulating a very thick inflexible bus cable, routing heavy AUI cables, attaching transceivers, and lack of cable management mean that thicknet installations simply cannot cope with the rate of change and general wear and tear that is expected on most LANs today. The use of multiport transceivers with a thinner and more flexible 5 m transceiver cable has made it somewhat easier to add and remove nodes without having to manipulate the thick coaxial cable. Today, 10Base5 is deployed only in situations where relatively few attachments are required and frequent change is unlikely.

10Base2

10Base2 (also referred to as thin Ethernet, thin-wire Ethernet, or cheaper-net) specifies 10-Mbps operation over baseband Ethernet with a maximum segment length of 185 m (607 ft) and up to 30 nodes per segment, with a separation distance of 0.5 m (19.7 in). The segment length is reduced due to a lower propagation velocity of 0.65 c. 10Base2 was introduced to address the problems associated with 10Base5. 10Base2 uses a cheaper, lower-grade 50-ohm RG58 coaxial cable, much thinner and considerably more flexible than 10Base5, with a minimum bend radius of 50.8 mm (2 in). As with 10Base5, terminators are used at both ends of a segment to prevent the signal from being reflected back. The topology is bus based, linked extended by repeaters. Figure 6.6 and Table 6.3 illustrate the basic design principles and physical characteristics. Note that many hubs feature an MDI/MDI-X configurable polarity port to avoid using crossover cables.

10Base2 segment comprises a number of thin coax cables connected via a number of T connectors, which makes it easy to install and allows the bus to be attached directly to a node interface card via simple BNC (Bayonet Neill Concelman) connectors on the T pieces. Since 10Base2 transceivers can be easily embedded into most NIC cards, this also avoids the use of AUI cable. Repeaters and/or bridges must be used to connect the segments. Because of its relative simplicity, 10Base2 is often used in preference to 10Base5 for floor distribution or for starter networks where flood-wiring UTP would be overkill. The ease of installation makes 10Base2 suitable for networks that are more dynamic in nature. Nowadays the low cost and wide availability of Ethernet UTP repeaters and switches are gradually phasing out the use of 10Base2.

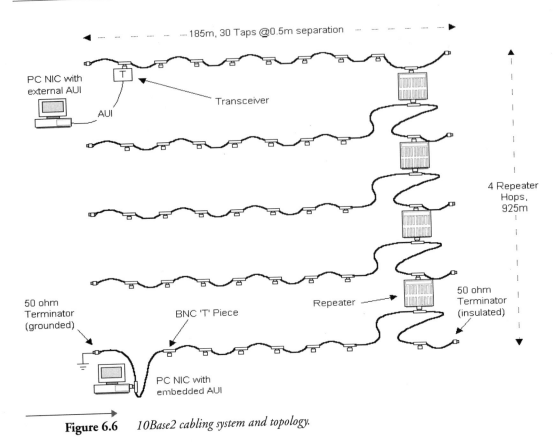

Figure 6.6   *10Base2 cabling system and topology.*

10Broad36

10Broad36 uses 75-ohm coaxial cable up to 75 km, similar to that used in Cable TV (CATV) and employs Frequency Division Multiplexing (FDM). Due to its rarity in modern networks we will discuss it no further. The interested reader is referred to reference [1].

10BaseT

10Base5 and 10Base2 do not scale or deploy well for large workstation populations such as those found in multistory buildings, and they do not offer a structured wiring capability. 10BaseT emerged in the 1980s to give Ethernet a low-cost, highly manageable, centrally distributed topology. The 10BaseT standard was defined by IEEE to address the requirement of running Ethernet over a structured cabling system using unshielded twisted-pair (UTP) copper (although shielded twisted pair [STP] may also be used). 10BaseT defines 10 Mbps transmission over two pairs of Cat-3 (or higher grade) 100-ohm twisted-pair UTP cable. By using Cat-5 cable a speed of

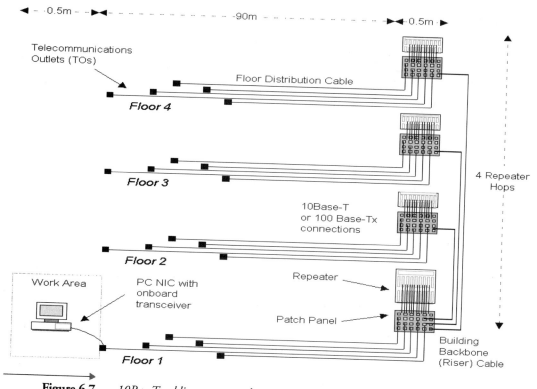

Figure 6.7   *10BaseT cabling system and topology.*

100 Mbps can be achieved (i.e., 100BaseTx). Note that higher-speed applications require the patch panel components and all connectors to be of high quality, and twisted-pair cabling must be used throughout (the use of flat silver satin cable for patch leads is precluded).

The topology comprises a star topology point-to-point network, extended by repeaters. In 10BaseT installations the cabling radiates out from a concentrator (hub) in a central wiring closet (floor distributor) to user access points (termination outlets) on the floor. The maximum distance for floor distribution wiring is 100 m (328 ft). Figure 6.7 and Table 6.3 illustrate the basic design principles and physical characteristics. Typically there is at least one wiring closet per floor, and the concentrators are linked together vertically up one or more risers to form a backbone (usually linked by fiber-optic cores, although it is possible to use point-to-point twisted-pair crossover cables between concentrator ports, subject to distance limitations and potential interference). The concentrator acts as a multiport repeater between all attached segments. Each segment is a point-to-point connection between a node (DTE) and a port on the concentrator. The

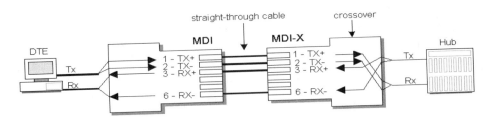

Figure 6.8   *10BaseT station (DTE) to hub (repeater) wiring connections.*

standard connector is the RJ45, which has eight contacts (although only four are used). The wiring for this connection is internally crossed inside the connector (referred to as MDI-X), which enables cheaper straight-through cables to be used, as illustrated in Figure 6.8.

802.3 over fiber-optic media

As outlined earlier, fiber-optic cable has many advantages for data networking, and there are a number of specifications for IEEE 802.3 operation over fiber media, including the following:

- FOIRL—Fiber-Optic Inter-Repeater Link (FOIRL) was the first standard to be defined for the use of fiber-optic cables in a 10-Mbps 802.3 LAN. It was intended as a repeater-to-repeater link only, providing a point-to-point long-distance connection of up to 1 km between two repeaters. FOIRL is similar to the 10BaseT standard in that it requires the use of a separate transmit and receive path and also requires the use of repeaters as the concentration point. An FOIRL MAU is also required to perform link integrity, by transmitting a 1-MHz link pulse signal when no data transmission is taking place. If the peer MAU fails to detect this signal, it enters link fail state and prevents the DTE from transmitting onto the network. Up to five repeaters are allowed in series.

- 10BaseFL—is the standardized version of FOIRL supporting up to 2 km of fiber at 10 Mbps. It is backward compatible with FOIRL (reducing the maximum distance to 2 km between stations). The use of FOIRL for desktop connectivity was excluded from the standard, but the 10BaseFL standard, which supersedes FOIRL, permits such connections. Up to five repeaters are allowed in series.

- 10BaseFP—is based on a passive star system, which links repeaters and stations together over a distance of 1 km. It is rarely used, being incompatible with other 10BaseF devices.

- 10BaseFB—is designed specifically for 10-Mbps backbone cabling applications; there is no support for desktop DTE connectivity. 10BaseFB is based on a superior technology using synchronous signaling techniques. A 2.5-MHz active idle signaling is used to indicate that the transmit path is idle. The transmit data from the repeater is synchronized to this idle signal, enabling the receiving MAU to remain locked to the active/idle packet data transition. 10BaseFB extends the allowable distance between two MAUs to 2 km. Up to 30 repeaters are allowed in series.

- 100BaseFx—is used for both repeater and desktop connectivity at 100 Mbps. It may be used in both shared and switched environments.

- 100BaseLx/100BaseSx—used for Gigabit Ethernet.

As with all other forms of Ethernet the maximum number of stations in a collision domain remains at 1,024. Several connectors are available for fiber-optic networks, including the Straight Tip (ST) connector, SubMiniature Assembly (SMA) connector, and the Subscriber Connector (SC). The ST connector is favored for many applications, while the SC connector is generally popular with 100BaseFx and Gigabit Ethernet vendors. Both the ST and SC connectors are generally accepted to be better optically and more reliable than the SMA connector. Fiber connectivity is always point to point, and since one fiber strand in a fiber pair is used for transmit and the other for receive, fiber pairs must be crossed between devices.

Attachment Unit Interface (AUI)

The connection between DTE and MAU (transceiver) is made by an Attachment Unit Interface (AUI) cable (commonly known as the transceiver cable).

AUI cables use individually screened AWG 22 wire for signal and power pairs. Since the 802.3 standard specifies that the DTE should have a female connector and MAU should have a male connector, the AUI cable requires opposite mating connectors to provide the connection between DTE and MAU. The connectors at the end of the AUI cable are 15-pin D-type connectors. The maximum allowed length for the AUI cable is 50 m. The AUI cables for Ethernet and 802.3 AUI attachments are not identical (see Figure 6.9). In IEEE 802.3 pin 1 is not used, and all shields of the signal and power pairs are connected to pin 4. The AUI cable shield is connected to the AUI connector shell to provide earthing. In Ethernet version 2, pin 4 is not used and all shields are connected to pin 1 and the AUI connector shell.

1	Shield Drain Wire
2	Collision +
3	Transmit +
5	Receive +
6	Power - [1]
9	Collision -
10	Transmit -
12	Receive -
13	Power +

(a)

2	Collision +
3	Transmit +
4	Shield Drain Wire
5	Receive +
6	Power - [1]
9	Collision -
10	Transmit -
12	Receive -
13	Power +

(b)

Figure 6.9   *AUI pinouts for (a) Ethernet version 2 and (b) IEEE 802.3.*

In Ethernet version 1 the point-to-point wiring is the same as for version 2, but the electrical requirements of the cable differ. Shielding of individual signal or power pairs is not required. The overall AUI cable shield provides both shielding and signal ground. It is connected to pin 1 and the AUI connector shell. AWG 22 is used for signal pairs and AWG 20 for the power pair. Most Ethernet equipment uses the version 2 cable due to its superior construction.

Key product manufacturers

The major vendors of Ethernet-based equipment include Cabletron, 3Com, Cisco, and Nortel/BAY. Many of the products used to build Ethernet are now commodity items and can be bought at computer stores or via mail-order equipment catalogs.

6.2.5   Performance considerations

The theoretical maximum frame rate for 64-byte frames is 14,880 fps (this figure is based on overheads imposed by the 64-bit preamble and the inter-frame gap of 9.6 ms). We have already seen that Ethernet begins to show performance degradation as load increases due to the increased probability of collisions. There are various myths about what level of load causes saturation, and the figure 37 percent is often stated as the saturation point. This is a widespread misconception, due largely to misinterpretation of well-intentioned theoretical studies of CSMA/CD and token-passing protocols performed by the IEEE. In reality Ethernet is capable of sustaining very high loads, and this varies according to how the network is being utilized. Aside from the fixed parameters of Ethernet, such as bit rate, slot time, and so on, variable factors that affect performance include the following:

- Packet length distribution—In many networks packet distribution is strongly bimodal (mainly short and long packets). Most theoretical studies use a Poisson distribution, which is unrealistic.

- Number of hosts in a collision domain—Obviously the fewer devices in a collision domain the less probability of collisions and the better probability of medium acquisition.

- Arrival rate of frames—Very few devices can currently transmit every 51.2 ms as allowed. Most devices can only send a few hundred frames per second. As described previously, the 9.6-ms interframe gap (IFG) must also be taken into account.

- Average length of cable—Often cable length can be far shorter than the maximum allowed. Collisions are therefore detected much sooner and performance is improved.

- Distance between nodes

- Average medium acquisition time

Boggs [6] documents experimental work on Ethernet and demonstrates scenarios where Ethernet is capable of handling over 90 percent load efficiently. For optimum performance, be aware of the following:

- Do not install long cables, since the time to detect collisions increases with cable length.

- Do not attach too many nodes to a segment.

- Configure the largest possible packet size, if possible. Large packets reduce the chances of a collision, since collisions can occur only during a fixed time window at the beginning of a packet.

- Try not to mix real-time and heavy bulk data traffic in the same collision domain.

Ethernet is most suited to bursty applications over relatively short distances (up to approximately 2 km). For large LANs with many hosts running highly parallel-distributed real-time applications, either a ring network technology or a higher-capacity switched Ethernet technology is better suited.

6.3   High-speed Ethernet and hybrid standards

There have been a number of high-speed Ethernet initiatives over recent years, designed to take Ethernet well beyond 10 Mbps while maintaining low-cost migration paths for existing Ethernet users. Most of these standards are aimed purely at the Ethernet installed base, although 100BaseVG-AnyLAN presents a possible migration path for both Ethernet and Token Ring users.

6.3.1   IEEE 802.3u Ethernet (100BaseX)

IEEE 802.3u covers three 100-Mbps systems, collectively known as 100BaseX (sometimes referred to as Fast Ethernet), which include 100BaseTx, 100BaseFx, and 100BaseT4. Their characteristics are as follows:

- 100BaseTx uses two pairs of Cat-5 balanced UTP copper cable, or 150-ohm balanced STP copper cable, and is based on the ANSI X3.263 standard (i.e., FDDI's TP-PMD). The standard connector for operation over UTP is the RJ45 (ISO 8877), using the same pin assignments as for other IEEE 802.3 implementations.

- 100BaseFx uses two multimode fiber strands, usually 62.5/125 μm, and is based on the ISO 9314-3 standard. In all cases the cable strands must be crossed. Standard connectors include the low-cost fiber-optical interface connector (or duplex Subscriber Connector [SC]), the Media Interface Connector—MIC (or Fixed Shroud Duplex [FSD]), and the medium connector plug and socket (the Straight Tip [ST] connector).

- 100BaseT4 uses four pairs of Cat-3, 4, or 5 balanced UTP copper cable.

100BaseX also introduced a feature referred to as autonegotiation. This enables a DTE and repeater (or switch) to negotiate various operational parameters on a link basis, saving on administration effort and providing a mechanism for backward compatibility. 100BaseX relies on a Reconciliation Sublayer (RS) and Media Independent Interface (MII) to facilitate negotiation over various media types and enable mixed-speed interworking (i.e., permutations of 10 Mbps, 100 Mbps, full-duplex, or half-duplex mode) [1]. Unlike other CSMA/CD standards, neither Jabber protection nor SQE testing is implemented with 100BaseX, since the design of 100BaseX renders them unnecessary.

100BaseX defines two classes of repeaters: Class I and Class II. Class I repeaters are designed to connect dissimilar signaling systems, and therefore the internal delays imposed by theses devices are much higher than Class II devices. Hence only one Class I repeater can be deployed within a collision domain between DTEs over a maximum length segment. Since Class II repeaters generally support a single signaling system, up to two Class II repeaters can be deployed within a collision domain between DTEs over a maximum-length segment. In both cases multiple repeaters can be deployed if the segment length is reduced [1]. Unlike 10-Mbps Ethernet, with 100BaseX repeater, port partitioning occurs on reception of 60 or more collisions. At the time of writing, 3Com, Cabletron and Synoptics have selected IEEE 802.3u as their standard for fast Ethernet.

6.3.2   100BaseT2 Ethernet (IEEE 802.3y)

100BaseT2/IEEE 802.3y supports 100-Mbps CSMA.CD over Cat-3 (or better) twisted pair, to a distance of up to 100 m. Support is also provided for 100BaseT MII (Medium Independent Interface) via autonegotiation, where a master-slave relationship is instigated. During repeater to DTE autonegotiation the repeater normally assumes the role of master, although this is configurable and negotiable. 100BaseT2 can run in half- or full-duplex mode and supports a maximum collision diameter of 200 m (i.e., using two repeaters). The standard connector with 100BaseT2 is the RJ45 (ISO 8877), using two-pair wiring.

6.3.3   Gigabit Ethernet (IEEE 802.3z)

Gigabit Ethernet, also referred to as 1,000BaseX, provides 1 Gbps (i.e., 1,000 Mbps) of bandwidth and is the fastest mode of Ethernet available at present. Gigabit Ethernet was formally ratified by the IEEE 802.3z Working Group as a standard in 1998 and has already gained wide industry support, with well over 100 companies joining the Gigabit Ethernet Alliance (GEA), an industry consortium founded to promote the standard and coordinate interoperability testing. One of the main attractions of Gigabit Ethernet is that it builds on a hugely successful install base of 10/100-Mbps Ethernet (described earlier in this chapter). Gigabit Ethernet retains many of the positive attributes of Ethernet, such as Ethernet's simplicity, manageability, and price-performance ratio. Network planners, managers, and support personnel are already familiar with Ethernet, and the adoption process for Gigabit Ethernet is therefore potentially shorter and far easier than that of other complementary technologies. The main barriers to adoption to date have been standardization and interoperability. For more information on Gigabit Ethernet see the Gigabit Ethernet Alliance (GEA) Web pages [7, 8].

Frame formats

Gigabit Ethernet uses the same packet format and frame sizes as standard IEEE 802.3. This means that migration from existing 10/100 Ethernet environments is straightforward; there is no need for fragmentation/reassembly or protocol conversion. Because of the high bit rate, two modifications to the access protocol—carrier extension and packet bursting—require small changes to access protocol, which affect the way frames are placed on the wire. The implications of these features are described in the next section.

Operation

Gigabit Ethernet operates in the same way as current Ethernet technology. Gigabit Ethernet embodies a new Media Access Control (MAC) and Physical (PHY) Layer technology. As with 100BaseX, Gigabit Ethernet relies on a Reconciliation Sublayer (RS) and a modified Media Independent Interface (MII) called the Gigabit Media Independent Interface (GMII) to facilitate negotiation and interworking over various media types and different speeds [1]. 1,000BaseT facilitates autonegotiation between 100 and 1,000 Mbps, enabling organizations to easily migrate from Fast Ethernet to Gigabit Ethernet in incremental steps. Standard Ethernet flow control is implemented with a modified Xon/Xoff protocol, specified by the IEEE 802.3x standards; however, this addresses flow control only at the port level. In order to expedite the standards process, the 802.3z Task Force used a modified version of the physical layer signaling protocol used by the ANSI Fibre Channel standard, since Fibre Channel was a proven technology that already operated at gigabit speeds (and also offered off-the-shelf, cost-effective, fiber-optic components from many suppliers). Another advantage is that Fibre Channel also supported short haul (25-m) connections over balanced, shielded copper cable (twinax or quad), used primarily in wiring closets for short jumper connections.

Gigabit Ethernet supports both half-duplex and full-duplex modes. However, there is a problem specific to half-duplex mode that requires enhancements to the media access protocol. Because of the increased bit rate of Gigabit Ethernet, and its shorter slot time (0.512 µs), the network diameter would be significantly reduced to enable collision detection to work (remember that a CSMA/CD station must still be transmitting when a collision is detected). At such high speeds a minimum-sized (64-byte) Ethernet frame would complete transmission before the transmitting station has the opportunity to detect a collision.

To resolve this timing problem CSMA/CD has been enhanced to maintain the 200-m collision diameter by extending the slot time from 64 bytes to 512 bytes. This requires that small frames be padded up to 512 bytes (4,096 bits), using a technique referred to as carrier extension. Padding is achieved with nondata symbols called extension bits. Frames larger than 512 bytes are left unmodified.

To avoid performance overheads with applications using small packets the CSMA/CD algorithm has been further modified to incorporate a feature called packet bursting, which allows switches and servers to send short bursts of small packets without relinquishing control of the media. In effect a station transmits the first frame, pads if necessary, fills the interframe gap with extension bits, and then transmits additional frames and continues to fill the interframe gaps until the burst limit is reached (65,536 bits). Note that only the first frame within a burst, if less than 512 bytes, requires extension, and the total burst frame size must not exceed the standard 1,518 bytes.

Clearly, in both cases the receiving station is required to strip off extension bits to reveal the original frame structure before passing to higher protocol layers. In full-duplex mode small frames are not subject to carrier extension, since there is no need for collision detection. The standard 96-bit InterFrame Gap (IFG) and 64-byte minimum frame size are supported. In practice most network implementations are expected to be full duplex.

Designing gigabit Ethernet networks

Gigabit Ethernet provides a means of upgrading or interconnecting legacy Ethernet networks where bandwidth is becoming saturated and response times are increasing. Alternative options such as ATM are considered by many to be either overcomplicated, expensive, or inflexible (ATM also introduces inefficiency by requiring fragmentation and reassembly unless it is used end to end). As prices continue to erode, Gigabit Ethernet may ultimately be rolled out to the desktop. Until such time the first wave of applications for Gigabit Ethernet include the following:

- High bandwidth aggregation of multiple Fast Ethernet segments

- Fast interfaces for high-speed server attachment

- Switched intrabuilding backbones, interswitch links, and high-speed workgroup networks

Gigabit Ethernet delivers very high bandwidth to aggregate multiple Fast Ethernet segments and to support high-speed server connections, switched intrabuilding backbones, interswitch links, and high-speed workgroup networks. Gigabit Ethernet is, therefore, currently best suited for data applications in enterprise environments. Although the bit rate of Gigabit Ethernet is clearly much faster than 100 Mbps Ethernet, cable delay budgets are similar. The primary topology choices for Gigabit Ethernet are as follows:

- 1,000BaseLX: Long-wavelength (1,300-nm) Multimode Fiber-Optic (MMF) link of maximum length 550 m (50/125 µm) or 550 m (62.5/125 µm). Also Single-Mode Fiber-Optic (SMF) link of maximum length 5,000 m (10/125 µm). 1,000BaseLX is known colloquially as long-haul fiber.

- 1,000BaseSX: Short-wavelength (850-nm) Multimode Fiber-Optic (MMF) link of maximum length 550 m (50/125 µm) or 275 m (62.5/125 µm). 1,000BaseSX is known colloquially as short-haul fiber.

- 1,000BaseCX: 150-ohm balanced shielded twisted-pair copper link (as specified by TIA 568A) of maximum length 25 m. 1,000BaseCX is known colloquially as short-haul copper.

- 1,000BaseT: Unshielded twisted-pair (four-pair Cat-5) copper link of maximum length 100 m.

1,000BaseSX is designed for low-cost, multimode fiber runs for horizontal or short intrabackbone (multistory riser) applications. 1,000BaseLX is designed for longer multimode intrabuilding backbones or monomode campus interbuilding backbones up to 3 km. Some vendors are already announcing their ability to run Gigabit Ethernet over distances of 100km or more (although this depends largely on the quality of the fiber, transmitter and receiver, and installation). With both 1,000BaseSX and 1,000BaseLX the standard connector used is the duplex SC connector.

1,000BaseCX is designed for short-haul, high-speed interconnection of equipment clusters and uses ANSI X3.230-1994 Fibre Channel–based 8B/10B encoding at the serial line rate of 1.25 Gbps. IBM Type 1 cable (ISO/IEC 11801:1995), also known as STP, is not recommended for 1,000BaseCX. Cables must be continuous (no joints or splices), and the standard MDI connector used is either the nine-pin D Subminiature connector or the eight-pin shielded ANSI Fibre Channel Style-2 connector. Use of this medium is also restricted to appliances with a common electrical ground. Since this conceivably limits its use to jumper connections between one or two equipment racks sharing common power, this raises questions about its applicability, since it would be easier to use a fiber jumper.

1,000BaseT is designed for structured horizontal cabling (i.e., floor distribution to the desktop) and will take advantage of legacy Cat-5 cabling infrastructures (although existing installations will either need to be recertified or must have passed a TSB-67 Level II scanner test). At present this solution is too expensive to deploy for most enterprises, and for many desktop applications 100 Mbps is currently ample, though this situation is bound to change with time and prices will eventually be eroded. Note that the 1,000BaseT standard is covered under IEEE 802.3ab.

The network topology for Gigabit Ethernet follows the traditional rules of Ethernet. However, only one 1,000BaseX repeater is allowed within a single collision domain. Domains may be linked in the conventional manner (i.e., via switches, bridges, and routers). With 1,000BaseX repeaters, as with 100BaseX, port partitioning occurs on reception of 60 or more collisions. The maximum round-trip delays for 1,000BaseT (100 m), 1,000Base-CX (25 m), and 1,000Base-SX/LX (316 m) are 1,112, 253, and 3,192 bit times, respectively.

Key product manufacturers

Gigabit Ethernet is applicable for all current Ethernet products (transceivers, switches, NICs, router/bridge/firewall interfaces) together with a new class of device called the buffered distributor. The buffered distributor is a full-duplex, multiport hub that interconnects multiple 802.3 links at 1 Gbps or faster. It operates similar to a conventional Ethernet repeater by providing a shared traffic domain (forwarding frames to all ports other than the source port) and does not filter on MAC addresses. However, it is allowed to buffer incoming frames before forwarding them and uses 802.x flow control to manage internal buffer congestion (hence it is a hybrid device, somewhere between a bridge and a repeater). The major vendors of Gigabit Ethernet–based equipment include Cabletron, 3Com, Cisco, and Nortel/BAY.

Performance considerations

Theoretical simulations performed by Intel indicate that Gigabit Ethernet exceeds the performance of Fast Ethernet by an order of magnitude as frame size increases. With packet bursting Gigabit Ethernet achieves greater efficiency with small frames (see Figure 6.10). AMD has performed experiments that demonstrate that in half-duplex mode (with collisions) a Gigabit Ethernet network will achieve throughput of over 720 Mbps with 100 per-

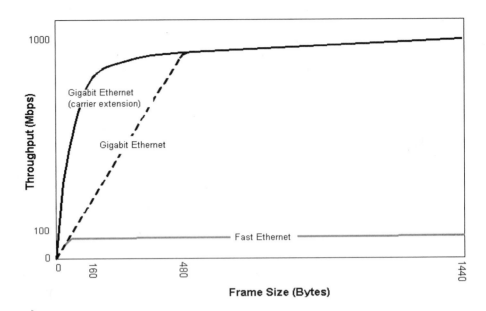

Figure 6.10   *Throughput for Gigabit Ethernet and Fast Ethernet as frame size increases. (Source: Intel)*

cent offered load. With full duplex (i.e., no collision) implementations this figure will be easily exceeded and should approach the 2 Gbps ceiling.

Gigabit Ethernet is optimized for high-speed raw data throughput; it has no inherent support for application, such as real-time voice or video traffic. It cannot prioritize traffic to deliver Class of Service (CoS) nor can it deliver specific bit rates or constrain jitter to deliver Quality of Service (QoS). CoS and QoS are to be supported through complementary technologies, such as IEEE 802.1p, 802.1Q, and the Resource Reservation Protocol (RSVP).

6.3.4   100VG-AnyLAN (IEEE 802.12)

100VG-AnyLAN is a relatively recent technology for transmitting either Ethernet or Token Ring frames at 100 Mbps [9]. 100BaseVG offers the ability to bridge to either 10 Mbps to standard Ethernet environments or 16 Mbps to standard Token Ring environments. 100VG-AnyLAN combines increased transmission speeds with a simple yet efficient media access control that operates over Cat-3, 4, or 5 unshielded twisted pair (UTP), shielded twisted pair (STP), and optical fiber. By supporting all of the network design rules and topologies of 10BaseT, as well as Token Ring, 100VG-AnyLAN allows organizations to leverage their existing network and cable infrastructure. In addition, 100VG-AnyLAN can provide guaranteed bandwidth for emerging time-sensitive applications such as multimedia. Relatively low costs, support for multimedia, and a straightforward migration path for existing 10BaseT and Token Ring networks make 100VG-AnyLAN an attractive alternative for upgrading both Ethernet 10BaseT and Token Ring users to 100-Mbps speeds. Although perhaps technically superior (no other 100-Mbps standard offers this level of flexibility), deployment of 100VG-AnyLAN lags behind that of 100BaseTx and 100BaseFx.

100VG-AnyLAN was ratified in 1995; however, the controlling committee for 100VG-AnyLAN was changed from 802.3 to 802.12 because it is technologically quite different from traditional 802.3 networking. 100BaseVG can carry Ethernet or Token Ring frames; however, the reality is that most existing 10BaseX users will migrate to 100BaseX and 1,000BaseX standards rather than 100VG-AnyLAN (even though 100VG-AnyLAN is technically superior in many respects). The main champion of 100VG-AnyLAN is Hewlett-Packard, together with a consortium of members including IBM.

Operation

The MAC protocol used with 100VG-AnyLAN is called demand priority protocol. Demand priority protocol enables data transfers with very low latency across a hub and supports two service priority levels: normal priority and high priority. Normal priority is used for general data, and high priority is used for time-sensitive data. This scheme enables quality-of-service mapping. A data transfer rate of 100 Mbps can be achieved over standard UTP copper wires without compromising on distance. 100VG-AnyLAN is a dedicated media; shared bandwidth network and all devices attached to the network share the 100-Mbps bandwidth.

Unlike traditional 802.3 repeaters, 100VG-AnyLAN hubs are intelligent network controllers. 100VG-AnyLAN hubs monitor link and end-node availability and also perform security functions (in 100VG-AnyLAN hubs, frames are not repeated to all ports as in traditional Ethernet/802.3 repeaters). Network access is managed by hubs using a simple round-robin algorithm. Media access in 802.12 LANs is, therefore, deterministic. Quartet coding is used in the transmission of 100VG-AnyLAN by segmenting transmissions into quartets, and then sending them concurrently across four pairs of copper wires. The hub performs arbitration by polling ports in turn to see if attached end nodes have data for transmission (end nodes signal the hub with either a request-high, request-normal, or up-idle). An end node is allowed to transmit only one frame during a scan; ports attached to other repeaters (described shortly) are allowed to send multiple packets during a scan. The priority setting determines the order in which port scanning takes place (i.e., priority requests are stacked at the head of the round-robin queue).

When the hub is ready to allow an end node to send data, it sends a grant signal to the attached end node and then issues an incoming signal to all other ports, informing all other attached devices to prepare for data reception. These devices then cease any pending requests until transmission is complete. On receiving a frame, the destination address is parsed, and once the hub has decided where the destination port is, it forwards a frame and at the same time issues an idle-down signal to all other ports. Once transmission is complete, an idle-up signal is sent to all ports. Hub ports can be either in normal or promiscuous mode. In normal mode, only frames addressed to the attached end node are forwarded. In promiscuous mode all frames are forwarded down the link. Note that data transmission always operates in half-duplex mode; signaling and control operate in full-duplex mode.

Since neither Ethernet nor Token Ring Media Access Control (MAC) is used to transmit a frame, this allows either frame type to go through a single switch. The only restriction is that all repeaters on the same segment must be configured to use the same format. The use of Ethernet or Token Ring frame formatting enables traffic to be transparent to applications running on today's Ethernet or Token Ring LANs. Note that this additional flexibility means that switches and bridges tend to be more complex, especially those that deal with native 802.3 and Token Ring networks as well as demand priority networks.

Designing networks with 100VG-AnyLAN

The topology for 100VG-AnyLAN is a hierarchical star (actually a star-wired ring). Simple topologies can be created from a single hub (i.e., a repeater) and a number of attached end nodes (e.g., workstation, switch, bridge, and routers). This topology can be enhanced by cascading hubs via special uplink ports to form a hierarchy, with a Level 1 root hub at the top and its subordinates (Level 2 hub and so on) to an arbitrary depth. In practice the tree depth is limited to five levels, due to timing constraints. Beyond this level the network may be extended via traditional switches, bridges, or routers.

100VG-AnyLAN requires new workstation adapter cards and concentrators to implement this technology, as well as support for various cable types, and drive distances vary between vendors. IEEE 802.12 specifies several media types (note that use of flat cable is precluded anywhere in the design), as follows:

- Four-pair Cat-3 and Cat-4 UTP up to 100 m. Note that Cat-3 support requires four cable pairs for each host. The standard connector for UTP connections is the eight-pin IEC 603-7 RJ45 modular plug.

- Four-pair Cat-5 UTP up to 200 m

- Two-pair STP up to 100 m

- Single and multimode fiber-optic cable up to 2,000 m

As with most traditional Ethernet/802.3 standards, the maximum number of nodes per segment is 1,024. Loops are not allowed unless bridges, switches, or routers are deployed to control them. The IEEE 802.12 Committee is considering several enhancements to the standard, including support for redundant link operations.

6.4   Token Ring/IEEE 802.5

6.4.1   Background

IBM developed the Token Ring protocol in the late 1960s, and the first networking products appeared in 1984. Token Ring networks operate at 1, 4, or 16 Mbps, depending on the actual implementation. Differential Manchester code is used to convert binary data into signal elements. Hosts must have their NIC cards configured for the appropriate speeds in order to communicate. The protocol is defined in the ISO 8802.5/IEEE 802.5 standard. The standard does not specify the type of cabling to be used. IBM recommends shielded twisted-pair (STP) cabling, although unshielded twisted pair (UTP) and optical fiber may be used, depending upon the performance, price, and environmental conditions. The token-passing protocol is deterministic and has been shown to be efficient under both light- and heavy-traffic conditions. It guarantees fair access to all attached stations and also supports traffic prioritization (with eight priority levels), based on priority reservations made in a passing token or frame. A major benefit of the token-passing protocol is its deterministic ability to deal with increased traffic loads and peaks. This makes it suitable for mission-critical applications and large, heavily loaded LANs. It may also be used for small to medium backbone networks at 16 Mbps, although FDDI and ATM are more common and Gigabit Ethernet is the next likely contender.

6.4.2   Frame formats

Token Ring networks specify two frame types: tokens and data/command frames. Both formats are illustrated in Figure 6.11.

Field definitions

- SD—The start delimiter is used for both tokens and normal frames and informs the receiving node of the arrival of a following frame or token.

- AC—The access control byte contains the priority and reservation fields, as well as a token bit (used to differentiate a token from a data/command frame) and a monitor bit (used by the Active Monitor [AM] to determine whether a frame is circling the ring endlessly).

- FC—The frame control byte indicates whether the frame contains data or control information. In control frames, this byte specifies the type of control information.

- DA (Destination Address) and SA (Source Address)—48-bit (six bytes), Media Access Control (MAC) addresses. The least significant bit of the most significant byte of this field is called the I/G (Individual/Group) bit. The type of address used is indicated by the state of this bit, as follows:

  - Unicast: The DA contains the unique address of one node on the network. I/G bit is not set.
  - Multicast: A group destination, where multiple devices will be listening on this address. I/G bit is set.

Figure 6.11
Token Ring frame formats. (a) A data/command frame. (b) A token.

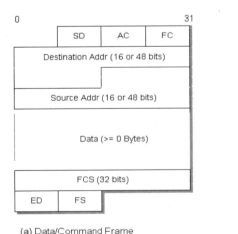

(a) Data/Command Frame   (b) Token

- Broadcast: When the DA field is set to all 1s (hence the I/G bit is also set), it indicates a broadcast. A broadcast is a special form of multicast. All nodes on the network must be capable of receiving a broadcast.

- DATA—The actual data being transmitted. The length of this field is limited by the ring token holding time, which defines the maximum time a ring node may hold the token.

- FCS, 32 bits, containing a Cyclic Redundancy Check (CRC) value, calculated by the transmitting node and recalculated by each receiving node to ensure that no damage has occurred in transit.

- ED—the end delimiter signals the end of the token or data/command frame. It also contains bits to indicate a damaged frame (the E bit). The ED field also contains an I bit to indicate intermediate frames in a multiframe sequence.

- FS—the frame status field contains the address recognized (A) and frame copied (C) bit flags. Since the A and C bits are not covered by the FCS, they are duplicated in this field as a redundancy check.

Tokens are three bytes (24 bits) in length and comprise a start delimiter, an access control field, and an end delimiter. The maximum frame size is 4,000 bytes at 4 Mbps and 17,800 bytes at 16 Mbps. The IEEE allows vendors to implement either 16-bit or 48-bit MAC addresses. The address field formats are shown in Figure 6.12.

Field definitions

- I/G—Individual or group address indicator. Used to differentiate between unicast MAC addresses and broadcast/multicasts.

  - 0—Individual address
  - 1—Group address

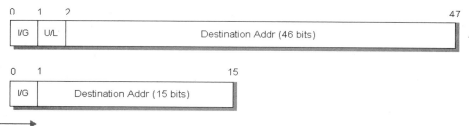

Figure 6.12   *Token Ring MAC address formats.*

- U/L—Universal or locally administered address

  - 0—Universal administered address
  - 1—Locally administered address

Two special destination address values have been defined. The value 0xffffffffffff is used for an all-stations broadcast group address and means that all ring stations are effectively destination nodes. The value 0x000000000000 means that the destination MAC address is not addressed to any ring node; it can be sent but not received.

6.4.3 Operation

In a Token Ring network nodes are physically connected to a wiring concentrator, usually in a star-wired ring topology, although logically the topology is a ring. Each station has driver/transmitter as well as receiver circuitry, and the transmission technique used is baseband. Contrary to the Ethernet, Token Ring transmits high-order bytes/bits first (i.e., byte 0 is transmitted before byte 1 and high-order bit 0 within a byte is transmitted first). You need to be aware of this when evaluating protocol traces from different LAN media because of the potential need to reorder bits. This translation requirement is also a feature that can significantly affect performance on bridge router products, as described later.

Before a station can communicate, it must be physically connected onto the ring via a Multistation Access Unit (MAU, or MSAU) and powered up. It will then go through a process called ring insertion, whereby the MAU tests and reconfigures its internal connections to the node, and the node performs a series of initialization checks and learns its Nearest Active Upstream Neighbor (NAUN) and advertises its own address to its nearest active downstream neighbor. Token Ring MAUs may be either active (i.e., have their own power supply) or passive (i.e., unpowered). Both types of MAU include Trunk Coupling Units (TCUs), which facilitate port interfacing for lobe (station) connections. Each TCU includes a bypass relay, which automatically closes if a station is either not inserted or not an active member of the ring. Relays are opened using DC current (termed phantom current, a maximum of 20 mA) emitted by the end station along the lobe cable when the station is activated. Phantom current is also useful for monitoring link integrity.

Frame transmission

In order to transmit data on the ring, a node must capture a special 24-bit sequence called a token that circulates the ring. Only one token may exist on a ring segment at any given time, and on a small ring with few nodes only a few bits of the token may be actually on the ring at a given point in time (i.e., the total transmission path may be shorter than 24 bit times). When a node captures the token and is ready to transmit, it must set the token bit in the Access Control (AC) field to signify that data are being transmitted. It also appends the destination and source MAC addresses, user data, a new Frame Check sequence (FCS), and the end delimiter and frame status fields.

Frames transmitted onto the ring are passed from one station to the next active downstream neighbor (termed normal repeat mode). A ring node in normal repeat mode will typically run a CRC check, and, if appropriate, set the error detected (E bit) flag. If the frame is destined for the receiving node, it will copy the frame as it passes it on and will mark the frame as copied by setting the address recognized (A bit) and frame copied (C bit) flags in the frame trailer FS field. Note that bridges vary in the way they use the AC bits. When the frame reaches the originating node, it checks the A and C bits and will remove the frame from the ring. As soon as the originating station receives the frame header, it must issue a new token so that other nodes can transmit. The priority reservation bits in the access control field of the received frame, together with stored priority levels in the originating station, determine the priority of the new token.

The protocol is called a single-token protocol, since only one token can circulate on the ring at any time, and a delay equivalent to the time it takes for a token to circulate the ring is required to ensure that no overrun occurs, which would result in a station receiving a token that it is transmitting and thinking that a second token exists on the ring. For a 24-bit token this means a minimum 24-bit delay. In addition to this delay an additional elastic buffer is introduced to support the token protocols and speed. In order to establish communication between any two-ring stations, addressing mechanisms are needed. At the same time the integrity of the transmitted frames between ring stations must be preserved. Therefore, data-checking capabilities are required at the medium access control level of a ring station.

Ring management and control

At any point in time one station per segment operates as the Active Monitor (AM). All other nodes on the ring that are not performing the active monitor function act as standby monitors. The AM provides overall clock synchronization and control. The AM creates a new token when a ring is started, detects and recovers lost tokens or frames, and supports ring purging and initiation of the neighbor notification process. Each time a token or frame is repeated, a standby monitor restarts its good-token timer to verify the presence of an active monitor. A second timer, the receive-notification timer, is restarted by a standby monitor every time it copies an active monitor present frame. If either of these two timers expires, the standby monitor station will initiate the token-claiming process. This process, also called the monitor-contention process, is the procedure by which ring nodes elect a new AM.

The AM also maintains two buffers to control frame and token timing: the fixed-latency buffer and the elasticity buffer. The fixed-latency buffer is used to ensure that a 24-bit token can exist in entirety, even where the overall transmission path cannot support 24-bit times. This buffer is placed in the data path and is 24 bits long. The elasticity buffer is used to maintain consistent delays.

Fault management

Token Ring classes errors as hard and soft, as follows:.

- A hard error is a permanent fault (such as a cable break) that prevents transmission on the ring. Token Ring uses an algorithm called beaconing to detect and attempt repairs for such failures. Whenever a node detects a serious problem with the network, such as a cable break, it sends a beacon frame at regular intervals. A beacon frame identifies the address of the node reporting the failure and the nearest active upstream neighbor (NAUN), as well as error information. A cable break, for example, would typically be detected first at the receive side of the ring station downstream from the fault. A change in ring topology would be required to bypass such a severe failure. Beaconing initiates a process called autoreconfiguration, where nodes within the failure domain automatically perform diagnostics in an attempt to reconfigure the network around the failed areas. Physically, the MSAU can accomplish this through electrical reconfiguration. Reconfiguration may require manual intervention depending upon the level of equipment used.

- A soft error is an intermittent fault that temporarily disrupts normal operation of the ring. Soft errors are usually tolerated by error recovery procedures, but they may impair normal ring operation if excessive or nonrandom. The most critical soft errors are monitored in each ring station by a set of counters. Every two seconds the values of the soft error counters are sent as a soft error report frame to the ring error monitor functional address (typically residing in a bridge or LAN Manager station), where the values for each counter are accumulated. If a soft-error counter exceeds a predefined threshold, a LAN Manager will be informed through its link with the LAN reporting mechanism. The LAN Manager may reconfigure the ring to bypass a faulty node, if the fault can be located. Soft errors are said to be isolating if a fault domain can be specified. If not, they are called nonisolating soft errors.

For further information about Token Ring operations refer to [1, 2].

Quality of service

Token Ring supports a simple packet prioritization scheme as an integral part of the token passing ring protocol.

6.4.4 Designing Token Ring networks

As described earlier, Token Ring nodes are connected to a wiring concentrator called a Multistation Access Unit (MAU, or MSAU), which may be either active or passive. MAUs have two distinct types of ports: Lobe ports are used for station connectivity, and trunk or ring in/out ports are used for connections to other MAUs. Trunk ports cannot be used for station connectivity, and not all MAUs include trunk ports. Passive MAUs typically use the MIC connector for trunk ports, since these are self-wrapping; the choice of interface for active MAUs is more varied. A simple Token Ring LAN design is illustrated in Figure 6.13. This figure shows three MAUs and their physically attached end station via lobe ports. When a node is powered up, phantom current from the NIC is transmitted to the concentrator and activates relays to allow the station to access the LAN. Note that Station-A is not powered up and therefore the associated relays stay in bypassed mode.

As a general rule active MAUs are preferable, although more expensive. Passive MAUs require careful design to ensure that drive distances are not exceeded; with active MAUs the maximum cable distance is often specified by the manufacturer's documentation and takes precedence. Active MAUs are typically managed (e.g., via SNMP) and also provide modular trunk ports, enabling more flexible interface options. They also typically support advanced features such as automatic ring speed detection, automated ring wrapping, and automatic beacon resolution. For example, in Figure 6.14 a cable between two concentrators fails. If passive wiring concentrators are used, then the MIC connector is responsible for wrapping the primary path to the backup path. Active wiring concentrators (such as the IBM 8230) have their own power supply and offer automatic recovery for all interface types. However, it is important to note that vendors of active MAUs may

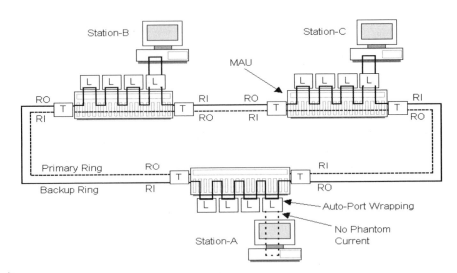

Figure 6.13   *A Token Ring network with hosts attached to three passive wiring concentrators. Station-A is not powered up, and the lack of phantom power means that port wrapping occurs within the MIC connector. In a stable topology the ring operates with both a primary and a backup ring.*

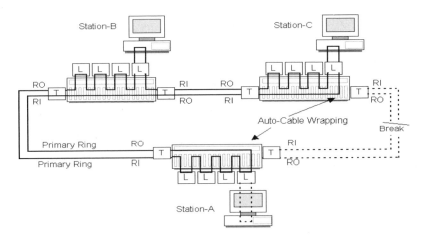

Figure 6.14   *A Token Ring network showing automated trunk cable wrapping when the link between Station-A and Station-C becomes faulty. The ring heals and wraps internally within the two MAUs terminating the breakage. Note that there is only one active ring.*

Table 6.4   *Maximum Number of Stations in Token Ring Networks*

Parameter	Passive MAUs		Active MAUs	
	4Mbps	16Mbps	4Mbps	16Mbps
Max Stations	250	250	144	180
Max Retiming TCU Ports	-	-	144	180
Additional Repeating Elements	50	125	12	15

implement different cable fault detection mechanisms, leading to potential inconsistencies, and therefore it is recommended that active rings should use equipment from the same vendor.

The use of bridges to provide additional capacity and distance is an attractive growth option, because the absence of collisions on Token Ring simplifies bridge processing and maintains the deterministic characteristics of the protocols. Fairness in the access protocol and high-priority utilization by the bridge helps avoid frame loss. Even if a frame is rejected due to bridge congestion, recovery is simplified by the access protocol.

Maximum station counts

The maximum station count for Token Ring networks is determined by attenuation (loss of signal power with distance) and aggregated jitter (variable delays introduced by retiming within Token Ring nodes). Jitter is particularly important and restricts the absolute maximum number of stations to 250 per ring. Depending upon the speed of the ring, and whether passive or active MAUs are deployed, the maximum number of stations varies below this figure, as illustrated in Table 6.4. Active MAUs have additional retiming circuitry within the Trunk Coupling Units (TCUs), which introduce increased jitter, thereby decreasing overall drive distances even further.

Note that these numbers are purely a guideline, since station counts can be reduced and additional repeaters deployed. Consult the manufacturer's guidelines for the equipment you have selected and ensure that you do not exceed the maximum thresholds quoted. In many cases the vendor thresholds will differ from the values listed in Table 6.4 (e.g., IBM states that up to 72 nodes can be supported per ring using UTP and up to 260 nodes using STP).

Media types and drive distances

Token Ring supports three main media types, as follows:

- 150-ohm Shielded Twisted Pair (STP) two-pair screened copper cable, introduced by IBM as part of its structured cabling system in 1984. The standard connector used is the IBM Media Interface Connector (MIC).

    - Type 1A—High-performance 22AWG cable for floor distribution and trunk applications.
    - Type 2A—Hybrid cable with four-pair UTP included between the outer braid and the PVC jacket as well as the central two-pair STP cable. Used for mixed data (STP) and voice (UTP) applications, primarily in the United States, since this mixed application is disliked by many international service providers.
    - Type 6A—Flexible 26AWG cable used for patching/jumper cables and fly leads in the work area.
    - Type 9A—Smaller version (26AWG) of Type 1A, with the same applications but supporting only 75 percent of the distance.

- 100-ohm Cat-5 Unshielded Twisted Pair (UTP) four-pair 24AWG copper cable. Although Cat-3 and Cat-4 are applicable for some 4-Mbps applications, only Cat-5 has the performance capabilities required to support all Token Ring applications. The standard connector used is the ISO/IEC 11801 (RJ45). Compared with STP, UTP offers reduced drive distances.

- Multimode 62.5/125 µm Fiber-Optic cable. Until 1988 fiber was available only for trunk connections such as campus building interconnections and building backbones. ISO 8802-5 now includes support for end-station attachment. Although the standard defines 62.5/125 µm, use of 50/125 µm is also possible. The standard connector was, until recently, the ST bayonet connector, although nowadays the smaller Subscriber Connector (SC) is becoming more common, as specified in ISO/IEC 11801.

The maximum drive distances for various Token Ring media types at speeds of 4 and 16 Mbps are listed in Table 6.5. Where the distance between Token Ring nodes exceeds the maximum drive distance, a repeater can be used (e.g., for 4-Mbps Token Ring a copper repeater will drive the signal 770 m for IBM Type 1 STP; an optical repeater will drive the signal up to 2 km). Multiple token rings can be interconnected via bridges.

Table 6.5 *Maximum Drive Distances for Various Token Ring Media Types (in meters)*

Media	4Mbps	16Mbps
IBM Type 1 and 2 STP	770	346
IBM Type 6 and 9 STP	579	260
Cat-5 UTP	400	100
Multi-mode Fibre Optic	2000	2000

Media filters

Since most standard Token Ring devices (NICs, bridges, switches, routers) are designed for 150-ohm operations, use of UTP requires the use of media filters to compensate for the differences in impedance. These are relatively small, unpowered devices, presented with a DB9 interface on the DTE side and an RJ45 interface on the cable side. Although relatively inexpensive, the overall port cost needs to be considered in large networks where UTP is to be deployed.

Cabling design rules

The physical design rules for Token Ring are complex and possibly contribute to the lack of willingness for many organizations to install and maintain Token Ring networks. IBM originally published a comprehensive set of tables to illustrate design requirements, but the rules vary for different speeds and different manufacturers (e.g., some MAUs impose more cable loss if they include transformers on each port). If in any doubt, the safest scenario is to request the applicable rules from your chosen supplier. Tables 6.6 through 6.9 can be used to calculate the appropriate cable distances for various Token Ring implementations. Essentially the cabling design boils down to the following four parameters:

- The number of MAUs
- The number of wiring closets
- The longest lobe cable
- The Adjusted Ring Length (ARL)

These parameters are determined by your physical design. The ARL represents the worst-case length of the ring in a wrapped condition and is, therefore, calculated as the sum of all cable distances between wiring closets,

Table 6.6   *Token Ring Cable Distances at 4 Mbps over Type 1 and Type 2 (All distances are in meters. If using Type 6 or Type 9 cable, divide the numbers in the table by 1.33.)*

	Number of Wiring Closets										
	2	3	4	5	6	7	8	9	10	11	12
MAUs											
2	367										
3	358	353									
4	349	345	340								
5	340	336	331	326							
6	332	327	322	318	313						
7	323	318	314	309	304	300					
8	314	309	305	300	295	291	286				
9	305	301	296	291	287	282	277	273			
10	296	292	287	282	278	273	269	264	259		
11	288	283	278	274	269	264	260	255	250	246	
12	279	274	270	265	260	256	251	246	242	237	232
13	270	266	261	256	251	247	242	238	233	228	224
14	261	257	252	247	243	238	234	229	224	219	215
15	252	248	243	238	234	229	225	220	215	211	206
16	244	239	234	230	225	221	216	211	206	202	197
17	235	230	226	221	216	212	207	202	198	193	189
18	226	222	217	212	208	203	198	194	189	184	180
19	218	213	208	203	199	194	190	185	180	176	171
20	209	204	199	195	190	186	181	176	171	167	162
21	200	195	190	186	181	177	172	167	163	158	154
22	191	186	182	177	173	168	163	158	154	149	145
23	182	178	173	168	164	159	154	150	145	141	136
24	173	169	164	160	155	150	146	141	136	132	127
25	164	160	155	151	146	142	137	132	128	123	118
26	155	151	147	142	137	133	128	123	119	114	110
27	146	142	138	129	129	124	119	115	110	105	101

minus the shortest distance (exclude the patch cables' lengths within the wiring closets). Depending upon the type of cable you are using and the speed of Token Ring selected, choose the appropriate value from Tables 6.6 through 6.9 to determine a valid cable design. The values represented in these tables are the combined distance of the ARL plus the longest lobe cable. To test whether the design will work use this calculation:

Result = TableValue – (ARL + MaxLobeCableLength)

If Result is negative, then the design is invalid and you will need to adjust the topology to produce a positive result. For example, assume a 4-Mbps Token Ring design running over Cat-2 cable with six MAUs and three wiring closets.

The distances between wiring closets are 150, 125, and 90 meters, so the ARL is calculated as (150 + 125 + 90 – 90) = 275 m. The longest lobe cable length is 15 m. Therefore, using the previous formulae we can calculate:

Result = 327 – (275 + 15) = 37 m

Table 6.7   *Token Ring Cable Distances at 16 Mbps over Type 1 and Type 2. (All distances are in meters. If using Type 6 or Type 9 cable, divide the numbers in the table by 1.33.)*

MAUs	Number of Wiring Closets								
	2	3	4	5	6	7	8	9	10
2	163								
3	157	151							
4	150	145	140						
5	143	138	133	128					
6	136	131	126	121	116				
7	130	125	120	114	110	105			
8	123	118	113	108	106	98	93		
9	116	111	106	101	96	91	86	81	
10	110	105	99	94	89	84	79	74	69
11	103	98	93	88	83	78	73	67	62
12	96	91	86	81	76	71	66	61	56
13	83	78	73	68	63	58	53	48	42
14	70	65	60	55	50	45	40	34	30
15	57	52	47	42	37	31	26	21	16
16	44	38	34	28	23	18	13	8	3
17	30	26	20	15	10	5			
18	17	12	7						

Since the result is positive, our design in this example will work. Clearly, you could also use these tables to determine either the ARL or maximum lobe length if either of these parameters were desired.

Key product manufacturers

The major vendors of Token Ring–based equipment include IBM, Madge Networks, Proteon Cisco, Cabletron, and Nortel/BAY.

Table 6.8   *Token Ring Cable Distances at 4 Mbps over UTP. (All distances are in meters.)*

MAUs	Number of Wiring Closets			
	1	2	3	4
1	225			
2	219	209		
3	213	203	198	
4	207	197	192	186
5	201	191	186	181
6	195	185	180	175
7	190	179	174	169
8	184	174	168	163
9	178	168	162	157
10	172	162	157	151

Table 6.9   *Token Ring Cable Distances at 16 Mbps over UTP. (All distances are in meters.)*

MAUs	Number of Wiring Closets		
	1	2	3
1	55		
2	46	39	
3	36	39	
4	26	20	23
5	16		

6.4.5   Performance considerations

Using an average frame size of 1,000 bits to simulate the performance of a 4-Mbps token-passing ring with 100 active LAN devices results in a maximum throughput of approximately 3.6 Mbps. The token-passing protocol is stable and efficient, even under high load conditions, and the impact of increased transmission speeds, increased numbers of attached stations, or increased transmission distances on a token-passing LAN is significantly less than similar changes on a CSMA/CD LAN. Because each station regenerates the signal, increased distances are easier to support, while transmission speed is primarily limited by the choice of medium.

Due to the nature of token passing, it is important to minimize latency as frames are passed and retimed from node to node. The total latency comprises the cumulative latency of the ring, plus the internal latency of the Active Monitor (AM), where the AM supplies clocking information for all attached nodes. The AM, therefore, maintains an elasticity buffer to cope with variations in cumulative latency on the ring. This buffer is tightly coupled with the AM's internal crystal clock and is placed in the data path. The buffer is initially 3 bits for 4-Mbps operations, and 15 bits for 16-Mbps operations and may be expanded to twice this length or contracted to zero as required to maintain consistent delays.

Early token release

If the originating node issues a new token only when the frame header has circulated around the ring back to the source and the frame transmission time is shorter than the ring transmit time, then the originating station must generate idles until a header is received. Token-passing ring protocols define the length of a token to be 24 bits (three bytes) and the shortest possible MAC frame to be 200 bits (25 bytes) long. On a 4-Mbps Token Ring LAN the length of 1 bit is approximately 50 meters; a complete token is 1,200 meters long while the shortest frame length would be 10,000 meters. Therefore, at 4 Mbps, the percentage of potential bandwidth that remains idle can be extremely small (i.e., high bandwidth utilization can be maintained at higher traffic levels). On a 16-Mbps ring, 1 bit is 12.5 meters long, and a complete token and the shortest possible MAC frame both become four times smaller (300 and 2,500 meters, respectively). It would be useful to reduce the idle time required waiting for a header in order to make better use of the bandwidth available. To assist this there is an option called early token release. This allows a transmitting node to issue the token after completing the transmission of a frame and before the receipt of the frame. This eliminates any idle time and allows multiple frames to be circulated but still at only one token at a time. This option is recommended for use on 16-Mbps rings.

6.5   FDDI/ANSI X3T9.5

6.5.1   Background

In 1982 the American National Standards Institute (ANSI) created the X3T9.5 committee, which began studies on high-speed communications and produced specifications for the Fiber Distributed Data Interface (FDDI). FDDI is a dual counter-rotating ring, which operates at a rate of 100 Mbps, and its protocol and operations are defined in the ISO 9314 and the ANSI X3T9.5 standards [10]. FDDI is defined by four separate specifications, as follows:

- Media Access Control (MAC)—Defines how the medium is accessed, including frame formats, token handling, addressing, the algorithm for calculating a CRC value, and error recovery mechanisms.

- Physical Layer Protocol (PHY)—Defines data encoding/decoding procedures, clocking requirements, framing, and other functions.

- Physical Layer Medium (PMD)—Defines the characteristics of the transmission medium, including the fiber-optic link, power levels, bit error rates, optical components, and physical connectors.

- Station Management (SMT)—Defines the FDDI station configuration, ring configuration, and control features, including station insertion and removal, initialization, fault isolation and recovery, scheduling, and statistics gathering.

FDDI is similar to IEEE 802.5 Token Ring in several respects but was originally targeted as a new standard for high-speed host attachment. FDDI subsequently emerged as a primary candidate for LAN trunking and interconnect applications, where the high cost of deploying optical fiber is outweighed by its tremendous benefits, such as support for high-speed networking and immunity to electromagnetic interference.

6.5.2 Frame formats

As with Token Ring, FDDI networks specify two frame types: tokens and data/command frames. Both formats are illustrated in Figure 6.15. Tokens are 20 bits in length plus a preamble and comprise a start delimiter, frame control field, and an end delimiter. The IEEE allows vendors to implement either 16-bit or 48-bit MAC addresses.

6.5.3 Operation

FDDI is similar to Token Ring in several ways: It uses a token-passing protocol over a dual-ring LAN using a fiber-optic transmission medium (with all the advantages that brings). An FDDI LAN comprises a number of nodes connected to each other to form a physical ring. Information is transmitted sequentially, as a stream of encoded symbols, and passed from one

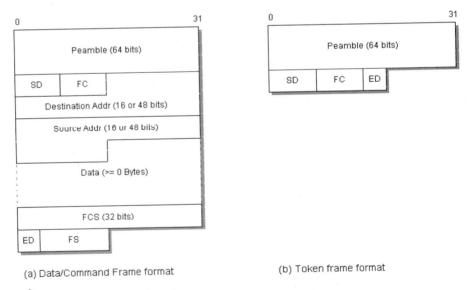

(a) Data/Command Frame format   (b) Token frame format

Figure 6.15   *FDDI frame formats. (a) A data or command frame. (b) A Token.*

active node to the next. Each node regenerates and repeats each symbol and has the opportunity to transmit frames when a token passes and can be claimed. Unlike Token Ring, an FDDI node can decide how many frames it will transmit using an algorithm that permits bandwidth allocation. FDDI also allows a node to transmit many frames without releasing the token.

FDDI uses two rings: the primary ring and the secondary ring (similar to the backup ring path in Token Ring). Each ring is a single fiber path comprising one pair of fibers (transmit and receive). FDDI permits attachment units (nodes/stations, concentrators, and bridge/routers) to be attached in several configurations.

Field definitions

- Preamble—used to synchronize a frame with each of the station clocks.

- SD—The start delimiter is used for both tokens and normal frames and informs the receiving node of the arrival of a following frame or token. It is coded as JK, where J and K are nondata symbols.

- FC—The frame control byte indicates whether the frame contains data or control information. It is encoded as CLFFZZZZ, where C specifies synchronous or asynchronous mode; L indicates 16- or 48-bit addressing; FF indicates LLC, MAC control, or a reserved frame; and ZZZZ is used by control frames.

- DA (Destination Address) and SA (Source Address)—48-bit (six bytes), Media Access Control (MAC) addresses. The least significant bit of the most significant byte of this field is called the I/G (Individual/Group) bit. The type of address used is indicated by the state of this bit, as follows:

  - Unicast: The DA contains the unique address of one node on the network. I/G bit is not set.
  - Multicast: A group destination, where multiple devices will be listening on this address. I/G bit is set.
  - Broadcast: When the DA field is set to all 1s (hence the I/G bit is also set), it indicates a broadcast. A broadcast is a special form of multicast. All nodes on the network must be capable of receiving a broadcast.

- DATA—The actual data being transmitted. The length of this field is limited by the ring token holding time, which defines the maximum time a ring node may hold the token.

- FCS—32 bits, containing a Cyclic Redundancy Check (CRC) value, calculated by the transmitting node based on the FC, DA, SA, and data fields.

- ED—the end delimiter signals the end of the token or data/command frame. It contains a nondata symbol, T.

- FS—the frame status field contains the address recognized (A) and frame copied (F) and error detected (E) bit flags. Since the A and C bits are not covered by the FCS, they are duplicated in this field as a redundancy check.

FDDI is similar to a fiber-optic Token Ring network from a cabling perspective, except that it offers much more flexibility. With FDDI a node can be attached directly to the ring without requiring a concentrator, and a node can be attached to either or both of the rings. To differentiate between nodes that attach to one or both rings, FDDI defines the following two classes of devices:

- Class A devices—attach to both of the rings directly. They may either be a station (Dual Attachment Station—DAS) or a concentrator (Dual Attachment Concentrator—DAC).

- Class B devices—attach to only one of the rings, either directly or through a concentrator. They may be a station (Single Attachment Station—SAS) or a concentrator (Single Attachment Concentrator—SAC).

Concentrators are active devices and are similar to active Token Ring access units. During normal ring operation, the primary ring is active while the secondary ring is idle. In the event of a failure on the primary ring, the secondary ring will become active when a DAS or DAC wraps the primary ring to the secondary ring to form a continuous single ring.

Quality of service

FDDI supports the real-time allocation of network bandwidth, making it suitable for a variety of different application types, including multimedia.

6.5.4   Designing FDDI networks

The FDDI network topology may be viewed both physically and logically. Physical topology describes the arrangement and interconnection of nodes with physical connections. The logical topology describes the paths through the network between MAC entities. An FDDI network forms one of two physical topologies: a dual ring of trees or a subset of dual ring of trees. The implication on the logical topology is that at the most, two logical sets of MAC entities (e.g., two independent token/data paths) exist in a single fault-free network. A set of MAC attachments can be called a logical ring. The two types of topologies are not necessarily similar.

Media support

FDDI specifies two types of optical fiber: single mode (monomode) and multimode. Multimode fiber uses light-emitting diodes (LEDs) as the light-generating devices, while single-mode fiber generally uses lasers. Single mode allows only one mode of light to propagate through the fiber, while multimode allows multiple modes of light to propagate through the fiber. Because multiple modes of light may travel different distances (depending on the entry angles), causing them to arrive at the destination at different times (a phenomenon called modal dispersion), single-mode fiber is capable of higher bandwidth and greater cable run distances than multimode fiber. Due to these characteristics, single-mode fiber is often used for interbuilding connectivity, while multimode fiber is often used for intrabuilding connectivity. In addition to optical fiber, FDDI supports copper (TP-PMD, sometimes called CDDI) in the form of unshielded twisted pair (only category 5) and shielded twisted-pair media at 100 Mbps.

The signal techniques used to encode data on copper and fiber are quite different. As indicated in Table 6.10, fiber utilizes NRZI4B/5B encoding (giving a signaling frequency of 125 MHz for a bit rate of 100 Mbps). Copper utilizes MLT-3 encoding (giving a signaling frequency of 31.25 MHz for the same bit rate). This allows existing cabling systems to be reused (as long as they are of sufficient quality) to provide significant cost savings. The FDDI signal is put on the copper wire as a baseband signal. A 1 bit is signaled as a voltage of between .35 V and .7 V and a 0 bit is the absence of

Table 6.10   *FDDI Fiber and Copper Specifications*

	FDDI - Fibre Optic	FDDI - Copper
FDDI Cable type	Optical Fibre	Twisted pair
Data Rate	100Mbps	100Mbps
Max Length Between Repeaters	2000m	100m
Max No of Repeaters	100	100
Signalling Technique	4B/5B/NRZI	MLT-3
Max Transceiver cable length	50m	50m

voltage. Transmission distance between workstation and hub (or between two directly connected workstations) is limited to 100 m.

Port connection rules

The FDDI standard differentiates four physical port types, and these determine what is possible in terms of physical attachment, as follows:

- A-Type—For dual attachment stations: primary ring-in, secondary ring-out

- B-Type—For dual attachment stations: secondary ring-in, primary ring-out

- M-Type—On a concentrator, to attach a single attachment station

- S-Type—On a single attachment station, to attach to a concentrator

Physically, FDDI ports are typically offered as ST, Fixed Shroud Duplex (FSD), or SMA connectors. SMA (screw) connectors are now rarely used due to the unreliability of mechanical interface; ST (bayonet) connectors are generally limited for use as patch cables. The connection rules for interfacing the various port classes differ, as follows:

- A-to-B and B-to-A are peer-to-peer trunk connections.

- M-to-S is a master-to-slave connection.

- M-to-A and B provide dual homing.

- S-to-S is a point-to-point connection.

In a dual ring topology, one end of the link is configured as an A-Type and the other end as a B-Type port. With a tree topology, one end of the link is an M (Master) port and the other end is an S (Slave) port. Only DAS nodes reside on both rings. SAS nodes reside on the FDDI tree and connect to the network via concentrators. In this case, the concentrator can be a DAC or an SAC. Table 6.11 illustrates the connection rules for SAS and DAS nodes.

Simple design based on a ring topology

The FDDI ring topology comprises the primary ring on which frames flow from port B on one station to port A on the next station and the secondary ring in which the frames flow in the opposite direction. In the stable topology the secondary ring has no data flow and simply provides a redundant backup path. Figure 6.16 shows an FDDI dual ring configuration comprising Single Attached Stations (SAS), Dual Attached Stations (DAS), and

Table 6.11   *FDDI Port Connection Rules for SAS and DAS Nodes*

Connection	Description
A to A	Undesirable peer connection. Creates twisted primary and secondary rings.
A to B	Normal trunk ring peer connection.
A to M	Tree connection with possible redundancy. Port B has precedence for connecting to port M in a single MAC node.
A to S	Undesirable peer connection. Creates a wrapped ring.
B to B	Undesirable peer connection. Creates twisted primary and secondary rings.
B to M	Tree connection with possible redundancy. Port B has precedence for connecting to port M in a single MAC node.
B to S	Undesirable peer connection. Creates a wrapped ring
M to M	Invalid Tree connection.
M to S	Normal tree connection.
S to S	Creates a single ring of two slave nodes.

Dual Attached Concentrators (DAC). Each station will have ports A and B directly attached to the primary and backup ring. The cabling between the stations can be all fiber or shielded twisted pair (STP).

If any device fails, or a cable failure occurs, the nearest ports on the adjacent stations will wrap the primary and secondary rings and the network will continue to operate as a single ring. For example, in Figure 6.16, if Node-1 fails, Node-2 will wrap its B port and Node-3 will wrap its A port, creating a single ring, which connects only nodes 2 and 3 and the concentrator. Note that if Node-3 were single attached to the primary only, it could not wrap and the concentrator would wrap, leaving Node-3 isolated. For this reason it is advisable to connect SAS nodes via concentrators or always dual attach mission-critical servers. Rings are fine for single points of failure, but they are potentially vulnerable to multiple failures, since this can cause isolation of groups of users and services. In the case of failures on non-adjacent parts of the ring (say between Node-1 and Node-2 and between Node-3 and the concentrator), the normal wrapping procedure ensures that the topology integrity is maintained, but the ring becomes fragmented, forming two rings. Optical bypass switches can be used to prevent ring segmentation by eliminating failed stations from the ring. These devices are obviously very useful but add cost to the design.

Note the configuration of the Dual Attached Concentrator (DAC) in the ring. In this case the signal will enter the concentrator at port A, then

Figure 6.16

FDDI ring with a combination of Dual Attached Stations (DAS), Dual Attached Concentrators (DAC), and Single Attached Stations (SAS).

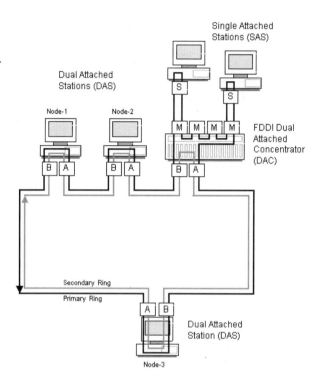

flow through the M ports, and finally exit the concentrator at the B port. If a Single Attached Station (SAS), such as a workstation, is attached via its S port to the concentrator's M port, then the signal extends through the M port up to the station and back. Note that SAS nodes in this configuration have no resilience if the S-M cable breaks. One benefit of a concentrator attachment is that it allows a workstation to enter and leave the network without disrupting the ring.

Design based on a tree topology with dual homing

Figure 6.17 shows a more complicated FDDI tree topology. Conc-1 is dual attached to the main FDDI ring, and below it three subordinate concentrators are single attached via their B ports. Some of the concentrators have single attached stations (SAS node) attached via the M ports. Note that Conc-4 is dual homed from both Conc-3 and Conc-2. A concentrator, which is not part of the main ring, can be dual attached via one or two other concentrators via the A and B ports to provide greater resilience. In this case Conc-4 is described as a Dual Homing Concentrator (DHC). The link from port A is passive until activated automatically by the failure of the

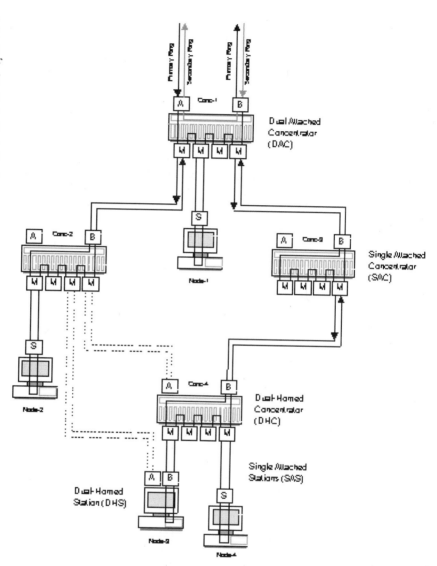

Figure 6.17
FDDI tree with a combination of Dual Attached Concentrators (DAC), Single Attached Concentrators (SAC), Dual Homing Concentrators (DHC), and Single Attached Stations (SAS).

port B connection. Should the connection from Conc-3 to port B on Conc-4 fail, port A will be activated automatically without affecting the attached users.

Mission-critical devices such as routers or mainframe hosts can also benefit from this fault-tolerant technique directly. A DAS can be connected to multiple concentrators using both A and B ports for additional resilience. In this case Node-3 is described as a Dual Homing Station (DHS). Again, only port B is active; the connection to port A remains in standby mode. Note that Node-3 will only switch links if its link to Conc-4 fails.

Key product manufacturers

The major vendors of FDDI-based equipment include Cisco, Cabletron, 3Com, and Nortel/BAY.

6.5.5   Performance considerations

It is important to remember that FDDI is a shared medium, so even though it is deterministic (being token based), as the number of nodes increases the available bandwidth per node decreases. This is important for FDDI applications, since it is often proposed as a LAN/MAN backbone or high-speed server interface and therefore may be carrying many flows concurrently. FDDI is traditionally configured with an active primary ring and a counter-rotating standby ring. It is possible to have data flowing on both rings concurrently to give an aggregate 200 Mbps, although the standards do not recommend this due to the lack of fault tolerance.

The theoretical maximum frame rate for 64-byte frames is 152,439 fps, representing about 78 percent utilization. With 1,518-byte frames the efficiency rises to almost 99 percent (8,138 fps). FDDI can support much larger frame sizes, but the MTU is often configured lower to match interconnecting LAN media (avoiding fragmentation inefficiency at the interface but at the expense of less efficient direct FDDI-to-FDDI communications).

6.6   Fibre Channel

Fibre Channel is not a LAN protocol in the conventional sense; it was developed to meet the demand for a standards-based, high-performance IO channel, capable of driving greater distances and including the flexibility for future performance improvements. The result is a technology that combines the best of both channel-oriented and protocol-oriented communications. Fibre Channel is important in the LAN environment because it is fast emerging as the preferred method for building Storage Area Networks (SANs). SANs are essentially LANs for online peripherals (such as hard disk arrays, magnetic tape libraries, CDs, and other media devices). Fibre Channel supports full-duplex, frame-based peer-to-peer connectivity between Fibre Channel interfaces. It comprises a five-layer protocol architecture (FC-0 through FC-4) defined by ANSI, as follows:

- FC-0—defines a number of physical media types and data rates, as listed in Table 6.12.

- FC-1—defines the transmission protocol, where the signal encoding technique used is 8B/10B (8 bits of data are converted into 10 bits for transmission).

- FC-2—defines the signaling protocol; it deals with frame transmission.

- FC-3—provides common services, which currently include striping (the ability to transmit in parallel across multiple links for better performance), hunt groups (the ability to alias a set of ports at a particular node, reducing latency by increasing port availability), and multicast (the ability to send data to multiple destinations concurrently).

- FC-4—defines mappings onto a number of legacy interfaces. Current protocol interface specifications support conventional I/O channel techniques, such as the Small Computer System Interface (SCSI), High-Performance Parallel Interface (HPPI), IPI-3, and network schemes such as IEEE 802, ATM, and IP.

A Fibre Channel network comprises end systems (nodes) connected to a collection of switching elements called the fabric. All devices are connected via point-to-point links; the node interface is referred to as an N-Port, and the switch fabric interface is referred to as an F-Port. All communication across these links is frame based; the fabric is responsible for buffering and routing frames between N-Ports (note that buffering allows mixed speed interfaces to be supported, with current data rates ranging from 100 to 800 Mbps).

Table 6.12   *Fibre Channel Media Types and Speeds, with Associated Maximum Cable Distances (specified in meters)*

Media Type	100 Mbps	200 Mbps	400 Mbps	800 Mbps
Single Mode Fibre (SMF)	-	10,000	10,000	10,000
Multimode Fibre (MMF) - 50 µm	10,000	2,000	1,000	500
Multimode Fibre (MMF) - 62.5 µm	1,500	1,500	350	175
Video Coaxial	100	75	50	25
Shielded Twisted Pair (STP)	100	50	-	-
Miniature Coaxial	35	25	15	10

Fibre Channel is very flexible in terms of topology; three main topologies are supported, as follows:

- Point-to-Point—where two nodes are attached directly by their N-Ports. Since there is no fabric, no F-Ports are required and no routing is required.

- Ring/Loop—up to 126 nodes can be connected in a ring topology. Ports on the nodes must combine both N-Port and F-Port functionality (called NL-Ports). No routing is required—the ring operates using token admission, in a manner similar to Token Ring and FDDI.

- Switched Fabric—an arbitrary mesh of up to 2^{24} switching nodes. The minimum fabric topology would be a single switch interconnecting a number of N-Ports. The fabric takes care of routing. Loop topologies can be combined with an arbitrary fabric; however, loop ports require additional functionality to participate in fabric routing (this functionality is provided by FL-Ports).

Fibre Channel supports a range of distances, up to 10 km, depending upon the medium type and speed, as listed in Table 6.12. The combined use of circuit- and packet-switched features and the ability to define a modular, arbitrary, buffered fabric, provide considerable flexibility and enable Fibre Channel to scale well.

6.7   Wireless LAN/IEEE 802.11

6.7.1   Background

So far we have been discussing networking implementations that are predominantly wired. These cable-based networks are potentially more expensive to install and maintain and are less adaptable to moves and changes compared with a wireless infrastructure. Until recently the applications of wireless LANs, based on microwave, infrared, or radio frequency technologies, have been restricted to niche applications (such as line-of-sight building interconnection and peripheral connectivity). The technology has either been too slow, too expensive, or too unreliable to consider for serious deployments, and much of the technology was proprietary. Recent developments, such as the emergence of the IEEE 802.11 standard, are now making this technology much more attractive and enable interoperability between different vendors. As performance and features improve, it is anticipated that wireless communications will begin to gain a serious foothold in the LAN market over the next decade, and some of the major vendors of data and voice products are already beginning to establish strong leadership positions.

The electromagnetic spectrum

The electromagnetic spectrum has been arbitrarily subdivided by wavelength, as illustrated in Figure 6.18. Over time, applications have been discovered for almost every part of the spectrum, and today each country regulates and licenses all or parts of the frequency range. In the developed parts of the world (such as the United States and much of Europe) the spectrum has effectively reached the stage of oversubscription, and there is now a broad consensus to standardize the use of specific frequency ranges for particular applications. Clearly, for applications such as mobile telephony and wireless networking there are significant benefits in standardizing the frequencies used around the world. So far, international agreement has been reached on the allocation of three common Industrial, Scientific, and Medical (ISM) bands, which do not require licensing. The middle band (the 2.4- to 2.48-GHz range) is available internationally for use by wireless systems; however, this band is widely used by many other applications, including consumer devices such as baby monitors, garage door openers, and microwave ovens. For wireless LAN applications (ranging from the top end of the UHF band at 900 MHz, through to the infrared band), a special transmission technique known as spread spectrum is used to minimize the interference with other devices in the vicinity. Wireless LANs fall into three main categories: UHF and microwave radio, microwave, and infrared. Figure 6.18 illustrates the parts of the electromagnetic spectrum occupied by these technologies. The frequency range that could potentially be used for wireless LAN communication ranges from approximately 200 kHz, through the microwave range, up to the top of the infrared range at approximately 200 THz. Efforts have been largely concentrated in supporting a few specific frequency bands that do not require licensing in the microwave and infrared regions.

Currently, the FCC and IEEE 802.11 have specified wireless LAN standards for the United States (at the 2,400–2,500 MHz and 2.4 GHz ranges, respectively). There are other bodies designated for Europe, such as CEPT and the ETSI workgroups (at the 2,400–2,500 MHz and 2.4–2.5 GHz ranges, respectively). Note that the ISM band is not universal in availability; notable exceptions include France and Spain. France uses the 2,446.5–2,483.5 MHz band, and Spain uses 2,445–2,475 MHz. Products relying on the ISM range would have to work with a reduced frequency band in such regions.

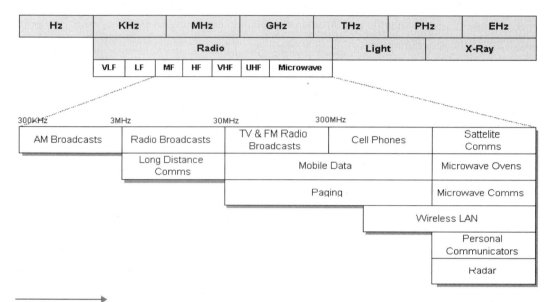

Figure 6.18   *Subdivision of the electromagnetic spectrum by application.*

Frequency and wavelength

Whereas wired LANs encode data onto an electrical impulse, wireless LANs encode data onto a radio or light wave. Theoretically, the amount of data that can be transmitted is directly proportional to the frequency of the wave (e.g., if a switching component within a transmitter is capable of modulating 1 bit of data per cycle, then a 10-kHz wavelength can carry five times as much data as a 2-kHz wavelength). Given the high frequencies available, and the ability of some modulating techniques to encode up to 4 bits per cycle, wireless LANs have the potential to transmit data at very high speeds.

Frequency, f (measured in cycles per second or Hertz [Hz]) and wavelength, λ, (measured in meters) are related to each other and to the speed of light, s (a constant = 300,000,000 meters per second) by the following expression:

$$f \times \lambda = 3 \times 10s$$

Frequency and wavelength are said to be in inverse proportion to one another; as frequency increases wavelength must decrease and vice versa. It turns out that the physical characteristics of energy waves at different frequencies vary. The higher the frequency (and therefore the shorter the wavelength), the more the wave takes on the properties of light and the more it is absorbed or reflected by most materials, including air (this is why FM broadcasts do not have the same reach as AM signals; given the same power they attenuate much more rapidly). In general, the shorter the wavelength, the easier it is for the wave to be reflected, focused, and controlled. At frequencies higher than 300 MHz, signals can be focused using a parabolic reflector (i.e., the type commonly seen on building rooftops) and directed toward a destination. This means that the transmitting device needs far less power than if it were transmitting in all directions. Focusing an incoming signal in the same way means that a far weaker signal can be detected than with a conventional antenna. These properties are very useful for wireless networking and have a number of implications, the key one being that that as the frequency increases and wavelength decreases, the physical range of a wireless LAN decreases due to increased signal attenuation. This range can be increased at any frequency by simply increasing the transmission power; however, most governments impose strict controls on power output (both for health reasons and to minimize interference). This effectively limits the range to a maximum of 400 m, so the emphasis is generally on improving the efficiency and design of the antenna to maximize reach.

Transmission techniques

There are several transmission techniques of particular interest in wireless LANs, the key ones being spread spectrum and infrared. Microwave links may also be used for line-of-sight applications, so we will discuss that briefly also.

Spread spectrum

Spread spectrum uses broadband techniques and spreads transmission over multiple available frequencies within a given band (the intention being to have a low watts-to-hertz ratio). The technology has been around since the late 1940s and was originally developed for United States military applications. The sender and receiver must be synchronized with regard to the parameters used to define frequency use during transmission; otherwise, the receiver will not be correctly tuned and the signal will appear as background noise (this also makes signal jamming and eavesdropping easy—without all of the transmission parameters only a small portion of a transmission could be intercepted). DSSS uses more bandwidth than a conventional narrowband RF transmission would require, resulting in a signal that is louder and easier to track (as a result the transmission is relatively insensitive to the effects of background noise/radio interference, even when that noise is at quite high levels). Two spread spectrum techniques are generally employed in wireless LANs (the third, Time Hopped Spread Spectrum [THSS] is not discussed here).

Direct Sequence Spread Spectrum (DSSS) (also referred to as CDMA) uses direct sequencing to artificially spread the signal over a range of frequencies. The carrier is modulated using a digital chipping code, where the code bit rate is higher than the data rate. In effect the chipping bits are redundant bits that are applied to each data bit transmitted; this technique, therefore, requires more bandwidth than would normally be the case. However, this also enables the receiver to recover the original data even if bits are damaged during transmission. Receivers without the chipping code see the transmission as wideband noise. As well as being used in wireless LAN technologies such as IEEE 802.11, DSSS is also used in mobile wireless communications.

Frequency Hopping Spread Spectrum (FHSS) divides up the available bandwidth into a number of discrete frequencies, or channels. The transmitter shifts frequency (hops) during transmission, using a predefined code sequence (a pseudorandom pattern) to determine the hopping sequence over a wide frequency band. The receiver must be aware of the code sequence in order to pick out the transmission from background noise. The duration of transmission at each frequency is constant, and the rate at which frequency switching occurs leads to two broad differentiations called fast hopping and slow hopping. With fast hopping frequency hopping occurs at a rate faster than the bit rate; the converse is true for slow hopping. Slow hopping is the most widely implemented and stipulates that hopping must occur at least every 400 ms and must cover all available frequencies. In practice, either CSMA or TDMA can be used for channel access.

Infrared

Infrared (IR) communications systems use very high frequencies (just below visible light), and there are no licensing requirements for infrared use. As discussed earlier, as the wavelength of an energy wave decreases, the wave takes on more of the properties of light. High-frequency IR radiation cannot penetrate opaque objects and, therefore, requires a direct line of sight between transmitter and receiver in order to function (failing that diffuse or reflective techniques must be employed). Transmission distance is also limited in comparison with spread spectrum techniques due to signal attenuation. Within networking equipment, optical transceivers can be constructed using two technologies, as follows:

- Laser Diodes (LDs)—produce a focused beam of light and are therefore used for line-of-sight applications, where the transmitter and receiver need to be precisely aligned for communication to take place (referred to as focused infrared). Typically these cover short-haul distances of up to a mile, although atmospheric conditions can impair communications.

- Light Emitting Diodes (LEDs)—produce a spread of light and are therefore applicable for communications via diffusion (where the beam is transmitted over quite a wide angle). Since the beam may be reflected off multiple surfaces before reaching the receiver, the same signal can arrive at the receiver from different directions and at different times, a phenomenon referred to as the multipath effect.

IR technology has been used for remote control applications since the 1960s, and today it is widely deployed in notebook and laptop computers for simple peripheral interconnection or close-proximity, point-to-point data transfer. IR is being used for wireless LAN applications, although its distance and deployment limitations mean that it is not ideally suited for use in mobile LAN environments within buildings, other than for small open plan spaces. The diffuse use of IR does have the advantage that users can move around relatively unimpeded within a local area without losing contact with the base station, and features such as roaming can be supported (where users are handed off transparently to different base stations as they move through a local area, without losing communications). IR also has the potential for very high transmission rates; there are some systems already available that emulate Token Ring at 4 Mbps, with media conversion facilities that enable integration with wired LANs. Note that the IR frequency range is also used by a number of domestic appliances (television remote controls, motion detectors, and door openers).

Microwave

Microwave is a directed line-of-sight radio transmission technique. It can be used for radar and wideband communication systems and has been used extensively for long-distance trunk connections in the telephone network. The first commercial microwave system was used across the English Channel in the 1930s. Microwave covers quite a wide range of frequencies in the electromagnetic spectrum (see Figure 6.18), ranging from 2 to 40 GHz. Most systems operate below 18 GHz. Low-power microwave systems are available at approximately the 9–18-GHz range. These devices have good reach (some offering up to 5,000 sqm). A data rate of approximately 12 Mbps can be obtained at 2 GHz, with up to 274 Mbps at 18 GHz [11]. For LAN applications, speeds are currently up to 4 Mbps. Individual licensing is typically required for this equipment, although some vendors have corporate licenses in place that can be passed on to the user.

We will now discuss some of the common implementations of wireless LANs.

6.7.2   Wireless LAN technologies

IEEE 802.11

The IEEE 802.11 Committee has developed a set of standards for wireless LAN products. The architecture of the 802.11 wireless LAN is similar to that of the cellular phone network. An 802.11 LAN is divided into cells, referred to as Basic Service Sets (BSS). Each BSS is controlled by a base station called an Access Point (AP). This acts rather like a wireless concentrator or repeater. Since APs themselves have a finite range, several APs may be connected to a common wired or wireless backbone, forming what is called a Distribution System (DS). A DS is viewed as a single 802 LAN as far as upper-layer protocols are concerned. In terms of geographic reach, the standard supports two types of coverage: Basic Service Areas (BSAs) and Extended Service Areas (ESAs). The BSA effectively covers a single cell; the ESA covers a distribution system that has one or more extension points (these act like wireless line drivers and are used to extend the range of the wireless network where a wired backbone cannot be deployed).

End stations (PCs, laptops, PDAs, etc.) are equipped with a wireless LAN adapter, which has a small antenna (in devices such as PDAs this may be integrated into the main circuit board). Stations typically communicate through the AP rather than directly (although this is possible, as will be discussed shortly). In an 802.11 environment the AP normally interfaces with a wired LAN uplink. The IEEE 802.11 standard unfortunately defines this 802.11 to 802.x translation bridge functionality as a portal (just to confuse matters). Most vendors of access points include portal functionality as standard (e.g., 802.11 to 802.3 is the most common form). IEEE 802.11a supports three physical layers: Frequency Hopping Spread Spectrum (FHSS), Direct Sequence Spread Spectrum (DSSS), and infrared. Both radio frequency methods use the unlicensed 2.4-GHz ISM frequency band (typically occupying 83 MHz of bandwidth between 2.4 and 2.483 GHz, although this may vary in some countries, as well as vary by permissible power levels). Speeds of up to 1 or 2 Mbps are supported. The more recent IEEE 802.11b standard specifies higher-speed access at 5.5 or 11 Mbps using only DSSS.

IEEE 802.11 uses an access control algorithm called Distributed Foundation Wireless MAC (DFWMAC), which is essentially a distributed access control mechanism (a variant of CSMA/CD) with optional centralized control (for time-sensitive or mission-critical traffic). This scheme relies on explicit acknowledgments to avoid the need for expensive collision detection mechanisms and uses a technique referred to as Virtual Carrier Sense (VCS) to reduce the probability of collisions.

HomeRF

HomeRF is targeted at SOHO environments. It is defined by the HomeRF Working Group and uses the Shared Wireless Access Protocol (SWAP), based on Frequency Hopping Spread Spectrum (FHSS) access techniques. As with IEEE 802.11, it, too, uses the 2.4-GHz ISM band for wireless transmissions. In HomeRF terminology the distribution node is called a Connection Point (CP). Up to 127 devices can be supported, at distances of up to 150 ft (45 m). In a HomeRF environment the CP normally interfaces with a PSTN uplink rather than a LAN.

Bluetooth

Bluetooth is not a wireless LAN technology in the conventional sense. The primary role of this technology is to provide wireless interoperability between a wide range of digital electronic devices over very short distances (e.g., PDAs, mobile phones, laptops, notebooks, peripherals, photocopiers, faxes, and consumer goods). The Bluetooth SIG was formed by a consortium of mobile phone manufacturers and silicon manufacturers, including Nokia and Ericsson (note that Bluetooth is the nickname of the Viking king, Harald Gormssøn, who united Denmark and Norway by force of arms in the tenth century). The first version of the Bluetooth specification was released in 1999.

Bluetooth uses low-power radio frequency transmission and operates in the 2.4–2.5-GHz SIM band. It uses frequency hopping, at a rate of 1,600 hops per second, to avoid interference with other devices and signal fading. There are 79 channels spaced 1 MHz apart, with a hop duration of 625 µs. Bluetooth defines a master-slave relationship between components; communication is full-duplex based on TDM techniques. Four physical interfaces are currently supported (Universal Serial Bus [USB], RS232, PC Card, and Universal Asynchronous Receiver Transmitter [UART]). Bluetooth defines the following three classes of devices based on power requirements:

- Class 1: Maximum output 100 mW, power –20 dBm
- Class 2: Maximum output 2.5 mW, power –4 dBm
- Class 3: Maximum output 1.0 mW, power 0 dBm

The maximum range for low-power Class 3 devices is approximately 10 m (roughly 30 ft), while Class 1 devices will be able to communicate at distances up to 100 m (roughly 300 ft). It is conceivable that Class 3 devices could compete with IEEE 802.11 for part of the wireless LAN market (e.g., SOHO and possibly SME).

During 2000 the cost per component of integrating Bluetooth was approximately $20, quite expensive for consumer goods. This is expected to drop significantly over the next few years as volume increases and Bluetooth is integrated further into both business and consumer products. One of the initial aims of Bluetooth is to eliminate the clutter of spaghetti cabling around user devices, replacing infrared for synchronizing devices such as PDAs, and as a solution for home wireless networks. It will be applicable for applications such as hotels, airports, libraries, and training. Eventually this should lead to smart home integration among products such as electronic security alarms, washing machines, ovens, refrigerators, etc.; it could easily be introduced into toys and children's games. Bluetooth is an exciting technology that is likely to directly impact many of our lives over the next few years. Bluetooth is likely to become ubiquitous in developed countries by 2005. It is fast becoming a de facto international standard with support from over 1,000 manufacturers.

6.7.3   Designing wireless LANs

For the purpose of network design we are primarily interested here in IEEE 802.11 LANs. There are three main topologies supported, as illustrated in Figure 6.19. The topologies are as follows:

- Peer to peer—Figure 6.19(a). Two stations with wireless LAN adaptors can create a direct wireless connection between them. This configuration requires very basic configuration but is only really suitable for applications such as short-distance file transfers, since it does not scale and requires all stations to be within the airwave distance.

- Single LAN access point—Figure 6.19(b). A peer-to-peer LAN can be extended by installing a single AP. This reduces the power requirements for stations and extends the radius of the LAN, since the AP is now responsible for relaying signals (although the bandwidth requirement is doubled, since traffic must traverse the airwaves twice from source to destination). This design improves scalability, since stations communicate via the AP, so this is effectively a wireless star topology rather than a full mesh (which would be required with the peer-to-peer model).

- Multiple LAN access point—Figure 6.19(c). The previous network can be further extended by installing multiple access points, connected either via a wireless or wired backbone. This enables a campus network or industrial complex network to be designed with some areas wireless and a common wired backbone. If required, WLANs can be extended through the use of extension points.

Wireless LANs are generally deployed with a wired backbone and a number of wireless distribution points, as illustrated in Figure 6.19(c). Some systems may allow users to roam between APs (e.g., online stock traders armed with wireless PDAs could wander across a trading floor, transparently connecting to different APs as they move through different floor areas). In IEEE 802.11 each station is associated with a particular AP; stations are allowed to move between cells without losing their connection (as is the case with cellular phone networks). As stations near the edge of a cell, they note that signal strength is deteriorating and begin scanning to locate a new AP (or use previously cached AP location data to associate themselves with a new AP). At the transition point some packet loss may occur, so higher-layer protocols are required to handle any retransmissions.

The number of clients supported by an AP varies between 10 and 50, depending upon the volume of traffic required to pass through to the wired LAN. Most APs can support a transmission radius of 100–200 ft, although this varies by site layout (there may be solid obstacles in transmission paths,

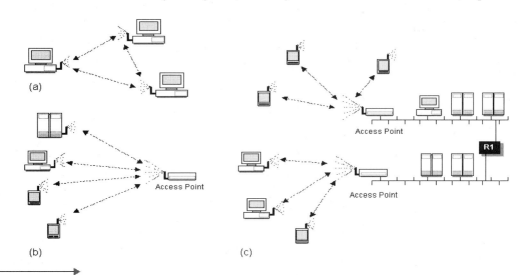

Figure 6.19   *Wireless LAN application topologies. (a) Peer to peer. (b) Shared single access point. (c) Multiple access points with extension points.*

etc.) and by the transmission technology used. One potential problem with using the ISM band is that many non-LAN devices have to use similar frequencies (microwaves, generators, welding equipment, and transformers can all produce frequencies in this range). Operating a wireless LAN in industrial complexes or sites with active construction requires special design considerations to overcome sources of strong radiation. For these reasons a site survey is always strongly recommended when deploying a wireless LAN.

Suitable applications

Early wireless LAN products operating the 2-Mbps shared access scheme have very limited applications (e.g., airports, SOHO, hotels, and conference/training functions). It is unlikely that these technologies will displace the bulk of existing wired solutions because of the very limited bandwidth. The new 11-Mbps DSSS IEEE 802.11b solution is more attractive; however, features such as switching, VLAN support, security, and network management may all need to be improved if these products are to seriously invade traditional wired LAN territory. There is no doubt, however, that these products continue to improve.

With the miniaturization of personal computers, such as laptops and notebooks, and the growth of wireless networks, more commercial applications are being developed to take advantage of the benefits wireless communication has to offer. Wireless LANs are particularly attractive for small, remote office networks (which are unlikely to have skilled staff onsite) and financial applications (such as an online trading floor, where traders can freely roam about with portable communicators). In most cases there will be a wired backbone network terminated at several points by wireless hubs.

6.8   Summary

This chapter discussed the basics of internetworking media types, including the following:

- Ethernet is the dominant access protocol in non-IBM environments. It ease of use, low cost, and vendor choice makes it the preferred medium for most networks today. Higher-speed variants of Ethernet, such as 100BaseX and 1,000BaseX, now offer a credible migration path for Ethernet LANs to higher-speed LAN and MAN backbone topologies.

- Token Ring provides efficient use under both light and heavy traffic loads. It guarantees fair access to all participating stations. This fairness is enhanced by an eight-level priority mechanism, based on priority reservations made in a passing token or frame. A key benefit of the token-passing ring protocol is its ability to handle increased traffic loads or peaks, making it an ideal protocol for larger and/or more heavily used LANs (including backbone rings). While perhaps technically superior to Ethernet, Token Ring has effectively lost the battle for dominance in the local area.

- FDDI is largely based on the token-passing features of Token Ring. It provides an excellent LAN backbone medium with built-in resilience features. Its shared access mechanism, limited capacity, and lack of scalability make ATM an attractive alternative. The fact that FDDI is a shared medium means that other technologies, such as full-duplex Gigabit Ethernet, are the likely contenders for LAN trunking and campus interconnect applications.

- 100VG-AnyLAN represents a highly flexible hybrid technology that supports both Ethernet and Token Ring transparently. Although 100VG-AnyLAN is technically superior in many respects to 100BaseX, most existing 10BaseX users appear to be migrating to 100BaseX and 1,000BaseX standards instead of 100VG-AnyLAN.

- Wireless LANs have the potential to greatly simplify installation and reduce costs in the enterprise. At present bandwidth, segmentation and interoperability are the key factors holding back this new technology, but the emergence of the IEEE 802.11 standard and new initiatives such as Bluetooth bode well for the future.

References

[1]   P. Miller and M. Cummins, *LAN Technologies Explained* (Woburn, MA: Digital Press, 2000).

[2]   W. Stallings, *Local and Metropolitan Area Networks* 5th ed. (Englewood Cliffs, NJ: Prentice Hall, 1997).

[3]   W. Stallings, *Local and Metropolitan Area Networks* 4th ed. (New York: Macmillan, 1993).

[4]   U. D. Black, *Data Networks: Concepts, Theory, and Practice* (Englewood Cliffs, NJ: Prentice Hall, 1989).

[5]   G. Keiser, *Local Area Networks* (New York: McGraw-Hill, 1989).

[6]   R. Boggs, *Measure Capacity of an Ethernet: Myths and Reality* (Digital Equipment Corporation, Western Research Lab).

[7]   www.gigabit-ethernet.org/, Gigabit Ethernet Alliance (GEA) home Web pages.

[8]   www.gigabit-ethernet.org/technology/whitepapers/, Gigabit Ethernet Alliance (GEA) white papers.

[9]   IEEE Standards for Local and Metropolitan Area Networks: Demand Priority Access Method, Physical Layer, and Repeater Specification for 100 Mb/s Operation, IEEE Std 802.12, 1995.

[10]   Fiber Distributed Data Interface MAC, ANSI Std. X3.139, 1987.

[11]   R. Pickens, "Wideband Transmission Media I: Radio Communication" in *Computer Communications*, vol. I: *Principles* (Englewood Cliffs, NJ: Prentice Hall, 1983).

7

WAN Technology and Design

Wide area networks (WANs) have been traditionally very easy to distinguish from LANs, but this differentiation is becoming increasingly fuzzy, with the emergence of technologies such as ATM and Gigabit Ethernet. Historically WANs tended to be built with one or more orders of magnitude less bandwidth than LANs (see Table 7.1). This is partly because of the high cost per bandwidth incurred and also due to the different techniques required in order to propagate traffic over much greater distances. Wide area networks connect cities or continents rather than buildings, and central to wide area networking are the issues of cost and ownership. While some large organizations have built their own private networks, this not the norm. Wide area networks are typically leased from PTTs and telcos for one or more years, since they require a huge investment and infrastructure to install and maintain. Wide area billing is, therefore, much more mature for wide area applications; until recently LANs have been seen as effectively free access, and only now are companies starting to examine the potential for billing users for local area network time and possibly outsourcing the local infrastructure to service providers. All of this would be impractical without the convergence toward a common protocol, IP, and a new breed of high-performance data collection products.

In this chapter, we discuss both the technology and design issues for wide area internetworks, specifically point-to-point networks such as leased and satellite links, circuit-switched networks such as ISDN, and packet-switched networks such as X.25, Frame Relay, and SMDS. The following subjects are covered in this chapter:

- Wide area network technologies
- Topology design and configuration issues
- Traffic management issues
- Performance issues

Table 7.1   *Commonly Used Wide Area Interfaces*

Interface	Applique	Sex
V.24/V.28	25-pin D-Subminiature	Male
V.35/V.36	37-pin D-Subminiature	Male
V.11/X.21	15-pin D-Subminiature	Male
HSSI	50-pin D-Subminiature	Male

An increasingly important element of wide area design is Quality of Service (QoS). Due to the complexity and variety of technologies involved we will not discuss it in this book.

7.1   Wide area network design principles

7.1.1   Basic concepts and terminology

The telephone network

The terminology used in wide area networking is extensive, and for those of us who were baptized in data networks in the 1980s and 1990s, much of this terminology appears archaic, with its roots firmly planted in telephony. Nevertheless, it is worth revisiting the source of this terminology briefly, since these terms frequently appear in material concerning the migration from circuit-switched to packet-switched networking.

Telephone networks were originally designed as a rigid hierarchy, as illustrated in Figure 7.1, and many of the components of this model have

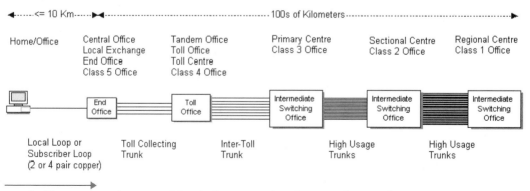

Figure 7.1   *Structure of the telephone network and associated terminology.*

alternate names, as shown, sometimes adding to the confusion. At the core of the network are a handful of regional centers. High-capacity trunks distribute call traffic through progressively smaller switching offices, until we reach the Central Office (CO). Between the larger switching offices, coaxial cable, microwave, and fiber-optic cables are used. Cable distribution is defined by a tree topology; as we near the subscriber, large, multipair copper is spliced and joined to form many smaller bundles (e.g., 900-pair to 3 × 300-pair to 6 × 150-pair to 18 × 50-pair and so on). From the central office, 2-pair unshielded copper cable is delivered to individual subscriber premises over what is termed the local loop.

Point of Presence (PoP)

A Point of Presence (PoP) is a provider location where DCE equipment is deployed to terminate user access from a variety of link technologies and speeds (e.g., switching nodes, modem banks, multiplexing equipment, and dial termination services such as Remote Access Servers [RAS] or Network Access Servers [NAS]). PoPs are normally located in major population centers (i.e., large towns and cities), since services are rolled out across a region. As service uptake expands, PoP density and reach is extended, increasing capacity to meet the demand, increasing resilience, and improving competition by lowering prices. By adding more PoPs the average access circuit length between a subscriber and a PoP decreases, enabling more cost-effective access. Note that individual technologies may use their own specific definition of the term PoP.

Interface definitions

Devices are connected to wide area networks through a variety of physical and electrical interfaces, partly due to the numerous standards that have emerged over the years, the differences between United States, European, and Far East standardization, and technological innovation by manufacturers. Table 7.1 illustrates the most familiar interfaces you are likely to come across today. From both the vendor and customer perspective this diversity represents yet another layer of complexity and unnecessary expense. When designing an international network, you need to bear in mind that different interface specifications and approvals are typically mandated for different countries, and you will need to provide adequate spares for each region. Manufacturers may have to submit products through several different approval bodies, each using different test criteria, in order to release essentially the same product internationally.

The DTE/DCE interface

At the physical layer there is also a logical interface definition, first introduced by X.21, called the Data Terminal Equipment (DTE)/Data Communication Equipment (DCE) interface. The DTE/DCE interface definition is now widely used as a generic definition throughout telecommunications industry and standards documentation. In practice, DTE equipment refers to Customer Premises Equipment (CPE), such as routers, gateways, bridges, terminals, or personal computers. DCE refers to carrier equipment, typically switching equipment residing at the provider's Point of Presence (PoP).

Multiplexing

Multiplexing is a technique commonly employed within wide area network infrastructures that enables multiple smaller input signals or data channels to be packed into larger channels for efficient transmission. Demultiplexing (or inverse multiplexing) is the converse process. There are several broad classes of technology available, as follows:

- Frequency Division Multiplexing (FDM)—FDM is an analog technique for aggregating multiple voice (or low-speed data) channels for high-speed transport. The total bandwidth is divided among subscribers, and each subscriber is allocated a fixed portion of the frequency spectrum. Frequencies are assigned to channels, and channels are separated by unused frequency bands called guard bands. FDM is still widely used in satellite, microwave, telephone, radio, and cable TV (CATV) systems.

- Time Division Multiplexing (TDM)—TDM is a synchronous technology and works by allocating channels divided into time slots, one slot for each user. Slots are encapsulated in TDM frames. This system is inherently fair, but inefficient, since even if empty time slots are available, a TDM user must wait for an allocated slot. Therefore, TDM represents wasted bandwidth unless the network is fully subscribed on all links; high bandwidth or bursty applications cannot make use of spare bandwidth dynamically. TDM was originally developed in the 1950s to eliminate the filtering and noise problems associated with the public telephone network. Since the 1980s, TDMs have been employed in private and corporate networks as a way of distributing asynchronous and synchronous traffic such as data, voice, and video.

- Statistical Time Division Multiplexing (STDM)—provides much more effective use of bandwidth than either TDM or FDM. STDM employs a more efficient (averaging 4:1) multiplexing technique, where slots are not dedicated but are divided dynamically among active subscribers. One variant of STDM is Asynchronous Time Division Multiplexing (ATDM), where the multiplexer allocates blocks of data for each user as required (a form of packet switching over a point-to-point circuit). Another variant is Statistical Packet Multiplexing (SPM), which combines features of X.25 packet switching with STDM. Because of the flexibility and efficiency of statistical multiplexers, these devices have essentially displaced FDM and TDM multiplexers in the marketplace.

- Dense Wave Division Multiplexing (DWDM)—is a relatively new technique for multiplexing many optical wavelengths (referred to as channels) onto a single fiber strand. DWDM optical multiplexers can handle up to 80 Gbps today, with a potential for 800 Gbps. This technique is already revolutionizing core network design.

T1/E1 digital multiplexing systems

In the early 1960s, engineers at Bell Labs invented a multiplexing system based on TDM techniques by first digitising a voice signal into a 64-Kbps data stream (at 8,000 voltage samples per second, with each sample expressed in 8 bits—called a slot). Bell organized 24 of these channels into a framed data stream. The resulting frame was 193 bits long and created an equivalent data rate of 1.544 Mbps. This structured signal was referred to as a DS1, although it is commonly referred to as a T1 (to be precise, T1 defines only the raw data rate, not the formatting). AT&T deployed DS1 in the interoffice plant starting in the late 1960s, although since then almost all of it has been replaced by optical fiber. By the mid-1970s DS1 was being used in the feeder segment of the outside loop plant. In Europe, the ITU/T adopted and modified the Bell Labs approach, introducing a system called E1. By contrast, E1 multiplexes 30 voice channels to provide a data rate of 2.048 Mbps. Furthermore, E1 defines both the format and the raw data rate (i.e., there is no equivalent of DS1).

Until recently, T1 and E1 circuits were implemented over copper wire by using crude transceivers with a self-clocking Alternate Mark Inversion (AMI) protocol. AMI requires repeaters 3,000 ft (914.4 m) from the central office and every 6,000 ft (1828.8 m) thereafter; it takes 1.5 MHz of bandwidth, with a signal peak at 750 kHz (U.S. systems). To a transmission purist, this is hardly elegant, but it has worked well for many years and hundreds of thousands of lines (T1 and E1) have been deployed around the world today.

Types of multiplexer

There are a number of basic multiplexer types that can be used to construct a complete network hierarchy, as illustrated in Figure 7.2. These include the following:

- Access or channel band multiplexers—Typically CPE equipment. They provide asynchronous and synchronous support for combined voice and data support. They may also integrate PBX, LAN, Frame Relay, X.25, SDLC/DDLC, and provide support for low-speed video and host attachment. Access multiplexers typically provide one or more T1 or E1 trunks. Fractional T1/E1 multiplexers enable the trunk to be channelized in increments of 56 or 64 Kbps. Subrate Data Multiplexers (SRDM) enable a DS0 to be channelized into smaller bandwidths (down to 2,400 bps).

- Network or backbone multiplexers—take inputs from one or more access multiplexers, typically offering many T1 interfaces on the access side and one or more T3 interfaces on the backbone side. Network multiplexers include basic routing functionality, either through static routing tables or dynamic routing algorithms.

- Aggregator multiplexers or hubs—aggregate multiple T1s onto high-speed trunks. They may also support switched 56/64 K dial termination. There are several variants. M12 multiplexers aggregate four T1s onto two T2s. M23 multiplexers aggregate seven T2s onto a T3. M13 multiplexers aggregate 28 T1s onto a T3. M22 and M44 multiplexers provide routing and configuration management for 22 and 44 channels. MX3 multiplexers aggregate combinations of T1 and T2 onto a T3.

- Drop and insert multiplexers—designed to drop and insert lower-speed channels into higher-speed trunks—for example, 56/64-Kbps channels dropped or inserted into T1/E1 trunks. They may also include some circuit-switching support.

These devices have been used for many years to build public and private data networks; however, there has been a major shift away from multiplexers in the 1990s, since there is an increasing need for more efficient, scalable solutions and some form of overall traffic engineering as the demand for bandwidth increases. Consequently, many vendors of multiplexing equipment have integrated switching, routing, and LAN access products into their chassis in an effort to at least stay in the game with hybrid solutions in the short term. However, more efficient, dynamic, high-speed switching

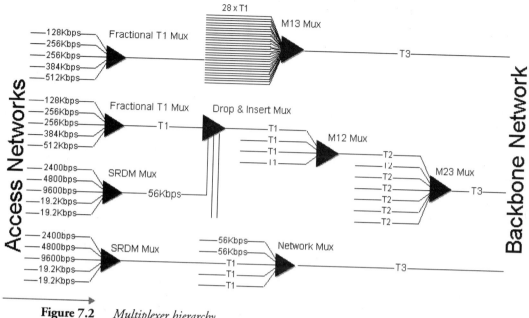

Figure 7.2   *Multiplexer hierarchy.*

solutions have emerged in the forms of FDDI, SONET, SMDS, Frame Relay, and ATM. For more information on multiplexing techniques the interested reader is referred to reference [1].

Wide area technologies

Wide area network technologies can be divided into three broad categories, as illustrated in Figure 7.3. This classification has a fundamental influence on the network design you choose to adopt, since the performance, traffic characteristics, reliability, and cost implications differ significantly for each technology.

Wide area network hierarchy

As with local area network design, wide area network design has a range of tools and technologies available to suit different applications, and unlike local area network design, recurring bandwidth charges are an important component of the design choices. Wide area network technology can be broadly aligned with two classes of networks, based on proximity to the user and function, as follows:

- Access networks—enable small-office, home-office (SOHO) users and remote office users to access a wide area backbone, either through

Figure 7.3
Wide area service network classifications.

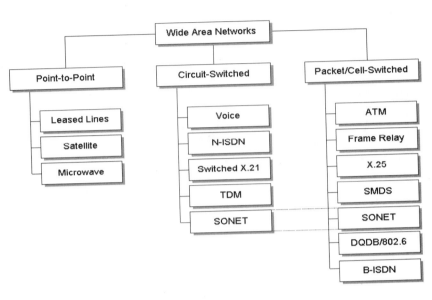

lower-cost, fixed access such as a Digital Subscriber Line (DSL) and cable modems, or dial-up access through Integrated Services Digital Network (ISDN) or PPP/SLIP running over modem links.

- Backbone networks—provide regional or international services, typically through one or more technologies, such as leased lines, satellite links, Synchronous Optical Network (SONET), Switched Multi-megabit Data Services (SMDS), Frame Relay, X.25, or Asynchronous Transfer Mode (ATM).

Note that there is no strict mapping of technology to either of the two applications; the main differentiator is cost. It is technically possible to have a 45-Mbps leased line directly wired to your home; chances are, however, that you would not be able to afford the $300,000 annual bill.

Figure 7.4 illustrates some of the concepts in wide area network design. On the periphery of the backbone are a number of access networks, broadly divided into local and metropolitan area networks and dial-up access from SOHO or remote office environments. These networks provide access to the backbone. Large backbones tend to be hierarchical, broadly divided into short-haul regional backbones and the core, with different technologies often selected for different levels of hierarchy. Large metropolitan areas, spanning many miles, are typically served by a number of central offices, head ends, and other facilities where customer access traffic is aggregated onto short-haul transport networks. Nowadays the transport network is typically implemented over optical fiber, and, as bandwidth demand

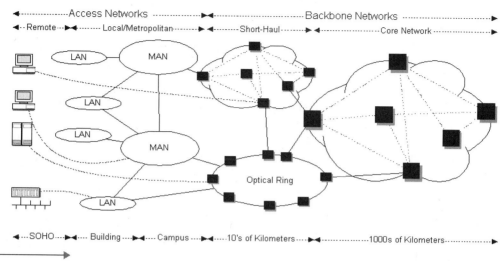

Figure 7.4   *Wide area network hierarchy.*

increases, the short-haul optical transport network is moving closer to the subscriber. Core networks may span hundreds or thousands of miles, with hundreds of miles between switching nodes. Again, the physical infrastructure is moving toward an all-optical-fiber core.

Backbones may be public (i.e., a service offered by an operator at a price) or private. On public backbones the service provider will deploy several Points of Presence (PoP) to facilitate cost-effective, short-haul access to the backbone. From the PoP, traffic is switched or routed through the backbone, potentially over many hops and a number of long-haul links.

Wide area network design issues

In wide area networking, and especially in packet-switched networks, there are several issues to resolve during the design phase, including the following:

- Physical topology—When designing any wide area internetwork, either packet switched, circuit switched, or point to point, there are three basic design models you can use: star topology and partial-meshed and full-meshed topologies.

- Logical topology—Depending upon the wide area technology employed, the design may comprise physical and possibly Virtual Circuits (VCs). For example, point-to-point networks such as leased lines can be used to design any topology; however, in each case all links require a physical end-to-end cable connection. On the other hand, packet-switched networks such as Frame Relay can use a physical connection at the user's premises to connect logically to many sites over the Packet-Switched Network (PSN). Circuit meshing is provided by a set of interconnected backbone switches, and data connections may be virtually routed by different switches at different times depending upon factors such as congestion and path failures.

- Performance—In a large internetwork, many local and campus networks may be interconnected over the backbone, and the issues in capacity planning become increasingly complex as the number of devices, buffers, and varying transmission speeds all impact on the traffic dynamics. Packets may traverse multiple hubs, buses, switches, and routers, often competing for bandwidth through a variety of links and buffers. Understanding performance on a LAN is relatively straightforward, but in the wide area you cannot readily assume that data will reach their destination in a timely manner, and this is particularly true of public networks. Users may experience significant delays and/or variable delays, and packets may be routinely discarded or corrupted. Even though end-system protocols will typically retransmit any lost data, in real terms this means more variable delay. In complex internetworks you may need to tune particular applications according to the transmission path characteristics. For example, client software running on a local workstation, connected via switched Ethernet to a database server, may have a default five-second timeout for database access (typically ample). A remote access user coming in via a satellite link may need a ten-second timeout (or more) to make up for the delays introduced by the link.

- Virtual circuit handling—You must consider how virtual circuits are handled by the specific WAN technology and hardware used. Some protocols may require special handling as traffic is queued and streamed from one node to the next. It may be necessary to assign specific virtual circuit identifiers to specific protocol types. For example, with Frame Relay we might choose different Data Link Connection Identifiers (DLCIs for IP traffic and NetWare traffic). In this way each VC could be tuned with different committed information rates and excess information rates. In this way we could allocate different bandwidth or service guarantees to individual VCs.

- Broadcast handling—Since wide area links are often an order of magnitude slower than LAN links, and most WAN technologies are essentially point to point in nature, we must pay special attention to broadcast (and multicast) traffic. Broadcasts are, unfortunately, a major component of many legacy applications and services, where a shared LAN medium is assumed. The magnitude of broadcast traffic produced depends on several factors, as follows:

- The type of protocols and services enabled, and how these services are configured (hello timers, routing updates, service advertisements, queries, etc.).
- The size and speed of the internetwork (number of services, number of routes to advertise, number of DHCP and BOOTP requests, available bandwidths, etc.).
- The mechanisms employed for broadcast distribution when integrating broadcast LANs such as Ethernet with nonbroadcast, multiaccess networks such as ATM, X.25, and Frame Relay.

In the WAN environment it is especially important to control and minimize broadcasts, because of the potential scope of distribution. On point-to-point networks it is possible to emulate a shared medium environment, however, since many VCs are often configured at a single physical interface, the additional processing required on routing and switching elements can be considerable, especially in highly meshed environments. In effect, each broadcast must be replicated down many virtual circuits, and this can significantly impair scalability. Despite the advantages that highly meshed topologies can offer, they may be impractical for large packet-switching internetworks where packet replication is high. Clearly, some level of meshing is always desirable, even in these circumstances, to ensure better availability. In reality, there is a direct trade-off between performance and the requirements for physical path redundancy.

- Quality of service—Due to the performance variability described previously, and the special problems associated with public wide area backbones such as the Internet, increasingly Service-Level Agreements (SLAs) are being demanded by users. A whole new architecture is emerging to provide service guarantees.

- Scalability—With any large internetwork scalability is a key issue for the network designer, and this issue is determined by many factors, including hardware devices, protocols, buffering schemes, broadcast handling, VC architecture, addressing models, broadcast delivery, routing architectures, and switch architectures.

7.1.2   Access networks

During the 1990s organizations became much more mobile, and the increased use of laptop computers, together with increased reliance on intranets for Web, e-mail, calendar, and order-entry applications, meant that demand for remote access networking was huge. At present the majority of mobile users are still using dial-up, voice-grade data modems (termed asynchronous routing), primarily due to the high tariffs imposed by providers for fixed access. Voice-grade dial-up links are inappropriate, however, for site-to-site applications other than remote out-of-band management or backup.

Dial-up access

Voice-grade modems may be installed at the user's premises and connected via voice-grade lines (i.e., the plain old telephone system to the core-switching network). Data signals are transmitted through the network unaltered; the network treats them exactly like voice signals. This has been a significant advantage to date, despite being low bandwidth, since a user can be easily connected wherever a telephone point exists (and there are literally millions of them). Voice-grade modems currently transmit up to 33.6 Kbps symmetric (or 56–28 Kbps asymmetric), with voice-grade bandwidth not exceeding 3.3 kHz. V.34 modems achieve 10 bits per hertz of bandwidth, an impressive number seeing as it approaches theoretical limits, and they can also transmit and receive simultaneously within the same band. Nowadays the most widely used modems adhere to the V.90 specifications.

For higher-speed dial-up access the ISDN Basic Rate Interface (BRI), offering up to 128 Kbps, can be an attractive option, since it offers circuit-switched channelized access for both voice and data capability over existing telephone lines. For additional bandwidth there is an ISDN Primary Rate Interface (PRI), offering over 1 Mbps of channelized access. ISDN service availability and tariffs vary significantly by country; it may not be suitable or even an option for all users. Increasingly, mobile phone technology (either attached to, or built into personal computers) is becoming the preferred way to access the network for many mobile users. This enables a user to access the network from anywhere that a signal can be reached. In Europe this is particularly attractive, since the standardized use of digital GSM technology means that users can roam around Europe without ever having to plug into a physical socket. The next logical step for mobile users is Internet access built directly into mobile handsets. Already we are seeing the first generation of Wireless Application Protocol (WAP) phones made available for Internet access, although there are limitations in link speed (typically 9.6 Kbps) and the quality of content displayed (i.e., small, mainly text-oriented screens). Over the next five years there will be a huge push to so-called third-generation (3G) mobile phone technology, providing improved handset displays, and running at speeds of anywhere between 115 Kbps and 2 Mbps.

Higher speed and permanent access

The imminent demise of the modem has been predicted many times over the past two decades; needless to say it is still going strong. However, even with considerable advances in the algorithm, digital signal processing (DSP), and semiconductor technology, it is likely that speeds will progress way beyond current levels. Modems are also notoriously slow to connect, and the nature of dial-up means that information must be polled and cannot be easily pushed to the user dynamically. For example, to check for incoming e-mail a user must incur a call charge, even if just to establish that no mail has arrived. With the massive demand for Internet access, the increased application demands for bandwidth, and the gradual erosion of access charges through competition, there is now a perceived requirement for cost-effective permanent online access. Users are becoming increasingly frustrated with dial-up connectivity, and a number of technologies have emerged and are already being deployed. The main contenders are the ISDN BRI, plus newer technologies such as cable modems and various flavors of DSL. Note that although ISDN is a dial-up technology, it does have the capability for low-bandwidth online data applications (such as checking your mailbox status) via X.25 running over the D-Channel, although few service providers offer this capability at present.

It is clear that we are finally heading toward multimegabit service direct to the home, with permanent online network access, most probably accessed through next-generation multimedia televisions and mobile phones. This will provide a massive impetus to a wide range of e-commerce and group-oriented Internet applications, such as home shopping, video e-mail, online gaming, online dating, and so on. With the home wired up permanently there will be a new generation of smart houses with the ability to remotely control appliances, heating systems, alarm systems, and so on. In the future it is harder to see what will not be done via home Internet access.

Distance limitations

As with all wired technologies, there are constraints on bandwidth and distance. The bandwidth limitations associated with voice band lines, however, have more to do with the network equipment than the subscriber line; filters at the edge of the network limit voice grade bandwidth to 3.3 kHz. Without these filters, copper access lines could pass frequencies into the

Table 7.2 *Data Rate Limitations (One Way) and Distance Constraints on 24-Gauge Twisted Pair for Popular Wide Area Circuit Technologies*

Type	Circuit Speed	Max Distance (ft)
DS1 (T1)	1.544 Mbps	18000
E1	2.048 Mbps	16000
DS2 (T2)	6.312 Mbps	12000
E2	8.448 Mbps	9000
1/4 STS-1	12.960 Mbps	4500
1/2 STS-1	25.920 Mbps	3000
STS-1	51.840 Mbps	1000

MHz range, although the next problem they would face is attenuation. Attenuation increases with line length and frequency and is a major factor limiting data rates over twisted-pair wire. Practical limits on unidirectional data rates compared with distance (using 24-gauge twisted pair) are listed in Table 7.2.

The configuration of local loop plant varies from country to country. In some countries a local loop of 18,000 ft (5486.4 m) is enough to reach virtually all subscribers; in other countries, such as the United States, this distance covers less than 80 percent of subscribers, and the other 20 percent have lines with loading coils, which cannot be used for DSL service (including ISDN) without removing the coils. Most telephone companies have been running programs to reduce the average local loop length for several years, largely to increase the capacity of existing central offices. Typically this involves the deployment of access nodes as satellites of central offices, creating Distribution Areas with maximum subscriber loops of 6,000 ft (1,828.8 m) from the access node. Remote access nodes are usually fed by T1/E1 lines and more recently via HDSL and fiber. A distribution area may connect an average of 1,500 customer premises in the suburbs, and approximately 3,000 customer premises in urban areas. As one would expect, the number of premises served diminishes as service data rates increase; for example, a fiber-to-the-curb system offering STS-1 data rates may be within reach of only 20 customer premises in some suburban areas.

Selecting the right access technology

When planning any wide area access network, it is important to provide sufficient bandwidth to meet the demands of the applications expected to run into the customer's premises. These applications include the following:

- Occasional Internet and e-mail access—A voice-grade modem will suffice, at speeds of between 9.6 and 33.6 Kbps.

- Frequent Internet and e-mail access plus file transfer—For higher bandwidth and relatively short duration use (e.g., three to four hours of network access per day, typical of a remote office worker) ISDN is a good choice, though tariffs vary significantly by country. On a BRI interface data rates of either 64 Kbps or 128 Kbps (provisioned dynamically) are available. Frame Relay might also be an option here.

- Video-on-demand—For video applications a downstream data rate of approximately 1.5 Mbps per subscriber terminal is required, and you should be able to supply many subscribers within 18,000 ft. For subscribers with shorter lines (either to a central office or remote access node), you can offer more than one channel to more than one premise's terminal. ISDN PRI or Frame Relay would be an option here, although likely to be expensive. DSL and cable modem technology would be an attractive option.

- Digital live television—You must provision at least 6 Mbps, and you may be limited to 4,500-ft distances to supply more than one channel at a time (hence telco interest in wireless broadcast digital TV technology). HDTV requires up to 20 Mbps and is supported only over the shortest loop length. Again, DSL and cable modem technology would be an attractive option.

Note that the provisioning of digital services over legacy twisted-pair copper lines requires transceivers and special modems capable of very high data rates.

7.1.3   Backbone networks

Today there are a diverse number of technologies available to build backbone networks, including SONET/SDH, Frame Relay, ATM, SMDS, leased and satellite circuits, TDM, and X.25. The network designer needs to be aware of the merits and limitations of each of these technologies, together with the bandwidth, availability, and performance characteristics they offer.

Available bandwidths

Leased circuits are available in both analog and digital formats and a range of fixed bandwidths. Typically they require a single physical interface at each end of the circuit to terminate the connection. For large networks this impairs scalability unless channelized circuits are used, since the central site may require dozens of expensive ports over multiple concentrators. For large backbone applications the traffic dynamics may vary considerably, and fixed-access technologies such as leased circuits and satellite links may be inappropriate. More efficient and flexible technologies such as Frame Relay, SMDS, and ATM are becoming increasingly attractive, from both an operational and a financial perspective. Note that short-haul leased circuits are also commonly used as an integral part of packet- or cell-switching services such as Frame Relay, providing access links from the customer's premises to the nearest PoP.

It is worth remembering that the communications infrastructure available in different parts of the world varies significantly, largely dependent upon the size and cash available to those regions. X.25, for example, may effectively be dead in most of the Western Hemisphere, but in parts of Eastern Europe it is still alive and kicking. Even deployment of Frame Relay and ATM technology varies significantly around the globe, and there are also marked differences in the technology choices for public and private backbones. All of these differences should illustrate the point that it is unwise to generalize, and even more unwise to ignore the installed base. After all, ATM was almost universally expected to have conquered both LAN and WAN environments by 2000. That proposition seems no longer remotely likely, at least not in the near term.

There are a range of higher-bandwidth solutions available for higher-speed permanent connections as listed in Table 7.3. Many of these physical interfaces use framed transmission structures. This principle was developed from Time Division Multiplexing (TDM) techniques used to transport digitally encoded voice. The European E1 system transmits data at 2.048 Mbps, while the U.S. T1 system transmits data at 1.544 Mbps. As faster transmission link technology became available, there was a requirement to multiplex many E1 and T1 systems onto the faster bearer circuit. This was achieved using a hierarchical multiplexing scheme known as the Plesiochronous Digital Hierarchy (PDH). Note that plesio is Greek for "almost"; so plesiochronous means almost synchronous. PDH is the digital hierarchy that was used before the advent of the SONET/SDH standards.

Note in Table 7.3 that ISDN BRI includes 2 × 64-Kbps data/voice channels plus a 16-Kbps signaling channel. ISDN PRI varies by region. In the United States this is provisioned as 23 × 64-Kbps data/voice channels plus a 64-Kbps signaling channel. In Europe there are 30 × 64-Kbps data/voice channels plus a 64-Kbps signaling channel. STS is synchronous transport signal for optical fiber (also referred to as OC-n, where OC means

Table 7.3   *Typical Wide Area Service Bandwidths*

Service	Bandwidth
Europe	
ISDB Basic rate Interface (BRI)	144 Kbps
ISDB Primary Rate Interface (PRI)	1.984 Mbps
E0	64 Kbps
E1	2.048 Mbps
E2	8.448 Mbps
E3	34.368 Mbs
E4	139.264 Mbps
USA	
ISDB BRI	144 Kbps
ISDN PRI	1.544 Mpbs
DS-0	64 Kbps
DS-1 / T1	1.544 Mpbs
DS-1C / T1C	3.142 Mbps
DS-2 / T2	6.312 Mbps
DS-3 / T3	44.736 Mbps
DS-4 / T4	274.176 Mbps
Generic	
STS-1 & OC-1	51.84 Mbps
STS-3 & OC-3	155.52 Mbps
STS-9 & OC-9	466.56 Mbps
STS-12 & OC-12	622.08 Mbps
STS-24 & OC-24	1.24416 Gbps
STS-36 & OC-36	1.86624 Gbps
STS-48 & OC-48 (STM-16)	2.48832 Gbps
STS-n & OC-n (STM-n/3)	n * 51.84 Mbps
SMDS	56 Kbps to 34 Mbps

optical carrier). Note that the theoretical maximum speed for SONET OC-n is OC-255.

Backbone technology strengths and weaknesses

Table 7.4 summarizes some of the main strengths and weaknesses of the various wide area technologies available for backbone design. While it is always useful to encapsulate the key points in a concise form, the differences between these technologies and selection for a particular network design are rarely black and white and depend on many factors, such as service availability in different regions of the world, bandwidth flexibility, cost, traffic characteristics, error handling, and the desired quality of service. We cover

Table 7.4   *WAN Technology Comparison*

Technology	Bandwidth	Strengths	Weaknesses
Leased Lines	64Kbps to 45Mbps	Dedicated bandwidth Simple to deploy Wide availability	Bandwidth allocation static & inefficient Does not scale
X.25	2.4Kbps to 2Mbps	Excellent for poor quality lines Protocol Independent Guaranteed Delivery	No performance guarantees Large latency and jitter Typically data only Future decline predicted
TDM	64Kbps to 45Mbps	Predictable Performance Protocol Independent Mixed voice and data	Bandwidth allocation static & inefficient Future decline predicted Circuit switching does not scale
Frame Relay	64Kbps to 45Mbps	Dynamic flexible bandwidth Limited QoS Wide Service offering	Poor multiservice performance Relatively Large latency and jitter Typically data only
ATM	1.5Mbps to 2.5Gbps	Dynamic flexible bandwidth Predictable Performance Low latency and jitter Layer 2 multiservice capability	Cell overhead quite high Patchy service availability Generally available at T1 or higher Complex
SONET	45Mbps to 9.6Gbps+	Very High Performance Guranteed low latency Good Physical layer resilience Dynamic Bandwidth Allocation	Cell overhead quite high Expensive Patchy service availability Generally only OC-3c/OC-12c or higher

the detailed operations and applications of these technologies in subsequent sections of this chapter.

Network overlays

Many public core networks have a huge amount of legacy circuit-switched equipment in place, which will take significant time and money to displace. To remain competitive, operators are rolling out new data services (such as Voice over IP and IP VPNs) over more efficient and scalable transports such as ATM, Frame Relay, and SONET. These services must coexist with legacy circuit-switched applications and in many cases exhibit the same reach. In practice this means data network services and associated switching equipment may need to be transposed on this existing infrastructure to form a layered overlay network. Each data service typically runs over its own overlay network.

Network overlays may comprise several layers, each typically requiring different physical equipment, different management infrastructures, and dedicated maintenance staff. Clearly, from the transmission perspective, there is the potential for major inefficiency, since user data are encapsulated and possibly segmented and reassembled many times before they are placed on the physical cable. All of these factors affect the overall cost and the ability of a service provider to deploy new services and react to change. For older, established operators much of this layering may be historical, necessitated because of the installed base of legacy equipment and cable plant. Newer operators have the opportunity to minimize the depth of overlays through judicious technology choices and in doing so gain competitive advantage in the future.

Core networking issues

Historically, the majority of public backbones today have been built using core TDM technology—a technology that is now over 20 years old and primarily designed for voice traffic. TDM standardizes on DS-0 (64 Kbps) voice channels. These channels are aggregated by TDMs at Central Offices (COs) into bigger pipes such as DS-1s (1.544 Mbps) and DS-3s (45 Mbps) and then switched across the core via cross-connect switches. TDMs are then required to demultiplex these large pipes back into DS-0s.

There has been a dramatic rise in data traffic generated by the Internet. Since the mid-1990s the Internet has begun to attract significant volumes of data traffic onto public networks. Some operators are experiencing growth as high as 800 percent annually. By contrast, voice is increasing at a mere 4 percent worldwide. It is now generally accepted that conventional circuit switching is inadequate for delivering the anticipated volumes of mixed-media traffic cost effectively in the twenty-first century. The circuit-switched model has several inherent problems. The TDM model is based on a rigid compromise of 64-Kbps channels. With modern compression techniques voice can be compressed into 16 Kbps or less without sacrificing quality, so 64 Kbps is too much for voice, and 64 Kbps is far from optimal for bursty LAN and multimedia traffic. Also, TDM does not scale. Multiplexers are expensive and typically have to be configured manually. This slows down the provider's ability to roll out new services quickly and increases labor costs. Since 64-Kbps channels do not scale efficiently, some carriers find it more economical to overprovision bandwidth (e.g., by running a single T1 over a T3 circuit rather than deploy more TDMs). Finally, there is the problem of overlays. Large established carriers typically have many overlay networks (as many as 20), either inherited or accumulated over the years through multiple technology changes. Aside from the overheads on messaging, this leads to serious operating inefficiencies through redundant equipment, additional maintenance staff, dedicated management systems, and so on. Ultimately these inefficiencies constrain the ability of a provider to roll out new services quickly, and additional costs are passed on to the user.

All of these technology choices represent a series of compromises for data traffic, and a complete overhaul is required to meet the new demands for IP networking. To remain competitive, public wide area network backbones are undergoing a dramatic reshaping, and both operators and equipment vendors are beginning to construct converged packet- and cell-based infrastructures that will handle mixed data and voice and video traffic, while accommodating quality of service and security guarantees. In recent years the design of core networks has been revolutionized by the convergence on IP as the unifying transport protocol, the emergence of very high performance terabit routers, and the introduction of Dense Wavelength Division Multiplexers (DWDMs). In comparison to Time Division Multiplexing (TDM) technology, the need for and cost of electrical regeneration over long distances has been reduced through DWDM, and far more information per fiber can be transmitted. These changes have fundamentally changed the economics of core optical networks. Consequently, virtually all operators of long-distance, fiber-optic networks have implemented or expect to implement DWDM. Forward-thinking operators are already replacing circuit-switched networks with IP, enabling them to carry mixed media traffic with potentially huge cost savings. The changes required are substantial, and for larger operators with a large installed based the cost implications are huge as follows:

- Backbone network infrastructure products—TDMs in the backbone need to be displaced by advanced switching and routing equipment, enabling more flexible bandwidth configurations, better utilization, and lower cost. Next-generation backbones will incorporate IP running over terabit routers and ATM switches, which will aggregate traffic into very large pipes (currently 10 Gbit/s on SONET OC192, but this will increase as Dense Wavelength Division Multiplexers (DWDMs) are deployed). Even higher speeds may be achieved in the future as this technology matures, with so-called metaswitches eliminating the need for DWDM and SONET, enabling carriers to transmit ATM and IP directly over the optical layer.

- Access network infrastructure products—In access networks, a new class of Integrated Access Device (IAD) is required, incorporating

DSL modems and CSU/DSUs and interfacing with legacy PBXs, hubs, Ethernet switches, and routing equipment. IADs are CPE equipment provisioned and managed by the operator.

- Minimizing overlays—All existing data services must be migrated onto a dynamic, high-performance switching infrastructure, which can be traffic engineered to meet the demands for mixed-media applications.

- Value-added PoPs—Operators are expected to increase the functionality provided at PoPs—for example, VOIP gateways, cache servers for Web traffic and directory-enabled service provisioning, and high-capacity call termination equipment with policy management via LDAP directory access.

- Advanced traffic engineering—More powerful and granular solutions to traffic engineering are required to maximize utilization, avoid the costs of overprovisions, and adapt rapidly to change. Several solutions are emerging, such as MPLS and constraint-based routing.

- Quality of service—With increased reliance of business on the network, users are demanding increasingly tighter service guarantees. In a large internetwork environment this requires substantial changes to the infrastructure and support for signaling and tagging protocols, flow classification, label distribution, and advanced routing.

- Virtual Private Networks (VPNs)—Another major change likely to occur is in service presentation. Users are already being offered a range of customized Virtual Private Network (VPN) services running over managed backbones, each tuned to deliver a different class of service securely for an appropriate price.

From a pragmatic standpoint, however, circuit switching is likely to remain part of the infrastructure for some time yet. First, there is the issue of installed base. There are over 13 million fiber circuits and over 120 million copper lines in North America alone; upgrading this infrastructure and all associated equipment is likely to take time and considerable cost. This may be further hampered at the access level (i.e., the local loop) by the virtual monopoly exercised by some of the larger PTTs and Incumbent Local-Exchange Carriers (ILECs). Since these organizations control most of the connections to customer sites, they can effectively stifle competition and delay progress, as has been demonstrated on occasions in the past when new technology became available (e.g., ISDN). Another key piece in the jigsaw is Quality of Service (QoS). This also requires potentially huge infrastructure changes to enable applications such as voice and video to be delivered in a timely manner and to enable mission-critical data to be prioritized appropriately. For the foreseeable future, a new breed of hybrid TDM/data network equipment is being deployed in established backbones to support both circuit-switched and packet-switched traffic. For greenfield designs, data network equipment based on cell- and packet-switching technologies is available for data-optimized networks or to supplement existing circuit-based infrastructure.

7.2   **Encapsulation techniques**

Packet- and cell-switched data are moved over wide area circuits by first encapsulating these data. This encapsulation typically embodies addressing and control information pertinent to the underlying transport media and, optionally, basic error checking. There are several encapsulation techniques of interest, including the following:

- Binary Synchronous Control (BSC or Bisync)—developed by IBM in the mid-1960s. A half-duplex, point-to-point or multipoint, character-oriented protocol used for bidirectional transfer of character-oriented data.

- Data Communications Message Protocol (DCMP)—similar to BSC, but developed by Digital Equipment Corporation (DEC). A half-duplex or full-duplex, point-to-point or multipoint, synchronous or asynchronous byte-count-oriented protocol.

- Synchronous Data Link Control (SDLC)—developed by IBM in the early 1970s. The first true bit-oriented protocol, subsequently modified and adopted by the ISO as the ISO 4335 High-Level Data Link Protocol (HDLC) protocol and by ANSI as the ANSI X3.66 Advanced Data Communications Control Protocol (ADCCP).

- High-Level Data Link Control (HDLC)—an international standard based on IBM's SDLC and very widely deployed in various forms. HDLC is a bit-oriented, simple, half-duplex or full-duplex, synchronous protocol for point-to-point or multipoint links.

- Serial Line Protocol (SLIP)—the first encapsulation protocol to become widely used on simple dial-up serial lines. A subset of HDLC, now largely displaced by PPP, since it is limited to IP and limited in flexibility.

- Point-to-Point (PPP)—based on HDLC and created in 1988 by the IETF and now the most popular encapsulation for point-to-point and dial-up links. PPP offers multiprotocol support and strong peer negotiation capabilities and is widely supported, offering excellent multivendor capabilities.

As indicated, many modern wide area technologies use derivatives or subsets of the HDLC protocol (it forms the basis of several protocols introduced by the CCITT including X.25's LAPB and ISDN's LAPD). Before examining wide area technologies in detail, we will first review three of the most popular encapsulation types—HDLC, SLIP, and PPP—in more depth.

7.2.1 High-level data link control (HDLC)

High-level data link control (HDLC), documented in ISO 3309, specifies a packet encapsulation standard for serial links. HDLC supports several modes of operation and includes a simple sliding window mode for reliable transmission. The basic encapsulation format is illustrated in Figure 7.5.

PPP field definitions

- Flag (one byte)—proprietary bit patterns used to indicate the start and end of a frame.

- Addr (one byte)—secondary station address (not required on point-to-point links).

- Ctrl (one or two bytes)—the most significant 2 bits identify the frame type: 0 = information (I), 10 = supervisory (S) and 11 = unnumbered information (UI). All frames include a Poll/Final (P/F) bit. Information frames include sequence (N[S]) and acknowledgment numbers (N[R]). Supervisory frames manage flow control and error detection and can be one of four types: Receiver Ready (RR), Receiver Not Ready (RNR), Reject (REJ), and Selective Reject (SREJ).

- Data (variable)—user data (zero or more octets).

- FCS (two bytes)—the Frame Check Sequence (FCS) is used to verify the data integrity. The FCS is a CRC calculated using polynomial $x^{16} + x^{12} + x^5 + 1$.

| Flag | Addr | Ctrl | Data... | FCS | Flag |

Figure 7.5 *HDLC encapsulation.*

In order to provide framing on serial links, the start and end of an HDLC frame is indicated by the special flag character (0x3f, binary 0111111). These bit sequences must not appear within HDLC user data; therefore, any user data using the same bit sequence must be modified during transmission. This process must be transparent to higher-level protocols, and the original must be recovered at the remote HDLC peer. On bit-synchronous links, a binary zero is inserted after every sequence of five ones (a process called bit stuffing). Thus, the longest sequence of ones that may appear of the link is 0111110—one less than the flag character. The receiver, upon seeing five ones, examines the next bit. If zero, the bit is discarded and the frame continues. If one, then this must be the flag sequence at the end of the frame. Between HDLC frames, the link idles. Most synchronous links constantly transmit data, usually by transmitting all ones during the interframe period (mark idle) or all flag characters (flag idle).

Since an HDLC connection is a Layer 2 hop, an end-to-end connection over a public network such as the Internet is extremely unlikely to guarantee reliable delivery across all intermediate hops. Higher-level, connection-oriented transport protocols such as TCP are, therefore, typically used to provide reliable delivery, and most Internet applications employ HDLC's unreliable delivery mode (i.e., using unnumbered information frame). For private point-to-point links, HDLC's reliable mode (i.e., information frame) may be used to support connectionless protocols such as UDP if data are deemed to be mission-critical (e.g., an IP multicast stock trading stream). HDLC has also been used successfully in satellite transmissions, where its large window size (2 to 127 bytes) can be used to offset the large delays incurred (typically 500ms). Note that Cisco uses a variant of HDLC as its default serial link encapsulation on its router range.

7.2.2 Serial line protocol (SLIP)

Standards for the encapsulation of IP packets have been defined for most network media technologies, but there is to date no standard for serial lines. SLIP is a de facto standard (not a true Internet standard) and is documented in RFC 1055 [2]. SLIP is a relatively simple packet-framing protocol. It defines a sequence of characters that frame IP packets when transmitted over a serial line. SLIP is widely deployed for historical reasons; many host IP implementations incorporate SLIP, and SLIP is simple and cheap to implement, especially for remote connection or dial-in access and point-to-point serial TCP/IP connections. SLIP is not suitable for router-to-router links and is not recommended for use in dynamic internetwork environments, since it has several major shortcomings, as follows:

- No multiprotocol support—SLIP has no support for protocol types; only a single protocol (IP) is supported across a link.

- Addressing—Both computers on a SLIP link need to know each other's IP address for routing purposes. SLIP defines only the encapsulation protocol; there is no negotiation or address learning capability. SLIP connections are, therefore, manually configured, including the specification of the IP address.

- No error detection/correction—SLIP does not include error detection; it relies on higher-level protocols (or intelligent modems) to detect and correct bad packets. This can lead to very poor performance on noisy lines.

- Limited or no compression—SLIP originally had no data compression mechanisms and did not compress frequently used protocol fields in the TCP or IP headers.

A typical use of SLIP would be a PC dial-up link, via a modem attached to the COM1 interface, enabling asynchronous communication over existing telephone lines. SLIP's lack of compression meant that poor performance was commonly experienced on low-speed links with interactive applications such as Telnet. Telnet sessions are characterized by a large number of small packet transmissions with a relatively large protocol overhead (a user key stroke will typically generate one byte of data with 40 bytes of TCP/IP encapsulation). Character-oriented TCP/IP applications also include repetition in both data and protocol fields. Subsequent SLIP implementations incorporate the Van Jacobsen (VJ) Header Compression standard. This reduces the size of the TCP/IP header to only eight bytes by maintaining data structures for TCP connection states at each end of the link and replacing static fields (or fields with simple increments) with small encoded updates. Refer to RFC 1144 [3] for full details. SLIP is now largely replaced by the Point-to-Point Protocol (PPP), as described in the next section.

7.2.3 Point-to-Point Protocol (PPP)

The Point-to-Point Protocol (PPP) is a more sophisticated serial line protocol developed by the IETF to overcome the shortcomings of SLIP. Note that SLIP and PPP are incompatible. When PPP was first introduced, it enabled many different router vendors to interoperate readily over point-to-point links for the first time, a major bonus for network designers and customers. PPP is an Internet standard, uses STD 51, and is described in RFC 1661 [4] and RFC 1662 [5]. There are a large number of proposed standards, which specify the operation of PPP over various point-to-point link media and various extensions to PPP. The main features of PPP include the following:

- Network layer protocol multiplexing

- Link configuration and parameter negotiation between peers

- Peer authentication

- Compression

- Error detection and link quality monitoring

    PPP is composed of three main components, as follows:

- Link Control Protocol (LCP)—for setting up, configuring, authenticating, monitoring, and maintaining the data link connection.

- Network Control Protocol (NCP)—a family of protocols used for configuring, enabling, and disabling various network protocols to be multiplexed over the link. For example, the NCP for IP is called IP Control Protocol (IPCP). PPP can also support multiplexing of other protocols such as Spanning Tree BPDUs.

- Data encapsulation—PPP includes a method for encapsulating datagrams over serial links based on HDLC.

    It is likely that many networks will continue to support a mixture of SLIP and PPP for historical reasons, even though PPP clearly has several major advantages. Specifically, PPP enables addresses to be negotiated across the link instead of being statically configured at both ends. PPP also implements reliable delivery of datagrams over both synchronous and asynchronous serial lines and can be used to encapsulate a wide variety of routed or bridged protocols. Finally, PPP supports a number of standard compression techniques, which may be negotiated by peers to maximize link efficiency.

Message format

The basic PPP encapsulation is illustrated in Figure 7.6. On a serial link PPP is normally preceded by the address and control bytes $0 \times ff$ and 0×03, respectively.

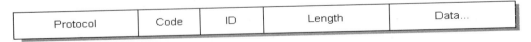

Figure 7.6   *PPP encapsulation.*

Operations

Before a link is considered to be ready for use by Network-Layer protocols, a sequence of events must happen. The LCP provides a method of establishing, configuring, maintaining, and terminating the connection. LCP goes through the following phases:

- Link establishment and configuration negotiation—In this phase, link control packets are exchanged, and link configuration options are negotiated. Once options are agreed upon, the link is open but not necessarily ready for network layer protocols to be started.

- Link quality determination—This phase is optional. PPP does not specify the policy for determining quality but does provide low-level tools, such as echo request and reply.

- Authentication—This phase is optional. Each end of the link authenticates itself with the remote end using authentication methods agreed to during phase 1.

- Network layer protocol configuration negotiation—Once LCP has finished the previous phase, Network-Layer protocols may be separately configured by the appropriate NCP.

- Link termination—LCP may terminate the link at any time. This will usually be done at the request of a user but may happen because of a physical event.

The example trace shown in Figure 7.7 illustrates two PPP peers negotiating a configuration set across a serial link.

PPP field definitions

- Protocol—The protocol field is one or two octets, and its value identifies the datagram encapsulated in the information field of the packet. Up-to-date values of the protocol field are specified in RFC 1700 [6]. Examples include the following:
  - 0021—Internet Protocol
  - 002d—Van Jacobson Compressed TCP/IP
  - 0201—802.1d Hello Packets
  - C021—Link Control Protocol
  - c023—Password Authentication Protocol
  - c025—Link Quality Report
  - c223—Challenge Handshake Authentication Protocol

```
File:PPPONLY1.SYC    Type:SNIFFER_SYC  Mode:•••••••  Records:144   A:[0•00000]
==============================================================================
FRAME HH:MM:SS:ms   LEN S PACKET CONTENT
----- -----------   --- - ------------------------------------------------------
  22: 08:56:47:634   12   DTE->DCE PPP LCP CTRL CFG Req Type=MRU (1518)
  23: 08:56:47:637   12   DCE->DTE PPP LCP CTRL CFG Ack Type=MRU (1518)
  24: 08:56:47:639   11   DCE->DTE PPP NCP Bridge PDU CFG Req
  25: 08:56:47:641   11   DTE->DCE PPP NCP Bridge PDU CFG Req
  26: 08:56:47:643   18   DCE->DTE PPP NCP Xyplex XCCP CFG Req
  27: 08:56:47:644   18   DTE->DCE PPP NCP Xyplex XCCP CFG Req
  28: 08:56:47:645   11   DCE->DTE PPP NCP Bridge PDU CFG Ack
  29: 08:56:47:646   11   DTE->DCE PPP NCP Bridge PDU CFG Ack
  30: 08:56:47:649   18   DCE->DTE PPP NCP Xyplex XCCP CFG Ack
  31: 08:56:47:650   18   DTE->DCE PPP NCP Xyplex XCCP CFG Ack
  32: 08:56:47:822   46   DTE->DCE PPP PID Xyplex XCCP
  33: 08:56:47:831   46   DCE->DTE PPP PID Xyplex XCCP
  34: 08:56:47:836   14   DTE->DCE PPP PID Xyplex XCCP
  35: 08:56:48:029   43   DCE->DTE PPP PID Xyplex XCCP
  36: 08:56:48:083   12   DCE->DTE PPP LCP CTRL ECHO Reply   Magic=00000000
  37: 08:56:48:086   12   DTE->DCE PPP LCP CTRL ECHO Request Magic=00000000
  38: 08:56:48:633   12   DTE->DCE PPP LCP CTRL ECHO Reply   Magic=00000000
  39: 08:56:48:636   12   DCE->DTE PPP LCP CTRL ECHO Request Magic=00000000
  40: 08:56:49:083   12   DCE->DTE PPP LCP CTRL ECHO Reply   Magic=00000000
  41: 08:56:49:086   12   DTE->DCE PPP LCP CTRL ECHO Request Magic=00000000
  42: 08:56:49:633   12   DTE->DCE PPP LCP CTRL ECHO Reply   Magic=00000000
  43: 08:56:49:636   12   DCE->DTE PPP LCP CTRL ECHO Request Magic=00000000
  44: 08:56:50:026   22   DCE->DTE PPP PID Xyplex XCCP
  45: 08:56:50:083   12   DCE->DTE PPP LCP CTRL ECHO Reply   Magic=00000000
  46: 08:56:50:086   12   DTE->DCE PPP LCP CTRL ECHO Request Magic=00000000
  47: 08:56:50:633   12   DTE->DCE PPP LCP CTRL ECHO Reply   Magic=00000000
  48: 08:56:50:636   12   DCE->DTE PPP LCP CTRL ECHO Request Magic=00000000
  49: 08:56:51:083   12   DCE->DTE PPP LCP CTRL ECHO Reply   Magic=00000000
  50: 08:56:51:086   12   DTE->DCE PPP LCP CTRL ECHO Request Magic=00000000
  51: 08:56:51:633   12   DTE->DCE PPP LCP CTRL ECHO Reply   Magic=00000000
  52: 08:56:51:636   12   DCE->DTE PPP LCP CTRL ECHO Request Magic=00000000
  53: 08:56:52:026   18   DCE->DTE PPP PID Xyplex XCCP
=-=-=-=-=-=-=-=-=-=-=-=-=-==-=-=-=-=-=-=-=-=-=-=-=-=-=-=-=-=-=-=-=-=-=-=-=-=-=
```

Figure 7.7 *PPP link establishment and protocol negotiation.*

- Code—The code field is one octet and identifies the kind of LCP packet. LCP Codes are assigned as follows:

  - 1—Configure-Request
  - 2—Configure-Ack
  - 3—Configure-Nak
  - 4—Configure-Reject
  - 5—Terminate-Request
  - 6—Terminate-Ack
  - 7—Code-Reject
  - 8—Protocol-Reject

- 9—Echo-Request
- 10—Echo-Reply
- 11—Discard-Request

- Data—The data field is zero or more octets. The information field contains the datagram for the protocol specified in the protocol field. The maximum length for the information field, including padding but not including the protocol field, is termed the Maximum Receive Unit (MRU), which defaults to 1,500 octets. By negotiation, other values can be used for the MRU.

- Padding—On transmission, the information field may be padded with an arbitrary number of octets up to the MRU. It is the responsibility of each protocol to distinguish padding octets from real information.

IPCP supports Van Jacobson header compression, as described in RFC 1144 [3].

As indicated, PPP is designed to encapsulate and transfer a number of network protocols as negotiated by the relevant NCP; for example, IP traffic is identified by 0×0021 in the protocol field. In addition to Network Layer protocols, PPP is capable of handling bridge management traffic, as illustrated in Figure 7.8, where an IEEE bridge Spanning Tree BPDU is encapsulated directly within a PPP.

PPP is a small, highly versatile protocol with powerful negotiating abilities and a standard mechanism for encapsulating many protocol types. It is,

```
File:PPLOT1.SYC        Type:SNIFFER_SYC  Mode:•••••••  Records:480
================================================================================
Frame    : 11            Len     : 39              Error     : None
T Elapsed: 12:58:05:331  T Delta : 00:00:00:003
----------------------------[WAN]-----------------------------------------------
Dst Addr : DTE           Src Addr : DCE
----------------------------[ppp encap]----------------------------------------
Address  : FF            Control  : 03
----------------------------[ppp]----------------------------------------------
Type     : PID           Protocol : 802.1d Hello
----------------------------[ieee stp]-----------------------------------------
STA Pri  : 0             STA Ver  : 0             BPDU Type: CONFIG_BPDU
Flags    : 0             Root Pri : 256           Root ID  : This Bridge
Root Cost: 00000000      Brdge Pri: 256           Bridge ID: 08008701ff84
Port ID  : 0x8002        Msg Age  : 0    secs     Max Age  : 20    secs
T_Hello  : 2    secs     Forw Del : 15   secs
============================[data:   0]=========================================
```

Figure 7.8 *PPP encapsulated spanning tree BPDU.*

therefore, frequently used in wide area applications running on analog and digital lines above or below popular wide area transports. For example, in addition to running PPP directly over a leased line, PPP can be deployed over a diverse range of protocols and media, including ISDN [7], Frame Relay [8], SONET [9], ATM AAL5 [10], FUNI [11], and Ethernet [12].

Multilink PPP (MPPP)

Multilink PPP (MPPP) enables two or more channels to be aggregated between peers (sometimes referred to as channel aggregation) and is specified in RFC 1990 [13]. MPPP uses load balancing to enable overall bandwidth to be increased and is particularly useful with dynamic channelized technologies such as ISDN. MPP distributes packets over all links available and reorders them at the remote device through the use of sequence numbers in the MPPP header. MPPP load-balancing operations are, therefore, transparent to higher-layer protocols. As indicated, the standard application of MPPP requires parallel links between two directly connected peers. Some vendors have implemented enhanced functionality, which enables MPPP to spread operations over multiple terminating devices (e.g., Cisco promotes a feature called multichassis MPPP).

Authentication

PPP supports two authentication techniques: Password Authentication Protocol (PAP) and Challenge Handshake Protocol (CHAP).

Link Quality Monitoring (LQM)

PPP offers an additional facility called Link Quality Monitoring (LQM). LQM is used to send regular messages that include a number of objects exchanged between PPP peers on a point-to-point link, as follows:

MagicNumber	PeerInLQRs	PeerInOctets
LastOutLQRs	PeerInPackets	PeerOutLQRs
LastOutPackets	PeerInDiscards	PeerOutPackets
LastOutOctets	PeerInErrors	PeerOutOctets

Most of these objects are basic statistics, which can be used for debugging the wide area link state or measuring link quality. These parameters are typically exposed via the system's command-line interface. For further information refer to RFC 1989 [14] and your equipment vendor's user documentation.

7.3 Access technologies

7.3.1 Digital Subscriber Line (DSL)

Digital Subscriber Line (DSL) is a relatively new, medium bandwidth, remote access service running over standard telephone wiring. It is currently targeted at SOHO applications for Internet access; access to the service provider's central office is enabled using a DSL modem on the customer's premises. Upstream bandwidth is available at speeds of between 16 Kbps and 1.5 Mbps. Downstream speeds may be as high as 32 Mbps. Service offering at present is patchy; many parts of the United States still do not have access to DSL, and the service is just beginning to be deployed across Europe at the time of writing. DSL is not a single service; it comprises a number of services designed to cope with different kinds of applications, as follows (most of these acronyms were originally defined by Bellcore):

- IDSL—ISDN DSL

- ADSL—Asymmetric DSL

- HDSL—High Bit Rate DSL

- VDSL—Very High Bit Rate DSL (sometimes referred to as BDSL)

- SDSL—Single-Line DSL (or symmetric DSL)

- CDSL—Consumer DSL

- RDSL—Rate-Adaptive DSL

Because of the variety of flavors on offer, DSL is often referred to as xDSL. At present the two main services of interest being deployed are ADSL and HDSL. It is expected that some of the other services may disappear and new ones emerge as the service and technology matures.

ISDN Digital Subscriber Line (IDSL)

DSL uses the same modem technology used for Basic Rate ISDN (BRI). A DSL modem transmits full-duplex data, at 160 Kbps over copper lines up to 18,000 ft (5,029.2 m) using 24-gauge, twisted-pair copper. DSL modems use twisted-pair bandwidth from 0 to 80 kHz. (Some European systems use 120 kHz of bandwidth.) They, therefore, preclude the simultaneous provisioning of analog telephone lines. However, DSL modems are being used today for so-called pair gain applications, in which DSL modems convert a single telephone line to two telephone lines, obviating the physical installation of the second line wiring. The provider just installs the analog/digital voice functions at the customer's premises for both lines. Multiplexing and demultiplexing of the data stream into two 64-Kbps B channels and a 16-Kbps D channel, takes place in attached terminal equipment. The standard ANSI T1.601 and ITU I.431DSL implementations both employ echo cancellation to separate the transmit signal from the received signal at both ends.

Asymmetric Digital Subscriber Line (ADSL)

ADSL is designed for remote user access and is ideal for SOHO applications. ADSL offers an asymmetric data stream; upstream bandwidth from the subscriber ranges from 16 Kbps to 640 Kbps, whereas downstream bandwidth is significantly larger. ADSL has a range of downstream speeds, depending on distance (note that the bandwidth rates will vary, depending not just upon the circuit length and quality of the cable plant but also upon the type of DSL modem used and the service provider's offering). Distance and speed are shown in the following chart.

Distance	Speed
18,000 ft (5,486.5 m)	1.544 Mbps (T1)
16,000 ft (4,876.8 m)	2.048 Mbps (E1)
12,000 ft (3,657.6 m)	6.312 Mbps (DS2)
9,000 ft (2,743.2 m)	8.448 Mbps

ADSL also includes support for a 64-Kbps telephone channel for circuit-switched voice; data signaling is designed to operate at a higher-frequency band than telephone lines, so voice services are independent and should continue to operate even if the subscriber DSL modem fails. ADSL includes optional error correction capabilities designed to reduce the effect of impulse noise on video signals (this service is not required for most LAN- and IP-based applications, since it introduces an additional 20 ms latency).

ADSL's asymmetry is determined more by the quality of cable plant itself rather than clever design, since ADSL is expected to run over legacy telephone-grade twisted pair from the central office to the customer's premises. Twisted-pair wiring is designed to minimize signal interference caused by radiation or capacitive coupling between cables, but the process is not perfect. Signals unfortunately do couple, and coupling increases as frequencies and the length of line increase. As a result, if you try to send symmetric signals in many pairs within a cable, you significantly limit the data rate and length of line you can attain. This effect is further amplified by the fact that twisted-pair telephone wires are routinely bundled together into large cables. Cables coming out of a central office may have hundreds or even thousands of pairs bundled together, and further out toward the subscriber 50-pair cable is typical. An individual line from a central office to a subscriber is created by splicing together many cable sections (Bellcore claims that the average U.S. subscriber line has 22 splices).

The majority of target applications for DSL services are, therefore, characterized by relatively high data rates downstream to the subscriber and low data rates upstream (upstream traffic is expected to comprise mainly key presses and acknowledgment traffic)—for example, home shopping, Internet/WWW access, remote LAN access, interactive multimedia, and video on demand. An interactive MPEG movie requires 1.5 to 3.0 Mbps downstream but can function with only 16 Kbps upstream. Internet or remote LAN access can demand larger upstream rates, but a 10:1 ratio of downstream to upstream bandwidth is currently adequate. ADSL is not suitable for heavier client/server applications or peer-to-peer applications, where significantly more upstream bandwidth is required.

High data rate Digital Subscriber Line (HDSL)

HDSL is the most mature xDSL technology; it has been available as a service since the mid-1990s as a cost-effective alternative to T1/E1. Typical applications include PBX network connections, cellular antenna stations, digital loop carrier systems, interexchange PoPs, Internet servers, and private data networks. HDSL is symmetric, offering 1.544 Mbps (T1) or 2.048 Mbps (E1) in bandwidths ranging from 80 kHz to 240 kHz. HDSL uses sophisticated modulation techniques for transmission over relatively poor grade 24-gauge, twisted-pair copper lines without the need for line conditioning. In practice it uses two wire pairs for T1 (each operating at half speed up to 15,000 ft (4,572 m)) and three wire pairs for E1 (each operating at one-third speed up to 12,000 ft [2,657.6 m]). Signal repeaters may be used to extend the range of HDSL. Since HDSL was the first DSL service to offer rates above one megabit, it has been used for early adopters of Internet and remote LAN access. However, this application will be better targeted by ADSL and SDSL, as these services begin to roll out.

Single-line Digital Subscriber Line (SDSL)

SDSL is effectively HDSL, transmitting symmetric T1 or E1 signals over a single twisted pair, typically over telephone lines. SDSL is attractive for subscriber premises that are equipped with only a single telephone line (i.e., most SOHO users). It is suited to applications requiring more symmetric access (such as servers and remote LAN users). The downside is that SDSL operates over quite a short range (approximately10,000 ft [3,048 m]).

Very high data rate Digital Subscriber Line (VDSL)

VDSL offers asymmetric bandwidth at data rates higher than ADSL but over shorter lines. While no general standards exist yet for VDSL, upstream speeds lie in a range of 1.6 Mbps to 2.3 Mbps, and downstream speeds are likely to be as shown in the following chart.

Distance	Speed
4,500 ft (1,371.6 m)	12.96 Mbps (25 percent of STS-1)
3,000 ft (914.4 m)	25.82 Mbps (50 percent of STS-1)
1,000 ft (304.8 m)	51.84 Mbps (STS-1)

Even though VDSL is ten times faster than ADSL, it is much less complex, since shorter cable length means there are fewer transmission constraints, and the transceiver technology is, therefore, relatively simple. At present VDSL only targets ATM network architectures and does not include the channelization and packet-handling requirements of ADSL. VDSL does provide error correction. VDSL also admits passive network terminations, allowing multiple VDSL modems to be connected to the same line at a customer's premises (in the same way as telephone extensions). VDSL will operate over telephone lines and ISDN, with both separated from VDSL signals by passive filtering. Standards in this area are still in a state of flux, but there are two main standards: T1E1.4 in the United States and ETSI TM3 in Europe.

7.3.2 Cable modems

A cable modem provides access over the same shared coaxial cable used by cable TV (CATV) service providers. It operates more like a LAN transceiver than a classical dial modem. Coaxial cable supports higher data rates than telephone cable, and the user is permanently online, since there is no requirement to dial. The standards for this technology are still immature; hence, there are still interoperability issues to resolve. Currently, the main technology options include the following:

- IP over Cable Data Network (IPCDN)—The IETF IPCDN Working Group is now working on standardizing IP over CATV networks.

- IEEE 802.14—This IEEE Working Group is defining MAC and PHY standards for cable modems.

- Digital Audio Visual Council/Digital Video Broadcasting (DAVIC/ DVB)—A European standard now being adopted in several parts of the world, such as the Far East and Australia.

- Multimedia Cable Network System/Data Over Cable Service Interface Specification (MCNS/DOCSIS)—A U.S. standard also being adopted in other parts of the world.

One of the issues with CATV networks is that they are designed primarily for highly asymmetrical applications (i.e., high-volume TV/video broadcast traffic downstream to the consumer with relatively little traffic coming upstream). Typically this means up to 50 Mbps downstream and roughly 3 Mbps upstream. While this is fine for the current wave of interactive data applications such as Web access and e-mail, it may not be suitable for more intensive client/server applications and distributed or peer-to-peer applications.

All downstream broadcasts are received by all cable modems, where each modem must filter out unwanted traffic (the broadcast nature of this technology also means that it is inherently insecure unless some form of encryption is employed). Upstream traffic is delivered by the modems using contention time slots. When two or more modems attempt to transmit during the same time slot, a collision occurs and the modems must back off for a random interval (much like the CSMA/CD operation of Ethernet). The head-end system on the cable also allocates reserved time slots (for bandwidth allocation) and ranging time slots (for clocking).

Although the bandwidths on offer appear relatively high for remote access applications, a key point to appreciate about cable modem networks is that they offer shared access. Performance may, therefore, vary over time and may degrade as more users sign up. You must, therefore, discuss with the service provider how many users are likely to share the medium, how many are likely to be concurrent, what applications are running on the medium, and what the current traffic profile is. Some systems have the ability to guarantee a certain level of bandwidth for high-bandwidth applications. Another factor you should take into account is that you may have little choice over the ISP.

7.3.3   Narrowband Integrated Services Digital Network (N-ISDN)

Narrowband Integrated Services Digital Network (N-ISDN) is basically a fast-dial digital telephone service. ISDN was designed to enable telephone companies to provide integrated services capable of handling voice, data, and video over the same circuits, with a channel size geared for digitized voice (64 Kbps). The core of the telephone network is now almost all digital, so most analog telephone calls are now converted into bits, carried through digital circuits, and then converted back into analog at the remote end. The international standard for communication between switches on the digital telephone network is Signaling System 7 (SS-7) [1], a protocol suite roughly comparable to TCP/IP. ISDN provides a fully digital user interface to the SS-7 network, capable of transporting either voice or data. B-ISDN (Broadband ISDN) uses ATM instead of SS-7 as the underlying networking technology.

ISDN is a complete networking technology, providing clearly defined Physical, Data Link, Network, and Presentation Layer protocols. However, for most internetwork applications ISDN is regarded as just another Data Link protocol used to transport IP packets. ISDN is defined in several international standards, as follows:

- I.430 Protocol—ITU I.430 documents the Physical Layer and lower Data Link Layer of the ISDN BRI interface. The specification defines a number of reference points between the telco switch and the end system. The most important of these are S/T and U. The U interface is the local loop between the telephone company and the customer's premises. At the customer site, the two-wire U interface is converted to a four-wire S/T interface by an NT-1. Originally, the T interface was point-to-point and could be converted to a point-to-multipoint S interface by an NT-2. However, the electrical specification of the S and T interfaces was almost identical, so most modern NT-1s include built-in NT-2 functionality and can support either single or multiple ISDN devices on what is now called the S/T interface. The rarely used R interface is a normal serial connection, which allows non-ISDN devices to be connected via a terminal adapter.

- I.431 Protocol—ITU I.431 documents the Physical Layer and lower Data Link Layer of the ISDN PRI interface, as described previously.

- Q.921 Protocol—Q.921, also referred to as LAPD (Link Access Protocol—D Channel) and a close cousin of HDLC, is the Data Link protocol used over ISDN's D channel.

- Q.931 Protocol—Q.931 is ISDN's connection control protocol, roughly comparable to TCP in the Internet protocol stack. Q.931 is one of the most important ISO standards and documents the Network Layer user-to-network interface, providing call setup and breakdown, channel allocation, and a variety of optional services. Q.931

doesn't provide flow control or perform retransmission, since the underlying layers are assumed to be reliable and the circuit-oriented nature of ISDN allocates bandwidth in fixed increments of 64 Kbps. As with TCP, Q.931 documents both the protocol itself and a protocol state machine. Variants of Q.931 are used in both ATM and voice-over-IP.

- G.711 Protocol—G.711 is the international standard for encoding telephone audio on a 64-Kbps channel and is used by telcos throughout the world. It is a Pulse Code Modulation (PCM) scheme operating at an 8-kHz sample rate, with 8 bits per sample. According to the Nyquist theorem, which states that a signal must be sampled at twice its highest frequency component, G.711 can encode frequencies between 0 and 4 kHz. Telcos can select between two different variants of G.711: A-law and mu-law. A-law is the standard for international circuits. (Note that several equipment vendors have been caught out with interoperability issues between the two.)

Terminal adapter standards for serial interfaces include the following:

- V110 (Europe, Japan for V.24, V.35)

- V.120 (United States for V.24, V.35)

- DMI-1 (United States AT&T for V.35)

- DMI-2 (United States AT&T for V.24)

- T-LINK (United States, Canada for NorTel V.24, V.35)

- X.30 (Germany, United Kingdom, Scandinavia, Japan for X.21)

When deploying ISDN it is always worth checking the interfaces offered by the provider. For example, for historical reasons British Telecom in the United Kingdom still employs proprietary DASS-2 in some areas.

Operation

An ISDN interface is time division multiplexed into channels. In accordance with SS-7 convention, control and data signals are separated onto different channels. In ISDN, the D-channel is used for control, and the B-channel is for data. The two main variants of ISDN are Basic Rate Interface (BRI) and Primary Rate Interface (PRI). BRI, sometimes referred to as 2B+D, provides two bidirectional 64-Kbps B-channels and a 16-Kbps D-channel over a single 192-Kbps circuit (the remaining bandwidth is used for framing). BRI is the ISDN equivalent of a single phone line, though it can handle two calls simultaneously over its two B-channels. PRI is essentially ISDN over a T1 or E1 link (23B+D in the United States, Canada, Japan, and South Korea, and 30B+D in Europe), where the D-channel uses a full 64-Kbps circuit. ISDN multiplexing equipment combines all of these channels into a single combined data stream (144 Kbps for BRI and 1.536 Mbps [United States] or 1.984 Mbps [Europe] for PRI). PRI is intended for use by large concentrator sites, targeted at organizations such as an ISP.

The ISDN Reference Model is well documented, so I will not dwell on it here, since it has little relevance for most internetwork designers and bears more than a passing resemblance to OSI standards documentation. The interested reader (surely an oxymoron) is directed to reference [15], which at least attempts to liven things up. To keep things simple all you need to know is that ISDN terminal equipment includes devices such as digital telephones, routers, and bridges, and ISDN terminal adapters are devices that enable nodes that do not have a direct ISDN interface to access the ISDN.

Physical connectors

Interfaces for BRI and PRI are typically presented as follows:

- BRI ports are presented as standard RJ45 (ISO/IS 8877) jack plug. ISDN requires a mandatory minimum of four pairs (differential Tx and Rx). Two additional power and power sink wires may optionally be added (making a total of eight wires). The latter configuration enables telephone equipment to be powered from the network but is not normally implemented, since modern data equipment often exceeds the power requirements originally defined by ISDN standards.

- PRI ports should be presented as RJ45 (120 ohm) or twin coax BNC G.703 connectors (identical to most European E1 service interfaces).

Encapsulation

There is no RFC specifically defining the encapsulation format to be used over ISDN. Since an ISDN B-channel is essentially a point-to-point serial connection, PPP encapsulation is commonly used (documented by RFC 1618 [7]). The PPP LCP and NCP mechanisms are particularly useful for simplifying channel configuration and setup and negotiating setup parameters between multivendor implementations. The ISDN D-channel can be used for low-bandwidth transmission of PPP frames, but often this is not available, being restricted to communication with the local switch. Some router implementations support Multilink PPP (MPPP, see Section 7.2), which enables several ISDN B-channels to be aggregated if connected in parallel between the same source and destination site.

Levels of ISDN support

When designing internetworks with ISDN it is important to understand that there are various levels of ISDN integration on devices such as routers, as follows:

- ISDN ignorant
- ISDN aware
- ISDN enabled

ISDN-ignorant routers make use of ISDN Backup Adapters (BA), which spoof the serial line connection. These devices are available from some of the TA manufacturers. This configuration is transparent to the router (it looks just like a leased line), and the routing table is not affected. There is only one physical interface between the router and the BA. No approvals are needed on the router for this application. This option is more expensive than a TA solution, and the BAs need to be installed in pairs, so on a large site this does not scale very well.

ISDN-aware routers require at least the ability to interface with an ISDN Terminal Adapter (TA) via either DTR dial or V.25bis software support. In ISDN parlance this equates to the TE2 terminal equipment definition. The routing table needs to be aware of the transient nature of the ISDN link. In this configuration no serial interface is required, so simple ISDN dial-up routing can be implemented for SOHO configurations relatively cheaply. DTR dial can be used for backup or dial-up and is relatively simple to implement. The remote TA telephone number must be configured in the TA, so this approach has limited flexibility. V.25bis is an ITU/T standard, which uses in-band signaling and can handle dialing dynamically. V.25bis can handle only one B-channel at a time; once a channel is established, signaling cannot take place to establish the second channel. V.25bis is obviously more complicated to implement but is a major improvement over DTR dial. V.25bis can support backup, dial on demand, and bandwidth on demand functionality.

ISDN-enabled routers have a native ISDN S/T interface installed inside the router. In ISDN parlance this equates to the TE1 terminal equipment definition. This approach has maximum flexibility and least cost. In the United States, routers are also available with a U interface, since it is the end user's responsibility to supply the NT1 (in Europe this is supplied by the PTO), and the NT1 may be built into the router I/O. Mature, competitive products are available from Cisco, NorTel/BAY, 3Com, Ascend, Spider Systems, and Xyplex.

Security considerations

Security is important in ISDN design because of its dial anywhere nature. We need to make sure that the sites we are connecting into, and the sites connecting into us, are trusted. There are three primary security features typically offered with ISDN devices: Password Authentication Protocol (PAP), Challenge Handshake Protocol (CHAP), and Call Line Identification (CLID), as follows.

- PAP and CHAP—PAP and CHAP authentication are typically negotiable via PPP. Both techniques employ relatively straightforward password techniques to ensure that both ends of the ISDN circuit can be trusted. PAP offers very weak security, since the password is sent only at startup and in cleartext mode. It is better than nothing, but only just. CHAP offers stronger security, since a challenge-response handshake is initiated both at the start and at several points within the session via a hashed number (generated from information already known to both parties), so the password itself does not have to be sent.

- CLID—When an ISDN call is made, the caller ID can be passed to the destination. We can use this information to vet the call. Devices such as routers and bridges often implement call filtering based on known or unknown caller IDs and this can be a good security feature. For example, there may be blacklists of CLIDs not trusted, or the device could be configured not to accept any incoming calls from unknown CLIDs. Another secure application here would be to dial back the trusted site using its CLID (remember there are cost implications here, though, as the charging point will be the site initiating the call). Unfortunately, even for trusted sites, CLIDs may not always be passed through multiple carriers and therefore CHAP could be used as a supplementary security mechanism.

Design considerations

From the network designer's perspective there are several features of ISDN and its implementation to understand. The two most important are as follows:

- Cost—We know that ISDN tariffs vary considerably internationally. Keeping a call open costs money, so we need to minimize circuit uptime where appropriate.

- Application—Only in a few countries will ISDN be priced low enough to consider as the primary WAN technology. Therefore, you will typically be considering it for Bandwidth on Demand (BoD), backup, or dial-up operations.

There is a wide regional and international variation in ISDN tariffs and many subtleties in the charging model that could influence how you configure ISDN. For example, some countries impose a minimum call charge (e.g., four minutes); in some cases it could be cheaper to leave a call open for the full four minutes rather than make multiple short calls within a minimum charge period. Another cost-related design issue is how you intend to attach devices to the ISDN, since this depends upon the level of ISDN integration present in the router, gateway, or switch. For example, a router that has no ISDN support at all will be required to interface with an external device such as a terminal adapter or backup adapter. On a large network this could considerably inflate the cost of the design while adding complexity and reducing the overall MTBF.

Other issues that should be considered as part of the design include the following:

- Maximum frame size—A receiver connected to the ISDN link is likely to have a Maximum Receive Unit (MRU) size of either 1,500 or 2,048 bytes or greater. To avoid fragmentation, the Maximum Transmission Unit (MTU) at the sender's network layer should not exceed 1,500, unless a peer MRU of 2,048 or greater is specifically negotiated.

- Unnumbered links—Unnumbered interfaces for routing protocols are extremely useful in resilient network designs where remote dial-up routers may use ISDN to connect into different sites dynamically. If addressing schemes need to be consistent or known when a dial-up connection is made, then unnumbered interfaces can greatly simplify matters and allow much more flexibility.

- Address mapping—Currently translation between IP addresses and ISDN dial codes is done via static address tables configured by the system administrator. ISDN uses the ITU/T E.164 addressing structure and you need to map these addresses onto remote network IP addresses.

- Time-of-day support—Accurate time support and time/day awareness is critical for efficient bandwidth management. ISDN tariffs are sensitive to time of day and day of week. Several European countries, such as France, have quite sophisticated cost bands throughout the working day. You may want to tune your network to open up circuits from particular locations at specific times of day to get the best use of the tariff bands. For example, it should be possible to set up the following scenarios:

- Interface A is marked as ON_DEMAND for Monday through Friday, 8:30 A.M. through 9:00 P.M.
- Between 9:00 P.M. and 8:30 A.M., Monday through Friday, Interface A is marked for BACKUP only.
- Saturday through Sunday, all hours, Interface A is marked as DISABLED.

- Interoperability—As described previously, the encapsulation format commonly used over ISDN B-channels is PPP; although there is no mandatory standard, proprietary solutions still exist and should be avoided. If you are using ISDN solutions from multiple vendors, make sure you test interoperability first, even at the PPP level. When you connect your ISDN device into the ISDN service, you must also be aware that the relevant switch profiles are supported (so that the D-channel can exchange signaling with the service provider's particular brand of switch). Another area to ensure you have fully covered is approvals, especially in a large international network.

Dial-on-demand applications

For sites with traffic demands that are typically characterized as short bursts of remote activity throughout the day, dial-up ISDN can be considerably cheaper and more flexible than a leased line service. For example, a site may need to send 10 MB of data to three other sites once a day and wants the transaction to be less than one hour for each. Assuming we can send 1,500-byte frames, and 40 bytes of TCP/IP overhead are present, this means we will need to send:

Total Frames = $(10 \times 1,024,000)/(1,500 - 40) = 7,013.7$

With this overhead this means that we are actually sending the following load over the network:

Total Frame Data = $(7,013.7 \times 8 \times 1,500) = 84,164,400$ bits

So we can roughly calculate the latency over a 64-Kbps circuit as:

Duration = $84,164,400/(64,000 \times 60) = 21.92$ minutes

We need approximately 22 minutes for each file transfer, excluding acknowledgments and queuing considerations. In total for all three sites we need about 66 minutes. We could introduce a low-speed serial link, but the latency introduced is going to slow things down considerably unless we go to 64 Kbps (which would simply be overkill). Here we can simply install ISDN dial-up BRI circuits between the sites. If we have MPPP, then we could even halve the time taken.

If, however, we have an application that requires frequent terminal access throughout the day (even if it represents very low traffic levels), then ISDN dial-up can become prohibitive. Each transaction will require time to initiate call setup, transfer the data, sense idle, and complete circuit tear down. This could represent up to 30 seconds of overhead per data transfer, plus the additional latency incurred by the user each time he or she waits for the call to be set up. Assuming an average transaction time of 60 seconds and 250 transactions per day, this represents approximately 6.25 hours call time [(60 + 30) × 250 seconds]. In some countries this would be more expensive than a leased line solution at comparable speed. Dial-up ISDN is a useful design approach for businesses such as car dealerships, where there are relatively low-volume inquiries to a main site throughout the day. Once the call frequency and duration increase you need to examine possible alternatives, since costs can become prohibitive.

Bandwidth-on-demand applications

In LAN and many leased line applications, peak utilization is often an order of magnitude greater than average load. Since ISDN enables channels to be dialled up on demand, it could be used to great effect to cope with average and worst-case conditions. This feature is called Bandwidth on Demand (BoD). Either ISDN can be used as the primary transport (a 64-Kbps channel up continuously with more available on demand), or it can be used to top-up a leased line. It is usually recommended to limit ISDN channel aggregation (a maximum of seven circuits is often recommended), due to the potential for skew between individual call-routing processes (this can lead to additional latency via reassembly overheads at the termination point).

To configure BoD you would typically identify the primary circuit to be monitored and set various thresholds for that circuit. So, for example, we could monitor a 128-Kbps leased line between London and Paris, and open up ISDN B-channels on a PRI interface (multiples will require MLPP) if the current utilization levels step above 80 percent. Figure 7.9 illustrates how BoD works with such a design. A primary link (a 128-Kbps leased line) is monitored between two major sites. When utilization exceeds a preset level, a primary rate ISDN link is used to top-up the bandwidth with n × 64 channels. When utilization drops, the channels are torn down. Note

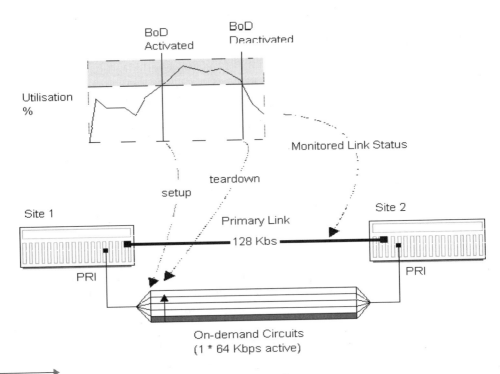

Figure 7.9   *ISDN Bandwidth on Demand (BoD) application.*

that the PRI circuits could also be configured to come up under other conditions (e.g., if the leased line fails). You could achieve the same result if the leased line were replaced by an X.25 or Frame Relay virtual circuit, depending upon the implementation. You should be aware that implementations of BoD are still quite immature, and you will need to clarify the exact capabilities with your equipment supplier.

Circuit backup applications

ISDN can be extremely useful for network designers when providing circuit backup for conventional WAN links. For example, a leased line (a 64-Kbps leased circuit) can be backed up by an ISDN BRI circuit, as illustrated in the case of Router-3 and Router-2 in Figure 7.10. If MPPP is used, then both B-channels can also be used to provide an additional 128-Kbps top-up bandwidth on demand. In this case, you would pay only the connection and rental charge for ISDN (typically very low), since no use costs are incurred in normal operation. ISDN can also be used to back up other WAN technologies such as Frame Relay and X.25. In Figure 7.10, Router-1 interfaces with an external Terminal Adaptor (TA) via V.25bis and is able to

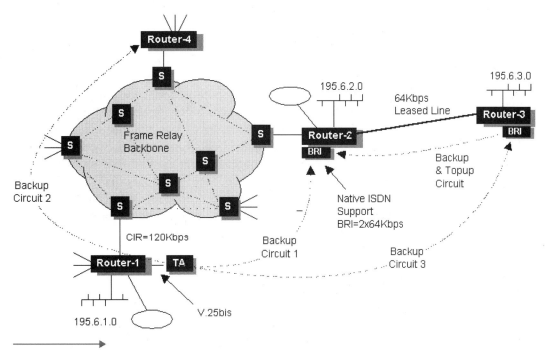

Figure 7.10   *ISDN backup and top-up applications.*

automatically provide a backup circuit on demand for a failed Frame Relay uplink. Router-3 has native ISDN support and is able to automatically provide a backup for a failed leased line connection. By using MPPP the ISDN circuit could also offer an additional 128-Kbps bandwidth on demand during periods of congestion.

Another variant of this application can be achieved via an external Terminal Adapter (TA), as illustrated in Figure 7.10. For example, at site 195.6.1.0 we may require a resilient backup connection in the event that the link to the Frame Relay switch, or the switch itself, fails. The requirements may also specify that Router-2, Router-4, and Router-3 should be attempted in sequence until a successful connection is found. The cost of backing up this topology with conventional leased circuits would be huge, but we can use a spare serial port to interface with the TA. When the switch uplink goes down, a V.25bis call is made via the TA, specifying the ISDN address of Router-2 as its first preference. The TA then dials the number and connectivity is reestablished. Note that DTR dial is not sufficient for this application, since the TA needs to dynamically call from a range of addresses.

Performance considerations

There are several performance-related issues that should be considered in any ISDN design, including the following:

- Call setup and teardown—The amount of time taken to set up and tear down a call is important for both performance and cost reasons. With some tariff schemes it may be highly desirable for applications to make the call, pass a small amount of data, and then tear down the call within a matter of seconds. Call setup time is partly determined by the amount of negotiation handled at the PPP level, so switching off unnecessary options can help. Teardown time is partly controlled by the algorithm used to detect an idle state on the circuit. If the idle condition is set too early, you risk losing data and having to open up a new call to retransmit. Therefore, handle with care.

- Low demand routing and spoofing support—ISDN lines should be kept in use for as little time as possible due to their tariff structure. Unfortunately, many LAN protocols and services assume permanent bandwidth availability, so ISDN devices need to counteract this by acting as if the circuit is up when it is really down. For specific protocols, ISDN-aware routers can spoof protocol events such as TCP acknowledgments, IPX Watchdog packets, NetWare Server licensing checks, IP and IPX RIP advertisements, and IPX SAP announcements. In addition to this, special low-demand variants of routing protocols, such as RIP and OSPF [16], are available for implementation over ISDN.

- Compression—Since ISDN is based on 64-Kbps channels, compression is usually available and can improve performance by reducing latency, thereby reducing uptime cost. Typically it is negotiable as part of the PPP offering and includes support for VJ header compression [3] or the more sophisticated Stac LZS compression [17].

7.4   Backbone technologies

7.4.1   Leased lines and satellite links

Leased lines are point-to-point, duplex, dedicated links, which are permanently available, typically at speeds between 64 Kbps and 45 Mbps. Leased lines may be used for both voice or data traffic. Data traffic is normally encapsulated in PPP or HDLC. Leased lines assure privacy, since none of the bandwidth provided is shared with other users. Typically the customer pays an installation cost and a monthly rental (usually based on distance) to the provider. Leased lines are available in both analog and digital formats, at a range of speeds. Typically they require a single interface at each end of the circuit to terminate the connection. Private leased lines and satellite links are a mature, established, reliable technology and have been used for many years in the core of large international and regional backbone networks. They form a natural extension for LAN-LAN internetworking and for many applications still represent a good choice.

If utilized efficiently, leased lines represent a reasonable way to build a small to medium-sized network, and they are particularly good for LAN extension applications. However, wherever there is a lull in traffic you are effectively still paying for use. For large networks this limits scalability, since the central site may require dozens of expensive ports over multiple concentrators. One of the more flexible technologies to emerge is the use of channelized circuits, where high-bandwidth circuits are broken up into increments (typically 64-Kbps chunks) and may terminate at different destinations. In large, modern internetworks, however, there is often a requirement for considerable site meshing, and the traffic dynamics can vary considerably by application. In these environments leased lines simply do not scale. Switched technologies such as Frame Relay, SMDS, and ATM are now often more attractive, both from an operational and a financial perspective, and often leased lines are simply used for short-haul tail circuits from the core (i.e., telco service) to the customer's premises. There are also substantial price differentials between different countries, which means that in some regions of the world alternative technologies are the only cost-effective option. Another subtle issue here is that, since many manufacturers of routers are United States–based, these devices often lack the features that make them suitable for optimizing leased circuit use in Europe (such as G.703 and G.704 channelized access).

Service offerings

Leased lines come in various grades and bandwidths, starting with the most basic offering: the analog leased line through to dedicated, point-to-point, multimegabit leased data circuits. Analog leased lines require modems at either end for analog-to-digital conversion and offer the lowest grade of quality and the slowest speeds, but they are the least expensive. The next grade of service is the Digital Data Service (DDS), offering a digital solution at speeds of 2,400, 4,800, 9,600, and 19,200 bps. DDS is more expensive than analog leased lines. Higher-speed lines are available as part of the Subrate Digital Multiplexing (SRDM), which supports the same access speeds as DDS but enables aggregation of many low-bandwidth channels into a single DS0 channel for better cost efficiency. Above this fractional T1/E1 offers features similar to SRDM but uses higher-bandwidth DS1 aggregation. Beyond these services there are high-bandwidth dedicated solutions such as T1/E1, T2/E2, and T3/E3. At these service levels prices rise dramatically, especially for long-distance circuits, and, depending upon the network topology, it may be worth considering switched services such as Frame Relay.

T1 and E1

T1 is a United States service and offers a data rate of 1.544 Mbps (24 channels of 64 Kbps). E1 is a European service and offers a data rate of 2.048 Mbps (30 channels of 64 Kbps). The origins of the T1/E1 digital multiplexing system were outlined in Section 7.1.1. Telephone companies originally used T1/E1 circuits for transmission between offices in the core-switching network. Over time they tariffed T1/E1 services and offered them for private networks, connecting PBXs and T1 multiplexers together over the wide area. Today T1/E1 circuits can be used for many other applications, such as connecting Internet routers, bringing traffic from a cellular antenna site to a central office, or connecting multimedia servers into a central office. An increasingly important application is the so-called feeder plant, the section of a telephone network radiating from a central office to remote access nodes, which, in turn, service premises over individual copper lines. T1/E1 circuits feed Digital Loop Carrier (DLC) systems, which concentrate 24 or 30 voice lines over two twisted-pair lines from a central office, thereby saving copper lines and reducing the distance between an access point and the final subscriber.

T1/E1 is not suitable for connecting to individual residences (even if the user could afford it). First of all, AMI is so demanding of bandwidth, and corrupts cable spectrum so much, that telephone companies cannot put more than one circuit in a single 50-pair cable and must put none in any adjacent cables. Offering such a system to residences would be equivalent to pulling new wire to most of them. Second, until recently no application going to the home demanded such a data rate. Third, even now, as data rate requirements accelerate with the hope of movies and high-speed data for everyone, the demands are highly asymmetric—bundles downstream to the subscriber and very little upstream in return—and many situations will require rates above T1 or E1. In general, high-speed data rate services to the home will be carried by ADSL, VDSL, or similar types of modems over CATV lines.

Channelized E1

Channelized or fractional leased circuits are attractive to ISPs and service providers in Europe. For example, a 2.0428-Mbps E1 circuit may be split into one or more multiples of 64-Kbps channels, with a central site using a single, higher-speed interface, terminated at several remote sites by lower-speed interfaces. This provides much more flexibility and reduced cost for concentrator sites. Typically, G.703 provides a means of connecting standard serial interfaces such as V.35 to telephone lines or PTT networks. Vendors often offer a G.703/G.704 port adapter, which supports point to point from 2.048-Mbps, E1 leased-line services, eliminating the need for a separate, external data termination unit, which is typically used to convert standard serial interfaces, such as V.35, to E1-G.703/G.704.

The E1 interface is available in either balanced or unbalanced mode, and this varies by country across Europe and internationally. E1 is also available in framed mode (G.704) and unframed mode (G.703). These modes are described as follows:

- Balanced and unbalanced modes—A unique port adapter supports each type and availability varies by location. Neither the modes nor the cables are interchangeable; you cannot configure a balanced port to support an unbalanced line; nor can you attach an interface cable intended for a balanced port to an unbalanced port. Balanced interfaces typically use three conductors and three signal states: high, low, and ground. The high and low signals mirror each other. Unbalanced interfaces use only two signals: signal and ground.

- Unframed mode—The G.703 interface is divided into 32 time slots or frames. Each of the 32 time slots is an 8-bit frame, which transmits data at 64 Kbps. Each of these time slots can be configured to carry data or to remain empty. (The port adapter inserts an idle pattern into empty time slots.) Time slot 0, or the first 8 bits, is reserved as overhead. The remaining 248 bits (31 frames with 8 bits each) are designated time slots 1 through 31. Time slot 16 is also designated as a framing slot when using framed mode. When you use unframed mode (G.703), the default, you can configure time slot 16 to carry data and operate as any of the other slots—therefore, in framed mode time slot 0 must be designated as a framing signal; time slot 16 can be configured for either data or framing. Unframed mode uses all 32 time slots for data (data are also called payload). None of the 32 time slots is used for framing signals. This allows each of the 32 time slots to transmit at 64 Kbps. (For example, 32 time slots $\times$ 64 Kbps = 2.048 Mbps).

- Framed mode—G.704 allows you to specify a bandwidth for the interface by designating a number of the 32 time slots for data and reserving others for framing (timing). When you use framed mode, you must designate start and stop time slots; the slots within these boundaries are used for data, and the remaining slots are left idle. For example, on an interface with framing set on time slots 1 through 8, the interface will carry data within the specified eight frames, and frames 9 through 31 will remain idle. Because each time slot transmits at 64 Kbps, the interface will operate at 512 Kbps (8 frames × 64 Kbps = 512 Kbps). By configuring 16 of the time slots to carry data and the remaining 16 to remain empty, you can essentially configure the interface for 1.024 Mbps (by leaving half the time slots empty and unable to carry data). The FSIP inserts an idle pattern into unused time slots to identify them as overhead (unused for data). Only one contiguous time slot range can be used. In PABX systems, time slot 16 is always left unused. By default, time slot 16 is often not enabled for data in the G.703/G.704 interface. Time slot 16 is used for data if it is included in the specified range of data slots. Also, the command time slot 16 overrides the default and enables time slot 16 to carry data. Framed mode supports a 4-bit CRC (CRC4), which you typically enable with a software command. The default is usually no CRC.

The E1 G.703/G.704 interface does not operate in the conventional DTE and DCE modes typical of data communication interfaces, especially with respect to timing. By default, the interface recovers the line clock signal from the received data stream. The interface may use an internal clock signal (typically generated by the E1-G.703/G.704 port adapter). When testing equipment in a back-to-back mode (i.e., in the lab, with simulated wide area links), E1 interfaces may, therefore, require special external simulation devices to generate clock signals if this is not available from an internal source.

T3 and E3

E3 is one of the highest (34.816 Mbps) transmission rates available in a European digital infrastructure. The equivalent in the United States is T3 (44.736 Mbps).

HSSI

High-Speed Serial Interface (HSSI) is a network standard for high-speed (up to 52 Mbps) serial communications over WAN links. It is commonly used by providers at the central office for high-bandwidth concentration.

Operation

The PTT uses Time Division Multiplexing (TDM) or Digital Access Cross-Connect Switch (DACS) technology to divide backbone bandwidth into smaller circuits suitable for use by a typical site. Multiplexers are placed in key locations around the country to act as local concentrators for users; these sites are known as Points of Presence (PoPs). Leased lines are serial links, where bits are transmitted a single bit at a time in each direction. The stream of bits is assembled into bytes and then packets. The speed of a serial line is rated in bits per second (bps). Table 7.5 illustrates the typical bandwidths available. Leased circuits can be broken into two broad categories: synchronous and asynchronous.

Typically, lower-speed synchronous leased lines operate over the RS232 interface. Higher bandwidths require higher-specification interfaces, such as the V.35, X.21, or even the HSSI interface.

Synchronous links require some form of timing to synchronize data transfer between the sender and receiver (called clocking). A clock signal is transmitted along with the data, and this can take many forms. For example, the sender could transmit each bit on the rising edge of the clock. The receiver latches the data signal on the trailing edge of the clock. In this manner, race conditions between the two are avoided. Every clock cycle, a single bit is transferred. It is also possible to combine the clock and data signals together into one. For example, every 0 bit is encoded as a full clock cycle, while 1 bits are encoded by skipping a transition in the middle of the cycle. The decoding circuitry is more complex, but fewer wires are required in this scheme. In any event, such serial links are termed synchronous because the data signal is synchronized with a clock signal. In fact most serial links are synchronous; typically, one side of the link provides clocking (gives clock) for data traveling in both directions. The other side of the link takes clock.

Table 7.5 *Typical Leased Line Service Bandwidths by Interface Type*

Interface	Bandwidth
RS232, V.24/V.28, X.21bis	up to 19.2 Kbps
V.35	up to 8 Mbps
X.21	up to 10 Mbps
HSSI	up to 52 Mbps

If a telco leased line is involved, the telco will provide the clock, since data must be carefully synchronized as they moves through the telco's network..

Asynchronous links, characterized by lower-speed, dial-up modem links, lack any form of clock signal. Rather, a start bit is used to signal the beginning of a transmission. Once the receiver has seen the start bit, it begins counting bit times according to the preconfigured line speed. Without an explicit clock signal, the receiver risks gradually losing synchronization with the sender. For this reason, almost all asynchronous links transmit only a single byte at a time. The next byte requires a new start bit to resynchronize the sender and receiver. Asynchronous links require the sender and receiver to agree on the bit speed of the link; otherwise, both ends could talk at different speeds and communication would be impossible.

In serial lines data transferred must be formed into frames. The beginning and end of each packet must be clearly delineated, and typically a checksum will be included to ensure the frame is undamaged. Most serial links use HDLC or some variant of it. Dial-up asynchronous modem lines initially used SLIP, but PPP is now the preferred encapsulation. Both SLIP and PPP are HDLC-based, but PPP is more sophisticated, supporting dynamic address assignment, negotiable data compression, and multiple Network Layer protocols. PPP is also the preferred encapsulation over synchronous router connections, since it enables multivendor interworking. Typically router vendors default to their proprietary encapsulations (usually HDLC derived), which are optimized for peering with their own routers only.

Lower-speed circuits up to 64 Kbps are presented as a single data pipe with no additional framing imposed. At higher speeds the circuit is channelized. In the United States a T1 connection comprises 24 channels of 56 Kbps (aggregate 1.544 Mbps). Internationally an E1 circuit comprises 32 channels of 64 Kbps (aggregate 2.048 Mbps). One channel is always reserved for signaling, and a second can be reserved by the carrier for management traffic. Users may choose to aggregate one or more channels and have channels terminate at different destinations. For example, an E1 circuit could be terminated in London as a single physical interface, with various $N \times 64$ configurations (such as 64, 128, and 384 Kbps) terminating at different destination sites throughout the United Kingdom.

Framed interfaces such as E1 are presented via a G.703 interface (a duplex connection usually via dual BNC connectors, or an RJ-45 120-ohm twisted-pair connector). ITU/T G.704 and G.732 define framing and signaling conventions. Several router vendors, such as Cisco, BAY, and Xyplex, support G.703 interfaces directly. G.703 is also used as an interface for ISDN primary rate (which typically uses the RJ-45 presentation).

Design considerations

Leased lines are a reasonable choice for small to intermediate networks with limited meshing and medium to high consistent traffic levels. For simple point-to-point applications they may still be the best design option. One key point to remember when considering alternatives is that leased lines and satellite circuits offer dedicated bandwidth (services such as Frame Relay, ATM, xDSL, etc. are still essentially shared resources). Leased circuits are easy to understand, easy to implement, and easy to maintain. In highly centralized sites you may want to consider channelized leased circuit bandwidth, since the cost of equipment for providing multiple interfaces at the central site can soon become prohibitive. Even so, the granularity (minimum of 56/64 Kbps) of channelized T1/E1 may be too coarse for your network. As the number of sites increases, and the benefits of meshing become more apparent, other technologies such as Frame Relay may become much more attractive, especially in Europe. (See Figure 7.11.)

Leased lines can be multiplexed together onto a single interface, a technique known as inverse multiplexing. This can save valuable port costs and provide much more flexibility in the backbone bandwidth design. However,

Figure 7.11
Typical leased line network topology with ISDN backup links (higher-bandwidth circuits are indicated by thicker lines).

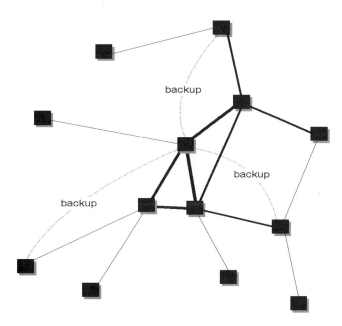

inverse multiplexing can be unattractive financially. In Europe the cost of about 7×64-Kbps multiplexed circuits is about the same as a 2-Mbps circuit. In the United States it can be lower.

In large meshed internetworks leased circuits can chew up valuable IP address space (two per circuit), and you should make use of Variable-Length Subnet Masks (VLSM) or better still unnumbered links. Unnumbered links are supported by advanced routing protocols such as OSPF. Since leased lines operate as a two-node point-to-point LAN, ARP and RARP do not present any problems.

Performance considerations

Leased circuits are the simplest of WAN technology to characterize in performance. Since data transmission is serial, and frames are sent on a frame-by-frame basis, the longer a frame is, the greater its latency over the link. We call this store-and-forward delay. Frames of different protocol types are effectively multiplexed over the circuit in a serial stream. The order in which they are placed onto the circuit is determined by the queuing mechanisms available at the terminating devices; in its simplest form this will be FIFO.

Table 7.6 illustrates the latency associated with various frame sizes as bandwidth is increased. Notice that a maximum-sized Ethernet frame (1,500 bytes) takes at least five seconds to transfer over a 2,400-bps circuit. With this degree of latency a router is likely to start dropping packets in the queue as they age out, leading to retransmissions. With the store-and-forward technique bursty protocols may also cause timeouts in other protocols on relatively slow links as they monopolize the queue for periods. For example, NFS may require tuning for WAN operations, since it uses UDP for its

Table 7.6   *Link Latency (Seconds) for Various Leased Circuit Speeds and Frame Sizes (larger packets have a larger latency)*

Frame Size (Bytes)	Link Speed (Kbps)							T1 1,544	E1 2,048
	2.4	9.6	56	64	128	256	512		
64	0.21333	0.05333	0.00914	0.00800	0.00400	0.00200	0.00100	0.00033	0.00025
128	0.42667	0.10667	0.01829	0.01600	0.00800	0.00400	0.00200	0.00066	0.00050
256	0.85333	0.21333	0.03657	0.03200	0.01600	0.00800	0.00400	0.00133	0.00100
512	1.70667	0.42667	0.07314	0.06400	0.03200	0.01600	0.00800	0.00265	0.00200
1024	3.41333	0.85333	0.14629	0.12800	0.06400	0.03200	0.01600	0.00531	0.00400
1500	5.00000	1.25000	0.21429	0.18750	0.09375	0.04688	0.02344	0.00777	0.00586
2048	6.82667	1.70667	0.29257	0.25600	0.12800	0.06400	0.03200	0.01061	0.00800

transport protocol. UDP has a timeout of 700 ms for a complete UDP message block (8 KB), and this may be insufficient for NFS on slower links. Clearly, store and forward is not ideal for sending mixed voice, video, and legacy data without virtually unlimited bandwidth.

7.4.2 X.25

X.25 and Frame Relay are conceptually similar, and both can be set up to encapsulate IP datagrams for transmission across the backbone network. X.25 is a very mature technology and has seen wide deployment, especially in Europe. X.25 is still popular in Eastern Europe, although availability in the United States can be patchy. X.25 was designed to operate over lower-quality lines with potentially higher bit error rates than Frame Relay (which assumes a BER of 1 in 10^6). X.25, therefore, includes three layers of protocol, including a connection-oriented network service, the Packet Layer Protocol (PLP), and a connection-oriented link layer service, Link Access Protocol Balanced (LAPB). PLP is run end to end over the network; LAPB is used between the user's Data Terminal Equipment (DTE) and the Data Communication Equipment (DCE) at the edge of the X.25 cloud. In recent years X.25 has been offered at higher bandwidths (up to 2 Mbps in France and Germany), but this can induce significant overhead on X.25 attached devices such as routers.

Operation

X.25 is deployed as a Switched Virtual Circuit (SVC) network, although Permanent Virtual Circuit (PVC) mode is possible. An X.25 virtual circuit is identified by a Logical Channel Number (LCN). One or more X.25 virtual circuits are opened on demand when datagrams arrive at the network interface for transmission. For example, if a packet is being queued for transmission over an open VC, and if a second packet arrives, another VC is established. Whenever a new packet arrives, the existing VCs are examined to see if their queues are empty; if so, then the new packet is forwarded down an existing VC or a new VC is established. Typically the number of open VCs between two sites is limited to four. This operation came about because X.25 originally supported only seven outstanding packets, and this is a way of effectively increasing the window size, since each VC has its own window. Nowadays window sizes can be opened up to 127 packets [18]. If multiple packet encapsulations are used (e.g., IP, CLNP, SNAP), then each encapsulation requires a separate VC. Multiple VCs for a single encapsulation can be used between systems to increase throughput.

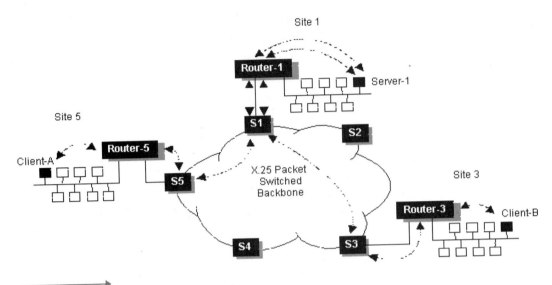

Figure 7.12   *An X.25 wide area network.*

X.25 can establish VCs to multiple destinations, forming highly flexible mesh topologies, as illustrated in Figure 7.12. The number of active VCs is typically dependent on the device's installed memory and CPU. On access routers we would expect to see up to 32 or 64 active VCs; on a backbone router there could be hundreds. X.25's SVC mode poses problems for LAN address resolution with protocols such as ARP. In Figure 7.12, Client-A and Client-B initiate IP connections to Server-1 on Site 1. The routers map these X.121 addresses and open switched virtual circuits across the X.25 cloud. IP datagrams are likely to be fragmented over the cloud as multiple X.25 PDUs (using the M-bit). At Site 1 Router-1 unpacks and reassembles the IP data and forwards the IP packets onto the server. A complete logical meshed topology can be achieved using X.25.

Some X.25 networks charge for virtual circuit holding time. For this reason virtual circuits are typically closed automatically after a specified period of inactivity to minimize costs (the period depends on the tariff used). If multiple circuits are open and idle, then all of them will be cleared down immediately, except for one VC, which remains open until an inactivity timer expires. Some X.25 networks also charge by the byte (especially for excess traffic over previously agreed limits). An open VC may also be closed automatically to free up resources if an interface runs out of circuits and a new call is attempted. In this case the closed VC would typically form part of a group of VCs to a common destination, and the new call would be targeted for a different destination.

X.25 connections can be made between routers (or bridges, etc.) directly or from a host to a router. A host running TCP/IP can simply install an X.25 adapter card (such as Eicon's PC card) to enable direct connection into an RFC 877/1356–equipped router via X.25 packet-switched network. Since X.25 is widespread, especially across Europe, this could be a useful option, but potentially expensive; hence, most configurations employ routers to multiplex user traffic between sites.

IP encapsulation over X.25

Multiprotocol encapsulation over X.25 networks is documented by RFC 1356 [18], which supersedes RFC 877 [19]. The main enhancements are an increase in the IP datagram MTU, the X.25 maximum data packet size, changes to VC management, and the encapsulation of more protocol types. A one-byte Network Layer Protocol Identifier (NLPID) (contained in the call user data field) identifies which Network Layer protocol is encapsulated over the X.25 virtual circuit. The NLPID has several values; the following are of interest:

- 0x00—Null encapsulation

- 0xC5—Blacker X.25

- 0xCC—IP

- 0xCD—Blacker X.25

- 0x81—ISO/IEC 8473 (CLNP)

- 0x82—ISO/IEC 9542 (ES-IS)

- 0x80—IEEE Subnetwork Access Protocol (SNAP)

SNAP is used as a generic encapsulation and identifies a single Network-Layer protocol. The SNAP header is sent as part of the CUD field; it is not sent in subsequent X.25 data packets. Only one SNAP-encapsulated protocol is allowed per VC. Null encapsulation is used to multiplex multiple Network Layer protocols over the same circuit. 0xC5 and 0xCD may continue to be used for Blacker X.25 but only by prior negotiation. X.25-attached Internet devices must support 0xCC encapsulation for IP datagrams. Systems that support other NLPIDs must negotiate with their peers.

Null encapsulation for multiplexing is useful when a system for any reason (such as implementation restrictions or network cost considerations) may only open a limited number of VCs simultaneously. This is the method most likely to be used by a multiprotocol router to avoid using an unreasonable number of active VCs. If performing IEEE 802.1d bridging across

X.25, then the Null encapsulation must be used. Implementations may support four possible encapsulations of IP, as follows:

- IP datagrams must by default be encapsulated on a VC opened with the 0xCC CUD.

- IP datagrams may be encapsulated in multiplexed data packets on a circuit using the Null encapsulation. These data packets have an NLPID of 0xCC.

- IP may be encapsulated within the SNAP encapsulation. This encapsulation is identified by an OUI of 0x000000 followed by the PID 0x0800.

- On a circuit using the Null encapsulation, IP may be encapsulated within the SNAP header of IP in multiplexed data packets.

Design considerations

When interconnecting LANs over X.25 there is trade-off between performance and cost. You will also need to consider how this design will scale in the future and how manageable the design is. X.25 can provide a highly redundant meshed topology, but there are potential latency issues and bandwidth inefficiencies, which could lead you to examine other choices. One of the prime motivations for using X.25 is its relatively low cost, especially in less developed regions where high-speed reliable bandwidth may simply not be available. The following design considerations are worth noting:

- Hierarchy—Adopting a hierarchical approach to the overall backbone and access design can reduce the overall complexity of an internetwork by dividing the network into smaller logical domains. This makes troubleshooting easier, while providing protection against the propagation of broadcast storms and routing loops. Hierarchical internetworks provide greater flexibility in the use of WAN packet services. You may choose to use a hybrid approach, with leased lines implemented in parts of the backbone, and packet-switching services, used in the distribution and access networks. With the use of a layered, hierarchical approach the complexity of individual router configurations can be substantially reduced, since each router has fewer peers.

- NBMA issues—X.25 and Frame Relay are examples of multiaccess networks that do not include broadcast facilities; hence, they are referred to as NonBroadcast MultiAccess (NBMA) networks. In these environments functions such as ARP are not available, and packet replication down multiple virtual circuits is required. Since X.25 is SVC based, this situation is worse than for Frame Relay, which is PVC based.

- Optimization of broadcast traffic—The adverse effects of broadcasting in packet-service networks mean that you will want to consider a hierarchical approach to limit the size of router groups. Typical examples of broadcast traffic are the routing updates from protocols such as RIP and broadcast between routers over a PSDN (the same applies to multicast routing updates). A high population of peered routers can result in traffic bottlenecks brought on by broadcast replication. A hierarchical design allows you to limit the level of broadcasting between regions and into your backbone.

- X.32 asynchronous packet mode—X.25 supports dial-up access via a standard called X.32. This enables applications such as home offices or mobile work forces to be considered (similar to ISDN dial-up). The user dials into a modem pool run by the service provider over the plain old telephone network (POTS). The client PC runs standard client software such as DEC PathWorks and has an off-the-shelf async modem. At the modem pool the async modem stream is converted by an X.32 Packet Assembler/Disassembler (PAD) into packetized synchronous X.25 traffic and forwarded over X.25 to an RFC 877/1356-equipped router. X.32 has several advantages for home offices but as yet appears to be slow to take off. At present higher speed modems (such as V.34) are not supported until higher-performance PADs are deployed.

- Interoperability—RFC 877 is a mature standard (in place since 1982) and many routers, hosts, and other X.25-enabled devices support it. Examples include Eicon X.25PC cards, DEC PathWorks, Cisco, BAY, and Xyplex routers and gateways. Because of the longevity of this standard interoperability is almost guaranteed. The new standard for multiprotocol operation over X.25 (RFC 1356) has been around since 1992. Since the IP formats are identical to RFC 877, backward compatibility for IP internetworks should be transparent.

Performance considerations

There are several areas of concern with X.25 performance in modern internetworks. These include the following:

- Latency—Given the low bit error rates on modern transmission media, much of the error-checking protocol in X.25 is now considered redundant. These protocols add significantly to the latency experienced by users working over an X.25 service, and this is particularly evident in LAN-to-LAN applications. Interactive applications such as Telnet can be more problematic for users than bulk file transfer operations.

■ High-speed access issues—As mentioned, X.25 is now available at speeds up to 2 Mbps. This is a very CPU-intensive protocol and typically can be supported only on high-end products from router manufacturers. Therefore, equipment costs can be higher than anticipated. In contrast Frame Relay can be supported by access router products to fill a 2-Mbps link.

■ Optimizing MTU and window size—It would be natural to assume that larger X.25 packet sizes would result in increased performance, but this is not necessarily true, and, in fact, the opposite may result. Most X.25 networks store complete data packets in each switch before forwarding them. If the network requires a path through a number of switches, and low-speed trunks are used, then negotiating and using large data packets could result in large transit delays through the network as a result of the time required to clock the data packets over each low-speed trunk. If a small end-to-end window size is also used, this may also adversely affect the end-to-end throughput of the X.25 circuit. For this reason, segmenting large IP datagrams in the X.25 layer into complete packet sequences of smaller X.25 data packets allows a greater amount of pipelining through the X.25 switches, with subsequent improvements in end-to-end throughput. Large X.25 data packet size combined with slow (e.g., 9.6 Kbps) physical circuits will also increase individual packet latency for other virtual circuits on the same path; this may cause unacceptable effects on, for example, X.29 connections. This discussion is further complicated by the fact that X.25 networks are free to internally combine or split X.25 data packets as long as the complete packet sequence is preserved. The optimum X.25 data packet size is, therefore, dependent on the network and is not necessarily the largest size offered by that network.

■ MTU size and fragmentation—RFC 1356 [18] states: Every system MUST be able to receive and transmit PDUs up to at least 1,600 octets in length. For compatibility and interoperability the default transmit MTU for IP datagrams is typically defaulted to 1,500 bytes and must be configurable in at least the range of 576 to 1,600. On older networks the MTU is often set to 128 or 256 bytes for performance reasons, and you should note that X.25 Protocol Data Units (PDUs) are sent as complete packet sequences, with the M-bit (within the PLP) set in fragments to indicate more data and cleared on the last fragment. PDUs that are larger than an X.25 data packet are fragmented and sent down the same VC (i.e., they cannot be load balanced). The fragmentation processes are actually quite efficient.

- Optimizing VC use—Another method of increasing performance is to open multiple virtual circuits to the same destination, specifying the same CUD. This is not always the best method of improving performance. When the throughput limitation is due to X.25 window size, opening multiple circuits effectively multiplies the window and may increase performance. However, opening multiple circuits also competes more effectively for the physical path, by taking more shares of the available bandwidth. While this may be desirable to the user of the encapsulation, it may be somewhat less desirable to the other users of the path. Opening multiple circuits may also cause datagram sequencing and reordering problems in end systems with limited buffering (e.g., at the TCP level, receiving segments out of order, when a single circuit would have delivered them in order). This will affect only performance, not correctness of operation. Opening multiple circuits may also increase the cost of delivering datagrams across a public data network.

- Packet-switch node performance—X.25 performance is heavily dependent on queue behavior of X.25 packet switches inside the X.25 cloud. Some X.25 packet switches degrade in performance as their queues fill up, causing decreases in throughput and an increase in response times. Errors in the X.25 transport protocols can increase delays and add more queuing. Another major issue with X.25 is the protocol overhead imposed by the X.25 layers. Typical overheads are between 64 and 256 bits per packet, and since the average message size is likely to be approximately 256 to 1,028 bits, this can represent up to 25 percent of the overall transmission bandwidth. Clearly, this has an adverse effect on efficiency. In a packet-switched network performance is measured in packets per second (pps) throughput and the delay between the points of ingress (entry) to a packet-switch node and egress (exit) from a packet-switch node. In the purchase of a packet switch the vendor should easily be able to produce graphs showing the characteristic curves or throughput and delay. In a typical packet-switch node the average delay would be in the range of 50 to 200 ms due to packet processing, and the average throughput would be between 300 and 10,000 pps. When selecting a packet-switch node it is advisable to choose one with a constant performance regardless of packet size. Some packet switches degrade very quickly with larger packet sizes, and this can adversely affect applications such as batch processing and file transfer.

7.4.3   Frame Relay

Frame Relay is a packet-switched data network service that supports public and private WAN backbone applications, such as connecting LAN-based enterprises (the majority of frame networks deployed today are public). Frame Relay emerged in the early 1990s as the panacea for packet-switched networking, the successor to X.25. Frame Relay was designed to take advantage of the latest generation of digital high-performance/low bit error rate fiber technology being installed at the time. This meant a radical approach, effectively stripping out most of X.25's error correction and packet buffering protocol to leave a fairly straightforward multiprotocol encapsulation scheme supporting virtual circuits and limited error detection.

Frame Relay packets are largely transmitted over high-speed leased lines; however, the design of Frame Relay enables straightforward migration to future network architectures via software changes. Frame Relay is designed to handle bursty, unpredictable data traffic (typical of LAN applications) and provide multiple, individually configured, logical connections to one or multiple destinations over a single physical interface. This enables the network designer to use minimal hardware to construct a highly flexible bandwidth-optimized network design, with reduced operating costs. Over the last decade Frame Relay bearer services have become increasingly popular, as has dedicated Internet access. Connection speeds are typically from 64 Kbps to 1.522 or 2.048 Mbps. Frame Relay is specified in RFC 2427 [20] and ANSI T1.606.

Frame format

With standard Frame Relay, higher-level protocols are encapsulated within a Q.922 Annex A frame. Frames contain a protocol identifier (NLPID) to enable multiprotocol support. Routed and bridged packets are differentiated by the NLPID and SNAP header information. The frame format is shown in Figure 7.13. Note that a different frame format is used by LMI packets, as will be discussed shortly.

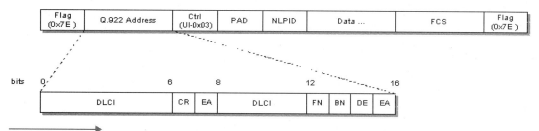

Figure 7.13   *Frame Relay message format.*

Field definitions

- Flags—Delimit the beginning and end of the frame. The value of this field is always the same and is represented either as the hexadecimal number 7E or the binary number 01111110.

- Q.922 address—Contains the following information:

  - DLCI—The 10-bit Data Link Circuit Identifier (DLCI) uniquely identifies the virtual connection between the DTE and the DCE (switch). DLCI values have local significance only; therefore, devices at opposite ends of a connection can use different DLCI values to refer to the same virtual connection.

  - CR—Undefined

  - EA—The Extended Address bit indicates whether further bytes are used to create a larger DLCI. If the value is 1, then this indicates that this is the byte containing the EA bit that is the final byte of the DLCI.

  - FN—The Forward Explicit Congestion Notification (FECN) bit is set to 1 by a switch to indicate to a source DTE device that congestion was experienced in the direction of the frame transmission from source to destination. FECN relies on the ability of higher-layer protocols to react intelligently to these congestion indicators. Currently, DECnet and OSI are the only higher-layer protocols that support these capabilities effectively.

  - BN—The Backward Explicit Congestion Notification (BECN) bit is set to a value of 1 by a switch, indicating that congestion was experienced in the network in the opposite direction of the frame transmission from source to destination.

  - DE—The Discard Eligibility (DE) bit is set by the DTE device to indicate that the frame is of lower priority relative to other frames being transmitted. Such frames will be discarded before any other frames during periods of congestion.

- Control—The control field is the Q.922 control field. The UI (0x03) value is used unless it is negotiated otherwise. The use of XID (0xAF or 0xBF) is permitted.

- Pad—The pad field is used to align the data portion (beyond the encapsulation header) of the frame to a two-byte boundary. If present, the pad is a single octet and must have a value of zero.

- NLPID—The Network Level Protocol ID (NLPID) field is administered by ISO and the ITU. It contains values for many different protocols, including IP, CLNP, and IEEE Subnetwork Access Protocol (SNAP). This field tells the receiver which encapsulation or which protocol follows. Values for this field are defined in ISO/IEC TR 9577. An NLPID value of 0x00 is defined within ISO/IEC TR 9577 as the null network layer or inactive set. Since it cannot be distinguished from a pad field, and because it has no significance within the context of this encapsulation scheme, an NLPID value of 0x00 is invalid under the Frame Relay encapsulation.

- Data—Comprises user data, up to 16,000 bytes.

- FCS—The Frame Check Sequence ensures the integrity of user data. This value is computed by the source device and verified by the receiver.

Operation

A Frame Relay service comprises a number of switches connected together via leased lines to form a partial or full mesh. Instead of a single fixed pipe, the designer can carve up the access port into one or many different logical pipes of different sizes and with different traffic characteristics. Frame Relay uses Permanent Virtual Circuits (PVCs) as its primary delivery mechanism, although there is increasing support for Switched Virtual Circuits (SVCs). Devices interconnected via PVCs form a private Frame Relay group, which may be either fully or partially meshed. Each VC is identified at the Frame Relay interface by a logical number called a Data Link Connection Identifier (DLCI). DLCIs typically have only local significance and do not match end to end. When service providers set up the network to support a design, they will allocate bandwidth and establish PVCs between the locations specified by the client.

IP datagrams sent over a Frame Relay network conform to this encapsulation and therefore IP can be encapsulated with an NLPID of 0xCC, indicating IP, or with an NLPID indicating SNAP encapsulation.

```
File:FR-TRY.SYC        Type:SNIFFER_SYC  Mode:•••••••  Records:215
===============================================================================
Frame    : 2              Len      : 45               Error    : None
T Elapsed: 01:51:47:151   T Delta  : 00:00:00:500
------------------------------[WAN]--------------------------------------------
Dst Addr : DTE            Src Addr : DCE
-----------------------------[Frame Relay]------------------------------------
DLCI     : 220            Flags    : R:_EA1:xFCN:xBCN:xDE:xEA2:_
Padding  : 1              Q922 Ctrl: 0x03  (UI)
Protocol : SNAP
-----------------------------[ieee snap]-------------------------------------
SNAP OID : 0080c2         SNAP PID : BPDU
-----------------------------[ieee stp]--------------------------------------
STA Pri  : 0              STA Ver  : 0                BPDU Type: CONFIG_BPDU
Flags    : 0              Root Pri : 256              Root ID  : This Bridge
Root Cost: 00000000       Brdge Pri: 256             Bridge ID: 0800870216e5
Port ID  : 0x8016         Msg Age  : 0      secs      Max Age  : 20     secs
T_Hello  : 2      secs    Forw Del : 15     secs
=============================[data:    0]====================================
```

Figure 7.14   *Frame Relay SNAP encapsulation of a bridge BPDU packet.*

IP data should ideally be encapsulated using the NLPID = 0xCC. This is more efficient, since it transmits 48 more data bits than the SNAP header and is consistent with IP encapsulation over X.25. Figure 7.14 illustrates a protocol decode of a bridged packet using SNAP encapsulation.

As mentioned previously, PPP is sometimes used as an encapsulation protocol above Frame Relay because of its flexibility. Figure 7.15 illustrates a protocol decode of an IP packet using PPP encapsulation over Frame Relay encapsulation.

Bandwidth allocation

We previously discussed the concepts of Committed Information Rate (CIR), Excess Information Rate (EIR or Be), and Committed Burst Size (Bc). The parameters determine bandwidth allocation on a per virtual circuit basis. Note that the CIR does not necessarily guarantee bandwidth; Frame Relay is a shared switched network and therefore under extremely congested conditions even CIR traffic may be dropped at overloaded switching nodes. These parameters need to be estimated with care during the capacity-planning phase. Incorrect settings could lead to serious performance problems. Furthermore, in practice CIR is not actually guaranteed and may be misleading over extended periods of congestion. Therefore, some vendors have provided extensions to these parameters and additional algorithms to enable service providers to offer a more realistic measure of the bandwidth actually provided. Cisco, for example, adds two additional

```
File:FR-1DLCI.SYC      Type:SNIFFER_SYC  Mode:•••••••  Records:211
===================================================================================
Frame    : 13              Len    : 34               Error    : None
T Elapsed: 03:22:15:092    T Delta : 00:00:00:020
--------------------------------[WAN]----------------------------------------------
Dst Addr : DTE             Src Addr : DCE
--------------------------------[Frame Relay]-------------------------------------
DLCI    : 16               Flags    : R:_EA1:xFCN:xBCN:xDE:xEA2:_
Padding  : None            Q922 Ctrl: 0x03  (UI)
Protocol : PPP
--------------------------------[ppp]----------------------------------------------
Type    : PID              Protocol : IP
--------------------------------[ip]-----------------------------------------------
IP Ver  : 4                IP HLen : 20 Bytes
TOS     : 0x00             Pkt Len : 28           Seg ID   : 0x00c8
Flags   : FRAG:_.LAST      Frag Ptr : 0    (8 Octet) TTL     : 64
PID     : UDP ( 17)        Checksum : 0xb6c8 (Good)
Dest IP  : 255.255.255.255 Source IP: 195.0.0.65
--------------------------------[udp]----------------------------------------------
Dest Port: TIME [    37]              Src Port : GLOBE [ 2002]
Length   : 8                          Checksum : 0x0000
============================[data:    0]===========================================
```

Figure 7.15 *Frame Relay packet showing PPP encapsulation of an IP packet.*

parameters called Peak Information Rate (PIR) and Minimum Information Rate (MIR), where PIR = MIR × (1 + Be/Bc). MIR represents the lowest information rate to be expected when the network is congested, and this enables a provider to offer subscribers a minimal service level with some degree of certainty.

Frame Relay devices

Frame Relay devices fall into two general categories, as follows:

■ Data Terminal Equipment (DTE)—The DTE is terminating equipment usually classified as customer premises equipment (CPE). The DTE is typically the property of the customer, although service providers may deploy and maintain DTE equipment as part of the overall service. DTE devices normally attach into the service via leased lines to the nearest PoP. The most common example of a Frame Relay DTE is the router, although other devices such as terminals, personal computers, gateways, switches, and bridges may also operate as a DTE.

■ Data Circuit Terminating Equipment (DCE)—DCEs are internetworking devices deployed within the carrier network at the PoP or central office. The DCE equipment provides clocking and enables

DTE equipment to access switching services within the Frame Relay backbone. DCE equipment is a form of packet switch..

A DTE device interfaces with a DCE device via both a physical layer connection and a link layer connection. Perhaps the most common physical layer interface specification for Frame Relay attachment is the RS-232 specification. At the link layer, Frame Relay protocol establishes the connection between the DTE device and the DCE device, as will be described shortly. For the purpose of our discussion we will assume that a DTE is a router and a DCE is a switch, unless otherwise specified.

A Frame Relay Access Device (FRAD) is a special variant of a Subrate Data Multiplexer (SRDM), discussed previously.

Frame Relay Virtual Circuits

Frame Relay is connection oriented, and this functionality is implemented through the use of Virtual Circuits (VCs). A VC is a logical bidirectional data path created statically or dynamically between two routers across a Frame Relay Packet-Switched Network (PSN). In practice many VCs can be multiplexed into a single physical circuit, thereby reducing the need for additional equipment, ports or cabling, and reducing costs. A VC can traverse any number of switches over the Frame Relay PSN. There are two basic types of Frame Relay virtual circuits, as follows:

- Switched Virtual Circuits (SVCs)—are temporary connections used in situations requiring only sporadic data transfer between DTE devices across the Frame Relay network. A communication session across an SVC consists of four operational states: (1) During the call setup state, the VC between two Frame Relay DTEs is established; (2) Data may then be transferred over the SVC between DTEs during the data transfer state; (3) If the SVC is still active, but no data are transferred, then it is said to be idle (for SVCs there is an idle timer, which forces the VC to be terminated if inactive for too long); (4) The SVC is terminated during the call termination state. Note that for these dynamically switched connections the DTE must establish a new SVC if there are additional data to be transferred and a circuit has timed out. At the time of writing relatively few manufacturers of Frame Relay switches support SVCs.

- Permanent Virtual Circuits (PVCs)—are permanent connections that are configured for long-term data transfer applications between DTE devices across the Frame Relay PSN. One could think of this as Frame Relay's equivalent of a leased line. Since a PVC is statically configured by a network administrator, there is no requirement for the call setup and termination states used with SVCs. PVCs operate in one of two states: (1) During data transfer the PVC is said to be in the data transfer state; (2) During periods of inactivity the PVC is said to be in an idle state, but there is no idle timer as in the case of SVCs—the circuit stays up permanently. DTE devices can transfer data whenever they are ready, since the circuit is permanently available.

Frame Relay VCs are identified by Data Link Connection Identifiers (DLCIs). DLCI values are generally assigned by the service provider, and for PVCs they are statically configured. DLCIs have local significance and are, therefore, not unique in the Frame Relay PSN (unless LMI extensions are used, as described shortly). Two DTE devices connected by a virtual circuit, for example, may use a different DLCI value to refer to the same connection.

Frame Relay nodes may optionally support the Exchange Identification (XID) mechanism specified in Appendix III of Q.922. XID enables several parameters to be negotiated at the start of a VC, including the maximum frame size, retransmission timer, and the maximum number of outstanding information frames. If XID is not used, these values must be statically configured or must be defaulted to the values specified in Q.922. In practice routers often implement PPP over Frame Relay to take advantage of its facilities for negotiating features.

Address resolution

For LAN interconnect applications there are often situations in which a Frame Relay device may need to dynamically resolve an address over PVCs. This can be achieved using the Address Resolution Protocol (ARP) encapsulated within a SNAP-encoded Frame Relay packet. Because of the inefficiencies of emulating broadcasting in a Frame Relay environment, a technique called Inverse ARP is employed to enable a network address to be resolved when only the hardware address is known a priori (in this case the hardware address is effectively a DLCI). Support for Inverse ARP is not mandated, but it has proven useful, especially for interface autoconfiguration. If the peer cannot resolve addresses using either ARP or Inverse ARP, then you may need to configure static ARPs.

A common requirement is the ability to map multiple IP addresses onto a single DLCI. For example, remote access applications require servers to act as ARP proxies for many remote dial-up clients. Each client typically has a unique IP address but shares bandwidth with other clients on the same DLCI. The dynamic nature of this kind of application means that there are frequent address association changes, while the DLCI remains constant. Hosts may learn the associations between IP addresses and DLCIs by listening for unsolicited (gratuitous) ARP requests associated with the DLCI. If a node wants to inform a peer node on the other end of a Frame Relay connection of a new association between an IP address and that PVC, it should send a gratuitous ARP request. In this request the source and destination IP address should both be set to the new IP address being used on the DLCI. This allows a station to announce new client connections on a particular DLCI. The receiving node must cache the new association and flush any existing association from any other DLCI on the interface.

Frame Relay Local Management Interface (LMI)

The Local Management Interface (LMI) was developed in 1990 by a consortium of Cisco/StrataCom, Northern Telecom, and Digital Equipment Corporation and comprises a set of extensions to the Frame Relay specification geared to managing more complex internetworks. Some of the main extensions include the following:

- Global addressing—gives DLCI values global rather than local significance. DLCI values effectively become DTE addresses that are unique within the Frame Relay PSN. This assists with the manageability of Frame Relay internetworks—for example, network interfaces and the end stations attached to them can be identified by using standard address-resolution and discovery techniques. Furthermore, the Frame Relay network is presented as a typical LAN to routers on its periphery.

- Virtual circuit status messages—provide additional communication and synchronization between Frame Relay DTE and DCE devices and periodically generate PVC status reports to prevent data from being sent into black holes (i.e., to PVCs that either no longer exist or are no longer functioning correctly).

- Multicasting—allows multicast groups to be assigned. This extension preserves bandwidth by enabling routing updates and address-resolution messages to be sent only to specific groups of routers; it also generates status reports for multicast groups.

Design considerations

Frame Relay is now one of the key technologies used to design backbones, and as such one of the major concerns when designing a Frame Relay network is scalability. As the number of remote connections increases, the design must be able to accommodate these changes without compromising performance or reliability, while still remaining manageable. As in any packet-switching network, another major issue in the design of a Frame Relay network is congestion control. Since Frame Relay is circuit based, there are also issues concerning broadcast replication and address resolution.

The following guidelines are intended to provide a foundation for constructing scalable Frame Relay internetworks that trade off performance, resilience, manageability, and cost.

Design issues with DLCIs

Before we discuss example design strategies, we must first examine some issues concerned with the use of DLCIs, since these are fundamental to the design strategy adopted. From the design perspective there are two chief concerns in the implementation of DLCIs; the number of DLCIs assigned to each interface and the use of broadcast replication down DLCIs. These issues affect cost and scalability and are discussed in the following text.

Service providers typically tariff Frame Relay services by DLCI, since a DLCI identifies a Frame Relay PVC. For any given design, the number of Frame Relay PVCs is dependent on the protocols in use and traffic dynamics. In general, Frame Relay designs should allow a maximum of between 10 and 50 DLCIs per interface. The threshold you choose depends upon several factors, to be considered together, as follows:

- Protocols being routed—Any broadcast-intensive protocol constrains the number of assignable DLCIs. For example, AppleTalk and Novell IPX are known to produce high levels of broadcast overhead. In contrast, IGRP is less broadcast intensive because it sends routing updates less often (by default, every 90 seconds). However, IGRP can become broadcast intensive if its IGRP timers are modified so that updates are sent more frequently.

- Broadcast traffic—Broadcasts, such as routing updates, are the single most important consideration in determining the maximum number of DLCIs per interface. The amount and type of broadcast traffic will influence your ability to allocate DLCIs.

- Speed of circuits—If broadcast traffic levels are expected to be high, you should consider faster circuits and DLCIs with higher CIR and excess burst (B_e) limits. You should also implement fewer DLCIs per interface.

- Static routes—If static routing is implemented, you can use a larger number of DLCIs per interface, since a larger number of DLCIs reduce the level of broadcasting.

- Size of routing and service updates—The larger the internetwork, the larger the size of these updates. The larger the updates, the fewer the number of DLCIs that you can assign.

Broadcast issues for Frame Relay internetworks

Routers treat Frame Relay as a broadcast medium, which means that each time the router sends a broadcast or multicast frame (such as a routing update, Spanning Tree update, or SAP update), the router must replicate the frame to each DLCI for that Frame Relay interface. Frame replication results in substantial overhead for the router and for the physical interface. One way to reduce broadcasts is to implement more efficient routing protocols and to adjust timers on lower-speed Frame Relay services.

Multiprotocol traffic management

With multiple protocols being transmitted into a Frame Relay internetwork through a single physical interface, it can be useful to separate traffic among different DLCIs based on protocol type. In order to split traffic in this way, you must assign specific protocols to specific DLCIs. This can be done by specifying static mapping on a per virtual interface basis or by defining only specific types of encapsulations for specific virtual interfaces.

Congestion control

A Frame Relay network is basically a network of queues. At each switch node, there is a queue of frames for each outgoing link. If the rate at which frames arrive and queue up exceeds the rate at which frames can be transmitted, the queue length increases and the delay experienced by a frame approaches infinity (in reality frames will be dropped, since the queue will be of finite size). Even if the arrival rate is less than the transmission rate, queue length will grow dramatically as the arrival rate approaches the transmission rate. As a rule of thumb, when the line for which frames are queuing exceeds 80 percent utilization, the queue length growth rate becomes a problem.

In a Frame Relay network there is much less queuing compared with X.25, since Frame Relay is designed to discard frames when congestion occurs and warn both the sender and receiver that congestion is occurring. In effect the responsibility is placed on the end systems to throttle back or risk further packet loss. Some switch vendors implement queuing in the switch node to cope with short-lived (milliseconds) traffic bursts. This can adversely affect session-oriented applications such as SNA, and ideally any queuing should be restricted to user access devices (the PAD or FRAD). If queuing is restricted to the access device, then data can be discarded before they hit the network in periods of congestion. Implementations that allow large, sustained bursts above the CIR and discard packets based upon the DE settings, together with the ability to carry large MTUs, are more likely to provide good throughput.

The purpose of congestion control is to avoid catastrophic traffic events by limiting queue lengths at the switching nodes by using a number of techniques. Congestion control is the responsibility of both the network and end users. The network is in the best position to monitor the degree of congestion, while the end users are in the best position to control congestion by limiting the flow of traffic. There are two basic components to congestion control, as follows:

- Congestion avoidance is applied at the early signs of congestion to prevent congestion from progressing throughout the network and escalating. Since at this stage users would be unlikely to be aware of any congestion increase, this requires explicit signaling mechanisms from the network to trigger congestion avoidance.

- Congestion recovery is applied to prevent network failure given a state of severe congestion. Recovery is typically initiated when the network has begun to discard frames due to buffer overflows. Discards are reported by some higher layer of software and thereby serve as an implicit signaling mechanism.

Frame Relay embodies several techniques to provide a measure of congestion avoidance and recovery, as follows:

- Committed Information Rate (CIR)—To provide for a fairer allocation of resources, the Frame Relay bearer service includes the concept of a Committed Information Rate (CIR). This is a rate that the network agrees to support for a particular frame-mode connection. Data transmitted in excess of the CIR are vulnerable to discard in the event of congestion. Despite the use of the term committed, there is no guarantee that even the CIR will be met. In cases of extreme congestion, the network may be forced to provide service at less than the CIR for a given connection; however, the network will choose to discard frames on connections that are exceeding their CIR before discarding frames on those that are not.

- Discard strategy (DE bit)—Frames that are deemed less important may be marked for discard eligibility using the DE bit. This does not mean that they will be automatically discarded; however, the DE bit provides some guidance to the network on which frames to select first when the information rate cannot be supported.

- Explicit congestion avoidance—It is desirable to use as much of the available capacity in a Frame Relay network as possible but still react to congestion in a controlled and fair manner. This is the purpose of explicit congestion-avoidance techniques, wherein the network alerts end systems to growing congestion within the network and the end systems take steps to reduce the offered load to the network. As the standards for explicit congestion avoidance were being developed, two general strategies were considered. One group believed that congestion always occurred slowly and almost always in the network egress nodes. Another group had seen cases in which congestion grew very quickly in the internal nodes and required quick, decisive action to prevent network congestion. These two approaches are reflected in the forward and backward explicit congestion-avoidance techniques, respectively. With congestion-avoidance techniques, the network signals congestion to those end users with affected Frame Relay connections. This explicit signaling may make use of one of two bits in the LAPF address field of each frame or a special LAPF control message. Either bit may be set by any frame handler that detects congestion. If a frame handler receives a frame in which one or both of these bits are set, it must not clear the bits before forwarding the frame. Thus, the bits constitute signals from the network to the end user. The two bits are as follows:

  - Backward Explicit Congestion Notification (BECN) bit—The user is notified that congestion-avoidance procedures should be initiated where applicable for traffic in the opposite direction of the received frame. BECN indicates that the frames the user transmits on this logical connection may encounter congested resources.
  - Forward Explicit Congestion Notification (FECN) bit—The user is notified that congestion-avoidance procedures should be initiated where applicable for traffic in the same direction as the received frame. FECN indicates that this frame, on this logical connection, has encountered congested resources.

Note that congestion control in higher-level protocols is generally decoupled of these measures. TCP, for example, will use its sliding-window control mechanism to deal with packet loss—decreasing its window size and then gradually reopening the window if packet loss is detected. There is no explicit signaling defined for this purpose within Frame Relay.

Reliability

Frame Relay networks have proven to be highly reliable on the whole; hence, when there are problems, they often attract significant attention. The main problems to date seem to occur from software or hardware device failures throughout the network. For a large provider this can be both embarrassing and costly. With a leased line backbone problems are typically localized to specific links or exchanges. With more intelligent switching technologies such as Frame Relay, software or hardware faults can manifest themselves throughout large parts of the network, often at the same time. This could effectively bring service to a halt and may require a complete system reboot and possible software patches. For example, a software bug may occur under certain traffic conditions (such as high load with a certain mix of QoS parameters). This could start by affecting one switch and then spread quickly throughout part, or all, of the network. Designing around such problems generally incurs additional costs. There are several potential options, including the following:

- Using multiple carriers and load balancing between them. If one network fails, then the second network should be able to carry most of the load with minimal disruption.

- Design backup features into the network. For example, ISDN BRI dial-up links could be utilized at the access routers and larger PRI (or multiple BRI) interfaces at core routers. With ISDN the main costs are in use, so this is a good solution for a quick workaround, assuming that the problems can be fixed in the core relatively quickly.

Another option to consider would be to ensure that switch suppliers give sufficient advanced notice of any software upgrades so that you can make contingency plans (such as pulling in extra staff for a month and training them about how to quickly downgrade software should problems occur).

Design strategies for Frame Relay access networks

For Frame Relay–based regional access networks there are three basic choices in topology: star topology, fully meshed, and partially meshed. In general, emphasis is placed on partially meshed topologies integrated into a hierarchical environment. Star and fully meshed topologies are discussed for structural context, as follows.

- Star topologies—Star topologies are attractive with Frame Relay because they minimize the number of DLCIs and result in a lower-cost design. However, a star topology presents some inherent bandwidth limitations. Consider an environment where a backbone router is attached to a Frame Relay PSN at 256 Kbps, while the remote sites are attached at 56 Kbps. Such a topology will throttle traffic coming off the backbone intended for the remote sites. A simple star topology does not offer the fault tolerance needed for many commercial networks. If the link from the hub router to a specific leaf router is lost, all connectivity to the leaf router is lost.

- Fully meshed topologies—In a fully meshed topology every routing node is logically connected via an assigned DLCI to every other node on the cloud. This topology is simply not scalable for larger Frame Relay internetworks. As discussed previously, a large, fully meshed Frame Relay topology requires many DLCIs—in fact $[n(n-1)]/2$ DLCIs, where n is the number of routers to be directly connected. Routers treat Frame Relay as a broadcast medium, so every time a router sends a broadcast or multicast (e.g., a routing update), the router must copy the frame to each DLCI for that Frame Relay interface. Broadcast replication will seriously degrade such networks. Fully meshed topologies are only conceivable for small Frame Relay networks.

- Partially meshed topologies—A partial mesh is basically a hybrid between a star and a fully connected topology. In essence it forms multiple redundant star topologies. This topology is recommended for Frame Relay regional designs because it offers good fault tolerance and is less expensive than a fully connected network. In general, you should implement the minimum meshing to eliminate a single point-of-failure risk while maintaining the performance requirements. You should check with your router vendor whether this form of topology can be fully supported, since interfaces need to be capable of connecting remote routers virtually over the same physical interface if they do not have a direct PVC connection. Cisco uses a technique called virtual interfaces to achieve full connectivity over limited PVCs.

Design strategies for Frame Relay backbone networks

The case for hierarchical design for packet-switching networks has already been discussed and this applies equally well to Frame Relay internetworks. Three factors drive the recommendation for implementing hierarchy in the design—namely, scalability, manageability, and the optimization of broadcast and multicast control traffic. You can choose to implement a Frame Relay design in a number of ways, as follows:

- Hub-and-spoke, point-to-point network

- A single meshed Frame Relay internetwork

- A hierarchical meshed Frame Relay internetwork

- A hybrid hierarchical meshed internetwork using a combination of Frame Relay and other core media

The pros and cons of these techniques are discussed in the following text.

Hub-and-spoke topologies

Hub-and-spoke topologies are common for simple applications involving a small number of interconnected sites. A central switching node may have many logical circuits running to different destinations over a single physical interface. Installation, configuration, management, and maintenance are relatively simple. In a hub-and-spoke design the CIR at the central hub should be at least equal to the sum of all CIRs set for each leaf network spoke (and should ideally be higher to cope better with bursting). (See Figure 7.16).

There are a number of issues associated with the hub-and-spoke design, as follows:

- Scalability—For larger backbone applications the hub-and-spoke design does not scale. The processing and memory requirements on the central site switch node become untenable, and some level of meshing is required.

Figure 7.16
Frame Relay hub-and-spoke design.

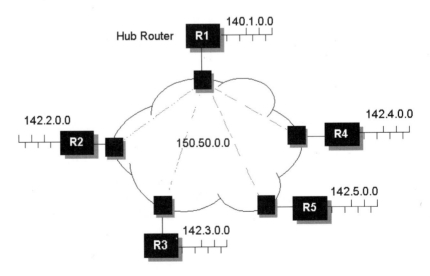

- Resilience—The Hub-and-spoke design embodies a single point of failure (i.e., the central switching node and central site). If such a failure occurs, then the whole network is broken.

- Split horizon routing problems—with distance-vector routing protocols such as RIP, the split-horizon feature can cause routing problems. Leaf networks cannot learn about other leaf networks because the routing updates distributed by the central site router do not advertise any leaf networks (since they are all received down the same physical interface and must therefore be ignored).

- Poison reverse routing problems—A problem similar to the split horizon issue occurs with the poison reverse feature. This time, all leaf networks are advertised at a cost of infinity.

Distance vector routing problems could be resolved through full meshing; however, the increased cost would be prohibitive. Some routing protocol implementations may allow the administrator to disable split horizon and poison reverse (ideally on a per interface basis) to work around this problem (note that some non-IP protocols such as Novell RIP and Apple-Talk Routing Table Maintenance Protocol (RTMP) require split horizon).

Another possible solution is the use of logical subinterfaces, where each subinterface emulates a physical point-to-point interface between the central router and a remote site, over a single physical interface. The central router could then apply split horizon/poison reverse rules on a subinterface basis rather than a physical interface basis. The drawbacks of subinterfaces are that they increase complexity, increase the amount of broadcasting, and a network number (i.e., IP address) must be allocated to every subinterface. With this design it is generally recommended that you limit broadcast traffic to no more than 20 percent of the total bandwidth; otherwise, some meshing must be considered. In Figure 7.17, we see a fully meshed Frame Relay backbone. Regional networks are connected into the backbone via routers, and this hierarchy reduces the amount of meshing required and consequently the number of DLCIs. The regional networks attach access networks (LANs), typically broadcast domains. Note that the regional networks show various degrees of meshing; this is a trade-off between cost, resilience, and performance. Note also that some networks may require dual connections to the backbone via alternate switches for additional resilience.

Hierarchical meshed Frame Relay internetworks

For large backbone applications a meshed topology is required. Clearly, for such applications a single meshed design does not scale, requiring up to

$[n(n-1)]/2$ DLCIs, where n is the number of routers to be directly connected. Broadcast replication and high circuit costs can be a serious concern for such a flat design. By implementing a hierarchical Frame Relay mesh, where the network is broken up into a Frame Relay backbone with regional Frame Relay networks attached onto the backbone via routers, we can reduce the number of DLCIs and provide a manageable, segmented environment. The hierarchy is created by strategically placing routers in the hierarchy. Figure 7.17 illustrates such a design. The design illustrates a three-tiered hierarchy, with a fully meshed backbone, partially meshed regional internetworks, and broadcast access networks at the periphery. This design is modular and manageable and scales well. Routers limit the num-

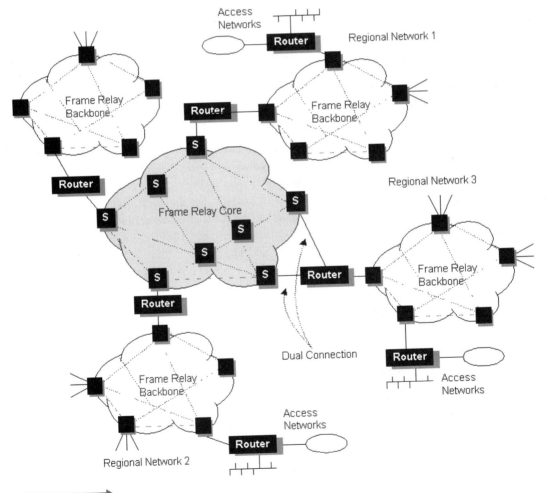

Figure 7.17 *Frame Relay hierarchical backbone design.*

ber of DLCIs per interface and segment the internetwork to contain traffic locally.

There are, however, two issues to consider when implementing such a design: broadcast packet replication and increased costs associated with additional router interfaces. The more meshing you add to the design, the more DLCIs are required per router interface. In networks with a large number of DLCIs per interface, excessive broadcast and packet replication can degrade overall performance; this is especially important for the backbone. Furthermore, compared with a simple fully meshed topology, additional routers are needed to enforce hierarchy, adding to the overall cost of the design. The trade-off is that these routers enable you to create much larger internetworks that scale well.

Hybrid meshed Frame Relay internetworks

The strategic importance of backbone design often leads network designers to consider a more optimal hybrid approach. Such designs may employ redundant, meshed leased lines in the backbone and partial or fully meshed Frame Relay internetworks for regional access. Once again, routers are used to enforce hierarchy, as illustrated in Figure 7.18. Hybrid leased line designs can lead to better traffic management on the backbone, providing higher performance on the backbone and easier scalability. Since the backbone is also constructed from dedicated point-to-point links, it will be more stable and less prone to failure. The disadvantages of this approach are higher backbone costs, together with the same broadcast and packet replication issues as in the regional access networks.

There are other alternate technologies that could be employed for the core, for example: ATM over SONET/SDH over optical fiber or IP over MPLS over DWDM over optical fiber.

Performance considerations

Since the transmission network used for Frame Relay is based on digital fiber optics, we should expect very low error rates, approaching zero. The performance of Frame Relay over this medium should be superior to X.25, since Frame Relay has no Layer 3 protocol and does not buffer packets at Layer 2 (similar to LAPB). Typical node delays due to data transport should be in the order of 5 or 10 ms. Frame Relay also provides fast reconnect and statistical multiplexing. The following additional issues should be considered when designing Frame Relay internetworks:

- MTU and fragmentation—MTU can affect performance by degrading throughput if it is set too low. There is no commonly imple-

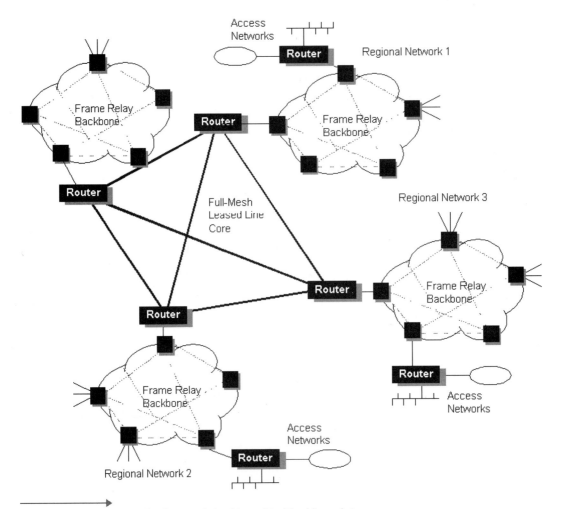

Figure 7.18   *Hybrid Frame Relay hierarchical backbone design.*

mented minimum or maximum frame size for Frame Relay. A network must, however, support at least a 262-byte minimum. Generally, the maximum will be greater than or equal to 1,600 bytes, but each Frame Relay provider will specify an appropriate value for its network. Frame Relay Data Terminal Equipment (DTE), therefore, must allow the maximum acceptable frame size to be configurable.

- Burst size—Setting burst sizes too high can adversely affect performance when the network becomes congested and starts to drop DE tagged packets. Networks are expected to have some oversized capacity, since it is expected that switches should attempt to pass as much DE tagged traffic as possible, even in congestion conditions.

- Delay—In Frame Relay packet sizes are variable, and so the total transmission delay is also variable (i.e., jitter). Multimedia applications such as voice and compressed video do not tolerate variable delay and therefore Frame Relay is not suited to these kinds of applications. Frame Relay is suitable for applications that can tolerate some jitter and the possibility of retransmissions (e.g., typical characteristics of bursty LAN traffic). The main performance criterion for Frame Relay is transit delay (specified in ANSI T1.606-1990). The transit delay of a Frame Relay PDU is expressed as:

$$T_{\text{TransitDelay}} = T_{\text{Transmit}} - T_{\text{Receive}}$$

where the delay is measured from the time the first bit of the packet crosses the point of ingress to the time where the last bit crosses the point of egress (sometimes referred to in the specifications as boundaries).

Transit delays are typically of the order of 5 to 10 ms. A typical cross-country transit delay for a 128-byte frame should be no more than 300 ms. The switching nodes within the network incur very little delay, essentially limited to DLCI switching and packet processing in hardware. The main delays are likely to be due to protocol and address conversion, as well as data insertion. These typically occur in the user access devices.

- Error rates—Frame Relay assumes a very low bit error rate on the transmission medium, preferring fiber-optic cables with error rates of 10^{-13}. This is the main reason for not including X.25's bulky transport services. When bit errors do occur inside the Frame Relay cloud, they have the same impact as congestion, since frames in error must be discarded and cannot be repaired inside the network itself. The network relies on higher-level protocols at the access nodes or inside the user network to perform packet recovery procedures. Frame Relay should not be run over poor transmission facilities. ANSI T1.606-1990 defines two performance measurements of interest: Residual Error Rate (RER) and lost frames. Residual Error Rate is defined as:

RER = 1 − (Total correct FPDUs delivered/Total offered FPDUs)

- The counters are measured from the same ingress and egress boundaries previously defined. Lost frames are those incurred in a given period of time between boundaries, measured in frame loss per second.

- Statistical multiplexing—As discussed, Frame Relay provides statistical multiplexing (typically of magnitudes from 4:1 to 1:1, depending upon traffic patterns). Statistical multiplexing improves performance by providing the ability to multiplex data over several physical channels as if they were a single logical channel. Frame Relay also has the ability to quickly redirect logical channels if one or more physical channel fails. Throughput can be controlled by the switch, allowing no more traffic than can be handled by the network.

- Efficiency—Frame Relay imposes very little protocol overhead, since it relies on the end-system protocols to provide packet recovery procedures. The efficiency and performance of the network are, therefore, much higher than with X.25, since a higher proportion of the packet is data, not protocol. It follows that the larger the MTU supported by the network, the greater the throughput. Throughput is measured as the number of successful packet transfers between the ingress and egress boundaries over a specified time.

7.4.4 Switched Multimegabit Data Stream (SMDS)

SMDS emerged in 1989 from research done by Bell Communications Research (Bellcore) into a high-speed data service for LAN interconnect, another alternative for leased lines. SMDS is designed to offer LAN services over the wide area, via a packet-switched datagram service designed for very–high-speed wide area data communications. It was developed in response to two emerging trends: the requirement for high-performance site-to-site networking and the decreasing cost and bandwidth potential of fiber-optic media for WAN applications. SMDS services were introduced in 1992 by the regional Bell operating companies (RBOCs) at access speeds of DS-1/T1 (1.544 Mbps, 1.17 Mbps data rate) and DS-3/T3 (44.736 Mbps, 34 Mbps data rate), although lower-speed access is available (typically starting at 0.5 Mbps). SMDS is expected to be available at much higher rates over SONET. SMDS is now deployed in public networks by many of the major carriers across the United States and Europe.

SMDS roughly corresponds to the first three layers of the OSI model. Layer 1 provides a physical interface to the digital network. Layer 2 specifies a cell structure similar to ATM (using 53-byte cells) and performs error detection, and Layer 3 deals with addressing and routing issues. SMDS is defined by Bellcore specifications in the United States, and by the European SMDS Special Interest Group (ESIG) in Europe.

Operation

The SMDS service provides a connectionless datagram packet service. Each data unit is handled and switched separately without the prior establishment of a network connection. The SMDS service is designed to offer high throughput and low latency and delivers up to 9,188 bytes of data in a single transmission. No explicit flow control mechanisms are provided; instead, SMDS uses access classes to control the data flow on both the ingress and egress points of the SMDS network. Both unicast and multicast packets are supported. In addition to these LAN-like features, several additional features (source address validation, source/destination address screening) are provided to enable the creation of logical private networks, or Closed User Groups (CUGs), over the public SMDS service. The SMDS provider is responsible for setting up these private networks [21].

SMDS Interface Protocol (SIP)

The protocol used between the customer premises equipment and SMDS network equipment is called the SMDS Interface Protocol (SIP). Devices such as routers use SIP to attach to an SMDS network for high-speed internetworking. SIP is based on the IEEE 802.6 Distributed Queue Dual Bus (DQDB) MAN standard. The DQDB protocol defines a MAC protocol that allows many systems to interconnect via two unidirectional logical buses. As designed by IEEE 802.6, the DQDB standard can be used to construct private, fiber-based MANs supporting a variety of applications, including data, voice, and video. This protocol was chosen as the basis for SIP because it is an open standard, could support all the SMDS service features, is designed for compatibility with carrier transmission standards, and is aligned with emerging standards for Broadband ISDN (BISDN). As BISDN technology matures and is deployed, the carriers intend to support not only SMDS but broadband video and voice services as well. To interface to SMDS networks, only the connectionless data portion of the IEEE 802.6 protocol is needed. Therefore, SIP does not define voice or video application support. When used to access an SMDS network, operation of the DQDB protocol across the Subscriber Network Interface (SNI) results in an access DQDB. The term access DQDB distinguishes operation of DQDB across the SNI from operation of DQDB in any other environment (such as inside the SMDS network). A switch in the SMDS network operates as one station on an access DQDB, while customer equipment operates as one or more stations on the access DQDB. Because the DQDB protocol was designed to support a variety of data and nondata applications, and because it is a shared medium access control protocol, it is relatively complex. It has two parts: the protocol syntax and the distributed queuing algorithm, which constitutes the shared medium access control.

SIP is logically partitioned into three levels: SIP Level 3 corresponds to the MAC level, and SIP Levels 1 and 2 occupy the physical layer. SIP Level 1 provides the physical link protocol, which operates between the CPE and the network. SIP Level 1 is divided into two parts: the transmission system sublayer and the Physical Layer Convergence Protocol (PLCP). The transmission system sublayer defines the characteristics and method of attachment to the transmission link. The PLCP specifies how the Level 2 PDUs are to be organized in relation to the DS-3 or DS-1 frame and defines management information.

SIP-3 field definitions

- Res—The two reserved fields must be populated with zeros.

- BEtag—The two BEtag fields contain an identical value and are used to form an association between the first and last segments or Level 2 PDUs of a SIP Level 3 PDU. These fields can be used to detect the condition where the last segment of one Level 3 PDU and the first segment of the next Level 3 PDU are both lost, resulting in receipt of an invalid Level 3 PDU.

- BAsize—Contains the buffer allocation size.

- destination and source addresses—The addresses comprise two parts: an address type and an address. In both cases, the address type occupies the four most significant bits of the field. If the address is a destination address, the address type may be either 1100 or 1110. The former indicates a 60-bit individual address; the latter indicates a 60-bit group address. If the address is a source address, the address type field can indicate only an individual address. Bellcore Technical Advisories specify how addresses consistent in format with the North American Numbering Plan (NANP) are to be encoded in the source and destination address fields. In this case, the four most significant bits of each of the source and destination address subfields contain the value 0001, which is the internationally defined country code for North America. The next 40 bits contain the binary coded decimal (BCD) encoded values of the ten-digit SMDS, NANP-aligned addresses. The final 16 (least-significant) bits are populated with ones for padding.

- X+—Fields marked X+ are used to ensure alignment of the SIP format with the DQDB protocol format. Values placed in these fields by the CPE must be delivered unchanged by the network.

- Higher-layer protocol identifier—Indicates what type of protocol is encapsulated in the information field. This value is important to systems using the SMDS network (such as Cisco routers) but is not processed or changed by the SMDS network.

- Header Extension Length (HEL)—Indicates the number of 32-bit words in the header extension field. Currently, the size of this field for SMDS is fixed at 12 bytes. Therefore, the HEL value is always 0011.

- Header Extension (HE)—Currently has two uses. One is to contain an SMDS version number, which is used to determine what version of the protocol is being used. The other use is to convey a carrier selection value providing the ability to select a particular interexchange carrier to carry SMDS traffic from one local carrier network to another. In the future, other information may be defined to be conveyed in the header extension field, if required.

- CRC—The CRC field contains a cyclic redundancy check value.

SMDS data units are encapsulated within the IEEE 802.2 LLC and IEEE 802.1A Sub-Network Access Protocol (SNAP), LLC Data Link Layer, and the SIP headers. The SNAP OID code indicates the EtherType code. The total length of the LLC header and the SNAP header is eight bytes. LLC encapsulated PDUs are encapsulated within SIP Level 3 headers and trailers, as illustrated in Figure 7.19. SIP Level 3 PDUs are segmented into SIP Level 2 PDUs to conform to Level 2 specifications.

Level 3 PDUs are segmented into uniformly sized (53-byte) Level 2 PDUs, often referred to as slots or cells. The format of the SIP Level 2 PDU is shown in Figure 7.20.

SIP 2 field definitions

- Access control—Contains different values depending on the direction of information flow. If the slot is sent from the switch to the CPE, only the indication of whether the PDU contains information or not is important. If the slot was sent from the CPE to the switch, and if the configuration is multi-CPE, this field can also carry request bits that indicate bids for slots on the bus going from the switch to the CPE. Further detail on how these request bits are used to implement

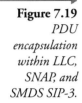

Figure 7.19
PDU encapsulation within LLC, SNAP, and SMDS SIP-3.

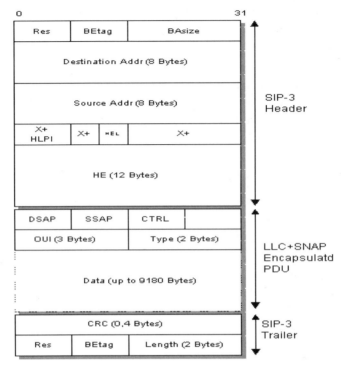

distributed queuing media access control can be obtained from the IEEE 802.6 standard.

■ Network control information—Can contain only two possible values. One particular bit pattern is included when the PDU contains information; another is used when it does not.

■ Segment type (2 bits)—Indicates whether this Level 2 PDU is the beginning slot, the last slot, or a slot from the middle of a Level 3 PDU.

■ Message ID (14 bits)—Allows association of Level 2 PDUs with a Level 3 PDU. The message ID is the same for all segments of a given Level 3 PDU. On a multi-CPE access DQDB, Level 3 PDUs originating from different CPEs must have different message IDs. This allows the SMDS network receiving interleaved slots from different Level 3 PDUs to associate each Level 2 PDU with the correct Level 3 PDU. Successive Level 3 PDUs from the same CPE may have identical message IDs. This presents no ambiguity, because any single CPE must send all Level 2 PDUs from one Level 3 PDU before it begins sending Level 2 PDUs of a different Level 3 PDU.

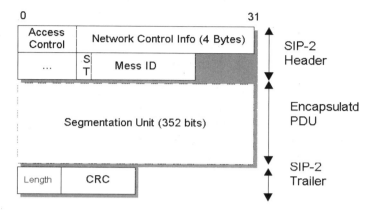

Figure 7.20
PDU encapsulation within SIP 2.

- Segmentation unit (44 bytes)—Is the data portion of the PDU. In the event of an empty Level 2 PDU, this field is populated with zeros.

- Payload length (6 bits)—Indicates how many bytes of a Level 3 PDU are actually contained in the segmentation unit field. If the Level 2 PDU is empty, this field is also populated with zeros.

- Payload CRC (10 bits)—Contains a Cyclic Redundancy Check (CRC) value used to detect errors over the segment type, message ID, segmentation unit, payload length, and payload CRC fields. This CRC does not cover the access control or network control information fields.

Addressing

SMDS addresses are represented by 15 Binary Coded Decimal (BCD) digit numbers, which resemble conventional telephone numbers. Addresses are encoded in 60 bits plus a 4-bit address type. The address type field occupies the four most significant bits of both the destination and source address fields in SIP L3 PDUs. SMDS supports both unicast and group addresses (analogous to multicasts). The address type value 0xC0 is used to indicate a unicast and the value 0xE0 indicates a group address. Since SMDS is datagram based, both the source and a destination address are present in each data unit. The receiver of a data unit can use the source address to return data to the sender and for functions such as address resolution. Group addresses are configured at the time of subscription to the SMDS service.

Design considerations

SMDS offers a high-speed, low-latency, cost-effective solution for integrating LANs ands MANs over a cell-relay WAN. SMDS offers connectionless

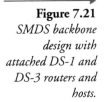

Figure 7.21
SMDS backbone design with attached DS-1 and DS-3 routers and hosts.

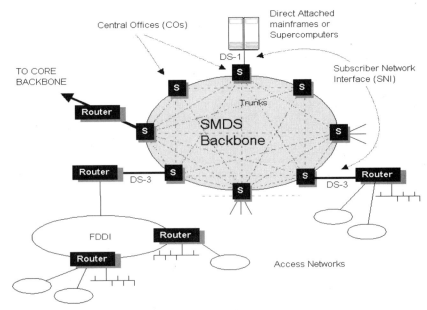

access to many destinations over a single physical interface, and this connectionless mode makes it far easier to administer and maintain than a connection-oriented Frame Relay or ATM network, especially as the number of nodes increases. Connectionless mode also makes SMDS more applicable for LAN access network integration onto the backbone. A typical SMDS network design is illustrated in Figure 7.21.

Inside the carrier network, the high-speed packet-switching capability required by SMDS can be provided by a number of different technologies. In the near term, switches based on MAN technology such as the DQDB standard are being included in a number of networks. There are two ways to configure CPE (such as routers) on the SMDS access DQDB, as follows:

- Single-CPE configuration—In this configuration, the access DQDB connects the switch in the provider network and one device located at the subscriber's premises. Here, the access DQDB is essentially just a two-node DQDB subnetwork. Both the switch and the CPE transfer data to each other via a unidirectional logical bus. There is no contention for this bus because there are no other stations, and therefore the distributed queuing algorithm is not required (hence, SIP for single-CPE configurations is much simpler than SIP for multi-CPE configurations).

- Multi-CPE configuration—In this configuration, the access DQDB comprises the switch in the provider network and multiple interconnected CPEs at the subscriber's premises. All CPEs must belong to the same subscriber.

Logical IP Subnetwork (LIS) configuration

Network designers can build multiple Logical IP Subnetworks (LIS) over SMDS. In this section, we discuss the implications for IP hosts or routers only. Hosts can be assigned within a closed logical IP subnetwork. All hosts within the LIS have the same IP network/subnet number. Each LIS operates independently of other LISs over the same SMDS network, so hosts in an LIS can only communicate directly with each other. For each LIS a single SMDS group address is configured that identifies all members of the LIS. Any packet transmitted with this address is delivered by SMDS to all members of the LIS. External communication to hosts outside of an LIS is achieved via an IP router, configured to be a member of multiple LISs. Even if a direct path is available between hosts, all inter-LIS communication currently has to go via the router. This situation may change in the future, but for now the issues of scalability of address resolution or propagation of routing updates means that this strict hierarchy is enforced.

Media support

Although SMDS is generally associated with fiber-optic media, DS-1 access can be provided over either fiber or copper (with good error characteristics). The demarcation point between the carrier's SMDS network and the CPE is referred to as the Subscriber Network Interface (SNI).

Multicast and broadcast handling

As described previously, MAC layer broadcasts and multicasts are supported over SMDS without additional software configuration in routers. This greatly simplifies the design issues. In reality there is no facility for complete hardware broadcast addressing over the SMDS service. An SMDS group address is configured to include all stations in the same LIS, and the broadcast IP address (all binary ones) is mapped to this group address. Currently all multicast addresses are also mapped to this LIS group address, and group filtering is the responsibility of the destination. RFC 1209 [22] discusses the ability to dynamically join and leave multicast groups, but this facility is not yet available.

Address resolution

The mapping of IP addresses to SMDS addresses is handled dynamically by ARP [22]. The hardware type code assigned to SMDS addresses is 0x0E, and the hardware address length for SMDS is 8. The SMDS hardware addresses are carried in SMDS native address format in ARP packets, with the most significant bit of the address type subfield as the high-order bit of the first byte.

Traditionally, ARP requests are broadcast to all directly connected stations. For the SMDS service, the ARP request packet is sent to the Logical IP Subnet (LIS) group address, which identifies all members of the LIS. RFC 1209 [22] specifies a special ARP request address, but this is currently mapped onto the LIS group address. In the future, a large-scale public network could use this as the address of an ARP server, acting as a relay for multiple LISs.

Quality of Service

SMDS provides mechanisms to address the Quality of Service (QoS) issue for data traffic through a number of access classes.

Security features

SMDS offers several additional addressing features, which enable network security at a low level. These features include the following:

- Antispoofing—Source addresses are validated by the network to ensure that the address is legitimately assigned to the SNI from which it originated. In effect, this protects against *address spoofing* (a sender pretending to be another user).

- Source and destination address screening—Source address screening is used on addresses as data units leave the network, while destination address screening acts on addresses as data units enter the network. If the address is disallowed, the data unit is not delivered. This feature allows a subscriber to establish a secure private virtual network and saves valuable bandwidth by excluding unwanted traffic.

SMDS screening tables do not have to be used when attaching to SMDS. However, if they are used, then both source and destination tables (for each SNI) must be configured to allow, at minimum, direct communication between all hosts in the LIS and use of the LIS group address.

Performance considerations

The IEEE 802.6 protocol and SIP were intentionally designed to align with the principal B-ISDN protocol, ATM. ATM and IEEE 802.6 belong to a class of protocols often referred to as fast packet-switching or cell-relay protocols. These protocols organize information into small, fixed-size cells (Level 2 PDUs in SIP terminology). Fixed-size cells can be processed and switched in hardware at very high speeds. This tightly constrains delay characteristics, making cell-relay protocols useful for video and voice applications. As ATM-based switching equipment becomes available, this technology will also be introduced into networks providing SMDS. Because the SIP is based on IEEE 802.6 DQDB, it has the advantage of compatibility with future B-ISDN interfaces that will support video and voice applications in addition to data. However, this compatibility does incur significant protocol overhead. When calculating overall data throughput using SIP over DQDB, DS-3 access provides approximately 34 Mbps total bandwidth for L3 PDU user data, and over a DS-1 access, approximately 1.17 Mbps.

MTU and fragmentation

SMDS refers to packets as data units. SMDS data units are capable of containing up to 9,188 bytes of user data, leaving 9,180 bytes for user data after the LLC SNAP header is taken into account. The MTU for IP stations operating over SMDS is 9,180 bytes, and there is no minimum packet size restriction.

SMDS is, therefore, capable of encapsulating complete IEEE 802.3, IEEE 802.4, IEEE 802.5, and FDDI frames. The large packet size is designed to optimize this high-performance service. RFC 1209 [22] specifies how IP datagrams should be transported over SMDS. The standard encapsulation used is SNAP. Datagrams are segmented into IEEE 802.6 cells by a Segmentation and Reassembly Service (SAR), identical to ATM. Each L2 PDU is 53 bytes long and contains 44 bytes of L3 PDU payload. Since L2 PDUs do not hold full addressing information, they cannot be routed independently. In effect a virtual circuit is set up to transfer each L3 PDU identified for the L3 PDU message ID.

7.4.5   Synchronous Optical Network (SONET)

The Synchronous Optical Network (SONET) is an international standard first proposed by Bellcore in the mid-1980s. SONET is a Physical Layer specification for high-speed, full-duplex synchronous transmission over fiber-optic media. SONET is not, however, restricted to optical links; electrical specifications have been defined for single-mode fiber, multimode fiber, and CATV 75-ohm coaxial copper cable. SONET is an octet-synchronous multiplexing scheme; it uses the ITU/T Synchronous Digital Hierarchy (SDH) system with STS-1 as the basic building block. The transmission rates are, therefore, integral multiples of 51.840 Mbps, which may be used to carry T3/E3 bit-synchronous signals. SONET is designed to operate at speeds well above the conventional T and E hierarchies indicated in Table 7.3 and is also designed to be compatible in both Europe and the United States. Services start at 51.84 Mbps STS-1. SONET offers a high-speed, low-latency, low–error-rate backbone service. SONET is widely deployed in public backbone networks, and is increasingly being used in private backbones for LAN-WAN integration or MAN applications. SONET defines four protocol layers, as follows:

- Photonic layer—specifies the physical characteristics of the optical devices

- Section layer—specifies frame formats and the translation of frames to optical signals

- Line layer—specifies timing and multiplexing

- Path layer—specifies end-to-end transport

Both cell-switched and packet-switched networks can run over SONET. Packet over SONET (POS) mode is becoming increasingly attractive for applications such as Voice over IP (VOIP) and intranet/Internet access. In POS mode, IP is normally encapsulated over PPP. You should be aware of the following:

- The basic rate for PPP over SONET/SDH is 155.52 Mbps (i.e., STS-3c/STM). The available information bandwidth is 149.76 Mbps, which is the STS-3c/STM-1 SPE with section, line, and path overhead removed (this is the same upper-layer mapping that is used for ATM and FDDI).

- Lower signal rates must use the Virtual Tributary (VT) mechanism of SONET/SDH. This maps existing signals up to T3/E3 rates asynchronously into the SPE or uses available clocks for bit-synchronous and byte-synchronous mapping.

- Higher signal rates should conform to the SDH STM series rather than the SONET STS series, as equipment becomes available. The STM series progresses in powers of four instead of three and employs fewer steps, which is likely to simplify multiplexing and integration.

Access to SONET is via optical interfaces provided by multiplexers, typically implemented in switch/router line cards. SONET is normally deployed as a dual-ring topology over two pairs of fiber strands. One ring pair acts as the active primary path, the other as a backup (i.e., idle). Failover in the event of primary ring failure is automatic and achieved in milliseconds. If both rings fail, then the ring self-heals (with 50 ms) by auto-wrapping at the two stations at the end of the break (as in Token Ring).

Increasingly, short-haul transport networks and core networks are being deployed over fiberoptic media, often based on SONET/SDH network elements and self-healing fiber rings. SONET/SDH networks can carry different types of traffic, including voice, leased line, and mixed data services, generally back-hauled as circuits to centralized service nodes. The service nodes may include voice switches, ATM switches, and IP routers, either located inside the facilities of the short-haul service provider or handled through a long-distance network operator, with traffic handed off via circuits.

7.4.6   Dense Wave Division Multiplexing (DWDM)

DWDM is an optical transmission technique where multiple optical signals are optically multiplexed onto a single optical fiber at different wavelengths, where each wavelength can be thought of as a channel. The original definition of dense referred to the ability to multiplex more than eight wavelengths per fiber, although nowadays it is possible to multiplex hundreds of wavelengths per fiber. Today's high-end DWDM systems enable each channel to operate at speeds of up to 2.5 Gbps or 10 Gbps and support up to 100 channels per fiber, enabling a single fiber to carry several hundred gigabits of information. Systems supporting terabits per fiber have been demonstrated in laboratories and will eventually become available for commercial deployment.

Long-haul DWDM systems (see Figure 7.22) take standard optical signals from clients, such as SONET/SDH equipment, IP routers, or ATM switches, and convert each signal to a distinct, precise wavelength in the 1,530–1,610 nm range. These individual wavelengths are then multiplexed onto a single fiber. At the destination, wavelengths are filtered and converted back to a standard SONET/SDH optical signal to the client. The complete DWDM system typically includes modules for each client interface in addition to equipment for multistage optical combining or splitting of wavelengths, amplification, and management/control, comprising several racks of equipment. Most DWDM systems support standard SONET/

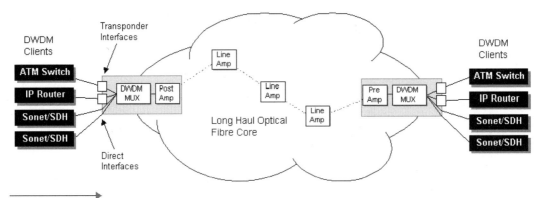

Figure 7.22   *Long-haul DWDM model.*

SDH optical interfaces to which any SONET/SDH-compliant client device can attach. In today's long-haul DWDM systems, this is most often an OC-48/STM-16 short-reach interface operating at 1,310 nm wavelength, as specified by ITU standards.

As with copper transmission, optical signals become attenuated with distance and must be regenerated periodically within the core. Prior to the introduction of DWDM, in SONET/ SDH optical networks, each separate fiber carrying a single optical signal, typically at 2.5 Gbps, required a separate electrical regenerator every 60 to 100 km. As additional fibers are enabled (lighted) in a core network, the total cost of deploying regenerators can become significant. The need to add regenerators also increases the time required to light new fibers. For example, a long-haul span of 600 km over 12 fibers requires 108 regenerators [(600/60 − 1) × 12]. However, the introduction of optical amplifiers (known as Erbium Doped Fiber Amplifiers [EDFAs]) and DWDM equipment have significantly reduced the total cost of long-haul transmission. A single optical amplifier can reamplify all the channels on a DWDM fiber without demultiplexing and processing them individually, at a cost close to that of a single regenerator. Since the optical amplifier merely amplifies the signals (it does not reshape, retime, or retransmit them as a regenerator does), signals may still need to be regenerated periodically depending upon the distance. However, depending on system design, signals can now be transmitted anywhere from 600 to thousands of kilometers without regeneration.

Another major advantage of DWDM systems is that they greatly simplify the expansion of network capacity; the only requirement is to install additional interfaces in the DWDM systems at either end of the fiber. The existing optical amplifiers amplify the new channel without the need for additional regenerators. The overall cost benefit and efficiencies gained by using DWDM generally more than offset the cost of deploying the new DWDM equipment; consequently, most core network operators are already adopting this technology.

Designing issues

Although ITU recommendations define a standard wavelength grid, core DWDM systems today use proprietary multiplexing and management schemes. Some of the potential areas of conflict include the portion of the optical spectrum used, power and amplification schemes, mechanisms for adjusting optical amplifier gain, and the methods used for forward error correction. Until standards are fully defined, DWDM systems must either be selected from a single vendor or from those with proven interoperability. This restriction also applies to DWDM client integration components, such as SONET/SDH terminal and multiplexer equipment, ATM switches, and IP routers. As a general rule look for standard optical and electrical interfaces that allow for straightforward integration of client elements from different vendors. Some DWDM equipment may offer proprietary interfaces, which need to be supported by all clients; clearly, this is undesirable. The majority of current long-haul DWDM networks are implemented with open systems; the most common interface is the ITU-compliant OC-48/STM-16 short-reach optical interface (supported by practically all networking equipment that operates at line speeds of 2.5 Gbps).

In order to maintain open interfaces between clients and proprietary optical technologies, low-cost, standardized interfaces must become available, especially as operators begin to deploy 10-Gbps channels. Unfortunately, the only standardized 10-Gbps interfaces available today are SONET/SDH serial interfaces, which have extremely high component costs. To address this problem, some vendors are developing very–low-cost interfaces such as the OC-192/STM-16 Very Short Reach (VSR) interface.

7.5 Summary

This chapter discussed the basics of wide area network design, including the following:

- Traditional dial-up modems, used for decades for remote access, are reaching the end of their usefulness. The need for greater bandwidth and so-called permanent online access means that users will increasingly turn to technologies such as cable modems, ADSL, and ISDN.

- Leased lines are the traditional way to build internetworks; they are simple to manage and easy to implement for LAN interconnect and are still possibly the best solution for simple site-to-site networks. As networks grow in size, leased lines may not be scalable or financially attractive, and other packet-switched technologies should be considered.

- ISDN is gaining acceptance for certain applications across Europe and in Japan. The major applications are currently leased line backup and remote dial-up for home or mobile use.

- Frame Relay is seen as an attractive alternative to leased lines. It effectively emulates leased line attributes over multiplexed logical interfaces and provides good performance, flexible bandwidth options, and a measure of congestion control.

- X.25 is a mature protocol, the predecessor of Frame Relay. Although still widely used across Europe, it is very top-heavy as a protocol and not ideal for interactive use. The demands placed on access devices such as routers are nontrivial. X.25 is still applicable for use over poor transmission lines due to its error recovery and buffering capabilities.

- SMDS provides a high-speed LAN interconnection optimized for LAN data traffic, with access speeds at DS-1/E1 and DS-3/E3. Take-up has been patchy due to general confusion about WAN strategy and availability.

- The introduction of optical amplifiers (known as Erbium Doped Fiber Amplifiers [EDFAs]) and Dense Wave Division Multiplexers (DWDMs) has significantly reduced the total cost of long-haul transmission and dramatically increased capacities.

References

[1]   U. D. Black, *Data Networks: Concepts, Theory, and Practice* (Englewood Cliffs, NJ: Prentice Hall, 1989).

[2]   Nonstandard for Transmission of IP Datagrams over Serial Lines: SLIP, RFC 1055.

[3]   Compressing TCP/IP Headers for Low-Speed Serial Links, RFC 1144.

[4]   The Point-to-Point Protocol (PPP), RFC 1661.

[5]   PPP in HDLC-Like Framing, RFC 1662.

[6]   Assigned Numbers, RFC 1700.

[7]   PPP over ISDN, RFC 1618 (May 1994).

[8]   PPP in Frame Relay, RFC 1973 (June 1996).

[9]   PPP over SONET/SDH, RFC 2615 (June 1999).

[10]   PPP over AAL5, RFC 2364 (July 1998).

[11]   PPP over FUNI, RFC 2363 (July 1998).

[12]   Method for Transmitting PPP over Ethernet (PPPoE), RFC 2364 (February 1999).

[13]   The PPP Multilink Protocol (MP), RFC 1990 (August 1996).

[14]   PPP Link Quality Monitoring, RFC 1989 (August 1996).

[15]   Charles K. Summer, *ISDN Implementer's Guide, Standards, Protocols, and Services* (New York: McGraw-Hill, 1995).

[16]   Extending OSPF to Support Demand Circuits, RFC 1793 (April 1995).

[17]   R. Friend, W. Simson, "PPP Stac LZS Compression Protocol," RFC 1974.

[18]   Multiprotocol Interconnect on X.25 and ISDN in the Packet Mode, RFC 1356.

[19]   A Standard for the Transmission of IP Datagrams over Public Data Networks, RFC 877.

[20]   Multiprotocol Interconnect over Frame Relay, RFC 2427 (September 1998).

[21]   Generic Systems Requirements in Support of Switched Multimegabit Data Service, Technical Advisory TA-TSY-000772, Bellcore Technical Advisory, Issue 3 (October 1989).

[22]   D. Piscitello and J. Lawrence, "Transmission of IP Datagrams over the SMDS Service," RFC 1209, Bell Communications Research (March 1991).

8

ATM Technology and Design

Asynchronous Transfer Mode (ATM) emerged in the late 1980s as a new switching technology based on the earlier development of Broadband Integrated Services Digital Network (B-ISDN). Unlike many competing frame-based technologies, ATM is a cell-relay technology. ATM builds on some of the benefits of fast packet switching and provides basic multiplexing and circuit switching. Multimedia applications require high bandwidth and real-time transfer of information with minimal delay variation, and ATM has the required characteristics (guaranteed delay, bounded jitter rate) to support these applications, together with true bandwidth scalability. Cell relay combines the high throughput and bandwidth optimization of Frame Relay with the predictability characteristics of time division multiplexing, making it suitable for bursty legacy data traffic and isochronous voice and video traffic. ATM is based on work done by the International Telecommunications Union, the Telecommunications Standardization Sector (ITU-T), and the American National Standards Institute (ANSI) to apply Very Large-Scale Integration (VLSI) technology to the transfer of data within public networks. The ATM Forum is the body responsible for defining enabling technologies that guarantee interoperability between public and private networks. This forum has over 300 members comprising users, carriers, service providers, and network equipment manufacturers.

ATM technology is applicable for both local and wide area applications and for high-speed interconnection of campus environments. The ATM architecture is still relatively new and differs in significant ways from existing LAN architectures. This means that new techniques are required to integrate traditional LAN systems (both protocols and applications). Significant effort has been made to support the huge installed base of LAN protocols and services as transparently as possible. For IP-based networking there are several integration techniques currently available, including Classical IP over ATM and ATM LAN Emulation (described later in this chapter).

ATM technology is being deployed in public networks and by service providers for a new generation of scalable backbone networks, with built-in
QoS. At the interface between public and private networks a new breed of
WAN switches has emerged. These devices use high-speed switching fabrics
to provide self-routing, nonblocking, and scalable switching at multigigabit
throughput rates, and they have the potential to support gigabit port
speeds.

8.1   Architecture

8.1.1   Overview

ATM end stations, including workstations, servers, and routers, may be
directly attached to ATM. ATM is based on the concept of end stations
communicating via end-to-end Virtual Channel Connections (VCCs, analogous to X.25 or Frame Relay virtual circuits) through one or more intermediate switches. There are two basic types of interface in an ATM
network: the User-to-Network Interface (UNI) and the Network-to-Node
Interface (NNI). The UNI is the interface between an end-station device
and a private or public ATM switch. The NNI is the interface between
ATM switches. All information (voice, video, data, etc.) in an ATM network is transported in short (53-byte) fixed message blocks called cells. At
the edge of the ATM network, where ATM interfaces with traditional
frame-based LANs and WANs, frame-based traffic is segmented into cells at
the ingress and later reassembled back into frames at the egress. Cells are
routed along VCCs; the cell header contains identifiers that associate the
cell with a particular path. Once a VCC is established, cell traffic always follows the same path through the network and is delivered to the destination
in order. Circuits can be either permanent (PVC) or dynamically switched
(SVC) connections.

8.1.2   Functional layers

ATM is a layered architecture but is still very much in development; Figure
8.1 illustrates the current status of the ATM protocol stack. Note that the
mapping of ATM against the OSI seven-layer reference model is arbitrary;
there is no exact fit. In the ATM data plane standards are currently only
defined up to the Network Layer. In the control plane the semantics for
UNI and NNI are defined. The UNI specification is based on Q.2931, a

	User Plane	Control Plane	Management Plane
Application		UNI, PNNI	
Presentation		Q.2931	
Session			
Transport		SSCOP	ILMI
Network	ATM Adaption Layer (AAL 1-5)	S-AAL (AAL5)	
Data Link	ATM Layer	ATM Layer	
Physical	ATM Physical Layer	ATM Physical Layer	
	Various	Various	

Figure 8.1   *ATM protocol stack. ATM defines a data (or user) plane, a control plane, and a management plane.*

public network signaling protocol developed by the ITU-T. Q.2931 is effectively used for connection setup (note that Q.2931 was itself based on the Q.931 signaling protocol used with Narrowband ISDN). The ATM signaling protocols run on top of a Service-Specific Convergence Protocol (SSCOP), defined by ITU-T recommendations Q.2100, Q.2110, and Q.2130. SSCOP effectively provides a reliable transport, offering guaranteed delivery through the use of windows and retransmissions. At the lower levels, the ATM protocol model comprises three functional layers roughly corresponding to Layer 1 and parts of Layer 2 (i.e., error control and data framing) of the OSI reference model. The ATM Adaption Layer (AAL) provides segmentation and reassembly and offers a number of service classes to support different types of traffic. The physical layer offers a diverse range of media, including fiber optic, twisted-pair copper, and wireless networking. The management plane is still under development and is currently occupied by the ATM Forum's Interim Layer Management Interface (ILMI).

ATM Physical Layer

The ATM Physical Layer controls transmission and receipt of bits on the physical medium, keeps track of ATM cell boundaries, and packages cells into the appropriate type of frame for the physical medium being used (coax, copper, single-mode and multimode fiber). ATM is designed so that the Physical Layer is transparent to ATM switching functions and higher-layer protocols. All currently defined ATM physical interface protocols have the following in common:

- Point-to-point—Connections between an ATM end point and an ATM switch or between two ATM switches are all point-to-point. No multipoint or LAN-type connections have been defined.

- Full-duplex—Data can be transferred simultaneously in both directions (half-duplex mode is also possible, with some restrictions).

- Asymmetric—The bandwidth defined for a particular circuit may differ in each direction, enabling capacity to be more efficiently aligned to the application, reducing overall costs.

Clearly, this degree of flexibility poses some interesting problems for circuit cost modeling.

ATM operates over a wide variety of physical media and link speeds. Table 8.1 summarizes the media that have either been accepted by standards bodies or are current proposals. Existing standards that can carry ATM cells include the following:

- 155.520-Mbps STS-3c Synchronous Optical Network (SONET)/ SDH, running on single-mode fiber (SMF) or multimode fiber (MMF)

- 44.736-Mbps DS-3/T3/E3 over coaxial copper cable

- 100-Mbps FDDI using 4B/5B encoding and based on multimode fiber (referred to as TAXI)

- 155.520-Mbps fiber channel using 8B/10B encoding over fiber of shielded twisted-pair copper cable

The ATM Forum has defined several standards for encoding ATM over various types of media. Due to the widespread acceptance of the FDDI TAXI (Transparent Asynchronous Exchange Interface) 4B/5B chipset standard, the ATM Forum encouraged initial ATM development efforts by endorsing TAXI 4B/5B as one of the first ATM media encoding standards (nowadays the most common fiber interface is STS3c/STM). ATM also provides interfaces for unshielded twisted-pair (UTP) and shielded twisted-pair (STP) copper cable. There are two UTP interface standards: The UTP-5 specification supports 155 Mbps with NRZI encoding, while the UTP-3 specification supports 51 Mbps with CAP-16 encoding. CAP-16 is more difficult to implement, so, while it may be cheaper to wire with UTP-3 cable, workstation cards designed for CAP-16-based UTP-3 may be more expensive and will offer less bandwidth.

Table 8.1 *ATM UNI Physical Interface Options*

Link Type	Speed (Mbps)	Cell Throughput	Encoding	Physical Medium	Application	Standards Body
DS1 (T1)	1.544	1.536	PDH	Copper	LAN-WAN	ANSI
E1	2.048	1.920	PDH	Copper	LAN-WAN	ETSI
SONET 'Lite'	12.960	12.384	SONET Frame	Cat 3/5 Copper	LAN	ATM Forum
Raw Cells	25.600	25.600	Clear Channel	Cat 3/5 Copper	LAN	ATM Forum
SONET 'Lite'	25.920	24.768	SONET Frame	Cat 3/5 Copper	LAN	ATM Forum
E3	34.368	33.984	PDH	Copper	WAN	ETSI
DS3 (T3)	44.736	40.704	PDH	Copper	WAN	ANSI
DXI (RVX)	0-50	0-50	Clear Channel	Copper	LAN	ATM Forum
SONET 'Lite'	51.840	49.536	SONET Frame	Cat 3/5 Copper	LAN	ATM Forum
FDDI-PMD	100.000	100.000	Block Encoded	Fibre-MM, STP	LAN	ATM Forum
Raw Cells	100.000	100.000	Clear Channel	Cat 3 Copper	LAN	Proposed
E4	139.264	138.240	PDH	Copper	WAN	ETSI
SDH STM-1, SONET, ST3-3c	155.520	149.760	SONET/SDH	Fibre-SM	WAN	ITU-T
Fibre Channel	155.520	150.340	Block Encoded	Fibre-MM	LAN	ATM Forum
Raw Cells	155.520	155.520	Clear Channel	Fibre-SM	WAN	ITU-T
SONET 'Lite'	155.520	149.760	SONET/SDH	Fibre-MM	LAN	ATM Forum
Raw Cells	155.520	155.520	Clear Channel	UTP/STP	LAN	ATM Forum
SDH, STM-4c, SONET, STS-sc	622.080	599.040	SONET/SDH	Fibre-SM	WAN	ITU-T
Raw Cells	622.080	622.080	Clear Channel	Fibre-SM	WAN	ITU-T

ATM layer

Virtual circuits are a key element of ATM, and a method is required to set up and tear down these circuits, which is a key function of the ATM layer. The ATM layer establishes virtual connections and passes ATM cells through the ATM network, using information contained in each ATM cell header. The cell header includes the Virtual Channel Identifier (VCI) and/or Virtual Path Identifier (VPI). In an ATM network, voice traffic can be carried on one circuit, video on another, and data on another. Cells for each traffic type can also be intermixed. ATM intermediate nodes ignore the least significant bits of the VCI, so a range of virtual circuits is carried between end systems. End systems operate using full VCI.

ATM Adaptation Layer (AAL)

The network characteristics required by different types of traffic flow are serviced by an ATM Adaptation Layer (AAL). The AAL is deployed in ATM end systems and switches. Part of the AAL's function is to perform segmentation and reassembly (SAR); when it receives packets from upper-level protocols (e.g., IPX, IP, or AppleTalk), it breaks them into the 48-byte segments that form the payload field of an ATM cell. There are currently six AAL types defined, as follows:

- AAL0—Null type

- AAL1—Circuit Emulation (CBR)

- AAL2—Video/Audio (VBR)

- AAL3—Connection-oriented data

- AAL4—Connectionless data

- AAL5—Simple and efficient connection-oriented data

The AAL type is specified by end systems at cell setup time (i.e., the AAL type is not carried in the ATM cell header). For PVCs the AAL type is administratively configured at the end points when the circuit is initially defined. For SVCs, the AAL type is communicated along the VC path via Q.93B as part of call setup, and the end points use the signaled information for configuration. Each AAL type is designed to handle a specific application scenario, as follows:

- AAL0—is used for cell-relay services that are inherently cell based and so require adaption now.

- AAL1—is used for synchronous bits streams, typically for mapping E1/T1 and other Pleisiochronous Digital Hierarchy (PDH) frames across an ATM network. AAL1 is appropriate for transporting telephone traffic and uncompressed video traffic. It requires timing synchronization between the source and destination and therefore relies upon media types that support clocking (e.g., SONET). The SAR-PDU is 48 bytes long, and includes a 1-byte SAR-PDU header, comprising the Sequence Number field (SN) and Sequence Number Protection (SNP) fields, which enable the receiving AAL1 node to verify that it has received cells in the correct order. The remaining 47 bytes are available as payload.

- AAL2—was designed for ATM class B services (connection oriented, variable bit rate, and time sensitive), such as compressed video, audio, or voice (using compression techniques automatically makes a constant bit rate application variable rate, depending upon the efficiency of the compression techniques). The problems encountered in defining and standardizing this AAL type have been significant and hinge on the issue of maintaining timing relationships between source and destinations, where the bit rate is highly variable, often resulting in no bit rate for indeterminate periods. Work is still progressing on this standard.

- AAL3/4—AAL3 no longer exists and is, therefore, always combined with AAL4 to form a type called AAL3/4 (used for time-sensitive, connection-oriented services). The only difference between types 3 and 4 was the use of a 10-bit field called Multiplexing Identifier (MID), which was used by AAL4 for connectionless operations (AAL3 is connection oriented); instead of deploying additional resources to support both types, they were merged. Use of the MID field indicates whether AAL3/4 is in connection-oriented or connectionless mode, although nowadays the MID field is seen as a substantial overhead (raising the total overhead to 20 percent); AAL3/4 is used almost exclusively in connectionless mode (AAL5 offers connection-oriented service). AAL3/4 is designed for use by network service providers. Applications range from circuit emulation to compressed video, and AAL3/4 is also closely aligned with Switched Multimegabit Data Service (SMDS). AAL3/4 is used to transmit SMDS packets over an ATM network.

- AAL5—AAL5 offers a very simple, low-overhead (short trailers and no additional AAL headers), connection-oriented data transfer service. It is sometimes referred to as the Simple and Efficient Adaption Layer (SEAL). AAL5 excludes the sequencing and integrity checking functions of AAL3/4, placing that responsibility on the end systems. AAL5 also significantly reduces the protocol overhead (all overhead is contained in a small trailer in the last cell of a sequence) and is better aligned to 32- and 64-bit processor architecture (with both 4 and 8 being factors of the 48-byte payload). AAL5 is intended for class C services (connection oriented, variable bit rate, and time insensitive). AAL5 is used to transfer most non-SMDS data, such as router connectivity over ATM (via Classical IP over ATM and LANE). The omission of the MID field means that multiplexing of the AAL layer is precluded. AAL5 specifies user data of up to 64 KB, with 0–47 bytes of padding to force the complete CPSC-PDU trailer into the last cell. The trailer includes the length of the frame plus a 32-bit CRC computed across the entire PDU, enabling AAL5 to detect bit errors, lost cells, or cells out of sequence. AAL5 supports a form of congestion notification (similar to Frame Relay's FECN), referred to as Explicit Forward Congestion Notification (EFCN).

The various AAL types are intended to support a number of ATM service classes. A detailed description of the various AAL types is provided in reference [1].

8.1.3   Virtual channels and virtual paths

As already indicated, ATM is a connection-oriented technology. Cells are forwarded down preestablished virtual channels (either switched or permanent), between switching nodes. Virtual channels are established dynamically and concatenated over multiple hops to form an end-to-end Virtual Channel Connection (VCC). In effect a VCC performs the same function as an X.25 or Frame Relay virtual circuit. To promote scalability and flexibility, VCs are aggregated into a number of Virtual Paths (VP). Virtual paths form the ATM mesh topology and can be dynamically created, enabling the logical routing topology to be changed to reflect changes in the physical topology or even time-of-day requirements (although in ATM Forum networks it is more likely that VPIs will be statically configured for user sites at the time of provisioning, in the form of a Permanent Virtual

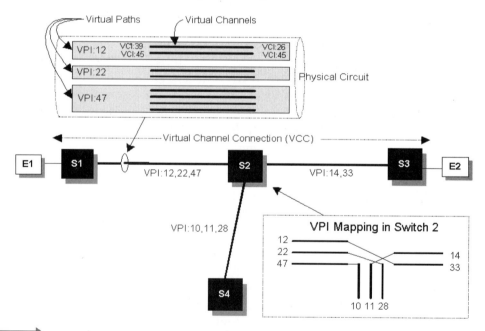

Figure 8.2   *ATM Virtual Paths and Virtual Channels over a single physical link between two switches.*

Circuit [PVC]). The main concepts of this connection model are illustrated in Figure 8.2. As can be seen in Figure 8.2, multiple virtual paths can be supported over a single physical circuit, each identified by a Virtual Path Identifier (VPI). Within each virtual path, multiple virtual channels can be supported, each identified by a Virtual Circuit Identifier (VCI). The figure also illustrates the VPI mapping within Switch 2. Note that VCI mapping also takes place within each switching node.

Several VPI and VCI values are reserved for special uses, as shown in the following chart:

VPI-VCI Label	*Application*
[VPI = 0]	Normally allocate to UNI connections by ATM switch nodes
[VPI = 0, VCI = 5]	Reserved for ATM signaling packets
[VPI = 0, VCI = 8]	Reserved for SSI
[VPI = 0, VCI = 15]	Reserved for connectionless calls over UNI
[VPI = 0, VCI = 16]	Normally allocated for ILMI SNMP flows

In general, all VCI below 32 are reserved within each VPI for control purposes; so data connections are allocated VCI values above this range.

Terminology

For reference, the terminology used for the ATM connection model is as follows:

- Virtual Path (VP) and Virtual Path Indicator (VPI)—A virtual path is an aggregate logical pipe representing a group of Virtual Channels (VCs). VPs may exist between ATM end systems, between end systems and switch nodes, and between switch nodes. The virtual path indicator identifies a virtual path to be used by a particular cell and is a field contained within the cell header.

- Permanent Virtual Path (PVP)—A statically configured VP (i.e., similar to a Frame Relay PVC).

- Virtual Path Link (VPL)—A virtual path link exists between the points where a VPI value is assigned or where it is translated or determined. Typically these points would be switches in the ATM network.

- Virtual Path Connection (VPC)—A virtual path connection is the concatenation (sequence) of VPLs that extends between virtual path terminations.

- Virtual Path Switch (VPS)—A virtual path switch is the processing function that interconnects VPLs to form VPCs. This function translates VPI values (label swapping) and directs cells to the appropriate output link within an ATM switch.

- Virtual Path Terminator (VPT)—The virtual path terminator is a processing function that terminates each VP and makes the associated VCs available for separate and independent connection routing.

- Virtual Path Connection Identifier (VPCI)—This is the 16-bit identifier of a VP connection and is returned by the ATM network when call setup is performed by a user device. It is used by the signaling protocol instead of the VPI, which is unique only within a single ATM link.

- Virtual Channel (VC) and Virtual Channel Indicator (VCI)—A virtual channel is defined in ATM as a unidirectional connection between user devices. The Virtual Channel Indicator (VCI) is the indication of the virtual channel to be used by a cell and is contained within each cell in the network.

- Virtual Channel Connection (VCC)—A virtual channel connection is the end-to-end connection along which a user device sends data. Because, strictly speaking, virtual channels are unidirectional, a VCC would normally consist of two virtual channels to provide full-duplex data transfer.

- Virtual Channel Link (VCL)—A virtual channel link exists between the points where a VCI value is assigned or where it is translated or determined. Typically these points would be switches in the ATM network. A virtual channel link is a separately defined data flow within a link or virtual path. A Virtual Channel Connection (VCC) through a network is a sequence of interconnected (concatenated) VCLs.

- Virtual Channel Switch (VCS)—The virtual channel switch is the VC switching function, where VCLs are connected together to form VCCs. To do this they terminate VPCs and translate VCI values.

As illustrated in Figure 8.2, it is important to note that neither the VCI nor the VPI have end-to-end significance; they are significant only between switching nodes. For example, the VPI may be changed by a cross-connect switch between two switching nodes. The routing table of a cross-connect switch only deals with VPIs and physical port IDs. Switching nodes must also deal with VCIs.

8.1.4   ATM interface definitions

This section briefly reviews some of the key interfaces defined by ATM, as illustrated in Figure 8.3.

The UNI interface

The UNI specification defines the interface between ATM end stations (ATM-enabled terminals, routers, bridges, servers, or concentrators) and the ATM network. The UNI comprises two parts, as follows:

- Private UNI—defines interfaces between an end system and a private switch, as specified by the ATM Forum. Private networks will generally use addressing from LAN or OSI environments.

- Public UNI—defines interfaces between a private switch and a switch owned by a service provider (since these switches do not typically exchange NNI information) and is specified by the ITU-T. Public ATM networks will use the E.164 addresses.

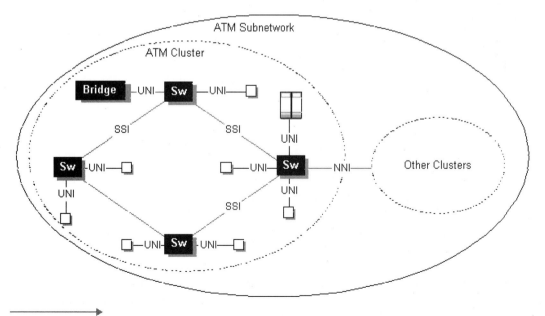

Figure 8.3   *Key ATM interfaces.*

ATM campus network devices typically use the private UNI, based on UNIv3.0 and UNIv3.1. (Note that UNIv3.0 and UNIv3.1 are incompatible—the major differences being the signaling procedures and a different data link protocol.) Some of the media types supported by the private UNI use protocols that operate over short distances and are, therefore, unsuitable for public network interfaces. For stations that support a full Interim Local Management Interface (ILMI), the UNI version will be used; if not, the UNI version of the adjacent station must be predefined. Basic UNI signaling information, such as connection setup, uses the reserved channel VPI = 0, VCI = 5. The ILMI protocol (part of the UNI specification) is used by switches to communicate their network address prefixes to end systems and by the end systems to communicate the ESI portion of their network address for the switches at initialization time. The ILMI protocol uses the VPI = 0, VCI = 16 channel for address registration.

Generic Flow Control (GFC)

The header of the UNI cell contains a field called Generic Flow Control (GFC); note that in NNI cells there is no GFC field, and the first 4 bits of the cell are used by an expanded (12-bit) VPI field. The GFC field enables one-way flow control to be defined from the ATM end system to the ATM switch. There is no control in the opposite direction. According to the UNI specification, three queues may be defined at the end system: one for uncontrolled and two for controlled traffic. Typically only one queue is used for controlled traffic.

Controlled traffic refers to traffic for which the GFC mechanism is defined. It is usually all the nonreserved bandwidth traffic on the interface. Controlled traffic is distinguished in the cell header by the presence of a nonzero GFC field.

Uncontrolled traffic refers to traffic that is not subject to GFC control and is treated as having a higher priority than the controlled traffic. Typically this would be reserved bandwidth traffic.

The flow-control mechanism utilizes windowing. Each queue has a window that represents the number of cells it is allowed to transmit before the network must acknowledge. The window is maintained as a counter in the end system; every time a cell is transmitted the counter is decremented. The end system is allowed to transmit until the counter reaches zero, at which point the end system must wait until the counter has been reset to its initial value. During normal operation the switch sends reset signals frequently so that the counter never reaches zero.

System-to-System Interface (SSI)

The System-to-System Interface (SSI) defines the interface operating over a link between two ATM hubs in the same cluster. There is currently no standard for SSI, so implementations are proprietary, and interoperability problems could result when grouping equipment from different vendors within a single cluster. The SSI procedures used by vendors may be based on the Interim Interswitch Signaling Protocol (IISP). The SSI uses the same signaling mechanism as the UNI. Topology information flows over the VPI = 0, VCI = 8 channel.

Private Network-to-Network Interface (PNNI)

The Private Network Node Interface or Private Network-to-Network Interface (PNNI) protocol is used between ATM switches, or logical groups of switches, called a cluster, in a private ATM network. By private we mean networks that use NSAP format ATM addresses (public networks that use E.164 numbers for addressing will be interconnected using a different NNI protocol stack based upon the ITU-T B-ISUP signaling protocol and the ITU-T MTP Level 3 routing protocol, not covered here). Clusters are effectively logical switches connected internally via private SSIs. A cluster interfaces with other switches via PNNI. The NNI currently supported by many ATM campus switches is based on the Interim Interswitch Signaling Protocol (IISP), referred to as PNNI Phase 0. IISP is a technique for using UNI 3.0 signaling protocols (Q.2931 and Q.SAAL) between switches and is really only suitable for small network topologies. Static routes are required to manage network topology across NNI interfaces, so clearly this interim solution does not scale. IISP is superseded by the ATM Forum PNNI Phase 1 specification [2]; since this specification comprises 365 pages, we can only briefly review some of its key features here. The main functions of PNNI are summarized as follows:

- Topology routing and signaling—PNNI routing is designed to support efficient loop-free routing of end-to-end SVC requests by maintaining and distributing topology state information throughout the ATM network

- Traffic management—Although PNNI is not primarily concerned with traffic management, at the time of connection setup the PNNI uses link state information to calculate optimum routes (this can be thought of as one-time traffic management per VC).

- Network management—Network management standards for PNNI are being developed as part of the wider suite of network management specifications; however, the PNNI Management Information Base (MIB) objects are defined within the PNNI specifications.

PNNI routing and signaling are discussed in more detail later in the chapter. For further details of PNNI refer to references [1, 2].

ATM Data Exchange Interface (DXI)

In order to escalate ATM deployment cost effectively, the ATM Forum introduced a standard known as the *Data Exchange Interface* (DXI). DXI defines a local interface between a packet-based router and an ATM-capable Digital Service Unit (ADSU). This allows routers to connect into ATM networks via the UNI interface of an ADSU. The DTE-to-DCE physical interface can be either V.35 or HSSI, enabling a DXI port and an HDLC port of a router to be directly connected. The router sends packets to the ATM-capable DSU (ADSU) using MultiProtocol Over ATM (MPOA) encapsulation. The ADSU performs cell-level processing, SAR, and virtual connection termination. ATM DXI is available in several modes, as follows:

- Mode 1a—Supports AAL5 only. Offers a 9,232-byte maximum, a 16-bit FCS, and 1,023 VCs.

- Mode 1b—Supports AAL3/4 and AAL5. Offers a 9,224-byte maximum and a 16-bit FCS. AAL5 offers 1,023 VCs; AAL3/4 offers only a single VC.

- Mode 2—Supports AAL3/4 and AAL5. Offers a 65,535-byte maximum, a 32-bit FCS, and 16,777,215 VCs.

Within a router, data from higher-level protocols are encapsulated into ATM DXI frame format, and the router (DTE) is connected directly to an ADSU (DCE) device. The router sends ATM DXI frames to the ADSU, which converts the frames to ATM cells by processing them through the AAL5 CS and the SAR sublayer. The ATM layer attaches the header, and the cells are sent out the ATM UNI interface. ATM DXI addressing consists of a DXI Frame Address (DFA), which is equivalent to a Frame Relay Data Link Connection Identifier (DLCI). The DSU maps the DFA into appropriate VPI and VCI values in the ATM cell [1].

The Interim Local Management Interface (ILMI)

The ATM Forum Interim Local Management Interface (ILMI) specification is an interim standard that enables existing SNMP technology to be used to manage ATM networks. The ILMI protocol uses SNMP format packets across the UNI and NNI links to access an ILMI Management Information Base (MIB) within each node. ILMI SNMP flows are encapsulated in AAL5 across a well-known virtual channel, VPI = 0, VCI = 16 (the ILMI specification indicates that this should be configurable). Message formats are as defined in SNMPv1 format. The ILMI protocol enables ATM nodes to determine various characteristics of adjacent ATM nodes (e.g., the configuration of VP and VC connections available at the UNI, the size of each other's connection space, and the type of signaling employed). ILMI provides access to a range of information provided by the ILMI MIB. Examples of the categories of information held within the MIB include the following:

- Physical Layer

- ATM Layer

- ATM Layer statistics

- Virtual Path (VP) connections

- Virtual Channel (VC) connections

- Address registration information

Address registration is perhaps one of its most useful features, since it greatly facilitates the administration of ATM addresses. The ILMI will likely be extended in the future to support other autoconfiguration and autodiscovery capabilities and possibly group addressing.

8.1.5 Cell formats

ATM uses a fixed-length, 53-byte packet or cell, which comprises a 5-byte header and 48-byte payload. The VPI and VCI fields in the ATM header are used to route cells through ATM networks and identify the next network segment that a cell needs to transmit on its way to its ultimate destination. (See Figure 8.4.)

Field definitions

- GFC—4 bits of generic flow control that can be used to provide local functions, such as identifying multiple stations that share a single ATM interface. The GFC field is typically not used and is set to a default value. The GFC field is not present in the format of the NNI header. Instead, the VPI field occupies the first 12 bits, which allows ATM switches to assign larger VPI values. With that exception, the format of the NNI header is identical to the format of the UNI header.

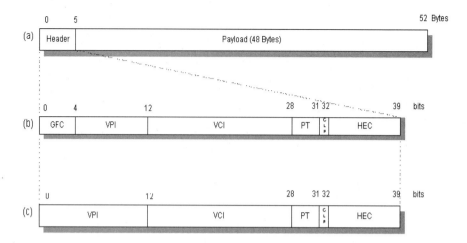

Figure 8.4   *ATM cell formats. (a) 53-byte cell format; the 5-byte header is presented in two almost identical formats. (b) The UNI header format. (c) The NNI header format.*

- VPI—bits of virtual path identifier, which are used, in conjunction with the VCI, to identify the next destination of a cell as it passes through a series of ATM switches on its way to its destination.

- VCI—16 bits of virtual channel identifier, which are used, in conjunction with the VPI, to identify the next destination of a cell as it passes through a series of ATM switches on its way to its destination.

- PT—3 bits of payload type. The first bit indicates whether the cell contains user data or control data. If the cell contains user data, the second bit indicates congestion, and the third bit indicates whether the cell is the last in a series of cells that represent a single AAL5 frame.

- CLP—1 bit of congestion loss priority, which indicates whether the cell should be discarded if it encounters severe congestion as it moves through the network.

- HEC—8 bits of header error control, which is a checksum, calculated only on the header itself.

8.1.6 Addressing

ATM end points are addressed using the Network Service Access Point (NSAP) format specified by ISO. An NSAP is variable in length (between 7 and 20 bytes), and the length field normally precedes an NSAP in the frame header.

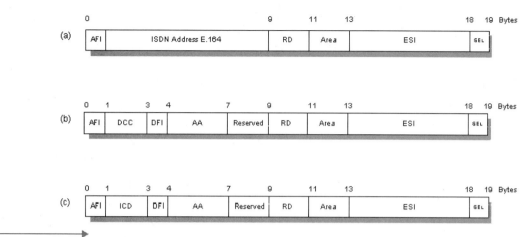

Figure 8.5   *ATM address formats, each 20 bytes in length. (a) ITU-T format (E.164). (b) IEEE 802 LAN format (DCC). (c) OSI format (ICD).*

NSAPs comprise two parts: an Initial Domain Part (IDP) and a Domain-Specific Part (DSP). The IDP is made up of two subfields: the Authority and Format Indicator (AFI) and the Initial Domain Identifier (IDI). NSAPs are designed to be self-administered and extremely customizable. The basic idea is that ISO gives a naming authority a unique AFI identifier (e.g., the U.S. government has AFI 47); the naming authority then defines the remaining NSAP format. The naming authority itself hands off part of the address space (a range within the IDI) to an addressing domain. (See Figure 8.5.)

ATM addressing field definitions

- AFI—1 byte of authority and format identifier. The AFI field identifies the type of address. The defined values are 45, 47, and 39 for E.164, ICD, and DCC addresses, respectively.

- DCC—2 bytes of data country code.

- DFI—1 byte of domain-specific part (DSP) format identifier.

- AA—3 bytes of administrative authority.

- RD—2 bytes of routing domain.

- Area—2 bytes of area identifier.

- ESI—6 bytes of end-system identifier, which is an IEEE 802 Media Access Control (MAC) address.

- Sel—1 byte of Network Service Access Point (NSAP) selector. This field has local significance to the end station and is not used in routing.

- ICD—2 bytes of international code designator.

- E.164—8 bytes of Integrated Services Digital Network (ISDN) telephone number.

There are three different formats for ATM addresses, each controlled by a different authority, as follows:

- ITU-T (E.164) format—This format is specified by the ITU-T and is essentially the same as telephone-style addressing. It is used by public ATM networks and by Narrowband ISDN (N-ISDN) networks.

- DCC (Data Country Code) format—This format carries LAN addresses, as specified in IEEE 802 recommendations.

- ICD (International Code Designator) format—This format is specified by the ISO for OSI.

The ATM Forum specifies that equipment in a private network must support all three formats. Figure 8.5 illustrates the three formats. The IDI specifies the particular network addressing scheme to which the DSP relates. The DSP is also hierarchical and contains the DTE NSAP address. In effect the NSAP comprises a <Network><Host> address pair:

- The end-system address is seven bytes long and comprises an ATM end-system address (the ESI), analogous to a MAC address, plus a single byte selector (SEL) field that identifies a subcomponent of an end system (i.e., it has only local significance). The ATM address formats are modeled on ISO NSAP addresses, but they identify SubNetwork Point of Attachment (SNPA) addresses by incorporating the MAC address into the ATM address. This makes it easy to map ATM addresses into existing LANs.

- The other 13 bytes of the NSAP are network address, including fields for hub number, cluster number, routing domain, and the standard network prefix.

8.1.7   Quality of Service

One of the key benefits of ATM is its ability to support QoS requests on a virtual channel basis. The type of service required and a description of the expected service constraints (e.g., average data rate, peak data rate, cell loss ratio, cell delay, and cell delay variation) are specified by the user at virtual channel setup time. Once a channel is established, there is an agreement that the network will provide the desired service as long as the user stays within the specified Service Level Agreement (SLA). Connections are categorized into several ATM QoS types, depending upon the nature of the QoS guarantee requested and the characteristics of the expected traffic types.

Service types

ATM offers the following types of services:

- Constant Bit Rate (CBR)—End systems use CBR connection types to carry constant bit rate traffic with a fixed timing relationship between data samples, typically for circuit emulation.

- Variable Bit Rate—Real Time (VBR[RT])—Used for connections that carry variable bit rate traffic, in which there is a fixed timing relationship between samples; for instance, for applications such as variable bit rate video compression.

- Variable Bit Rate—Non-Real Time (VBR(NRT))—Used for connections that carry variable bit rate traffic in which there is no timing relationship between data samples, but a guarantee of QoS (on bandwidth or latency) is still required. Such a service class might be used for Frame Relay internetworking, in which the Committed Information Rate (CIR) of the Frame Relay connection is mapped into a bandwidth guarantee within the ATM network.

- Available Bit Rate (ABR)—As with VBR(NRT), ABR supports variable rate data transmissions and does not preserve any timing relationships between source and destination. Unlike the VBR(NRT) service, however, the ABR service does not provide any guaranteed bandwidth to the user. Rather, the network provides a best-effort service, in which feedback (flow control mechanisms) is used to increase the bandwidth available to the user—the Allowed Cell Rate (ACR)— if the network is not congested and to reduce the bandwidth when there is congestion. Through such flow control mechanisms, the network can control the amount of traffic that it allows into the network and minimize cell loss within the network due to congestion.

- Unspecified Bit Rate (UBR)—The UBR service does not offer any service guarantees. The user is free to send any amount of data up to a specified maximum while the network makes no guarantees at all on the cell loss rate, delay, or delay variation that might be experienced.

Of these, only CBR, VBR, and UBR are generally available today. ABR is designed to map to existing bursty LAN protocols that attempt to use as much available bandwidth as is available from the network but can either back off or be buffered in the presence of congestion. ABR is ideal for carrying LAN traffic (e.g., using LAN Emulation) across ATM networks. The ABR service can optionally provide a guaranteed Minimum Cell Rate (MCR) for an ABR connection, but the exact nature of this guarantee is currently a matter of debate within the ATM Forum. The UBR service was initially introduced to support LAN protocols while the ABR specification was being developed.

Service classes

The ITU-T has defined four different generic service classes for network traffic, each of which must be treated differently by an ATM network. These classes are designated Class A through Class D, with an additional user-defined class referred to as Class X. The four classes are an attempt to group the three parameters—bit rate (i.e., constant or variable), connection mode (i.e., connection-oriented or connectionless), and timing compensation (i.e., the timing relationship between cells)—into meaningful scenarios for application traffic. These classes are defined as follows:

- Class A (Circuit Emulation)—A constant bit rate service with timing. This service is intended to emulate a leased line for traditional digital voice and video and other applications needing constant bandwidth and timing guarantees.

- Class B (Variable Bit Rate Services)—A connection-oriented, variable bit rate with timing. This is intended for isochronous voice and video traffic (packet video or silence-compressed voice) or other bursty applications that require timing guarantees. The service is strictly connection oriented. Note that some video applications (such as videoconferencing) require tight synchronization between voice and video, while others can be transmitted in multicast mode and are much less sensitive to network delay. To design and control a network for Class B traffic is very challenging because of the unpredictable way high bandwidth is required and because the data rates are often near to the peak rate capability of the network.

- Class C (Connection-Oriented Data)—A connection-oriented variable bit rate without timing. Class C supports traditional data traffic, such as SNA and X.25. The service offered for it is connection oriented, and it supports variable rate information flow.

- Class D (Connectionless Data)—A connectionless variable bit rate without timing. It is intended to support connectionless protocols such as TCP/IP.

- Class X (User Defined)—A connection-oriented ATM transport service where the network characteristics are user defined. Only the required bandwidth and the QoS parameters are used by the network.

Each service class is supported by an appropriate ATM Adaption Layer (AAL), configured as part of the call setup procedure, or at least that was the original intention. The four ITU classes, A through D, were intended to map directly onto AAL types as follows: A = Type 1, B = Type 2, C = Type 3, and D=Type 4. As with many good intentions in networking, things got a little more complicated, and today there is no fixed relationship between classes and AAL types.

In order to deliver QoS, ATM switches implement a function referred to as *Connection Admission Control* (CAC). The CAC function is invoked for every new connection request. Depending upon the traffic characteristics and requested QoS for the new connection, the switch determines whether the additional resources required for the connection can be met without violating the QoS guarantees of established connections. The switch accepts the connection only if QoS guarantees are still met. Note that CAC is a local switch function and is dependent on the architecture of the switch and implementation decisions such as the granularity of QoS guarantees. CAC is discussed further in Section 8.2.2.

8.2   Operation

8.2.1   ATM connections

ATM differs from traditional LAN network technologies in that it uses connection-oriented technology. From the end-system perspective, the connection is a point-to-point or point-to-multipoint link across a series of ATM switches in a network.

Point-to-point connections are peer connections between two ATM end systems. These connections can be unidirectional or bidirectional.

Point-to-multipoint connections are one-to-many connections, where a single source node (known as the root node) connects to multiple destination nodes (known as leaves). Cell replication is performed automatically by ATM switching nodes at the point where the connection splits into two or more branches. Note that this is not the same as multicasting; these connections are unidirectional, enabling the root to transmit to the leaves but not vice versa. Furthermore, end stations cannot transmit to each other on this connection.

Before any data can be transferred over an ATM network, a virtual connection needs to be established between end systems, either by using a predetermined path or created dynamically using ATM signaling protocol. For example, a connection may be permanently configured by the network operator (PVC) or temporarily established on demand (SVC). To facilitate such connections, ATM uses the concepts of virtual paths and virtual channels, as described earlier. This connection-oriented model greatly simplifies and speeds up the routing of cells across the ATM network. Once a VC is established, end-system addressing information does not need to be carried in each ATM cell; only the circuit IDs are required by ATM switching nodes to route the cell correctly. This VC-based model also means that cells arrive in sequence (especially useful for voice and video traffic and greatly simplifies the processing of conventional data traffic).

ATM signaling

ATM signaling at the end system is required for the dynamic setup and clearing of ATM switched virtual connections at the UNI interface (PVCs are configured by a network operator and, therefore, do not require signaling). In the event of network or system failures, permanent virtual connections are simply restarted, but switched virtual connections are lost. The key elements of ATM signaling are as follows:

- Signaling takes place on VCCs separate from those used by user data. This is similar to narrowband ISDN's use of the D channel.

- The default signaling method is point to point; however, broadcast signaling may be implemented in the future. Point-to-multipoint connections are established using point-to-point signaling.

- Connection setup by third-party equipment that is not involved in the data transfer is not supported.

- There is a mechanism to set up additional signaling channels besides the predefined channels (although this is not used in current ATM implementations).

Since Class B (AAL2) services are yet to be defined, there is no support for Class B. Class D is also not supported, since clients have connections to connectionless servers (i.e., the calling signaling procedures are, therefore, not required). The following functions and subfunctions are defined for ATM signaling:

- Call establishment—setup, call processing, connect, connect acknowledge

- Call clearing—disconnect, release, release complete

- Status—status enquiry, status

- Point-to-multipoint messages—add party, add party acknowledge, add party reject, drop party, drop party acknowledge

Through PNNI source routing, connection paths can be precomputed in advance; the route computation process is independent of the connection setup procedure, leading to short connection setup times and a higher connection setup rate. During connection setup, the only checking required is whether there is resource available bandwidth for the new connection in order to meet its QoS requirements.

Label swapping

An ATM cell is transmitted along a virtual channel connection according to the VCI/VPI routing information encapsulated in its header. This routing information is swapped at every intermediate switch along the path of the connection, using simple mapping tables held on each switch node. This enables rapid cell forwarding to the next switch along the chosen path. This process is referred to as label swapping. The mapping table comprises VPI/VCI input and port input fields and associated VPI/VCI output and port output fields, as shown in the following chart:

Input Port	VPI	VCI	Output Port	VPI	VCI
1	12	43	4	7	36
1	12	37	3	19	42
2	18	41	4	7	36
3	10	54	2	17	38

Therefore, each VPI/VCI pair is associated directly with a corresponding input and output port on a switch. Unlike conventional routing, there is no expensive prefix match lookup operation to perform to find an output port. This is the principle upon which MultiProtocol Label Switching (MPLS) was developed. An example VC connection is shown in Figure 8.6. Note that S1's initial path selection was via switch S4, but S4 is overloaded and

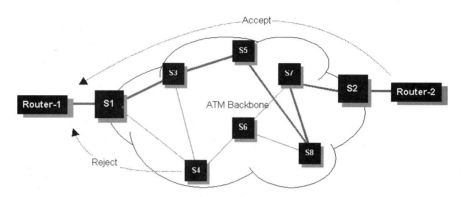

Figure 8.6   *VC establishment between two ATM-attached routers.*

the request is rejected by the CAC algorithm. After cranking back, a new route is selected via switch S3, and Router-2 finally accepts the connection. The final path selected for the VC is shown in bold.

Let us assume we have two ATM-attached routers: Router-1 and Router-2. Both routers have ATM interfaces to ATM switching nodes, as illustrated in Figure 8.6. If Router-1 wishes to establish a connection (SVC) to Router-2, then the sequence of events can be summarized as follows:

- Router-1 sends a signaling request packet to its directly connected ATM switch (S1). This request contains the ATM address of Router-2 as well as any QoS parameters required for the connection.

- S1 reassembles the signaling packet from Router-1 and then examines it.

- If S1 has an entry for Router-2's ATM address in its forwarding table, and it can accommodate the QoS requested for the connection, it sets up the virtual connection and forwards the request to the next switch along the path, in this case S4.

- Each switch along the selected path reassembles and examines the signaling packet and then forwards it to the next switch if the QoS parameters can be met. Each switch also sets up the virtual connection as the signaling packet is forwarded. If any switch cannot accommodate the requested QoS, then a reject message is sent back to Router-1. In this case S4 rejects the connection based on the results of its local Connection Admission Control (CAC) calculation, and S1 must crankback to restart the connection request, this time choosing a path via switch S3.

- Assuming all switches in the path accept the connection, the request finally arrives at Router-2, via switch S2. Router-2 reassembles the request, and, if it is able to support the requested QoS, responds with an accept message. As the accept message is forwarded back to Router-1, the switches establish the virtual circuit.

- Router-1 receives the accept message from its directly connected ATM switch (S1), as well as the Virtual Path Identifier (VPI) and Virtual Channel Identifier (VCI) values that it should use for traffic to be forwarded to Router-2.

In the next section we discuss ATM routing and signaling in more detail.

8.2.2   Routing and signaling

PNNI Phase 1 supports a dynamic shortest path routing protocol called PNNI routing, designed to support efficient loop-free routing of end-to-end SVC requests. The VC routing protocol must ensure that a connection request is routed along a path to the destination that has a high probability of meeting the QoS requested in the connection set up. In order to achieve this, PNNI uses source routing, maintains a topology database on each switch node, and provides signaling mechanisms and protocols to distribute topology and reachability information among neighboring switches (the specific route determination algorithm does not need to be standardized, and this is a potential area for vendor differentiation). It is important to note that PNNI routing is not required to route individual cells (as would be the case for a traditional routing protocol in a packet-switched environment, such as OSPF or IGRP); once the VC is established all cells follow the predetermined path and the routing tables no longer need to be consulted. PNNI Phase 1 is designed to enable the construction of very large ATM networks (potentially thousands of nodes) by taking advantage of logical group hierarchies. It confines the flow of topology information within the logical groups and enables route summarization among them.

Addressing

Components of the routing hierarchy are identified via ATM 20-byte addresses. PNNI routing uses address prefixes up to 19 bytes long (up to 152 bits). As illustrated in Figure 8.5, the twentieth byte is the selector field and is ignored by PNNI routing. In general PNNI will advertise reachability to ATM end systems using an address prefix rather than advertising

ATM end-system address. Nodes within a peer group use the same address prefix. Hierarchy is determined by two values, as follows:

- Peer group identifier—A 14-byte value, the first byte being a level indicator, which defines which of the next 104 leftmost bits are shared by switches in the peer group. Peer group IDs are ATM address prefixes and are specified at configuration time. Neighboring nodes exchange peer group IDs in hello packets.

- Node identifier—A 22-byte value composed of a 1-byte level indicator and a unique 21-byte value. The node ID is unique for each PNNI node in the routing domain. A PNNI node that advertises topology information in PNNI Topology State Packets (PTSP) will include the node ID and the peer group ID.

Route computation

The main objective of PNNI is to compute an efficient route from a source to a destination based on a called ATM address. The PNNI signaling protocol is based on a subset of UNI 4.0. The called ATM address is carried within the SETUP message (part of the connection request) sent over the UNI from the initiating device to a switch. The SETUP message is forwarded from switch to switch along the preselected route (as per source routing). Each switch should have an entry in its topology database that matches a prefix of the 20-byte ATM address contained in the SETUP message. Since PNNI performs source routing, the first switch to receive the connection request (i.e., the originating switch, nearest to the ATM end station) computes the best available route in advance. However, the topology database may vary in its detail between switches (since route summarization necessarily leads to inaccuracies) and may occasionally be out of synchronization (due to imposed latencies and periodicity in topology state flooding). This means that the path calculated by the originating switch may be suboptimal, so this issue is resolved as the connection setup request is forwarded and processed by switches along the selected path. Each switch along the path has the capability to update the original route selection, if its path tables indicate that a superior route is available.

Signaling

As indicated earlier, PNNI signaling is based on a subset of UNI 4.0 signaling. It does not support features such as proxy signaling, leaf-initiated joins, or user-to-user supplementary but does support QoS parameters, ATM anycast addressing, scoping, and ABR. PNNI signaling also differs from UNI 4.0 signaling in that it is symmetric (for switch-to-switch peer signaling operations). PNNI signaling uses information maintained by the PNNI routing process (e.g., route calculations, connectivity, and resource state information). PNNI signaling defines a number of unique capabilities, including Designated Transit Lists (DTLs), crankback, and alternate routing. DTLs are used to carry hierarchically complete source routes. Crankback and alternate routing enable an SVC request to be rerouted around failed components as a connection request is forwarded to the destination switch.

Flooding topology state information

PNNI is a topology state routing protocol where nodes flood QoS and reachability information throughout the network. A PNNI switching node advertises both link state and node state parameters to neighbors in its peer group. This information is carried within PNNI Topology State Packets (PTSP), which contain various type-length-value (TLV) encoded PNNI Topology State Elements (PTSE). Each switch advertises the following:

- Nodal information—This includes the switch's ATM address, peer group identifier, leadership priority, and other aspects about the switch itself.

- Topology state information—This covers outbound link and switch resources and comprises various metrics and attributes. This includes performance-related attributes and policy-related attributes.

- Reachability—This includes ATM addresses and address prefixes that the switch has learned about or is configured with.

This process is similar to that performed by link state routing protocols such as IS-IS and OSPF; however, PNNI provides much richer support for QoS routing through a large number of link and node state parameters.

CAC

Connection Admission Control (CAC) was introduced in Section 8.1.7 as part of the discussion about ATM QoS. CAC is important for route calculations in that it directly influences whether or not routes are viable through particular switches, depending upon current resource utilization. CAC is implementation dependent, and different switch vendors may differentiate their products based on the sophistications of the algorithms used. In order to provide some degree of normalization, the PNNI protocol defines a Generic CAC (GCAC) algorithm. This is a standard function that any node can employ to estimate the anticipated CAC behavior of another switch node, given the target node's advertised additive link metrics and the requested QoS for the connection request. GCAC requires only a small number of link state metrics, and switch nodes can influence the accuracy of the GCAC calculation via the offered metrics. The PNNI Phase 1 GCAC algorithm is primarily designed for CBR and VBR connections, although variants are used depending upon the type of QoS guarantees requested and the types of link metrics available, yielding varying degrees of accuracy. For UBR connections the only GCAC performed is to determine whether a node can support such connections. For ABR connections a check is performed to determine whether the link or node is authorized to support any additional ABR connections and to ensure that the node's ACR for the ABR traffic class is greater than the minimum cell rate specified for the connection.

Scalability

In order to promote scalability, the PNNI protocol uses the 20-byte NSAP addresses to identify levels in the network hierarchy to support an almost limitless number of levels: a maximum of 105 (the number of bits in the 13 high-order bytes of the NSAP address, excluding the ESI and SEL fields), though no more than a half dozen or so will likely ever need to be used, and even then only within the very largest, global networks [1, 2].

8.2.3   Address resolution

In this section we briefly review the specific application in an ATM environment. ATM uses variants of ARP and Inverse ARP to resolve addresses with Logical IP Subnets (LIS, described in Section 8.3.2). ATMARP is based on RFC 826 [3], and InATMARP is based on RFC 2390; both are covered in RFC 2225 [4]. ATMARP extends ARP to support ARP in an ATM unicast server environment. InATMARP simply enables ARP to run on the new ATM interface type. Inverse ARP uses the same frame format as the ARP but with two additional operation codes (8 = InARP request, 9 = InARP reply). The operation of these protocols differs depending on whether PVCs or SVCs are used. The hardware type value for ATM is 19 decimal and the EtherType field is set to 0x806.

PVC and SVC environments can be describes as follows:

- PVC environment—In a PVC environment each station uses the InATMARP protocol to dynamically resolve the IP addresses of all other connected stations. Remember that Inverse ARP is used to dynamically resolve a host's IP address when the hardware address is known. The resolution is done for those PVCs that are configured for

LLC/SNAP encapsulation. It is the responsibility of each IP station supporting PVCs to revalidate ARP table entries as part of the aging process. In a PVC environment a virtual circuit needs to be established before any communication can occur. Since the hardware address of the destination station is already known, a requesting station simply formats the InATMARP request by inserting its source hardware and IP address and the known target hardware address. It then zero fills the target protocol address field and sends it directly to the target station. The receiving station formats a reply using the request information and inserts its IP address. Both sides update their ARP tables accordingly.

- SVC environment—SVCs require support for ATMARP in the non-broadcast environment of ATM. To meet this need, a single ATMARP server must be located within the Logical IP Subnetwork (LIS). The ATMARP server mechanism requires that each client be administratively configured with the ATM address of the ATMARP server. This server has authoritative responsibility for resolving the ATMARP requests of all IP members within the LIS. The server itself does not actively establish connections. It depends on the clients in the LIS to initiate the ATMARP registration procedure. An individual client connects to the ATMARP server using a point-to-point VC. The server, upon the completion of an ATM call/connection of a new VC specifying LLC/SNAP encapsulation, will transmit an InATMARP request to determine the IP address of the client. The InATMARP reply from the client contains the information necessary for the ATMARP server to build its ATMARP table cache. This table comprises the IP address, ATM address, timestamp, and associated VC. This information is used to generate replies to the ATMARP requests it receives.

ATMARP table operations

Within an ATM environment, the ARP cache is updated according to the following rules:

- If the ATMARP server receives a new IP address in an InATMARP reply, the IP address is added to the ATMARP table.

- If the InATMARP IP address duplicates a table entry IP address, the InATMARP ATM address does not match the table entry ATM address, and there is an open VC associated with that table entry, the InATMARP information is simply discarded.

- When the server receives an ATMARP request over a VC, where the source IP and ATM address match the association already in the ATMARP table and the ATM address matches that associated with the VC, the server updates the timeout on the source ATMARP table entry. For example, if the client is sending ATMARP requests to the server over the same VC that it used to register its ATMARP entry, the server notes that the client is still alive and updates the timeout on the client's ATMARP table entry.

- When the server receives an ARP_REQUEST over a VC, it examines the source information. If there is no IP address associated with the VC, and if the source IP address is not associated with any other connection, then the server adds this station to its ATMARP table. This is not the normal way, because, as mentioned previously, it is the responsibility of the client to register at the ATMARP server.

ATMARP table entries are valid according to ARP timing rules, and vary depending upon whether the device is a client or server, as follows:

- Client operations—ARP entries in clients are valid for a maximum time of 15 minutes. When an ATMARP table entry ages, the ATMARP client invalidates this table entry. If there is no open VC associated with the invalidated entry, that entry is deleted. In the case of an invalidated entry and an open VC, the ATMARP client revalidates the entry prior to transmitting any nonaddress resolution traffic on that VC. There are two possibilities: In the case of a PVC, the client validates the entry by transmitting an InARP_REQUEST and updating the entry on receipt of an InARP_REPLY, and in the case of an SVC, the client validates the entry by transmitting an ARP_REQUEST to the ATMARP server and updating the entry on receipt of an ARP_REPLY. If a VC with an associated invalidated ATMARP table entry is closed, that table entry is removed.

- Server operations—ARP entries in servers are valid for a minimum time of 20 minutes. Prior to aging an ATMARP table entry, the ATMARP server generates an InARP_REQUEST on any open VC associated with that entry and then does one of the following actions: If an InARP_REPLY is received, that table entry is updated and not deleted; if there is no open VC associated with the table entry, the entry is deleted. Therefore, if the client does not maintain an open VC to the server, the client must refresh its ATMARP information with the server at least once every 20 minutes. This is done by opening a VC to the server and exchanging the initial InATMARP packets.

Every ATM IP client that uses SVCs must know its ATMARP server's ATM address for the particular LIS. This address must be named at every client during customization. There is at present no well-known ATMARP server address defined. The use of address resolution for multicast services is described in Section 8.3.4.

8.2.4   Multicast operations

A significant omission from the ATM connection model is direct support for multicasting and broadcasting, as required by many shared-medium LAN technologies. AAL5 (the most widely used ATM adaptation layer) cannot offer bidirectional support for multicast through its point-to-multipoint connections; they must be unidirectional. AAL5 has no support within its cell format (such as AAL3/4's message identifier field) for the interleaving of cells from different AAL5 packets on a single connection. This means that all AAL5 packets for a particular destination must be received in sequence, with no interleaving between the cells of different packets on the same connection; otherwise, the destination reassembly will fail to reconstruct the packets. If a leaf node were to transmit an AAL5 packet onto the connection, it would be received by both the root node and all other leaf nodes, where the packet would be interleaved with packets sent by the root (and possibly other leaf nodes); this would preclude the reassembly of any of the interleaved packets. Note that AAL3/4 is unlikely to be used for this purpose, since it is a much more complex protocol than AAL5.

Since ATM is intended to run all LAN applications transparently, ATM must provide some form of multicast support. In effect, ATM must simulate multicasting and broadcasting by some form of cell replication down multiple circuits. Three methods have been proposed for resolving this problem, as follows:

- VP multicasting—Here, a multipoint-to-multipoint VP is used to connect all nodes in the multicast group, and each node is allocated a unique VCI, so interleaved packets can, therefore, be identified by VCI.

- Multicast server—Here, all nodes wanting to transmit within a multicast group set up a point-to-point connection with a device known as a multicast server (sometimes described as a resequencer or serializer). The multicast server is also connected to all nodes wanting to receive the multicasts through a point-to-multipoint connection. The multicast server receives packets across the point-to-point connections and then retransmits them across the point-to-multipoint connection after first ensuring that the packets are serialized, thereby precluding the issue of cell interleaving.

- Overlaid point-to-multipoint connections—Here, all nodes in the multicast group establish a point-to-multipoint connection with every other node in the multicast group. All nodes can, therefore, both transmit and receive multicasts from all other nodes.

VP multicasting requires protocol mechanisms for VCI allocation that are as yet unavailable. It is also unclear whether current Segmentation and Reassembly (SAR) devices could easily support such interleaving operations. The overlay mechanism is not scalable, since it requires each node to maintain $N - 1$ connections for each group of N nodes. It also requires some form of registration mechanism to distribute group membership information dynamically so that nodes can set up or tear down circuits as required. In contrast, the multicast server mechanism requires only two connections per node but relies on a central resequencer, which could represent both a potential bottleneck and a single point of failure. To date there is no ideal solution within ATM for multicast, and higher-layer protocols within ATM networks use both the latter two solutions for multicast. This is one of the reasons why ATM interworking is so complex, and we discuss this topic further in Section 8.3. Another issue with multicasts is address resolution; we deal with this specifically in Section 8.3.4.

8.2.5 Switching architectures

The basic operation of an ATM switch is quite straightforward: It must receive a cell across a link on a known VCI or VPI value, perform a lookup using VPI/VCI in a local translation table to determine the outgoing port(s) of the connection, map a new VPI/VCI value of the connection on that link, and retransmit the cell on that outgoing link with the appropriate connection identifiers. Since VPI/VCI mappings directly determine the output port, the forwarding lookup operation is extremely fast and does not require expensive operations such as prefix matching, as required by router operations. Note that MPLS uses this technique to provide scalability in large routed backbones. The fact that cells are of fixed size also greatly simplifies and speeds up switch operations (since queue insertion and retrieval operations are much simpler to implement).

An ATM switch fabric is a cell-forwarding device implemented in silicon, based on some form of a matrix switch or multiplexer design. A switch fabric generally provides self-routing capabilities to ATM cells based on the

ATM header's VPI/VCI values and is optimized to minimize cell-switching latency. There are many types of switch architectures. The most common ones are the single bus, self-routing blocking and nonblocking, and the multiple bus architectures. The switch architecture determines a switch's characteristics, such as complexity, speed, scalability, blocking, multicast support, and cost.

Blocking characteristics

An important characteristic of an ATM switch architecture is the degree to which it is nonblocking or virtually nonblocking. The term cell loss ratio is more commonly used in the ATM paradigm to mean blocking. In some switch designs there is a trade-off between the maximum switch utilization and the probability of cell loss. Lower values may guarantee nonblocking. The ATM switch-blocking figure is derived from the switch architecture and the source traffic assumptions. This can be an important practical consideration, since, depending upon the source traffic patterns, one switch may be better than another.

Buffering method and capacity

Buffering method in a switch determines its performance and has an impact on the switch blocking or cell loss ratio. Cells can be buffered at the input port, output port, or the fabric. Buffering capacity refers to the total amount of storage (input, output, fabric) available in a switch. In general, the greater the buffer capacity the smaller the probability that a cell may be dropped; however, buffering also generally increases latency at high loads. Often buffer capacity is specified on a port basis. Buffer capacities can vary widely depending upon the switch type. Typically they are in several tens of thousand cells (4,096 to 65,536). The port buffers can vary between 2,000 to 5,000 cells in size. Port buffers are more important at the output side because traffic from a number of incoming ports may all map into the same output port. Shared memory allows the ports to share a common pool of memory, thus reducing the chance that a cell will be dropped due to lack of cell space at the dedicated port buffer.

8.2.6   Performance considerations

In this section, we cover some of the key issues in considering ATM performance. For a good introduction to ATM performance modeling techniques refer to reference [5].

Performance parameters

The performance of an ATM network can be characterized by the following parameters:

- Cell loss ratio—The ratio of the number of lost cells to the number of lost and delivered cells.

- Cell insertion rate—The number of cells inserted into an ATM network within a specified time, as defined by the ITU. Since it is difficult to define a standard time period for all ATM networks, the ATM Forum has redefined this parameter as a ratio of the total number of undelivered cells on a connection divided by the total number of undelivered cells plus delivered cells for that connection.

- Severely errored cell ratio—The ratio of severely errored cells (e.g., more than one bit error in the header) to the number of successfully delivered cells.

- Cell transfer capacity—The maximum number of successfully delivered cells over an ATM connection during a specified time (e.g., one second).

- Cell transfer delay—Comprises the mean transfer delay and the average of a specified number of cell delays.

- Cell Delay Variation (CDV)—This is the difference between a specific cell delay observation and the average. CDV is a phenomenon wherein some cells may be switched rapidly through an ATM network, whereas other cells may take longer due to the effects of congestion and queuing. CDV is particularly important for Constant Bit Rate (CBR) applications (such as real-time videoconferencing applications).

The ATM Forum has proposed several enhancements to these parameters; the interested reader is referred to reference [6].

Switching speed

ATM switch capacity refers to the switching speed of the device. These speeds range in value from 120 Mbps to over 10 Gbps depending on the switch type. ATM is designed so that simple hardware-based logic elements can be used at each switching node to perform cell processing extremely quickly; this is particularly important for backbone switches. For example, on a link of 1 Gbps a new cell arrives and a cell is transmitted every .43 μsec.

Switch latency

Switch latency is the total one-way delay through the switch. This delay varies widely and depends on the switch fabric design. Minimum switching delays can vary from values as low as 1.2 µsec to over 50 µsec. Average switching delays tend to be much higher in value (e.g., 250 µsec average delay). Excessive switching delay can adversely impact some forms of traffic such as video and voice.

Throughput

The information payload capacity (i.e., user data, excluding all ATM protocol headers) of ATM links is typically 60 to 87 percent of the rated capacity, primarily due to protocol overhead. A general rule of thumb is to assume 75 percent of rated capacity as an upper limit on what an ATM link should be expected to carry. For example, assuming ATM is run over a SONET OC-3c link (rated 155.52 Mbps) we should expect throughput of approximately 116 Mbps in each direction. There are several additional factors that constrain throughput to less than the theoretical information payload capacity, as follows:

- Effective processing and I/O capacities—Many ATM end stations cannot transit or receive data from an ATM network at anywhere near the offered capacity of the ATM physical link. In particular, multiuser devices typically sustain far lower throughput than special-purpose terminals such as routers or ATM multiplexers. Although measurements have demonstrated that high-end workstations can sustain in excess of 100 Mbps over a 155 Mbps ATM/SONET port, these measurements were taken under special traffic conditions and do not represent real application throughput rates.

- Bursty traffic and queuing problems—ATM was originally designed to accommodate traffic sources that were quite predictable (e.g., constant bit rate or variable bit rate with known variance). However, data traffic from general-purpose workstations and LAN environments tends to be extremely bursty. Unless link utilization is kept quite low (suggestions of 60 percent of information payload capacity have been made), cell loss may occur. This problem should be resolved over time through a combination of traffic shaping, buffering, management, and end-to-end flow control, and some switch vendors already have reasonably effective proprietary mechanisms to handle bursty traffic sources.

- Virtual circuit setup delay—We have seen that SVC setup latency in ATM should be very short. However, in large, busy ATM networks, with high connection rates and periods of congestion, and particularly where setup requests include very stringent QoS requirements, circuit setup could require rerouting. This may become an additional factor that could limit throughput.

Since ATM is a switching technology, terminals will most likely be attached via dedicated links to switches. Because switches can be interconnected with several high-capacity links, ATM's aggregate throughput should theoretically scale well (up to at least low-gigabit levels). However, there will be practical deployment and use issues that will make it unlikely that any ATM network will achieve anything close to its theoretical aggregate throughput in actual operation.

Delay

The ATM standards currently mandate no absolute delay or jitter requirements on ATM networks or ATM equipment. Consequently, the amount of delay and delay variance in ATM networks is largely a function of architecture, equipment selection, and utilization patterns. A reasonable lower bound on best-case, end-to-end single-cell delay for a simple terminal-switch-terminal configuration today is 18 to 50 μsec. This is for an otherwise unloaded system. Delay under load will largely be a function of buffering in Network Interface Cards (NICs), and switches, and the data rates of the links; thus, it is very architecture and implementation specific. Similarly, it is very difficult to give a reasonable general bound on delay variance without knowing the specific topology, choices of equipment, and anticipated workload. Bellcore has suggested a DS1 circuit emulation Cell Delay Variation (CDV) of 750 μsec across a six-switch configuration (TA-001110) and a value of 1 msec across a single Local Access and Transport Area (LATA) ATM network (TA-001409). The ATM Forum BICI specification gives an approximation of how CDV accumulates across multiple nodes.

IP versus ATM performance

Once of the specific design goals of ATM was to promote implementation of simple, inexpensive switches. VCIs can be rapidly looked up, and fixed-size cells are both easy to switch (using a fast parallel fabric) and easy to schedule. This was seen as a major advantage over the traditional slow Layer 3 switched environment of IP, where variable-length packets and a tough longest prefix match operation are used when forwarding. Consequently, IP routers are significantly more expensive than ATM per switched Mbps of bandwidth. However, advances in route lookup technology have now given IP a real edge over ATM. Using fast route lookup algorithms, routers can perform a longest prefix match almost as fast, and almost as cheaply, as ATM VCI lookup. ATM-like switching fabrics are now fairly commonplace within IP routers, and recent advances have reduced the cost of complex scheduling algorithms sufficiently that the overhead for scheduling variable-size packets has decreased to a level comparable with cell switching (especially when one considers the relative inefficiency of small cell payloads). In the very near future, the cost of IP bandwidth is likely to be only marginally higher than that of ATM, and the ubiquitous role of ATM in internetwork environments is clearly under threat.

8.3   Interworking with ATM

ATM is connection oriented and cell based and therefore does not map easily onto many traditional LAN and WAN technologies. The dominant Layer 3 technology, IP, is connectionless and based on variable-length datagrams; the dominant LAN technology is connectionless frame-based Ethernet. There are significant problems to resolve when integrating these technologies with ATM, not the least of which are how to encapsulate traffic prior to segmentation, how to handle address resolution, how to handle broadcast and multicasts, and how to deal with traffic scalability and logical subnetwork mapping. Clearly, ATM is not going to take over the world overnight (if ever), and customers do not want to throw away a huge installed base of physical, protocol, and application technologies. The ATM Forum has been especially active in trying to gain general acceptance for migration and interworking strategies. Leading vendors have also been active in the IETF standards committees in an effort to enable potential customers to access the benefits of ATM for specific design applications. To date there are several strategies for bridged and routed protocol interworking between existing networks and pure ATM environments, including the following:

- Multiprotocol encapsulation over AAL5—Has been used to provide a simple point-to-point link between bridges and routers over ATM PVCs. Some amount of manual configuration (e.g., in lieu of INARP) was necessary in these scenarios.

- Classical IP over ATM (CIOA)—Proposed by the IETF in RFC 2225 [4]. CIOA provides an environment where the ATM network serves as a Logical IP Subnet (LIS). ATM PVCs are supported with address resolution provided by Inverse ARP. For ATM SVCs, a new form of

ARP operates over the ATM network between a host (or router) and an ARP server. Where servers are replicated to provide higher availability or performance, a Server Synchronization Cache Protocol (SCSP) is used. CIOA defaults to the LLC/SNAP encapsulation.

- LAN Emulation (LANE)—The ATM Forum specification for transparent bridged interworking between ATM and traditional LANs (Token Ring, Ethernet, etc.). LANE provides an environment where the ATM network is enhanced by LAN emulation server(s) to behave as a bridged LAN. Stations obtain configuration information from, and register with, a LAN emulation configuration server; they resolve MAC addresses to ATM addresses through the services of a LAN emulation server. They can send broadcast and multicast frames and also send unicast frames for which they have no direct VC to a broadcast and unicast server.

- Next-Hop Resolution Protocol (NHRP)—In some cases, the constraint that CIOA serves a single LIS limits performance. NHRP, as defined in RFC 2332 [7], extends Classical IP to allow shortcuts over an ATM network that supports several LISs.

- MultiProtocol over ATM (MPOA)—The ATM Forum multiprotocol over ATM specification. Effectively an evolution of LANE, which integrates LANE and NHRP to provide a generic bridging/routing environment.

- IP Multicast—RFC 2022 [8] extends Classical IP to support IP multicast. A Multicast Address Resolution Server (MARS) is used, possibly in conjunction with a multicast server to provide IP multicast behavior over ATM point-to-multipoint and/or point-to-point virtual connections.

- PPP over ATM—RFC 2364 extends multiprotocol over ATM to the case where the encapsulated protocol is the Point-to-Point Protocol (PPP). Both the VC-based multiplexing and LLC/SNAP encapsulations are used. This approach is used when the ATM network is used as a point-to-point link and PPP functions are required.

For specific data transport technologies such as SMDS and Frame Relay there are also architectures developed for interworking via gateway facilities. These approaches all provide migration paths and interworking with ATM but were made with different goals in mind. There are, therefore, various trade-offs depending upon the environments you are designing around and the functionality required. Some of the key technologies are discussed in the following text.

8.3.1 Multiprotocol encapsulation over AAL5

In order to transport protocols over ATM we need a generic encapsulation format that will sit directly over the ATM Adaption Layer (AAL). The simplest way to carry IP would be to encapsulate it directly in the data portion of an AAL5 cell. If you want to transport more than one protocol type (e.g., IP, AppleTalk, and IPX) concurrently over the same physical link (say, between LANs), you need a method of multiplexing the different protocols. RFC 2684 [9] defines two methods for achieving this: VC-based multiplexing and LLC encapsulation.

The VC multiplexing scheme specifies that a different VC must be established for each protocol type transferred between two hosts.

The LLC encapsulation scheme provides multiplexing at the LLC layer, via eight-byte SNAP encapsulation and, therefore, needs only one VC to carry multiple protocols. The IP PDU is encapsulated in an IEEE 802.2 LLC header followed by an IEEE 802.1a SubNetwork Access Protocol (SNAP) header and then transported within the payload field of an AAL5 CPCS-PDU (Common Part Convergence Sublayer).

RFC 2225 [4] and RFC 2684 [9] specify that IP uses LLC encapsulation, since this scheme was already defined in RFC 1042 for all other LAN types, such as Ethernet, Token-Ring and FDDI. The multiplexing header for an IP packet is, therefore, 0xAAAA030000000800. Considering the high cell tax already imposed by ATM, this compromise seems a costly choice for the benefit of compatibility (a simple two-byte header would have been more than sufficient, since the first six bytes of the LLC/SNAP header don't exactly add much value here).

This encapsulation scheme means that IP is effectively insulated from ATM. None of the benefits ATM has to offer (QoS, transportation of isochronous traffic, etc.) are employed. This is an area of active research by both the IETF and the ATM Forum. The advantage of this approach is that ATM is treated as a Data Link Layer with a large MTU and can operate in either bridged or multiplexed mode. Since we are not providing LAN emulation, the default MTU for ATM-attached IP hosts can be 9,180 bytes, which can significantly improve host performance. Since the LLC/SNAP header is eight bytes, the default ATM AAL5 PDU size is 9,188 bytes. In fact, ATM allows MTUs between 0 and 65,535, though all members of an LIS must be set to the same MTU value. RFC 1755 [10] recommends that all implementations should support MTU sizes up to and including 64 KB.

8.3.2   Classical IP over ATM (CIOA)

Multiprotocol encapsulation over AAL5 provides a way of encapsulating IP (and other protocols) over ATM but does not deal with the problem of mapping ATM variable-length NSAPs onto IP addresses. Classical IP over ATM (CIOA), described in RFC 2225 [4], is designed to provide native IP support over ATM with support for address resolution. CIOA treats ATM as a NonBroadcast MultiAccess network (NBMA), rather like Frame Relay. NBMAs are assumed to contain multiple hosts, which cannot communicate using conventional broadcasts and so require special address resolution and broadcast workarounds. There are several standards pertinent to CIOA operations, as follows:

- Multiprotocol encapsulation over AAL5 [9]

- Classical IP and ARP over ATM

- ATM signaling support for IP over ATM [10]

- Multicast Address Resolution (MARS) protocol [8]

The CIOA specifies that the NBMA (perhaps a single Layer 2 network) can be broken up into several Logical IP Subnetworks (LISs), joined by routers. An LIS is a collection of ATM-attached hosts and ATM-attached IP routers that form part of a common subnetwork. Policy is set at the router interfaces, since ATM is seen as just a piece of virtual cable.

Logical IP Subnetwork (LIS)

The term LIS was introduced to map the logical IP structure to the ATM network. In the LIS scenario, each separate administrative entity configures its hosts and routers within a closed logical IP subnetwork (with the same IP network, subnet number, and mask). Each LIS operates and communicates independently of other LISs on the same ATM network. RFC 1577 specifies the requirements for IP members (hosts, routers) operating in an ATM LIS configuration. Specifically, all members of an LIS must have the same IP network/subnet number and address mask and be directly connected to the ATM network. They must have a mechanism for resolving IP addresses to ATM addresses via ATMARP and vice versa via InATMARP when using SVCs. They must have a mechanism for resolving VCs to IP addresses via InATMARP when using PVCs and must be able to communicate via ATM with all other members in the same LIS—that is, the virtual connection topology underlying the intercommunication among the members must be fully meshed.

Hosts that are connected to an ATM network communicate directly to other hosts within the same LIS. This implies that all members of an LIS are able to communicate via ATM with all other members in the same LIS (VC topology is fully meshed). Communication to hosts outside of the local LIS is provided via an IP router. This router is an ATM end point attached to the ATM network that is configured as a member of one or more LISs. This configuration may result in a number of separate LISs operating over the same ATM network. Hosts on different IP subnets must communicate via an intermediate IP router even though it may be possible to open a direct VC between the two IP members over the ATM network (refer to Figure 8.7).

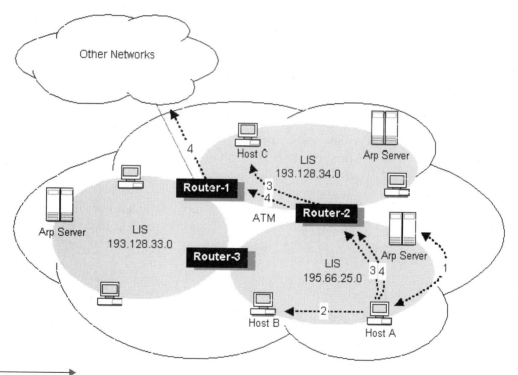

Figure 8.7 *Classical IP over ATM architecture. Host A is establishing a number of communication channels. (1) To reach Host B, it must first query the local ARP server to resolve Host B's ATM NSAP address from the IP address. (2) Once Host A has Host B's NSAP address it can set up a direct VC. (3) To communicate with Host C, Host A must go via Router-2 (even though it could set up a direct ATM VC). (4) To communicate with non-ATM hosts, Host A must use routers.*

Operation

Address resolution is handled by special server processes (referred to as the ARP server) typically run on ATM-attached routers. Each LIS has one ARP server, which is responsible for resolving addressing queries within the LIS domain. A modified ARP (ATMARP) and Inverse ARP message (InAT-MARP) are specified in RFC 2225 [4] for use over ATM.

The ARP server itself does not actively establish connections in order to build its ARP table; it relies on the clients within the LIS to initiate ARP requests. When an IP host wishes to send data to another IP host (for which it does not have an ATM address), it must send an ARP request to the ARP server. In order to reach the server the client must first set up a VC to that server (specifying LLC/SNAP encapsulation). As soon as the ARP server completes the circuit setup, it preemptively sends an inverse ARP request to the client to obtain its IP address (i.e., before the client has time to issue the ARP). The reply from the client is cached (or refreshed) in the server's ARP cache. The server then services the ARP request. In this way the ARP server dynamically updates its mapping database at the expense of doubling the ARP traffic down a VC. Clients cache address resolutions locally in their ARP tables, and entries must be renewed every 15 minutes. On the ARP server the timeout is 20 minutes. Clients are responsible for updating the ARP server. Once a client receives an ARP reply, it can set up a VC directly with the target system over the ATM subnetwork. IP PDUs sent between these systems will be fragmented into cells and do not have to be reassembled and examined at each hop, just at the VC termination point. IP is encapsulated using LLC/SNAP prior to segmentation, as defined in RFC 2684 [9].

Issues

The simplicity of this model and the ability to break up traffic domains means that broadcast traffic is reduced, as is the number of interactions between various servers (compared with LANE). For a pure IP environment it can work well. Having said that, this simplicity does mean that some functionality is lost, as follows.

- CIOA supports only IP, since the ARP servers know about IP only. It is not a solution for IPX, AppleTalk, or SNA.

- CIOA cannot leverage key ATM features such as QoS provision.

- All communication between LISs and subnetworks must be via ATM-attached routers. Direct VC setup is not possible. This can degrade throughput and increase delay.

- The current implementation of ARP servers has no inherent redundancy. If a single ARP server on an LIS fails, then all new (noncached) ARP requests will fail and communication is prevented.

- Each ATM host needs to be manually configured with the address of the ARP server.

A host on a CIOA network has no way of knowing whether it has a direct path to another host on a different LIS; it must establish a VC to a router on the LIS. The router then decides whether to set up a VC to the destination host (if the target LIS is in the same ATM network) or use conventional routing (destination not reachable via ATM).

8.3.3 Next-Hop Routing Protocol (NHRP)

We have just seen that with CIOA the only way to communicate between LISs is via a router. Clearly, this is inefficient where direct ATM paths are possible, and this problem is resolved with the Next-Hop Resolution Protocol (NHRP) and one or more Next-Hop Servers (NHS) [7]. An NHS (replacing the ARP server) is responsible for mapping and caching IP to ATM addresses for all hosts in the ATM network that register with it. It also caches IP address prefixes reachable through routers.

Nodes are locally configured with the ATM address of their NHS. They each register their own ATM and IP addresses with the NHS (using registration packets) so that the NHS can automatically build its cache tables. In effect all registered hosts become part of a NonBroadcast MultiAccess network (NBMA) subnetwork that replaces the LIS concept. A single NBMA network can support multiple administrative domains.

When a host needs to set up a connection to another host, it queries the NHS to see if it can resolve the target IP address into an ATM address. An NHS can query other NHSs if the address is nonlocal, much like the operation of a DNS server. If the address is resolvable, then the host is guaranteed that a direct connection is possible over the ATM network. The host can, therefore, use ATM signaling to set up a VC directly to the resolved ATM address and has no need to contact the router. This is referred to as cut-through routing. If the address cannot be resolved, then it must be assumed that the target host cannot be reached over ATM, and, therefore, the connection must be established via the router. If the local NBMA network has multiple routers, then the NHS can determine which router is the best choice for a particular target.

8.3.4   **Multicast Address Resolution Server (MARS)**

There is no specific support in the CIOA for IP multicast operation, and this is viewed as a critical weakness of RFC 1577 when compared with LANE. With CIOA the ARP server works fine for unicast IP addresses but does not deal with multicast (class D) IP addresses and the need for dynamic group registration. Multicasting is becoming more important for applications such as online trading and is also key to advanced routing protocols such as OSPF. Since ATM is a nonbroadcast environment, proving support for broadcasts and multicasts is not straightforward. In effect, we must translate a class D address into a group of ATM addresses, and this set may change dynamically with time. This means that the process for distributing multicasts must be an active process. With ATM there are effectively two ways of simulating multicast distribution: All stations that need to send multicasts communicate with a well-known multicast server, which sets up point-to-multipoint VCs to the simulated destination multicast groups and handles distribution transparently; and each station must itself set up point-to-multipoint VCs to each simulated destination multicast group.

In Figure 8.8, IP hosts are grouped into logical IP subnetworks (LISs) on the ATM network. Each LIS has its own MARS, which is used to resolve an IP multicast into a set of ATM addresses.

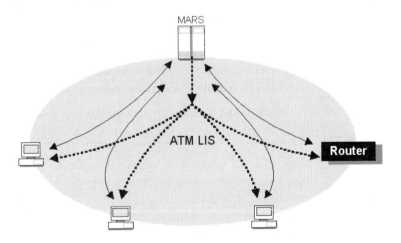

Figure 8.8   *MARS Architecture. The MARS maintains a cluster control multicast VC (shown as dashed lines) to all group members, updating them dynamically on membership status. Stations set up control VCs (shown as solid lines) to the MARS for address requests and responses.*

In either case the class D IP address needs to be resolved into a set of ATM addresses, and this is handled by a Multicast Address Resolution Server (MARS), an IETF initiative defined in RFC 2022 [8]. MARS is used to resolve internetwork layer multicast and broadcast addresses to either a list of ATM addresses or to the ATM address of a Multicast Server (MCS), which is responsible for distributing these data to the appropriate end systems. A MARS serves a logical group of ATM-attached end systems in a MARS cluster, which is currently equivalent to an LIS. There is one MARS per LIS, and each station is configured with the ATM address of its MARS. A MARS maintains a point-to-multipoint ATM connection to every ATM destination in the LIS (referred to as the cluster control VC). This VC is used to dynamically update mapping tables as stations join or exit the group. The MARS distributes multicasts via multicast meshes of overlaid point-to-multipoint connections or through multicast servers.

8.3.5   LAN Emulation service (LANE)

So far we have concentrated on providing support for IP over ATM. If we take a more generic approach and can constrain our topology to a bridged LAN domain, then another integration strategy is possible via the ATM Forum's LAN Emulation (LANE) specifications. The prime goal of LANE is to run Layer 3 and higher protocols unmodified over ATM. This means that existing protocols, such as TCP/IP, IPX, AppleTalk, NetBIOS, and SNA, together with all supported applications, can reap the benefits of a high-speed ATM network without any changes. There are several components in the LANE architecture, as follows:

- LAN Emulation Client (LEC)

- LAN Emulation Server (LES)

- LAN Emulation Configuration Server (LECS)

- Broadcast Unknown Server (BUS)

An Emulated LAN (ELAN) comprises a LES-BUS pair and several LECs and is dedicated to a single type of LAN emulation (i.e., either Ethernet or Token Ring). Each ELAN can be equated to a broadcast domain. One or multiple ELANs can run on the same ATM network; however, each ELAN operates independently, and users on one ELAN cannot communicate directly with those on another ELAN. ATM switches handle intra-ELAN communication; routers deal with all inter-ELAN communication. Most LANE networks consist of multiple ATM switches and typically employ the PNNI protocol.

Operation

LANE achieves Layer 3 transparency by operating below the MAC layer, inserting an extra layer of protocol, called the LAN Emulation Client (LEC), below the Data Link Layer and over the AAL5 stack. LEC software is typically implemented in host ATM NICs, LAN switches with ATM uplinks, and routers that support ATM attachment. The LEC communicates with other LECs via ATM VCs. During initialization the LEC establishes the default VC with the LES, registers its MAC addresses, and discovers its own ATM address. The LES provides centralized coordination of directory, multicast, and address resolution services for LECs. Each LEC maintains a control direct VC to the LES to facilitate sending of registration and control information. The LES maintains a point-to-multipoint VC, known as the control distribute VC, to all LECs. As new LECs join the ELAN, each LEC is added as a leaf to the control distribution tree.

ATM has no inherent support for broadcasts. LANE solves this problem by centralizing the broadcast support in a device called the Broadcast Unknown Server (BUS). Each LEC must set up a multicast send VC to the BUS. The BUS then adds the LEC as a leaf to its point-to-multipoint VC (known as the multicast forward VCC). The BUS also acts as a multicast server. The BUS takes the sequence of cells on each multicast send VC and reassembles the cells into frames. When a full frame is received, it is queued for distribution to all LECs on the multicast forward VCC. An entity called the LAN Emulation Configuration Server (LECS) maintains a database of ELANs and the ATM addresses of the LESs that control the ELANs. It accepts queries from LECs and responds with the ATM address of the LES serving the attached ELAN. The database is defined and maintained by the network administrator.

When a frame arrives at the LEC interface for transmission, it first checks whether the destination address is multicast or unicast.

Multicast frames are sent to a broadcast server (which is responsible for multicast distribution). The LANE multicast function can reside either within the LANE server or within a separate multicast server. If it resides in the LANE server, then default VCs can be used by the end systems for transferring their multicast frames to the server. If a dedicated multicast server is used, point-to-point VCs have to be established between the end systems and the server for this purpose.

Unicast frames are sent directly down an SVC to their ATM destination. When sending unicasts, the LEC will first examine its ARP cache to see if it has a translation from the MAC address to an ATM address. If no mapping exists locally, the LEC sends an ARP request to the LES on the control direct VC. The LES forwards the request on the control distribute VC, so all LECs hear it. In parallel, the unicast data packets are forwarded from the LEC to the BUS, which then distributes these frames to all LECs. Clearly this flooding mechanism is not optimal for unicasts, and the LANE standard dictates that it should be rate controlled at ten frames per second. Unicast packets continue to be flooded until the ARP request has been resolved. One of the LECs should eventually respond to the ARP and reply to the LES, which forwards the reply on the control distribute VC so that all LECs learn and cache the new address mapping. When the transmitting LEC receives the ARP response, it can signal the other LEC directly and set up a data direct VC for unicast data flow. Clearly, if the LEC switches immediately to the new path, there is the possibility of packets arriving out of order, so LANE provides a flushing mechanism. Before using the optimal path, the transmitting LEC generates a flush packet and sends it to the BUS. When the LEC receives its own flush packet on the multicast forward VC (from the BUS), it knows that all outstanding unicasts have been forwarded and it is safe to switch over to a direct VC.

The LEC and LES allow any Network Layer protocol to run over ATM transparently. This makes it easy to integrate or possibly replace Ethernet and Token Ring LANs with ATM (FDDI is not directly supported and requires integration via a translation bridge). LANE enables devices attached to legacy LANs and devices attached to ATM to communicate freely, via transparent and source-route bridging. All devices attached to an emulated LAN appear to be on one bridged segment and should exhibit performance characteristics similar to those in a traditional bridged environment. LANE protocols such as TCP/IP, IPX, and OSI should have performance characteristics similar to those in a traditional bridged environment.

LANE issues

There are several issues regarding the current LANE standards including the following:

- LANE's transparency means that one of the key benefits of ATM, QoS guarantees, is hidden from the overlying protocol. All cells are sent as undefined bit rate. Over time, this mapping is likely to be improved to take advantage of some of the key features of ATM.

- There is no current standard for virtual LAN (VLAN) operation over ATM. Cisco supports the mapping of VLANs to ELANs via the interswitch link, or 802.10.

- LANE requires end systems to install expensive ATM host adapter cards. There is some work done by Cornell University to support existing LAN cards via an external multiplexing device referred to as a Cells In Frame Attachment Device (CIF-AD) [11].

- Once a LEC knows where to find the LES and has successfully joined the ELAN, it is free to send any traffic into the bridged ELAN. The only place for any OSI Layer 3 security filters is in the router that routes between ELANs. Therefore, the larger the ELAN, the greater the likelihood and scope of security violations.

- Intersubnet traffic still needs to be sent via routers, even though direct ATM paths may be available.

8.3.6   MultiProtocol over ATM (MPOA)

LANE offers significant functionality, but there is still a requirement to use routers for intersubnet traffic, even where direct ATM paths are available. LANE also does not support VLANs. MultiProtocol over ATM (MPOA) is an ATM Forum initiative [12]. MPOA is designed to optimize the transfer of intersubnet unicast data in a LANE environment by integrating LANE v2.0 and NHRP to enable intersubnet, internetwork layer protocol communication over direct ATM VCs (using UNI signaling). MPOA provides end-to-end Layer 3 internetworking connectivity across an ATM network for hosts that are attached either directly or indirectly (via a legacy LAN). MPOA allows LANE edge devices to perform internetwork layer forwarding and establish direct communications without requiring that the edge devices be full routers. MPOA merges bridging and routing functionality with ATM and supports diverse protocols, network technologies, and IEEE 802.1 VLANs. MPOA is intended to provide a unified framework for overlaying internetwork layer protocols on ATM. MPOA is capable of using both routing and bridging information to locate the optimal exit from the ATM cloud. MPOA allows the physical separation of internetwork layer route calculation and forwarding, a technique known as virtual routing. This separation provides a number of key benefits, including the following:

- Enables efficient intersubnet communication

- Increases manageability by decreasing the number of devices that must be configured to perform a Layer 3 route calculation

- Increases scalability by reducing the number of devices participating in internetwork layer route calculation

■ Reduces the complexity of edge devices by eliminating the need to perform Layer 3 route calculation

Client/server architecture

The MPOA framework is designed as a client/server architecture, with MPOA Clients (MPCs) and MPOA Servers (MPSs) connected via LANE (see Figure 8.9). MPOA also defines the protocols used for communication between MPCs and MPSs. An MPC sends requests for shortcut ATM addresses and receives replies from the MPS. MPSs use routers that run standard routing protocols, such as OSPF, enabling integration with existing networks. MPOA-enabled devices can be edge devices (including the MPC, the LEC, and a bridge port), hosts (including the MPC, the LEC, and an internal host stack.), and routers (including the MPS, which in turn includes a Next-Hop Server (NHS), the LEC, and the routing function). There are other ways to create MPOA-enabled devices, including locating the MPS and MPC in a router and thereby creating a device that is capable of internetwork routing/forwarding, detecting flows, and creating ATM shortcuts for flows.

MPOA clients maintain local caches of mappings (from packet prefix to ATM information). These caches are populated by requesting the information from the appropriate MPOA server on an as-needed basis. The Layer 3 addresses associated with an MPOA client would represent either the Layer 3 address of the client itself or the Layer 3 addresses reachable through the client. (The client has an edge device or router.) An MPOA client will connect to its MPOA server to register the client's ATM address and the Layer 3 addresses reachable via the client. The primary function of the MPOA client is to create and terminate internetwork shortcuts. To achieve this an MPC performs Layer 3 forwarding but does not run a Layer 3 routing

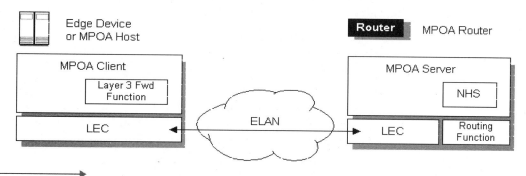

Figure 8.9   *MPOA client/server architecture.*

protocol. In its ingress role, an MPC detects flows of packets that are being forwarded over an ELAN to a router that contains an MPS. When it recognizes a flow that could benefit from a shortcut that bypasses the routed path, it uses an NHRP-based query-response protocol to request the information required to establish a shortcut to the destination. If a shortcut is available, the MPC caches the information in its ingress cache, sets up a shortcut VCC, and forwards frames for the destination over the shortcut. In its egress role the MPC receives internetwork data frames from other MPCs to be forwarded to its local interfaces/users. For frames received over a shortcut, the MPC adds the appropriate DLL encapsulation and forwards them to the higher layers (e.g., a bridge port or an internal host stack). The DLL encapsulation information is provided to the MPC by an egress MPS and stored in the MPC's egress cache. An MPC can service one or more LECs and communicates with one or more MPSs.

An MPOA server is the logical component of a router that provides Layer 3 forwarding information to MPCs, since it includes a full Next-Hop Server (NHS). MPOA servers maintain complete knowledge of the topologies they serve. To accomplish this, they exchange information among themselves and with MPOA clients. The MPS interacts with its local NHS and routing functions to answer MPOA queries from ingress MPCs and provide DLL encapsulation information to egress MPCs. An MPS services MPOA and NHRP queries on behalf of MPCs.

Control and data flows

The MPOA solution involves a number of control and data flows. By default, all control and data flows are carried over ATM VCs using LLC/SNAP [9] encapsulation. MPOA control flows include the following:

- Configuration flows—By default, MPSs and MPCs communicate with the LECS to retrieve configuration information.

- MPC-MPS control flows—Used for MPC cache management. The MPOA resolution request/reply allows the ingress MPC to obtain shortcut information. The ingress MPS may trigger the ingress MPC to make a request by sending the MPOA trigger message. The MPOA cache imposition request/reply allows the egress MPS to give the egress MPC egress cache information. Finally, either the egress MPC or an MPS may send a purge message if it discovers that cached information has become invalid.

- MPS-MPS control flows—These are handled by standard internetwork layer routing protocols and NHRP. MPOA does not define any new MPS-MPS protocols. MPOA requires no new replication techniques and relies upon the standard replication techniques provided by LANE and internetwork layer routing protocols.

■ MPC-MPC control flows—An egress MPC may send a data plane purge to an ingress MPC if it receives misdirected packets from that MPC. This message causes the ingress MPC to flush its bad cache information.

MPOA data flows include the following:

■ MPC-MPC data flow—MPC-MPC flows are used primarily for the transfer of data between MPCs over MPOA shortcut VCs.

■ MPC-NHC data flows—An MPC may send unicast data to an NHC, and an NHC may send unicast data to an MPC.

MPOA operations

MPOA performs the following operations:

■ Configuration—MPCs and MPSs each require configuration. By default, MPOA components retrieve their configuration parameter from the LECS. MPOA components must be capable of configuration via the LECS, although they may be administered to obtain their configuration by some other means. Other methods for obtaining configuration may include manipulation of the MPOA MIB, or through unspecified mechanisms.

■ Registration and discovery—To reduce operational complexity, MPOA components automatically discover each other using extensions to the LANE LE_ARP protocol that carry the MPOA device type (MPC or MPS) and ATM address. This information is discovered dynamically and used as needed. This information may change and must be periodically verified. MPCs are not NHCs and do not register host internetwork layer addresses with NHSs using NHRP registration.

■ Destination resolution—MPOA uses an extended NHRP resolution request protocol to allow MPCs to determine the ATM address for the end points of a shortcut. In the following sections, the protocol is described from the perspectives of the ingress MPC, the ingress MPS, the egress MPS, and the egress MPC.

■ Connection management—MPOA components establish VCs between each other as necessary to transfer data and control messages over an ATM network. For the purpose of establishing control VCs,

MPOA components learn of each other's existence by the discovery process. For the purpose of establishing data VCs, MPOA components learn of each other's existence by the resolution process.

■ Data transfer—The primary goal of MPOA is the efficient transfer of unicast data. Unicast data flow through the MPOA system, which has two primary modes of operation: the default flow and the shortcut flow. The default flow follows the routed path over the ATM network. In the default case, the MPOA edge device acts as a Layer 2 bridge. Shortcuts are established by using the MPOA target resolution and cache management mechanisms. When an MPC has an internetwork protocol packet to send for which it has a shortcut, the MPOA edge device acts as an internetwork-level forwarder and sends the packet over the shortcut.

■ Intra-IASG coordination—The function that enables IASGs to be spread across multiple physical interfaces; it provides the following support:

  ▪ Routing protocol support: Enables the MPOA system to interact with traditional internetworks.
  ▪ Spanning Tree support: Enables the MPOA system to interact with existing extended LANs.
  ▪ Replication support: Provides for replication of key components for reasons of capacity or resilience.

Routing information is supplied to MPOA via the NHS and its associated routing function. MPSs interact with NHSs to initiate and answer resolution requests. Ingress and egress NHSs (associated with MPSs) must maintain state on NHRP resolution requests that they have initiated or answered so that they can update forwarding appropriately if routing information changes. MPSs receive these updates from their collocated router/NHS and update or purge relevant MPC caches as appropriate [12].

Key benefits of MPOA

MPOA represents a transition from the LANE specifications to more explicit exploitation of native ATM features by the Layer 3 protocols. This enables protocols to view ATM as more than just a fast bit pipe and eliminates the overhead of the legacy LAN frame structure. An MPOA solution has several benefits over both CIOA and LANE, including the following:

■ Provides lower latency across subnet boundaries by allowing direct connectivity between end systems instead of the requirement to transit via ATM routers.

- Provides higher aggregate Layer 3 forwarding capacity by distributing processing functions to the edge of the network.

- Allows mapping of specific flows to specific ATM QoS characteristics.

- Allows a Layer 3 subnet to be distributed across a physical network.

- Provides support for VLANs.

8.3.7   ATM interworking with WANs

Frame Relay

Frame Relay is now a well-established broadband networking protocol, and in many cases there will be a need to migrate from or interwork with existing Frame Relay infrastructures as customers wish to preserve their investment. An architecture that solves this problem has been refined by the ATM and Frame Relay Forums [13–15]. Some of the key items for conversion include the following:

- Frame Relay UNI or NNI and ATM UNI connections need to be mapped (Frame Relay DLCIs are mapped onto an ATM VPI/VCI).

- Frame Relay variable-length frames must also be segmented and reassembled to and from 53-byte cells over AAL5.

- The congestion bits must be mapped to ATM EFCI bits.

- The DE bit must be mapped to the ATM CLP bit. Frame Relay's CIR is mapped to ATM's VRB traffic parameters.

- Local management information needs to be mapped (Frame Relay LMI to ATM ILMI).

The device providing this mapping runs Q.922 core protocols over the Physical Layer at the frame relay interface and the Frame Relay Specific Convergence Sublayer (FR-SCS) over AAL5 at the ATM interface.

SMDS

SMDS is a connectionless data transport service. The ATM and SMDS Interest Group have worked together on this issue, and Bellcore has defined a document for a Broadband Switching System (BSS) that would support ATM, Frame Relay, and SMDS concurrently [16]. There are two basic interworking models offered, SNI and UNI access. In the SNI model the user runs the SMDS SIP 1–3 stack over an SNI interface, and protocol conversion occurs within the BSS. With the UNI model the SMDS user runs

the SIP Connectionless Protocol (SIP_CLS) over AAL3/4 on a UNI interface (SIP_CLS includes SIP Level 3 functionality).

8.4   ATM network design

Before working through some example designs, we will cover some generic
issues for ATM deployment.

8.4.1   Media flexibility

ATM is closely associated with fiber-optic media, but, as we have already
discussed, it has far more flexibility, and this is particularly important in the
campus environment, as follows:

- There are ITU-T recommendations for ATM at 155 Mbps (SONET
  OC-3 over single-mode fiber) and 622 Mbps (SONET OC-12 over
  single-mode fiber).

- The ATM Forum has developed interoperability agreements for ATM
  at 1.544 Mbps DS1 over twisted pair, 45 Mbps DS-3 over coax, 51
  Mbps over twisted pair, 100 Mbps (FDDI PHY-based over multimode fiber), and 155 Mbps over multimode fiber and twisted pair.

- The Secure Survivable Communications Network (SSCN) program
  has defined the transport of ATM cells over military-unique TRI-
  TAC digital rates of 512, 1,024, 2,048, and 4,096 Kbps. There has
  been discussion in military contexts of defining ATM over rates as
  low as 2.4 Kbps.

8.4.2   Scalability

There are several factors that affect ATM scalability, including topology, distance, circuit thresholds, and performance.

Topology

Local ATM topologies tend to be star, with multiple terminals attached via
dedicated media to a switch or hub. Larger configurations offer more resilience, with multiple stars interconnected via switches in a mesh or ring.
These large ATM networks could employ path switches, which operate only
on the virtual path identifier of cells. ATM, when used over SDH, may also
involve SDH add/drop multiplexers in addition to ATM switches. These
would allow the flexible interconnection of ATM switches to support (for
example) a self-healing dual-ring topology.

Distance

Some of the media supported by ATM have distance limitations (e.g., coax, unshielded twisted pair, and multimode fiber). ATM over SDH can be extended over extremely long distances with repeaters.

Number of terminals

Theoretically, there is no real limit on the number of terminals on an ATM network. Practically, however, the number of terminals will be limited by the numbers of ports or switches. Today, this number ranges from 4 to 96. Larger numbers of terminals may be accommodated by collocating and interconnecting switches. Of course, it is highly likely that many terminals supported by ATM will not be directly attached to an ATM switch; rather, they will be directly attached to a local area networking technology such as 802.3 or FDDI, which, in turn, is connected via a router or bridge into an ATM switch.

Number of circuits per terminal

Theoretically, the only limitations on the number of circuits per attached terminal is the number of possible VPI/VCI combinations. The maximum number of VPs on links is determined by the number of bits allocated to address the VPs in the cell header (VPI). This is either 8 or 12 bits. The maximum number of VCs within a VP is determined by the number of bits allocated to address the VCs in the cell header (VCI). This is 16 bits.

In practice, however, ATM equipment such as Network Interface Cards (NICs) and ports have implementation-specific limits on the number of supported circuits. In some early implementations, this number was quite low, but many current implementations offer hundreds or thousands of circuits per terminal (e.g., Hughes ATM Enterprise switch and 3Com's CELL-plex 2000 switch both support a maximum of 4,096 virtual channels per port; Efficient Network's adapter supports 1,024 VCIs).

8.4.3   LAN backbone design

ATM can be used to interconnect traditional LANs such as Ethernet and Token Ring. In this design we assume no directly attached ATM users; ATM is used purely as a transparent intersite bit pipe connected via conventional bridges or routers (or both), with LAN protocols effectively tunneled across the ATM network.

ATM can be used as a bridged backbone by installing two half-bridges at the LAN/ATM interfaces (see Figure 8.10). The bridges may connect to an

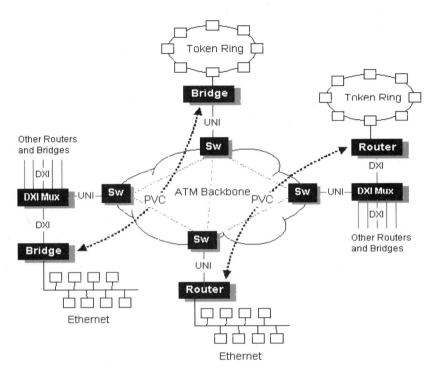

Figure 8.10
Simple ATM backbone interconnecting bridged and routed legacy LANs.

ATM network directly, via UNI, or indirectly via the DXI. You may recall that UNI is a direct cell interface into the ATM network, whereas DXI is a frame-based interface to an external device that provides the cell interface. The physical layer for the UNI is one of those specified by the ATM Forum (currently DS1, E1, DS3, 51-Mbps twisted pair, 100-Mbps multimode fiber, 155-Mbps multimode fiber, and 155-Mbps single-mode fiber, with more in work). The physical layer for the DXI is either V.35, HSSI, or RS449. The bridges perform SAR functionality at the ATM ingress and egress interfaces if UNI is used. All frames are segmented and carried inside AAL5 headers. The exact method of transport varies. There are some proprietary bridging solutions, which require that peer bridges must be from the same vendor. A growing number of bridge vendors now support multiprotocol encapsulation over ATM adaptation Layer 5 [9]. Another possibility is LAN Emulation (LANE).

An ATM routed backbone is in many ways similar to an ATM bridging backbone. Routers connect to the ATM network either directly, via standard ATM UNI, or indirectly with ATM DXI and an external DSU or ATM multiplexer containing an ATM UNI. For IP internetworking we can use Classical IP over ATM, selecting either of the two LLC encapsulation methods offered. Non-IP layer packets can be transported either via proprietary encapsulation or preferably using the encapsulation for bridging backbone use as specified in RFC 2684 [9].

A bridging backbone is useful where there are large numbers of LANs to interconnect; IP and non-IP protocols are widely used, unless the additional latency or operational issues introduced by routers is unacceptable. A routing backbone is useful where high-performance router interconnection is required, and IP is the Layer 3 protocol. In either topology the virtual channel between peers can also be established in several ways. PVCs could be preconfigured by a system administrator. SVCs would currently require proprietary (or RFC 2684) setup and would almost certainly require both peers to be of the same type, since there are currently no standard signaling standards. Alternatively, SVCs could be set up according to the LANE specification. ATM Forum's LANE specification does specify signaling for SVCs, and this could be used for bridging Ethernet and Token Ring LANs. The LANE specification also shows how a server can resolve MAC addresses to ATM addresses; this would support greater autoconfiguration than if proprietary or RFC 1483–based bridging were used.

The type of ATM service that best matches the requirements for bridging or routing among LANs is Available Bit Rate (ABR) service. ABR service will allow ATM users to contend continuously in a statistically fair way for available bandwidth, similar to the way shared medium LAN users do today. The decision as to which option to choose really boils down to the age-old bridge versus router argument, since ATM is effectively transparent in this design. The choice of direct UNI interfaces or external DXI interfaces boils down essentially to cost, performance, and reliability, as follows:

- Cost—DXI will probably be cheaper if you have several ATM bridges/routers to attach to ATM at the same location. For a single bridge/router it will probably be cheaper to install a native UNI interface. UNI prices are, however, falling, so this decision will depend on the number of devices and the vendor equipment cost.

- Performance—DXI should provide adequate bandwidth for traditional low- to medium-bandwidth LAN backbone applications. If there are large numbers of networks connected to the bridges/routers, or if some interfaces are FDDI or 100-Mbps Ethernet, then direct ATM UNIs are preferred.

- Reliability—With more devices in the end-to-end path the DXI solution is less reliable.

Using ATM as a LAN backbone (either bridging or routing) does work and represents a useful short-term migration strategy. In the long term it is probably not the best technical or most cost-effective solution, since it makes little use of native ATM features. ATM is still relatively expensive and new and is proving relatively difficult to operate and manage in comparison with high-speed alternatives for this environment, such as Gigabit Ethernet (or lower-speed options such as FDDI or Frame Relay).

8.4.4   Campus network design

Design approach

In an ATM campus network design, you need to consider how many switches are required and how they should be connected to offer the best performance, reliability, and availability. The following issues need to be considered:

- Whether or not to reuse existing cabling

- The number of ATM devices that will be connected to the network

- Bandwidth and virtual circuit requirements of ATM-attached devices (e.g., servers and bridges)

- The need to distribute heavy traffic in hub-to-hub connections and hub-to-server connections

- Requirements for performance, reliability, and availability of key resources

- Making sure you have a full understanding of the topology and routing services used on the ATM switches. For example, ATM campus switches make routing decisions using the widest path available (typically using a variant of OSPF).

In Figure 8.11, we note the UNI interface connections to ATM end systems (workstations, servers, bridges, routers, etc.) via an ATM adapter in the station. Each ATM adapter has one or more ATM addresses. Using ATM switching, the end stations communicate over virtual circuits. PVCs are preconfigured; SVCs are dynamically established using UNI procedures. Adapter flow control is used for nonreserved bandwidth connections to regulate data transmitted on UNI links. ATM switches are clustered together using the Switch-to-Switch Interface (SSI). Adapter flow control is used for nonreserved bandwidth connections to regulate data transmitted on SSI links. All switches within a cluster exchange network status information using Link State Update (LSU) messages. LSUs enable each switch to main-

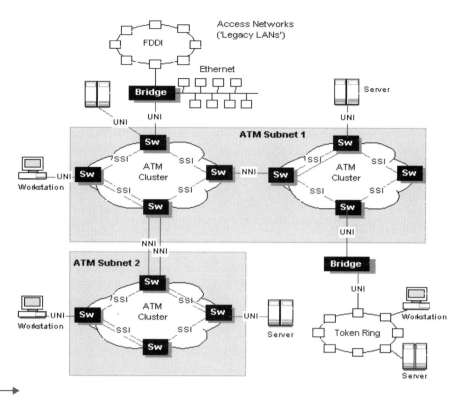

Figure 8.11 *ATM campus network design.*

tain its own live network topology database. Information contained within the network topology database enables switches to calculate optimum routes for virtual circuits established within the network. ATM clusters are connected using the Network-to-Network Interface (NNI). Depending on the addressing structure used, clusters can be part of the same or part of different subnetworks. End-to-end routes are a concatenation of optimized routes calculated per cluster. Parallel NNI and SSI links increase the availability and performance of the network. For route calculation, these parallel links are seen as single aggregated links.

In campus networks it may be desirable to reuse existing cabling wherever possible. ATM can be run over Cat-5 UTP or STP, 150-ohm STP (IBM Type 1A), or fiber optic (multimode fiber for up to 2 km and single-mode fiber for up to 20 km). Cat-5 is normally considered the minimum copper specification for supporting ATM up to 155 Mbps. The SC connector has become the ATM standard for interfacing. Scalability and management issues can be addressed by using hub clustering and link aggregation.

Hub clustering

In an ATM campus network, individual ATM switches are identified by a hub number. Hubs can be logically grouped together into clusters, linked by the Switch-to-Switch Interface (SSI). Clusters can be interconnected via the NNI interface to form ATM subnetworks. SSI supports topology and routing services, allowing optimal route selection. This means that all the devices connected to the same ATM hub have the same first 13 bytes in their ATM addresses. In the same way, all the devices connected to the same hub cluster have the same first 12 bytes in their addresses, and those connected to the same ATM subnetwork have the same first 11 bytes. By grouping ATM switches into logical clusters you can improve performance and scalability. Clustering achieves the following:

■ Reduces network restart time

■ Reduces the number of topology updates sent (topology information remains inside a cluster)

■ Reduces the resources required on each node to maintain the network topology

The way in which clusters are interconnected is also important. We will now briefly discuss some of the topology choices available.

Cluster topologies

As illustrated in Figure 8.12, ATM switches can be clustered into various topologies, including fully meshed (any to any), ring, and star topologies.

A fully meshed topology optimizes performance and availability as the number of intermediate hops between two communicating end stations is minimized. A drawback is that a larger number of links increase the size of the cluster network topology, which results in longer restart times due to a

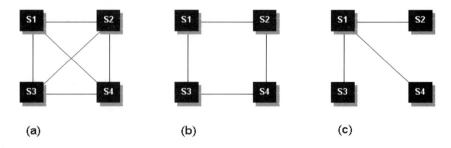

(a)   (b)   (c)

Figure 8.12   *ATM cluster topologies. (a) Fully meshed any-to-any topology. (b) Ring topology. (c) Star topology.*

higher number of LSUs advertised and routes precomputed. During steady state, however, no increased number of LSUs or route computations are required. A more important drawback is the high number of links and ATM ports required for the interhub connections. Adding a node to an n any-to-any node cluster requires $2 \times n$ extra ports and n additional links. Especially for larger networks, ≥ 4 nodes, an any-to-any topology will in most cases not be feasible, as it simply does not scale.

A ring topology limits the number of links and ports for interhub connectivity. Adding a node to an *n* ring node cluster requires two extra ports and two additional links. In addition, an alternate route, enabling service continuation during link or node failure, is available. The ring topology is less suited for large networks. As within ATM networks the transit delays are caused by hub latency rather than link transmission delays, so it is advisable to make sure that your VCs in general do not traverse more than five hubs.

A star topology is most suited for networks in which all application, LAN, and other servers are attached to a single or a limited number of ATM switches, and traffic is predominantly to and from the servers. The main advantage of a star topology is that it is cheap, because it requires a minimum of backbone links and ATM ports, and it allows you to use smaller switches with a limited number of high-speed (≥ 100 Mbps) ports. Furthermore, a star topology is easily expandable. Adding a switch to an *n* node cluster requires only two extra ports and one additional link. Due to its simplicity, this topology is easy to define and maintain. Drawbacks are that all communication between end stations attached to the downstream hubs will flow through the upstream node, which may lead to excessive load on the upstream links and adapters, without any backup during failure of the upstream node or components.

The recommended topology for your network depends on your traffic patterns, availability, and performance requirements, as well as your budget. If your servers are predominantly attached to a single ATM switch and the traffic between downstream hubs is minimal, a star topology could be considered. If there is considerable node-to-node communication and your performance and availability requirements are high, a fully meshed topology is more suitable.

ATM cluster interconnection

ATM clusters can be interconnected into larger, logical structures called subnetworks. Subnetworks can themselves be interconnected to form ATM networks. Clusters can be directly adjacent, connected via an intermediate cluster, or even connected over a WAN. Hybrid forms (e.g., a direct link with an intercluster connection) are also possible. Two clusters can be interconnected via multiple links using NNI link aggregation (multiple parallel links appear as a single link as far as topology and routing are concerned). This improves performance and availability through load balancing and link redundancy. Physical links should ideally be connected on different interface modules for better resilience. Campus switches may mandate that all NNI links connecting two clusters must originate from the same nodes (one within each cluster); these nodes are referred to as border nodes. To connect to multiple clusters, the border node function can be distributed on multiple nodes or can be concentrated in a single node.

Cluster interconnection is most likely to be required when connecting ATM clusters in different geographic locations (i.e., WAN connectivity). A key design factor is line costs, since WAN connections are much more expensive than local connections. PNNI-0 is not particularly flexible for joining ATM clusters, when compared with the job of hub clustering itself. PNNI-0 imposes the following limitations:

- NNI interfaces can be defined only between adjacent clusters or, for nonadjacent clusters, through a single intermediate cluster.

- NNI interfaces between nonadjacent clusters require an NNI/UNI link to and a Permanent Virtual Path (PVP) within an intermediate cluster.

- On the NNI/UNI interfaces you can define a maximum of 16 PVPs.

- Static routes are an alternative for any-to-any NNI connectivity.

You should not only define NNI interfaces between adjacent clusters but also between nonadjacent clusters. The latter allows SVCs to be established between end stations that reside in nonadjacent clusters, without static routes in the border nodes and the switches to which the end stations connect. It is not possible to define an NNI interface between two nonadjacent clusters when the number of intermediate clusters is larger than one. For complex cases such as these, static routes are required. (The issue of either having to define NNI interfaces or rely on static routes is fixed in PNNI phase 1.) With PNN phase 1 only NNI interfaces are required between adjacent clusters.

Multiple nonadjacent clusters can be connected using a third cluster; remember that an NNI between two nonadjacent clusters requires nonsymmetrical links (i.e., one end NNI, the other end UNI, within the intermediate clusters). The UNI links are connected together using Permanent Virtual Paths (PVP). On some campus switches, it is not possible to define

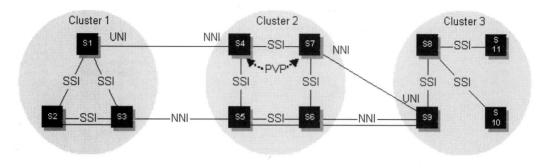

Figure 8.13 *ATM cluster interconnection.*

an ATM physical interface as UNI and NNI simultaneously (separate physical links are required for the NNI interfaces between adjacent and nonadjacent clusters). Since 16 PVPs can be defined on a single UNI connection, up to 16 cluster interconnections are possible on the same physical link.

A PVP allows switching of all virtual connections within the virtual path, enabling transparent connectivity between the nonadjacent clusters. Multiple, aggregated, NNI links can be defined. See, for example, the two links originating between S6 and S9 in Figure 8.13. Within each cluster, the NNI end of the links must originate from a single border node; the UNI side of the links, however, may terminate on separate nodes (providing PVPs have been defined). To maintain physical connectivity between the two nonadjacent clusters (1 and 3) a PVP is set up between S4 and S7 and nonsymmetrical UNI-NNI links between S1 and S4 and S9 and S7.

8.4.5 Wide area backbone design

In addition to using ATM to combine multiple networks into one multiservice network, network designers are deploying ATM technology to migrate from traditional TDM networks to reduce WAN bandwidth cost, improve performance and scalability, and reduce downtime. In this section we will run through some of the backbone decisions made by ISPs.

Internet backbone migration to ATM

In the early 1990s the majority of ISP networks were constructed over E1/T1 and E3/T3 links, and traffic was controlled by manipulating IGP routing metrics. This approach was reasonable at the time, because Internet backbones were much smaller than today (i.e., number of routers, links, and the volume of traffic handled). Figure 8.14 illustrates how metric-based traffic management operates. Assume that Router-1 in Figure 8.14 sends a

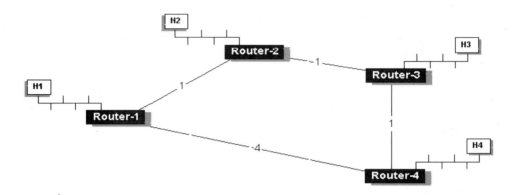

Figure 8.14   *Simple IGP router network with circuit metrics configured.*

large amount of traffic to Routers-3/4. With the metrics as they stand, Routers-1/2, and Routers-2/3 circuits may get congested because both Routers-1/3 and the Routers-1/4 flows go over those circuits. If the metric on the Routers-3/4 link were changed to 3, the Routers-1/4 flow would be moved to the Routers-1/4 link, but the Routers-1/3 flow would stay on the Routers-1/2/3 links. The result is that the hot spot is fixed without breaking anything else on the network. This is an example of conventional but effective traffic control through manipulating IGP metrics.

By the mid-1990s the load on many ISP networks was increasing to the point where they needed faster links than E3/T3 in order to remain competitive. At that time, OC-3 interfaces (155 Mbps) were available only on ATM switches; they were not yet available on routers. ISPs had to decide whether to continue with a routed core or migrate to an ATM core. In general, ISPs that chose to migrate to ATM continued to experience good growth, while some ISPs that remained with a traditional router core experienced problems (partly because of the late delivery and poor performance of OC-3 SONET interfaces for routers). In the following sections, we'll discuss the advantages and disadvantages of each of these choices.

Traffic management on a routed core

Basic traffic management was achieved over a routed core in the early 1990s by using routing metric manipulation. Unfortunately, this approach has very little granularity and simply does not scale. As the size and sophistication of carrier networks increased, metric-based traffic control became more and more complex to the point where it was simply unmanageable. On large internetworks it becomes increasingly difficult to ensure that a metric change in one part of the network does not create a new problem in another part of the network. If the only method of traffic management is to manip-

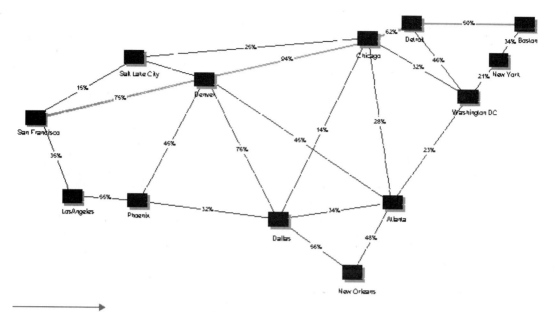

Figure 8.15 *A simulated network design for a U.S.–based ISP.*

ulate routing metrics, it is possible for some of a network's links to be underutilized while other links become heavily congested. This is simply not cost-effective for anyone running a large wide area network.

Figure 8.15 illustrates a simulated network topology for a U.S.–based ISP with PoPs in several major cities. There are several possible paths between the San Francisco PoP and the Boston PoP. The shortest path chosen by the IGP (shown in bold) is currently heavily utilized, and the IGP does not have the flexibility to choose longer but underutilized paths. If the network is only capable of selecting links based on the IGP metrics, situations like this can often occur. Reliance on IGP metrics creates paths that become traffic magnets. The result is congestion and poor performance and a design that does not exploit the economies of the bandwidth provisioned across the wide area network.

Advantages and disadvantages of a routed core

There are a number of benefits gained by remaining with a routed core when compared with migrating to an ATM core. These benefits include the following:

- In a routed core, the flexibility of a partially meshed physical and logical topology means that there is no *n*-squared problem (associated with ATM networks) when adding new edge nodes.

- There is no cell tax in a routed core. If you assume 20 percent overhead for ATM when factoring in framing and realistic distribution of packet sizes, this means that on a 155-Mbps OC-3 link, 124 Mbps is available for data while 31 Mbps is consumed by the ATM overhead. However, if you consider a 2.488-Gbps OC-48 link, 1.990 Gbps is available for data and 498 Mbps is required for the ATM overhead (almost a full OC-12!). The lack of a cell tax in a routed core means that the provisioned bandwidth is used much more efficiently.

- Routed cores, by virtue of their connectionless operation, are more resilient in failure modes. In an ATM circuit-based network, backup Permanent Virtual Circuits (PVCs) must be designed and installed in the switches before a failure occurs. Because failures have the potential of occurring at any point in a network, it is extremely difficult to design secondary PVCs to provide the same level of resilience offered by IP routing.

Despite these advantages, traditional routed cores have a number of significant disadvantages, including the following:

- In a routed core, the traffic load is not equally distributed across the network's links, causing inefficient use of network resources. Some of the links can become congested, while other links remain underutilized. This may be satisfactory in a sparsely connected network, but in a richly connected network it is necessary to control the paths that traffic takes in order to load the links equally.

- Metric-based traffic control does not offer an adequate solution to perform traffic engineering. As ISP networks become more richly connected (i.e., bigger, more thickly meshed, and more redundant), it is difficult to ensure that a metric adjustment in one part of the network does not cause problems in another part of the network.

PVC-based traffic control in an ATM core

When IP runs over an ATM backbone, routers interface directly with ATM switches at the edge of the ATM cloud. Routers communicate with each other using preconfigured PVCs across the ATM core. The ATM physical topology is transparent to the routers; they see only the specific PVCs that are presented to them as simple point-to-point circuits between other routers. Figure 8.16 illustrates how the physical topology across the ATM core differs from the logical topology across the ATM core.

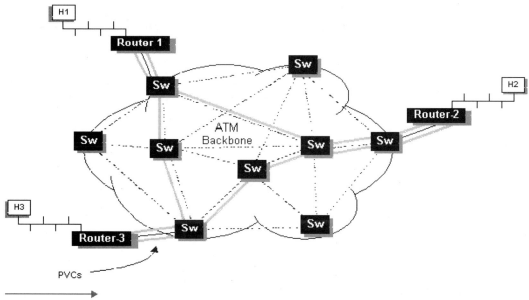

Figure 8.16 *ATM physical and logical topology.*

ISPs with an ATM backbone typically calculate the paths that the PVCs take through the network using an offline design tool. Some ATM switch vendors offer proprietary techniques for routing PVCs online while taking some traffic engineering concerns into account. However, these features are immature, and an ISP frequently has to resort to full offline path calculation. After the PVC mesh has been calculated, the supporting configurations are downloaded into the routers and the ATM switches to implement the full mesh logical topology. For some ISPs, each router not only participates in a full mesh of PVCs with the other routers, but also participates in a full mesh of backup PVCs with every other router. Figure 8.17 illustrates the logical topology for an ISP network with an ATM core. Note that only the primary PVCs are illustrated, not the secondary PVCs. PVCs are integrated into an IP network by running an IGP across each PVC. Between any two routers, the IGP metric for the primary PVC is set such that it is more preferred than the backup PVC. This guarantees that the backup PVC is used only when the primary PVC is not available.

ATM PVCs enable precise traffic engineering to be specified. The ISP determines the path for the PVCs based on measured traffic patterns so that traffic flows are distributed across different physical links. Each PVC is provisioned so that it can accommodate the anticipated load. As the network's

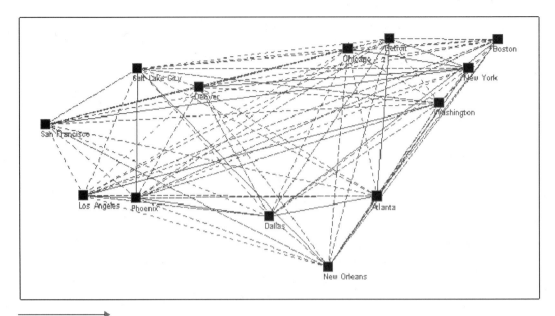

Figure 8.17   *Logical ISP topology over an ATM core with fully meshed PVCs.*

traffic matrix evolves over time, paths can be modified to accommodate
shifting traffic loads across the physical links.

The n-squared problem over ATM backbones

One of ATM's limitations in backbone designs is that it requires a fully
meshed overlay of PVCs to provide Layer 3 connectivity. This full mesh of
PVCs leads to an *n*-squared problem [$n \times (n - 1)$], whenever edge routers
are added to the design and place excessive stress on routing protocols. For
example, in our simulated network of 13 nodes in Figure 8.17, we need 156
PVCs to provide a full mesh (13×12). To add another router to the network we need to increase the number of PVCs from 156 to 182, an increase
of 26 PVCs. Not only is this laborious and expensive, but it does start to
impact on scalability. In a 50-node network adding a single additional
router requires another 100 PVCs to be configured. Furthermore, the stress
placed on routing protocols in larger networks becomes intolerable and further impacts scalability. With link state protocols such as OSPF the flooding of LSPs becomes inefficient, and each router has too many adjacencies
to maintain. The Dijkstra calculation becomes inefficient because of the
large number of logical links.

Advantages and disadvantages of an ATM core

Despite the *"n*-squared" problem, there are a number of advantages to deploying an ATM-based core in an ISP network, including the following:

- An ATM-based core fully supports traffic engineering via PVC configuration. This permits the ISPs to precisely distribute traffic across all of their links so the trunks are evenly used. This eliminates the traffic magnet effect of least-cost routing, which creates overutilized and underutilized links. Traffic engineering makes the ISP more competitive within its market, permitting it to provide lower costs and better service to its customers.

- In an ATM-based core, the per-PVC statistics provided by the switches facilitate the monitoring of traffic patterns. Network designers provision each PVC to support specific traffic-engineering objectives. They constantly monitor traffic on the PVCs. If a particular PVC begins to experience congestion, the service provider has all the information it needs to remedy the situation.

Despite the significant advantage of supporting traffic engineering, ATM-based cores still have a number of substantial limitations, including the following:

- The full mesh of ATM PVCs exhibits the *n*-squared problem.

- The ATM cell tax can consume a significant amount of bandwidth. As discussed earlier, the cell tax on an OC-48 can be as much as a full OC-12. The elimination of the cell tax in a routed core means that bandwidth is used as efficiently as possible and not wasted on unnecessary overhead.

- ATM-based cores, being connection oriented, are less resilient in failure modes. In a routed core, alternate paths are calculated on demand whenever a link or peer fails. In an ATM-based core, backup paths have to be calculated in advance and then installed in the switches to provide an immediate backup capability.

ATM-based cores require the management of two different networks: an ATM infrastructure and a logical IP overlay. The task of managing any given network has a specific amount of associated cost. By running an IP network over an ATM network, an ISP doubles its overhead because it needs to manage two separate networks. Also, routing and traffic engineering occur on different sets of boxes (i.e., routing happens on the routers and traffic engineering happens on the ATM switches). As a result, there are two configuration processes to design, operate, and debug.

8.5   Summary

This chapter discussed the basics of ATM and ATM design issues, including the following:

- ATM has emerged as perhaps the first technology that can claim to integrate LANs and WANs, voice and data. ATM can also scale to very high speeds and has been adopted by all the leading equipment manufacturers for LAN, WAN, and PBX products. ATM is viewed by many as the solution to the ever-growing demand for bandwidth. This demand is being generated by increasingly more sophisticated applications that integrate various combinations of voice, data, video, and image. An important characteristic of ATM is that it is both a local and wide area transport technology. It has been generally acknowledged that the initial implementation of ATM will address the local environment, where its use of switched, rather than shared, media will make it the high-speed LAN of choice.

- Traditional LAN/MAN technologies such as FDDI, Ethernet, and Token Ring are based on the concept of a shared medium of fixed bandwidth. Each node contends for bandwidth, and each adapter must run at the same speed (100, 16, or 10 Mbps) even though the average usable bandwidth per node is less. ATM connections are switched and the bandwidth is dedicated per connection. Key advantages of ATM are its scalability, high network throughput, low latency, and multimedia support and speed adaptation.

- ATM reduces WAN bandwidth cost through voice compression, silence compression, repetitive pattern suppression, and dynamic bandwidth allocation. ATM combines the strengths of TDM with the strengths of packet-switching data networks to deliver data efficiently. While building on the strengths of TDM, ATM avoids the weaknesses of TDM (which wastes bandwidth by transmitting the fixed time slots even when no one is speaking) and PSDNs (which cannot accommodate time-sensitive traffic, such as voice and video, because PSDNs are designed for transmitting bursty data). By using fixed-size cells, ATM combines the isochronicity of TDM with the efficiency of PSDN.

- ATM offers high reliability (99.99 percent uptime), thereby reducing downtime. This high reliability is available because of the ATM's ability to support redundant components (processors, port and trunk interfaces, and power supplies), and its ability to rapidly reroute around failed trunks.

- During the mid-1990s ATM looked unstoppable. Today its future is less certain and deployment has been sporadic. The arguments for migrating all WAN and LAN installations over to ATM seemed rational and compelling in many ways, but several issues have dogged mass deployment—specifically, the size of an existing install base; the fact that managers, designers, and users all hate complexity; the relatively high cost of ATM (especially to the desktop); and the emergence of new technologies in user-friendly guise (such as Gigabit Ethernet). In the LAN/WAN arena ATM is currently still seen as overly complex, expensive, and difficult to debug. The cell versus frame argument also seems less solid than at first proposed, with advances in IP route lookup performance. In the LAN/MAN base Gigabit Ethernet is roughly the same price per port as ATM and viewed as considerably easier to implement and manage.

- MPOA represents a transition from the LANE specifications to more explicit exploitation of native ATM features by the Layer 3 protocols. This enables protocols to view ATM as more than just a fast bit pipe and eliminates the overhead of the legacy LAN frame structure. MPOA offers lower latency and higher throughput for intersubnet communications and includes support for VLANs.

References

[1]   W. J. Goralsk, *Introduction to ATM Networking* (New York: McGraw-Hill, 1995).

[2]   The ATM Forum, Private Network-Network Interface Specification, version 1.0 (PNNI 1.0), af-pnni-0055.000 (March 1996).

[3]   Ethernet Address Resolution Protocol: Converting Network Protocol Addresses to 48-bit Ethernet Address for Transmission on Ethernet Hardware, RFC 826 (November 1982).

[4]   Classical IP and ARP over ATM, RFC 2225 (April 1998).

[5]   J. M. Pitts and J. A. Schormans, *Introduction to ATM Design and Performance* (New York: John Wiley & Sons, 1996).

[6]   www.atmforum.com, ATM Forum's home page.

[7]   NBMA Next-Hop Resolution Protocol (NHRP), RFC 2332 (April 1998).

[8]   Support for Multicast over UNI 3.0/3.1–Based ATM Networks, RFC 2022 (November 1996).

[9]   Multiprotocol Encapsulation over ATM Adaptation Layer 5, RFC 2684 (September 1999).

[10]   ATM Signaling Support for IP over ATM, RFC 1755 (February 1995).

[11]   S. Brim, "Cells in Frames, version 1.0: Specification, Analysis, and Discussion," www.cif.cornell.edu (October 1996).

[12]   The ATM Forum, "MultiProtocol over ATM," version 1.0, af-mpoa-0087.000 (May 29, 1997).

[13]   The Frame Relay Forum, "Frame Relay/ATM PVC Network Internetworking Implementation Agreement, FRF.5" (1994).

[14]   The Frame Relay Forum, "Frame Relay/ATM PVC Service Internetworking Implementation Agreement, FRF.8" (1995).

[15]   International Telecommunications Union–Telecommunication Standardization Sector (ITU-T), "Frame Relay Bearer Service Interworking," Recommendation I.555 (1993).

[16]   Bell Communications Research Inc., "Broadband ISDN Switching System Generic Requirements," GR-1110-CORE (September 1994).

9

Designing Bridged and Switched Networks

This chapter discusses the design of flat (nonhierarchical or Layer 2) networks, using devices such as bridges and switches. These devices are not, strictly speaking, internetworking devices but are commonly used in network design, mostly in campus-based local area networks (although they may support wide area interfaces also). We will focus on the following issues:

- Bridging mechanisms and applications

- Switch mechanisms and applications

- Virtual LANs (VLANS)

Previously, we discussed how to build local and campus area networks, and one of the key features introduced was the idea that LAN segments are constrained in both length and the number of stations that may be attached. Many of these LAN technologies also employ shared bandwidth schemes, where overall traffic levels are directly related to the number of nodes added. Regarding IEEE 802.3/Ethernet networks we also discussed the concept of the collision domain, which introduces further constraints on network growth.

Bridging was the first real tool for improving scalability in local area networks, and in the early 1980s bridging technology was (hard to believe now) at the cutting edge. Bridges were also used to build wide area networks, though thankfully these applications are now rare (for reasons we will discuss later). Bridges have been largely eclipsed nowadays by their faster, slicker offspring—switches and general-purpose multiprotocol bridge-routers. Bridging is actually still very much alive but now working in disguise.

9.1   Overview of bridging and switching

Previously, we focused primarily on media characteristics and cabling design issues. The device used for extended and distributing local area segments at the physical layer is referred to as a repeater. Repeater functionality is the most basic transmission facility for data networking and is today integrated into many network products. Figure 9.1 illustrates how repeaters have evolved into increasingly sophisticated bridging and switching products since the early 1980s.

One of the key differences between a repeater and a classical bridge or switch is that the latter two devices are store-and-forward devices (we will discuss the special case of cut-through switching shortly). In Ethernet-style networks, for example, repeaters transfer packets between interfaces while maintaining frame timing on both receive and transmit interfaces. This is achieved by removing leading bits from the preamble field (the so-called bit budget delay) as each new repeater hop is traversed. In effect the preamble field is nibbled away to ensure that the start of frame is synchronized on transmit interfaces. By contrast, bridges and repeaters store incoming frames into buffers, so that they may be processed more intelligently. This means that interfaces on multiport switches and bridges are attached to separate timing domains (or collision domains in the Ethernet sense). As a result of buffering, it is possible (through additional protocol functions) to entirely interconnect different types of local or wide area technology via a bridge or switch; something that is not practical on a repeater.

Performance also improves in bridged or switched Ethernet LANs, because overall traffic levels are lowered through filtering, and collision levels are also lowered (by the act of filtering bad frames and the fact that traffic levels are lower—reducing the probability of collisions). All of this means more bandwidth is available for data.

9.1.1   Bridging

In essence, a bridge is a semiintelligent buffered device that connects two or more similar or dissimilar LAN media types and may also support wide area interfaces (although wide area applications are now becoming far less common since the introduction of high-performance multiprotocol routers). If the bridge connects LAN segments of the same type (say Ethernet), then the task is relatively straightforward. If mixed media or mixed local and remote interfaces are supported, then the task is more complex (the bridge

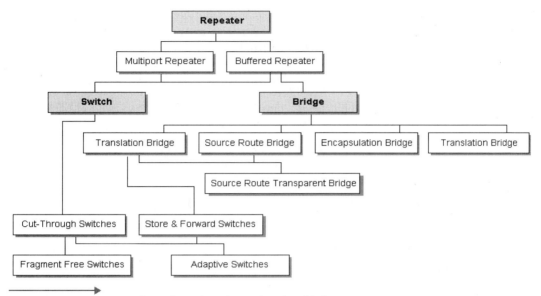

Figure 9.1   *Bridge and switch evolution from humble beginnings.*

must resolve factors such as bit ordering, addressing, MTU, differences in line speeds, etc.). There are also areas here where standards are simply not defined. Unlike a repeater, the main benefit of bridging is that it contains local traffic by filtering out traffic that it knows (through a learning process) to be local. Bridges also extend segments beyond the normal media limitations, since frames are buffered and retimed (on Ethernet networks the preamble will also be reinstated). Bridges also limit the scope of errors to an interface (e.g., short frames [runts] and CRC errors will not be forwarded to other interfaces). They can achieve this because they have much more time than repeaters to examine frames and make sensible filtering decisions.

There are various types of bridges, depending upon the interfaces offered, the media types supported, and the level of functionality supported, as follows:

- Local bridge—supports one or more LAN media types, such as Ethernet, Token Ring, and FDDI.

- Remote bridge—supports one or more LAN interfaces plus one or more WAN interfaces, such as T1/E1, ATM, and Frame Relay.

- Transparent bridge—operates without modifying frames in any way or interacting with end systems. Primarily associated with IEEE 802.3/Ethernet LANs.

- Spanning Tree bridge—a bridge that operates using the IEEE 802.1d Spanning Tree protocol for loop resolution (most standard bridges support some form of Spanning Tree operation).

- Source Routing Bridge (SRB)—a bridge that performs source routing operations by using the Token Ring Routing Information Field (RIF) to make forwarding decisions. Primarily associated with IEEE 802.5/ Token Ring LANs.

- Source Routing Transparent Bridge (SRT)—a bridge that combines both transparent and source routing functions concurrently.

- Source Routing Translation Bridge (SR-TB)—a bridge that performs complete translation at the Data Link and Physical Layers (currently for Token Ring and Ethernet networks only).

- Encapsulation bridge or tunnel bridge—a bridge that performs IP encapsulation of either source route bridging frames or transparent bridge frames in order to perform Layer 3 forwarding.

Bridges examine each incoming frame and, depending upon forwarding decisions, either copy the frame into local buffers or discard it. Forwarding knowledge is based on a process called learning in transparent bridge environments or implicit topology information contained within frames in the source routing environment. Bridges are Layer 2 devices; therefore, forwarding decisions are based on Media Access Control (MAC) addresses; there is no visibility of the Layer 3 IP address space.

9.1.2   Switching

The term switching was originally used to describe wide area technologies such as X.25, Frame Relay, and SMDS; however, LAN switching has evolved from bridging and multiport repeater techniques. LAN switches are designed for high-performance, high port density station attachment, as well as the classic media extension role performed by bridges. Just like bridges, LAN switches are designed to work with existing cable infrastructures transparently, so that they can be installed with minimal disruption to existing networks. Switches also construct MAC address filter tables for use in forwarding decisions, in essentially the same way as bridges. There are various types of switches, depending upon the level functionality supported, including the following:

- Store-and-forward switch—sometimes called classical switching. Effectively this is a high-performance multiport bridge. It has all the characteristics of a standard bridge (such as buffering complete frames and limiting frame errors to an interface).

- Cut-through switch—a hybrid switch with some bridge and repeater-like functionality. Since the destination MAC address appears first in a frame, this device can make a forwarding decision very quickly by buffering only the first six bytes of the frame (not the whole frame as in a bridge). In effect, forwarding can take place while the frame is still arriving, enabling very high performance. The problems associated with cut-through switches are that the act of forwarding while receiving means that frame errors (such as runts, pygmies, giants, collision fragments, alignment errors, and FCS failures) are also propagated.

- Fragment-free switch—a cut-through switch with additional buffering. Up to 64 bytes are buffered, meaning that some important errors can be avoided (collision fragments, runts, pygmies, etc.). Clearly, problems experienced beyond 64 bytes (such as giants, FCS failures, and alignment errors) cannot be detected, since cut-through switching has already started.

- Adaptive switch—another hybrid switch. Here the switch behaves by default like a cut-through switch but continuously monitors the level of bad frames experienced (and therefore propagated). When bad frame counts reach a threshold, the bridge changes behavior to operate like a classic store-and-forward switch until the error rate drops to acceptable levels.

Another problem with cut-through switching is the lack of Spanning Tree support. If frames are not buffered, it is not possible to operate the Spanning Tree protocol to resolve loops. This can be a serious design issue in a large, flat network. Of course, a combination of cut-through and classical bridges could be used as long as the designer pays attention to detail in configuring the failure modes of the topology (i.e., in normal operating conditions the slower Spanning Tree bridges would all be blocking to maintain topological integrity).

9.1.3   Traffic management

Traffic segmentation

Bridges are a simple and effective way of isolating intrasegment traffic and, therefore, a good way of reducing the traffic seen on each individual LAN segment. This generally improves network response times, as observed by users. The extent of the improvement depends very much on the volume of intersegment traffic relative to the total traffic, as well as the volume of broadcast and multicast traffic. Bridge placement is, therefore, key to the effectiveness of traffic segmentation. If, for example, you place a bridge between a central host and a client base, where all communication is to and from the host, then you could actually make things worse, since, in effect, you have only added latency. If there is significant interclient traffic, then there will be some benefit, since the host LAN segment will be less utilized and the response time of the host could be improved.

The main use of bridges in network designs is to create partitions (discrete traffic domains) when the traffic on a repeated network begins to affect users or business-critical applications. Bridges may also be used for basic interconnection between remote offices or to transfer protocols that have no Layer 3 address and routing capabilities (such as DEC's LAT). Traditional bridges are now dying out as a useful network device—first, because of the emergence of the router network and second, because the price of switches has come down. Routers generally offer much better security and traffic management features, while switches effectively provide the same functionality but with much higher throughput.

When installed in a repeated network, the first thing a bridge will do is start to manage traffic. It uses fairly simple technology to listen to the network and work out whether to forward packets or drop them. When a bridge forwards a frame, it first makes a complete copy of it in an internal buffer and then queues the frame up on one or more output queues. Bad frames are dropped (such as frames with bad CRCs) and usually error counters are maintained.

Since frames are being buffered, we may improve network reliability by ensuring that bad frames are not propagated. Clearly, however, there is increased latency, since a frame is now copied and queued, but in practice this latency is usually very small.

Broadcast domains and scalability

It is important to understand that bridges propagate broadcasts everywhere, and this can be a serious issue that limits the scalability of bridged networks. For example, on a single LAN segment broadcasts from protocols such as ARP typically represent a small percentage of the overall traffic. As more segments are joined together via bridges, this broadcast traffic is forwarded to every segment and so begins to multiply. Since each device on a bridged network typically has to process broadcasts, this can start to degrade host performance as well as reduce available bandwidth. In order to scale Layer 2

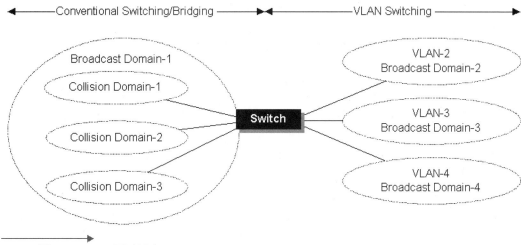

Figure 9.2   *VLAN domains.*

networks more effectively, a technique known as Virtual LANs (VLANs) was introduced to enable broadcast domains to be segregated in flat networks; this concept is illustrated in Figure 9.2. VLANs are described later in Section 9.7. Note that in conventional bridging or switching each interface represents a separate collision domain, but all physical ports belong to a single broadcast domain. VLAN ports, on the other hand, are logical interfaces with a discrete broadcast domain per interface.

Layer 2 access lists

Most bridges today implement a range of user-configurable filtering (Access Control List [ACL]) capabilities to enable the network designer to fine-tune traffic management and impose basic security. For example, you may want to stop hosts on a particular LAN from broadcasting boot requests across the entire subnet. Note that on some Layer 2 products, filtering capabilities may extend beyond the range of the Data Link Layer header. As a general rule you should try to avoid filtering above Level 2 header. This requires expert protocol knowledge, is hard to maintain, and in practice often results in subtle problems, that are hard to debug. High-level filtering is best handled using advanced switching and routing products.

Compression techniques

Traffic compression techniques are often employed on wide area bridge links. Nowadays this is primarily via standard PPP mechanisms. For historical reasons there are a variety of proprietary techniques, several of which will work only with peer bridges from the same manufacturer. Examples include the following:

- Ethernet packet compression, such as frame header compression (typically compresses 14 bytes to 2 bytes)

- Specific protocol optimizations, such as LAT announcement compression techniques, LAT header compression (typically compresses 18 bytes to 2 bytes)

- Zero fill padding suppression (to reduce minimum packet size)

9.1.4   Load-balancing techniques

In Source Route Bridging (SRB) the ability to send data down multiple paths is built into the architecture. In transparent bridging load-balancing techniques are either dependent on lower-level data-link operations (such as multilink PPP for parallel bridge links) or proprietary implementations, since the use of multiple paths is precluded by the use of the Spanning Tree Algorithm (STA). This is a particular problem for wide area networks, since it may be beneficial for performance, reliability, and cost issues to forward traffic over several wide area links concurrently.

Proprietary techniques generally require peer bridges to be from the same vendor (with very few exceptions) and may be restricted to specific WAN media. Xyplex, for example, employs a technique called Fully Distributed Redundant Bridging (FDRB), which works transparently in cooperation with Spanning Tree bridging. Up to 32 bridge pairs are supported in parallel, and all of these links form a logical group, presented to the network as a single Spanning Tree link. Load balancing is achieved dynamically via a simple hashing algorithm based on flow attributes, using the IP addresses and port numbers to route flows over different bridges. FDRB automatically redistributes flows between bridges, as more or fewer bridge pairs are available. Vitalink also employs a technique called DLS, which enables triangulation between remote sites by allowing traffic to be forwarded down a point-to-point link between bridges. This technique is rather complicated and imposes several constraints on the design that restrict its application [1].

9.1.5   Multicast support

One of the design issues raised by multiport bridges and switches in a multicast environment is a phenomenon referred to as multicast leakage. We know that a bridge must propagate broadcasts and multicasts to all ports other than the receiving port. In the case of IP multicasts there are several Layer 3 protocols used to distribute multicasts efficiently, so that specific multicasts are directed only to those users who require them. All of this good work is wasted if a Layer 2 switch or bridge blindly forwards these frames to its interfaces without knowledge of user subscriptions. A special class of multicast-aware bridges and switches has emerged to resolve this problem by implementing additional protocols and functionality that can transparently assist the device in acquiring multicast group status information. The three key protocols of interest are, as follows:

- Generic Attribute Registration Protocol (GARP)

- GARP Multicast Registration Protocol (GMRP)

- GARP VLAN Registration Protocol (GVRP)

GARP

The Generic Attribute Registration Protocol (GARP) is designed to allow GARP applications to propagate status information throughout the network. GARP is standardized under IEEE 802.1P. Currently there are two GARP applications: GMRP and GVRP. A GARP application makes declarations or withdrawals in order to communicate the status via a number of attributes. At present there are five attribute-specific messages and a general message supported, as follows:

- JoinEmpty (operator type 0)—a device is declaring an attribute value. At this stage the device has not registered the attribute or is interested to see if other participants wish to declare.

- JoinIn (operator type 1)—a device is declaring an attribute value and has either registered the attribute or does not care if other participants wish to declare.

- LeaveEmpty (operator type 2)—the opposite actions of JoinEmpty.

- LeaveIn (operator type 3)—the opposite actions of JoinIn.

- Empty (operator type 4)—a device is simply interested to see if other participants wish to declare.

- LeaveAll (generic)—indicates that registrations will be terminated shortly, either by specifying all attributes (by setting attribute type to 0) or by identifying the specific attributes. If participants wish to remain registered, they must explicitly rejoin.

Each GARP application is allocated a unique group multicast MAC address referred to as the GARP Application Address. GARP does, however, use the same LLC address as Spanning Tree, relying on the combination of the unique MAC address and a specific GARP to ensure that the protocol is correctly handled on reception.

GMRP

The GARP Multicast Registration Protocol (GMRP) enables multicast group membership information to be propagated throughout a bridged or switched network. GARP is also standardized under IEEE 802.1P. In operation GMRP is similar to the combination of IGMRP (which supports dynamic group membership activities) and MOSPF (which supports multicast distribution). GMRP carries two types of information, as follows:

- Group membership information—is used to indicate whether a participant wishes to subscribe to or unsubscribe from a specific multicast group. Upon receipt of this message a multicast-aware switch or bridge can decide whether to graft or prune a port onto the distribution tree for a specific multicast group address.

- Service requirement information—specifies that the default behavior of the receiving interface should be either to forward all groups or to forward unregistered groups. This mechanism is used to enable GMRP-aware switches to interact with GMRP-unaware switches.

GMRP uses the MAC destination multicast address 01-80-c2-00-00-20. GMRP defines two attribute types: the group attribute contains group membership information, and the service requirement contains service requirement information for all groups or all unregistered groups.

GVRP

The GARP VLAN Registration Protocol (GVRP) supports the distribution of VLAN registration over a bridged or switched network. GARP is standardized under IEEE 802.1Q. GVRP uses the MAC destination multicast address 01-80-c2-00-00-21. GVRP operates in a manner similar to GARP/ GMRP except that it distributes 12-bit VLAN Identifiers (VIDs) rather than 48-bit multicast group MAC addresses. VLANs are described in Section 9.7.

9.1.6   Applicability in internetwork design

Bridges and switches are tools that alleviate congestion in local area networks (Ethernet, Token Ring, and FDDI) by reducing traffic and preserving valuable bandwidth. The relative simplicity and utility of these devices,

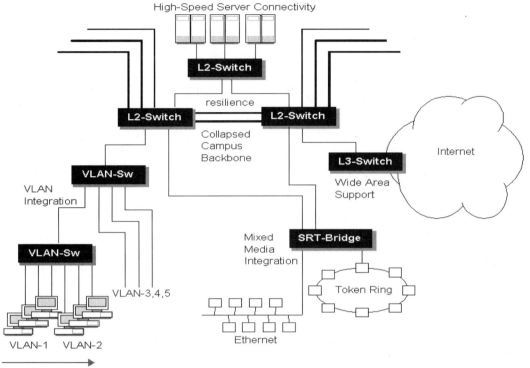

Figure 9.3   *Typical applications of bridges and switches.*

as well as their maturity, performance, and reliability, make them useful in many network designs. Protocol transparency is also a useful asset in some networks; there are still several LAN protocols in use that were not developed with routing in mind (such as NetBIOS and DEC LAT). For this reason bridging functionality is commonly employed within multiprotocol routers to handle any nonroutable protocols.

On the downside, since neither bridges nor switches are aware of Network Layer addressing, there is no concept of network hierarchy. Therefore, bridged or switched networks are not inherently scalable, and their ability to direct traffic efficiently is far from optimal. Figure 9.3 illustrates common applications of bridges and switches today. Bridging and switching applications are generally limited to the following:

- Startup or pilot networks

- Interconnecting local area networks in campus environments

- Simple, remote office interconnect

- High-speed server attachment

- Collapsed local area backbones

- Bulk high-performance user attachment

In order to impose some form of hierarchy at Layer 2, a technology known as Virtual LANs (VLANs) was introduced in the late 1980s. Essentially, VLANs introduced an addressing scheme between Layer 2 and Layer 3, which operates transparently as far as users are concerned.

Classical bridges have declined in popularity since the early 1990s. In the wide area, the flexibility, resilience, and better traffic management capabilities of multiprotocol bridge routers mean that bridges are now rarely used for LAN interconnect. In campus networks, LAN switches have effectively displaced bridges almost entirely. Switches typically offer much greater port density, flexible media support, a low price per port, and wire speed forwarding rates on a per-user basis. While specialist bridges, such as those required for protocol translation, are still in use in many IBM environments, switches have gone from strength to strength, incorporating additional functions such as Layer 2, Layer 3, Layer 4, LAN, WAN, Virtual LAN (VLAN), and even security functions.

9.2   Transparent bridging

Transparent bridges were first developed at Digital Equipment Corporation (DEC) in the early 1980s. This work was subsequently adopted by the IEEE and ISO, culminating in the IEEE 802.1 and ISO 8802-1 standards. An IEEE 802.1d transparent bridge is characterized by store-and-forward operation, the ability to listen to all traffic on all ports, the ability to learn and cache topology information transparently, and the ability to resolve topology loops through the implementation of the Spanning Tree algorithm. Transparent bridges are commonly used in Ethernet/IEEE 802.3 networks to connect LAN segments. Transparent bridging may also be used to connect Token Ring LAN segments, although this application is not common.

9.2.1   Operation

Transparent bridging relies on the principle that a node should be able to transmit a frame to another node on a LAN without any knowledge of the location of that node. Transparent bridges are completely transparent to network hosts, and this makes their use in network designs relatively simple. When transparent bridges are powered on, they begin to build up a picture of the network topology by listening to packets on the network and learning which source addresses are associated with which physical interfaces. To provide transparent operation, a bridge will assume that the intended destination of a packet could be on any interface until it has proof. This means that any frame that has a destination address not recognized by the bridge will be forwarded to all interfaces other than the receiving interface. In essence a transparent bridge acts like a buffered repeater until it can start to make smart decisions, and only the source address of a packet is proof of location.

Transparent bridges are constantly listening and learning. Each frame received at an interface will cause the bridge to either make a new association of a source MAC address with an interface (meaning a new entry in a filter table) or cause an aging timer to be refreshed for an existing table entry. This filtering database acts as a forwarding table for any received frames. Whenever a new packet is received, these tables are examined for any entries matching the destination address. If the destination address is matched against a particular interface, then the packet will be forwarded to that interface only; otherwise, it will be sent to all interfaces. Packets are never sent out on the interfaces on which they are received. To summarize, a packet received at an interface will go through the following process:

- If the destination address is broadcast or multicast, then the packet will always be forwarded to all interfaces except the receiving interface.

- If the destination address is not in the database, the frame is forwarded to each interface except the receiving interface.

- If the destination address is in the database and the frame was received on an interface associated with the destination address, the frame is discarded.

- If the destination address is in the database and the frame was received on an interface not associated with the destination address, the frame is forwarded to the associated interface for this destination address in the database.

Figure 9.4 illustrates how a transparent bridge will build up its filtering database. Let's assume that the network has been inactive for a long time and there are no entries in the bridge filter tables. In the morning the bridge will start to build a new picture of the topology, as follows:

- At 8:30 A.M. Node-A sends a packet destined for Node-B. When the bridge receives this packet on interface 1, it learns from the source address that Node-A is reachable via interface 1. It then adds Node-A to its filter tables, associating it with interface 1 and setting a timer

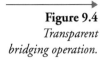

Figure 9.4
Transparent bridging operation.

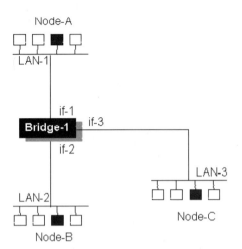

Bridge Filter Table			08:30:00
Node	**If**	**Age**	
A	1	60	

Bridge Filter Table			08:30:02
Node	**If**	**Age**	
A	1	58	
B	2	60	

Bridge Filter Table			08:30:08
Node	**If**	**Age**	
A	1	52	
B	2	54	
C	3	60	

(let's assume a 60-second timer for this example). The packet is then forwarded to both interface 2 and interface 3, since the bridge has no idea where Node-B is at this point.

- Two seconds later, at 8:30:02 A.M., Node-B sends a reply to Node-A. When the bridge receives this packet, it learns from the source address that Node-B is reachable via interface 2. It then adds Node-B to its filter tables, associating it with interface 2 and setting a timer. The bridge examines the destination address in the packet and scans its filter tables, finding a match on interface 1. The bridge then forwards this packet only to interface 1. Note that by now the Node-A filter table entry is aging.

- Six seconds later, Node-C sends a packet to Node-D. When the bridge receives this packet, it learns from the source address that Node-C is reachable via interface 3. It then adds Node-C to its filter tables, associating it with interface 3 and setting a timer. The bridge examines the destination address in the packet and scans its filter tables, finding no match. The bridge then forwards this packet only to interfaces 1 and 2. If Node-C continues to send packets to this address, they will continue to be forwarded out of both interfaces, and Node-C's aging timer will simply be reset.

The principle that the bridge's memory of the topology is constantly being eroded is important. First, it is possible that the topology will change, and therefore a bridge must be capable of responding to such changes. Second, filter tables consume memory and there is typically a finite limit on the number of learning table entries (usually a power of 2, such as 1,024, 2,048, or 4,096). On large, flat networks the number of hosts may exceed the number of available table space, so it is useful to age out any hosts that have not communicated for some time. Clearly, if you have a very large network and limited bridge memory, then you could have a real problem, since any destination addresses that are not in the tables cause packets to be flooded out of multiple interfaces. For the same reason it is not a good idea to set this aging timer too low. To avoid unnecessary surges of traffic, especially on large or busy networks, transparent bridges implement a simple state machine that starts off by blocking all traffic and precharges its filter tables.

The bridge state machine

IEEE 802.1d transparent bridges implement the Spanning Tree Protocol (STP), which relies on a simple state machine to determine how to communicate with peers, learn addresses, prevent loops, and recover from topology failures. The basic operational states are illustrated in Figure 9.5. Note that state 4, in particular, differentiates Spanning Tree bridges from simple transparent bridges (now quite rare). Note that these states also refer to ports

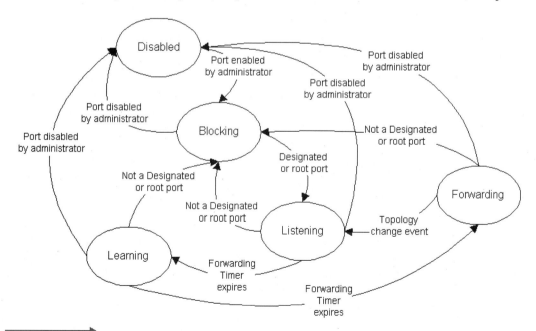

Figure 9.5   *Spanning Tree state transition diagram for a bridge port.*

(interfaces). On a multiport bridge or switch the device may be in several states concurrently on different ports.

In states 1, 2, and 4 the network is effectively broken for all users who need to reach destinations across a bridge (local communications on a segment, for example, are still active). A timer called the forward delay timer (a form of hold-down timer) is implemented to ensure that user data frames do not circulate while a bridge is reconfiguring. This timer is normally configurable by a network administrator (typically the default is 15 seconds, maximum 255 seconds). The main features of the various states are highlighted as follows:

- Listening—A port enters this state if it has been classified as either a designated or root port. In this state STP is still configuring, and a forward delay timer is initialized. Ports may receive and act upon bridge management frames (i.e., Hello-BPDUs) but will not pass or process user data frames. The listening state allows each bridge to take part in an election process, where a master, or root, bridge will be elected. Once elected the root bridge begins sending out Hello messages at regular intervals, and all other bridges will align themselves with the new root bridge; some will forward on all ports while others may decide to block certain ports to stop loops forming. Once the forward delay timer has expired, the bridge will enter a learning state. Any ports deemed to be not designated or root at this point would go into the blocking state.

- Learning—In the learning state a forward delay timer is again initialized. The bridge will then receive and process all user data frames but will still not forward them. This enables the bridge to precharge its filter database by caching any source address to port mappings it learns (i.e., each new source MAC address observed by the bridge is placed in a table together with the ID of the receiving port). Upon expiration of the forward delay timer, the bridge will enter either the forwarding or the blocking state.

- Forwarding—The bridge becomes fully activated. User traffic is forwarded using the filter tables to determine which ports to send packets to. Even when the bridge starts to forward frames, it is always updating this filter database with new or updated information on station locations. A bridge makes essentially three forwarding decisions, as follows:

  - Local destination—If the bridge knows that the destination station is on the same segment as the source address in the frame, it will discard the frame (there is no need to transmit it, since both stations can see each other's traffic).

■ Remote destination—If the bridge knows that the destination station is on another segment, it forwards the frame only to the interface attached to that segment.

■ Unknown destination—If the bridge has no knowledge of where the destination station resides (e.g., if that station has not transmitted any data so far), then the bridge forwards the frame on all segments except the interface attached to the source segment and any ports in the blocking state (a technique known as flooding).

● Blocking—In this phase only bridge management frames are received; no user traffic is forwarded, and no bridge management frames are forwarded, since the port is neither a designated nor a root port. Once ports are determined to be either root or designated ports the port enters the listening state.

● Disabled—The port is disabled through software by the system administrator.

The precharging stage (learning) is important in busy networks. During the forwarding state the bridge knows nothing of the whereabouts of end-station devices. If the bridge were to go straight into a forwarding condition, then it would have no choice but to send all packets to every other port except the received port (rather like a multicast or broadcast packet). On a busy network this would result in an unhealthy surge of traffic until sufficient knowledge is acquired to discard packets intelligently.

Loop avoidance

IEEE 802.1d–compliant transparent bridges require that there be only a single active path between any two LANs in an internetwork. This ensures that frames do not loop around the topology and multiply. Transparent bridges rely on the Spanning Tree Protocol (STP) to resolve potential loops and provide automatic topology recovery from network or bridge failures. Without STP, the transparent bridge algorithm fails when there are multiple paths between bridges connected subnetworks. Consider the bridging loops created in Figure 9.6.

In Figure 9.6(a), we have a bridging loop created by two non-STA bridges. Let's suppose that Node-A transmits a frame destined for Node-B. Both Bridge-1 and Bridge-2 receive the frame from Network-1 and correctly conclude that Node-A is on Network-1. Both bridges cache Node-A's source address against if-1. Node-B subsequently receives two copies of

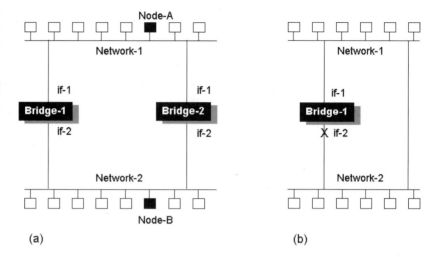

Figure 9.6
*(a) Bridging loop
created by two non-
STA bridges.
(b) Loop created
with a simple
Spanning Tree
topology.*

Node-A's frame, so we have doubled the traffic on Network-2 and possibly confused Node-B. Worse still, both bridges now see the frame propagated from their peer on their Network-2. At this point we should expect both bridges to immediately change their internal tables so that Node-A is now cached on if-2, and the entry associated with if-1 should be flushed (you might want to check this with your bridges, since I have come across some that do not!). If this is the case, when Node-B replies to Node-A's frame, both bridges receive and subsequently drop the reply, since their mapping tables now indicate that the destination address (Node-A) is local (i.e., on the same interface as the source address). So we will not see a reply at Node-A, since we have lost communication (even though we have plenty of it physically). Note that the situation could be worse; if the bridges do not flush old address-interface associations, then traffic could simply loop and multiply exponentially, causing a network meltdown.

In addition to basic connectivity issues, we can see some even more crippling problems with broadcasts and multicasts. Assume that Node-A's initial frame is an ARP broadcast. After the initial replication of the frame, both bridges will forward the frames continuously, using all available network bandwidth and inhibiting the transmission of other packets on both segments. We call this a broadcast storm, the networking equivalent of acoustic feedback.

In Figure 9.6(b) we see a single Spanning Tree bridge connecting two LANs. The fact that there is a parallel loop means that a loop is created. In this example the bridge will automatically elect itself as root, detect the loop, and close down one of its ports (by placing it into a blocking state). The process by which this is achieved is explained in the next section.

Spanning Tree Algorithm (STA)

The Spanning Tree Protocol (STP) uses a Spanning Tree Algorithm (STA) to eliminate logical loops in a bridged network topology, while providing automatic rerouting around failures to preserve the network integrity. You may remember that a Spanning Tree is a loop-free subset of a graph (i.e., the network topology), which includes all nodes. Graph theory states: For any connected graph consisting of nodes and edges connecting pairs of nodes, there is a Spanning Tree of edges that maintains the connectivity of the graph but contains no loops.

The STP algorithm works by automatically configuring a loop-free subset of the network topology, a single Spanning Tree. It achieves this by placing all bridge interfaces, which, if forwarding, would create loops, into a standby, or blocking, state. Blocked ports can be switched to forward in the event of link failure to provide an alternate path through the internetwork. STP is relatively simple in that, unlike more sophisticated routing protocols such as RIP and OSPF, it does not distribute sufficient information for bridges to know what the actual topology is. In effect, it works by aligning bridges based on relatively simple messages passed from an elected master (called the root bridge) and implements fairly long hold-down timers to ensure that all bridges have sufficient time to realign themselves after a failure.

Spanning Tree bridges communicate with their neighbors using configuration messages called Bridge Protocol Data Units (BPDUs). Bridges are constantly listening on all ports to each other's transmissions. All bridge topology decisions are made locally; there is no central authority on network topology or administration. The Spanning Tree calculation occurs when the bridge is powered up and whenever a topology change is detected. The calculation requires communication between the Spanning Tree bridges, which is accomplished through configuration messages (BPDUs). Configuration messages contain information identifying the bridge that is presumed to be the root (root identifier) and the distance from the sending bridge to the root bridge (root path cost). Configuration messages also contain the bridge and port identifier of the sending bridge and the age of information contained in the configuration message.

The Spanning Tree algorithm calls for each bridge to be assigned a unique identifier. Typically, this identifier is one of the bridge's MAC

Figure 9.7
*Starting
topology—only
STA BPDUs are
circulating at this
time.*

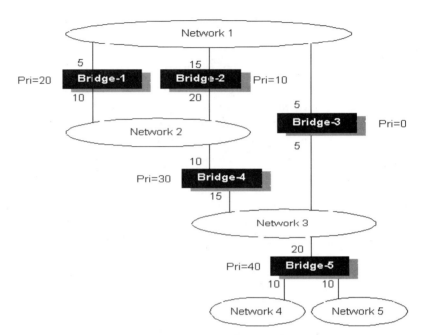

addresses plus a priority. Each port in every bridge is also assigned a unique (within that bridge) identifier (typically, its own MAC address). Finally, each bridge port is associated with a path cost. The path cost is the cost of transmitting a frame onto a LAN through that interface. In Figure 9.7, path costs are noted on the lines emanating from each bridge. Path costs are usually defaulted but can be assigned manually by network administrators.

The first activity in the Spanning Tree algorithm is the election of the root bridge, which is the bridge with the lowest value bridge identifier. The root bridge transmits periodic Hello-BPDUs.

Next, the root port on all other bridges is determined. A root port is the port through which the root bridge can be reached (i.e., the upstream port) with the least aggregate path cost. This value (the least aggregate path cost to the root) is called the root path cost. All bridges append their path costs to the BPDUs received on their root ports and send them out of their downstream ports. At this stage the network still has loops, but there is still no regular traffic being forwarded other than BPDUs.

Finally, designated bridges and their designated ports are determined. A designated bridge is the bridge on each LAN that provides the minimum path cost back to the root bridge. A LAN's designated bridge is the only bridge allowed to forward frames to and from the LAN for which it is the

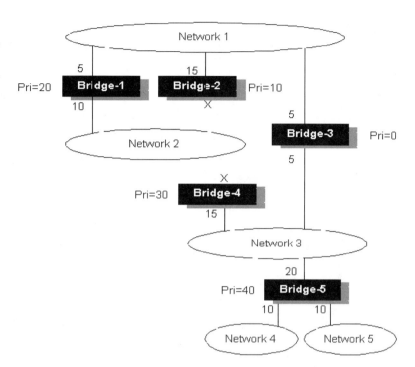

Figure 9.8
Loop-free bridged network after Bridge-3 is elected root.

designated bridge. A designated port is the root port on a designated bridge. All highest-cost downstream ports are blocked, leaving only the least-cost paths available.

The result is a single Spanning Tree with lowest-path costs aligned toward the current root bridge. It is important to note that if a different root bridge is subsequently elected, then, depending where that bridge is, the entire topology could change considerably. In the example network in Figure 9.7, Bridge-3 has the lowest priority and so is elected root (all bridges attached to the same LANs defer when they hear BPDUs of lower priority). The resulting topology is shown in Figure 9.8.

In some cases, two or more bridges can have the same root path cost. For example, in Figure 9.7, Bridges-2 and -4 both have a root path cost of 15. If Bridge-1 were to fail, then these two bridges would tie, and the lowest priority bridge would win (Bridge-2).

Bridges exchange configuration messages at regular intervals (typically two seconds). If a bridge fails, then neighboring bridges will quickly detect the absence of configuration messages and initiate a Spanning Tree recalculation. In Figure 9.9 we see a different way of representing the topology.

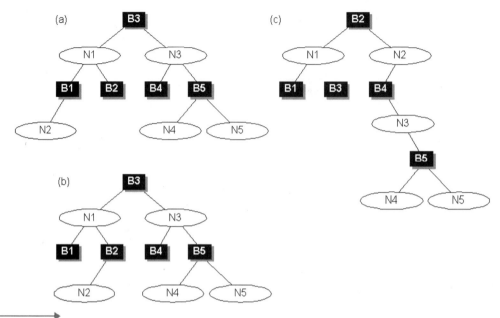

Figure 9.9   *Changes in Spanning Tree topology. (a) Stable topology with Bridge-3 as root. (b) Stable topology after Bridge-1 loses its interface to Network 1. (c) Stable topology after Bridge-3 dies, forcing the election of Bridge-2 as root bridge.*

Figure 9.9(a) shows the same stable topology shown in Figure 9.8. Figure 9.9(b) shows the result of Bridge-1 losing its interface with Network 2. Figure 9.9(c) illustrates a completely new topology, resulting from Bridge-3 dying. In this case Bridge-2 takes over (next lowest priority) and the whole network is realigned.

For this reason it is important to consider the order in which roots are to be prioritized to minimize disruption throughout the network. If bridges with priorities similar to the root are located closest to the root, then peripheral bridges do not necessarily have to reorient themselves if the root is subsequently reelected. For example, in Figure 9.9(c), Bridge-4 has to swap designated and root ports completely after Bridge-2 becomes root.

BPDU frame format

Field definitions

- Protocol identifier—Set to zero.

- Version—Set to zero.

- Message type—Set to zero.

- Flag—A one-byte field, of which only the first two bits are used. The topology change (TC) bit signals a topology change. The Topology Change Acknowledgment (TCA) bit is set to acknowledge receipt of a configuration message with the TC bit set.

- Root ID—Identifies the root bridge by listing its two-byte priority followed by its six-byte ID.

- Root path cost—Contains the cost of the path from the bridge sending the configuration message to the root bridge.

- Bridge ID—Identifies the priority and ID of the bridge sending the message.

- Port ID—Identifies the port from which the configuration message was sent. This field allows loops created by multiple attached bridges to be detected and dealt with.

- Message age—Specifies the amount of time since the root sent the configuration message on which the current configuration message is based.

- Maximum age—Indicates when the current configuration message should be deleted.

- Hello time—Provides the time period between root bridge configuration messages.

- Forward delay—Provides the length of time that bridges should wait before transitioning to a new state after a topology change. If a bridge transitions too soon, not all network links may be ready to change their state, and loops can result.

Transparent bridges exchange configuration messages and topology change messages. Configuration messages are sent between bridges to establish a network topology. Topology change messages are sent after a topology change has been detected to indicate that the STA should be rerun. The IEEE 802.1d configuration message format is shown in Figure 9.10.

Topological change messages consist of only four bytes. They include a protocol identifier field, which contains the value 0; a version field, which contains the value 0; and a message type field, which contains the value 128. An example Hello-BPDU is shown in Figure 9.11. For further information on the Spanning Tree algorithm and protocol the interested reader is referred to reference [1].

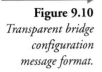

Figure 9.10
*Transparent bridge
configuration
message format.*

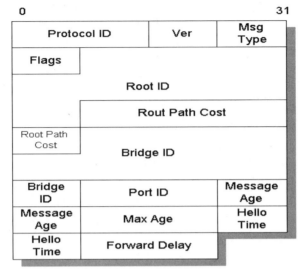

Timers

The key timers used to control Spanning Tree protocol operations are
Forwarding_Delay, Message_Age, Root_Hello_Time, and Max_Age. A
Spanning Tree BPDU is considered valid only if:

Message_Age + Root_Hello_Time < Max_Age

So with a Root_Hello_Time of 2 seconds and a Max_Age of 20 seconds,
the Message_Age must be less than 18 seconds for the frame to remain

```
File:PPLOT1.SYC      Type:SNIFFER_SYC  Mode:•••••••  Records:480
==============================================================================
Frame    : 1                 Len     : 39            Error    : None
T Elapsed: 12:58:03:331      T Delta : 00:00:00:003
-----------------------------[WAN]--------------------------------------------
Dst Addr : DTE               Src Addr : DCE
-----------------------------[ppp encap]--------------------------------------
Address  : FF                Control  : 03
-----------------------------[ppp]--------------------------------------------
Type     : PID               Protocol : 802.1D Hello
-----------------------------[ieee stp]---------------------------------------
STA Pri  : 0                 STA Ver  : 0          BPDU Type: CONFIG_BPDU
Flags    : 0                 Root Pri : 256        Root ID  : This Bridge
Root Cost: 00000000          Brdge Pri: 256        Bridge ID: 08008701ff84
Port ID  : 0x8002            Msg Age  : 0    secs  Max Age  : 20    secs
T_Hello  : 2    secs         Forw Del : 15   secs
=============================[data:   0]======================================
```

Figure 9.11   *Typical STA Hello-BPDU.*

valid. Note that even though bridges throughout the network may be configured with different local Hello times (this is not recommended), the Hello interval used by all bridges in a Spanning Tree is determined by the active root bridge. All bridges synchronize with the Root_Hello_Time passed in its Hello-BPDUs.

The minimum forwarding delay should be consistent with the formula:

$$2 \times (\text{Forwarding\_Delay} - 1 \text{ sec}) = \text{Max\_Age}$$

So a Forwarding_Delay of 15 seconds would result in a Max_Age of 28 seconds.

The DEC Spanning Tree algorithm

The Spanning Tree protocol was originally developed by Digital Equipment Corporation, one of the founding Ethernet vendors. DEC's algorithm was subsequently revised by the IEEE 802 committee and published in the IEEE 802.1d specification. It is important to note that the DEC algorithm and the subsequent IEEE 802.1d algorithm are not the same, nor are they compatible. If both algorithms are implemented in the same network, then you will need to be extra careful to avoid some potentially nasty looping problems. Key points to understand are as follows:

- Typically the two algorithms use different destination multicast addresses by default, and, if both are activated, they will be invisible to each other (causing potential loops on the network, which may be difficult to debug).

- It is possible to run both algorithms together if you really must, but you should only do this by isolating the parts of the topology to be controlled by each algorithm with a well-defined interface between the two domains. Specifically, do not allow Spanning Tree domains to overlap.

- You should also check the filter configuration on non-DEC bridges, since there may be default filters configured to block DEC multicast addresses, and this can cause problems when troubleshooting loops in multivendor bridged environments.

9.2.2 Design guidelines

The following guidelines are provided:

- Maximum bridges in series—Bridges do incur some delay, and therefore there are guidelines to the number you should install in series in a network design. For transparent bridges such as Ethernet bridges the recommended maximum number in series is seven.

- Bridge placement—I have seen several real examples of bridges being positioned where they either do more harm than good or no good at all.

  - In general you should aim to get at least a rough idea of where the major sources and sinks of traffic are, and use bridges to isolate users and devices into sensible partitions.
  - Placing a bridge in between a server and a user group generally does nothing but slow things down. This could be a valid thing to do if there is significant client-to-client traffic or significant or sensitive server-to-server traffic and you want to protect each segment and thereby lower the overall traffic. Another possible justification is the case where the device is a multiport switch (each port representing a user or server), where internal filtering processes enable traffic to be forwarded quickly and efficiently.

- Bridge timers—In general you should avoid changing the default timers unless absolutely necessary, or you are prepared to document and manage your network proactively. On a network where topology convergence is paramount, you may want to speed up Spanning Tree reconfigurations by shortening the Hello timer and decreasing the listening and learning periods. One important trade-off here is that on busy networks decreasing the learning period significantly can result in a large traffic surge once the forwarding bridges kick in.

- Control root bridge election—On any reasonably sized bridge network (i.e., more than just a couple of bridges), you should proactively configure which bridges will become root. Try to aim for a bridge in the center of the topology (i.e., a bridge with roughly the same number of hops to all other bridges).

- Control backup root bridges—Often overlooked, but nevertheless important is the election of a new root bridge when the primary bridge fails. In this case try to ensure that you nominate bridges closest to the primary root bridge in the topology; this way if the main root bridge dies many of the remaining bridges will maintain the same orientation with the new root. This will speed up convergence after a root bridge failure by minimizing the impact of the new election process on all other bridges.

- STA bridges should not be underpowered, since they are doing considerably more than just forwarding traffic. There have been examples of early STA bridges with insufficient processing power to handle heavy traffic conditions and STA concurrently; the results are potentially chaotic, leading to network meltdown (imagine if a bridge starts to drop BPDUs or cannot forward them in time under load; we would see oscillations in the Spanning Tree, loops, and potentially broadcast storms).

- Potential address conflicts must be dealt with prior to joining LANs via bridges. When two LANs are interconnected via bridges, they effectively become one single address space. If you have poorly administered IP addressing schemes on one or both of these LANs, you could waste considerable time tracking down duplicate address issues. Either resolve possible problems beforehand, or ensure that addressing is handled centrally (from a common DHCP server, for example).

- Interoperability—In the LAN environment most bridges should work with each other quite well. There may be some issues with older bridges running prestandard Spanning Tree, or bridges running proprietary Spanning Tree, but most of the time you should not see any issues. In the WAN environment different vendors' bridges often will not interoperate, or interwork, with reduced functionality. Typically the only choice for interoperability is via the PPP protocol over a serial link. In general it is advisable to run bridges in pairs, with the same vendor at each end of the wide area link.

9.3   Source Route Bridging (SRB)

Source Route Bridging (SRB) is covered by IEEE 802.5d and implemented by IBM and several of the major bridge vendors for use over Token Ring LANs. SRB is a Layer 2 function (the term routing is somewhat misleading) and operates between two Token Ring LANs, connected via either a local or a wide area link. Both 4 Mbps and 16 Mbps ring speeds are supported. SRB is far more popular in Token Ring environments than either translation bridging or Source Route Transparent (SRT) bridging (described later).

Source routing is fundamentally different from transparent bridging in that the onus is placed on hosts (rather than the bridges) to provide and maintain routing information when transmitting frames. This enables source routing to offer more flexibility and several distinct advantages over transparent bridging. For example, source routing enables multiple active routes to be used to forward traffic rather than the single Spanning Tree, increasing both the throughput and overall efficiency of the network (each host uses a specific path between source and destination, but different source-destination pairs may use different paths concurrently). Source routing also allows a host to determine the MTU for any given path.

9.3.1   Operation

In source route bridging the node transmitting a frame specifies the path that should be taken over an internetwork and includes the path in every frame sent in a special field called the Routing Information Field (RIF), illustrated in Figure 9.12. This is in contrast to transparent bridging, where the bridges make the routing decision. In order to forward packets efficiently, the transmitting node must first establish the best path to a specific destination, using a discovery process. To facilitate this, networks and bridges are configured with a 12-bit and 4-bit address, respectively. Bridge IDs can be reused within the same extended LAN as long as the bridges with the same ID are not running in parallel.

The Routing Information Field (RIF)

The RIF (see Figure 9.12) is an extension of the source MAC address field. The RIF starts with a 16-bit Route Control Field (RCF) header, followed by zero or more 16-bit Route Descriptor Fields (RDFs—sometimes called a route designator). The RCF contains key information on the type of frame being sent and how the information should be handled. The RDF contains pairs of ring and bridge numbers (12 and 4 bits, respectively). The size of the RIF, and hence the number of RDF ring-bridge pairs, is theoretically constrained by the length field within the RCF header. The length field is 5 bits wide, allowing up to 32 bytes in total. Subtracting the 2 bytes of the RCF itself leaves 30 bytes, equivalent to 15 RDF fields of 2 bytes each. In

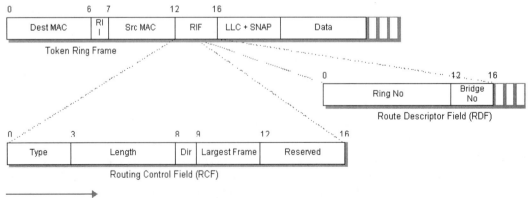

Figure 9.12   *Structure of the RIF field.*

practice the number of RDFs is constrained to meet the seven-bridge constraint on network diameter (primarily a limitation imposed by IBM, which effectively controls the SR bridging standards).

Field definitions

- Routing control field (16 bits)

  - Type (3 bits)—The routing type field identifies the frame as either an explorer frame or an explicitly routed frame. Values (in binary) are as follows:

    001 Specifically Routed Frame (SRF)

    100 All Routes Explorer (ARE)

    110 Spanning Tree Explorer, All Routes Explorer return

    111 Spanning Tree Explorer, Spanning Tree return

  - Length (5 bits)—Total length of the RIF field in bytes. The minimum value is 2 (just the RCF present), and the maximum value is 30. In practice some implementations limit the maximum value to support only seven RDFs, which determine the radius on a Token Ring network.

  - Direction (1 bit)—Used to indicate in which direction to read the RDF entries. Cleared equals left to right and vice versa.

  - Largest frame (3 bits)—Indicates the MTU size supported over a particular path, in binary this can be:

    000 Up to 516 bytes, IEEE 802.2 LLC and ISO 8473 CLNP

    001 Up to 1,500 bytes, IEEE 802.3 Ethernet

    010 Up to 2,052 bytes, an 80 × 24 character screen plus control information

    011 Up to 4,472 bytes, IEEE 802.5 Token Ring 4 Mbps and FDDI

    100 Up to 8,144 bytes, IEEE 802.4 Token Bus

    101 Up to 11,407 bytes, IEEE 802.5 Token Ring 4 Mbps burst errors unprotected

    110 Up to 17,800 bytes, IEEE 802.5 Token Ring 16 Mbps

    111 Up to 65,535 bytes, Interpreted as ANY size and used in an all routes broadcast frame.

  - Reserved (4 bits)—Unused

- Route descriptor (or route designator) field—A 16-bit field containing ring/bridge ID pairs

    - Ring number (12 bits)—The ring ID. This is configurable on all SRBs.
    - Bridge number (4 bits)—The bridge ID

    If a frame is received by a bridge with the RDF field full, it must be discarded.

Since there was no place for the Route Information Indicator (RII) bit in the original IBM specifications, the bit selected is the group/individual bit of the source MAC address field. Clearly, if this were set in the destination address, it would indicate a multicast frame, but in the source address field there is no such convention, so it was commandeered for this use by IBM. If the RII bit is set, an SRB will forward the frame; if cleared, then an SRB will assume that the two stations communicating are local to the ring.

Host-to-host communications

When a Token Ring station wishes to transmit data to another station for which it does not have routing information, it will first issue a probe, in the form of an Exchange Identification (XID) frame, onto the local ring. For example, in Figure 9.13 Node-A wishes to transmit data to Node-B, so Node-A sends out a local XID probe onto network 100. In this case the XID frame circulates the ring and is returned back to Node-A without any positive indication that Node-B has seen it (i.e., the AR and AC bits are not set). Node-A must therefore assume that Node-B resides on a remote network, and a route discovery process is initiated.

The next step varies depending upon the implementation, since the standards were never entirely clear on the various applications of Spanning Tree explorer frames. In essence an explorer frame must be sent, addressed to the destination node, to discover a path to that destination. As the explorer frame crosses bridges and networks, it grows in size by aggregating ring numbers and bridge IDs in the Routing Information Field (RIF). The explorer frame can also collect other useful information on a path, such as the minimum MTU required. The difference in implementations lies in the type of explorer issued and whether or not Spanning Tree is enabled on intermediate bridges, as described in the following scenarios:

- Scenario 1—In this scenario the generally accepted doctrine is that the source node sends out an All Routes Explorer (ARE) with a length set to two bytes (since there are no router descriptor fields

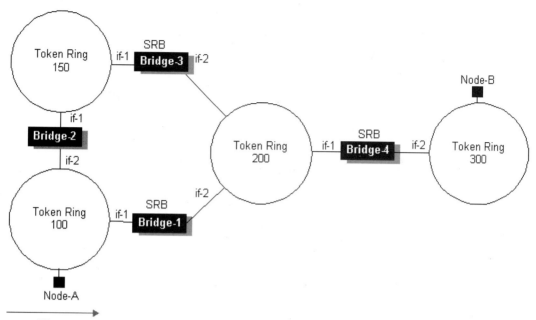

Figure 9.13   *Source route bridging.*

within the RIF field at this stage). In this case Node-B should receive multiple copies of the discovery frame, since there are multiple paths from Node-A to Node-B. Once ARE frames reach the destination, Node-B caches any routes (from the RIF fields), and then returns each frame as a specifically routed frame with the direction bit in the RCF flipped to 1 to indicate that the route should be interpreted backwards. In this way a frame is returned down each available path back to the source.

- Scenario 2—In this scenario (typically the IBM implementation) the transmitting node issues a single-route broadcast (i.e., RCF type 6— Spanning Tree Explorer, All Routes Explorer return). In this case Node-B should, therefore, receive only one copy of the discovery frame. When explorer frames arrive at Node-B, it must respond with a discovery response frame marked all-routes broadcast. This will contain the most significant bit; the Route Information Indicator (RII), set in the source MAC address field; and a single RDF entry with the bridge number set to 0, and the ring number set to 300. The direction bit (Dir) is normally flipped in the RCF for the return path. Since the response frame is marked all-routes broadcast, it will pass through all bridges and rings on its way to Node-A. Each bridge must insert its bridge and associated ring number, so in effect the route is built up in reverse (contrary to scenario 1).

In both scenarios Node-A will receive several response frames, and it is Node-A's responsibility to cache the most efficient route based on predetermined criteria. In our example Node-A will receive frames indicating two paths to Node-B, as follows:

- Route 1—Ring 100 to Bridge-1 to Ring 200 to Bridge-4 to Ring 300

- Route 2—Ring 100 to Bridge-2 to Ring 150 to Bridge-3 to Ring 200 to Bridge-4 to Ring 300

The IEEE 802.5 specification does not mandate the criteria Node-A should use in choosing a route, but it does include several suggestions, as follows:

- First frame received

- The response with the minimum number of hops

- The response with the largest allowed frame size

- Combinations of the above criteria

In most cases, the path contained in the first frame received will be used, and in this case we are most likely to choose Route 1, all bridge and link performances being equal. Once a route is cached at the hosts, the same path will be used for all subsequent traffic between them. In practice stations do not cache routing information for long periods to keep routing table sizes small and ensure that topology information is reasonably dynamic. If both hosts were on the same ring, then the Route Information Indicator (RII) bit is cleared to stop traffic leaking through bridges unnecessarily.

Spanning Tree operations

We described the Spanning Tree Algorithm (STA) in Section 9.2. Spanning Tree may be disabled by default in some SRB implementations. When enabled, however, there is a subtle difference between the way that the STA works in an SRB environment. Unlike transparent bridging, in SRB networks STA ports in the blocking state only block non–source-routed traffic and Spanning Tree Explorer frames. This enables source-routed traffic to employ the RIF field to provide alternate paths and maximize bandwidth efficiency, as described previously. This also means that broadcast and multicast traffic can be forwarded down a single multicast tree, rather than duplicating such traffic through all paths.

Extended source route bridging

BAY Networks, Inc. (now part of Northern Telecom) has implemented an extension to basic source route bridging in its router product line. Extended source routing enables end systems to support both local source route bridging and internetwork routing and eliminates the seven-hop bridge restrictions imposed by implementations such as that offered by IBM. Routers use source route Explorer packets to build the routing tables dynamically, and each router can reset the hop count to zero as it forwards packets onto the next router. This protocol improves reliability, improves scalability, and decreases network response time.

9.3.2 Design guidelines

In a Token Ring environment there are several reasons why a network designer would consider extended the LAN via bridging. These include the following:

- To create separate traffic domains—The classic justification for installing any bridge; this has minimal impact on the design.

- To avoid accumulated jitter—In Token Ring LANs frames travel down different sections of the cable at slightly different speeds and this results in jitter. To counteract this Token Ring networks limit the number of hosts that can be attached to a LAN (260 for STP or fiber and 72 for UTP, although some vendors may support larger numbers). When a bridge is installed, the jitter is effectively zeroed across bridged interfaces.

- To transport nonroutable protocols over extended LANs—Token Ring environments are typically users of IBM protocols, such as SNA, LU6.2, and NetBIOS. None of these protocols incorporates a routing layer.

The following guidelines are provided when designing SRB extended LANs:

- Bridge IDs—Bridge IDs are a limited resource (a 4-bit quantity). You can use more than 16 bridge IDs by using duplicate bridge IDs, so long as the bridges with the same ID are not running directly in parallel (i.e., not connecting the same two rings directly). In smaller networks it is recommended that you choose unique bridge IDs to simplify the design and avoid routing issues.

- Ring numbers—Ring numbers do not have to be unique within a Token Ring LAN; however, where multiple bridges are attached to a ring, all bridge ports must use the same ring number. Within a single bridge all ports should be assigned different ring numbers.

- Maximum bridges in series—In implementations where the network radius is constrained to bridge seven hops, this limitation should not be exceeded. Nodes more than seven hops away will not be able to communicate.

- Shortest paths in source routing are response based. In source routing, the shortest path is determined by the fastest response to an Explorer frame. Regardless of the number of hops involved, the fastest response will be chosen.

- Parallel bridges are supported. So long as bridge IDs can be differentiated between two rings it is possible to support multiple bridge paths. Since the paths chosen are based on response time, this can allow both resilient links and some measure of load sharing to be implemented between Token Ring LANs (session based rather than packet based). Source routing enables logical meshing of the traffic.

- Source routing does not scale. Aside from the seven-hop limit, broadcasts from protocols such as ARP, RARP, and BOOTP will propagate throughout the extended LAN, so SRB networks have the same inherent scalability problems of transparent bridging.

- Be aware of performance trade-offs. SRB adds more traffic overhead than conventional bridging, since each frame will contain complete routing information as well as protocol data. On the plus side, SRB bridges have to do very little work when making frame-forwarding decisions.

The designer should be aware that there are potential problems with the A and C bits (MAC layer acknowledgments) when interconnecting with transparent bridges, since the standards have never quite resolved these issues for Token Ring bridges (the FDDI bridging standards do). These issues are discussed in the next section.

9.4   Source Route Transparent Bridging (SRT)

The IEEE 802.1 committee identified the need for source route bridges to interoperate with transparent bridges in the same internetwork. The result was a standard called Source Route Transparent Bridging (SRT). Note, however, that SRT bridges operate only between two Token Ring LANs and are covered in an unapproved IEEE 802.1m standard. SRT bridges do not perform conversion between Token Ring and Ethernet LANs.

9.4.1 Operation

The basic operation of SRT bridges is quite simple. The bridge inspects all received frames and checks the Routing Information Indicator (RII). If the RII is set, the bridge acts as a source route bridge and inspects the Routing Information Field (RIF). If not set, the bridge operates in transparent mode and forwards frames based on their MAC destination address (using information built up in the learning tables). In order to achieve this the Token Ring chipset in the bridge has to be in mixed mode.

SRT bridges do not allow source route bridge nodes to communicate with transparent bridge nodes; even though an SRT bridge can understand both source route bridging and transparent bridging, it does not perform translation between frame types (in effect an SRT bridge has a split personality). SRT bridges also introduce a problem with the A (address recognized) and C (frame copied) bits in the Token Ring frame status field. Source routing bridges use the RIF fields to decide how to set A and C, but bridges in transparent mode do not look at the RIF. This leads to several possible solutions, none of which is perfect, as follows:

- Never set A and C. This means that any frames forwarded by the bridge for remote nodes will return around the ring and be interpreted by the sender as unacknowledged. The sender will continue to retransmit and may subsequently get a response. The sending node may then get very confused, since the reply is good, but there is no record of the receiver acknowledging and copying the original frame (since A and C were never set). Needless to say this can cause a variety of problems.

- Always set A and C. If both the source and destination nodes are on the same ring, this will result in a duplicate address error being sent to the ring error monitor (often the bridge itself) for every frame modified.

- Conditionally set A and C. This is the smarter way of doing things but still problematic. The bridge will set A and C if it forwards frames with the knowledge that the destination node is not on the local ring. The problem is that it can learn of a station's whereabouts only by listening for traffic, and if the receiver has not transmitted any packets to date, then there is the possibility that the bridge forwards the frame, sets A and C, and the local host receives the frame. Again, a duplicate address event is generated, but the scale of the problem is much smaller.

The IEEE 802.1m standard suggests that A and C are always set by the bridge. The error reports for duplicate addresses can be disabled, but this will need to be configured for all rings in the network.

Spanning Tree

Spanning Tree on the transparent bridge interfaces runs independently from the source route Spanning Tree and supports all the traditional functionality. This means that multiple SRT bridges can be placed in parallel, but be aware that any interring source route traffic passing over the transparent network will only go down the active path, and load balancing is not supported.

9.4.2   Design guidelines

The following guidelines are provided when designing SRT extended LANs:

- Applications—Because of the many limitations of SRT, in real life these bridges are often used in source route only mode. SRT bridges can be used to enable interring communication between hosts whose drivers cannot support source route Explorer traffic. Figure 9.14 shows an example where SRT is required between ring 400 and 200.

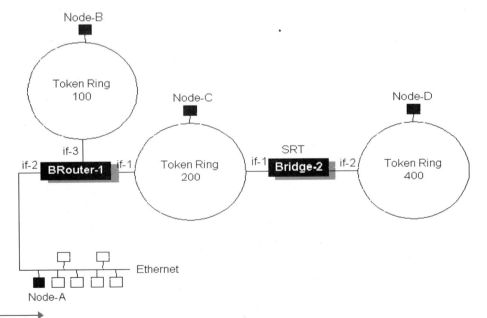

Figure 9.14   *SRT bridges enable interring communication.*

Traffic between ring 100 and 200 does not require SRT; frames have the RII bit set and are source routed by Brouter-1. Traffic between rings 100, 200, and the Ethernet LAN does not require SRT, since the RII bit will be cleared; frames will be sent transparently. Traffic between ring 200 and 400 is source routed as normal. SRT bridging is required where node D, on ring 400, has old drivers that do not support source route Explorer frames.

- Plug-and-play mode—SRT bridges do not need to have ring or bridge IDs configured if they are to operate only in transparent mode (i.e., as transparent Token Ring bridges). In small networks this can be very attractive, since they are quick and easy to deploy.

- SRT and SR bridges in parallel—If you design an SRT bridge and SR bridge in parallel, then the SR bridge will operate only in backup mode (assuming that hosts on the rings can send source route Explorer frames). Since all hosts transmit their first frame with the RII bit clear, the SRT bridge will always forward the traffic.

- End-to-end paths must be consistent—SRT bridges do not perform any frame translation between transparent and source route formats. A pure translation mode frame can never pass through a pure SRB ring, and the end-to-end path must be supported by SRT bridges.

9.5   Translation bridging

Given the huge range of issues that translation bridges need to resolve, some commentators have classified translation bridges as an engineering triumph over common sense. The basic idea with translation bridging is that different MAC layers must be completely translated so that interworking between different media types on different interfaces is entirely transparent and requires no setup by the user. Stations on either side of the bridge communicate as if they were directly connected. Considering that we are talking about media such as Ethernet, Token Ring, and FDDI, each with different MTU sizes, frame formats, and bit ordering, this is no mean feat, especially when you consider that this must all be achieved at wire speed forwarding rates. A translation bridge must deal with a number of difficult issues when converting between different media, as follows:

- Interface speeds

- Bit ordering (Big Endian or Little Endian)

- MAC address formats

- MTU sizes

- Routing mechanism (source routing, transparent, etc.)

- Frame formats (type/length, LSAPs, SNAP)

- Protocol irregularities (e.g., embedded addressing)

- Spanning Tree operations

We will now look at how Token Ring and Ethernet networks can be connected and how FDDI and Ethernet networks can be connected via translation bridges. Note that there is no current standard for translation between FDDI and Token Ring, so most network designers will use either encapsulation bridging or native source route bridging techniques.

9.5.1   FDDI-to-Ethernet translation

In this scenario, translation bridging passes packets between FDDI and Ethernet so that on either medium the packets appear to be from a locally attached device. This operation is covered by the IEEE 802.1h standard. Figure 9.15 shows an example network with an FDDI backbone and two Ethernet LANs attached via translation bridges. IEEE 802.h operates the same Spanning Tree for Ethernet and Token Ring. In Figure 9.15 both the FDDI and Ethernet interfaces act as independent transparent tree bridges, compatible with IEEE 802.1.

In this example, hosts A, B, C, and D can all communicate transparently. Frames in transit between the Ethernet LANs are placed on the FDDI ring and forwarded between the two bridges. To comply with FDDI MAC procedures, these transit frames must be removed from the ring; however, since the frames do not have source MAC addresses that match any device

Figure 9.15
Ethernet-to-FDDI translation bridging.

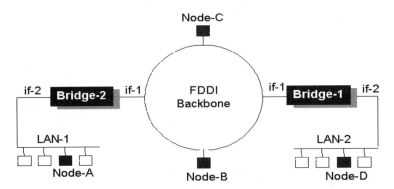

on the ring, they cannot be removed in the normal way (usually this would be done by the sending device on the ring). To complicate matters further, the standards in this area specify only that frames should be removed but do not specify the mechanism. In practice, bridges either maintain a database of source addresses for frames transmitted or transmit a marker frame on the ring to indicate when the bridge should remove frames.

As with any IEEE 802.1–compliant bridge, all interfaces of the bridges operate in mixed learning mode. On the FDDI interfaces this requires a very high filtering rate from the FDDI chipset, so these bridges typically use Content Addressable Memory (CAM) to optimize forwarding lookups. The maximum rate for an FDDI ring is 446,000 fps using 28-byte frames. On real networks the frame size is typically much larger and frame rates lower, since FDDI is usually employed as a backbone interconnect between LANs for remote file transfer client/server interaction. Another issue is the size of the learning table, which tends to be large on such bridges, since they are typically used as backbone devices and stored in CAM. Table size can limit scalability, since bridge networks have a flat address space, so some high-end vendors allow the tables to be extended.

Design issues

There are several nontrivial issues to be resolved in the translation process, including the following:

- Bit ordering—Ethernet uses noncanonical bit ordering (least significant bit first), and FDDI uses canonical ordering (least significant bit last). Translation is resolved by the bridge internally and is not a concern for the network designer. However, one potential area of conflict arising from bit reversal is address translation.

- Address resolution—ARP and RARP pose particular problems in this environment and require specific software enhancements in the bridges to cope. The problem here is that these protocols carry addressing information in their data fields, and, since bit ordering is reversed between media types, this addressing information becomes reversed on a byte level. For example, 1.1.1.1 becomes 128.128.128.128 when bit reversed. Either the bridge must explicitly deal with ARP and RARP by reversing the relevant data fields, or the drivers must automatically translate addresses recovered from data fields according to the bit order preference of the interface. The latter option is recommended by RFC 1042 [2] and adopted by 802.1h bridges, which somewhat simplifies matters.

- Encapsulation—Frame formats on IEEE 802.3 and FDDI differ in several ways. A native EtherType encapsulated protocol would typically be translated into SNAP format on the FDDI, which is straightforward enough. Things may get problematic when the frame comes back off the FDDI onto the LAN, since it could be converted back into either EtherType, IEEE 802.2 encapsulation (length field plus LSAPs), or SNAP. Typically the bridge will allow you to configure the preferred encapsulation per interface. In reality you may have an application that uses IEEE 802.2 encapsulation at the server end, uses SNAP encapsulation on the backbone, and uses EtherType encapsulation at the client. Debugging such a session might prove interesting.

- MTU size—MTU size is an issue between Ethernet and FDDI. FDDI supports up to 4,352-byte frames, whereas Ethernet supports only 1,518-byte frames. Bridges cannot handle fragmentation and reassembly, so the only real course of action is to limit the MTU size on the end systems, which is consistent with IEEE 802.3h and RFC1042 [2].

- Mixed-speed buffering—FDDI and basic Ethernet operate at different speeds (100 Mbps versus 10 Mbps). Bridges do not offer any form of flow control but should have large buffers available to cope with most reasonable conditions. Under sufficient load an 802.1h bridge will silently discard packets (typically from FDDI to Ethernet). For example, a Sun workstation directly attached to an FDDI backbone could easily outpace an Ethernet-attached receiver with a UDP stream (TCP will typically back off according to the prevailing conditions).

MTU inconsistencies are a typical problem for the network designer. For example, the FDDI hosts in Figure 9.15 would have their MTU reduced to 1,500 bytes. This resolves the problem but can degrade performance on the FDDI; in particular, it penalizes high-bandwidth applications between native FDDI devices unnecessarily. The only other sensible option would be to use routing between the FDDI and Ethernet LANs and let the routing protocol use MTU Discovery to resolve the different MTU sizes optimally.

Encapsulation is also a likely area of conflict. Most translation bridges will by default translate all FDDI 802.2/SNAP frames to EtherType format (except for AppleTalk EtherTypes). On Ethernet it is, therefore, important not to have interfaces configured in 802.2./SNAP format; otherwise, communications will be lost. On older networks there may also be the issue with Novell raw frame-type encapsulation to contend with (a broken form of LLC whereby a length field is used instead of the EtherType field, but no

LSAPs). Another potential issue here is when routers and bridges are used on the same ring. Routers should be configured to use both the FDDI 802.2 and FDDI 802.2/SNAP encapsulations if stations on the Ethernet segments are configured to use different Ethernet encapsulation types.

9.5.2   Token Ring to Ethernet translation

This type of bridging is often called Source Route Translation Bridging (or SRTB) and is synonymous with the IBM 8209 translation bridge [3]. IBM 8209 is a two-port device that allows Ethernet and Token Ring hosts to communicate transparently using nonroutable protocols such as LU6.2 and NetBIOS. This, in effect, allows IBM SNA networks to deploy Ethernet LANs for workgroup users, while connecting SNA hosts onto Token Ring via cluster controllers and Front-End Processors (FEPs). Table 9.1 presents an Ethernet to Token Ring translation bridging example.

In Figure 9.16 we see two Token Ring LANs connected via a source routing bridge and an Ethernet LAN attached via a source route translation bridge. On Bridge-1, interface 2 must use mixed learning mode to build up its forwarding tables and operates as a standard Spanning Tree transparent bridge. On interface 1 Bridge-1 must use source routing; forwarding is determined by sending all-routes Explorer frames and caching the RIF responses. On the Token Ring interface the Spanning Tree protocol is used to create a single path for Explorer traffic. Note that the two Spanning Tree processes are independent of each other; there is no interaction. Spanning Tree BPDUs from either side are carried over each media type. The bridge uses its internal mapping database to make forwarding decisions between the two different media types. From the perspective of an Ethernet node the Token Ring networks appear as if they were a single Ethernet segment. From the Token Ring perspective the Ethernet appears to be a single virtual ring segment.

Table 9.1   *Ethernet to Token Ring Translation Bridging*

Ethernet				Token Ring			
if	NodeID	Encap	Age	if	NodeID	RIF	Age
2	A	V2	32	1	C		24
2	B	802	12	1	D		6
				1	E	[200]+[1]+[400]	45
				1	F	[200]+[1]+[400]	17

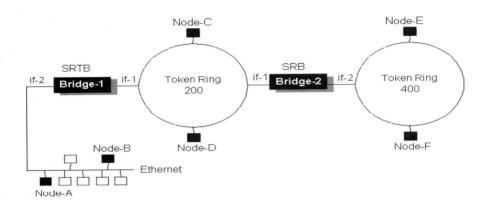

Figure 9.16   *Ethernet to Token Ring translation database mapping for Bridge-1.*

Design issues

■ Bit ordering—Ethernet uses noncanonical bit ordering (least significant bit first), and Token Ring uses canonical ordering (least significant bit last). Translation is resolved by the bridge internally and is
not a concern for the network designer.

■ MTU size—As with FDDI translation, MTU size is potentially a
major problem between Ethernet and Token Ring. Token Ring supports up to 4,500 bytes at 4 Mbps and 17,749 bytes at 16 Mbps,
whereas Ethernet supports only 1,518-byte frames. Fragmentation
and reassembly are not sensible solutions for bridging, so we should
limit the MTU size on the end systems (potentially degrading performance for some Token Ring hosts). IBM 8209 gets around this issue
by dynamically overwriting the 3-bit largest frame field within the
Token Ring Explorer frame's Route Control Field (RCF) with the
binary value 001 (indicating 1,500 bytes). This field specifies the
maximum frame size to be used, and since it is set dynamically there
is no need to configure all hosts to this value.

■ Encapsulation—Frame formats on Ethernet/802.3 and Token Ring
differ in several ways. EtherType frames being forwarded from Ethernet to the Token Ring interface are SNAP encoded. Going back the
other way the bridge will examine its internal database and see which
encapsulation the host is using before converting back into EtherType
or IEEE 802.3 encapsulation. If the bridge does not know the correct
encapsulation (e.g., the destination host may have aged out), then it
can transmit duplicate frames with both types until the database is
updated.

- Address resolution—As with FDDI we have the same problem with ARP and RARP. In this case IBM 8209 checks all packets of type 0x806 (ARP) or 0x8035 (RARP) and dynamically changes the bit order of embedded addressing data (located at fixed offsets) according to the bit order used on the appropriate interfaces. Novell IPX also embeds host MAC addresses in the Layer 3 address field (avoiding the need to ARP). Since these addresses appear in several places and under several different encapsulations, it would be very tedious to dig all these addresses out and convert on the fly. IBM 8209 enables the user to configure a feature called NetWare Awareness, which basically means that the bridge will not convert the MAC addresses portion of NetWare frames received. This can cause further problems, since frames on one side of the bridge will appear inverted and in some cases will appear as multicasts. There is no easy solution to this; in some cases the network administrator may have to identify specific problem MAC addresses and configure new soft addresses in those hosts. At the time of writing IBM 8209 did not forward AppleTalk, DECnet (Phase IV and Phase V), or OSI packets, since these would require similar fixes. Clearly, it would be advantageous for any IBM 8209–compatible products to implement multiprotocol routing to handle these protocols appropriately.

There is no real standard for translation bridging between Token Ring and Ethernet; it is an industry standard defined effectively by IBM 8209. The IEEE specifications 802.1d, 802.5d, and 802.1h cover part of the functionality required, but since IBM 8209 is neither a transparent bridge nor a source route bridge, there are features not specified in the standards. Several major bridge vendors have implemented the SRTB because of the requirement to interwork between source route bridge domains and transparent bridge domains. Some of the key vendors are IBM, Cisco, Proteon, and BAY. Many of these devices are multiport devices with support for wide area interfaces (remember that 8209 has only two LAN interfaces). In wide area translation devices there is an additional issue to solve—namely, where to perform the translation. Most devices from the main manufacturers will perform conditional translation on either incoming or outgoing interfaces according to the source and destination media types.

9.5.3 Token Ring to FDDI translation

In practice these devices are rarely deployed in networks today, although this functionality may be embedded in multiprotocol bridge router platforms. The translation process is generally far simpler than for FDDI to Ethernet translation, since FDDI and Token Ring share many similarities, not the least of which are bit order and encapsulation types. Clearly, MTU size is a potential issue, with 16-Mbps Token Ring supporting an MTU nearly four times larger than FDDI (17,749 bytes versus 4,500 bytes). To resolve this problem either Token Ring stations must be configured to use the FDDI MTU, or routing must be enabled to support fragmentation.

Another major area of conflict is the use of Source Route Bridging (SRB) and the presence of the RIF field in Token Ring frames. To resolve this problem translation bridges typically implement both a forwarding database (for transparent bridging) and a routing database (for source route bridging) and map between the two environments. In this case the source-routed environment treats the whole of the transparent environment as a single ring, with its own ring ID. Implementations may vary in this area, and you should consult the manufacturer's documentation on this matter.

9.6   Encapsulation/tunnel bridging

Encapsulation bridges come in a number of forms; we will briefly review the more important ones here.

9.6.1   Data Link Switching (DLSw)

Encapsulation (or tunnel) bridges can be used to enable Source Route Bridging (SRB) domains or transparent bridging domains to communicate across an IP internetwork. This feature is generally referred to as Data Link Switching (DLSw). The encapsulation bridge encapsulates bridged frames (from either an SRB or TB domain) inside IP packets and forwards them to the destination IP address, via standard Layer 3 IP routing protocols. The destination IP address is, in fact, another encapsulation bridge. The destination target encapsulation bridge removes the IP encapsulation to reveal the original frame, and then forwards these frames to its attached SRB domain or TB domain, as if the domain were local. From the SRB perspective the IP network is perceived as a single LAN segment, and only one hop is added to cross this IP network. The end-to-end hop count must not exceed the seven-hop count limitation imposed by some SRB implementations (this includes the number of hops from the source node to the source IP encapsulation bridge, plus one hop to cross the IP network, plus the number of hops from the destination IP encapsulation bridge to the destination node).

9.6.2   FDDI encapsulation bridging

Encapsulation bridges were the first types of bridges used to interconnect Ethernet and FDDI LANs, since the standards available at that time were too immature to consider translation. In effect, the entire Ethernet frame is simply encapsulated inside an FDDI frame, passed over the ring, and then deencapsulated by a remote FDDI bridge before forwarding onto another Ethernet LAN. Most FDDI encapsulation bridges run proprietary protocols over the FDDI ring between bridges to ensure that bridges are aware of each other. They may also advertise forwarding tables between bridges.

Encapsulation avoids many of the pitfalls and complications of translation bridging but at the expense of any communication between Ethernet and FDDI-attached stations (only Ethernet-to-Ethernet communications are supported, with the FDDI treated as a high-speed transit LAN). This could be a nonstarter if high-speed servers are attached to the FDDI ring and need to be accessible by Ethernet clients. Interoperability is also clearly one of the main concerns for a network designer; bridges typically need to be supplied from a single vendor. As a result this method of bridging is rarely used for this application, with translation bridges being the preferred option.

9.7   Virtual LANs (VLANs)

This section examines the design issues of using LAN switches when implementing virtual LANs (VLANs) and switched internetworks. VLANs are mainly applicable for campus network designs, but they are unlikely to be used exclusively. A good campus internetworking solution must combine the benefits of both routers and switches. The main benefits of incorporating switches in campus network designs (as opposed to pure bridged or routed environments) include the following:

- Higher bandwidth

- Better performance

- Lower costs

- Simplified configuration

VLAN switches impose a logical hierarchy on flat networks (unlike bridges), but they require routers to deal with interdomain traffic. VLANs resolve several major problems in flat networks, including the following:

- Scalability—A flat LAN (i.e., nonhierarchical) is a single broadcast domain and, hence, inherently not scalable because broadcast traffic becomes a much more significant proportion of the bandwidth as the number of hosts and services increases. VLANs resolve scalability problems by breaking this broadcast domain into several smaller broadcast domains called virtual LANs (essentially similar to IP subnets but based on logical addresses transparent to the user, rather than IP addresses). Broadcasts are, therefore, localized within each VLAN, and this logical segmentation is commonly referred to as VLAN communication. For example, in a broadcast domain consisting of 100 users, if the broadcast traffic is intended only for 30 of the users, then placing those 30 users on a separate VLAN will better optimize bandwidth. When compared with switches, routers have to do more processing on incoming packets. As the volume of traffic increases, so does latency, which results in performance degradation. The use of VLANs reduces the number of routers required, since VLANs create broadcast domains using Layer 2 switches instead of routers.

- The ability to form virtual workgroups—The ability to move users around easily, transparently, and cost-effectively has become an essential requirement for many enterprise networks. Since physical hardware addresses are typically fixed, the other problem VLANs are designed to resolve is how to handle moves and changes in an enterprise environment without having to constantly reassign addresses or reconfigure user workstations and ports (or worse still, reconfigure bridge filter tables). Consider the situation where the whole finance department is to be relocated to another building on a campus at short notice, and one-third of them will remain in the original office for a week. To create virtual LANs, a VLAN ID is associated with each interface on the switch, so when a user workstation is plugged into that interface, the VLAN ID is automatically associated with the user but centrally controlled by the network administrator. In this way two users located next to one another could be physically connected to the same switch but logically connected to different sets of resources. This technology would, for example, enable virtual teams to be set up without the need to physically locate everybody in the same physical workspace.

- Simplified administration—Some sources report that as much as 70 percent of network costs is a result of adds, moves, and changes of users in the network. Every time a user is moved the administrator potentially has to rewire, change station addressing, reconfigure hubs and routers, and so on. VLANs simplify most of these tasks. If a user is moved within a VLAN, reconfiguration of routers is unnecessary. In addition, depending on the type of VLAN, other administrative work can be reduced or eliminated. Despite this saving, VLANs do add an extra layer of administrative complexity.

- LAN security—Sensitive data may be compromised by the broadcast nature of a local area network, and installing firewalls at the departmental layer may be viewed as prohibitively expensive. In such cases, placing only those users who can have access to that data on a VLAN improves security. VLANs can also be used to control broadcast domains, set up firewalls, restrict access, and inform the network manager of an intrusion.

9.7.1 Operation

VLANs are a relatively new abstraction of the way traffic domains are created in LAN environments. Essentially it was thought that a transparent mechanism was required to offer Layer 3 functionality within Layer 2 environments. Switches and routers each play an important role in VLAN design.

- Switches provide connectivity and communication for individual VLAN users, while routers provide inter-VLAN communication. VLAN switches free the designer from the physical constraints imposed by shared-hub architectures (within each wiring closet). On a VLAN users and ports are grouped logically across the LAN, irrespective of their actual location or physical connectivity.

- Routers provide inter-VLAN communication, as well as VLAN access to shared resources such as servers and external services. In addition routers may also provide firewall functionality, broadcast suppression, policy-based control, broadcast management, and route processing and distribution.

LAN switches are typically used to segment networks into virtual workgroups, and each workgroup VLAN is typically associated with a VLAN ID—for example, VLAN 3. When a VLAN switch or bridge receives data from a workstation, it tags these data with a VLAN identifier indicating the VLAN from which these data originated. This is called explicit tagging. It is also possible to determine to which VLAN data received belong by using implicit tagging. In implicit tagging the frame is not tagged, but the source VLAN is determined based on other information such as the port on which these data arrived. Note that it is not always necessary to have a router to provide access to shared resources. For example, a server port on a security VLAN switch may be configured with several VLAN IDs, thus providing service to more than one group of users. The overlapping VLANs are still effectively separated within the switch, but each has access to the server. Note that the overlapping VLANs configured at the server port cannot communicate directly (there is no path between different VLANs other than through the server).

Figure 9.17 illustrates several VLAN design concepts. VLANs are defined at the switch port level; physical location is transparent. In this example Cisco's Inter-Switch Link (ISL) protocol is used between switches to multiplex VLANs over higher-speed campus backbone links (this could equally be another vendor-specific protocol such as Cabletron's ISMP). Spanning Tree is run on a per-VLAN basis, and this can be configured

Figure 9.17
VLAN design concepts.

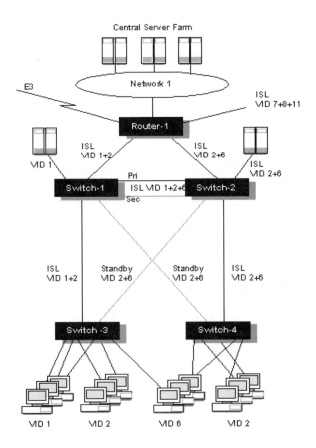

either on physical links (for high resilience) or over existing ISL links. The router enables inter-VLAN communications and access to the central server farm and external services. Some servers are directly attached to switches, either tied to a specific VLAN or via NIC cards that support multiple VLANs. Note the primary and backup ISL links between Switch-1 and -2. This ensures that VLAN 2 is contiguous and does not require the router in the forwarding path. These links could also be configured with alternative VLAN IDs to load-balance and maintain both links live.

In general the majority of end systems are not aware of tagging mechanisms (such as 802.1Q [4]). One of the key advantages of VLANs is that they are totally transparent to the end user, so tagging is not normally seen outside of VLAN trunk ports, which connect Inter-Switch VLANs (ISV-LANs). In general, switches will use tagging on dedicated trunk ports and will strip the tags before forwarding the frame into a user segment. Another reason for this is that tagging increases the frame size and may, therefore, create an illegal frame (i.e., exceeding the MTU), which would be rejected by most end-station stack drivers (particularly if using 802/LLC or SNAP encapsulations).

Tagging can be based on the port from which it came, the source MAC address, the source network address, or some other field or combination of fields. VLANs are classified based on the method used. To be able to do the tagging of data using any of the methods, the switch would have to keep an updated database containing a mapping between VLANs and whichever field is used for tagging. For example, if tagging is by port, the database should indicate which ports belong to which VLAN. This database is called a filtering database. Switches would have to be able to maintain this database and also to make sure that all the bridges on the LAN have the same information in each of their databases. The switch determines where data are to go next based on normal LAN operations. Once the switch determines where these data are to go, it now needs to determine whether the VLAN identifier should be added to these data and sent. If these data are to go to a device that is VLAN-aware, the VLAN identifier is added to these data. If these data are to go to a device that has no knowledge of VLANs, the bridge sends these data without the VLAN identifier.

In order to understand how VLANs work, we need to look at the types of VLANs; the types of connections between devices on VLANs; the filtering database that is used to send traffic to the correct VLAN; and tagging, a process used to identify the VLAN originating data.

Types of VLAN

VLAN membership can be classified by port, MAC address, and protocol type, as follows:

- Layer 1 VLAN: Membership by port—Membership in a VLAN can be defined based on the ports that belong to the VLAN. For example, in a VLAN bridge with four ports, ports 1, 2, and 4 could be assigned to VLAN 1, and port 3 could be assigned to VLAN 2. One disadvantage of this method is that user mobility may be compromised if the number of spare switch ports configured with the appropriate VLAN ID is small. If a user moves to a different location away from the assigned bridge, the network manager may have to reconfigure VLAN ports if free ports are in short supply and not configured with the correct VLAN ID.

- Layer 2 VLAN: Membership by MAC address—Here, membership in a VLAN is associated with the MAC address of the workstation. The switch tracks the MAC addresses that belong to each VLAN. Since MAC addresses form a part of the workstation's network interface card, when a workstation is moved, no reconfiguration is needed to allow the workstation to remain in the same VLAN. This is unlike Layer 1 VLANs where membership tables must be reconfigured. The main problem with this method is that VLAN membership must be assigned initially. In networks with thousands of users, this is no easy task. Also, in environments where notebook PCs are used, the MAC address is associated with the docking station and not with the notebook PC. Consequently, when a notebook PC is moved to a different docking station, its VLAN membership must be reconfigured.

- Layer 2 VLAN: Membership by protocol type—VLAN membership for Layer 2 VLANs can also be based on the protocol type field found in the Layer 2 header. For example, IP could be associated with VLAN 1, IPX could be associated with VLAN 3, and so on.

- Layer 3 VLAN: Membership by IP subnet address—Membership is based on the Layer 3 header. The network IP subnet address can be used to classify VLAN membership. For example, subnet 193.127.34.128 could be associated with VLAN 1, and subnet 140.5.64.0 with VLAN 2. Although VLAN membership is based on Layer 3 information, this has nothing to do with network routing and should not be confused with router functions. In this method, IP addresses are used only as a mapping to determine membership in VLANs. No other processing of IP addresses is done. In Layer 3

VLANs, users can move their workstations without reconfiguring their network addresses. The only problem is that it generally takes longer to forward packets using Layer 3 information than using MAC addresses.

- Higher-layer VLANs—It is also possible to define VLAN membership based on applications or service, or any combination thereof. For example, File Transfer Protocol (FTP) applications can be executed on one VLAN and Telnet applications on another VLAN.

Types of connection

Devices on a VLAN can be connected in three ways, based on whether the connected devices are VLAN-aware or VLAN-unaware. Recall that a VLAN-aware device is one that understands VLAN memberships (i.e., which users belong to a VLAN) and VLAN formats. The three connection methods are as follows:

- Trunk link—All the devices connected to a trunk link, including workstations, must be VLAN-aware. All frames on a trunk link must have a special header attached. These special frames are called tagged frames.

- Access link—An access link connects a VLAN-unaware device to the port of a VLAN-aware bridge. All frames on access links must be implicitly tagged (untagged). The VLAN-unaware device can be a LAN segment with VLAN-unaware workstations, or it can be a number of LAN segments containing VLAN-unaware devices (legacy LAN).

- Hybrid link—This is a combination of the previous two links. This is a link where both VLAN-aware and VLAN-unaware devices are attached. A hybrid link can have both tagged and untagged frames, but all the frames for a specific VLAN must be either tagged or untagged.

It should be noted that the network could have a combination of all three types of link.

VLAN protocols

VLAN switches require mechanisms to discover neighbor and topological information. VLAN switches also require a mechanism to ensure that VLAN traffic passed between them is distributed to the relevant interfaces. Since VLAN IDs are transparent to users, this requires that the IDs be inserted and removed from the LAN protocol stack by VLAN equipment.

There are several approaches that can be taken, and typically this involves tagging frames with VLAN information. There are a number of standard and proprietary protocols used to support VLAN operations. These include the following:

- IEEE 802.1Q tagging

- An adaptation of the IEEE 802.10 security protocol—Cisco et al. proprietary

- VLAN Hello protocol—Cabletron proprietary

- Virtual LAN Link State Protocol (VLSP)—Cabletron proprietary

- The Inter-Switch Link (ISL) protocol—Cisco proprietary

- VLAN Trunk Protocol (VTP)—Cisco proprietary

This list is not exhaustive, and a brief overview is provided in the following list:

- IEEE 802.1Q—IEEE 802.1Q reflects a move toward developing a common set of standards for VLAN products. In the past, VLAN standards were incomplete, and products typically interoperated via proprietary protocols, meaning that a customer wanting to install VLANs would have to purchase all products from the same vendor. IEEE 802.1Q is a VLAN tagging protocol that effectively provides the same functionality as Cisco's ISL. 802.1Q requires that a tag be inserted between the source MAC address and the EtherType or length field. The tag also carries a flag to indicate a Token Ring frame, so that Token Ring frames can be carried in native format over Ethernet, without requiring 802.1H translation. The 802.1Q draft standard defines Layer 1 and Layer 2 VLANs only. Protocol type–based VLANs and higher-layer VLANs have been allowed for but are not defined in the standard. Note that 802.1Q defines only the VLAN ID; 802.1P defines VLAN membership. Both 802.1P and 802.1Q share common tagging. Most of the major vendors now support these standards and either have released or are planning on releasing products based on them.

- IEEE 802.10—Several vendors have adapted the IEEE 802.10 security protocol so that VLAN IDs can be carried within LAN frames between the MAC and LLC headers. This information is inserted and stripped off by IEEE 802.10–compliant switches at the ingress and egress switch nodes, respectively. End systems send and receive standard frames so that VLAN operation is handled transparently within the switched cloud.

- VLAN Hello protocol—The VLAN Hello protocol is defined by Cabletron in RFC2641 [5]. This RFC is informational. VLAN Hello is part of the InterSwitch Message Protocol (ISMP), which provides interswitch communication between switches running Cabletron's SecureFast VLAN (SFVLAN) product RFC2643 [6]. Switches use the VLAN Hello protocol to discover their neighboring switches and establish the topology of the switch fabric.

- Virtual LAN Link State Protocol (VLSP)—Developed by Cabletron and defined in RFC2641 [5]. This RFC is informational. VLSP is part of the InterSwitch Message Protocol (ISMP), which provides interswitch communication between switches running Cabletron's SecureFast VLAN (SFVLAN) product RFC2643 [6]. VLSP is used to determine and maintain a fully connected mesh topology graph of the switch fabric. Each switch maintains an identical database describing the topology. Call-originating switches use the topology database to determine the path over which to route a call connection. VLSP provides support for equal-cost multipath routing and recalculates routes quickly in the face of topological changes, utilizing a minimum of routing protocol traffic. VLSP is derived from the OSPF link-state routing protocol.

- Inter-Switch Link (ISL) protocol—This protocol was developed by Kalpana, Inc. (a pioneer of switches) and subsequently acquired by Cisco. ISL is designed to carry VLAN information over 100-Mbps Ethernet switch-to-switch or switch-to-router links (called trunks) between access and distribution layer switches in a campus environment. ISL maintains VLAN information as traffic flows between switches. With ISL, an Ethernet frame is encapsulated with a 30-byte header that contains a 2-byte VLAN ID. ISL can multiplex multiple VLANs over a single link or distribute VLANs over multiple links. Some server NICs support native ISL operation and so enable application servers and file servers to participate in multiple VLANs directly with the switch.

- VLAN Trunk Protocol (VTP)—Cisco has implemented the proprietary VLAN Trunk Protocol (VTP), which is used to automate VLAN tagging in multimedia (ATM, Ethernet, FDDI, etc.) switching environments. VTP is a switch-to-switch and switch-to-router protocol that automatically configures VLANs over campus networks regardless of the physical media types. VTP also enables managers to move users easily without service disruption by allowing the addition, deletion, and renaming of VLANs on a campus-wide basis without the need to manually configure each switch. VTP also enables new switches and routers to be automatically configured with VLAN information as they are brought online.

Frame processing

A bridge, on receiving data, determines to which VLAN data belong either by implicit or explicit tagging. In explicit tagging a tag header is added to data. The bridge also keeps track of VLAN members in a filtering database, which it uses to determine where data are to be sent. Following is an explanation of the contents of the filtering database and the format and purpose of the tag header [4].

Filtering database

Membership information for a VLAN is stored in a filtering database. The filtering database consists of the following types of entries:

- Static entries—Static information is added, modified, and deleted by management only. Entries are not automatically removed after some time (aging), but must be explicitly removed by management. There are two types of static entries: Static filtering entries specify for every port whether frames to be sent to a specific MAC address or group address and on a specific VLAN should be forwarded or discarded, or should follow the dynamic entry. Static registration entries specify whether frames to be sent to a specific VLAN are to be tagged or untagged and which ports are registered for that VLAN.

- Dynamic entries—Dynamic entries are learned by the bridge and cannot be created or updated by management. The learning process observes the port from which a frame with a given source address and VLAN ID (VID) is received and updates the filtering database. The entry is updated only if all the following three conditions are satisfied: the port allows learning, the source address is a workstation address and not a group address, and there is space available in the database.

Entries are removed from the database by the aging-out process, where, after a certain amount of time specified by management (10 to 1,000,000 seconds), entries allow automatic reconfiguration of the filtering database if the topology of the network changes. There are three types of dynamic entry, as follows:

- Dynamic filtering entries.—specify whether frames to be sent to a specific MAC address and on a certain VLAN should be forwarded or discarded.

- Group registration entries—indicate for each port whether frames to be sent to a group MAC address and on a certain VLAN should be filtered or discarded. These entries are added and deleted using Group Multicast Registration Protocol (GMRP). This allows multicasts to be sent on a single VLAN without affecting other VLANs.

- Dynamic registration entries—specify which ports are registered for a specific VLAN. Entries are added and deleted using Generic Attribute Registration Protocol (GARP) and Generic VLAN Registration Protocol (GVRP), as described in Section 9.1.5.

GVRP is used not only to update dynamic registration entries but also to communicate the information to other VLAN-aware bridges. In order for VLANs to forward information to the correct destination, all the bridges in the VLAN should contain the same information in their respective filtering databases. GVRP allows both VLAN-aware workstations and bridges to issue and revoke VLAN memberships. VLAN-aware bridges register and propagate VLAN membership to all ports that are a part of the active topology of the VLAN. The active loop-free network topology is determined via the Spanning Tree algorithm. Once an active topology (which may comprise several VLANs) is determined, the bridges determine an active topology for each VLAN. This may result in a different topology for each VLAN or a common topology for several VLANs. In either case, the VLAN topology will be a subset of the active topology of the network.

Tagging

VLAN operations require that frames carry some form of identification to indicate the VLAN to which they belong. To achieve this, a field called a tag header is added to standard LAN frames between Layer 2 and Layer 3. The tag format is specified by IEEE 802.1Q [4] and IEEE 802.3ac [7]. The tagged frames that are sent across hybrid and trunk links; it is the responsibility of VLAN-aware devices to tag and untag frames accordingly so that these operations are transparent to the user. There are two formats of the tag header, as follows:

- Ethernet tag header—In Ethernet frames the tag header comprises a two-byte Tag Protocol Identifier (TPID) and a two-byte Tag Control Information (TCI) field. The TPI is transposed over the standard EtherType field with a special value of 0x8100, and the EtherType field is shifted so that it follows the TCI field.

- Token Ring and FDDI tag header—In Token Ring and FDDI networks the tag headers comprise a SNAP-encoded TPID and TCI.

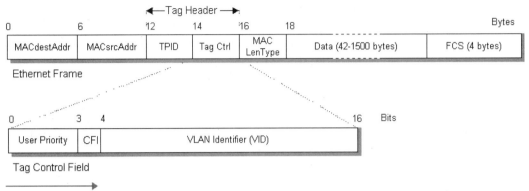

Figure 9.18   *VLAN tagging with Ethernet.*

The SNAP header is set to 0xAAAA03, and the SNAP PID is set to 0x000000. These are followed by the TPI, which is set to 0x8100, and then the TCI.

The format of the Ethernet tag header is shown in Figure 9.18.

TCI field definitions

- User priority (3 bits)—enables priority information to be encoded in the frame. Eight levels of priority are allowed (zero is the lowest priority and seven is the highest priority).

- CFI (1 bit)—used to indicate that all MAC addresses present in the data field are in canonical format (used to decode encapsulated frames that may be present in the data field, such as a Token Ring frame). This field is interpreted differently depending on whether it is an Ethernet-encoded tag header or a SNAP-encoded tag header.
  - In SNAP-encoded TPID the field indicates the presence or absence of the canonical format of addresses.
  - In Ethernet-encoded TPID, it indicates the presence of the source routing information field after the length field. This field indicates routing on Ethernet frames.

- VID (12 bits)—an unsigned binary value used to uniquely identify the VLAN to which the frame belongs. There can be a maximum of $(2^{12} - 1)$ VLANs, with the exception of the following reserved values:
  - 0x000—The NULL VID. Although no VID is used, this allows priority to be encoded in nonpriority LANs.
  - 0x001—The default VID. This is the default VID set on switch ports, which may be reconfigured.

- 0xFFF—Reserved for implementation use. Has significance inside a VLAN-aware device but should not be used externally.

9.7.2   Design guidelines

Network designers can use switches and routers to evolve their shared-media networks to a campus switched internetwork architecture. Typically, this evolution involves the following stages:

- Microsegmentation—existing hubs and routers are maintained; however, a LAN switch is added to enhance connectivity to improve performance.

- High-speed backbone technology—is added (such as ATM, Fast Ethernet, or Gigabit Ethernet), together with routing between switches. LAN switches perform switch processing and provide dedicated bandwidth to the desktop and to shared-media hubs. Backbone routers are attached to either Fast Ethernet or ATM switches. The increase in backbone bandwidth matches the increased bandwidth in the wiring closet.

- Router distribution—between the LAN switches in the wiring closet and the high-speed core switch. The network backbone is now strictly a high-speed transport mechanism with all other devices, such as the distributed routers, at the periphery.

- End-to-end switching—with integral VLANs and multilayer switching capability. Layer 2 and Layer 3 integrated switching is distributed across the network and is connected to the high-speed core.

However, despite the advantages of VLAN networks they can prove hard to manage and optimize. If logical VLANs are widely distributed across a physical LAN infrastructure, then intra-VLAN traffic needs to be dispersed to all physical connections. In a large, well-distributed campus VLAN this can lead to serious traffic overheads and subsequent performance degradation. Other design issues with VLANs include the following:

- Virtual workgroup resources—One of the problems with virtual workgroups is that shared resources may not be conveniently located for all users. A virtual workgroup may be spread over multiple floors and between buildings, whereas the main printing and server resources may be housed centrally. Without duplicating resources this is an unavoidable issue.

- Server farms—Another problem with virtual workgroups is the implementation of centralized server farms. Server farms can be problematic if servers cannot access more than one VLAN. In such a case, there are three options: The server farm would sit on a single VLAN, and all other VLANs needing to access the server would have to go through a router, with reduced performance; a special server NIC card would need to be installed to support multiple VLAN Ids; overlapping VLAN IDs would need to be configured at the server switch ports.

- Multiple Spanning Trees—Standard switching and bridging can often result in nonoptimal forwarding of packets, since every packet must travel down the minimum Spanning Tree, regardless of the physical proximity of the source and destination node. Routers generally offer more optimal paths, since each path is typically a least-cost path for each source and destination pair. To counter this, some VLAN vendors (such as Cisco) provide support for improved routing and redundancy in switched environments by supporting a single Spanning Tree per VLAN. Note that standard Spanning Tree bridges can implement separate Spanning Trees, but this requires the configuration of different Spanning Tree multicast addresses and very careful topological implementation to avoid loops.

VLANs can provide major benefits in key areas such as LAN administration, security, and network management in enterprise LANs. They require a fundamental change in the way that LANs are designed and managed, and there are several issues network designers should consider prior to large-scale VLAN deployment. VLANs have been heavily promoted by the main enterprise equipment vendors (such as Cisco, Cabletron, and 3Com). They are more commonly implemented in larger enterprises (such as financial institutions). However, as router technology improves in performance (approaching wire speed forwarding rates) and switches begin to incorporate more and more Layer 3 functionality, fewer organizations will need to implement large, flat networks, and, consequently, VLANs are likely to be less attractive for the network designer in the future.

9.8   Summary

In this chapter, we discussed the following:

- Repeaters are Physical Layer devices, which simply forward frames over extended LANs and offer no traffic management capabilities. Bridges and switches use Layer 2 MAC addressing to make forwarding decisions and in so doing perform a limited form of traffic management. A number of different switching models have emerged, including classic store-and-forward switching, cut-through switching, adaptive switching, and fragment-free switching.

- Since neither bridges nor switches are aware of Network Layer addressing, there is no concept of network hierarchy, and as such networks designed with these devices are not scalable and are limited in their ability to engineer traffic efficiently. Their use is primarily for extended local area networks and simple remote office interconnects. A new logical network architecture called the Virtual LAN (VLAN) has emerged in recent years, which enables hierarchy in bridged or switched networks.

- The Spanning Tree algorithm is implemented in bridges to provide automated loop avoidance. In practice it is slow to converge and potentially expensive to deploy, especially in wide area networks.

- The IBM 8209 translation bridge is a hybrid device, not fully covered by the standards, which enables Ethernet and Token Ring users to coexist. It uses brute-force techniques to convert frame formats from one media type to another. Typically there are protocols that are unsupported for bridging across these devices.

- Encapsulation bridging for Ethernet-to-FDDI applications is simple but limited to Ethernet-to-Ethernet communications only, with the FDDI ring used merely for transit. The use of proprietary protocols between bridges means that this form of bridging is now rarely used. The preferred method is translation bridging, which enables both FDDI and Ethernet/Token Ring stations to communicate directly.

- VLANs allow the formation of virtual workgroups, better security, improved performance, simplified administration, and reduced costs. VLANs are formed by the logical segmentation of a network and can be classified into Layers 1, 2, 3, and higher layers. Only Layers 1 and 2 are specified in IEEE 802.1Q. Tagging and the filtering database allow a bridge to determine the source and destination VLAN for received data.

- VLANs, if implemented effectively, offer an effective and transparent mechanism to scale flat networks. However, as router technology improves in performance (approaching wire speed forwarding rates) and switches begin to incorporate more and more Layer 3 functionality, fewer organizations will need to implement large, flat networks, and, consequently, VLANs are likely to be less attractive for the network designer in the future.

References

[1]   R. Perlman, *Interconnections, Bridges, and Routers* (Reading, MA: Addison-Wesley, 1993).

[2]   Standards for the Transmission of IP Datagrams over IEEE 802 Networks, RFC 1042 (February 1988).

[3]   A. Latif, E. J. Rowlance, and R. H. Adams, "The IBM 8209 LAN Bridge," *IEEE Network* (May 1992).

[4]   IEEE Standards for Local and Metropolitan Area Networks: Virtual Bridged Local Area Networks, IEEE Std 802.1Q-1998 (1998).

[5]   Cabletron's VLAN Hello Protocol Specification, version 4, RFC 2641 (August 1999).

[6]   Cabletron's SecureFast VLAN Operational Model, RFC 2643 (August 1999).

[7]   ISO/IEC 15802-3 Information Technology, Telecommunications and Information Exchange between Systems, Local and Metropolitan Area Networks, Specific Requirements, Supplement to Carrier Sense Multiple Access with Collision Detection (CSMA/CD) Access Method and Physical Layer Specifications, Frame Extensions for Virtual Bridged Local Area Network (VLAN) Tagging on 802.3 Networks, IEEE Std 802.3ac-1998 (supplement to IEEE 802.3 1998 edition) (1998).

UDP and TCP Port Numbers

The following list of port numbers comprises information derived mainly from RFC 1700. Any errors or omissions are, therefore, my own. The port numbers are divided into three ranges, as follows:

- Well-known ports are those from 0 through 1,023.

- Registered ports are those from 1,024 through 49,151.

- Dynamic and/or private ports are those from 49,152 through 65,535.

The list provided here is not exhaustive. For a complete up-to-date list of port assignments see the IANA URL: URL = ftp://ftp.isi.edu/in-notes/iana/assignments/port-numbers.

A.1 Well-known port numbers

Ports are used in protocols such as TCP and UDP to identify the end points of logical connections that carry long-term conversations. For many applications it is useful to have the service port predefined, so that clients connecting to a server know what port to connect to for widely used applications such as FTP, Telnet, DNS, and so on. These ports are sometimes called well-known ports or assigned ports. These ports are controlled and assigned by the IANA, and on most systems can be used only by system (or root) processes or by programs executed by privileged users. The assigned ports take only a small part of the available port space, for many years restricted to the range 0–255. Recently, the range has been expanded by the IANA to 0–1,023.

Keyword	Decimal	Protocol	Description
0	TCP, UDP	Reserved	
tcpmux	1	TCP, UDP	TCP Port Service Multiplexer
compressnet	2	TCP, UDP	Management Utility
compressnet	3	TCP, UDP	Compression Process
#	4	TCP, UDP	Unassigned
rje	5	TCP, UDP	Remote Job Entry
#	6	TCP, UDP	Unassigned
echo	7	TCP, UDP	Echo
#	8	TCP, UDP	Unassigned
discard	9	TCP, UDP	Discard
#	10	TCP, UDP	Unassigned
systat	11	TCP, UDP	Active Users
#	12	TCP, UDP	Unassigned
daytime	13	TCP, UDP	Daytime
#	14	TCP, UDP	Unassigned
#	15	TCP	Unassigned [was netstat]
#	15	UDP	Unassigned
#	16	TCP, UDP	Unassigned
qotd	17	TCP, UDP	Quote of the Day
msp	18	TCP, UDP	Message Send Protocol
chargen	19	TCP, UDP	Character Generator
ftp-data	20	TCP, UDP	File Transfer [Default Data]
ftp	21	TCP, UDP	File Transfer [Control]
#	22	TCP, UDP	Unassigned
telnet	23	TCP, UDP	Telnet
	24	TCP, UDP	any private mail system
smtp	25	TCP, UDP	Simple Mail Transfer
#	26	TCP, UDP	Unassigned
nsw-fe	27	TCP, UDP	NSW User System FE

Keyword	Decimal	Protocol	Description
#	28	TCP, UDP	Unassigned
msg-icp	29	TCP, UDP	MSG ICP
#	30	TCP, UDP	Unassigned
msg-auth	31	TCP, UDP	MSG Authentication
#	32	TCP, UDP	Unassigned
dsp	33	TCP, UDP	Display Support Protocol
#	34	TCP, UDP	Unassigned
	35	TCP, UDP	any private printer server
#	36	TCP, UDP	Unassigned
time	37	TCP, UDP	Time
rap	38	TCP, UDP	Route Access Protocol
rlp	39	TCP, UDP	Resource Location Protocol
#	40	TCP, UDP	Unassigned
graphics	41	TCP, UDP	Graphics
nameserver	42	TCP, UDP	Host Name Server
nicname	43	TCP, UDP	Who Is
mpm-flags	44	TCP, UDP	MPM FLAGS Protocol
mpm	45	TCP, UDP	Message Processing Module [recv]
mpm-snd	46	TCP, UDP	MPM [default send]
ni-ftp	47	TCP, UDP	NI FTP
auditd	48	TCP, UDP	Digital Audit Daemon
login	49	TCP, UDP	Login Host Protocol
re-mail-ck	50	TCP, UDP	Remote Mail Checking Protocol
la-maint	51	TCP, UDP	IMP Logical Address Maintenance
xns-time	52	TCP, UDP	XNS Time Protocol
domain	53	TCP, UDP	Domain Name Server
xns-ch	54	TCP, UDP	XNS Clearinghouse
isi-gl	55	TCP, UDP	ISI Graphics Language
xns-auth	56	TCP, UDP	XNS Authentication

Keyword	Decimal	Protocol	Description
	57	TCP, UDP	any private terminal access
xns-mail	58	TCP, UDP	XNS Mail
	59	TCP, UDP	any private file service
	60	TCP, UDP	Unassigned
ni-mail	61	TCP, UDP	NI MAIL
acas	62	TCP, UDP	ACA Services
#	63	TCP, UDP	Unassigned
covia	64	TCP, UDP	Communications Integrator (CI)
tacacs-ds	65	TCP, UDP	TACACS-Database Service
sql*net	66	TCP, UDP	Oracle SQL*NET
bootps	67	TCP, UDP	Bootstrap Protocol Server
bootpc	68	TCP, UDP	Bootstrap Protocol Client
tftp	69	TCP, UDP	Trivial File Transfer
gopher	70	TCP, UDP	Gopher
netrjs-1	71	TCP, UDP	Remote Job Service
netrjs-2	72	TCP, UDP	Remote Job Service
netrjs-3	73	TCP, UDP	Remote Job Service
netrjs-4	74	TCP, UDP	Remote Job Service
	75	TCP, UDP	any private dial-out service
deos	76	TCP, UDP	Distributed External Object Store
	77	TCP, UDP	any private RJE service
vettcp	78	TCP, UDP	vettcp
finger	79	TCP, UDP	Finger
www-http	80	TCP, UDP	World Wide Web HTTP
hosts2-ns	81	TCP, UDP	HOSTS2 Name Server
xfer	82	TCP, UDP	XFER Utility
mit-ml-dev	83	TCP, UDP	MIT ML Device
ctf	84	TCP, UDP	Common Trace Facility
mit-ml-dev	85	TCP, UDP	MIT ML Device

Keyword	Decimal	Protocol	Description
mfcobol	86	TCP, UDP	Micro Focus Cobol
	87	TCP, UDP	any private terminal link
kerberos	88	TCP, UDP	Kerberos
su-mit-tg	89	TCP, UDP	SU/MIT Telnet Gateway
dnsix	90	TCP, UDP	DNSIX Security Attribute Token Map
mit-dov	91	TCP, UDP	MIT Dover Spooler
npp	92	TCP, UDP	Network Printing Protocol
dcp	93	TCP, UDP	Device Control Protocol
objcall	94	TCP, UDP	Tivoli Object Dispatcher
supdup	95	TCP, UDP	SUPDUP
dixie	96	TCP, UDP	DIXIE Protocol Specification
swift-rvf	97	TCP, UDP	Swift Remote Vitural File Protocol
tacnews	98	TCP, UDP	TAC News
metagram	99	TCP, UDP	Metagram Relay
newacct	100	TCP, UDP	[unauthorized use]
hostname	101	TCP, UDP	NIC Host Name Server
iso-tsap	102	TCP, UDP	ISO-TSAP
gppitnp	103	TCP, UDP	Genesis Point-to-Point Trans Net
acr-nema	104	TCP, UDP	ACR-NEMA Digital Imag. & Comm. 300
csnet-ns	105	TCP, UDP	Mailbox Name Nameserver
3com-tsmux	106	TCP, UDP	3COM-TSMUX
rtelnet	107	TCP, UDP	Remote Telnet Service
snagas	108	TCP, UDP	SNA Gateway Access Server
pop2	109	TCP, UDP	Post Office Protocol - Version 2
pop3	110	TCP, UDP	Post Office Protocol - Version 3
sunrpc	111	TCP, UDP	SUN Remote Procedure Call
mcidas	112	TCP, UDP	McIDAS Data Transmission Protocol
auth	113	TCP, UDP	Authentication Service
audionews	114	TCP, UDP	Audio News Multicast

Keyword	Decimal	Protocol	Description
sftp	115	TCP, UDP	Simple File Transfer Protocol
ansanotify	116	TCP, UDP	ANSA REX Notify
uucp-path	117	TCP, UDP	UUCP Path Service
sqlserv	118	TCP, UDP	SQL Services
nntp	119	TCP, UDP	Network News Transfer Protocol
cfdptkt	120	TCP, UDP	CFDPTKT
erpc	121	TCP, UDP	Encore Expedited Remote Pro.Call
smakynet	122	TCP, UDP	SMAKYNET
ntp	123	TCP, UDP	Network Time Protocol
ansatrader	124	TCP, UDP	ANSA REX Trader
locus-map	125	TCP, UDP	Locus PC-Interface Net Map Ser
unitary	126	TCP, UDP	Unisys Unitary Login
locus-con	127	TCP, UDP	Locus PC-Interface Conn Server
gss-xlicen	128	TCP, UDP	GSS X License Verification
pwdgen	129	TCP, UDP	Password Generator Protocol
cisco-fna	130	TCP, UDP	Cisco FNATIVE
cisco-tna	131	TCP, UDP	Cisco TNATIVE
cisco-sys	132	TCP, UDP	Cisco SYSMAINT
statsrv	133	TCP, UDP	Statistics Service
ingres-net	134	TCP, UDP	INGRES-NET Service
loc-srv	135	TCP, UDP	Location Service
profile	136	TCP, UDP	PROFILE Naming System
netbios-ns	137	TCP, UDP	NETBIOS Name Service
netbios-dgm	138	TCP, UDP	NETBIOS Datagram Service
netbios-ssn	139	TCP, UDP	NETBIOS Session Service
emfis-data	140	TCP, UDP	EMFIS Data Service
emfis-cntl	141	TCP, UDP	EMFIS Control Service
bl-idm	142	TCP, UDP	Britton-Lee IDM
imap2	143	TCP, UDP	Interim Mail Access Protocol v2

Keyword	Decimal	Protocol	Description
news	144	TCP, UDP	NewS
uaac	145	TCP, UDP	UAAC Protocol
iso-tp0	146	TCP, UDP	ISO-IP0
iso-ip	147	TCP, UDP	ISO-IP
cronus	148	TCP, UDP	CRONUS-SUPPORT
aed-512	149	TCP, UDP	AED 512 Emulation Service
sql-net	150	TCP, UDP	SQL-NET
hems	151	TCP, UDP	HEMS
bftp	152	TCP, UDP	Background File Transfer Program
sgmp	153	TCP, UDP	SGMP
netsc-prod	154	TCP, UDP	NETSC
netsc-dev	155	TCP, UDP	NETSC
sqlsrv	156	TCP, UDP	SQL Service
knet-cmp	157	TCP, UDP	KNET/VM Command/Message Protocol
pcmail-srv	158	TCP, UDP	PCMail Server
nss-routing	159	TCP, UDP	NSS-Routing
sgmp-traps	160	TCP, UDP	SGMP-TRAPS
snmp	161	TCP, UDP	SNMP
snmptrap	162	TCP, UDP	SNMPTRAP
cmip-man	163	TCP, UDP	CMIP TCP Manager
cmip-agent	164	TCP, UDP	CMIP TCP Agent
xns-courier	165	TCP, UDP	Xerox
s-net	166	TCP, UDP	Sirius Systems
namp	167	TCP, UDP	NAMP
rsvd	168	TCP, UDP	RSVD
send	169	TCP, UDP	SEND
print-srv	170	TCP, UDP	Network PostScript
multiplex	171	TCP, UDP	Network Innovations Multiplex
cl/1	172	TCP, UDP	Network Innovations CL/1

Keyword	Decimal	Protocol	Description
xyplex-mux	173	TCP, UDP	Xyplex
mailq	174	TCP, UDP	MAILQ
vmnet	175	TCP, UDP	VMNET
genrad-mux	176	TCP, UDP	GENRAD-MUX
xdmcp	177	TCP, UDP	X Display Manager Control Protocol
nextstep	178	TCP, UDP	NextStep Window Server
bgp	179	TCP, UDP	Border Gateway Protocol
ris	180	TCP, UDP	Intergraph
unify	181	TCP, UDP	Unify
audit	182	TCP, UDP	Unisys Audit SITP
ocbinder	183	TCP, UDP	OCBinder
ocserver	184	TCP, UDP	OCServer
remote-kis	185	TCP, UDP	Remote-KIS
kis	186	TCP, UDP	KIS Protocol
aci	187	TCP, UDP	Application Communication Interface
mumps	188	TCP, UDP	Plus Five's MUMPS
qft	189	TCP, UDP	Queued File Transport
gacp	190	TCP, UDP	Gateway Access Control Protocol
prospero	191	TCP, UDP	Prospero Directory Service
osu-nms	192	TCP, UDP	OSU Network Monitoring System
srmp	193	TCP, UDP	Spider Remote Monitoring Protocol
irc	194	TCP, UDP	Internet Relay Chat Protocol
dn6-nlm-aud	195	TCP, UDP	DNSIX Network Level Module Audit
dn6-smm-red	196	TCP, UDP	DNSIX Session Mgt Module Audit Redir
dls	197	TCP, UDP	Directory Location Service
dls-mon	198	TCP, UDP	Directory Location Service Monitor
smux	199	TCP, UDP	SMUX
src	200	TCP, UDP	IBM System Resource Controller
at-rtmp	201	TCP, UDP	AppleTalk Routing Maintenance

Keyword	Decimal	Protocol	Description
at-nbp	202	TCP, UDP	AppleTalk Name Binding
at-3	203	TCP, UDP	AppleTalk Unused
at-echo	204	TCP, UDP	AppleTalk Echo
at-5	205	TCP, UDP	AppleTalk Unused
at-zis	206	TCP, UDP	AppleTalk Zone Information
at-7	207	TCP, UDP	AppleTalk Unused
at-8	208	TCP, UDP	AppleTalk Unused
tam	209	TCP, UDP	Trivial Authenticated Mail Protocol
z39.50	210	TCP, UDP	ANSI Z39.50
914c/g	211	TCP, UDP	Texas Instruments 914C/G Terminal
anet	212	TCP, UDP	ATEXSSTR
ipx	213	TCP, UDP	IPX
vmpwscs	214	TCP, UDP	VM PWSCS
softpc	215	TCP, UDP	Insignia Solutions
atls	216	TCP, UDP	Access Technology License Server
dbase	217	TCP, UDP	dBASE Unix
mpp	218	TCP, UDP	Netix Message Posting Protocol
uarps	219	TCP, UDP	Unisys ARPs
imap3	220	TCP, UDP	Interactive Mail Access Protocol v3
fln-spx	221	TCP, UDP	Berkeley rlogind with SPX auth
rsh-spx	222	TCP, UDP	Berkeley rshd with SPX auth
cdc	223	TCP, UDP	Certificate Distribution Center
#	224–241	TCP, UDP	Reserved
#	242	TCP, UDP	Unassigned
sur-meas	243	TCP, UDP	Survey Measurement
#	244	TCP, UDP	Unassigned
link	245	TCP, UDP	LINK
dsp3270	246	TCP, UDP	Display Systems Protocol
#	247–255	TCP, UDP	Reserved

Keyword	Decimal	Protocol	Description
#	256–343	TCP, UDP	Unassigned
pdap	344	TCP, UDP	Prospero Data Access Protocol
pawserv	345	TCP, UDP	Perf Analysis Workbench
zserv	346	TCP, UDP	Zebra server
fatserv	347	TCP, UDP	Fatmen Server
csi-sgwp	348	TCP, UDP	Cabletron Management Protocol
#	349–370	TCP, UDP	Unassigned
clearcase	371	TCP, UDP	Clearcase
ulistserv	372	TCP, UDP	UNIX Listserv
legent-1	373	TCP, UDP	Legent Corporation
legent-2	374	TCP, UDP	Legent Corporation
hassle	375	TCP, UDP	Hassle
nip	376	TCP, UDP	Amiga Envoy Network Inquiry Protocol
tnETOS	377	TCP, UDP	NEC Corporation
dsETOS	378	TCP, UDP	NEC Corporation
is99c	379	TCP, UDP	TIA/EIA/IS-99 modem client
is99s	380	TCP, UDP	TIA/EIA/IS-99 modem server
hp-collector	381	TCP, UDP	hp performance data collector
hp-managed-node	382	TCP, UDP	hp performance data managed node
hp-alarm-mgr	383	TCP, UDP	hp performance data alarm manager
arns	384	TCP, UDP	A Remote Network Server System
ibm-app	385	TCP, UDP	IBM Application
asa	386	TCP, UDP	ASA Message Router Object Def.
aurp	387	TCP, UDP	Appletalk Update-Based Routing Protocol
unidata-ldm	388	TCP, UDP	Unidata LDM Version 4
ldap	389	TCP, UDP	Lightweight Directory Access Protocol
uis	390	TCP, UDP	UIS
synotics-relay	391	TCP, UDP	SynOptics SNMP Relay Port
synotics-broker	392	TCP, UDP	SynOptics Port Broker Port

Keyword	Decimal	Protocol	Description
dis	393	TCP, UDP	Data Interpretation System
embl-ndt	394	TCP, UDP	EMBL Nucleic Data Transfer
netcp	395	TCP, UDP	NETscout Control Protocol
netware-ip	396	TCP, UDP	Novell Netware over IP
mptn	397	TCP, UDP	Multi Protocol Trans. Net.
kryptolan	398	TCP, UDP	Kryptolan
#	399	TCP, UDP	Unassigned
work-sol	400	TCP, UDP	Workstation Solutions
ups	401	TCP, UDP	Uninterruptible Power Supply
genie	402	TCP, UDP	Genie Protocol
decap	403	TCP, UDP	decap
nced	404	TCP, UDP	nced
ncld	405	TCP, UDP	ncld
imsp	406	TCP, UDP	Interactive Mail Support Protocol
timbuktu	407	TCP, UDP	Timbuktu
prm-sm	408	TCP, UDP	Prospero Resource Manager Sys. Man.
prm-nm	409	TCP, UDP	Prospero Resource Manager Node Man.
decladebug	410	TCP, UDP	DECLadebug Remote Debug Protocol
rmt	411	TCP, UDP	Remote MT Protocol
synoptics-trap	412	TCP, UDP	Trap Convention Port
smsp	413	TCP, UDP	SMSP
infoseek	414	TCP, UDP	InfoSeek
bnet	415	TCP, UDP	Bnet
silverplatter	416	TCP, UDP	Silverplatter
onmux	417	TCP, UDP	Onmux
hyper-g	418	TCP, UDP	Hyper-G
ariel1	419	TCP, UDP	Ariel
smpte	420	TCP, UDP	SMPTE
ariel2	421	TCP, UDP	Ariel

Keyword	Decimal	Protocol	Description
ariel3	422	TCP, UDP	Ariel
opc-job-start	423	TCP, UDP	IBM Operations Planning and Control Start
opc-job-track	424	TCP, UDP	IBM Operations Planning and Control Track
icad-el	425	TCP, UDP	ICAD
smartsdp	426	TCP, UDP	smartsdp
svrloc	427	TCP, UDP	Server Location
ocs_cmu	428	TCP, UDP	OCS_CMU
ocs_amu	429	TCP, UDP	OCS_AMU
utmpsd	430	TCP, UDP	UTMPSD
utmpcd	431	TCP, UDP	UTMPCD
iasd	432	TCP, UDP	IASD
nnsp	433	TCP, UDP	NNSP
mobileip-agent	434	TCP, UDP	MobileIP-Agent
mobilip-mn	435	TCP, UDP	MobilIP-MN
dna-cml	436	TCP, UDP	DNA-CML
comscm	437	TCP, UDP	comscm
dsfgw	438	TCP, UDP	dsfgw
dasp	439	TCP, UDP	dasp
sgcp	440	TCP, UDP	sgcp
decvms-sysmgt	441	TCP, UDP	decvms-sysmgt
cvc_hostd	442	TCP, UDP	cvc_hostd
https	443	TCP, UDP	https Mcom
snpp	444	TCP, UDP	Simple Network Paging Protocol
microsoft-ds	445	TCP, UDP	Microsoft-DS
ddm-rdb	446	TCP, UDP	DDM-RDB
ddm-dfm	447	TCP, UDP	DDM-RFM
ddm-byte	448	TCP, UDP	DDM-BYTE
as-servermap	449	TCP, UDP	AS Server Mapper
tserver	450	TCP, UDP	Tserver

Keyword	Decimal	Protocol	Description
#	451–511	TCP, UDP	Unassigned
exec	512	TCP	remote process execution; authentication via passwords and UNIX login names
biff	512	UDP	used by mail system to notify users of new mail received; currently receives messages only from processes on the same machine
login	513	TCP	remote login a la Telnet; automatic authentication performed based on priviledged port numbers and distributed databases which identify "authentication domains"
who	513	UDP	maintains data bases showing who's logged into machines on a local net and the load average of the machine
cmd	514	TCP	like exec, but automatic authentication is performed as for login server
syslog	514	UDP	syslog
printer	515	TCP, UDP	spooler
#	516	TCP, UDP	Unassigned
talk	517	TCP, UDP	like tenex link, but across machine—unfortunately, doesn't use link protocol (this is actually just a rendezvous port from which a tcp connection is established)
ntalk	518	TCP, UDP	
utime	519	TCP, UDP	unixtime
efs	520	TCP	extended file name server
router	520	UDP	local routing process (on site); uses variant of Xerox NS routing information protocol
#	521-524	TCP, UDP	Unassigned
timed	525	TCP, UDP	timeserver
tempo	526	TCP, UDP	newdate
#	527-529	TCP, UDP	Unassigned
courier	530	TCP, UDP	rpc
conference	531	TCP, UDP	chat
netnews	532	TCP, UDP	readnews

Appendix A

Keyword	Decimal	Protocol	Description
netwall	533	TCP, UDP	for emergency broadcasts
#	534-538	TCP, UDP	Unassigned
apertus-ldp	539	TCP, UDP	Apertus Technologies Load Determination
uucp	540	TCP, UDP	uucpd
uucp-rlogin	541	TCP, UDP	uucp-rlogin
#	542	TCP, UDP	Unassigned
klogin	543	TCP, UDP	
kshell	544	TCP, UDP	krcmd
#	545-549	TCP, UDP	Unassigned
new-rwho	550	TCP, UDP	new-who
#	551-555	TCP, UDP	Unassigned
dsf	555	TCP, UDP	
remotefs	556	TCP, UDP	rfs server
#	557-559	TCP, UDP	Unassigned
rmonitor	560	TCP, UDP	rmonitord
monitor	561	TCP, UDP	
chshell	562	TCP, UDP	chcmd
#	563	TCP, UDP	Unassigned
9pfs	564	TCP, UDP	plan 9 file service
whoami	565	TCP, UDP	whoami
#	566-569	TCP, UDP	Unassigned
meter	570	TCP, UDP	demon
meter	571	TCP, UDP	udemon
#	572-599	TCP, UDP	Unassigned
ipcserver	600	TCP, UDP	Sun IPC server
nqs	607	TCP, UDP	nqs
urm	606	TCP, UDP	Cray Unified Resource Manager
sift-uft	608	TCP, UDP	Sender-Initiated/Unsolicited File Transfer
npmp-trap	609	TCP, UDP	npmp-trap

Keyword	Decimal	Protocol	Description
npmp-local	610	TCP, UDP	npmp-local
npmp-gui	611	TCP, UDP	npmp-gui
ginad	634	TCP, UDP	ginad
mdqs	666	TCP, UDP	
doom	666	TCP, UDP	doom Id Software
elcsd	704	TCP, UDP	errlog copy/server daemon
entrustmanager	709	TCP, UDP	EntrustManager
netviewdm1	729	TCP, UDP	IBM NetView DM/6000 Server/Client
netviewdm2	730	TCP, UDP	IBM NetView DM/6000 send TCP
netviewdm3	731	TCP, UDP	IBM NetView DM/6000 receive TCP
netgw	741	TCP, UDP	netGW
netrcs	742	TCP, UDP	Network-based Rev. Cont. Sys.
flexlm	744	TCP, UDP	Flexible License Manager
fujitsu-dev	747	TCP, UDP	Fujitsu Device Control
ris-cm	748	TCP, UDP	Russell Info Sci Calendar Manager
kerberos-adm	749	TCP, UDP	kerberos administration
rfile	750	TCP	
loadav	750	UDP	
pump	751	TCP, UDP	
qrh	752	TCP, UDP	
rrh	753	TCP, UDP	
tell	754	TCP, UDP	send
nlogin	758	TCP, UDP	
con	759	TCP, UDP	
ns	760	TCP, UDP	
rxe	761	TCP, UDP	
quotad	762	TCP, UDP	
cycleserv	763	TCP, UDP	
omserv	764	TCP, UDP	

Keyword	Decimal	Protocol	Description
webster	765	TCP, UDP	
phonebook	767	TCP, UDP	phone
vid	769	TCP, UDP	
cadlock	770	TCP, UDP	
rtip	771	TCP, UDP	
cycleserv2	772	TCP, UDP	
submit	773	TCP	
notify	773	UDP	
rpasswd	774	TCP	
acmaint_dbd	774	UDP	
entomb	775	TCP	
acmaint_transd	775	UDP	
wpages	776	TCP, UDP	
wpgs	780	TCP, UDP	
concert	786	TCP, UDP	Concert
mdbs_daemon	800	TCP, UDP	
device	801	TCP, UDP	
xtreelic	996	TCP, UDP	Central Point Software
maitrd	997	TCP, UDP	
busboy	998	TCP	
puparp	998	UDP	
garcon	999	TCP	
applix	999	UDP	Applix ac
puprouter	999	TCP	
??????/			
cadlock	1000	TCP	
ock	1000	UDP	
	1023	TCP	Reserved
	1024	UDP	Reserved

A.2   Registered port numbers

The registered ports are in the range 1,024–65,535. These ports are not controlled by the IANA and on most systems can be used by ordinary user processes or programs executed by ordinary users. While the IANA cannot control use of these ports, it does register use of these ports as a convenience to the community.

Keyword	Decimal	Protocol	Description
	1024	TCP, UDP	Reserved
blackjack	1025	TCP, UDP	network blackjack
iad1	1030	TCP, UDP	BBN IAD
iad2	1031	TCP, UDP	BBN IAD
iad3	1032	TCP, UDP	BBN IAD
instl_boots	1067	TCP, UDP	Installation Bootstrap Proto. Serv.
instl_bootc	1068	TCP, UDP	Installation Bootstrap Proto. Cli.
socks	1080	TCP, UDP	Socks
ansoft-lm-1	1083	TCP, UDP	Anasoft License Manager
ansoft-lm-2	1084	TCP, UDP	Anasoft License Manager
nfa	1155	TCP, UDP	Network File Access
nerv	1222	TCP, UDP	SNI R&D network
hermes	1248	TCP, UDP	
alta-ana-lm	1346	TCP, UDP	Alta Analytics License Manager
bbn-mmc	1347	TCP, UDP	multimedia conferencing
bbn-mmx	1348	TCP, UDP	multimedia conferencing
sbook	1349	TCP, UDP	Registration Network Protocol
editbench	1350	TCP, UDP	Registration Network Protocol
equationbuilder	1351	TCP, UDP	Digital Tool Works (MIT)
lotusnote	1352	TCP, UDP	Lotus Note
relief	1353	TCP, UDP	Relief Consulting
rightbrain	1354	TCP, UDP	RightBrain Software
intuitive edge	1355	TCP, UDP	Intuitive Edge

Keyword	Decimal	Protocol	Description
cuillamartin	1356	TCP, UDP	CuillaMartin Company
pegboard	1357	TCP, UDP	Electronic PegBoard
connlcli	1358	TCP, UDP	CONNLCLI
ftsrv	1359	TCP, UDP	FTSRV
mimer	1360	TCP, UDP	MIMER
linx	1361	TCP, UDP	LinX
timeflies	1362	TCP, UDP	TimeFlies
ndm-requester	1363	TCP, UDP	Network DataMover Requester
ndm-server	1364	TCP, UDP	Network DataMover Server
adapt-sna	1365	TCP, UDP	Network Software Associates
netware-csp	1366	TCP, UDP	Novell NetWare Comm Service Platform
dcs	1367	TCP, UDP	DCS
screencast	1368	TCP, UDP	ScreenCast
gv-us	1369	TCP, UDP	GlobalView to Unix Shell
us-gv	1370	TCP, UDP	UNIX Shell to GlobalView
fc-cli	1371	TCP, UDP	Fujitsu Config Protocol
fc-ser	1372	TCP, UDP	Fujitsu Config Protocol
chromagrafx	1373	TCP, UDP	Chromagrafx
molly	1374	TCP, UDP	EPI Software Systems
bytex	1375	TCP, UDP	Bytex
ibm-pps	1376	TCP, UDP	IBM Person-to-Person Software
cichlid	1377	TCP, UDP	Cichlid License Manager
elan	1378	TCP, UDP	Elan License Manager
dbreporter	1379	TCP, UDP	Integrity Solutions
telesis-licman	1380	TCP, UDP	Telesis Network License Manager
apple-licman	1381	TCP, UDP	Apple Network License Manager
udt_os	1382	TCP, UDP	
gwha	1383	TCP, UDP	GW Hannaway Network License Manager
os-licman	1384	TCP, UDP	Objective Solutions License Manager

Keyword	Decimal	Protocol	Description
atex_elmd	1385	TCP, UDP	Atex Publishing License Manager
checksum	1386	TCP, UDP	CheckSum License Manager
cadsi-lm	1387	TCP, UDP	Computer Aided Design Software Inc LM
objective-dbc	1388	TCP, UDP	Objective Solutions DataBase Cache
iclpv-dm	1389	TCP, UDP	Document Manager
iclpv-sc	1390	TCP, UDP	Storage Controller
iclpv-sas	1391	TCP, UDP	Storage Access Server
iclpv-pm	1392	TCP, UDP	Print Manager
iclpv-nls	1393	TCP, UDP	Network Log Server
iclpv-nlc	1394	TCP, UDP	Network Log Client
iclpv-wsm	1395	TCP, UDP	PC Workstation Manager software
dvl-activemail	1396	TCP, UDP	DVL Active Mail
audio-activmail	1397	TCP, UDP	Audio Active Mail
video-activmail	1398	TCP, UDP	Video Active Mail
cadkey-licman	1399	TCP, UDP	Cadkey License Manager
cadkey-tablet	1400	TCP, UDP	Cadkey Tablet Daemon
goldleaf-licman	1401	TCP, UDP	Goldleaf License Manager
prm-sm-np	1402	TCP, UDP	Prospero Resource Manager
prm-nm-np	1403	TCP, UDP	Prospero Resource Manager
igi-lm	1404	TCP, UDP	Infinite Graphics License Manager
ibm-res	1405	TCP, UDP	IBM Remote Execution Starter
netlabs-lm	1406	TCP, UDP	NetLabs License Manager
dbsa-lm	1407	TCP, UDP	DBSA License Manager
sophia-lm	1408	TCP, UDP	Sophia License Manager
here-lm	1409	TCP, UDP	Here License Manager
hiq	1410	TCP, UDP	HiQ License Manager
af	1411	TCP, UDP	AudioFile
innosys	1412	TCP, UDP	InnoSys
innosys-acl	1413	TCP, UDP	Innosys-ACL

Keyword	Decimal	Protocol	Description
ibm-mqseries	1414	TCP, UDP	IBM MQSeries
dbstar	1415	TCP, UDP	DBStar
novell-lu6.2	1416	TCP, UDP	Novell LU6.2
timbuktu-srv1	1417	TCP, UDP	Timbuktu Service 1 Port
timbuktu-srv2	1418	TCP, UDP	Timbuktu Service 2 Port
timbuktu-srv3	1419	TCP, UDP	Timbuktu Service 3 Port
timbuktu-srv4	1420	TCP, UDP	Timbuktu Service 4 Port
gandalf-lm	1421	TCP, UDP	Gandalf License Manager
autodesk-lm	1422	TCP, UDP	Autodesk License Manager
essbase	1423	TCP, UDP	Essbase Arbor Software
hybrid	1424	TCP, UDP	Hybrid Encryption Protocol
zion-lm	1425	TCP, UDP	Zion Software License Manager
sas-1	1426	TCP, UDP	Satellite-data Acquisition System 1
mloadd	1427	TCP, UDP	mloadd monitoring tool
informatik-lm	1428	TCP, UDP	Informatik License Manager
nms	1429	TCP, UDP	Hypercom NMS
tpdu	1430	TCP, UDP	Hypercom TPDU
rgtp	1431	TCP, UDP	Reverse Gosip Transport
blueberry-lm	1432	TCP, UDP	Blueberry Software License Manager
ms-sql-s	1433	TCP, UDP	Microsoft-SQL-Server
ms-sql-m	1434	TCP, UDP	Microsoft-SQL-Monitor
ibm-cics	1435	TCP, UDP	IBM CISC
sas-2	1436	TCP, UDP	Satellite-data Acquisition System 2
tabula	1437	TCP, UDP	Tabula
eicon-server	1438	TCP, UDP	Eicon Security Agent/Server
eicon-x25	1439	TCP, UDP	Eicon X25/SNA Gateway
eicon-slp	1440	TCP, UDP	Eicon Service Location Protocol
cadis-1	1441	TCP, UDP	Cadis License Management
cadis-2	1442	TCP, UDP	Cadis License Management

Keyword	Decimal	Protocol	Description
ies-lm	1443	TCP, UDP	Integrated Engineering Software
marcam-lm	1444	TCP, UDP	Marcam License Management
proxima-lm	1445	TCP, UDP	Proxima License Manager
ora-lm	1446	TCP, UDP	Optical Research Associates License Manager
apri-lm	1447	TCP, UDP	Applied Parallel Research LM
oc-lm	1448	TCP, UDP	OpenConnect License Manager
peport	1449	TCP, UDP	Peport
dwf	1450	TCP, UDP	Tandem Distributed Workbench Facility
infoman	1451	TCP, UDP	IBM Information Management
gtegsc-lm	1452	TCP, UDP	GTE Government Systems License Man
genie-lm	1453	TCP, UDP	Genie License Manager
interhdl_elmd	1454	TCP, UDP	interHDL License Manager
esl-lm	1455	TCP, UDP	ESL License Manager
dca	1456	TCP, UDP	DCA
valisys-lm	1457	TCP, UDP	Valisys License Manager
nrcabq-lm	1458	TCP, UDP	Nichols Research Corp.
proshare1	1459	TCP, UDP	Proshare Notebook Application
proshare2	1460	TCP, UDP	Proshare Notebook Application
ibm_wrless_lan	1461	TCP, UDP	IBM Wireless LAN
world-lm	1462	TCP, UDP	World License Manager
nucleus	1463	TCP, UDP	Nucleus
msl_lmd	1464	TCP, UDP	MSL License Manager
pipes	1465	TCP, UDP	Pipes Platform
oceansoft-lm	1466	TCP, UDP	Ocean Software License Manager
csdmbase	1467	TCP, UDP	CSDMBASE
csdm	1468	TCP, UDP	CSDM
aal-lm	1469	TCP, UDP	Active Analysis Limited License Manager
uaiact	1470	TCP, UDP	Universal Analytics
csdmbase	1471	TCP, UDP	csdmbase

Keyword	Decimal	Protocol	Description
csdm	1472	TCP, UDP	csdm
openmath	1473	TCP, UDP	OpenMath
telefinder	1474	TCP, UDP	Telefinder
taligent-lm	1475	TCP, UDP	Taligent License Manager
clvm-cfg	1476	TCP, UDP	clvm-cfg
ms-sna-server	1477	TCP, UDP	ms-sna-server
ms-sna-base	1478	TCP, UDP	ms-sna-base
dberegister	1479	TCP, UDP	dberegister
pacerforum	1480	TCP, UDP	PacerForum
airs	1481	TCP, UDP	AIRS
miteksys-lm	1482	TCP, UDP	Miteksys License Manager
afs	1483	TCP, UDP	AFS License Manager
confluent	1484	TCP, UDP	Confluent License Manager
lansource	1485	TCP, UDP	LANSource
nms_topo_serv	1486	TCP, UDP	nms_topo_serv
localinfosrvr	1487	TCP, UDP	LocalInfoSrvr
docstor	1488	TCP, UDP	DocStor
dmdocbroker	1489	TCP, UDP	dmdocbroker
insitu-conf	1490	TCP, UDP	insitu-conf
anynetgateway	1491	TCP, UDP	anynetgateway
stone-design-1	1492	TCP, UDP	stone-design-1
netmap_lm	1493	TCP, UDP	netmap_lm
ica	1494	TCP, UDP	ica
cvc	1495	TCP, UDP	cvc
liberty-lm	1496	TCP, UDP	liberty-lm
rfx-lm	1497	TCP, UDP	rfx-lm
watcom-sql	1498	TCP, UDP	Watcom-SQL
fhc	1499	TCP, UDP	Federico Heinz Consultora
vlsi-lm	1500	TCP, UDP	VLSI License Manager

Keyword	Decimal	Protocol	Description
sas-3	1501	TCP, UDP	Satellite-data Acquisition System 3
shivadiscovery	1502	TCP, UDP	Shiva
imtc-mcs	1503	TCP, UDP	Databeam
evb-elm	1504	TCP, UDP	EVB Software Engineering License Manager
funkproxy	1505	TCP, UDP	Funk Software, Inc.
#	1506-1523	TCP, UDP	Unassigned
ingreslock	1524	TCP, UDP	ingres
orasrv	1525	TCP, UDP	oracle
prospero-np	1525	TCP, UDP	Prospero Directory Service non-priv
pdap-np	1526	TCP, UDP	Prospero Data Access Prot non-priv
tlisrv	1527	TCP, UDP	Oracle
coauthor	1529	TCP, UDP	Oracle
issd	1600	TCP, UDP	
nkd	1650	TCP, UDP	
proshareaudio	1651	TCP, UDP	proshare conf audio
prosharevideo	1652	TCP, UDP	proshare conf video
prosharedata	1653	TCP, UDP	proshare conf data
prosharerequest	1654	TCP, UDP	proshare conf request
prosharenotify	1655	TCP, UDP	proshare conf notify
netview-aix-1	1661	TCP, UDP	netview-aix-1
netview-aix-2	1662	TCP, UDP	netview-aix-2
netview-aix-3	1663	TCP, UDP	netview-aix-3
netview-aix-4	1664	TCP, UDP	netview-aix-4
netview-aix-5	1665	TCP, UDP	netview-aix-5
netview-aix-6	1666	TCP, UDP	netview-aix-6
licensedaemon	1986	TCP, UDP	Cisco license management
tr-rsrb-p1	1987	TCP, UDP	Cisco RSRB Priority 1 port
tr-rsrb-p2	1988	TCP, UDP	Cisco RSRB Priority 2 port
tr-rsrb-p3	1989	TCP, UDP	Cisco RSRB Priority 3 port

Keyword	Decimal	Protocol	Description
mshnet	1989	TCP, UDP	MHSnet system
stun-p1	1990	TCP, UDP	Cisco STUN Priority 1 port
stun-p2	1991	TCP, UDP	Cisco STUN Priority 2 port
stun-p3	1992	TCP, UDP	Cisco STUN Priority 3 port
ipsendmsg	1992	TCP, UDP	Ipsendmsg
snmp-TCP-port	1993	TCP	Cisco SNMP TCP, UDP port
snmp-UDP-port	1993	UDP	Cisco SNMP TCP, UDP port
stun-port	1994	TCP, UDP	Cisco serial tunnel port
perf-port	1995	TCP, UDP	Cisco perf port
tr-rsrb-port	1996	TCP, UDP	Cisco Remote SRB port
gdp-port	1997	TCP, UDP	Cisco Gateway Discovery Protocol
x25-svc-port	1998	TCP, UDP	Cisco X.25 service (XOT)
TCP-id-port	1999	TCP	Cisco identification port
UDP-id-port	1999	UDP	Cisco identification port
callbook	2000	TCP, UDP	
dc	2001	TCP	
wizard	2001	UDP	curry
globe	2002	TCP	
mailbox	2004	TCP	
emce	2004	UDP	CCWS mm conf
berknet	2005	TCP	
oracle	2005	UDP	
invokator	2006	TCP	
raid-cc	2006	UDP	raid
dectalk	2007	TCP	
raid-am	2007	UDP	
conf	2008	TCP	
terminaldb	2008	UDP	
news	2009	TCP	

Keyword	Decimal	Protocol	Description
whosockami	2009	UDP	
search	2010	TCP	
pipe_server	2010	UDP	
raid-cc	2011	TCP	raid
servserv	2011	UDP	
ttyinfo	2012	TCP	
raid-ac	2012	UDP	
raid-am	2013	TCP	
raid-cd	2013	UDP	
troff	2014	TCP	
raid-sf	2014	UDP	
cypress	2015	TCP	
raid-cs	2015	UDP	
bootserver	2016	TCP, UDP	
cypress-stat	2017	TCP	
bootclient	2017	UDP	
terminaldb	2018	TCP	
rellpack	2018	UDP	
whosockami	2019	TCP	
about	2019	UDP	
xinupageserver	2020	TCP, UDP	
servexec	2021	TCP	
xinuexpansion1	2021	UDP	
down	2022	TCP	
xinuexpansion2	2022	UDP	
xinuexpansion3	2023	TCP, UDP	
xinuexpansion4	2024	TCP, UDP	
ellpack	2025	TCP	
xribs	2025	UDP	

Keyword	Decimal	Protocol	Description
scrabble	2026	TCP, UDP	
shadowserver	2027	TCP, UDP	
submitserver	2028	TCP, UDP	
device2	2030	TCP, UDP	
blackboard	2032	TCP, UDP	
glogger	2033	TCP, UDP	
scoremgr	2034	TCP, UDP	
imsldoc	2035	TCP, UDP	
objectmanager	2038	TCP, UDP	
lam	2040	TCP, UDP	
interbase	2041	TCP, UDP	
isis	2042	TCP, UDP	
isis-bcast	2043	TCP, UDP	
rimsl	2044	TCP, UDP	
cdfunc	2045	TCP, UDP	
sdfunc	2046	TCP, UDP	
dls	2047	TCP, UDP	
dls-monitor	2048	TCP, UDP	
shilp	2049	TCP, UDP	
dlsrpn	2065	TCP, UDP	Data Link Switch Read Port Number
dlswpn	2067	TCP, UDP	Data Link Switch Write Port Number
ats	2201	TCP, UDP	Advanced Training System Program
rtsserv	2500	TCP, UDP	Resource Tracking system server
rtsclient	2501	TCP, UDP	Resource Tracking system client
hp-3000-telnet	2564	TCP	HP 3000 NS/VT block mode telnet
www-dev	2784	TCP, UDP	World Wide Web – development
NSWS	3049	TCP, UDP	
ccmail	3264	TCP, UDP	cc:mail/lotus
dec-notes	3333	TCP, UDP	DEC Notes

Keyword	Decimal	Protocol	Description
mapper-nodemgr	3984	TCP, UDP	MAPPER network node manager
mapper-mapethd	3985	TCP, UDP	MAPPER TCP, UDP/IP server
mapper-ws_ethd	3986	TCP, UDP	MAPPER workstation server
bmap	3421	TCP, UDP	Bull Apprise portmapper
udt_os	3900	TCP, UDP	Unidata UDT OS
nuts_dem	4132	TCP, UDP	NUTS Daemon
nuts_bootp	4133	TCP, UDP	NUTS Bootp Server
unicall	4343	TCP, UDP	UNICALL
krb524	4444	TCP, UDP	KRB524
rfa	4672	TCP, UDP	remote file access server
commplex-main	5000	TCP, UDP	
commplex-link	5001	TCP, UDP	
rfe	5002	TCP, UDP	radio free ethernet
telelpathstart	5010	TCP, UDP	TelepathStart
telelpathattack	5011	TCP, UDP	TelepathAttack
mmcc	5050	TCP, UDP	multimedia conference control tool
rmonitor_secure	5145	TCP, UDP	
aol	5190	TCP, UDP	America-Online
padl2sim	5236	TCP, UDP	
hacl-hb	5300	TCP, UDP	# HA cluster heartbeat
hacl-gs	5301	TCP, UDP	# HA cluster general services
hacl-cfg	5302	TCP, UDP	# HA cluster configuration
hacl-probe	5303	TCP, UDP	# HA cluster probing
hacl-local	5304	TCP, UDP	
hacl-test	5305	TCP, UDP	
x11	6000-6063	TCP, UDP	X Window System
sub-process	6111	TCP, UDP	HP SoftBench Sub-Process Control
meta-corp	6141	TCP, UDP	Meta Corporation License Manager
aspentec-lm	6142	TCP, UDP	Aspen Technology License Manager

| Appendix A

Keyword	Decimal	Protocol	Description
watershed-lm	6143	TCP, UDP	Watershed License Manager
statsci1-lm	6144	TCP, UDP	StatSci License Manager – 1
statsci2-lm	6145	TCP, UDP	StatSci License Manager – 2
lonewolf-lm	6146	TCP, UDP	Lone Wolf Systems License Manager
montage-lm	6147	TCP, UDP	Montage License Manager
xdsxdm	6558	UDP	
afs3-fileserver	7000	TCP, UDP	file server itself
afs3-callback	7001	TCP, UDP	callbacks to cache managers
afs3-prserver	7002	TCP, UDP	users & groups database
afs3-vlserver	7003	TCP, UDP	volume location database
afs3-kaserver	7004	TCP, UDP	AFS/Kerberos authentication service
afs3-volser	7005	TCP, UDP	volume managment server
afs3-errors	7006	TCP, UDP	error interpretation service
afs3-bos	7007	TCP, UDP	basic overseer process
afs3-update	7008	TCP, UDP	server-to-server updater
afs3-rmtsys	7009	TCP, UDP	remote cache manager service
ups-onlinet	7010	TCP, UDP	onlinet uninterruptable power supplies
font-service	7100	TCP, UDP	X Font Service
fodms	7200	TCP, UDP	FODMS FLIP
man	9535	TCP, UDP	
isode-dual	17007	TCP, UDP	

A.3   Dynamic and/or private ports

These ports lie within the range 49,152 through 65,535 and are for private or on-demand use by applications and user-defined services.

B
Mathematical Review

Much of the research literature available to the network designer may often appear impenetrable; since the language used to express ideas involves advanced mathematical notation. Although this book is not heavily numerical, it is assumed that the reader has a basic grasp of mathematics, as the use of mathematical conventions in some areas of network design is unavoidable. In this appendix we will briefly review a selection of the more common techniques applicable to data communications design theory.

B.1   Operators

$+$	Add	$\times$	Multiply
$-$	Subtract	$\div$	Divide
$=$	Equals	$\neq$	Note equal to
$\cong$	or $\approx$ Approximately equal to	$<$	Less than
$>$	Greater than	$\leq$	Less than or equal to
$\geq$	Greater or equal to	$\wedge$	Raised to the power of
$\sqrt{}$	The square root of	$\rightarrow$	Tends to or approaches

B.2   Numbers

Real numbers are numbers that can take a positive, negative, or zero value. For example:

$-400, -20, -11.75, -3, 0, +1, +3.76, +1000$

Integers are whole numbers, positive or negative, that have no fractional parts. For example:

−400, −20, −11, −3, 0, +1, +3, +1000

Rational Numbers are fractional numbers and may be positive or negative. Rational numbers include fractions that are less than one, those that are greater than one (so-called *improper* fractions). Formally stated rational numbers have the form a/b, where a and b are integers, b cannot be zero, and there are no common factors (i.e., 4/6 should be reduced to 2/3). Note that b can equal 1, so all integers, including zero, can be seen as rational numbers with a value of b equal to 1. For example:

−7/2, −1/4, 0/1, +1/8, +1/4, +3/2, +16/1

Irrational Numbers are a form of rational numbers where a and b are non-integer. Irrational numbers can be produced in a number of ways; for example π is irrational, and the square root of any *prime* number is irrational (e.g., $\sqrt{2}$ or $\sqrt{13}$). For example:

2.2360679, 3.1415926

Prime Number is a whole numbers that is greater than 1 and has no common factors other than 1 and itself (i.e., it cannot be divided by two integers that are greater than 1). Every natural number greater than 1 is either prime, or can be expressed as a product of primes (e.g., $28 = 2 \times 2 \times 7$). Prime numbers have many useful applications in cryptography, as discussed in Chapter 15. Examples include:

2, 3, ..., 17, 19, 23, ..., 47, ..., 101, ..., 1093,

Infinity is itself not a number. In effect it is an unbounded value; we may therefore use the phrase *infinitely large* or *infinitely small* to represent inconceivably large or small values respectively. The term *infinitesimal* means a value whose limit is zero. Infinity is normally represented by the symbol ∞.

B.3   Summation

Summation of a series of numbers is frequently used in statistical and communication theory. A shorthand notation is used to represent a series of additions:

$\sum$ (Sigma), used to denote "the sum of."

where the general form is:

$$\overset{Termination\_Condition}{\underset{Initialization\_Condition}{\sum}} \left(variable\ expression\right)$$

For example:

$$\sum_{i=1}^{n} x_i$$

Represents the sum of the series $X_1 + X_2 + X_3 + \ldots X_n$. For example, if $n = 4$, and the series of numbers is $\{1, 2, 3, 4\}$ then this operation would produce the result 10. Note that the variable expression must be summed before any external operator can be applied; so for example:

$$\sum_{i=0}^{n} x_i^2 \neq \left(\sum_{i=0}^{n} x_i\right)^2$$

This is clearly demonstrated using the previous example series $\{1, 2, 3, 4\}$ and $n = 4$.

$$1^2 + 2^2 + 3^2 + 4^2 \neq (1 + 2 + 3 + 4)^2$$

$$30 \neq 100$$

Summation is frequently used with more complex variable expressions, such as summation of a series of products:

$$\sum_{i=1}^{n} x_i y_i$$

It is important to recognize here that the *first* instance of x is multiplied by the first instance of y and so on through the series. There are a number of other basic rules applicable to summation operations, these include:

Rule 1: The summation of sum of two variables is equal to the sum of the two summations of those variables:

$$\sum_{i=1}^{n} \left(x_i + y_i\right) = \sum_{i=1}^{n} x_i + \sum_{i=1}^{n} y_i$$

Rule 2: The summation of the subtraction of two variables is equal to the difference between the two summations of those variables:

$$\sum_{i=1}^{n} \left(x_i - y_i\right) = \sum_{i=1}^{n} x_i - \sum_{i=1}^{n} y_i$$

Rule 3: The summation of a constant n times is equal to the product of n and that constant:

$$\sum_{i=1}^{n} c = cn$$

Rule 4: The summation of the product of a constant and a variable is equal to the product of the constant and the summation of that variable:

$$\sum_{i=1}^{n} cx_i = c\sum_{i=1}^{n} x_i$$

B.4   Sets

A collection, class, or listing of mathematical objects is called a set. The objects in the set are referred to as *elements* or *members*. The *universal set* is the complete set of objects applicable to the object context (for example, if we were interested in performing operations on sets of *prime* numbers between 0 and 20, then the universal set would be {2, 3, 5, 7, 11, 13, 17, 19}. For statistical applications we are largely interested in sets of *numbers*, however in areas of design such as topology analysis we may wish to manipulate set of *objects* such as *edges* or *adjacencies* (described in Chapters 4 and 6). A set can be described using precise mathematical notation. Once described, there are algebraic operations that can be performed on sets using additional notation.

$\{a,b,c,d,e, \dots z\}$	the set of elements from a to z
ϕ	the empty set
A′	the complement of set A (i.e., A becomes the *universal set* minus the intersection of set A and universal set)
n(A)	the number of elements in set A
$\cup$	union of two sets (i.e., those elements common or unique to both sets)
$\cap$	intersection of two sets (i.e., those elements common to both sets)
$\in$	is a member/element of (e.g., $3 \in \{1, 2, 3\}$).

$\notin$	is not a member/element of (e.g., $3 \notin \{1, 2, 4, 8\}$).
$\subseteq$	is a subset of (e.g., if every element of set T is a member of set S, then $\mathsf{T} \subseteq \mathsf{S}$).
$\subset$	is a proper subset of (e.g., $\mathsf{T} \subset \mathsf{S}$ in the above example, if an element $s \in \mathsf{S}$, and $s \notin \mathsf{T}$).

For example: the set containing 0 and 1 is denoted as $\{0, 1\}$. The set of even numbers between 2 and 500 is denoted as $\{2, 4, 6, \ldots, 500\}$. Regarding subsets, set S = $\{2, 4, 6\}$ has 8 distinct subsets: $\{2, 4, 6\}$, $\{2\}$, $\{4\}$, $\{6\}$, $\{2, 4\}$, $\{2, 6\}$, $\{4, 6\}$, plus the empty set $\{\}$, denoted as ϕ.

Index

10Base2, 275, 279–80
  cabling illustration, 280
  defined, 279
  segments, 279
  See also Ethernet
10Base5, 275, 277–79
  cabling illustration, 278
  defined, 277
  deployment, 279
  propagation velocity, 277
  transceivers, 278–79
  See also Ethernet
10BaseFB, 283
10BaseFL, 275, 282
10BaseFP, 282
10BaseT, 275, 280–82
  cabling illustration, 281
  defined, 280
  station to hub wiring connection, 282
  See also Ethernet
10Broad36, 280
100BaseFx, 283
100BaseT2, 287
100BaseX, 286–87
100VG-AnyLAN (IEEE 802.12), 292–95, 331
  defined, 292
  deployment, 293
  hubs, 293
  network design, 294–95
  operation, 293–94
  ratification, 293
1000BaseCX, 290–91
1000BaseSX, 290
1000BaseT, 291
1000BaseX. *See* Gigabit Ethernet (IEEE 802.3z)

Abstract cost, 207
Access layer, 94
Access networks
  collapsing sites in distribution concentrators, 192–95
  defined, 187
  design, 191–98, 245
  dial-up, 344–45
  distance limitations, 345–46
  Frame Relay design strategies, 406–7
  high-speed, 345
  infrastructure products, 352–53
  locating distribution concentrators, 195–97
  selecting, 346–47
  site layout, 197–98
  WAN, 343–47
Access technologies (WAN), 363–78
  cable modems, 366–67
  DSL, 363–66
  N-ISDN, 367–78
Accounting rate of return, 148
Accuracy, 67

Active research, 231–32
Adaptive routing, 206
Adaptive switches, 507
ADD heuristic, 196
Addresses
    data link, 17
    ISDN mapping, 373
    MAC, 16
    network, 17
    transport, 17
Addressing, 16–17
    ATM, 446–48, 455–56
    SMDS, 419
Address Resolution Protocol (ARP), 22,
        400–401
Alternate paths, 98–99
American National Standards Institute
        (ANSI), 14, 263, 431
    defined, 14
    X3T9.3 committee, 309
Analytical modeling, 107–28
    circuit-switched traffic, 121–24
    classical queuing analysis, 107–24
    defined, 107
    interconnecting remote LANs, 120–21
    overview, 107
    packetized traffic, 118–21
    packet train model, 125–26
    self-similarity, 126–27
    tools, 127–28
    X.25 packet switch, 118–20
    See also Modeling
Application maps, 82–83
    defined, 82
    example, 83
    flow, 85
Application profiles, 86
Applications
    bandwidth requirements, 55–58
    behavior, quantifying, 48
    data rates, 57

network delay sensitivity, 55–56
    storage space, 55
    thresholds and limitations, 58–59
Application simulators, 136
Asymmetrical traffic, 87–88
Asymmetric Digital Subscriber Line (ADSL),
        364–65
    defined, 364
    downstream speeds, 364
    target applications, 365
    See also Digital Subscriber Line (DSL)
Asynchronous Transfer Mode. See ATM
ATM, 173–75, 340, 431–501
    addressing, 446–48, 455–56
    address resolution, 458–61
    architecture, 431, 432–51
    ATM Adaptation Layer (AAL), 435–38
    ATM Layer, 435
    Available Bit Rate (ABR), 449
    CAC, 451, 457–58
    cell formats, 445–46
    Classical IP over (CIOA), 431, 467–68,
        470–73
    cluster interconnection, 491–93
    cluster topologies, 490–91
    connections, 451–55
    Constant Bit Rate (CBR), 449
    cost, 488
    costing complexity, 173–74
    defined, 531
    distance, 485
    end stations, 432
    examples, 175
    flooding topology state information, 457
    Frame Relay and, 483
    functional layers, 432–38
    hub clustering, 490
    interface definitions, 441–45
    Internet backbone migration to, 493–94
    interworking with, 467–84
    interworking with WANs, 483–84

label swapping, 453–55
LANE, 431, 468, 475–78
MARS, 474–75
MPOA, 468, 478–83
multicast operations, 461–62
multiprotocol encapsulation over AAL5, 467, 469
NHRP, 468, 473
number of circuits per terminal, 485
number of terminals, 485
operation, 451–67
overview, 432
Physical Layer, 433–35
PPP over, 468
protocol stack, 433
route computation, 456
routing, 455–58
scalability, 458, 484–85
service classes, 450–51
service types, 449–50
signaling, 452–53, 456–57
SMDS and, 483–84
summary, 500–501
switching architectures, 462–63
tariff structure, 174–75
technology, 431
topology, 484
UNI prices, 175
Unspecified Bit Rate (UBR), 449
Variable Bit Rate (VBR), 449
VCs, 438–41
VPs, 438–41
See also Private network charging models
ATM Adaptation Layer (AAL), 435–38
AAL0, 436
AAL1, 436
AAL2, 436–37
AAL3/4, 437
AAL5, 437
defined, 435

deployment, 435
service class support, 438
ATMARP, 458–61
defined, 458
PVC/SVC environments, 458–59
requests, 460
table entries, 460–61
table operations, 459–61
ATM core
advantages/disadvantages of, 499–500
failure modes and, 499
logical ISP topology over, 498
logical topology, 496, 497
network management, 499
n-squared problem, 498
per-PVC statistics, 499
physical topology, 496, 497
PVC-based traffic control in, 496–98
traffic engineering, 499
See also Wide area backbone design
ATM Forum, 434
ATM interfaces, 432
DXI, 444
ILMI, 444–45
NNI, 432, 492
PNNI, 443–44, 492
SSI, 443
UNI, 432, 441–42, 492
ATM network design, 484–500
campus, 488–93
LAN backbone, 485–88
media flexibility, 484
scalability, 484–85
wide area, 493–500
ATM performance, 463–67
Cell Delay Variation (CDV), 464
cell insertion rate, 464
cell loss ratio, 464
cell transfer delay, 464
delay, 466
IP vs., 466–67

ATM performance *(cont'd.)*
  parameters, 464
  severely errored cell ratio, 464
  switching speed, 464
  switch latency, 465
  throughput, 465–66
ATM switch(es), 31
  architecture, 462–63
  blocking characteristics, 463
  buffering method/capacity, 463
  CAC, 451
  capacity, 464
  fabric, 462
  latency, 465
  speed, 464
Attachment Unit Interface (AUI), 283–84
Availability analysis, 190–91
Available Bit Rate (ABR), 449

Backbone
  cabling, 265
  defined, 187
  layer, 93
Backbone design, 187–90, 198–232
  basic algorithm, 200–202
  capacity assignment, 213–17
  costing, 217
  dynamic programming method, 189
  genetic algorithms (GAs), 189–90, 225–32
  gradient methods, 189
  input data, 199–200
  localized iterative approach, 202–3
  MENTOR, 223–25
  optimal, 198
  perturbation algorithms, 217–23
  process, 199–203
  process illustration, 201
  random-restart gradient methods, 189
  random search approach, 188
  routing/traffic flows, 205–13
  simulated annealing method, 189

SMDS, 420
  starting topography algorithm, 203–5
  swarming algorithms, 190, 232
Backbone design case study, 236–44
  cost matrix, 236–37
  defined, 236
  design output, 240–44
  design variables, 239–40
  site list, 236
  traffic matrix, 237–39
Backbone design tools, 233–44
  commercial, 234–36
  Delite, 233
  iSIM+, 236–44
  NetMaker MainStation, 235–36
  publicly available, 233–34
  WANDL Network Planning and Analysis
    Tools (NPAT), 235
Backbone networks, 347–64
  available bandwidths, 347–49
  core issues, 351–54
  Frame Relay for, 407–11
  infrastructure products, 352
  network overlays, 350–51
  technology strengths/weaknesses,
    349–50
Backbone technologies (WAN), 378–427
  DWDM, 425–27
  Frame Relay, 394–414
  leased lines, 378–87
  satellite links, 378–87
  SMDS, 414–23
  SONET, 423–25
  X.25, 387–94
Balanced transmission line, 258–59
Bandwidth, 38–39, 68
  application requirements, 55–58
  choices, 37
  defined, 64
  Frame Relay allocation, 397–98
  network use, 56

  as routing metric, 207
  WAN, 347–49
Bandwidth charging model, 151–63
  calculation information, 154–55
  charge models, 152–53
  charge types, 151–52
  circuit cost, 156–59
  distance calculations, 154–55
  peak load pricing, 159–63
  piecewise linear, 156
  See also Charging models
Bandwidth on Demand (BoD), 375–76
Baselining, 48–52
  activities, 49
  sample interval and duration, 52
  tools, 50–52
  traffic profiles, 49–50
Bellman-Ford algorithm, 105–6
  defined, 105
  distributed asynchronous, 106
  implementations, 105
Bertsekas-Gallager (BG) algorithm,
    212–13
Billing systems, 182
Binary Synchronous Control (BSC), 354
Bit error rate (BER), 72–73
  for common media types, 73
  packet size and, 73
Bluetooth, 327–28
  defined, 327
  device classes, 327
  integration cost, 328
  See also Wireless LAN
BONeS, 132
Bottlenecks, 75–82
  client/server, 77–78
  examples, 77
  locating, 75
  network performance, 78–82
  typical, 75–77
  See also Performance

Branch exchange, 217–19
  defined, 217
  drawbacks, 218–19
  incremental nature of, 218
  modification/enhancement, 218
  operations, 219
  See also Perturbation algorithms
Bridges, 30–31
  applicability in internetwork design,
    512–14
  benefits, 32–33
  broadcast storms and, 34
  congestion feedback and, 34
  defined, 30, 504
  encapsulation/tunnel, 506, 546–47
  evolution, 505
  filters, 30
  interoperability, 529
  issues, 33–34
  local, 505
  manageability, 33
  maximum in a series, 527–28, 536
  multicast support, 510–12
  in network design, 508
  parallel, 536
  placement, 528
  price/performance, 33
  remote, 505
  in repeated network, 508
  Source Routing (SRB), 506, 529–36
  Source Routing Translation (SR-TB),
    506
  Source Routing Transparent (SRT), 506,
    536–39
  Spanning Tree, 506, 517
  STA, 528–29
  switches vs., 504
  timers, 528
  translation, 539–46
  transparency, 33
  transparent, 505

Bridging, 504–6
    encapsulation/tunnel, 546–47
    overview, 503
    translation, 539–46
    transparent, 514–29
Broadband ISDN (B-ISDN), 368, 431
Budgetary planning, 4
Buffering
    in packet-switched networks, 112–14
    requirements, growth of, 114
Building blocks, 13–39
    framework, 13–17
    hardware, 27–35
    physical connectivity, 35–39
    protocols, 17–27
Bus topology, 253–54

Cable modems, 366–67
    defined, 366
    downstream broadcasts, 367
    shared access, 367
    technology options, 366–67
Cabling
    backbone, 265
    centralized, 265–68
    distributed, 265–68
    horizontal, 264–65
    hybrid, 267–68
    standards, 263–65
    structured, 263–65
    Token Ring, 305–7
Campus network design, 488–93
    approach, 488–89
    ATM cluster interconnection,
        491–93
    cabling reuse, 489
    cluster topologies, 490–91
    hub clustering, 490
    illustrated, 489
    issues, 488
    See also ATM

Capacity
    assigning, 213–17
    constrained uniformly, 216
    defined, 64–65
    equal cost allocation, 214
    min-cost allocation, 214
    proportional allocation, 214
    square root allocation, 214
Capacity planning, 41–89
    defined, 42
    framework, 42–55
    need for, 42–44
    top-down framework, 44–54
Carrier Sense Multiple Access with Collision
        Detection (CSMA/CD), 270, 289
Cell Delay Variation (CDV), 464
Cells
    ATM, 445–46
    defined, 67
Centralized cabling, 265–68
    advantages/disadvantages, 266–67
    defined, 266
    illustrated, 266
    See also Cabling
Channel Service Unit (CSU).
        See CSU/DSUs
Charges
    by service type, 153
    congestion, 152
    distance calculations, 154–55
    fixed, 151
    models, 152–53
    service quality, 152
    types of, 151–52
    use, 151–52
Charging models
    bandwidth, 151–63
    Internet, 163–66
    piecewise linear, 156
    private network, 166–79
    See also Cost analysis

Chromosome encoding, 227–29
 advantages, 228
 disadvantages, 228
 tradeoffs, 228–29
 See also Genetic algorithms (GAs)
Circuit backup, 376–77
Circuit cost modeling, 156–59
 international circuits, 158–59
 location and, 156–59
 maximum costs, 158–59
 traffic and, 157
 zones, 158
Circuit switching, 37
 call abandonment, 124
 defined, 37
 packet vs., 38
 traffic modeling, 121–24
Classical IP over ATM, 431, 467–68, 470–73
 address resolution, 472
 architecture illustration, 471
 defined, 467–68, 470
 issues, 472–73
 LIS, 470–71
 lost functionality, 472–73
 operation, 472
 standards, 470
 See also ATM
Clients
 bottlenecks, 77–78
 DWDM integration components, 427
 MPOA, 479–80
 traffic, 84
Coaxial cable, 256, 259
 defined, 259
 Ethernet specifications, 276
 See also Cabling
Committed Information Rate (CIR), 404
Compression, 74–75
Congestion charge, 152
Congestion control, 403–5
 components, 404

 purpose, 404
 See also Frame Relay
Connection Admission Control (CAC), 451, 457–58
 defined, 457
 Generic (GCAC), 457–58
 implementation, 457
 See also ATM
Connectivity, 36
Constant Bit Rate (CBR), 449
Continuous models, 130
Cost
 abstract, 207
 ATM, 488
 backbone design, 217
 circuit modeling, 156–59
 equal allocation, 214
 exploring, 9
 matrix, 236–37
 monetary, 208
Cost analysis, 143–83
 bandwidth charging model, 151–63
 billing systems, 182
 Internet charging model, 163–66
 planning/billing tools, 179–82
 private network charging models, 166–79
 raw tariff data sources, 181–82
 summary, 182–83
Crossover and mutation, 230–31
Crosstalk, 257–58
CSU/DSUs, 30
Currency exchange rates, 150–51
Cut saturation algorithm, 219–22
 combined heuristic, 222
 defined, 219
 link addition, 221
 link deletion, 221
 process illustration, 221
 summary, 220
 See also Perturbation algorithms
Cut-through switches, 507

Data
    collation, 54–55
    environmental, 54–55
    input, summarizing, 53–54
    modeling, 82–88
    rate, 79
    transmit/receive, 273
Data Circuit Terminating Equipment (DCE),
        398–99
Data Communications Message Protocol
        (DCMP), 354
Data Exchange Interface (DXI), 444
Data Link Connection Identifiers (DLCIs),
        396, 403
    design issues, 402–3
    threshold factors, 402–3
    use of, 402
    See also Frame Relay
Data Link Layer, 16, 20–21
    LLC sublayer, 20–21
    MAC sublayer, 20
Data Link Switching (DLSw), 546
Data Service Unit (DSU).
        See CSU/DSUs
Data Terminal Equipment (DTE),
        398
Decision models, 147–50
    IRR, 148
    NVP, 147–50
    payback period, 148
Delay
    ATM, 466
    Frame Relay, 413
    media access, 66–67
    processing, 65
    propagation, 65
    routing metric, 207–8
    store-and-forward, 65
    total, 210
    transmission, 65
Delite tool, 233

Dense Wave Division Multiplexing
        (DWDM), 337, 352, 425–27, 428
    advantages, 426–27
    client integration components, 427
    defined, 425
    designing issues, 427
    long-haul, 425, 426
    SONET/SDH support, 425–26
Deployment, 13
Detailed Requirements Specification, 7
Dial-up access, 344–45, 427
Digital Subscriber Line (DSL), 340, 346,
        363–66
    Asymmetric (ADSL), 364–65
    defined, 363
    High data rate (HDSL), 365
    ISDN (IDSL), 363–64
    services, 363
    Single-line (SDSL), 365–66
    Very high data rate (VDSL), 366
Dijkstra's algorithm, 102–3
Discrete models, 129–30
Discussion groups, forming, 45–46
Distance calculations, 154–55
Distributed cabling, 265–68
    advantages/disadvantages, 267
    defined, 266
    illustrated, 266
    See also Cabling
Distributed entity traffic, 84
Distributed routing, 206
Distribution concentrators
    collapsing sites in, 192–95
    illustrated, 193
    locating, 195–97
Distribution functions, 109–10
    exponential, 110, 111
    Poisson, 110, 111
Distribution layer, 93–94
Divide-and-conquer approach, 186–87
Domain Name System (DNS), 26

DROP heuristic, 196–97
Dynamic ports, 590
Dynamic programming, 189

E1 lines, 380
    balanced/unbalanced modes, 381
    channelized, 381–82
    framed mode, 382
    interface, 381
    unframed mode, 381
    See also Leased lines
E3 lines, 382
E-commerce, 43
Economics, 144–51
    currency exchange rates and, 150–51
    decision models, 147–50
    taxes and, 150–51
    terminology, 144–47
    value of money and, 147
Electromagnetic Interface (EMI), 277
Electromagnetic spectrum, 321–22
Electronic Industries Association (EIA), 14
Elitism, 230
Empirical modeling, 133–37, 139
    benefits, 134
    links simulation, 137
    prototype testbed, 134
    routing tables, 136–37
    traffic generation, 134–36
    See also Modeling
Emulated LANs (ELANs), 475
Encapsulation techniques, 354–62
    BSC, 354
    DCMP, 354
    HDLC, 354, 355–56
    PPP, 354–55, 357–62
    SDLC, 354
    SLIP, 354, 356–57
    See also WANs
Encapsulation/tunnel bridges, 506
    DLSw, 546

FDDI, 547
    See also Bridges
End-to-end transaction delays, 59–60
End users, engaging, 5
Environmental data, 54–55
Equal cost allocation, 214
Erbium Doped Fiber Amplifiers (EDFAs).
        See Dense Wave Division Multiplexing
        (DWDM)
Erlang analysis, 122–23
Error probability, 72–74
Ethernet, 79–80, 250, 268–85, 330
    10Base2, 275, 279–80
    10Base5, 275, 277–79
    10BaseFB, 283
    10BaseFL, 275, 282
    10BaseFP, 282
    10BaseT, 275, 280–82
    10Broad36, 280
    100BaseFx, 283
    Attachment Unit Interface (AUI), 283–84
    background, 268
    defined, 268
    field definitions, 270–72
    frame format, 269
    frame types, 272
    generic design rules, 276–77
    high-speed, 286–95
    Inter-Repeater Links (IRLs), 277
    network design, 274–84
    node access rights, 272
    operation, 270–74
    performance considerations, 284–85
    quality of service, 274
    repeaters, 276
    specifications, 275
    transceiver operation, 272–74
    See also IEEE 802.3
European Computer Manufacturers
        Association (ECMA), 14
Event-driven simulation, 131

Explicit congestion avoidance, 405
Explicit routing, 206
Exponential distribution, 110, 111

FDDI, 81, 331
    Dual Attached Concentrators (DAC), 315,
        316
    Dual Attached Stations (DAS), 314, 316
    Dual Homing Concentrator (DHC), 216
    Dual Homing Station (DHS), 317
    encapsulation bridging, 547
    field definitions, 311–12
    frame formats, 310
    Media Access Control (MAC), 309
    media support, 313–14
    network design, 312–18
    operation, 310–11
    performance considerations, 318
    Physical Layer Medium (PMD), 309
    Physical Layer Protocol (PHY), 309
    port connection rules, 314
    product manufacturers, 318
    quality of service, 312
    rings, 311
    ring topology, 314–16
    Single Attached Stations (SAS), 214, 316
    Station Management (SMT), 309
    tree topology, 316–18
FDDI-to-Ethernet translation, 540–43
    address resolution, 541
    bit ordering, 541
    defined, 540
    design issues, 541–43
    encapsulation, 542
    illustrated, 540
    mixed-speed buffering, 542
    MTU size, 542
    See also Translation bridges
Fiber Distributed Data Interface. See FDDI
Fiber-optic cable, 256, 261–63
    advantages, 261–62

fiber grade, 263
reliability, 261
security, 262
sizes, 262
speed and drive distance, 261–62
Token Ring support, 304
See also LAN media
Fiber Optic Inter-Repeater Link (FOIRL),
    275, 282
Fibre Channel, 318–20
    defined, 318
    five-layer protocol architecture, 318–19
    interfaces, 318
    media types, 319
    topologies, 320
File Transfer Protocol (FTP), 25
Fitness evaluation, 229–30
Fixed charge, 151
Flat-rate pricing, 163–65
    capacity and, 165
    competitive pressure and, 164
    cost of capacity and, 164
    defined, 163
    tariff model, 164
    See also Internet charging model
Flooding, 205–6
Flow Deviation (FD) algorithm, 209–13
    complexity, 212
    defined, 209–10
    total delay and, 210
Flows
    characterizing, 83–86
    determining, 205–13
    in hierarchical model, 95
    types of, 84
    See also Traffic
Floyd-Warshall algorithm, 104–5
Forward delay timer, 518–19
    blocking, 519
    defined, 518
    disabled, 519

forwarding, 518–19
learning, 518
listening, 518
Fragment-free switches, 507
Frame Relay, 169–72, 340, 394–414, 428
    Access Device (FRAD), 399
    address resolution, 400–401
    ATM and, 483
    bandwidth allocation, 397–98
    broadcast issues, 403
    burst size, 412
    CIR, 169
    Committed Burst Size, 170
    congestion control, 403–5
    costing complexity, 170
    DCE, 398–99
    defined, 169, 394
    delay, 413
    design considerations, 401–6
    design strategies (access networks), 406–7
    design strategies (backbone networks),
        407–11
    devices, 398–99
    DTE, 398
    efficiency, 414
    EIR, 169
    error rates, 413
    examples, 171–72
    Excess Burst Size, 170
    field definitions, 395–96
    frame format, 394–95
    fully meshed topologies, 407
    hierarchical meshed internetworks, 409–11
    hub-and-spoke topologies, 408–9
    hybrid meshed internetworks, 411
    Local Management Interface (LMI), 401
    message format illustration, 395
    MTU and fragmentation, 412
    multiprotocol traffic management, 403
    operation, 396–400
    packets, 394

partially meshed topologies, 407
    performance considerations, 411–14
    pricing model, 170–71
    PVCs, 396, 399–400
    queuing, 403
    reliability, 406
    scalability, 401
    SNAP encapsulation, 397
    star topologies, 406–7
    statistical multiplexing, 414
    SVCs, 396, 399–400
    tariff structure, 169–71
    VCs, 399–400
    See also Private network charging
        models
Frames
    defined, 67
    size, 72–74
Framework, 13–17
Frequency Division Multiplexing (FDM), 336
Fully Distributed Redundant Bridging
        (FDRB), 510

GARP Multicast Registration Protocol
        (GMRP), 512
GARP VLAN Registration Protocol (GVRP),
        512
GASP, 133
Gateways, 32
Genetic algorithms (GAs), 189–90, 225–32
    active research, 231–32
    chromosome encoding, 227–29
    crossover and mutation, 230–31
    defined, 225
    elitism, 230
    features consideration, 227
    fitness evaluation, 229–30
    optimization techniques vs., 227
    population generation, 229
    problems, 226
    selection scheme, 230

Genetic Attribute Registration Protocol
    (GARP), 511–12
  applications, 511
  message support, 511
  Multicast Registration Protocol (GMRP),
    512
  VLAN Registration Protocol (GVRP), 512
Gigabit Ethernet (IEEE 802.3z), 287–92
  1000BaseCX, 290–91
  1000BaseSX, 290
  1000BaseT, 291
  Class of Service (CoS), 292
  defined, 287
  first wave applications, 289
  frame formats, 288
  half-duplex/full-duplex support, 288
  network design, 289–91
  operation, 288–89
  performance considerations, 291–92
  product manufacturers, 291
  resources, 288
  throughput, 292
  topologies, 290
  See also Ethernet; high-speed Ethernet
GPSS (General-Purpose Simulation System),
    132

Hardware, 27–35
  bridges, 30–31, 32–33
  CSU/DSUs, 30
  gateways, 32
  line drivers, 30
  MAUs, 28–29
  modems, 30
  repeaters, 29
  routers, 31–32, 34–35
  switches, 31
Hierarchical design model, 92–95
  access layer, 94
  advantages, 94–95
  backbone layer, 93

broadcast traffic segmentation, 94
  defined, 92
  distribution layer, 93–94
  illustrated, 92
  layers, 92–93
  manageability, 94
  scalability, 94
  traffic flows in, 95
Hierarchical network design, 186–91
  availability analysis, 190–91
  backbone, 187–90
  divide-and-conquer approach, 186–87
  three-level model, 188
High data rate DSL (HDSL), 365
High-Level Data Link Control (HDLC), 354,
    355–56
  connections, 356
  defined, 354
  encapsulation illustration, 355
  PPP field definitions, 355–56
  See also Encapsulation techniques
High-speed Ethernet, 286–95
  100BaseT2 Ethernet (IEEE 802.3y), 287
  100VG-AnyLAN (IEEE 802.12), 292–95
  Gigabit Ethernet (IEEE 802.3z), 287–92
  IEEE 802.3u (100BaseX), 286–87
  See also Ethernet
High-Speed Serial Interface (HSSI) lines, 382
HomeRF, 327
Hop count, 207
Horizontal cabling, 264–65
Hub-and-spoke topologies, 408–9
Hybrid cabling, 267–68

IEEE 802.10, 554
IEEE 802.1Q, 554
IEEE 802.11. See Wireless LAN
IEEE 802.3, 268–85
  background, 268
  defined, 268
  field definitions, 270–72

frame format, 269
frame types, 272
operation, 270–74
performance considerations, 284–85
quality of service, 274
transceiver operation, 272–74
See also Ethernet
IEEE 802.3u Ethernet, 286–87
IEEE 802.5. *See* Token Ring
Implementation, 12–13
CAC, 457
real-time, 100
SRB, 529
successful, 12
Information gathering, 10–11
Infrared (IR), 324–25
Institute of Electrical and Electronics
Engineering (IEEE), 13–14
Integrated Access Devices (IADs), 352
Integrated Services Digital Network. *See*
ISDN
Interim Local Management Interface (ILMI),
444–45
Internal Rate of Return (IRR) method, 148
International Organization for
Standardization (ISO), 13, 14–16
International Telecommunications Union
(ITU), 14, 431
Internet Advisory Board (IAB), 13
Internet charging model, 163–66
flat-rate pricing, 163–65
multi-tiered pricing, 165–66
See also Charging models
Internet Control Message Protocol (ICMP),
22
Internet Layer, 21–22
ARP, 22
defined, 21
ICMP, 22
IP, 21
Inter-Repeater Links (IRLs), 277

IP, 21–22, 39
ATM performance vs., 466–67
defined, 21
OSI model and, 18–20
protocol suite, 18
review, 18
ISDN, 177–79, 340, 346, 428
address mapping, 373
bandwidth-on-demand applications,
375–76
BRI, 177, 348, 369
Broadband (B-ISDN), 368, 431
circuit backup applications, 376–77
design considerations, 372–74
dial-on-demand applications, 374–75
DSL (ISDL), 363–64
encapsulation, 370
examples, 178–79
international standards, 368–69
interoperability, 374
levels of support, 371
maximum frame size, 373
Narrowband (N-ISDN), 367–78
operation, 369–70
performance considerations, 378
physical connectors, 370
PRI, 177, 369
security considerations, 372
tariffs, 372
tariff structure, 177–78
terminal adapter standards, 369
time-of-day support, 373–74
topology, 177
unnumbered links, 373
See also Private network charging models
ISIM+, 236–44
defined, 236
generated topology illustrations, 241–43
parameters, 239–40
running, 240
See also Backbone design tools

Jabber projection, 273
Jitter, 66

Kruskal's algorithm, 103–4

LAN backbone design, 485–88
  bridging backbone, 487
  illustrated, 486
  interface selection, 487
  routed backbone, 486–87
  See also ATM
LAN Emulation (LANE), 431, 468,
      475–78
  components, 475
  defined, 468
  goals, 475
  issues, 477–78
  multicast function, 476
  operation, 476–77
  transparency, 476, 477
  See also ATM
LAN media
  characteristics, 256–59
  coaxial, 256, 259
  fiber-optic, 256, 261–63
  STP, 256, 260–61
  transmission lines, 256–59
  types, 259–63
  UTP, 256, 259–60
LANs, 93, 94
  first, 249
  links, simulating, 137
  remote, 120–21
  shared, 79–81
  standards, 251–52
  switches, 31, 39
  virtual (VLANs), 547–60
  WANs vs., 333
LAN topologies, 252–56
  bus, 253–54
  mesh, 256

ring, 254–55
star, 255–56
tree, 254
See also Topologies
Latency, 65–66
  defined, 65
  MPOA, 482
  network contribution to, 65
Leased lines, 167–69, 378–87, 428
  asynchronous links, 384
  channelized E1, 381–82
  design consideration, 385–86
  Digital Data Service (DDS), 379, 380
  E1, 380
  examples, 167–69
  HSSI, 382
  for LAN extension applications, 379
  link latency, 386
  network topology, 385
  operation, 383–85
  performance considerations, 386–87
  service bandwidths, 383
  service offerings, 379–82
  Subrate Digital Multiplexing (SRDM),
      379–80
  synchronous links, 383
  T1, 380
  T3/E3, 382
  tariff structure, 167
  VLSM and, 386
Line drivers, 30
Link deficit algorithm, 204–5
Link Layer Service Access Points
      (LSAPs), 17
Link Quality Monitoring (LQM), 362
Links
  elimination, 223
  simulating, 137
  swapping, 222–23
Little's result, 112
Load, 207

Load balancing
   defined, 98
   techniques, 510
Local Access and Transport Area (LATA), 166
Local Area Networks. *See* LANs
Local bridges, 505
Local Management Interface (LMI), 401
Logical IP Subnetwork (LIS) configuration,
      421
Long-haul DWDM, 425, 426
Long-Range Dependent (LRD) model, 126,
      127, 138

MANs
   defined, 250
   standards, 252
   See also LANs; WANs
Mathematical review, 591–95
   numbers, 591–92
   operators, 591
   sets, 594–95
   summation, 592–94
Maximum Transmission Units (MTUs),
      69–70
Mean queue size, 112
Media access delay, 66–67
Media Attachment Units (MAUs), 28–29, 272
   defined, 28
   functions, 28–29
Medium Access Control (MAC) addresses, 16
MENTOR, 204, 223–25, 244
   defined, 223
   MENTOR-II, 225
   network characteristics, 224
   operation, 224–25
   problems, 225
   use of, 223–24
Mesh topology, 256
   ATM, 490–91
   Frame Relay, 407
   See also Topologies

Messages
   defined, 67
   size, 68–70
Metropolitan Area Networks. *See* MANs
Microwave, 325–26
Min-cost allocation, 214
Minimum Spanning Tree (MST),
      101–2, 243–44
M/M/I queues, 115–18, 213
   analysis, 115
   delay analysis, 117
   See also Queues
Modeling, 106–37
   analytical, 107–28, 138
   combining, techniques, 139
   empirical, 133–37, 139
   simulation, 128–33, 138–39
Modems, 30
Monetary cost, 208
Multicast
   ATM, 461–62
   LANE, 476
   server, 461–62
   support, 510–12
   VP, 461
Multicast Address Resolution Server (MARS),
      474–75
   architecture illustration, 474
   defined, 475
Multilink Point-to-Point (MPPP), 362
Multimedia applications, 44
Multipath-Constrained (MPC) routing
      problem, 208–9
Multiplexing, 336–39
   defined, 336
   Dense Wave Division (DWDM), 337, 352
   Frequency Division (FDM), 336
   multiplexer types, 338–39
   Statistical Time Division (STDM), 336–37
   T1/E1 digital systems, 337
   Time Division (TDM), 336, 348, 351

Multiprotocol bridge router, 31–32
Multiprotocol design, 96–97
Multiprotocol encapsulation over AAL5, 467,
        469
    defined, 467
    LLC encapsulation scheme, 469
    VC multiplexing scheme, 469
    See also ATM
MultiProtocol over ATM (MPOA), 468,
        478–83
    client/server architecture, 479–80
    configuration, 481
    configuration flows, 480
    connection management, 481–82
    control and data flow, 480–81
    data transfer, 482
    defined, 468, 478
    destination resolution, 481
    intra-IASG coordination, 482
    key benefits, 482–83
    latency, 482
    MPC-MPC control flows, 481
    MPC-MPC data flow, 481
    MPC-MPS control flows, 480
    MPC-NHC data flows, 481
    MPS-MPS control flows, 480–81
    operations, 481–82
    registration and discovery, 481
    routing/bridging functionality, 478
    virtual routing, 478
    See also ATM
Multiprotocol routing, 97
Multistation Access Unit (MAU),
        298, 301
Multi-tiered pricing, 165–66

Narrowband ISDN (N-ISDN), 367–78
National Bureau of Standard (NBS), 14
Nearest Active Upstream Neighbor (NAUN),
        298
NetMaker MainStation, 235–36

Net Present Value (NPV) method,
        147–50
    calculation, 149
    defined, 147–48
    example, 148–50
    value, 148
    See also Decision models
Network design
    100VG-AnyLAN, 294–95
    access, 191–98
    ATM, 484–500
    backbone, 198–232
    characteristics, 2
    elements, 1–2
    end users and, 5
    FDDI, 312–18
    fiber and copper specifications, 313
    Gigabit Ethernet, 289–91
    hierarchical, 186–91
    information gathering, 10–11
    as iterative process, 39
    life cycle, 3–4
    as living entities, 3
    planning, 11–12
    process illustration, 4
    process overview, 3–13
    requirements, 3, 4–10
    specification, 12
    Token Ring, 301–8
Network File System (NFS), 26
Network Interface Card (NIC), 78
Network Layer Protocol Identifier (NLPID),
        389
Networks
    availability, 43
    baselining, 48–52
    construction, 39
    cost, 9
    cost analysis, 143–83
    economics, 144–51
    performance, 2–3, 64–75

worst-case scenario, 62–63
X.25, 56
Network segmentation, 99
Network Service Access Points (NSAPs), 17
Network-to-Node Interface (NNI),
        432, 492
Next-Hop Resolution Protocol (NHRP),
        468, 473
    defined, 468
    Next-Hop Servers (NHS), 473
    See also ATM
Noise, 258
Null encapsulation, 389–90
Numbers, 591–92

Operators, 591
OPNET, 132
OSI reference model, 14–16
    Application Layer, 15
    Data Link Layer, 16
    defined, 14
    illustrated, 15
    IP and, 18–20
    Network Layer, 15
    Physical Layer, 16
    Presentation Layer, 15
    Session Layer, 15
    Transport Layer, 15

Packet over SONET (POS), 424
Packet rate, 71–72
    link speed relationship with, 72
    maximum, calculating, 71–72
Packets
    defined, 67
    generators, 136
    size, 73
Packet switching, 37–38
    buffer utilization in, 112–14
    circuit vs., 38
    defined, 37

theoretical delay, 74
See also Switching
Packet train model, 125–26
    arrivals in, 126
    defined, 125
    illustrated, 125
    implications, 126
    See also Analytical modeling
Pareto distribution, 138
Payback period method, 148
Payload, 70
    defined, 70
    maximum, 70
Peak load pricing, 159–63
    charging time bands, 161
    defined, 159
    relative utility modeling, 161–63
    See also Bandwidth charging model
Peer-to-peer traffic, 84
Performance, 2–3, 342
    ATM, 463–67
    bottlenecks, 75–82
    characterizing, 3
    definitions, 64–67
    FDDI, 318
    Frame Relay, 411–14
    Gigabit Ethernet, 291–92
    improvement techniques, 98–99
    ISDN, 378
    leased lines, 386–87
    network design tool, 100
    real-time implementation, 100
    relationships, 70–75
    SMDS, 423
    SRB, 536
    Token Ring, 308–9
    X.25 networks, 391–94
Permanent Virtual Circuits (PVCs), 396,
        399–400, 438–39
    ATM, 497
    defined, 399

Permanent Virtual Circuits (PVCs) *(cont'd.)*
    operation states, 400
Perturbation algorithms, 217–23
    branch exchange, 217–19
    cut saturation algorithm, 219–22
    defined, 217
    link elimination, 223
    link swapping, 222–23
Physical connectivity, 35–39
Physical topology design, 185–245
Pilot installation, 12
Planning, 11–12
    budgetary, 4
    capacity, 41–89
Planning/billing tools, 179–82
    billing systems, 182
    need for, 179–81
    raw tariff data sources, 181–82
    sample list of, 180
Point of Presence (PoP), 335
Point-to-Point (PPP), 354–55, 357–62
    authentication, 362
    defined, 354–55
    encapsulated spanning tree BPDU, 361
    encapsulation illustration, 358
    features, 358
    introduction, 357
    link establishment and protocol navigation,
        360
    Link Quality Monitoring (LQM), 362
    message format, 358
    Multilink (MPPP), 362
    operation, 359
    PPP field definitions, 359–62
    See also Encapsulation techniques
Poisson distribution, 110, 111
Population generation, 229
Port numbers, 563–90
    registered, 579–90
    well-known, 563–78
PPP over ATM, 468

Prim's algorithm, 103
Private network charging models, 166–79
    ATM, 173–75
    defined, 166
    Frame Relay, 169–72
    ISDN, 177–79
    leased lines, 167–69
    location/distance sensitivity, 166
    satellite services, 167–69
    SMDS, 172–73
    voice services, 176–77
    X.25 networks, 175–76
    See also Charging models
Private Network Node Interface (PNNI),
        443–44, 492
Private networks charging models, 166–79
Private ports, 590
Probes, 58
Processing delay, 65
Process interaction, 131
Product manufacturers
    FDDI, 318
    Gigabit Ethernet, 291
    Token Ring, 307–8
Propagation delay, 65
Proportional allocation, 214
Protocol analyzers, 58
Protocol Data Units (PDUs), 67
    defined, 68
    size, 68–69
Protocol design, 96–97
    multiprotocol, 96
    single-protocol, 97
Protocols, 17–27
    ARP, 22, 400–401
    ATM, 433
    common, 17–18
    DCMP, 354
    FTP, 25
    GARP, 511–12
    GMRP, 512

GVRP, 512
ICMP, 22
IP, 18–20, 21–22, 39, 466–67
NHRP, 468, 473
REXEC, 25–26
SLIP, 354, 356–57
SMTP, 26
SNMP, 26–27
STP, 517, 519, 521
TCP, 23–24
TFTP, 25
UDP, 23, 24–25
VLAN, 553–56
WAP, 44
Prototype testbed, 134, 135

Quality of Service (QoS), 34, 128
ATM, 448–51
Ethernet, 274
FDDI, 312
SMDS, 422
Token Ring, 301
WANs, 343
Quantifying
application behavior, 48
end-to-end transaction delays, 59–60
max packet rates, 63
server performance, 63
user behavior, 47
Queues
mean length, 113
M/M/I, 115–18, 213
Queuing, 88, 107–24
distribution functions, 109–10
Markovian systems, 108
metrics, 110–12
models, 108–9, 130, 138

Raw tariff data sources, 181–82
Real-Time Traffic Flow Measurement
Working Group, 88

Registered port numbers, 579–90
Relative utility modeling, 161–63
Reliability metric, 207
Remote bridges, 505
Remote Execution Protocol (REXEC),
25–26
Remote LANs
queuing analysis, 122
traffic modeling example, 120–21
See also LANs
Remote Procedure Call (RPC), 26
Repeaters, 276, 560
defined, 29, 560
interfaces, 29
Request for Information (RFI), 6–7
Request for Proposals (RFPs), 7
Requirements, 3
application bandwidth, 55–58
assessing, 8–10
designing, 7–8
Detailed Requirements Specification, 7
end users and, 5
establishing, 4–10
mandatory, 8
matrix of, 53
overspecifying, 6
phasing, 6–7
prioritizing, 8
Request for Information (RFI), 6–7
Request for Proposals (RFPs), 7
rolling process of, 4
sample analysis, 9
specification, 5, 6
structure, 8
translating, 5
weighting scheme, 9
RESQ (RESearch Queuing), 133
Ring topology, 254–55
ATM, 491
FDDI, 314–16
See also Topologies

Routed core, 494–96
  advantages/disadvantages, 495–96
  traffic management, 494–95
Routers, 31–32
  architecture, 32
  benefits, 34–35
  broadcasts, 35
  function, 31
  ISDN-aware, 371
  ISDN-enabled, 371
  ISDN-ignorant, 371
  issues, 35
  multiprotocol bridge, 31–32
  scalability, 35
  topological reconfiguration, 35
  VLAN, 549
Routing
  ATM, 455–58
  determining, 205–13
  FD algorithm, 209–13
  metric classes, 208
  metrics, 207–8
  MPC problems, 208–9
  multiprotocol, 97
  static, 202
  tables, populating, 136–37
  virtual, 478
Routing algorithms
  adaptive, 206
  distributed, 206
  explicit, 206
  flooding, 205–6
  shortest path, 206
  types of, 205–7

Satellite services, 167–69, 378–87
  examples, 167–69
  tariff structure, 167
Scalability
  ATM, 484–85
  broadcast domains and, 508–9

Frame Relay, 401
  hierarchical design model, 94
  router, 35
  Virtual LANs (VLANs), 548
  WAN, 343
Security, 44
  fiber-optic cable, 262
  ISDN, 372
  SMDS, 422
  VLANs and, 549
Selection scheme, 230
Self-similarity, 126–27
Serial Line Protocol (SLIP), 354, 356–57
  defined, 354
  deployment, 356
  shortcomings, 356–57
  uses, 357
  See also Encapsulation techniques
Servers
  bottlenecks, 77–78
  farms, 559–60
  multicast, 461–62
  performance, 63
Server-to-server traffic, 84
ServerTrak, 52
Service quality charge, 152
Sets, 594–95
Shared LANs, 79–81
Shared WANs, 81–82
Shielded twisted pair (STP), 256,
    260–61
  for broadband transmission, 261
  defined, 260
  Token Ring support, 304
  See also LAN media
Shortest-path algorithms, 99, 102–6
  Bellman-Ford algorithm, 105–6
  Dijkstra's algorithm, 102–3
  Floyd-Warshall algorithm, 104–5
  Kruskal's algorithm, 103–4
  Prim's algorithm, 103

routing, 206
stability issues, 106
SIMON, 133
Simple Mail Transfer Protocol (SMTP), 26
Simple Network Management Protocol
   (SNMP), 26–27
Simscript, 132
Simula, 132
Simulated annealing, 189
Simulation languages, 132–33
Simulation modeling, 128–33, 138–39
   applications, 128
   continuous models, 130
   discrete models, 129–30
   languages, 132–33
   outputs, 128–29
   process illustration, 129
   queuing models, 130
   simulation methods, 129–31
   tools, 131–32
   See also Modeling
Simulation tools, 53
Single-line DSL (SDSL), 365–66
Single-protocol design, 97
Site layout, 197–98
SLAM (Simulation Language for Alternative
   Modeling), 133
Source Routing Bridge (SRB), 506, 510,
   529–36
   bridge IDs, 535
   design guidelines, 535–36
   extended, 535
   field definitions, 531–32
   host-to-host communications, 532–34
   illustrated, 533
   implementation, 529
   maximum in a series, 536
   operation, 530–35
   parallel bridges, 536
   performance trade-offs, 536
   ring numbers, 535–36

Routing Information Field (RIF), 530–31
   Spanning Tree operations, 534
   transparent bridges vs., 529
   See also Bridges
Source Routing Translation Bridge (SR-TB),
   506
Source Routing Transparent Bridge (SRT),
   506, 536–39
   applications, 538–39
   bridges, 537
   defined, 536
   design guidelines, 538–39
   end-to-end paths, 539
   operation, 537–38
   plug-and-play mode, 539
   Routing Information Field (RIF), 537
   Spanning Tree, 538
   See also Bridges
Spanning Tree Algorithm (STA), 510,
   521–24, 561
   BPDUs, 522
   bridges, 528–29
   DEC, 527
   root bridge election, 522
Spanning Tree bridge, 506
   BPDUs, 521
   connecting two LANs, 520
   transparent bridges vs., 517
   See also Bridges
Spanning Tree Protocol (STP), 517
   functioning of, 521
   transparent bridge reliance on, 519
Spanning trees, 31
   minimum (MST), 101–2, 243–44
   multiple, 560
   use of, 102
Specialized application simulators, 136
Specialized packet generators, 136
Spread spectrum, 321, 323–24
SQE testing, 274
Square root allocation, 214

Standards
    cabling, 263–65
    CIOA, 470
    ISDN, 368–69
    LAN, 251–52
    MAN, 252
    organizations, 13–14
Star topology, 255–56
    ATM, 491
    Frame Relay, 406–7
    See also Topologies
Static routing, 202
Statistical Time Division Multiplexing
        (STDM), 336–37
Store-and-forward delay, 65
Store-and-forward switches, 506–7
Structured cabling system (SCS), 263–65
    backbone cabling, 265
    horizontal cabling, 264–65
Subnetworks, 491
Subscriber Network Interface (SNI), 421
Summation, 592–94
Swarming algorithms, 190, 232
Switched fabric topology, 320
Switched Multimegabit Data Service (SMDS),
        172–73, 340, 414–23, 428
    access, 173
    addressing, 419
    address resolution, 422
    ATM and, 483–84
    backbone design, 420
    defined, 172, 414
    design considerations, 419–21
    examples, 173
    Interface Protocol (SIP), 415–16
    LIS configuration, 421
    media support, 421
    MTU and fragmentation, 423
    multicast/broadcast handling, 421
    operation, 415–16
    performance considerations, 423

    quality of service, 422
    screening tables, 422
    security features, 422
    SIP 2 field definitions, 417–19
    SIP-3 field definitions, 416–17
    tariff structure, 173
    See also Private network charging models
Switched Virtual Circuits (SVCs), 396
    defined, 399
    termination, 399
Switches, 31
    adaptive, 507
    applicability in internetwork design,
        512–14
    ATM, 31, 462–65
    bridges vs., 504
    cut-through, 507
    evolution, 505
    fragment-free, 507
    LAN, 31, 39
    multicast support, 510–12
    store-and-forward, 506–7
    VLAN, 547, 549
Switching, 36–38, 506–7
    circuit, 37
    defined, 506
    packet, 37–38
Symmetrical traffic, 86–87
Synchronous Data Link Control (SDLC), 354
Synchronous Optical Network (SONET),
        340, 350, 423–25
    access, 425
    defined, 423
    octet-synchronous multiplexing scheme,
        424
    Packet over, 424
    protocol layers, 424
    SONET/SDH networks, 424, 425
SysMeter, 51
System Monitor, 51
System-to-System Interface (SSI), 443

T1 lines, 380
T3 lines, 372
Taxes, 150–51
TCP/IP applications, 24–27
    DNS, 26
    FTP, 25
    NFS, 26
    remote shell, 26
    REXEC, 25–26
    RPC, 26
    SMTP, 26
    SNMP, 26–27
    Telnet, 25
    TFTP, 25
    X Windows, 27
TCP/IP model
    Application Layer, 19
    Data Link Layer, 20–21
    illustrated, 19
    Internet Layer, 21–22
    Network Layer, 19–20
    Physical Layer, 20
    Transport Layer, 19, 22–24
Telephone networks, 334–35
Telnet, 25
Terminal-host traffic, 84
Three-phase event scheduling, 131
Throughput, 64–65
    ATM, 465–66
    calculating, 79
    defined, 64, 112
    expression, 112
    Gigabit Ethernet, 292
Time Division Multiplexing (TDM), 336, 348, 351
Token Ring, 80–81, 250, 295–309, 331
    background, 295
    cabling design rules, 305–7
    defined, 295
    drive distances, 304–5
    early token release, 308–9

fault management, 300–301
field definitions, 296–98
frame formats, 296–98
frame transmission, 298–99
hard error, 300
MAC address formats, 297
MAUs, 301
maximum number of stations, 303
media filters, 305
media types, 304–5
network design, 301–8
network illustrations, 302
network nodes, 298
operation, 298–301
performance considerations, 308–9
product manufacturers, 307–8
quality of service, 301
risk management and control, 299–300
soft error, 300–301
Token Ring-to-Ethernet translation, 543–45
    address resolution, 545
    bit ordering, 544
    database mapping, 544
    defined, 543
    design issues, 544–45
    encapsulation, 544
    illustrated, 543
    MTU size, 544
    See also Translation bridges
Token Ring-to-FDDI translation, 545–46
Top-down framework, 44–54
    application behavior quantification, 48
    discussion group formation, 45–46
    input data summary, 53–54
    network baseline, 48–52
    process, 44–45
    traffic projections, 52–53
    user behavior quantification, 47
    See also Capacity planning
Topologies
    ATM, 484

Topologies *(cont'd.)*
  backbone, 198–232
  bus, 253–54
  cluster, 490–91
  commercial modeling tools, 234
  design, 185–245
  FibreChannel, 320
  Gigabit Ethernet, 290
  hierarchical design, 186–91
  hub-and-spoke, 408–9
  initial, 203
  LAN, 252–56
  leased line, 385
  mesh, 256
  multiple LAN access point, 329
  optimization, 186
  peer-to-peer, 328
  point-to-point, 320
  ring, 254–55
  ring/loop, 320
  single LAN access point, 328
  star, 255–56
  switched fabric, 320
  tree, 254
  wireless LAN, 328–29
Traffic
  asymmetrical, 87–88
  characteristics, understanding, 63–75
  in circuit cost modeling, 157
  client/server, 84
  compression techniques, 509–10
  distributed entity, 84
  generation, 134–36
  intensity, 111
  peer-to-peer, 84
  profiles, 49–50
  projections, 52–53
  segmentation, 507–8
  server-to-server, 84
  symmetrical, 86–87
  terminal-host, 84

units of measurement, 68
  See also Flows
Traffic management, 494–95, 507–10
  broadcast domains/scalability, 508–9
  compression techniques, 509–10
  Layer 2 access lists, 509
  traffic segmentation, 507–8
Traffic matrix, 86–88
  backbone design case study, 237–39
  building, 87–88
  defined, 86
  illustrated, 87
Transaction delays, 59–60
Transceiver operation, 272–74
  collision detection, 273
  jabber projection, 273
  link integrity, 273–74
  SQE testing, 274
  transmit/receive data, 273
  See also Ethernet; IEEE 802.3
Translation bridges, 539–46
  defined, 539
  FDDI-to-Ethernet translation, 540–43
  issues, 539–40
  Token Ring-to-Ethernet translation,
    543–45
  Token Ring-to-FDDI translation, 545–46
  See also Bridges
Transmission (wireless LAN), 323–26
  infrared (IR), 324–25
  microwave, 325–26
  spread spectrum, 323–24
Transmission Control Protocol (TCP), 23–24
  defined, 23
  message format, 24
  See also TCP/IP applications; TCP/IP
    model
Transmission delay, 65
Transmission lines, 256–59
  balanced/unbalanced, 258–59
  crosstalk, 257–58

noise, 258
propagation velocity, 257
wire sizes, 256
See also LAN media
Transparent bridges, 505, 514–29
BPDU frame format, 524–26
bridge state machine, 517–19
configuration message format, 526
control backup root, 528
control root, 528
DEC Spanning Tree, 527
design guidelines, 527–29
development, 514
filtering database, 515
illustrated operation of, 516
interoperability, 529
listening/hearing, 515
loop avoidance, 519–21
maximum in a series, 527–28
operation, 514–27
placement, 528
principle, 514
SRB vs., 529
STA, 528–29
STP, 519
timers, 526–27, 528
uses, 514
See also Bridges
Transport Layer, 15, 19, 22–24
defined, 22–23
TCP, 23–24
UDP, 23
Transport Service Access Points (TSAPs), 17
Tree topology, 254
defined, 254
FDDI, 316–18
See also Topologies
TrendTrak, 52
Trivial File Transfer Protocol (TFTP), 25
Trunk Coupling Units (TCUs), 303
Two-phase event scheduling, 131

Unbalanced transmission line, 259
Universal Asynchronous Receiver Transmitter (UART), 327
Unshielded twisted pair (UTP), 256, 259–60
performance improvement, 259–60
specifications, 260
Token Ring support, 304
See also LAN media
Unspecified Bit Rate (UBR), 449
Use charge, 151–52
Use patterns, 60–62
Use profiles, 60–62
equipment supplier, 60–61
online brokerage, 62
User behavior, quantifying, 47
User Datagram Protocol (UDP), 23
for datagram services, 24–25
reliability, 25
User-to-Network Interface (UNI), 432, 441–42, 492
Generic Flow Control (GFC), 442
links, 492
private, 441
public, 441
Utilization factor, 111

Variable Bit Rate (VBR), 449
Variable-Length Subnet Masks (VLSM), 386
Very high data rate DSL (VDSL), 366
Virtual Channel Connection (VCC), 438, 440
Virtual Channel Link (VCL), 440
Virtual Channels (VCs), 438–41
Virtual Channel Switch (VCS), 440
Virtual Circuit Identifier (VCI), 439, 455
Virtual LANs (VLANs), 547–60, 561
access link, 553
advantages, 551
classification, 551
connection types, 553
defined, 509, 547

Virtual LANs (VLANs) *(cont'd.)*
  design concepts, 550
  design guidelines, 559–60
  domains illustration, 509
  end-to-end switching, 559
  filtering database, 556–57
  frame processing, 556–58
  Hello protocol, 555
  higher-layer, 553
  high-speed backbone technology, 559
  hybrid link, 553
  ID (VID), 556
  IEEE 802.10, 554
  IEEE 802.1Q, 554
  Inter-Switch Link (ISL) protocol, 555
  Layer 1, 552
  Layer 2, 552
  Layer 3, 552–53
  Link State Protocol (VLSP), 555
  microsegmentation, 559
  multiple spanning trees, 560
  operation, 549–59
  overlapping, 550
  protocols, 553–56
  router distribution, 559
  routers, 549
  scalability, 548
  security and, 549
  server farms, 559–60
  simplified administration, 548–49
  switches, 547, 549
  tagging, 557–58
  TCI field definitions, 558–59
  trunk link, 553
  Trunk Protocol (VTP), 555–56
  types, 552–53
  virtual workgroup resources, 559
Virtual Path Connection (VPC), 440
Virtual Path Connection Identifier (VPCI), 440
Virtual Path Identifier (VPI), 439, 455

Virtual Path Link (VPL), 439
Virtual Paths (VPs), 438–41
  defined, 439
  dynamic creation, 438
  illustrated, 438
  multicasting, 461
Virtual Path Switch (VPS), 440
Virtual Path Terminator (VPT), 440
Virtual Private Networks (VPNs), 44, 353
Virtual routing, 478
Voice services, 176–77

WANDL Network Planning and Analysis Tools (NPAT), 235
WANs, 333–428
  access networks, 343–47
  access technologies, 363–78
  ATM interworking with, 483–84
  backbone networks, 347–54
  backbone technologies, 378–427
  bandwidths, 347–49
  broadcast handling, 342–43
  concepts and terminology, 334–43
  design issues, 341–43
  design principles, 334–54
  dial-up access, 344–45
  distance limitations, 345–46
  DWDM, 425–27
  encapsulation techniques, 354–62
  Frame Relay, 394–414
  hierarchy, 341
  high-speed access, 345
  interfaces, 334, 335–36
  LANs vs., 333
  leased lines, 378–87
  links, simulating, 137
  logical topology, 341–42
  multiplexing, 336–39
  network hierarchy, 339–41
  networking issues, 351–54
  network overlays, 350–51

performance, 342
physical topology, 341
Point of Presence (PoP), 335
quality of service, 343
satellite links, 378–87
scalability, 343
service classifications, 340
shared, 81–82
SMDS, 414–23
SONET, 423–25
technologies, 339
technology comparison, 350
telephone networks, 334–35
virtual circuit handling, 342
X.25, 387–94
Well-known port numbers, 563–78
Wide area backbone design, 493–500
    ATM core advantages/disadvantages,
        499–500
    Internet backbone migration, 493–94
    n-squared problem, 498
    PVC-based traffic control, 496–98
    routed core, 494–96
    traffic management, 494
    See also ATM
Wireless Application Protocol (WAP), 44
Wireless LAN, 320–30, 331
    applications, 330
    background, 320–26
    Bluetooth, 327–28
    deployment, 329
    designing, 328–30
    frequency and wavelength, 322–23
    HomeRF, 327
    IEEE 802.11, 326–27

infrared (IR), 324–25
microwave, 325–26
spread spectrum, 321, 323–24
technologies, 326–28
topologies, 328–29
transmission techniques, 323–26
Wireless networking, 44
Worst-case scenario, 62–63

X.25 networks, 56, 240, 387–94, 428
    connections, 389
    defined, 175, 387
    deployment, 387
    hierarchy, 390
    high-speed access issues, 392
    interoperability, 391
    IP encapsulation over, 389–90
    LAN interconnection over, 390
    LAPB, 387
    latency, 391–92
    MTU size/fragmentation, 392–93
    NBMA issues, 390–91
    operation, 387–90
    optimization of broadcast traffic, 391
    packet-switch node performance, 393–94
    performance considerations, 391–94
    PLP, 387
    tariff structure, 176
    VC holding time, 388
    VC optimization, 393
    VCs, 388
    WAN illustration, 388
    X.32 asynchronous packet mode, 391
    See also Private network charging models
X Windows system, 27